European Business Strategy

Seventh Edition

European Business Strategy

Tutor's Manual

The **Tutor's Manual** contains notes and supporting documents,
chronologies, updates and other material to help the tutor in managing
effective learning and is designed to accompany
European Business Strategy
It is presented in a large A4 plastic-pocketed
binder for ease of consultation and copying.

ISBN 1 85450 251 4

* * * * * * * * * * * * *

Terry Garrison

Terry Garrison is Professor of International Business
and Leader of the Strategy Faculty
at Henley Management College.

* * * * * * * * * * * * *

European Business Strategy

Seventh Edition

Terry Garrison

This seventh edition of European Business Strategy is published September 2000 by Elm Publications, Seaton House, Kings Ripton, Huntingdon, Cambridgeshire PE17 2NJ England.

Tel: 01487 773254
website *www. elm-training.co.uk* email *elm@elm-training.co.uk*

Printed by St Edmundsbury Press, Bury St Edmunds, Suffolk, England.

Bound by Woolnough Bookbinding, Express Works, Church Street, Irthlingborough, Northants, England

---

ISBN 1 85450 237 9

British Library Cataloguing-in-Publication Data. A catalogue record for this publication is available from The British Library.

CONTENTS

STRATEGY ANALYSIS FRAMEWORK

DEDICATION

To my wife, Ann, and for Christopher and Kirsty, Alistair and Helen.

Ne ingrati videamur

PREFACE

This casebook seeks to meet a two-fold requirement that is as challenging as it is worthwhile:

- to increase students' knowledge of strategic moves being made by European businesses and
- to create greater familiarity with the economic and political context of Europe within which these strategies are played out.

There are many books on the politics and economics of the EU and the processes of integration but casebooks that are contemporaneous and data-rich are few and far between. The European Foundation for Management Development has long supported an annual competition to inspire the creation of just this sort of teaching material.

The seventh edition of *European Business Strategy* contains 30 major European business strategy cases covering the period 1988-2000. They are arranged chronologically, with many covering the period of the mid to late 1990s. Two industries which are undergoing huge amounts of mutation, financial services and telecommunications, are strongly featured.

The themes and the case studies that illustrate them are as follows:

- **the context of European Union development:** Europe Plc, GATT, ERM, Channel Tunnel, EMU and Mad Cow Disease
- **the context of business developments in central Europe:** Berlin Wall and Ikarus
- **the context of business developments in Russia:** Perestroika, Port of St Petersburg and Russia at the Crossroads
- **the changing face of the telecommunications industry:** Plessey, France Télécom and Cable and Wireless

- **the changing face of the financial services industry:** Banesto, Barings, Crédit Lyonnais, Canary Wharf and The World of Deutsche Bank
- **the aerospace industry in Europe:** European Space Agency, Air Europe, Eurofighter and Air France
- **European M&A:** Irish Distillers, Pirelli, Groupe Bull, DAF, Klockner, Renault and Thyssen Krupp

In each case study, material is provided relating to the political and economic backcloth behind the strategic move made and covering the industry. This is done in such a way that, not only can the book be used explicitly as a casebook on courses across Europe, such as MBA, Diplomkaufmann and DESCAF, but it can also serve as a reader on the integration of Europe over the period 1988-2000. As such it has an immediacy and usefulness to professors in campuses as distant from the European heartland as Pittsburgh and Calcutta.

Two caveats need to be entered about the style of writing of the cases, namely that
- the wealth of data about the industry context in which the strategic moves are made by companies often exceeds that about the company itself
- the cases are not written sequentially, Harvard-style, and cannot be cursorily read.

This gives a level of complexity to the cases which can be challenging. Yet there are also rich rewards to be had. A deeper and more practical understanding of business issues and strategic drivers in Europe can only be highly beneficial for all practititioners. It is to serve this powerful purpose that this casebook has been written.

Terry Garrison,
Henley Management College, July 2000

EUROPE PLC?

Abstract:

Europe Plc deals with the opportunities open to Britain as a result of its endorsement of the Single European Act (SEA) of 1986. The case contains data on the legislation itself and allows British attitudes to European integration to be reviewed in two dimensions; agricultural protectionism and fiscal harmonisation. In both cases the standpoints of Britain and its partners are seen to be opposed. The case then considers the implications for some mainland European and British businesses of SEA changes in the light of background developments in world trade. The case is complemented later in the book by the ERM, GATT and EMU case studies.

Question:

Do you agree with Kazuo Chiba's assessment of the attractiveness of Britain as an economic springboard into Europe for Japanese companies?

Case Timing: 1988

THE TASK AHEAD

European firms are wide-awake and ready to expand their sales in the United Kingdom. British firms must ensure that they are ready to meet this competition and expand their sales in Europe. If they do not prepare now to meet this challenge, they risk being forced out of business. Regardless of battles, we've got no choice. [1]

This stark warning came from John Owens, Deputy Director-General of the CBI, in April 1988, as the British government set in motion its publicity campaign to alert businessmen to the implications of the Single European Market. The passing of the Single European Act by all the parliaments of the 12 European Community (EC) countries committed each of them to the speedy execution of the steps to finally achieve the implementation in full of the Treaty of Rome. This was the Treaty which, in 1957, had originally set up the framework for working towards a true Economic Community in Europe.

So far as the precise consequences of each nation's endorsement of the Single European Act, 1986 (SEA) were concerned, it was too early to judge. Indeed, in 1988, questions were raised about whether and how quickly the EC's Council of Ministers would be capable of accepting the 300 steps thought necessary by the Commission, in its July 1985 White Paper, for the full actualisation of the Single European Market, particularly as some of them were highly contentious.

Where there was no room for question, however, was in the fact of what was being sought by the Commission: acceptance by all leaders of the European nations belonging to the EC of the need to change it from its existing situation to a truly free trading area, with as few obstacles in the way of internal competition as humanly possible.

Given that much of the industry policy thrust of successive British Conservative governments since 1979, all led by Prime Minister Margaret Thatcher, had been precisely in the area of achieving greater competitiveness, it is little wonder that the Commission's views on the purpose of the Single European Market were welcomed in Whitehall. The Department of Trade and Industry's advertising slogan *Europe Open for Business* had, therefore, no abnormal significance. Indeed the Conservative government, with its predecessors, had privatised substantial slices of British public sector industry. In addition, in 1980, 1982 and 1984, major pieces of legislation were passed limiting the powers and rights of trade unions. What was worrying, however, was Britain's preparedness for the changes which might arise. The conclusions in a report by Robert Kerr, of brokers CL-Alexanders Laing & Cruikshank, focused not a few minds:

a number of cross-border mergers, acquisitions and joint ventures in manufacturing, marketing and distribution are inevitable – and, most notably, for the British for whom it will be crucial because of their relative size, lack of muscle and dependence on the domestic market. [2]

SINGLE EUROPEAN MARKET : THE NAMING OF PARTS

Arguably the most important post-war politico-economic decision taken by each EC member was that of accepting and endorsing the principles of the Treaty of Rome. It is of importance to note that there is no divergence between the principles of the Treaty of Rome and the Single European Act.

Article 1

By this Treaty, the High Contracting Parties set up among themselves a EUROPEAN ECONOMIC COMMUNITY.

Article 2

The Community shall have as its task, by setting up a common market and progressively approximating the economic policies of member states, to promote throughout the Community an harmonious development of economic activities, a continuous and balanced expansion, an increase in stability, an accelerated raising of the standard of living and closer relations between member states belonging to it.

TABLE 1 : PRINCIPLES OF THE 1957 TREATY OF ROME

The practical implementation of the principles of the Treaty of Rome was based on the dismantling of internal trade barriers [Article 3(a)], the setting-up of a common external tariff [3(b)], the abolition of obstacles to the freedom of movement within the Community of persons, services and capital [3(c)] and the establishment of a system to ensure that competition was not distorted. Of special interest was signatories' acceptance of limitations on their future sovereignty. These were based on Article 3(f), the approximation of the laws of member states to the extent required for the proper functioning of the Common Market, and that of the acceptance of the notion of a timetable for the implementation of the Treaty's 248 Articles.

The Single European Act (1986) can be seen as not just another step along the unification road but also (to mix the metaphor) as a whip which the Commission might use to spur on European leaders to speed up the Euro-integration process. It was an Act which supporters claimed would look forward to the Europe of the twenty-first century and not backwards to the economic stagnation of the 1960s and dislocation of the 1970s, caused by oil price rises, which had slowed down the initial impetus of the Treaty of Rome.

---

(1) Removal of Physical Barriers to Trade
  * removal of internal customs controls
  * general removal of immigration/passport controls
  * speedier transit of goods: less documentation

(2) Removal of Technical Barriers to Trade
  * agreement on basic quality/safety standards
  * general acceptance of national testing/certification procedures, leading ultimately to an EC trademark.
  * dismantling of any residual barriers to free movement of capital, services and workers. Greater freedom of establishment for all financial and other professional institutions. Mutual recognition of educational qualifications
  * opening up public procurement to EC-wide tender. Achieving real "open-entry", even in telecommunications.

(3) Removal of Fiscal Barriers to Trade
  * approximation of indirect taxation rates
  * removal of fiscal checks at frontiers

(4) Consumer Protection
  * harmonisation of public health standards
  * harmonisation of consumer protection

(5) Lessening Barriers to Competitiveness
  * creation of up-graded EC system for vetting takeover or merger bids and government subsidies.

TABLE 2 : SINGLE EUROPEAN ACT CHANGES

As Table 2 suggests, the Single European Act (SEA) covered a process of liberalisation which allowed greater rein to market forces and curbed (or envisaged the dismantling of) many of the protectionist approaches so ingeniously built up by European businesses and even their governments over the years. For example, the setting-up of purely domestic product standards, by the British Standards Institute or the French AFNOR or the German DIN, had the effect of keeping foreign competition at bay.

There can also be seen in the SEA the Commission's intent to push more vigorously for the implementation of articles 85 and 86 of the Treaty of Rome. These stipulate:

* the prohibition of all business agreements affecting trade among members *the object or effect of which is to prevent, restrict or distort competition,* especially price-fixing, deals on the sharing of supplies or markets and discrimination against customers. (Art.85)

* that it would be unlawful for one or more undertaking *to exploit in an improper manner, a dominant position within the Common Market or within a substantial part of it.* (Art.86)

In this connection it is noteworthy that the EC's Merger Control Regulations, first introduced in 1973, were ear-marked for strengthening. Also there was a plan to set-up a new court to deal with merger/takeover cases to relieve pressure on the European Court of Justice.

The SEA was also intended, as its preamble states, to strengthen the political will for 'European Union'. However, a hard-headed Jacques Delors, Commission President, referred in a major speech in March 1988 less to political principle than to the economic plusses that would stem from the Single European Market. He was clearly anxious to make 1992 'irreversible' by passing as many of the 300 changes as possible through the Council of Ministers by the end of 1988. In his speech [3] he indicated that the attainment of the Single European Market by the end-1992 target date would add a further five per cent to Europe's industrial output through economies of scale, job creation and stabilised prices, brought about by healthier competition. Allied to this were statistics produced by the EC Commissioner for the Internal Market, ex-Cabinet Minister Lord Cockfield, to show that the scrapping of frontier formalities would save 1.8 per cent of the value of goods traded in the EC and that protectionist technical regulations added another two percentage points to company costs.

Surveys showed, however, that the British seemed hard put to recognise either principle or practice when it came to EC matters. In 1988, six months after the enactment of the SEA, studies revealed a parlous state of affairs of ignorance, even among the business fraternity, as to the meaning and significance of 1992, the Single European Market and the SEA. The UK government, worried by the comparison with France where there was wide awareness, based a long-running official *L'union fait la force* 1992 advertising campaign, had started its publicity moves only in April 1988.

FAILURE TO:	COST OF FAILURE [£B]
Complete the internal market	35
Complete the European Monetary System	20
Adapt the Common Agricultural Policy to market needs	10
Align macro-economic policies of member states	10
Create open market for public procurement	7

TABLE 3: THE COST OF POTENTIAL FAILURE
Source: Europe 1992 (Report by MEP Sir Fred Catherwood), Commission 1988.

There was much to do. It was now noted, for instance, that Britain seemed to be lacking political power through under-representation at chairman level in those EC committees where debate and decision-narrowing on European standards were taking place. What would the effect on British industry be if it had to accommodate itself to alien standards over a wide product range? Fortunately, it looked as though in certain categories there would be acceptable trade-offs. In food, for example, there was no danger of standardised *Eurobeer* or *Eurosausage* because of *mutual recognition, approximation* and, in the final analysis, *derogation* (making an exception from the rule).

Country	Percentage of respondents in survey in favour of granting the Euro-parliament power to pass laws applying directly to all members of the EC
Italy	69
France	58
Britain	47

TABLE 4 : STRASBOURG RULES?
Source: Eurobarometer Survey, Commission, December 1987.

DOWN ON THE FARM

It would be a mistake to think that, because Lord Young (Secretary of State for Trade and Industry in the 1988 Conservative government) was, like all his colleagues, strongly in favour of Single European Market moves, that all was sweetness and light in European circles. Indeed, it should not be forgotten that Britain did not join the EC until 1973, a full 15 years after its establishment by France, Germany, Italy, the Netherlands and Benelux, - and after experiencing two entry refusals. Also, once in, Britain had itself tested the European waters by holding a referendum on whether to stay in!

In fact, almost since the start of Margaret Thatcher's premiership in 1979, Britain's Euro-relations had been characterised by a ferocious running battle with its partners over the Common Agricultural Policy. In this all insults, like the 'housewife' epithet used by French PM Jacques Chirac in response to the British veto at the Bruxelles summit in July 1987, were treasured by the media.

However, it was not the need for farm support measures that divided the partners. Most industrial countries provide substantial help for their domestic agriculture. This is done by ensuring that domestic produce is bought, where necessary, at higher-than-world-price levels, by imposing suitable tariffs and/or quotas on imports, by subsidising exports or by a judicious combination of these measures. All were against the spirit, if not the practices, laid down in the protocol of the General Agreement on Tariffs and Trade (GATT). It was estimated by the OECD, in a 1987 report entitled *National Policies & Agricultural Trade*, that no less than one third of the value of agricultural output in Australia, Canada, the EC, Japan, New Zealand and the USA was made up of government subsidies. The EC was certainly, in the British government's view, guilty of some excesses in this regard.

The EC for too long imposed high prices as a means of supporting farm incomes without sufficient regard to costs of taxpayers and consumers.. Agriculture became 'isolated from market signals'

proclaimed the Treasury's Economic Progress Report of February 1988.

Indeed, the wide-ranging EC procedures for agricultural support specifically involved guaranteed or 'intervention' prices for farm produce that could not be sold at market prices (*deficiency payments*) and guaranteed acceptance and storage of any over-production, however achieved. Such a system evolved quite naturally out of articles 38-47 of the Treaty of Rome. The critical problem was not so much the principle of farm support as the practices pursued by the EC and the cost involved. Any government as ideologically committed to free enterprise, as those led by Mrs Thatcher, was bound to regard these as highly distasteful and to be wholly bent on the elimination of Common Agricultural Policy (CAP) fraud, wherever located.

Such fraud itself was estimated to be costing EC member states nearly ten per cent of the total yearly EC budget and covered every conceivable form of trickery. Those most widely known were the making of false claims for rebates on fictitious exports (fictitious in the sense that sometimes the goods were not, in fact, exported or, if so, were fraudulently re-imported, a system known as the 'carousel') and inflating output figures (or even falsifying the products) to gain greater subsidies.

The British government's hostility was only increased by the political clamour stemming from the spiralling need for budget finance to deal with the over-production that resulted in such things as *wine lakes* and *butter mountains* and the fact that agriculture support accounted for a staggering £20 billion in 1987. It was not helped either by revelations that in 1986 the EC farmer was being paid three times the world price for his wheat, barley, butter and sugar.

Clearly, any politician of Mrs Thatcher's persuasion would have been unhappy with the paradox that much of the technological advance in agriculture and changes in the level and intensity of cultivation (both associated with the increased profitability of European agriculture as a function of the CAP support mechanisms) was itself adding heavily to the apparently unstoppable rising cost of the CAP by creating huge extra volumes of unwanted food. A far cry from the Europe of 1957! Again the British government's viewpoint was unequivocal:

Policies have to be judged against the principle that the allocation of resources is generally best left to market forces.. Support should not be given indiscriminately through unnecessarily high prices. [4]

The most ferocious phase of the running battle stretched from the Fontainebleau summit of 1984, when Mrs Thatcher won a budget rebate or 'abatement' for Britain (paid ever since as, in the British view, a matter of principle), to the summit in Brussels in February 1988.

The Brussels summit culminated, after the climactic Copenhagen summit in 1987, in a major revision of the CAP in terms of:

☐ **Limits to the production of a variety of commodities**
A legally binding mechanism, called the 'automatic stabiliser' was agreed. By this mechanism, farmers who exceed the stipulated production quota in a given year suffer a drop in the intervention price in the following year. The percentage price fall is compounded by any failure to keep within production guidelines in the next year and so on.

☐ **An increase in Structural Funding**
This refers to the amount of money spent under the EC's Regional and

Social Fund on moves to further social cohesion and bring economic benefits to depressed or backward regions. In fact, it was agreed in 1987 to double the funding by 1992 to a level of £9 billion, of which £6m would be spent in Category 1 need areas, such as Portugal, Greece, French Overseas Territories, Spanish Andalucia and Galicia and Northern Ireland. A need area of this type is one where per capita income is only 75 per cent of the EC average.

☐ **Set-Aside**

Under this scheme farmers are compensated for taking 15 per cent of their land out of production for a specified period in order to reduce the production of, for instance, arable products, wine, sugar.

This deal was seen by Margaret Thatcher as a 95 per cent victory. Others were not quite so sure, particularly those concerned at the new deal agreed on budget contributions. This entailed not just a percentage of each state's VAT and excise duty receipts, as in the past, but also a levy on national output. This was sometimes difficult to compute, as in Italy and France, because of the size of the black economy. Some EC partners, by contrast, were much concerned with the effect of the deal on poorer commodity-exporting nations. Mentioning the fact that, in 1987, each of the EC's 25 million cows was subsidised to the tune of £156 per cow, Lord Plumb (President of the European Parliament and ex-President of the National Farmers' Union) lambasted the CAP in a speech given on the 18th March 1988. *A fetid air* he declared, *hangs behind the heavy trade barriers of protectionism. World agriculture is in the spotlight and we are witnessing a tragic and harrowing imbalance in world food production and consumption.* [5]

British Conservative MP Teddy Taylor took an even more jaundiced view:

A decision to give a real increase in spending of 25 per cent to an organisation now spending £233m/week on dumping and destroying food... is an insult. [6]

As if to underline these criticisms of the protectionist CAP system, the 27 nation, GATT talks about the freeing-up of world trade (and agriculture in particular) broke up in failure at the end of March.[7] It was a failure which persisted into the 1990s. Indeed only in 1994 was the Uruguay Round included.

THE NUB OF THE MATTER

The practicalities and cost of CAP was not the only EC subject about which feelings ran high at Westminster. Another was the issue of fiscal policy harmonisation.

In accepting the provisions of the Single European Act, each member state had agreed to a tightening up of the Council of Ministers' decision-making system. Now, post-SEA, some two-thirds of the White Paper's list of 300 items were to be the subject of qualified majority, as opposed to unanimity, decisions. Not only that, but the state sovereignty issue was further affected by the agreed changes in the role of the European Parliament. This would, through a re-structured and intensified co-operation procedure, play a much more active part in future in influencing EC legislation. The British government's concern here was with the political pressure being mounted by the Commission to try to win acceptance for its proposal of two rates for VAT throughout the EC, a reduced rate (4-9 per cent) and a standard rate (14-20 per cent), on which members would have a choice. This was seen in Westminster as a sovereignty matter transcending questions of economics.

Speaking at the Königswinter Conference in Cambridge in early 1988, Chancellor Nigel Lawson firmly rejected the Commission's two-tier VAT plan, which he labelled *a bureaucratic non-sequitur*, and stated that 1992 should be about de-regulation and not harmonisation. To back up this assertion, the Treasury issued a table of likely price rises and falls resulting from such change (See Table 5). With the British Prime Minister bound hand and foot by her election manifesto commitment not to change Britain's zero-level VAT rating on food and children's shoes, this hostility towards the commission's plan was not unexpected.

Commodity	price rise %/p	price fall %/p
Petrol (gallon)		12p
Cigarettes (packet of 20)	20p	
Spirits	4%	
Gas		85%
Wine	4%	

TABLE 5 : WINNERS & LOSERS

By contrast, the issue of Britain's full membership of the European Monetary System seemed to weigh low in the political scales. This would have meant Britain aligning the value of its currency tightly with those of other EC members to produce ultimately a sort of EC international trading currency. It appeared, at the same time, to be accorded little prominence, even though it could conceivably have entailed surrendering some operating freedom over the exchange rate of the pound sterling and its petro-currency status. In the 1990s the European Monetary System would become the subject of major political discord within EC ranks.

Imagine, therefore, the media attention that was focused on the ruling by the European Court of Justice (ECJ) in February 1988. This stated that Britain should impose VAT on two categories of product currently free of it, namely spectacles and medical goods. The Commission's action was brought under the 6th Eurodirective on Value Added Tax which had been accepted by Britain's 1974-79 Labour Government but from some of whose specifications it had been initially derogated. Worse, further rulings on coal, sewage and industrial construction products were known to be in the pipeline.

Conservative government leaders retained their *sangfroid* and insisted on the need for Britain to control its own VAT rates. They also reflected on the fact that the European Court of Justice had set no time limit for compliance with its ruling and that, anyway, all Council of Ministers' decisions on fiscal and employee rights matters had to be unanimous.

MP Teddy Taylor was again in the van of the more outspoken critics:

It is the first time since the Ship Tax in the seventeenth century that a body outside Parliament has told Parliament what taxes to levy.

In stark contrast, Lord Cockfield stoutly defended the Commission's plan on the grounds that VAT rate harmonisation was an integral and inescapable element in removing restrictions to cross-border trade and, thereby, improving competitiveness. Speaking of the 300 hundred items in his 1985 White Paper, he declared *One cannot simply pick and choose ... to do the things you like and block the things you don't.*[9]

	1987	1992
Agreed EC Budget (£ billion)	31	37
Budget as % of all countries' VAT receipts	1.4	1.9
Legally-binding spending limit on the CAP (£ billion)	19.2	20.7

TABLE 6 : THE COMMON MARKET BUDGET

Many agreed with the conclusion of a report entitled *Europe's Domestic Market* compiled by the Royal Institute of International Affairs. This stated that the harmonisation of indirect taxation rates was the greatest obstacle to the creation of the Single European Market.[10] Unlike in the USA, where Sales Taxes varied by 7.5 per cent points, the disparity between rates in Europe was between nought per cent (UK: children's shoes) and 38 per cent (Italy: luxury goods). [11]

A SHOPKEEPING NATION?

The launch of Britain's Single European Market campaign took place against the backcloth of increasingly strongly-felt, novel trends in the nation's industrial and commercial life. Many of these trends could be said to have originated in, or received much impetus from, the impact on Britain's economic and social situation of the reformist policies (fiscal, monetary and employee relations in particular) pursued by Conservative governments since 1979. They were clearly taking place at a time of severe world difficulties - the crippling level of third world indebtedness, currency instability and commodity price weakness for example, and at a time of unprecedented technological advances in information technology, robotics, biotechnology and so on.

Examples of industrial predicaments illustrating the effects of this maelstrom abounded. The 1970s and 1980s in Britain, for instance, had seen what appeared at times to be end-game steps in the sad decline of once vital mass-output, world-beating, British-owned 'smokestack' industries like ship building and motor cycles. Britain had seen massive falls in employment in other industries (coal and steel) as a precursor to equally dramatic rises in productivity. Greater economic reliance, market-led, was being placed on service industries to offset sectoral weaknesses in a manufacturing base which no longer provided the nation with a balance of payments surplus. South-east Britain enjoyed a heavy concentration of the mix of new high-technology 'sunrise' manufacturing industries and services. The trade unions were under siege from without (the government's anti-closed shop, anti-strike legislation) and from within (single union, no-strike agreements; inter-union job disputes). Britain in 1987 depended on mainland EC for almost 50 per cent of its entire exports. In 1972 this had been 33 per cent. Mainland EC accounted for 54 per cent of all UK imports in 1987 as against 36 per cent in 1972.

EC industrial change was symbolised in the form of company take-overs and mergers. In 1987 and 1988 these came big, strong and increasingly international. The Franco-British tie-up between CAP-Semametra-CGS in the computer systems field was one such. This was aimed at establishing a European company to rival the US majors like Martin Marietta.

Given the central 'increasing competition' thrust of the Single European Act, it is not surprising that the Commission intervened to scrutinise the largest merger moves. Their action was on top, quite naturally, of the investigations carried out by such national bodies as the British Monopolies and Mergers

Commission (MMC), the German Kartellamt and the French Competition Council. All had much to do. The latter, for instance, was deliberating in April 1988 whether:

* Beghin Say (the French No.1 sugar maker) and its Italian partner Ferruzzi should be allowed to hold a stake in the No.2 French sugar producer, St Louis and

* a joint venture between Colgate-Palmolive and Henkel of West Germany (two of the world's Big Four in washing powders, the others being Proctor & Gamble and Unilever) would lead to a dominant market position in the French market.

Whereas neither of these could be said to be capable of rousing protectionist passions unduly, one proposed take-over in 1988 did apparently do just that. It was the £88 million bid by Pearson (owner of the *Financial Times*) for France's leading financial daily, *Les Echos*. Despite the support of the latter's owner, Mme Jacqueline Beytout, the move was very strongly resisted by M Edouard Balladur, the French Finance Minister. Interestingly, it would have made Pearson (having just ingested the US' Addison Wesley) the fifth largest publisher in the world. The French government's objection was on grounds of foreign ownership. Twenty per cent of Pearson was, in fact, already owned by Rupert Murdoch's multi-national News Corporation, just one of whose range of owned newspapers was *The Times*.

The EC Commission was keen not only to supplement the role of national watchdogs but guard against distortion of competition in the EC-wide sense. Hence, the new guidelines for investigation it was proposing to the Council for Ministers in 1988 included scrutiny of any merger which:

* led to a combined company turnover of 1 billion ECU (£700m) or more

* involved, regardless of the size of the bidder, a target with annual sales of 500 million ECU or more.

If accepted, the guidelines would also have enabled the Commission to halt any merger which it thought, might inhibit competition or, on the other hand, to promote one if, despite the negative effects, the nature of world-wide competition warranted it.

Takeovers made by British Firms in	Jan-Mar 1987		Jan-Mar 1988	
	USA	EC	USA	EC
Number	57	25	98	47
Value: $ billion £ million	2.4	82	2.2	418

TABLE 7: TAKEOVER TRENDS?

There was another Commission power which was of great concern to member governments, its capacity (and willingness) to investigate state industry-support measures which were held to distort competition. There were three major interventions by the Commission in this sphere in 1987/8. The first was a study in respect of the planned de-nationalisation of Renault. This involved a French government write-off of £1.2 billion of the company's accumulated losses to the end of 1986 of almost £3 billion. The second covered British Airways' take-over of its competitor British Caledonian and resulted in the former's being subject to route restrictions not laid down in the MMC ruling. The third related to the announcement in 1988 of the takeover of the Rover Group by British Aerospace. In effect, the sale of the publicly-owned Rover was interpreted to be dependent on British government aid to the tune of a £1.1 billion write-off of losses (since 1974 what was the Rover Group had run up losses of £2.6 billion) and a grant-equivalent of £800 million to pay off bank debt and provide working capital.

The Commission study was aimed at finding whether this help could be interpreted as conferring an intolerable competition-distorting advantage. Interesting disclosures about so-called 'sweeteners' were made in late 1989 about this deal.

That the Commission had teeth was established beyond question when its enquiry into the British Government's sale of the British Leyland Bus & Truck Division (B&T) to DAF down-graded the Government's contribution to making it saleable from £750 million to £680 million. The privatisation of this division led to the creation of the Rover Group out of elements of the remaining car businesses.

It seemed beyond doubt that the Commission's work would also increase in scope since, according to *Acquisition Monthly* data, the number of EC mergers and take-overs had risen from 75 to 134 in number and from £425 million to £1,250 million over the two years to 1987.

FAIR'S FAIR

European leaders wished to usher in the Single European Market as a matter of urgency. Much of the rationale behind this was rooted in the global trade position after the first OPEC oil price rise in 1973. The competition between individual EC members and their larger and, in many areas, technologically more advanced rivals Japan and the USA was growing more intense at precisely the same time as the indebtedness and need for even more credit of lesser-developed countries was rising. Accompanying this disturbing trend was an apparently inexorable rise in the budgetary and trade deficits run by the USA and a parallel, almost commensurate, growth in Japan's trade surplus and its capability to finance overseas investments and provide trade credit. The interest rate and currency value instability produced by the combination of all these elements had much bearing on the confidence-shattering stock market crash of October 1987.

Against this backcloth all major trading nations fought desperately, according to their individual policy stances, to preserve industries, companies and jobs. At precisely the same time as the mid-'80s Uruguay round of GATT talks on measures to liberalise world trade were taking place at Punte del Este, protectionist feelings were running high in the industrial nations and hopelessness was growing in indebted nations (such as Mexico, Brazil, Poland). Their economies often appeared, from an industrial and/or agricultural production perspective, to be increasingly marginal. It was a time also when the ownership of, and ability to finance, new high-technology developments in products and processes was conferring enormously valuable advantages on some nations and some firms within them.

The EC, with its Single European Market of £320 million (larger than the USA and Japan combined), was embroiled in trading squabbles with the USA and Japan, just as these two were themselves taken up with bilateral protectionist arguments. Of these the most visible issues were:

(1) USA vs Japan

A strongly-supported Trade Bill passed through the US Congress in April 1988. It advocated tariff rises, quotas and bans specifically affecting Japanese high value-added, low-cost mass-produced consumer goods. Although President Reagan was thought likely to veto it, for other reasons, it was accompanied by a demand for increased access to the heavily-protected Japanese home market particularly in respect of beef and citrus fruit exports on which Japan had imposed quotas. Last minute concessions apparently ordered by the Japanese Prime Minister, Noboru Takeshita did not influence senators.

There was also apparent widespread concern in U.S. business circles about such factors as Japan's approach to targeting certain product sectors and seeking to establish world-wide unit cost and technology leadership in them The close strategic planning interlinkage between the corporate, banking and governmental sectors (MITI) and the pronounced level of cross-ownership of Japanese industrial shares, inhibited foreign (*Gaijin*) ownership and prevented the Nikkei Dow index from falling like its Wall Street counterpart in the 1987 share drop.

(2) Europe vs Japan

In a report entitled *Righting the Balance - A New Agenda for Euro-Japanese Trade* issued in August 1987, the Conservative Political Centre group spoke of the *dire* consequences of perpetuating the present Europe-Japan trade line-up. Even after 15 solid years of complaint the Japanese home market was 'virtually impenetrable' and Japan's overly-aggressive 'market domination' approach to trading was to be deplored. The report took special exception to what it called *screwdriver plants* set up to cope with markets into which the Japanese manufacturers could not directly import the 100 per cent finished product. Such assembly operations, which supplied only lower added-value local components and local labour, were not acceptable over the long haul. The authors went so far as to suggest a new 19 per cent tariff on a range of electronic products. So exasperated was the EC Commission on the issue of *screwdriver plants* that it called for anti-dumping duties on four Japanese typewriter manufacturers, Silver Reed, Sharp, Canon and Kyushu Matsushita, who between them had a 40 per cent share of the EC market.

(3) EC vs USA

Apart from what has been called the *pasta war*, hostility over the question of EC access for US cereal products, a major point of division between the EC and the USA was over the competition which the European 'plane-making consortium, Airbus Industrie, was giving the other world leaders, Boeing and McDonnell Douglas. Airbus, made up of France's Aerospatiale (37.9 per cent share), Deutsche Airbus (37.9 per cent), British Aerospace (20 per cent) and Spain's CASA (4.2 per cent), was heavily criticised at the start of 1988 for managerial shortcomings in the co-ordination of manufacturing and marketing operations on its product range, the A300-340 series. To compound these problems, it had to face a falling dollar and unremitting criticism from the Americans about governmental subsidies.

Perhaps Britain could not afford to complain too loudly because of the huge level of U.S. and Japanese in-bound investment that had been made in recent years. Over $4 billion had been spent by Japan alone on takeovers and establishing new manufacturing plants, like Nissan (cars) and JVC (consumer electronics). After the USA and Germany, Japan was the largest overseas investor in Britain. According to DTI figures, the level had more than doubled over the period 1980/1 – 1986/7. So far as jobs created are concerned, Japanese industrialists invested in 22 projects in 1986 which created 2499 new jobs (Invest in Britain Bureau data).

To avoid the EC tariff applicable to goods manufactured outside the EC, Japanese companies setting up in the EC needed to input a statutory 60 per cent local components into their products. This was calculated by comparing the cost of the local components used with the ex-works cost of the product.

The Japanese view was that its British investment would soar. Thus Kazuo Chiba, newly-appointed Japanese ambassador to Britain:

With 1992 in mind, Britain has come to be regarded as the spring-board for opportunity in Europe. What Japanese leaders see in the UK are the adaptability, high productivity and relative advantage in cost of your labour force - historically dependable and now proving to be very responsive.

Certainly, the excellent performance of the British economy and the death of the myth of Britain as a strike-prone casualty ward for industry have combined to make the UK a first on the client list of Japanese companies eager to expand overseas. [12]

* * * * * * * * * * * * * * * * * * *

APPENDIX 1: SELECTED STATISTICS

COUNTRY	A	B	C	D	E	F	G	H	I
USA			13.61	4195	17.3	123	1.39	140	42
JAPAN			11.02	1520	16.1	132	2.23	116	38
W. GERMANY	68	2.83	15.33	781	14.6	107	1.98	121	
ITALY	92	1.83		673	10.5	101	1.19	216	
FRANCE	163	1.91	11.57	670	13.0	105	.54	169	
UK	57	1.8	8.91	655	9.6	116	1.4	155	6.1

NOTES:

A = No. of complaints against individual EC countries in 1986 for possible infringement of EC rules [Implementing the European Internal Market, A. Butt, Royal Institute of International Affairs, 1987]

B = New car registrations in 1986 [M] [D.R.I. Europe]

C = 1987 Industrial Labour Rates in $/hour [Salomon Bros and US Dept of Labour]. Note S. Korea's hourly labour rate was $1.51/hour

D = GDP in $ billion for 1986 [OECD]

E = GDP ['000.$ per capita] in 1986 [OECD]

F = Index of industrial production in Dec '87 based on 1980 = 100 [Eurostat & Financial Times 7/3/88]

G = S. Africa's imports [$ billion] for Jan-July '87 [EMF] from listed countries

H = Index of World Retail Prices for November 1987 [1980 = 11] Eurostat & Financial Times 25/1/88

I = % share of turnover of world's 16 largest stockmarkets held by capitals of these countries in 1987. [FT 22/1/87]. Note that Japan's trade surplus rose from $1.5 billion in 1980 to $92 billion in 1986

NOTES & REFERENCES

1 *Firms Must Face up to the Challenge or Fail*, says CBI's Derek Harris, *The Times*, 24/3/88.
   Note: the significant conclusions in the 1987 report of the British Advisory, Conciliation and Arbitration Service that:
   (a) British managers are now increasingly questioning working practices and the whole issue of trade union recognition.
   (b) The percentage of employees belonging to trade unions had fallen from 55 per cent in 1979 to about 40 per cent in 1987.
   (c) secret ballots before any decision on industrial action were now well-established.

2 'Take-over Risk in EEC', Robert Matthews, *The Times* 23/3/88.
   Note: in this connection,
   (a) the enormous stress laid in the consumer product field on the importance of 'global' brands i.e. those like Mars Bars or Kit Kat with an actual or potential Europe-wide 'consumer franchise'
   (b) the aggressive nature of the European expansion strategy pursued by UK advertising firm WCRS to buy stakes in the French Belier & SGGMD groups aspiring to become larger than its rival Saatchi & Saatchi.

3 *The Times* 30/3/88. Note also
   (a) that 70 of the 300 steps had already been agreed by the end of March 1988 by the Council.
   (b) the precise wording of Article 99 of the Single European Act. That is:
   the Council of Ministers shall, acting unanimously on a proposal from the Commission and after consulting the European parliament, adopt provision for the harmonisation of legislation concerning turn-over taxes, excise duties and other forms of indirect taxation to the extent that such harmonisation is necessary to ensure the establishment and the functioning of the internal market within the time limit laid down.
   The wording was agreed by Mrs Thatcher at the Luxembourg summit in December, 1975.
   (c) the gradual increase in the power and authority of the Parliament from a purely deliberative and advisory body to one with capacity to influence (by, for example, delaying or stubborn insistence on modification) the proposals which the Commission puts up to the Council. Past instances of this, based on 1975 change, include the rejection of the Commission's budget proposals in 1979 and 1984.

4 *EPR*, Treasury, February 1988

5 *The Independent* 19/3/88. Note also
   (a) the estimate, by Derek Mercer (*Rural England*, Queen Anne Press, 1988) that Britain no longer needs an area equal to the size of Devon and Derbyshire for

food production.

(b) that the Animal Biotechnology Company (ABC) of Cambridge (*The Sunday Times* 1/5/88) estimate that, with the bio-technological technique of embryo transfer, the average natural lifetime calf production of a cow will increase from 3.5 to 17.5. The technique involves carrying the embryo to gestation in surrogate mothers.

(c) that the EC beef mountain in May 1988 weighed 686,000 tonnes; that of butter equalled 880,000 tonnes.

(d) that the 1988 EC Third World aid budget was £1.4 billion, of which the UK contribution was £223 million. One scheme, STABEX, was the target of special British government hostility (*The Times* 2/5/88). This was a scheme designed to protect countries in Africa, the Caribbean and the Pacific against unforeseen falls in their earnings from the sale of commodity produce.

6 *The Times* 6/2/88

7 *The Times* 22/3/88

8 'EEC Secures the Right to set the British Taxes', *The Times*, 24/2/88. The European Monetary System was a mechanism for full currency management under which currencies taking part in the Exchange rate Mechanism have fixed rates against the European Currency Unit (ECU). The rate was regularly re-aligned at bargaining sessions of European Finance Ministers.

9 'Cockfield Hits at Minister's failure to Grasp EEC Plan', Colin Narbrugh, *The Times* 11/12/87.

10 *Europe's Domestic Market*, Polkmans J., Winters A & Wallace H, Institute of International Affairs, April 1988.

11 Letter to *The Times*, Ben Patterson MEP for Kent West, 11/12/87

12 'Japan to Widen UK Investment for 1992 Trade', *The Sunday Times,* 3/4/88. Note that:

   (a) Japan is the world's largest creditor nation, foreign investor and holder of foreign currency reserves.

   (b) Britain's trade deficit in 1986 amounted to £1.6 billion

   (c) Japan's government debt (as percentage of GNP) rose from 32 per cent to 42 per cent in the period from 1981 to 1986.

   (d) Japan passed a new Labour Law at the start of 1988. Its provisions included a reduction in the working week from 48 to 40 hours and an increase in the length of paid annual holiday from six to ten days.
   Note also the launch by Prime Minister Takeshita during his visit to London in May 1988 of Japan's 'International Co-operation Initiative' involving increasing domestic spending reduced interest rates and a large rise in its Third World aid. Mrs Thatcher in her talks with Noboru Takeshita wished (*The Times* 5/5/88) to clear up 'the unfinished business' of Japan's tax on imported Scotch whisky and the number of seats available to British securities firms on the Tokyo exchange.

EUROPEAN SPACE AGENCY

Abstract:

The European Space Agency served throughout the 1980s and 1990s as one of the touchstones for European collaboration in a world under increasing technological domination by the USA. Indeed, by 1999, Britain was firmly established as a paid-up member (contributing 16% of the £1.8 billion or 2.7 billion euros over the period 1999-2003) and had joined in projects like Mars Express and the Earth Observation Science Programme. But membership remained always a challenge for the British and it had not participated in the Space Station project in the 1990s.

This case addresses the issue of Britain's threatened withdrawal from the European Space Agency, for reasons of economy and hostility towards the French plans for ESA, in 1988. The treatment of this question of ESA membership and that of HOTOL - a British breakthrough in space research - symbolised for many commentators the extent to which Britain was, in future, to be in the first or in the third division of global high technology work and a fully paid-up member of the new Europe, or not. British businesses were less concerned with symbolism than with the loss of lucrative contracts if the withdrawal went ahead.

Questions:

Do you accept the view that, as Robert Rhodes James put it, there was a danger that, if Britain did opt out of ESA, it was destined to become a "division three country"?

What would be the consequences for British companies if the government, did , in fact, opt out?

How powerful is the British government's reasoning on this issue.

Case Timing: 1988

GOOD EUROPEANS?

Our poor scientists, when they go to meetings now with other scientists, wear dark glasses and false beards in case they are recognised as being British. The atmosphere is really very bad in an area where we spent the past two or three years working up an influence that I think was in the very best of the national interest. The Europeans are quite puzzled by it, even more so than they usually are. [1]

Thus Roy Gibson, former Director-General of the European Space Agency (ESA) and, for the comparatively short time from job acceptance to resignation, Head of the British National Space Centre (BNSC). Doyen of European spacework and an able, long-serving administrator not given to exaggeration, he was speaking of the impact on his colleagues in ESA of the seeming about-turn that had taken place over the two previous years in Britain's policy towards space and, in particular, towards ESA's plans for its research and commercial exploitation.

Especially significant in this were, of course, the refusal by the Conservative Government led by Prime Minister Margaret Thatcher to accept the space plan put forward by BNSC and the subsequent critical policy statements made by the Secretary of State for Trade & Industry, Lord Young, and his Minister, Kenneth Clarke. These indicated that the Government now saw its role in this field as a decidedly minor one compared with that it foresaw for British private sector industry. The warmth of the UK relationship with ESA - an agency created and funded by 13 European governments and charged with independently planning and executing agreed space research and development missions on their behalf - had been boosted by the expansionist deal struck in Rome in late 1985 by Mrs Thatcher's envoy, Industry Minister Geoffrey (later Sir) Pattie. So the onset of such coolness in mid 1988 was viewed by some as politically incomprehensible. Especially as the awarding of contracts to European space firms for ESA work was strictly in accordance with the level of each government's funding of ESA.

Même si nos partenaires ne nous suivent pas, la France, grace à Hermès, enverra des hommes dans l'espace dès 1997. Personne ne doute d'ailleurs que nos partenaires suivront, et que l'ESA avalisera Hermes at européanisera l'aventure.

EXHIBIT 1 : ALLEZ FRANCE!
Source : President Mitterand, *Le Nouvel Observateur* 14-20/6/85
Translation, note 2 on page 42.
Note: please refer to the references for translations of French and German exhibits [2]

Mrs Thatcher's stance was regarded as highly questionable by some British industrialists. They saw lucrative contracts for ESA space-work slipping from their competent grasp and going willy-nilly to their mainland counterparts and, as a consequence, an alleged all-too-damaging erosion of Britain's long-run commercial prospects. One such was Peter Conchie, Director of Business Development at British Aerospace. Referring to ESA's programmes, he said:

It is very clear that they are going to drive technology through so that, by the end of the century, we will have something rather akin to an industrial revolution occurring. Now, either the UK is in it or it's not and that will have a big effect on the standard of living in the early part of next century.[3]

Could the British Government be persuaded to change its view on participating in ESA's growth plans? And, if it did, would the European governments making up ESA accept such a clear volte-face in the position adopted in February 1988? And what would it do about HOTOL, the technology-breakthrough spaceplane conceived by British Aerospace's Alan Bond, which promised much as a low-cost satellite launcher? Would it capitalise on the successful "proof of concept" studies and back, with a large volume of public money, further work on its power system, the revolutionary Rolls Royce RB 545 engine? Or would it, failing that, declassify what had been one of Britain's tightest-kept secrets and allow HOTOL development by the private sector in Europe, if not America. As of March 1988, these were burning questions...

STONY GROUND?

France's space agency - La Centre Nationale d'Etudes Spatiales (CNES) - was set up in 1961. Prestigiously situated near the Pompidou Centre in Paris, the CNES had been an inspiration for other national models like the Italian and the German. Feeding on France's defence position as a nuclear unilateralist and non-member of NATO, her industry had led Europe in the development of rockets. All the more so once Harold Macmillan's Conservative Government had cancelled the British Blue Streak programme (for economic as opposed to technology reasons, since it was technically highly successful) in the early 1960s and had, effectively, withdrawn from the space race. Thus, not only did the huge French state-owned Aerospatiale company, as a leading contractor for the ARIANE series of rockets, enjoy a European monopoly in the satellite launching field but its pioneering achievements also permitted, if not encouraged, French ambitions to the point of speaking of leading a drive for European 'autonomy' in space. It was in this context that the French plan to incorporate their HERMES minishuttle within the ESA programme (see Appendix 1) needed to be viewed.

Asked whether Britain, as a key ESA member, should support the concept of spatial independence bound up with the HERMES man-in-space endeavour, Roy Gibson declared:

> *Some of my best friends have second-class status... It doesn't worry me tremendously. We can't all have first-class status. One has to go for a logic in the thing... I wouldn't mortgage the future of our space programmes to be 7 or 8 or 9 years in getting a few men into space earlier. It's a false economy.*[4]

This notwithstanding, it had to be admitted that it was French élan and commitment that underlay the ESA advances that had begun in Rome in 1985. Here Geoffrey Pattie, with the Prime Minister's backing, had presented a powerful case for British participation in the programme based on an increase in our contribution to ESA and the establishment of the BNSC. It was, he said, *politically unthinkable* for Britain not to be involved.[5]

The Government's call for a British space plan was a real step forward. It gave the newly-appointed Roy Gibson, brought out of retirement (after directing ESA) on the recommendation of Mrs Thatcher's chief scientific advisor, a huge opportunity. This he used, he said, to address not only each of Britain's main space programmes but also, by looking across the board, to 'spot-target' areas of technology to really seek to develop in world markets and to attempt a balance between ESA and domestic programmes. In this, he recalled, he sought to change the previous philosophy, whereby what was paid to ESA was seen as *a complete absolution* of our obligations, and to actually influence ESA's choice of plans. Not, of course, that the French could be criticised for dictating the latter, he said

> *We should not in the least blame the French for having taken the initiative. There simply wasn't any other initiative around.*

Some of the UK's European partners welcomed the impetus for change which such developments implied. Especially the Germans. For Ernst Högenauer, Engineering VP of Germany's largest spacework contractor Messerschmidt-Bölkow-Blohm, it carried the hope of more balance in work-sharing. *I am fed up* he declared with much feeling *that I am always a second-hand 'people' ... that I am always a supplier of equipment and sub-systems.*[7]

Other industrialists on the European mainland (like the Toulouse-based Matra organisation) plainly might have been less charitable, since more British competition would have meant fewer ESA contracts for them. However, they could draw some comfort from Roy Gibson's assessment that:

The entrance fee for the big league gets bigger as the game goes on. There comes a point when it is better not to go in at all if you cannot put a certain minimum amount in. You get less and less proportionately as you reduce your expenditure.[8]

And from his concern to avoid the indecision and indecisiveness that led, in his view, not to *an integrated space plan* such as the BNSC put forward but to *narrow one-by-one decisions* which did not seem capable of giving a sound return.

CAPTAIN OVERBOARD!

Those seeking such comfort would not have been well-pleased by the rejection by the Prime Minister and her ministerial team, newly appointed after her substantial 1987 election victory, of the BNSC Space Plan. In her statement of the 23rd July 1987, she firmly turned down the proposal embodied in the Plan for a virtual tripling of the country's space spending from £112m (of which 80 per cent was spent on ESA projects) to £300m per year. This would have meant, had the Plan been accepted, a high level of participation in the ESA's COLUMBUS programme, a contribution to the US' SPACE STATION programme and heavy backing for HOTOL.

Industry has been awaiting the Government's decision on funding the space plan for nearly a year and the prevarication is now creating serious problems for effective industrial R & D. The long uncertainty over funding makes resource and financial planning at best a difficult task and one which is wasteful of Britain's highly trained manpower in this demanding sector of high technology. Britain's credibility in the ESA is being seriously damaged at a time when Britain should be strongly influencing European space policy.

EXHIBIT 2 : "TAKE A LETTER.."
Source : Letter to *The Times*, dated the 20th July 1987, from
Dr Raymond Harris, Software Sciences Ltd, Farnborough

Perhaps it was the Plan's apparent shortfall in economic analysis that caused the rejection. Certainly, the US' APOLLO programme was argued beforehand on the well-attested basis of a $7 return for every dollar of investment, and justified subsequently by reference to such estimable technological advances as non-scratch sunglasses, cordless tools and robotic pigs. Or perhaps it was the replacement of Sir Geoffrey Pattie as Minister in the Department of Trade &

Industry with a colleague who was, in Pattie's words, more agnostic about space, Kenneth Clarke.

During Prime Minister's Question Time in the Commons, Mrs Thatcher amplified her statement. It was a terse addition. *We spend* she declared *some £4.5 billion on R&D. We are not able to find any more resources without switching funds from one research or technology development to another. We feel we cannot make the switch. We shall continue our subscription to ESA but, at present, we are not able to find any more money.* [9] Minister Kenneth Clarke added the rider that all such investments needed comparison in terms of their contribution to Britain's economic performance and called for an increase in the level of private sector backing for them.

The Government had, in the view of Guardian commentator Peter Large, refused to accept *a top table gamble* and had taken a decision which flatly contradicted the *bright image of a logical long-term structure* for work in space so recently created. [10]

The turmoil created in the ranks of British industrialists was no whit reduced by Roy Gibson's resignation on the 4th August 1987. He was aged 63 and had been head of BNSC since its establishment in November 1985. Sir Geoffrey Pattie blamed it on Britain's *abdication from space and.. loss of nerve.* In the Government's scenario, he said, *short-term considerations must prevail at all costs.* [11]

If the Government thought that their refusal to back the BNSC would attract much support, they were to be sadly mistaken. The outcry over the Gibson resignation simply added to the feeling some Ministers must have had of being blockaded. Mrs Thatcher herself was attacked for not recognising the importance of *a strong science base* to Britain, a paradox since she was Britain's first scientist Prime Minister. It looked, as Labour spokesman Bryan Gould pointed out, *a pretty sad story.* [12]

It certainly looked peculiar. The ESA Council meeting scheduled for November 1987 was looming; inescapable decisions would have to be addressed at this meeting regarding the size of the ESA programme and its constituents, and involving a possible budget increase of 70 per cent. At the Rome meeting in 1985 the UK had agreed to a similar increase in the-then budget, thus enabling development work leading directly to the present choice of programme!

Another commentator, Peter Beaumont, referred to the *anger* of some British companies involved and spoke of the rejection of the plan as *a further body blow to the UK space programme after 20 years of vacillation by successive governments.* [13] He was also concerned at the possible knock-on effect on the Anglo-Russian space deal signed by the Prime Minister in early 1987.

Could there be any detriment to, for instance, the British Institute of Space Bio-medicine which had been set up as a joint venture, apparently at Mrs Thatcher's instigation? It was an issue of more than academic interest in the light of the *space medicine* research accord reached in 1985 between CNES, Aerospatiale and the French pharmaceutical manufacturers Rhone Poulenc and Roussel Uclaf.

> *I am sad to be leaving something unfinished. If there is no increase in funding, you do not need a British National Space Centre.[14] They, therefore, do not need someone of the rank of Deputy Secretary to run it.* [15]

EXHIBIT 3 : ROY GIBSON - SADDER & WISER

It was not only from the political left that criticism came. Many shared the view of the U.K. Industrial Space Committee that Britain would *lose out* unless it invested more in space technology; the pronouncement by Peter Wilmore, Chairman of the Space Science Board, that there were *no advantages to be gained in economics or efficiency*, unless BNSC played a broadened role within ESA, won wide support from lobbyists.[16]

The media were almost universally hostile. *The Times*, in a biting editorial on the 6th August 1987, entitled *No Place in Space*, spoke of *the big step backwards* that Britain was taking and the *embarrassment and despair* that Roy Gibson's resignation would cause to the scientific community. It bewailed the fact that just £200m of extra space spending would have assured us of a realistic role in the £1.25 billion COLUMBUS project and stated that *on this week's news...Britain's exclusion from the twenty-first century is already being mapped. The Financial Times'* editor contended that it was *difficult to make sense* of the government's approach which he described as *muddle-headed.* [17]

Despair? A strong term to use, but an apt one, at least in respect of the reaction to Roy Gibson's departure of Joerg Feustel-Buech, ESA's Director of Space Transportation. *We have lost* he declared *one of the captains of the space boat. The resignation is a poor sign for the cause of European unity in space.* [18]

BACK IN BUSINESS

Would the Government change its mind in the face of such a damning response? That was a key concern for senior executives at British Aerospace,[19] Marconi, Rolls Royce, Logica[20] and other leading British spacework companies.

Their hopes were strongly boosted by the successful launch from Kourou in French Guiana of a satellite-carrying ARIANE 3 on the 15th September 1987. It was a major comeback after the failure of the last rocket launch. Then, on the 31st May 1986, an upper third stage cryogenic motor had failed to ignite at blast-off. ESA was back in business, and with a vengeance since ARIANE had an order backlog of no less than 46 satellites to place in geosynchronous orbit over the coming five years.

For Professor Reimar Lüst, ESA Director-General, this period would give *a breathing space* allowing intensive R & D to consolidate an *autonomous* European space technology.[21] A possibility, certainly, but it was undeniable that there was big competition in the offing. The USSR, for instance, had just test-launched their enormous ENERGIA rocket whose payload capacity, at 270 tonnes, was equal to nine American Shuttles. Indeed, Glavcosmos, its space agency, was beginning to offer, much to the consternation of the U.S. State Department, a low-cost satellite launching facility. *The Times* remarked sagely:

If only half the potential of Energia is realised, the Soviets will be in a commanding position to embark on the large-scale exploitation of space. For Mrs Thatcher to maintain that the private sector, especially one so small as that in Britain, is sufficient to keep us in the business of space, is to defy the economics of space.[22]

The United States, with their SHUTTLE still grounded after the Challenger disaster, were contemplating the prospects outlined in the Ride Report [23] on the future of the US space programme. This report focused critical attention on what it saw as Washington's relinquished space leadership vis-a-vis the USSR For example, the minimal amount of earth-to-orbit transportation and long-distance manned spaceflights undertaken by NASA since the MARINER and VIKING missions or the vacating of SKYLAB in 1974 as compared with the USSR's use of eight orbiting space stations since the mid 1970s, the most recent being MIR. The report, from the US's first woman astronaut, Dr Sally Ride, also fore-shadowed the planned re-introduction to service of the SHUTTLE in June 1989 and its use in carrying out satellite launching for a projected Mission to Planet Earth, involving topography and vegetation mapping.

Despite the optimistic tone adopted by Dr Ride, the cost of space-work was known to be under close scrutiny in America. So much so that it was revealed that the Senate Appropriations Committee had cut $8.8m from the budget available to NASA in 1988/9 for the SPACE STATION programme. Admittedly small beer in terms of the giant $12 billion budget allocated overall to this, but still indicative.

The Germans, too, were beginning to get somewhat anxious about the rising cost of the package of decisions that awaited approval at the ESA Conference in

November. They were concerned at the downward revision in the HERMES payload capacity relative to its spiralling cost and the fact that this had underlined to the ESA's Coherence Task Force the need for two additional projects: ICE (Interconnecting Element) and LOVE (European Logistic Vehicle).

Still the pressure on the British Government mounted. At the Belfast Conference of the British Association for the Advancement of Science, held in late August 1987, calls for change came thick and fast. One particularly notable one was from no less a personage than the Astronomer Royal: he *had difficulty*, he said, in understanding the Government's decision.[24]

Media speculation that the *crisis* [25] facing Britain's space industry was causing concern in Washington also fuelled debate. It was held that U.K. manufacturers might not, after all and despite their stated requirements, be able to contribute to the POLAR PLATFORM section of the COLUMBUS project.

Von den technischen Schwierigkeiten und den politischen Querelen abgesehen, sind auch die Kostenentwürfe für eine eigene bemannte Raumfahrt der Europäer in den vergangenen Monaten drastisch gestiegen. Als der deutsche Beitrag noch in einstelligen Milliarden-betragen beziffert wurde, stellte sich Forschungsminister Heinz Riesen-huber schützend vor seinen Haushalt. Diese Summe könne er nicht abzweigen, weil sonst andere Forschungsgebiete Schaden erleiden würden.. Noch weiss niemand, wo die notwendigen Gelder herkommen sollen. Translation note 23 on page 42.

EXHIBIT 4 : NOT ENOUGH MARKS TO GO ROUND?
Source : Europa im Weltraum, Gunter Paul, *Frankfurter Allgemeine Zeitung*, 17/9/87

For the ESA's D-G Professor Reimar Lüst matters were also coming to a head. Interviewed after the ARIANE launch, he declared testily:

Britain has to choose between dependency on American technology or helping establish European autonomy in space technology. Britain is not needed any more on its present terms of membership. It would be a tragedy if Britain retired from the European space programme. But the UK has to recognise that it has to contribute its fair share to the European effort. [26]

In this he was making reference to the fact that the French had paid 60 per cent of the cost of developing the ARIANE facility, the Germans 20 per cent and the UK three per cent.

Whilst Roy Gibson himself dismissed speculation about American worries as *a load of nonsense*, he indicated that he shared the concern of the UK

Industrial Space Committee about the future prospects for ESA contracts that could be awarded, on the basis of development work already done, to Ferranti (guidance systems), British Aerospace (satellite cradles), GEC (avionics), Westland (new space materials) and Logica (software).

British Aerospace spoke for itself. On the 27th September 1987 a company spokesman announced:

The UK cannot afford to delay any longer. As long-established industries decline and N. Sea oil revenues fall we must emulate America, Japan and much of the rest of Europe. The UK must invest wholeheartedly in space taking advantage today of its technology advances and preparing for the new range of industries it will provide. [27]

On the first of October 1987 it was announced that the Government's funding of space ventures would be investigated by the new Advisory Council on Science and Technology. Under the chairmanship of the chairman of Rolls Royce, Sir Francis Tombs, the Council would study a wide range of submissions.

A TIME AND A PLACE...

In early October eminent scientists gathered in Brighton for the 38th International Aeronautical Federation Conference. Few can have been prepared for the hammer blow that Industry Minister Kenneth Clarke aimed at ESA when, in a TV interview, he called it *a highly expensive club* with *an overambitious programme.* [28] Nor for the flat rejection he gave, despite the forthcoming ACOST enquiry, of any possibility of a rise in the UK space budget and, hence, of more public spending on HOTOL. And this at a Conference honouring *Thirty Years of Progress in Space*!

Alan Bond was aghast at the news, coming as it did on the heels of the most recent successful HOTOL tests. Referring to the project's *Most Secret* classification, he said *I have been in prison for the past 5 years with this. If there is no more Government funding, I will take my experience elsewhere. My first step will be to Europe to try for support, probably from the French and the Germans. I am not going to stand by and watch the Government sit on something which is going to introduce a modern industrial revolution comparable to that of 150 years ago.* [31]

HOTOL

A radical project for a 'Horizontal Take-off and Landing' space plane. At its unveiling in 1985, it represented a first-order, unknown-technology breakthrough. Its capacity to fly at sub-sonic and hypersonic speed stems from the engine brilliantly conceived by its inventor Alan Bond. It carried a top-rate security classification, which, unless relaxed by the Government, precludes the inventor from developing it outside named contractors Rolls Royce and British Aerospace.

HOTOL promised to be, it is claimed, a relatively inexpensive satellite launcher/retriever and a highly cost-effective successor to ARIANE 5 as it did not have to be man-rated.

SÄNGER

The same sort of concept as HOTOL but using a different technology approach as did, incidentally, the US version - ORIENT EXPRESS - and its Japanese cousin. British Aerospace has a technical discussion deal with SANGER's manufacturer - Messerschmidt-Bolkow Blohm. [29]

TABLE 1 : EUROPEAN SPACEPLANES

Note: According to Dr Koelle, MBB's Director of Advanced Programmes, the estimated development costs of HOTOL (£6 billion) and SANGER (£10 billion) make it unlikely that they will both be developed. [30]

Again the editors fumed. *The Times* spoke of the Government's wearing *the mantle of Ned Ludd* and having to bear *the odium of Britons* for having turned its back on space.[32] *The Guardian* lambasted what it called a *myopic* decision and said it would be understandable if Britain were *the Poor Man of Europe*. But it was not. In fact, the paper wrote, *the Treasury's coffers are awash with money. The City is now predicting that the Treasury will make us the only country in surplus this year. What is holding things up is not money but the Prime Minister's stubborn belief that only private sector projects are any good. Having privatised the British economy, she now wants to privatise space.* It was, said the editorial, *a classic case where public pump-priming money is essential.* [33]

An opportunity for a somewhat softer line appeared when Kenneth Clarke's colleague, Junior Minister John Butcher, addressed the Conference. He picked the *British Day for Space* for his contribution, which not only re-iterated the previous line of argument, but also made clear that:

We don't think we are alone in this. We are saying publicly what other governments are saying privately. The time has come for Europe to review its space activities against likely future demands of the market. [34]

The main objection the Government had was, he pointed out, the HERMES shuttle. The estimated development cost of this had risen over the period 1986/7 from £1.5 billion to £4.5 billion; nothing if not a movable feast. Michael Heseltine, Secretary of State in Mrs Thatcher's previous Government, entered the fray. He took a broader and entirely contrary view:

A decision to give up a key role in the ESA is much more than a decision about the efficacy of an international quango. It is a statement about our attitude to Europe. The industrial consequences of failing to follow ESA are incalculable. [35]

As if to underline the point, a former US Defence Adviser and now President of the Institute for Space and Security Studies, Dr Robert Bowman warned against the UK's counting on getting rich contracts from President Reagan's Strategic Defence Initiative (Star Wars). Indeed, he stated, Europe and Canada had so far only won bids worth £53m out of the £2,650m worth of contracts awarded. The government so far as he was concerned was in danger of *shooting itself in the foot.* [36]

RE-CROSSING THE RUBICON?

What was to be the effect of this litany of complaint on Ministers' judgements? Not a lot, if Kenneth Clarke's performance at Question Time in the Commons on the 28th October 1987 was anything to go by:

*Mr Ernest Ross, Dundee West, Labour
Japan is considering increasing its quota of spending on space from 120 billion yen to 400 billion yen, with a further target to raise spending to 600 billion yen by the turn of the century. It would be silly for Mr Clarke to go to the space agency meeting on November 9 and 10 with such a low-spending programme.

*Mr Clarke
When I go to the space agency meeting at the Hague I shall explain that Britain wishes to play a constructive role in the agency but that we think projects should be related to financial, economic and scientific returns.

*Mr Gerald Bermingham, St Helens S., Labour
Unless we invest in the European programme, we shall not retain the scientists and engineers we trained in this country because the opportunities will be found in America, Europe and elsewhere.

*Mr Clarke
We encourage and have to maintain the undoubted lead which the industrial and scientific community has here, particularly for in-stance in space satellites. We shall continue to be members of the space agency but wish to question the

objective of HERMES, to get a European manned presence in space by the end of the century. In British industry there is real doubt about its commercial worth. [37]

Nor if we consider the letter from Julian Farrel (Kenneth Clarke's Private Secretary) to the House of Common's Committee which was preparing a report on the Government's space policy. In this letter he referred to the result of the ACOST review, that the Government should either modestly increase its subscription to ESA or, in effect, think of pulling out, and strongly reiterated the Government's refusal to increase their spending. This must have given the Committee food for serious thought, especially when coupled with Roy Gibson's own evidence. On the threshold of a new job as Special Adviser to the Director-General of INMAST, the marine satellite body, he had indicated to the Committee that the present approach was the *worst of all possible worlds* but that he himself did not support HERMES, having tried for the previous 18 months to try to get ESA to *tone down* its programme. In his view, it was no more than *a stop-gap* project to get *two men and a sandwich* into space for £6 billion. [38]

As the appointed day for the Hague ESA Council meeting approached, media and industry forecasts of any positive movement in the British government's spending position looked increasingly pessimistic. The auguries were soundly-based.

A report by Professor Keith Pavitt and Mr Pari Patel of Sussex University's Science Policy Research Unit showed that British firms were falling behind their foreign competitors in R & D spending, the low spot being micro-electronics. Indeed, the corporate leaders in Britain in semi-conductors, computers and image-sound equipment were foreign-owned. A figure of £3 billion on R & D spending would, in their view, be needed to restore the international parity.[39] Such expenditure was vital in the view of Dr John Mulvey (Secretary of the 'Save British Science' Campaign). *We must* he said *increase competitiveness in a high technology world if Britain is not to be reduced to the level of a third world economy, based on tourism and the supply of cheap labour for the assembly of goods designed.. elsewhere.*[40] An essential element in Britain's approach - apart, that is, from the urgent need for increases in Government spending on R & D pressed for by Association President, Sir Kenneth Durham, and Dr Mulvey who specified an increase to 2.5 per cent of GDP - was spelled out by speaker Dr Trevor Pinch, a York University sociologist. He called for the abandonment of what he referred to as the *Thatcher Model of Science - rigid, mechanistic* and solely concerned with *machines, manpower and money.*[41]

EXHIBIT 5: - VIEWS FROM THE 1987 B.A.A.S. CONFERENCE

GOING DUTCH

At the Hague the British side was completely on its own. In what *The Guardian* correspondent [42] defined as *a war of words* between Kenneth Clarke and his opposite French number Alain Madelin, the meeting was later described as *extremely friendly* by the former (43), the British Minister called point-blank for a freeze on any new work and a thorough review of ESA's aims. Alone among the 13 governments making up the ESA Council, the British refused to sign the plan to increase ESA's budget by 70 per cent. Possibly adding British insult to French injury, he labelled HERMES *an expensive frolic*, adding:

We are no longer in a space race but in a competition in technology, commercial exploitation and scientific discovery.[44]

As if to counter Roy Gibson's own description of the Hague meeting, *disastrous*, Kenneth Clarke also spoke of the possibility of creating another form of British space agency, this time with a significant equity stake.

On his return to the House of Commons the Industry Minister faced a hostile audience. He had, said Labour spokesman Bryan Gould in a striking piece of anatomical imagery, returned *with his tail between his legs and a flea in his ear*: the outcome was *the worst possible news for the 300 UK firms involved in space*. The attitude expressed as the Hague was described as *a prime example of Thatcherism in action: anti-investment, anti-scientist and characterised by short-term considerations.* [45] From Robert Rhodes James, Conservative MP for Cambridge, came the argument that the Government was wholly wrong to accept a situation in which *Britain was to become a division-three country.*[46]

Was Kenneth Clarke abashed by such attacks and by inferences that he had somehow mis-read the Hague line-up? Not a bit. He rounded on his detractors with an attacking speech. This laid down that, firstly, the budgetary increase called for by the ESA plan was equivalent to the NHS's building a dozen new hospitals per year and, secondly, that HERMES would achieve no more than the US had done twenty years before, save at enormous cost. The programme suffered from grandiose ambitions. Lastly he pointed out that we should not be prepared to join in an ESA project for an autonomous EUROPEAN SPACE PLATFORM in the event that the negotiations over ESA's Columbus contribution to the US' own programme were to founder.[47] In the event, these did not and a mutually satisfactory deal was signed by ESA and NASA in March 1988.

From Mr Claus Toksvig, MEP for Denmark, (European Democrat [KF])
Sir, ... European integration is not helped by the attitude of the British Government to the future of space exploration.

The European Space Agency is not a Community institution; but its immensely practical and professional effort since its inception has made Europe a space power fully competitive with other, major space users like the Unites States and the USSR. In some fields, notably the placement of satellites in geosynchronous orbit, ESA is the world leader.

For these reasons it was disappointing to see Great Britain pull out of future projects like the next generation launcher (ARIANE 5), the COLUMBUS space platform and the HERMES spacecraft.

The negotiating technique of Mr. Kenneth Clarke, while crystal clear, seems to suggest that Mr Dale Carnegie wrote his book 'How to Win Friends and Influence People' to no avail.

EXHIBIT 6 : TO SEE OURSELVES
Source :*The Times* 20/11/87

The effects on industry of the decision not to sign the ESA space plan can be imagined. The very notion that all the preparatory work done by potential contractors such as GEC Avionics and Singer Link Miles would have to be shipped to their mainland competitors (who would thus reap the ultimate success), was a bitter pill. It was one thing, declared E. Berks Conservative MP Andrew McKay, not to back the HERMES plan to put *a French midget astronaut* [48] in space but quite another to act as the Government had done.

FINIS?

Further political criticism came - to add weight to industrial grumbles - in the trenchant report 'UK Space Policy' produced by the Space Sub-committee of the House of Lords Select Committee on Science and Technology. Apart from disliking the current position on the BNSC's space plan and its funding, the report advocated support for the COLUMBUS and ARIANE 5 projects and recommended that ESA backing be sought for HOTOL. An increase to £200m in Government space spending was strongly advocated.[49] Sir Geoffrey Pattie added a further contribution by slating the Government's economic approach. This was in essence a potent compound of anti-inflationary control of the money supply, tight restriction in the rise in public spending, reduction in the level of public sector activity through privatisation/ deregulating and tax reduction. It was one which had been applied with consistency and vigour since the start of Mrs Thatcher's first administration in 1979. As applied to spacework it was, he

35

declared, a case of *the economics of the corner shop - penny pinching and lacking in vision.*[50]

Kenneth Clarke seemed to take no notice. Less than two weeks later he told the House of Commons that the Government had decided, after consideration of ESA programmes *as presently proposed* to opt out of ESA entirely. [51] Under ESA rules it had 3 months in which to change its mind...

* * * * * * * * * * * * * * * * * * *

APPENDIX 1 : ESA PROJECTS

COLUMBUS

This consists of three separate projects which plug into the US SPACE STATION planned for the 1990s. They are (a) the Polar Platform - a man-tended laboratory to be used mainly for remote sensing (b) Eureka - an automatic laboratory to be used mainly for micro-gravity experimentation work (c) the Man-Tended Free-Flyer (MTFF).

Transportation to and from the SPACE STATION will be by SHUTTLE.

ARIANE 5

The latest in the long-running ARIANE series of space rockets. To be used for the launching of satellites in high geosynchronous orbit (HIGH G) and for the launch of HERMES. Has a much higher pay-load capacity than previous ARIANE rockets and will reduce the cost of satellite launches. Fired from the ESA base in Kourou in French Guiana.

HERMES

This is a project for a reusable 'minishuttle' spaceplane to be launched from ARIANE. It aims at a capability of being able to transport to-and-from a Space Platform. Following the US CHALLENGER SHUTTLE disaster the HERMES design was changed to accommodate 2 astronauts instead of 6 - a heavy cut-back in load capacity. First conceived by the head of CNES in 1975, most of the technology to be used is already known.

Note:

The Times (11/11/87) put the estimated cost of developing COLUMBUS at £4,085m, ARIANE 5 at £3,845m and HERMES at £4,875m.

APPENDIX 2: THE NATIONAL COLLY-WOBBLES
STRIKE AGAIN?

The British Bulldog is characterised by its refusal to let go once it has its teeth in something. However, any attempt to use the bulldog as a symbol for any British high technology project would be a clear breach of the Trade Descriptions Act.

Britain has the world's worst record for starting high-tech projects and then cancelling them... The long-range jet transport market... the TSR2 fighter bomber... the light-and medium-lift helicopter market...

Now it seems projects like the UK HOTOL space plane are to become typical of innovations we have given, in every sense of the word, to the world.

Source : Giving up our Place in Space, Sir Geoffrey Pattie,
The Observer, 6/3/88.

APPENDIX 3: THE SATELLITE BUSINESS

WEATHER FORECASTING	Satellites like METEOSAT P2
REMOTE SENSING	Earth observation satellites like Radarsat and ESA's ERS 2. Used variously for oceanography, environmental control and mineral prospecting etc.
TELE-COMMUNICATIONS	Like PANAMSAT 1 or AMSAT 3C
TV RELAYING	The ASTRA satellite [launch date Nov 1988] is being used by SKY TV for direct broadcasting of 4 new TV channels for Britain. ECS 4 is the third in the EUTELSAT series etc.
EARLY WARNING	Satellites used to anticipate major hazards e.g. the UN FAO's locust plague spotting system.
INTELLIGENCE GATHERING	Like the KH 11 strategic reconnaissance satellite [the size of a school bus and reportedly costing $360m] launched from Vandenberg Airforce Base in California in October 1987. A TITAN 34D rocket was used.
SOLAR POWER	Satellites to be used in electricity generation are under intensive study in the USSR. The new ENERGIA rocket has given greater feasibility.
EARTH MAPPING	High resolution images of the earth are sold by the USA [30 metres], France's SPOT IMAGE [10 metres] and the USSR's SOYUZKARTA [5 metres].

Note: Authoritative estimates of the world-wide order book for satellite launches between 1990-2000 amount to some £10 billion. There is heavy competition to get the launch cost down and potential entrants to the rocket launch market include the Chinese [LONG MARCH rocket], Indian and Japan [NIPPON 1 & 2 rockets].

APPENDIX 4: ESTIMATED CIVIL SPENDING ON
SPACEWORK - $

Nation	Estimated Spending on Spacework in 1987 [$m]
USA	4500
France	600
Japan	550
Germany	440
Italy	300
India	150
Britain	112

Source: *The Times* 28/9/87

APPENDIX 5: SELECTED FINANCIAL DATA - £

	ROLLS ROYCE		BRITISH AEROSPACE	
	1984	1987	1984	1987
P&L ACCOUNT				
Turnover	1409	2059	2468	4075
Operating profit	164	347	196	217
R & D	101	187	51	42
Interest Payable	35	4	25	14
Profit before Tax	26	156	120	161
Tax	6	21	12	63
Profit after Tax	20	135	108	98
Profit after extra-				
ordinary items	20	135	108	[110]
BALANCE SHEET				
ASSETS				
Current	800	1106	1936	3333
Fixed	382	438	514	919
Total	1182	1544	2450	4252
LIABILITIES:				
Total Debt	872	689	1531	3233
Equity	310	855	919	1019
Total	1182	1544	2450	4252
Employees [000]	42	42	76	93
Earnings per Share [p]				
	3.0	20.1	53.5	[43.9]

Notes on the accounts:

(a) The figures given for R & D do not include Government funding. In the case of British Aerospace they cover Special Launch Costs, R&D spending being subsumed in other costs before the calculation of Operating profit.

(b) *1987 was a year of particular significance* for Rolls Royce Plc *since it saw the company's successful return to the private sector after 16 years of public ownership. The flotation was a great success in that it attracted over 2m shareholders.* The major part of the flotation was used to reduce the company's borrowings. One special redeemable preference share was allotted to a nominee of the Secretary of State for Trade & Industry. Source: Rolls Royce PLC *Annual Report* 1987.

(c) Rolls Royce Ltd was established as a state-owned company in 1971 following the company's bankruptcy, caused in no small measure by the cost of developing the RB 2 11 engine. The shares were vested in the National Enterprise Board in 1976.

(d) *British Aerospace is exposed to currency movements because the civil aircraft business is dollar-based. Much of the manufacturing cost is in sterling and the time cycle for the ultimate delivery of the products extends over several years. It is this latter feature of aerospace engineering which makes currency hedging especially difficult to manage.* On the basis of present currency forecasting, the BAe board has decided *to make an exceptional provision of £320m in the accounts to cover anticipated trading losses on civil aircraft orders and assumed sales* (BAe Annual Report 1987).

(e) BAe acquisitions from Government: Royal Ordnance (1987), Rover Group (1988)

NOTES & REFERENCES

1   *UK and the European Space Programme,* BBC's 'File on Four', 22/6/88
2   'A fond l'espace', *Le Nouvel Observateur,* 14-20/6/85
    Translation: *Even if our partners do not follow us, France, thanks to HERMES, will send men into space from 1997 onwards. No-one dobts that our partners will follow and that ESA will take HERMES on board and europeanise the venture.* **Note:** in 1988 Socialist Francois Mitterand began his second term as President of France.
3   As (1)
4   *A Giant Leap for Europe,* David Wheeler, Bbc's 'Analysis', 8/10/86
5   As (1).   Geoffrey Pattie also noted that BNSC's London premises did not compare at all with CNES' (being lodged inconspicuously in the DTI's offices at Millbank) and that, from the standpoint not a few within the DTI, BNSC was seen, organisationally, at least, as *a cuckoo in the nest.*
6   As 4
7   As 4
8   As 1
9   'Space plans shelved after budget delay', Sheila Gunn, *The Times,* 24/7/87
10 'There's life in space but, after Thatcher, Britain will not be on the Starship Enterprise', Peter Large, *The Guardian,* 25/7/87
11 'Attack on space cash policy', Philip Webster, *The Times* 6/8/87
12 'British space chief quits in cash row', Nigel Dudley and Roger Highfield, *The Daily Telegraph,* 5/8/87
13 'Space', Peter Beaumont, *The Guardian,* 6/8/87
14 'Europe loses one of the captains of its space boat', Peter Marsh, *The Financial Times,* 6/8/87
15 '£10m was space chief's last straw', Alan Travis, *The Guardian* 6/8/87
16 'British space projects in turmoil', Pearce Wright, *The Times,* 6/8/87
17 'Britain at sea in space', *The Financial Times,* 6/8/87
18 As 14
19 As 13
20 As 11
21 'Launch gives Europe a 4-year lead', *The Times,* 17/9/87
22 'Made in Space', *The Times,* 13/8/87
23 'Astronaut prompts debate on US space programme', Mohsin Ali, *The Times,* 2/9/87

EXHIBIT 4: translation:
Quite apart from technical difficulties and political quarrels, the estimated costs of a manned European spaceflight have also risen drastically in the past months. Even when the German contribution was still being measured

in single milliards, Research Minister Heinz Riesenhuber was becoming anxious about his budget. He couldn't earmark the sum involved since other research areas would suffer... We still do not know where the necessary money is going to come from.

24 'Space budget seen as a disaster', Pearce Wright, *The Times*, 27/8/87

25 'British role in space science under threat', Pearce Wright, *The Times*, 17/9/87

26 As 25

27 'Britain slips in world space race', Pearce Wright, *The Times*, 28/9/87

28 'Clarke rejects space proposal', Pearce Wright, *The Times*, 12/10/87

29 'Merger may rescue Hotol space plane', Jane Bird & Nick Rufford, *The Sunday Times*, 18/10/87

30 As 29

31 'Top scientist in threat to quit space project', Pearce Wright, *The Times*, 13/10/87

32 'No space in Britain', *The Times*, 13/10/87

33 'Opting out in space', *The Guardian*, 13/10/87

34 'Hint of extra cash for HOTOL space plane', Pearce Wright, *The Times*, 15/10/87.
    Note: that the 'proof of concept' development work had been funded jointly by the British Government (apparently 50 per cent) and by British Aerospace and Rolls Royce (equally sharing the balance).

35 'Little Britain ignores its space destiny', Michael Heseltine, *The Times*, 19/10/87

36 'High Tech industry put in danger', Pearce Wright, *The Times*, 21/10/87

37 'Clarke seeks economic return from space plans' Parliament, *The Times*, 29/10/87

38 'Ministers adamant on space budget freeze', Sheila Gunn, *The Times*, 29/10/87

39 'Low spending on research harms British firms', *The Independent*, 28/8/87

40 As 39

41 As 39

42 'Space talks on verge of collapse', Pearce Wright, *The Times*, 10/11/87

43 'Britain in a danger of becoming a Division Three country', Clarke told by Conservative MP, Parliament, *The Times*, 13/11/87

44 As 42

45 As 43

46 As 43

47 'European space projects are far too costly', *The Times*, 13/11/87

48 'Midget space plane rejected', Parliament, *The Times*, 26/11/87

49 'Peers urge £80m boost for space programme', Pearce Wright, *The Times*, 26/1/88

50 'Space cuts *a great betrayal*', Robin Oakley, *The Times*, 30/1/88.
    Note: that Mrs Thatcher was exceptionally bullish about the dramatic and factual improvements in British productivity, international competitiveness and

standard of living recorded since 1979 at the G7 Toronto summit meeting on the 19th of June, 1988; to the point of referring to *a golden age*.

51   'Britain withdraws from programme for manned station', Robert Matthews, *The Times*, 11/2/88.

IRISH DISTILLERS GROUP

Abstract:

This case features a takeover battle between two giants in the global drinks industry, both seeking to acquire Irish Distillers, the whisky producer. The protagonists were Grand Metropolitan and Pernod Ricard. The battle was fought under the spotlight of the development of Common Market take-over legislation and in the context of the economics of the drinks industry on a global basis. The controversial victory went to the French.

Question:

Analyse the take-over strategies of Grand Metropolitan and Pernod Ricard and the underlying logic for their approaches. In your view, and against the background of developments in the global drinks industry, was the take-over of Irish Distillers virtually inevitable?

Case Timing: 1988

THE CLOUD IN THE SKY

In early 1988, Pernod Ricard (PR), the eighth largest spirits corporation in the world - had only one cloud in its otherwise clear corporate sky: the potential loss of the French Coca Cola franchise. The Company's dramatic success over the giant Grand Metropolitan Group in the aggressively-fought take-over battle for the Irish Distillers Group lay over the horizon. The immediate challenge for the French giant was how to deal with the announcement by Coca Cola that it was withdrawing from PR the lucrative concession for its product in France and, like other drinks firms, it was going to set up its own direct marketing and distribution system. The fall in turnover for PR amounted to F1.4b and that of profits to in excess of F60m. As Coca Cola held a very substantial share of the French soft drinks market, the removal of the concession was a set-back to the company who were still in the throes of building up their own range in Europe (with brands like Orangina etc.).

Opinion was divided on the gravity of the problem. Some regarded it as not particularly significant, given founding family ownership of 40 per cent of PR equity, the Group's low gearing, its expanding product portfolio and distributive network (a strategic sine qua non for world ranking in the view of many analysts) and its financial track record. Had not PR's recent development comprised, all in 1987, such exciting steps forward as:

* the setting-up of a Japanese subsidiary and the establishment of a joint PR - Chinese company for wine production, the Beijing Friendship Winery.

* the acquisition of the Dutch number four in spirits, Cooymans, and the leading Italian food flavouring maker, San Georgio.

* the strengthening of its already powerful European distribution through the take-over of the Italian Ramazotti organisation.

Had not the pace continued with the buy-out of Yoohoo, US producer of chocolate milk with an annual turnover of $60m, in June 1988?

Nor was optimism about the Group's likely future likely to be diminished by such moves as PR's purchase of a three per cent stake in the giant French financial conglomerate Compagnie Financière de Suez or the company's buy-back of 515,000 of its own shares in early 1988.[1]

Nevertheless, others thought that the company had chosen a hard and highly competitive road to follow and that the loss of the Coca Cola concession would take a lot of making up.

There was little doubt, however, of PR's commitment to future growth. It was in mid 1987 that PR came to be widely recognised as a serious contender for top ranking in the world's drinks' league. The published growth plan for the company, with subsidiaries already covering Italy, Spain, Germany, Switzerland, Holland and Britain - indicated an ultimate 50:50 sales split between France and abroad. The entrepreneurial ambitions of 41 year old Company President Patrick Ricard (son of the founder of Ricard) and of his Director-General, Thierry Jacquillet, were well recognised.

Product & market		Pre-tax Turnover [Fm]		Profit on Sales: pre-tax, pre-interest [%]	
		1975	1987	1986	1987
France:	W & S	889	4997	14.2	16.3
	NAD	344	3035	9.7	10.4
Abroad:	W & S	187	1787	8.0	5.7
	NAD	14	885	10.2	neg
Totals		**1434**	**10704**	**11.0**	**11.5**

TABLE 1 : SELECTED PR FINANCIAL DATA
Source: Company Report 1987
[W&S = Wines & Spirits, NAD=Non-alcoholic drinks]

From the 1975 amalgamation of pastis manufacturers Pernod and Ricard and the subsequent absorption of Cusenier and House of Campbell - distillers of Clan Campbell, Aberlour Glenlivet and White Heather - PR had made giant strides. Why had it not, therefore, entered the lists with a bid for French cognac manufacturer Martell in 1987 against Grand Metropolitan and the Canadian Seagram Group (CSG were winners with a bid of £525m, 30x Martell earnings)?

The answer, as Exhibit 1 indicates, lies in PR's adherence to its growth plan.

> *Il y a des surenchères qui sont des surenchères d'image. On ne cherche pas à réaliser des OPA médiatiques. Pour P.R., racheter Martell n'était pas essentiel dans sa stratégie de developpement. Contrairement à Seagram nous acquérons des sociétés pour faire du profit et non du chiffre d'affaires.*

EXHIBIT 1: THE P.R. WAY, ACCORDING TO DENIS BERTHU, CORPORATE COMMUNICATIONS DIRECTOR [2]

Source: PR ne se noiera pas dans la mer d'Irelande Gilles Forestier,
Communication, 31/10/88

EMPIRES OF COMMERCE

However large Pernod Ricard had become by 1988, it was still dwarfed by its rival in the Irish Distillers bidding battle, Grand Metropolitan (GM). This was a multinational conglomerate of first rank which had just acquired the US' Heublein & Almaden Group (1987, £1.3 billion) and, in the UK, the William Hill's betting chain (1988, £331m). It was, in late 1988, in the process of bidding for Pillsbury, the US Green Giant-Burger King food conglomerate. The sale of its Intercontinental Hotels to the Japanese Saibu Saison Group also occurred in 1988 (£1.1 billion). As Table 2 shows, GM's trading results were truly impressive.

The logic behind such moves was seen as elementary by GM Chairman, Allen Shepherd. *The markets for drinks and food are becoming truly global. If one is to be a major player in consumer goods in the 1990s, one has to think internationally.* This was the rationale behind the addition of Smirnoff vodka (Heublein & Almaden) to the prestigious GM drinks stable of J & B Whisky, Le Piat d'Or, Gilbey's Gin and Bailey's Irish Cream and Croft Sherries. And behind the purchase of UK wine merchant Saccone & Speed (340 shops), a notable supplement to the 1,800 pubs, hotels and restaurants already owned in the UK by GM.

Territory	1986		1987	
	Sales T/O	Trading Profit	Sales T/O	Trading Profit
UK & Eire	3281	301	3559	331
USA	1566	143	1720	185
Rest of world	444	44	427	55
Total	5291	487	5705	572

TABLE 2: GM FINANCIAL DATA (£M, ROUNDED)
Source: Company Report 1987

It was also the rationale behind the distibution linkages which were wide-spread in the drinks industry - GM's being especially powerful as they would have to be in the light of the growing purchasing power of hypermarket and supermarket chains.

It was in the whisky area, however, that GM had to yield pride of place to its world rival, Guinness. This company held within its portfolio no less than 5 of the world's leading brands: Johnnie Walker Red, Johnnie Walker Black, Bell's, Dewar's and White Horse. This was thought to confer great strength in the static world market in which 35 brands (out of 400) accounted for sales of 97m cases (out of 157m) in 1986. Nonetheless, there could be little criticism of GM's 1987 wines and spirits performance with:

* T/O up to £1796m (1986 - £1076m)
* Trading profit up to £223m (1986 - £147m) and
* Capital employed up to £842m (1986 - £452m).

THE BRITISH PRIME MINISTER

If you believe some of the things said and written about my views on Europe, it must seem like inviting Genghis Khan to speak on the virtues of peaceful co-existence... We British have in a special way contributed to Europe for, over the centuries, we have fought and died for her freedom, fought to prevent Europe from falling under the dominance of a single power... The European Community belongs to all its members and must reflect the traditions and aspirations of all of them in full measure...

The Community is not an end in itself. It is not an institutional device to be constantly modified according to the dictates of some abstract theory...

Willing and active co-operation between independent sovereign states is the best way to build a successful European Community. To try to suppress nationhood and concentrate power at the centre of a European conglomerate would be highly damaging... Community policies must tackle present problems in a practical way, however difficult that may be... and reform those which are patently wrong or ineffective...

The need (is) for Community policies which encourage enterprise... The Treaty of Rome was intended as a charter for economic liberty... The lessons of the economic history of Europe in the 1970s and 1980s is that central planning and detailed control don't work and that personal endeavour and initiative do... Europe should not be protectionist.

Source: Mrs Thatcher's speech to the College of Europe, Bruges, 20/9/88.

THE BRITISH LABOUR PARTY LEADER

If the single market was to mean nothing other than a big finance free-for-all, it would be a social, industrial and environmental catastrophe.. If 1992 is focused purely upon the free movement of goods, capital and labour, it will actually create the free movement of poverty, unemployment and depression.

Source: Neil Kinnock's speech to the European Parliament Socialist Group, Glasgow, 7/9/88

EXHIBIT 2: EC DEVELOPMENT - THE VIEW FROM BRITAIN

THE COMMUNITY INTEREST

It is not surprising that such a high level of merger, take-over and link-up, with its unavoidable implications for even more concentration in world-wide drinks manufacture and distribution, should attract the special attention of the European Commission and, particularly, that of the incumbent (to end 1988) of the office of Competition Policy Commissioner, the Irishman Peter Sutherland. He was the custodian and official interpreter of Articles 85 & 86 of the Treaty of Rome which outlaw corporate moves to diminish competition. His track record over his five years of office revealed considerable willingness to intervene, in often difficult circumstances, to uphold the Treaty. He had taken action to limit governmental subsidies perceived to be excessive in France (Renault) and Britain (the DAF takeover of British Leyland Trucks; the British Aerospace takeover of the Rover Group). He had obliged British Airways, on buying up its rival British Caledonian, to divest itself of some BCal routes.

The parallel build-up of European business case law, European Court of Justice rulings, gave an additional impetus to the Commission's concern at possible breaches of competition rules. The Court had established clear benchmarks in, for example:

* The 1964 Grundig-Consten case (restraint-of-trade sole distributorship issue)
* The 1972 Continental Can case (abuse of a dominant market position to acquire a competitor)
* The Zoja laboratories case (abuse of dominant position to cut off supplies to actual/potential competitors).

Peter Sutherland's forceful interventionism was noteworthy in 1988 in action taken by the Commission against leading European manufacturers of plastics for having operated two illegal price-fixing and market-sharing cartels between 1980 and 1984. Those found guilty in the Commission's investigation, itself a by-product of a separate, successful inquiry into anti-competitive practices in polypropylene, included West Germany's BASF, ICI and British Petroleum. In all 22 major companies were fined more than £40m.

It should also be noted that in 1988 the Commission, having reached, in time terms, the half-way stage for the implementation of the Single European Act, was heavily involved in steps towards promoting the harmonisation of many aspects of corporate life in the community. Directives were in the course of preparation (consultation, draft, awaiting Parliamentary scrutiny and Council decision) in the key areas of banking, investment regulation and insurance liability. In each case the emphasis was on ensuring an equitable and harmonious working system throughout Europe. This was likely to be a difficult task given the British assertion that, in respect of investment regulation at least, any Community-wide system that was more relaxed than the tightly regulated British system would place British traders at a grave disadvantage. The Bank of England was also concerned at the extent to which the 2nd Banking Directive might, through an exaggerated concern with seeking international reciprocity in the setting up and the operations of banks, actually damage the international finance industry.

These were background concerns, however, to operators in the drinks field. Their central interest lay in the proposals (and ultimately, legislation) which would ensue from current discussions in respect of:

* the conditions under which the Commission would institute an enquiry into the desirability of allowing a proposed European merger/takeover bid to proceed, the terms of reference of such an enquiry and the nature of the judgement arrived at. This was a fraught issue, given the existence of such national organisations as the British Office of Fair Trading (and its investigative arm, The Monopolies & Mergers Commission) and the German Kartellamt. Questions of jurisdiction and the public interest - national or European - were at stake.

* the EC proposals to alter the level of indirect tax payable on goods and services throughout the Community by standardising it within two permissible bands (4-9 per cent and 14-20 per cent) and to alter the method of collection to a system where VAT was paid on each sales transaction not just on the final purchase by the ultimate consumer. Alongside the possible loss of business arising from the dismantling of the duty-free trade as part of moving towards a single market, this was also a major headache.

There was little surprise registered in the industry, therefore, when Peter Sutherland set up investigations into two mammoth drinks-related link-ups which took place in late 1988. The first was the friendly merger attempt (in October) between the MB Group (formerly Metal Box) and Carnaud, the leading French metal packaging group. The combination, created by the latter's proposed buy-out of the former for £780m, amounted to the largest food-drinks packaging group in Europe with an estimated £2 billion turnover. As such the new group would rank as the world number three, behind American National and Toyoseikan of Japan.

The second was the contested take-over bid launched by the Australian Elders IXL (interestingly, a five per cent shareholder in MB) for Edinburgh-based Scottish & National Breweries. According to John Elliott, Elder's chairman, it was a straightforward matter:

The issue is whether, by putting two and two together, you reduce competition. Our view is you increase it. Bass is just so far ahead of everybody else.. in Great Britain. It's got 22-23 per cent of the market now and rising. We'll make a more formidable competitor to Bass by being together. It's the irrefutable logic that Alick Rankin (S & N's chief executive) had when he wanted to buy Courage (acquired, in fact, by Elder's)... a couple of years ago. [3]

It was not quite so simple for the British Monopolies & Mergers Commission. They were already enquiring into the nature of the vertically-integrated industry at the time of the Elder's bid, a bid which would result in Elder's owning 20.6 per cent of British pubs, as against Bass' 22 per cent, Grand Metropolitan's 13 per cent and Whitbreads' 12 per cent. This was the third study of its kind in the last 20 years, one of them by the Commission itself.

ACTION STATIONS

High interest in the affairs of Carnaud and Elder's there might have been, but it was small beer compared with the furore aroused by the bid for the Irish Distillers Group that was mounted in mid-1988 by a consortium made up of the Irish subsidiaries of the British-based Allied Lyons, Grand Metropolitan, Guinness and Cantrell & Cochrane, the Irish distributors of Pepsi Cola. Only days before the closing date of the £170m, IR 350p/share offer, ID lodged a formal complaint that the bidder had broken the Community's competition law.

The immediate intervention by Commissioner Sutherland endorsed the ID board's conjecture.[4] Certainly, it was known the Allied Lyons and Grand Metropolitan had agreed to share out some ID brands and sell off others. In fact, the bid itself was not going well anyway. Since its unveiling on the 30th May, it had attracted acceptances from only 20.3 per cent of shares and, on the 9th August, it had been extended by another 60 days. ID chairman Joe McCabe and his board had been opposed to the bid from what they called *the unholy alliance* from the outset.[5]

On being advised that the bid had indeed been structured in such a way as to be illegal under European law, Grand Metropolitan bought out the interests of its consortium partners and proceeded to launch its own bid of IR400p/share. Joe McCabe was as hostile to this as he had been to the previous one:

The policy proposed by the bidder to fragment the Irish whiskey industry is ill-conceived. It stems from a lack of understanding and an absence of any real commitment to the Irish whiskey industry on the part of Grand Metropolitan, which intends to recoup half its outlay quickly by asset stripping, including the sale of brands. [6]

The despondency felt by ID was clearly a function of a sound comprehension of the mechanics of take-over bidding (Appendix 1, page 63) and brand valuation (Appendix 2, page 63). The Board's anger lay in the fact that any break-up of the Group would run exactly counter to all ID had ever stood for.

Irish whiskey brands command four per cent of the premium, de luxe and malt sectors in which they compete globally and it is these sectors that are growing while overall consumption is declining. In our main markets increased competition among lower-priced brands has been prevalent...
Your company has evolved a new export strategy which concentrates effort and investment behind a selected brand.. in the growth premium sector of the market.. The establishment of high quality premium brands in international markets is a long-term and expensive business and our brand names are the greatest assets of the company, even though they are not reflected on the balance sheet.

EXHIBIT 3 : THE ID APPROACH

Source: *ID Company Report* 1987

The Group, as the 1987 Annual Report pointed out, *was formed in 1966 by the merger of three distillers all dating from the 18th century (The Cork Distilleries Ltd, John Jameson & Son Ltd and John Power & Son Ltd), the objective being the creation of a strong group to develop export markets.*

Not only did ID enjoy, therefore, a monopoly of Irish whiskey production but, by owning the Old Bushmills distillery in County Antrim, the first licensed whisky distillery in the world, it had an ancestry dating back to 1608. And, as if that were not enough of a proud heritage, it is known that the distilling of UISCE

BEATHA (*The Water of Life*) from native barley was invented by the Irish more than a millennium ago.

EEC Country	Total Movement of investment Funds [£m] Year to end June 1988	
	Outflow from	**Inflow into**
UK	34041	13522
France	5255	3746
Italy	2741	856
W. Germany	1189	384
Ireland	848	157
Belgium	208	217
Netherlands	128	1202
Luxembourg	135	6
Denmark	62	227
Spain		773
Total	**44607**	**21090**

TABLE 3: EC COUNTRIES' INVESTMENT FLOWS
Source: KPMG Deal Watch, quoted in *The Times* 18/12/88

Note: *Britain, An Official Handbook*, (HMSO, 1989) points out that the service sector in Britain now accounts for 60 per cent of GDP and more than 66 per cent of employment. Manufacturing accounts for 25 per cent of each, as against its 1950 level of 33 per cent.

By GM's standards, Irish Distillers was clearly also a small business. With some 1,100 employees, 5,000 shareholders (80 per cent resident in Ireland) and a 1987 turnover of IR £229m, it was nonetheless a significant contributor to the economic performance of N. Ireland and Eire. Its product range included gins and vodkas but was chiefly reputed for its low-to-medium priced whiskies, of which the brand leaders were Jameson, Bushmill's, Power's Gold Label, Paddy and Tullamore Dew. New de luxe brands added in recent years were Middleton, Bushmill's Malt and Jameson 1780.

HOW LEVEL IS LEVEL?

The Grand Metropolitan bid also posed a problem for the UK's Office of Fair Trading and its investigative arm, the Monopolies & Mergers Commission. The inquiry being carried out by the latter's Take-over Panel (TP) was sandwiched between the studies sanctioned by Peter Sutherland and that being carried out by Ireland's own Fair Trade Commission. The TP was anxious to make clear that it was acting for Ireland *at the express wish of the Irish authorities*. It was *neutral as between the nationality or identity of rival offerors and as between both and the management of the offeree company*.[7] Albert Reynolds, Ireland's Industry Minister was also keen to make his country's position clear:

> *While the TP in London governs the Dublin Stock Exchange, we operate on a different statutory basis and, in this situation, it is my decisions that matter, not the London Takeover Panel's.* [8]

It was something of a paradox that the TP should be involved in adjudicating on a takeover bid for what was perhaps one of the most Irish of Irish institutions - the whiskey industry - at precisely the time the Commission was debating the trigger point for its own scrutiny of EC mergers (possibly a combined turnover of the partners of £700m) which would almost certainly involve multinational corporations. As can be easily imagined, there was tension in the air.

The atmosphere was certainly not eased by criticism of the British Government's policy (*a clear and predictable framework* leaving the market, on the whole *to get on with it* according to Industry Secretary, Lord Young) [9] from key British industrialists such as Derick Holden-Brown, Allied Lyons' chairman. He stated that he had no complaint about free market systems *no matter how brutal*, but he was unhappy with *the lack of clear guidance on monopolies and mergers policy*. The Government should, in his view, redefine its competition policy with *numbers which are relevant in the context of the single European market and not just the domestic market*. [10]

Another trenchant critic was United Biscuits' chairman, Sir Hector Laing who declared:

> *The 'shareholders' who make life-or-death decisions for British public companies are approximately 50-60 fund managers in major financial institutions... These managing agents probably believe that by maximising the value of their funds through short-term dealing, they are acting in their clients' best interests... I do not believe the vast majority of people want to see British industry sold abroad for jam today...*
>
> *If Britain loses its economic power base with the loss of ownership of its major businesses... we would be reduced to political serfdom, too.. It is said that chauvinism is wrong but the Germans, French and Japanese have free market economies. and they are certainly chauvinistic, much more so than we...*
>
> *Perhaps we could... block those speculators whose only interest is to make a quick killing by putting a company into play.* [11]

It was not so much the practicalities of take-over policy that were under attack. There seemed general agreement on such features as giving shareholders enough time to make up their minds and enough information, too, with obligatory disclosure by the bidder of basic intent (in the bidding prospectus), size of direct and nominee holdings and share trades (all above given minima). There was no contest, either, over the need to avoid regulation beyond such matters as adherence to the various stages in the bid timetable (when a fresh bid could take place: when a bid would lapse: when, after a lapsed bid, the offeror could bid afresh etc.).

What was causing dissension was the extent to which the British system was, and was seen to be by foreign predators, overly permissive and inequitable by comparison with those of some of our leading competitors. A particularly powerful attack was mounted by John Banham, Director-General of the Confederation of British Industry, at the 1988 CBI Conference in which he called for:

* Reciprocity. The Secretary of State should refer any in-bound bid if the bidder, in his home territory were seen as immune from a counter-bid.

* Safeguards. Like, for example, *postponing* (reducing the voting power of) shares transferred during a bid, reducing the present mandatory *trigger* ownership for a full bid from 30 per cent to 15 per cent, making the acceptance of a bid conditional on a 66 per cent shareholder assent at an Extraordinary General Meeting and obliging a failed bidder to divest himself of any holding above 15 per cent and make no rebid for 3 years.

For Lord Young, who considered Britain to be *the great overseas investor*,[12] such a call was misplaced. It smacked of what his Minister, Francis Maude, called a *defensive corporate culture*.[13] *The best defence* he said *is surely getting your company into good shape.. If we put up the shutters* he added *the barriers would go up quickly in the USA*.

He did, however, go some way to meeting demands for change when he announced a lowering of the mandatory stake disclosure level and, as a direct result of the Elder's bid for Scottish & Newcastle, made it illegal for bidders to acquire shares in their targets once their bid had been referred.

Lord Alexander of Weedon, Chairman of the Take-over Panel showed himself similarly averse to substantial policy change when he gave his reaction to the European Commission's publication of the 13th Company Law Directive on the 22nd December, 1988.

Operating Group Base [UK = UK] [F = France] [C = Canada]	Major Spirit Whisky [M = Straight Malt]	Brands Bourbon [B] Vodka [V] Gin [G] Cognac [C]	Wines & Spirits T/O 1987 [BF]	Sales of Alcohol 1987/8 [m cases]	Comment
Grand Metropolitan [UK]	J & B	Black Velvet [B] Smirnoff [V] Popov [V] Gilbey [G]	19.8	85	Controls 70% of its own world-wide distribution. Deal with Martell in France for distribution of some brands
Seagram [C]	Chivas, 7 Crown Crown Royal, V.O. Glenlivet [M]	4 Roses [B] Martell [C]	18.4	76	Owns Martell, distributes several Allied Lyons brands in France and Germany
Allied Lyons [UK]	Ballentines Teacher's Canadian Club Miltonduff [M] Glendronach [M]	Maker's Mark [B] High Tent [B] Courvoisier [C] Salignac [C]	15.8	50	Distributes own products world-wide except for France & Germany
Guinness [UK]	Johnnie Walker Black & White Haig, White Horse Dewar's Old, Parrs Dimple, Cardhu Malt, The Antiquary	Cossack [V] Gordons [G] Booths [G] Tanqueray [G]	14.3	47	Bought up Distillers Co. in bitter take-over battle. Controls 70% of its European distribution
Louis Vuitton Moet Hennessey [F]		Hennessey [C] Hine [C]	7.4	19.5	Growing distribution power in USA through its fused distributors Somerset & Schiefflein. Cross-holdings between Guinness & LVMH
Pernod Ricard [pre I.D. integration] [F]	Glen Campbell White Heather Aberlour Glenlivet	Wild Turkey [B] Bisquit [C]	6.8	5.7	Distributes Gilbey's Gin in France. Victory over Grand Metropolitan in the bid for Irish Distillers. Particularly strong European distribution network

TABLE 4: THE BIG 6 IN WINES AND SPIRITS IN THE WEST

Notes: This table extends one produced by Francoise Morin, in Grandes Manoeuvres, Science & Vie Economique, December 1988.

BF = Billion francs

The company with the largest world-wide sales of wines and spirits is the Japanese Suntory Group.

Many high-priced single malts are still manufactured independently of the above groups, e.g. Talisker, Laggavulin, Cragganmore, Glenkinchie, The Singleton of Auchroisk, Glenmorangie, Glenspey, The Macallan etc. They are becoming highly prized in European markets by connoiseurs and suppliers.

This proposed:

1. Greater disclosure of the bidder's plans for his target (assets, work-force, debts)

2. A statutory framework for the regulation of mergers and takeovers, as opposed to Britain's voluntary approach.

Lord Alexander gave an oblique, non-partisan welcome for the new Directive, which required European Parliament endorsement and qualified majority support in the Council of Ministers to put it into effect. *Our code* he stated *is a well-developed system that is internationally acknowledged as effective, arguably the world's most effective.* Avoidance of *a litigious culture*, which might arise from a statutory framework, was important. *In Britain* he continued *practitioners cannot evade regulation by designing round the letter of the rules so as to avoid complying with the principles. Nor can shareholders easily be deprived of their rights by others' resorting to the courts.* [15]

EC Country	VAT rate [%]	Excise duty [£ per bottle]	Consumption of pure Alcohol [litres per capita]	
			1975	1986
UK	15	4.75	NA	1.7
Ireland	25	5.2	2.03	1.76
Belgium	25	2.4	1.99	2.12
W. Germany	14	5.25	3.04	2.37
France	18.6	2.2	2.42	2.3
Denmark	22	6.7	1.74	1.61
Netherlands	20	2.5	3.4	2.2
Greece	-	.1	NA	NA
Italy	18	.5	1.8	1.2
Portugal	16	.5	.9	.8
Spain	12	.6	2.6	3.0

TABLE 5: EC TAX DISPARITIES

Source: L'Europe des Boissons, *PR Shareholders' Journal*, No. 14, Nov 1987 & Why Lord Cockfield got it wrong, *The Guardian*, 27/7/88

ROUND TWO

It was in early August 1988 that Pernod Ricard emerged as a possible rival for Irish Distillers. Under Take-over Panel rules it was recognised that, only if ID shareholders publicly received a competitive takeover bid, could Grand Metropolitan extend the deadline (beyond September 12th) for, and/or increase the value of, its IR400p/share bid. Hence many eyes were on the French.

Initial talks between ID and PR led to the well-publicised view that the GM offer was too low and that GM's apparent intention to sell off brands was a serious threat. As Michael Cummins, Irish Distillers' Marketing Director, put it:

Our policy is to promote Irish whiskey as a whole... If GM gets its way, individual brands will compete with one another that would lead to the demise of several of our products. [16]

Under such circumstances the company's KEEP THE SPIRIT IRISH campaign won not a few native supporters.

It was clear to PR that the key to success in obtaining control over Irish Distillers lay in acquiring the shares held by the fruit importing company FII-Fyffes (FIIF) - 20 per cent - and the eleven per cent held by the insurance company, Irish Life.

With PR's stake rising, on the second of September, to 5.5 per cent and GM's bid referred to the Irish Fair Trade Commission, the stage seemed set for a dramatic move on PR's part. And, indeed, that was what took place in Dublin over the weekend of the third and fourth of September.

Policy	Ger	Fra	Ita	Neth	UK
Regulatory Period during which the bid can be scrutinised?	N	Y	Y	N	N
National anti-trust laws?	Y	N	N	Y	Y
Controls on in-bound foreign investment?	N	Y	N	N	N
Public register of shares?	Y	N	N	N	Y

TABLE 6: EC COUNTRIES TAKE OVER CONTROLS
Source: Bidders Guide to Europe, *The Sunday Times,* 22/5/88

Note: A high level of intricate industrial ownership cross-holdings was an industry protection feature in Germany and Japan. French and British public companies were allowed the US' practice of trading in their own shares subject to certain conditions. In Switzerland, a company could issue new shares (e.g., a rights issue to pre-bid share holders) to preserve the ante-bid voting pattern & stop hostile takeovers.
N = No, Y = Yes.

On the morning of the third, it later transpired, a meeting between PR, FIIF and Irish Life Directors (at which other non-institutional shareholders were also present) had resulted in a verbal acceptance, sealed with a handshake, by FIIF of a PR offer of IR450p/share. This verbal acceptance was to be made into a written agreement to be signed by all parties at 4pm on Sunday the fourth. The Irish Life acceptance was stated as being conditional on FIIF's.

Imagine the furore in the Grand Metropolitan camp, when they were informed of the PR offer, so it was said, by some of the ID shareholders. They immediately contacted the Take-over Panel Executive (TP) to inform them that PR's action constituted, in their view, a *competitive situation* and requested permission (as, under TP rules, they had a perfect right to do) to make a new bid.

It was bloody close said GM chairman, Allen Sheppard, *They were just convening to sign up the big ID shareholders as we were allowed to make our bid.*[17] GM had just made it. At 3.55pm, with literally 5 minutes to spare, its new bid of IR525p was announced.

Pernod Ricard counter-attacked immediately. They appealed against the TP Executive's decision, took out an injunction against FIIF preventing them from taking any action on their ID holding until after the court hearing of PR's action for specific performance (i.e., carrying out the verbal contract made on the third of September) against them. The injunction was granted at 2am on the fifth and dealing in Irish Distillers' shares suspended.

Grand Metropolitan had no doubts as to the outcome. They were certainly not lacking in media support. *The Times*, for instance, referred to *the farcical happenings* of the weekend and the *extraordinary* position of the ID Board. It continued:

The industrial logic of splitting up the sleeping monopoly was impeccable. Undoing the series of mergers and takeovers that originally put ID to sleep would undoubtedly boost an industry that operates at only a fraction of its potential employment and world-wide sales. [18]

With the full Take-over Panel's backing for their Executive's ruling came GM's new offer and a call to the Irish Distillers' Board to recommend it to shareholders. After all, it was a IR75p improvement. The Board demurred, stating that it would await the outcome of the court case before acting. This led *The Times* Comment columnist to observe that it was just *more confusion in what must become a classic case study in takeover history.* [19]

Once dealing in ID shares resumed on the seventh of September, GM immediately lifted its stake to 12.1 per cent. By the tenth it stood at 20.1 per cent. This was the day on which GM lodged a formal complaint with Peter Sutherland about PR's tactics.

The case was heard on the 6th October in Dublin before Mr Justice Declan Costello. Details emerged of the discussions that had taken place between FIIF Directors Neil and Carl McCann and Jim Flavin and Pernod Ricard's Thierry Jacquillet. The case turned on the validity of the verbal contract that PR alleged had been well struck and on FIIF's argument that their acceptance had, in fact, been conditional on obtaining tax clearance from the Irish authorities. From PR's standpoint this was an empty argument. According to Robert Swannell, a director of PR advisers Schroder, Sean Mooney (FIIF's tax adviser) had indeed spoken at the meeting but *he did not recall when or what about*.[20]

Selected Financial Data	Consolidated Financial Results [rounded]					
	PR [BF]		ID [IR£m]		GM [£b]	
	'86	'87	'86	'87	'86	'87
Turnover	11.7	12.5	239	229	5.3	5.7
Net Profit after Tax	.54	.63	10	2	.27	.33
Total Assets	9.0	9.1	184	192	3.0	3.1
Total Equity	3.9	3.8	94	95	2.0	1.7

TABLE 7: GROUP FINANCIAL RESULTS
Source: Company Annual Reports

Note: ID suffered a loss in turnover in 1987 due to its sale of a 71 per cent holding in United Drug Plc. Its net profit fell substantially as a result of the start of a long term rationalisation exercise.
Conversion Rates: 1 UK £ = 10.77F, IR 1.17 punts. 1.68$

The verdict was that there had, in fact, been a contract even though Pernod Ricard's verbal offer had been made only on the specific condition that it would be accepted in advance of being formally uttered. It was also affirmed that both FIIF's and Irish Life's acceptances of the PR offer were irrevocable. Grand Metropolitan pressed ahead with their appeal to the Supreme Court and continued to build up their holding to 27.8 per cent. GM's appeal failed, as did its reference of the matter to the European Commission.

By the end of October everything hung on another appeal GM had made to the Takeover Panel. With a 33 per cent holding in ID, they felt confident of victory this time.

Their confidence was misplaced. In a Delphic judgement, the Takeover Panel agreed that Pernod Ricard & Irish Distillers had, in fact, breached a basic principle of the code but that *the breaches were not sufficiently serious nor of such a significant effect as to make it appropriate to release any shareholders from their undertakings to accept PR's offer.* [21]

Not until the 23rd November and after they had lost yet another appeal (for judicial review) did Grand Metropolitan acknowledge defeat. Patrick Ricard was ecstatic; the gain in turnover from Irish Distillers would, he reckoned, make up almost exactly for the threatened loss of the Coca Cola concession. [22]

* * * * * * * * * * * * * * * * * * *

APPENDIX 1: LEVERAGED BUY-OUTS

LBOs are successful takeover bids financed by debt which is secured against the assets of the target company. The new debt is serviced by the target company's cash flow and, once control is achieved by the bidder, by disposals of assets. This latter reduces the amount of principal on which interest must be paid.

During the late 70s and early 80s the US tax climate was seen as especially favourable to LBOs as tax was not liable on interest payments whereas it was levied on company profits. Hence the cost of debt, as a source of take-over capital, was viewed as lower than that of equity.

In the past entrepreneurs had tended to isolate under-utilised company assets and restructure/strip them. In the LBO 'game' the search was for a stable and under-utilised cash flow (as from a 'cash cow' in Boston Consulting Group jargon). Shareholders in the offeree company were typically given high-coupon bonds (derogatively called 'high flying paper' or 'junk bonds') in a 'leveraged ploy' which replaced the offeree's typical capital mix of low debt/high equity with one of heavy debt/low equity, thus also driving up the earnings per share. This approach, when coupled with a low-valued dollar, made take-over bids for US firms by British predators an exciting proposition.

On his inauguration in January 1989, President Bush underscored the concern felt in the US business community at the extent to which 'giant-killer' bids had become a matter of public concern. In Britain debt was also allowable for corporation tax whereas dividends on equity had to be paid out of taxed income and the Inland Revenue was showing concern at the tax position of some companies with a high debt/equity ratio.

APPENDIX 2: BRAND VALUATION

The take-over bid war between the UK's Rowntree and the Swiss Suchard and (the eventual winner) Nestle first focused attention on the question of the financial value of brands as corporate assets. Before the bids, Rowntree's shares stood at 477p: Nestlé's winning bid was for 1075p. The difference was held to be the value placed explicitly on the company's brands especially Kit Kat, Aero and Polo.

Historically, when a British company was acquired, the value of the assets was recorded on the balance sheet of the acquirer at the price paid. In 1981 Britain fell into line with the practice in other European countries of separating the price paid for a company (a) from the balance sheet value of its assets (b), describing the excess (a-b) as 'goodwill' and amortising it over time. Brand valuation (B.V.), by contrast, puts an explicit value on the brands owned by a company by treating them as identifiable and separate assets. In this it meets the conventional categorisation of assets given in the Accounting Standards' Committee's SSAP 23 & 24.

A UK leader in the practice was Grand Metropolitan. On advice from Interbrand Co and with the agreement of auditors Peat Marwick McClintock, GM valued all the brands it had acquired in takeovers since the start of 1985 in September 1988. The rationale could have been:

(1) a defensive exercise to ward off predators by making the company too expensive
(2) to help with obtaining future debt by increasing the size of the equity base
(3) to increase the value of a company that is to be sold
(4) to bring the company's value into line with reality

Factors involved in the B.V. exercise include longevity, brand leadership and loyalty, advertising and promotional support.

The BV actions by GM and by Rank Hovis McDougall, who added £678m to the value of their company in this way, was said to be causing great concern to the ASC who were considering issuing guidelines in January 1989.

APPENDIX 3: WHISKY SALES

Type of Whisky	Sales of Whisky by Type			
	1975		1986	
	m cases	%	m cases	%
Scotch	67.4	36.2	64.4	41.0
Japanese	25.5	13.7	27.5	17.5
Canadian	28.8	15.4	26.9	17.1
Bourbon/Tennessee	33.1	17.7	20.3	12.9
American Blended	24.4	13.1	11.5	7.3
Irish	1.6	.8	1.65	1.0
Other	4.9	2.6	4.4	2.8
Total	**186**	**100**	**157**	**100**

Source: Les Whiskies vers de nouveaux sommets,
Actualités No. 1088, 30/10/87

NOTES & REFERENCES

1 Pernod Ricard *Annual Report* 1987. PR must have been optimistic about its French whisky business since 1987 sales were up by 13 per cent on '86, a new House of Campbell product ('The Legendary', a 21-year old single malt) had been launched and Aberdour Glenlivet had just won the Gold Award of the International Wine and Spirit Competition in the 12 year-old single malt category. Sales of Glenlivet rose during the year by 43 per cent. The company's powerful European distribution system gave it access to new markets in Spain (Prac), Italy (Ramazotti) and the Low countries (Cooymans)

2 *There are some bids which amount to only really image purchases. We don't seek to carry out take-over bids in the media. For PR, buying Martell didn't fit into its strategy. Contrary to Seagram, we don't buy companies for turnover but for profit.*
The company is the world No 1 in anis and the leading French producer of branded French wines and alcohol-free drinks. Since 1975 Group turnover had gone up from F2.8 billion to F12.5 billion.

3 Experience teaches a global view, *The Sunday Times*, 13/11/88. Another version of this was given by Sylvie Hattemer in *Le Nouvel Economiste*, 2/9/88. She wrote of the choices facing Irish Distillers as being *grossir ou se faire manger* (*grow or get yourself eaten*). According to Elisabeth Chavelet (*La Vie Francaise*, 19/8/88), Pernod was *un géant trop petit* (*too small a giant*) in a world where *L'heure est donc aux mastodontes* (*It's the age of the mastodons*) in the view of Francoise Morin (*Science et Vie economique*, December 1988).

4 GM *Annual Report*, 1987

5 Brewing Strategy for Europe, Tony Jackson, *The Financial Times*, 9/11/88

6 Panel may extend bid, Colin Campbell, *The Times*, 11/8/88

7 ID rejects £210m bid, Colin Campbell, *The Times*, 31/8/88

8 Pragmatic panel fudges its tricky Irish question, *The Times,* 18/8/88

9 Irish refer GM offer, Colin Campbell, *The Times*, 31/8/88

10 Young's merger mix-up, Ian Williams and Jeff Randall, *The Sunday Times,* 13/11/88

11 Bids galore, Stella Shamoon, *The Observer*, 23/10/88

12 'At any price it is still prostitution', Sir Hector Laing, *The Times*, 2/6/88

13 'Who's buying whom', Ian Williams and Sue Thomas, *The Sunday Times*, 13/11/88

14 UK financial lead at risk, says Cockfield, Michael Dyness and Colin Narbrough, *The Times*, 22/11/88

15 Panel sees level playing field for European take-over games, Lord Alexander of Weedon, *The Times*, 3/1/88

16 Dash of Pernod may save Irish whiskey, Jeff Randall, *The Sunday Times*, 28/8/88

17   Panel allows GM to raise bid, Graham Searjent, *The Times*, 5/9/88

18   Why the panel cannot swallow PR tactics, *The Times*, 6/9/88

19   Lessons to be learned from the IDG saga, *The Times*, 8/9/88

20   FIIF denies sealed deal with Pernod, Frank Kane, *The Independent*, 8/10/88

21   IDG 'in breach of take-over code', Graham Searjent, *The Times*, 28/10/88

22   PR avec modération, *L'Express*, 2/12/88

Analysts concluded also that there was considerable room for expansion in European sales of Irish whisky. There was much scope for flexibility in the single malt and *top of the range - haut de gamme* products where a bright future could be seen. In the middle range blended whisky area throughout Europe discounting was heavy and promotion rising steeply. The French ad spend alone on Johnnie Walker, Ballantines, Chivas, J & B and Aberlour Glenlivet had risen from a total of F35.3m to F45.9m over the period 1985/6. Critical factors for success included, in their view, a match between price and brand image on a European scale. For triple-distilled (more than Scotch) Irish whisky, there were possibilities in this regard.

PERESTROIKA

Abstract:

Perestroika considers the USSR at a time of maximum stress and within an ace of its being dismantled. The case deals with the business systems created and used by a planned economy and the difficulty of re-shaping such systems to fit the needs of a resurgent Russia, however strong the thrust for ideological change. Indeed, perestroika makes plain that such changes - which may have significant opportunities for European businesses - cannot be made without upheavals in economic and social attitudes. Some of the tensions standing in the way of progress are in Russia's domestic politics. In this field major power struggles were taking place in 1989. This case can be read in conjunction with the Port of St Petersburg and Russia at the Crossroads cases.

Questions:

Review the factors which obliged the USSR's rulers to adopt the perestroika approach. What, in your view, stands in the way of success? Is success guaranteed?
What is the significance of perestroika for international trade relations between the USSR and the West?
What opportunities does it offer to European businesses?

Case Timing: 1989

OPEN SEASON?

On the tenth of April 1989 Cecil Parkinson, the British Government's Secretary of State for Energy, flew into Moscow on a mission to expand trade links between the UK and the USSR. His visit started in earnest on the 11th with the grand opening of the first industrial exhibition mounted by Britain in the USSR in 25 years and with detailed business discussions with Soviet prime minister Nikolai Ryzhkov and his deputy, Vladimir Kamentsev.

The European Commission was also most anxious to increase Europe's trading links with the USSR, especially since the fall in world oil prices in the mid-80's. This had dramatically affected the Soviet Union's revenues as a major oil exporter, (80 per cent of its hard currency earnings) and impacted adversely on Comecon imports. These were in fact, in 1987, at the same level as in 1981 – £22.1 billion as against the Comecon sales in 1987 of £27.9 billion. It was for this purpose that a Trade Convention was signed in Moscow in June 1988 between the EC Commission and the Comecon Secretariat to establish a framework for the expansion of trade on the basis of the exchange of economic, environmental and technical information. No change was foreseen in the system governing the continuation of existing bilateral trade relationships between individual EC members and their Comecon counterparts. A particularly interesting prospect for the EC would have been for the USSR to place its EC cereal purchases on the same sort of long-term contract basis as it had done with its massive imports of US grain used used to help feed its 286m inhabitants.

The 300 British exhibitors shared the UK government's high hopes of increasing the volume of trade between the two countries in line with the targets that had been laid down at the previous summit meeting in London between British Prime Minister Margaret Thatcher and Soviet president Mikhail Gorbachev. With British exports R220m below the figure reached in 1984 – a figure equal to Britain's 1988 trade deficit with the USSR – there was more than a touch of urgency about Cecil Parkinson's efforts to get trade moving to reach the 1990 goal of R2.5 billion. (1 Rouble = 1 Pound Sterling). Although Britain had been one of the first nations to sign a trade agreement with the young USSR in 1921, having already, in fact, signed a trade protocol with Russia during the reign of Elizabeth 1, it now ranked (1987) sixth in the league table for USSR trade with advanced capitalist countries, behind W. Germany, Finland, Japan, Italy and France.

Not that British efforts to date had been wanting. Quite apart from long-running, and often unsung, strategic trade relationships between major European companies and Soviet ministries, many UK companies had sought in recent times to penetrate a Soviet market made doubly difficult by a chronic shortage of hard currency and an elaborate, arbitrary and artificial system of rouble convertibility rates. This latter was based on a range of thousands of so-called 'coefficients', each applied to a different product sector. It was the cause of substantial disagreement among trading partners.

Company	Plant Type	USSR Partner	Plant Location
Courthaulds	Chemical	Techmashimport	Saratov
John Brown	Polypropylene	N/A	Budyonnovsk
Taylor Wood Row	Clothes	Tchnopromimport	Talinn, Riga & Minsk
Pechiney	Aluminium	N/A	Armenia

TABLE 1: EXAMPLES OF CURRENT STRATEGIC TRADE LINKS

One such British entrepreneur who had sought to establish new links with the USSR was Virgin Airways. Sensing a major opportunity, chairman Richard Branson had signed a co-operation deal with Intourist in January 1988 to take over, and run in conjunction with his airways business, the 121-bed Orianda hotel in Yalta, on the black Sea coast. It was formerly a Tsarist palace. There was certainly no shortage of optimism in the statement issued after the signing ceremony:

As long as Gorbachev is in power and is making positive moves to open up the country, said Richard Branson, *the more we can trade with Russia, the more it will encourage the politicians to come closer together...* [1] *He is making a tremendous effort to improve things in the Soviet Union and it is important we give him a chance... My decision is a gesture towards that change.* [2]

For the Virgin group much could stem from this initial break-through. Not only was Soviet youth eager to obtain the sort of pop music issued on the Virgin label but there was also the question of the 'Mates' condoms – manufactured by yet another Branson subsidiary. According to one seasoned USSR correspondent, the Soviet version was *thick and, therefore, not comfortable... and in short supply.* [3] Hence the expectation of great success for the British product.

Virgin was by no means alone in its hopes for the future. Francis Killingbeck Bain International, for example, had signed a marketing services agreement with Vneshtorgreklama for advertising and product design for Soviet firms and Ernst & Whinney, world-ranking financial analysts, had teamed up with Soviet Inaudit to offer a range of advanced consultancy and audit services. But these were by no means as visible as the joint USA-USSR venture deals made by the Macdonald's and the Pepsico subsidiary Astropizza to set up their fast-food businesses in Moscow.[4] Or those which resulted in the advertising of Pepsi Cola and Japan's Sony on Soviet television. Or the joint venture deal entered into by Tampax to build a factory in the Ukraine.

Date of loan	Bank Consortium	Value of loan [£ billion]
October 1988	W Germany	
	France	
	UK	
	Japan	
	Italy	9
November 1988	France	2
	Germany	1.7
April 1989	Italy	1

TABLE 2: EXAMPLES OF RECENT VNESHEKOMBANK BORROWINGS

Note: It is estimated that Western commercial bank lending to the USSR had grown, by the end of 1988, to £33 billion. This was twice the level outstanding at the end of 1984 but did not represent, in the view of *The Economist* (5/11/88), *a Russian borrowing splurge*, given the USSR' relatively low debt service burden (20 per cent of exports going on servicing foreign debt vs, for example, Brazil's 43 per cent) over the three-year period to mid-1988.

On the other hand there was much international competition at all levels to take advantage of the new trade conditions in the USSR which were based in part on the USSR's increased borrowings from the West. (See Table 2). Among the leaders in winning major construction contracts in recent years had been such prominent multinationals as the French construction group, Bouygues, and the Fiat subsidiary Telettra Espanola. Another Italian company, Ferruzzi, had been awarded in October 1988 a Gosagroprom contract to set up a huge 4-module agro-industrial complex in Stavropol (president Gorbachev's home town), Kursk, Odessa and Dniepropetrovsk. Nor were the Germans missing from the list. Siemens and Asea Brown Boveri (Switzerland) had signed an agreement also in October 1988, to construct a high temperature nuclear reactor, the first to be built in the Soviet Union since the catastrophic R8 billion Chernobyl disaster in 1986.[5]

The Japanese thrust was, by contrast, focussed upon Siberia. In December 1988 a consortium of Mitsubishi, Mitsui and Chioda announced the construction of a petrochemical complex worth £5 billion. Bilateral trade with Japan was bounding back after the setback sustained when Toshiba sold machinery designed to make submarine engines quieter. This action was against the regulations of the US-led Co-ordinating Committee for Multi-lateral Export Controls (COCOM) and much to the anger of the USA.

Four years ago we made a choice, asking ourselves the most difficult questions. We have firmly opted for overcoming ossified dogmas and stale patterns of thinking. This has produced perestroika... There is no turning back for anyone. The people have firmly linked their destiny with perestroika.. We launched perestroika with our eyes open...

As for the difficulties - and they do exist - we accept them as a natural expression of contradictions inherent in a transition period... We have chosen, definitively and irrevocably, the route leading to new forms of life - democratising our society in all its spheres... We are convinced that, only through democratisation, is it possible to build a well-functioning, healthy and dynamic economy. Radical economic reform which blends together planned regulation and the market will help us devise a new economic mechanism.

We have formulated a new agrarian policy seeking to tear down the adminsitrative command system in agriculture... The decisions adopted are of fundamental importance.

EXHIBIT 1: FROM PRESIDENT GORBACHEV'S GUILDHALL SPEECH
Source : Queen Invited to Moscow, *The Times* 7/4/89

Such massive capital investment projects were clearly aimed at stimulating the USSR's economy to a greater level of growth than that achieved over the period 1986-8, which the Economist put at an average of 2 per cent per year. They would be clearly helped by such infrastructural developments as the creation of the first foreign bank to be set up in the USSR - the International Moscow Bank - in May 1989. This was a joint venture spearheaded by Credit Lyonnais, Banca Commerciale Italiana, Bayerische Vereinsbank, Creditanstalt Bankverein (Austria) and Kansallis Osake Pankki (Finland), a consortium with 60 per cent control, and, from the Soviet side, Vnesheconombank, Promstroybank and Sberbank.

INVITATION TO TRADE

Many of the steps which president Gorbachev had initiated under the general heading of 'perestroika' (economic reconstruction) amounted to an open invitation to Western nations to try to increase trade. Among the most significant of these was the decree relating to the setting up of joint ventures (JV) involving Soviet and foreign organisations which was passed in September 1987. According to this, the Soviet partner had control of 51 per cent of the equity, the managing director had to be a Soviet citizen and any profit taken out of the USSR incurred a specially high rate of tax, a further 20 per cent on top of the standard rate of 30 per cent.

One of the first British companies to take advantage of this new departure was Rank Xerox who set up, in partnership with Vneshtorgizdat, a photocopying centre for public use at the Centre for Economic Achievement in Moscow. This began operations in March 1989. Another European company to seize the chances offered was Aer Rianta, the Irish Airports Authority, which formed a joint venture with the Soviet Aeroflot organisation to run duty-free shops in the USSR, starting with Moscow's Sheremetyevo airport in December 1988.

Bouygues, the French construction giant, was yet another leading entrepreneur in this field. The company announced, in October 1988, the creation of a F430m joint venture with a Soviet partner (43/57 per cent) to build a massive new hospital in Moscow. The funding of the F360m French element of IRIS, as the JV is called, was shared by Pullman Hotels (five per cent) and French banks like Credit Lyonnais (13 per cent).

Resistance to some of the conditions applying to joint ventures led later to some relaxation in the USSR's approach. For example, concessions made in December 1988 included the removal of restrictions with regard to foreign participation levels, the need for a Soviet MD and the reduction to a minimum of the customs duty levied on imported equipment to be used in the joint venture. The system whereby all payment for the accommodation of foreign workers was made in 'hard' currency was also changed, as was the inflexibility with which tax was levied on repatriated profit. Businessmen were also highly encouraged by the announcement, made in December 1988, that there would be a 50 per cent devaluation of the rouble for trade transactions as from the 1st January 1990.

By the end of March 1989, Britain had already set up 12 joint ventures and was negotiating for 40 more.

Another major change in the way in which business was done within the Soviet Union was bound up with the devastating critique of the Soviet Union's economic situation made by prime minister Nikolai Rhyzkov at the Supreme Soviet on the 29th June 1987. In his speech he urged his audience to give full backing to the Law on the State Enterprise, which he regarded as the corner-stone of the perestroika programme. It was certainly a dramatic innovation for through the bureacratic machinery of GOSPLAN and GOSNAB. (See Exhibit 4, page 76.)

> (1) Inadequacies in the operation of the USSR's industrial credit system. Soviet industry had a collective debt of 40 billion roubles and borrowings were being used by some 13 per cent of all organisations to cover losses instead of for investments. Such loss-makers faced the possibility of liquidation under new legislation coming into effect on 1/1/88 and the re-assignment of their workforces to new jobs.
>
> (2) Excessive bureacracy both at ministerial level and in terms of the nature of the systems for centrally setting all prices and for operating the newly-introduced GOSPRIOMKA industry-wide quality-control system. *Control* he said *should not be turned into a nerve-racking activity.*[6]

TABLE 3 : KEY POINTS IN THE SOVIET PM'S CRITIQUE

The main features of the new law, passed on the 5th February 1987 were to allow the decentralisation and freedom from state control of some 60 per cent of Soviet industry. These organisations were to be made responsible for their own accounting systems and for their own self-financing, to the point of negotiating price, quality and delivery with their customers. By January 1989 some five per cent of USSR industrial output was subject to freely-negotiated pricing, according to the Economist's estimate.

> *Some economic managers have assumed a passive position and, by force of habit, requested more money from the state instead of earning it. We must overcome habits of dependence on the national budget.. We must strengthen financial discipline throughout the economy. The practice of redistributing money between those enterprises with a good performance and those with a bad performance must be abandoned.*

EXHIBIT 2: FROM FINANCE MINISTER GOSTEV'S SPEECH TO THE SUPREME SOVIET 19/10/87

Note: Boris Gostev also disclosed that 13 per cent of Soviet enterprises were running at a loss, the total value of which was ten billion roubles.

The installation of the GOSPRIOMKA system of universal industrial quality control was intended as a parallel step. Sadly, some of the provisions of the system had to be relaxed in the spring of 1987 because of the huge rejection rate on industrial products, said to have reached 30 per cent in some sectors.[7] It was also clear that the new freedom of operation promised to Soviet enterprises was being frustrated by the continued placing of state orders (*goszakazi*) on them by state ministries. These often required the use of 100 per cent of a factory's capacity.

Another highly significant change in the Soviet economic system was the enactment of the Law on Co-operatives. Taking effect from the first of May 1987, the Law extended the provision, contained in the Law on Individual Labour Activity, for self-employment either directly or within a collaborative private framework. It did not extend so far as to breach article 17 of president Brezhnev's USSR Constitution of 1977. This prohibited workers' being employed by a private employer.

> *For at least three generations our people have grown up with the conviction that the country's economic success depends on a kind and clever General Secretary (of the Communist Party), on the wit and agility of our ministers, on the zeal of our planners, on good decrees and resolutions and, finally, on the honesty and loyalty of our police. In short on anything other than that which has always determined economic success anywhere else in the world; on the ability of a country's economic organism to produce blood and let it circulate freely in its veins and arteries.*

EXHIBIT 3 : THE SHMELYEV VIEW
Source: Nikolai Shmelyev, the economic monthly ECHO.
Quoted in 'Empty Shelves Mock Gorbachev Reforms', Angus Roxburgh,
The Sunday Times, 22/1/89.

Hence, the aim of the new legislation was focussed on the creation of a new form of economic enterprise, a co-operative which would have considerable autonomy in terms of managing its own affairs. By the middle of March 1989 the concept of co-operatives had taken root to the extent that it was increasingly being applied to the leasing of land from the state itself and from state collective farms by family groups and by individuals, the leaseholder being able to sell his produce at market prices. This made for the possibility of a much-needed supplement to the USSR's food resources. How necessary this was can be deduced from the facts that the five per cent of the USSR's land volume producing food destined for sale at market prices produced, in effect, 25 per cent of supplies [8] and that, as president Gorbachev himself pointed out in March 1989 'up to 20 per cent of everything raised in the countryside' was spoiled by the time it reached market.[9]

So popular was the concept that, according to Academy of Social Science statistics, the number of co-operatives rose from 14,000 in January 1988 to

77,000 in Jannuary 1989 and the number of people employed in them grew to 1.4m. This was seen by some to pose a strong threat to existing organisations and a decree published in January 1989 curbed the setting-up of co-operatives an a variety of areas, for example publishing, medicine, religion and co-operative schools. This was a reflection of the initial reaction of some of the Soviet Unions' 15 republics to the Co-operatives Law when it was first enacted. Indeed, less than eight of them had, at the time, specifically debarred the creation of co-operatives in the footwear manufacture and repair sector.

The liking for co-operatives was undeniably bound up with some of their built-in attractions like the lack of limits to individual earnings, the possibility of earnings' being specifically related to individual work contribution and the capacity for co-operatives to make their own plans and set their own prices.

The Law on Individual Labour Activity which came into effect on May Day 1987 gave the chance of limited freedom for private enterprise to such service-providers as doctors, hairdressers, cafe proprietors, car mechanics, freelance translators etc. provided they accepted the tax rate of up to 65 per cent on profits and the need to obtain operating permission from local authorities. The public debate on this law was a lively one. The magazine Sovetskaya Kultura was strongly in favour, commenting that *we ought to be defending the interests of the consumer, not the interests of the bureaucrat.* [10]

One Sovietskaya Rossiya reader, Nina Andreyeva, by contrast, wrote a bitter letter to the editor (Exhibit 5, page 77) claiming that *these people will become a new bourgeoisie and will strangle us with their profits.* [11]

FOR ALL THOSE WHO TRAVAIL

It is hardly surprising, given the tone of Mikhail Gorbachev's speech during his visit to the city of Murmansk at the start of October 1987, that the USSR was being subjected to such a barrage of economic change under the heading of perestroika. In his speech the Soviet president spoke of the fact that prices in the USSR had long remained unchanged, rents since 1928, communal services since 1946 and bread and sugar since 1954, and that, in his view, this matter was now critical. *It is impossible* he said *to solve the task of switching to new methods of management without getting to the bottom of things in the question of prices... One can see children using a loaf of bread as a football.. The value of meat consumed by a person annually is equal to that of a pair of boots. This is why no-one saves foodstuffs.*

In the light of the challenges ahead, there would, he stated, be no retreat in the clampdown of sales of vodka, a major problem for the Soviet consumer and one which had caused the virtual disappearance from Moscow shelves of sugar, one of the key ingredients for the home-made spirit, samogon. Nor, for that matter, in the plan to slash tens of thousands of effectively surplus bureaucratic jobs, the existence of which had contributed to economic inefficiency and to what president Gorbachev called the USSR's *bloated administrative apparatus*.[12] Such draconian action was perhaps not misplaced in a situation where Government subsidies on food amounted to no less than 57 billion roubles and where, as part of this, the state was paying - according to Valentin Pavlov, head of the State Price Commission (GOSKOMTSEN) - 1.8 times the consumer price for milk, 2.5 times for butter and 3.5 times for beef. [13]

Mikhail Gorbachev's Murmansk speech was wholly indicative of another facet of the sweeping reforms he was trying to introduce in the Soviet Union: the creation of a politically more open society. His strategy for achieving this was clearly to help promote realistic discussion of serious issues faced by the nation as well as institutional change. Here, as in the case of perestroika, there was opposition.

The state planning system consists of a variety of organisations, chief among which are GOSNAB (the state's supply arm) and GOSPLAN (the state's planning organisation). Together these constitute an all-embracing system for the procurement and supply of all salient consumer and capital goods within the USSR. On the basis of a comprehensive 5-Year Plan individual 1-Year Plans are set for all aspects of production, wholesaling, retailing, foreign trade and industrial financing. Naturally these also comprise plans for the management of the labour force and for the introduction of new technology. To create the massive inter-locking array of plans for a state as large as the USSR is a huge input-output analysis problem; overall coherence depends on the achievement of targets at each level in the planning hierarchy and in each plan sector.

The limited deregulation of the economy under perestroika is a direct challenge to this planning system.

EXHIBIT 4 : THE USSR'S CENTRALISED PLANNING SYSTEM

Take, for instance, the long-running political debate on Soviet history, begun in earnest and in the open with Mikhail Gorbachev's speech to mark the 70th anniversary of the Bolshevik Revolution.[14] In this, Gorbachev made remarks about Stalin which were construed by political conservatives, as intemperate and damaging. On the other hand, those committed to glasnost and perestroika, viewed them as inadequate to convey the enormity of the human tragedy the USSR had suffered during Stalin's leadership. Both sides were alert to the symbolism inherent in discussing publicly facets of Soviet history previously kept wholly secret.

The possibility of acrimonious debate was heightened by the announcement during the speech of the setting up of a Politburo Commission to enquire into the possible rehabilitation of some of the victims of Stalin's purges, men like Zinoviev, Kamenev and Bukharin. The last named was a particularly important figure to progressives since he had opposed Stalin's scheme for the collectivization of agriculture in the 1930s, with its attendant policy of destroying the land-owning small farmer class, the kulaks. He was shown in a never-before-seen film broadcast on peak time TV on the 17th May 1988 under bitter attack from Stalin's public prosecutor, the merciless Andrei Vyshinsky.

I cannot give up my principles... Just look at the sort of talk there is about the place - a multi-party system, freedom of religious propoganda, the right to settle abroad, the right to discuss sexual problems in the press, the need to decentralise, the ending of compulsory military service..

Letter from Nina Andreyeva (Leningrad Chemistry Lecturer) to the Editor of Sovietskaya Rossiya, March 1988.

This letter, commented Pravda, is *a manifesto of anti-perestroika forces. There is no alternative to perestroika, even delaying it is fraught with the most serious costs for the internal development of our society, for the international position of the Soviet state and for socialism as a whole.*

EXHIBIT 5 : THE ANDREYEVA LETTER
Source: *The Sunday Times* 4/11/88

Two men, Yegor Ligachev and Boris Yeltsin, were portrayed by the Soviet and Western media as key partisans in this debate. Politburo member Boris Yeltsin, the doyen of the progressives, had in fact threatened to resign two weeks before Mikhail Gorbachev's speech over the issue of opposition against reforms which was being mounted within the Communist hierarchy. As Moscow party boss his words carried weight.

They needed to, since opposition to excessive haste in the introduction of reforms was seen as emanating from Yegor Ligachev, the party ideologue and high-ranking Politburo member and, as if that were not enough, from his close ally, KGB chief Viktor Chebrikov.

To work with Yeltsin was torture. He kept dismissing people without reason. Some we managed to save by switching them to other jobs. But we still lost so many good officials. (Vladimir Skutyev, Chief of Moscow Communist Party's Organisation Dept)

Ambition, one of my most characteristic personal traits, showed itself. I tried to hold it in check, but without success. As a Communist, he said, *I am no longer worthy of being a political leader.* (Boris Yeltsin, Ex-Moscow Party Chief)

EXHIBIT 6: STATEMENTS FROM THE MOSCOW PARTY MEETING
OF 10/11/87. Source : Rupert Cornwell, *The Independent*, 11/11/87

Note: In August 1988 Boris Yeltsin was elected to the newly-instituted Congress of Peoples Deputies on a massive Muscovite vote. He was then elected, after a procedural quirk, to the new Supreme Soviet in May 1989.

In his first speech to the Congress, he criticised Mikhail Gorbachev's presidential powers which held potential for *a new totalitarian regime... a new dictatorship.* [15]

Time and time again, Mikhail Gorbachev showed himself aware of the dangers of excess in pushing his policies through; clearly the interests involved in promoting or resisting change were nothing if not entrenched. He needed this sensitivity in large measure when, at a meeting of the Central Committee in October 1987 Boris Yeltsin criticised the slow pace of perestroika and reportedly denounced Raisa Gorbachev, Mikhail's wife, for indulging in the development of a 'first lady' personality cult and was obliged to resign from his Moscow Party post. He later became deputy chairman of the State Construction Committee.

The leading figure in opposing haste was, undeniably, Ligachev. It was he who showed strong opposition to the increasing openness with which media editors, like Vitaly Korotich of Ogonyok and Viktor Afanasyev of Pravda, treated previously taboo topics. But the main pressure came from the massive 60,000 Moscow-based higher-level ministerial bureaucracy. Some 50 per cent of these were apparently faced with a possible perestroika-induced job loss by 1990 and re-deployment within industry. They would not be unemployed, since unemployment simply could not exist within the Soviet system as it did in the West, but they might have found themselves in the interesting situation of consulting one of the job centres which Leonid Kostin, deputy head of the State Labour Committee, was commanded by the Central Committee to create.[16] One of the first Ministries to be shut down was the Ministry of Foreign Trade, which, with the 37 trade organisations responsible to it, was, until 1985, in charge of handling 95 per cent of foreign trade. Another was the monster GOSAGROPROM which president Gorbachev had himself created, together with its regional bureaucratic tier (the RAPO) and its giant agricultural-industrial complexes, and which had been run by Yegor Ligachev.

This ceased to exist on the 15th March 1989.

So had preferential access to the BERIOZHKA shops where Ministry officials could buy, with the prized 'B Coupons' issued to all Soviet personnel working abroad, goods which were simply not available to ordinary citizens. Such coupons had been changing hands on the black market at five-times face value. The change was effected by government decree on the 1st July 1988.

From my brief observations, Moscow's stores - as they are quaintly known - are long on lacquered spoons and distinctly short on most other items. To mildly exaggerate the point: the shelves are bare. Russia's 71-year-old experiment has clearly fallen foul of gross bureaucratic management and corruption on a grand scale. No nation could have achieved economic stagnation on such a grand scale any other way.

EXHIBIT 7: THE LATEST FROM MOSCOW
Source: Melvyn Marcus, *The Observer*, 16/4/89

Note: that items in particularly short supply at the time were lettuces, apples and tomatoes. Soap was 'precious'.

PANDORA'S BOX?

There should be *no mistakes* in selecting candidates to attend the special Party conference called by Mikhail Gorbachev in Moscow in July 1988. Thus Pravda on the seventh of May 1988.[17]

Given that the next standard 5-yearly Conference was not due until 1991, this being the first Extraordinary Conference since 1941, and given that the subject matter for this event was to be major economic and political reform, Pravda's concern was clearly justified. The president's message to all Soviet newspaper editors about the delegates had spelled out what he wanted:

Our position is that it is committed stalwarts of perestroika, active Communists, who should be elected delegates... There must be no more quotas... specifying how many factory workers and farmers and how many women are to be elected. The principal political directive is to select active supporters of perestroika. [18]

Nation-wide voting by secret ballot began on the 13th May, the Conference having been scheduled since mid 1987. Boris Yeltsin was elected delegate by the region of Karelia, his abject apology for political 'misjudgements' whilst Moscow party boss having been, apparently, forgotten.

The proposals for 'theses' (topics) to be debated at the Conference also indicated sparks ahead. Matters such as command management and economic competitiveness, academic freedom and the *nomenklatura* (the list of Communist Party members suitable for high-'ranking' jobs; in a sense its aristocracy), price reform and even open debate - all these were relatively new conversational items in the USSR. The groundrules for handling the debates spoke volumes:

The formation of real pluralism of opinions and open comparison of ideas and interests are a characteristic feature of our time. While supporting a diversity of opinions, the CPSU's Central Committee emphasises that debates are fruitful only when conducted on the basis and in the name of, socialism. They must not lead to political confrontation or disunite social forces which would complicate the solution of tasks vital to our whole society. (19)

When, on the 28th June, president Mikhail Gorbachev opened the Conference with a stunning three-and-a-half hour address to the 4,900 delegates, he pulled no such punches, however. *We are learning democracy and openness, learning to argue and debate and to tell each other the truth* he declared. *The people demand democracy, full-blooded democracy and there can be no compromise.* On the basis of which he proposed no less a revolution than the use of a secret ballot to elect, still indirectly of course, both the parliament (The Congress of People's Deputies and the Supreme Soviet) and the president. The former would mean the overthrow of one of the founding principles of the Bolshevik revolution - the unopposed selection of the membership of the Supreme Soviet from among quotas of chosen, party-endorsed workers, peasants and intellectuals. Such people were, in fact, unelected and, possibly, unrepresentative of some of the critical interests of their putative electorate. Of course, all candidates for election had to be Communist party members.

His speech ranged far and wide. The Soviet economy's short-comings were dealt with, with reference alike to the inadequacy of Stalin's 'command methods', to Brezhnev's 'period of stagnation' and to the fact that the USSR was running a budget deficit, which had caused inflation and destabilised the rouble, which, one day, he hoped to make convertible. The reconstruction of the Soviet legal system was also called for to the point where there would be a presumption of innocence before trial and account taken of respect for freedom of conscience. Food and housing problems and the issue of the recent outbreaks of nationalist-democratic activism unrest, in Lithuania, Latvia, Estonia, Georgia, Azerbaidjan, Armenia, were not ignored.

The inalienable right to full and accurate information on any question with the exception of military or state secrets.

The rights to information and the process of administering justice to be enshrined in a new law. No use of such *glasnost* could be made to further sectional or corporate interests. So far as the bureaucracy was concerned there would be a new all-embracing principle that *everything that is not expressly forbidden is permitted.*

A new approach on inter-ethnic relations involving *not the dead hand of unification but full-blooded and dynamic unity in national multiplicity.* This would stretch to greater cultural and linguistic freedoms and more autonomy but not to any measure militating against *the strengthening and progress of our multi-national state.*

Changes in the political structure: a new, elected Congress of People's deputies, a reduced supreme Soviet with legislative powers and a new-style presidency, the election to one particular post for a 5 year term of office (renewable for a maximum second term) of all party and government officials.

EXHIBIT 8 : CONFERENCE DECISIONS
Source: *The Times* 4/7/88

It was 75 minutes before the President received the first round of applause; for most of the speech the audience remained silent.

He got what he wanted from the Conference, however, but not before a lot of ideological mud had been thrown. Speaker after speaker at the Conference seized the opportunity to openly air grievances against the system in their speeches. One of the most politically significant was from German Zagainov (head of department, Central Institute of Aero- and Hydrodynamics) who declared:

In no way do we doubt the correctness of the decision of the Central Committee on Yeltsin. But he is a well-known person in the Party with his resolute attitude in favour of restructuring. His incomprehensible repentance at the Plenum of the Moscow City Committee did not explain his position... we would like to hear his explanation at the Conference. If it is some crazy left-wing ideas, then they will get the appropriate assessment. [20]

Nearer to home was the complaint from the steel worker from the Urals:

Workers are asking plainly 'Where is the perestroika?'. For example, in the shops the situation with the foodstuffs is the same as it was and now coupons have been brought in for sugar. There used to be no meat and there is none now. Manufactured goods have disappeared somewhere altogether. [21]

Mikhail Ulyanov, president of the Theatre Workers Union, produced an oratorical tour de force on the subject of the freedom of the press. He referred particularly to the Stalinist values displayed in the now-celebrated Andreyeva letter and criticised the media for being *a tremulous hand maiden of a few party comrades who were used to living and ruling unchecked* and not *an independent and serious force*.

Perhaps the most serious issue was raised by academician Leonid Abalkin. Director of the Institute of Economics at the Academy of Sciences. Although his speech formally addressed the Soviet economy, his main thrust went deeper:

The chief question is whether we can organise society democratically and, at the same time, keep the organisation of society by the one party system? Yes or no? And, if yes, how can we do it? [22]

One contributor to the open debate at the Conference hailed from Stavropol, Gorbachev's home region. He had a very interesting tale to tell - especially in view of the proven corruption charges against President Brezhnev's son-in-law, Yuri Churbanov.

They say we do not have a mafia. I say that we do... This mafia, maybe it's not the Sicilian kind because they shoot at each other there. But here they plunder the state stealthily and daily and it is very difficult to do anything about it... [23]

As a political Pandora's Box the Conference augured much for the Congress of People's Deputies which sprang into existence in May 1989. Its birth followed after nation-wide elections and after (at a Central Committee plenum on the 25th April), Mikhail Gorbachev had received the resignations of no less than 110 of its members. These included the long-serving erstwhile Soviet Foreign Minister Andrei Gromyko and former Chief Commentator of Pravda, Yuri Zhukov. No less than 30 of these very senior party members had been voted down in the Congress election.

The election itself resulted from the adoption by the Supreme Soviet in December 1988 of modifications to the Soviet constitution whereby there was to be an end to over-arching rule by Central Committee and Politburo.

*The time has now come to take measures, perhaps extreme measures, through producing more consumer goods and increasing their importation.. We say to the ordinary industrial worker: try your best and you can earn more. But for what? To buy a car? For that he will have to save for 10 years.. In order to overcome this inertia, you should develop the demand to make such goods accessible - things we used to call objects of luxury.***(a)**

*There is a widespread opinion... that the situation in the produce and mass consumption markets has not only not improved but has deteriorated. There are queues in the shops and empty shelves as before... Our future ability does not depend on gold but on our ability to cope with technological change.***(b)**

*It's difficult (implementing perestroika) even if no-one interferes. But imagine there are people obstructing you. Someone holds your leg... your hand... pushes your head under water. You would lose interest in swimming.***(c)**

EXHIBIT 9: TOWARDS A NEW ECONOMIC POLICY?

Sources:

(a) Dr Leonid Abalkin (director of Economics Institute, Soviet Academy of Sciences quoted in *The Times* 3/11/88)

(b) Nikolai Shmelyev (writing in Novy Mir, quoted in *The Times* 12/4/88 and *The Independent* 16/4/88)

(c) Dr Abel Aganbegyan (chief economic adviser to President Gorbachev quoted in *The Observer* 10/4/88)

Note: Lenin, when introducing his 'limited free enterprise' New Economic Policy in 1921 at the height of post-war privation in the USSR, stated: *We are retreating in order to take a running start and make a bigger leap forward.*

The 2,150-strong Congress (of whom 1,500 were to be elected by constituencies and districts and 750 nominated) and the 542-member Supreme Soviet (elected from the ranks of the Congress according to a negative formula) (see Appendix 1, page 85) comprised the newly chosen governmental system. It did not necessarily reflect earlier electoral popularities at the Congress Level. It is noteworthy also that the president's executive role was to be strengthened as part of the constitutional change and that he (or she), too, was to be elected by Congress.

Mikhail Gorbachev was elated at the prospect of allowing *the master of the country,* [24] the people, to speak and of learning in a *school of democracy.* [25]

Since the April 1985 Central Committee plenum the Soviet press has actively been publishing materials reflecting different opinions in a phenomemon of democracy and glasnost (openness). But it is to be noted that some editors willingly publish that which accords with their own point of view. The result is one-way democracy and must be uprooted **(a)***...*

We must ensure that self-seeking ambitions, the cult of profit and individualism do not penetrate the souls of young people **(b)***...*

Foreign voices want there to be a political opposition in the USSR and toss us the idea of a multi-party system. If you add to that their "advice" about transforming our economy on to the lines of the West's market economy, then little remains of Socialism. **(c)***.*

EXHIBIT 10: LIGACHEV SPEAKS

Sources:

(a) Kremlin split on glasnost as Ligachev hits at press, Christopher Walker, *The Times*, 17/9/87.

(b) Socialism - a word in search of meaning, Angus Roxburgh, *The Sunday Times*, 21/2/88.

(c) Angus Roxburgh, *The Sunday Times*, 20/6/88

British businessmen, faced with the task of establishing the real facts about the Soviet economy - a budget deficit of R100 billion or eleven per cent of GNP was the Economist's estimate for 1988/1989, could be forgiven for not appreciating the small print of such constitutional amendments. One such was specialist London counter-trader, Peter Jankovich, who in mid-May 1989 had other, bigger concerns. *Barter deals* he said *are becoming more and more bizarre. The Russians have very few things which we really want but they imagine there are all sorts of things we would like.*[26] His international trading problem was not so much the demand for British goods in the USSR. It was how to deal with the latest Soviet offer he had received in exchange for what he had on offer, some 500,000 Soviet mouseskins.

* * * * * * * * * * * * * * * * * *

APPENDIX 1: MATTERS MILITARY

On the eighth of December 1987 US President Reagan and President Gorbachev signed an historic agreement to scrap all their countries' ground-based intermediate range nuclear missiles [US Pershing 1A, 1AB & 2 and BGM 109 G (Cruise); USSR SS 4, 5, 12, 20 & 23 and SSCX 4 (Cruise)]. It was more than 6 years since the zero-zero option had first been proposed and fifteen years since the Anti-Ballistic Missile Treaty covering the removal of medium-range missiles from Europe. This time 2,611 missiles (859 US and 1752 USSR) were involved in the deal. However, the USA's Strategic Defence Initiative (SDI), Intercontinental Ballistic Missiles (ICBMs), Submarine - launched Weapons (SLBMs) like Polaris and Trident and Long-range Bombers were left untouched. The spirit of the 1975 Helsinki Agreement on Human Rights was much in evidence as the signing took place.

President Gorbachev had had to endure much internal criticism in pushing for this deal with the USA. Yuri Andropov, his predecessor, had backed away from the zero-zero option, thinking that the USSR (Brezhnev) had given away too much to the USA (Nixon) in Salt 1.

The agreement was not an answer to all the superpowers' costly problems. Soviet troops were still in Afghanistan - although their extrication was being actively negotiated - and NATO was becoming concerned at the growth in output of the new Soviet T64 and T80 tanks, with their laminated-composite and explosive-reactive armour. This latter breakthrough gave a defensive capability against all NATO armour except the Leopard 2 and the new US' Abrams tank. New Soviet aircraft - MIG29 and 31 (*Fulcrum*) and SU27 (*Foxhound*) - were also coming into service. These too had a capability (look-down-shoot-down radar) which had long been a NATO monopoly.

NATO leaders had, therefore, much to ponder when President Gorbachev launched his offer to reduce the USSR's military strength in the European theatre by 10 per cent, provided that no provocative action was under-taken by the allies in respect of short-range Lance missiles in W. Germany. Of course, this was a massive step forward in terms of the possibility of change in the balance of conventional forces, as almost 15 years' non-stop dialogue in Vienna under the aegis of the Mutual and Balanced Force Reduction Talks (MBFR) had not affected it. NATO leaders were still unsure as the current balance was put (in favour of the Warsaw Pact) at 1.04 in ground troops, 2.35 in tanks and 3.3 in artillery to 1 and as Russia's military spending was put at 13 per cent of GNP (R122 billion) as against the US' six per cent.[27] Interestingly, President Gorbachev revealed that the current figure was 77.3 billion roubles (about 15 per cent of state spending) in his inaugural address to the Peoples' Congress on the 30th May 1989.

There was also the problems behind the tit-for-tat expulsion of diplomats and journalists from both Russia and the UK, one of them being the *Sunday Times'* Angus Roxburgh, in May 1989 which drew the comment from UK Prime Minister Margaret Thatcher that *things have not really changed much at all.* [27]

Despite this set-back, things had changed. The climacteric commitment to the ending of the long-running Sino-Soviet dispute made during the Peking talks between President Gorbachev and Deng Xiao Ping in May 1989 (against the background of the initial student demonstrations for democracy in Tiananmen Square and their horrific aftermath) was another supposed significant alteration in the world political balance. So was the degree of popular support given by the Polish people to Solidarnosc in the first 'party-political' election the nation had enjoyed since Communist rule under Soviet hegemony began. In fact, because the Polish voting system was, like the Russian one, in some aspects negative (you cross out the names of candidates you don't like), some of the Communist candidates, even in seats uncontested by Solidarnosc, had performed spectacularly badly. The knock-on effects of this June 1989 experiment in democracy on the USSR and other Eastern European countries are incalculable.

Another factor for change emanated from the White House in Washington. Imagine the international furore created when US President Bush in the W. German city of Mainz on the 31st May offered to help share in the building of what Mikhail Gorbachev had called *The Common European Home* by starting negotiations for reducing each pact's troop strength in Europe by 20 per cent and by achieving the tearing down of the *brutal* Berlin Wall - that *monument to the failure of Communism.* [29]

APPENDIX 2 : SELECTED STATISTICS

(1)	Average monthly rent [R] for a family of 4 in a Moscow flat of 50 sq metres with full central heating	11.39
(2)	Price of half a litre of vodka [R]	10.40
(3)	Average monthly take home pay [R]	189.00
(4)	Average monthly bus driver's pay [R]	300.00
(5)	Average monthly book-keeper's salary [R]	120.00
(6)	No. of working days lost in the USSR by people taking time off to shop for essentials [billion]	8.0
(7)	No. of retail & wholesale prices set yearly by the State Pricing Commission [GOSKOMTSEN] ['000s]	200
(8)	Cost to state of meat and milk subsidies in 1986 [R billion]	57.00
(9)	Economic Growth in the USSR 1981-5 [%pa]	-
(10)	Current annual rate of inflation [%]	5-7%
(11)	No. of people who do not have the privacy of their own separate apartment but who live with relatives or in communes [m]	50.0
(12)	Defence spending in 1986 per capita: USA [$]	1207.0
	France [$]	511.0
	UK [$]	492.0
	Germany [$]	458.0
	Italy [$]	238.0
	Spain [$]	117.0
(13)	Annual meat consumption per capita: USSR [k]	62.5
(14)	Russia's international credit-worthiness rating based on R30 billion gold reserves and debt repayment record	AAA
(15)	USSR's hard currency debt [R billion] at June '89	34
(16)	Cost of servicing this debt [R billion] '89/90	12
(17)	USSR exports to hard currency markets [R billion] in '89/90	16
(18)	USSR imports from hard currency markets [R billion] in 89/90 [including R5 billion on grain]	13.6

Sources of these estimates:

Trouble in store for Gorbachev, Christopher Walker, *The Times*, 19/10/87 [1, 2, 3, 6, 7, 11]
Monetarist Shadow over the Soviet Union, Martin Walker, *The Guardian*, 14/10/87 [4, 5]
Gorbachev Faces an Uphill Battle over Reform Programme, Rupert Cornwell, *The Independent*, 3/10/87 [8, 13]
The Economist 7/1/89 [14]
The Economist 28/1/89 [9, 10]
Defence paper Expounds on Need to Stay Nuclear, David Fairhall, *The Guardian*, 7/5/87 [12]

APPENDIX 3 : APPARATCHIKS BEWARE!

We have to learn to master the culture of democracy. The fate of our national reconstruction largely depends on this... We must solve the burning question of the Party cadres.. We cannot allow... illiterate people into party work... We will not achieve the national reconstruction without good Party workers and the question now is about Party cadres who are standing in the way of perestroika. It is not good enough for Party organisations just to sit in the palatial offices we have built for them, with carpets and polished floors and reception rooms and secretaries and visiting hours. We now have some experience of life under glasnost... of criticism and self-criticism... There may have been some excesses... We will not allow ourselves to be frightened nor to be seduced into the disease of trying to ban things. The only acceptable form for our debates is that of dialogue among equals with equal rights. [30]

Note: The Central Committee of the Communist Party and the Politburo are the policy-shaping mechanisms in Soviet government. The Congress and the Supreme Soviet now make up the legislative system. The Council of Ministers is the state's executive and administrative arm. The Communist Party is the engine which drives the USSR. Its cells, organised on a strictly hierarchical basis, operate at all levels in all organisations in the Soviet Union. It runs on the basis of the principle of democratic centralism (each party member is pledged to support policies adopted at a higher level) and has a strong aversion to bourgeois liberalism (despite the privileges, like dachas and official cars, enjoyed by well-placed Party members). Control is effected via the KGB whose ex-chief, Viktor Chebrikov, made a chilling comment about press freedom (*The Times* 1/10/87) in a speech commemorating the birth of Felix Derzhinsky, founder, in 1917, of the dreaded CHEKA. He said *We have among us people with alien ideas which are even openly hostile to Socialism.* By definition, all government in the USSR is Communist government... or, in his eyes, it should be.

The number of people employed in all aspects of government and state administration in the USSR was put, by president Gorbachev himself, at 18m and the annual cost was some 40 billion R.

NOTES & REFERENCES

1   Branson to join Intourist Board, Richard Palmer, *The Sunday Times*, 14/2/88
2   Branson Mates with Intourist, Richard Brooks, *The Observer*, 14/2/88
3   As 2
4   *The Wall Street Journal*, 24/5/89
5   Chernobyl costs Russians Eight Billion Pounds, Christopher Walker, 15/1/88
6   *The Times* 30/6/87
7   *The Economist* 25/3/89
8   Soviet party leaders vow food miracle after radical reform, *The Times*, 17/3/89
9   As 8
10 Slow May Day start for Soviet private enterprise, Martin Walker, *The Guardian* 2/5/87
11 As 10
12 *The Times* 3/10/87
13 Trouble in store for Gorbachev, Christopher Walker, *The Times*, 19/10/87
14 The *Times* 3/11/87
15 Yeltsin worries on new dictatorship, *The Times* 1/6/89
16 Gorbachev hands out the doleful news, Angus Roxburgh, *The Sunday Times*, 29/1/88
17 Gorbachev: democracy with a little help from Stalin, *The Times*, 8/5/88
18 Gorbachev woos editors in drive to press home reforms, Christopher Walker, *The Times*, 12/5/88
19 Party agenda highlights rift over Gorbachev reform, Mary Dejevsky, *The Times*, 8/6/88
20 The Great Debate, Mark Frankland, *The Sunday Times*, 3/7/88
21 As 20
22 Delegates revel in open debate with Gorbachev, Mary Dejevsky, 1/7/88
23 As 22
24 *The Times* 28/3/89
25 *The Times* 2/12/88
26 Russians float off their old subs on Pepsi, Chris Blackhurst and Mike Graham, *The Sunday Times*, 21/5/89
27 *The Economist* 28/1/89, quoting PlanEcon data
28 *The Times* 23/5/89
29 *The Times* Editorial 1/6/89
30 From Mikhail Gorbachev's speech at the Smolny Institute, Leningrad. Quoted in 'Gorbachev steps up glasnost campaign', Martin Walker, *The Guardian* 14/10/87
31 *The Times* 1/10/87

PLESSEY PLC

Abstract:

The telecommunications supply industry is the focus of this case which provides a good example of the take-over of a thrusting, yet small competitor by an industry giant. The case considers the dynamics of the industry and the moves under way within the European Community to deregulate the industry. This allows the logic of the take-over to be appraised.

Other telecommunications cases in this book are France Telecom and Cable and Wireless. They span developments up to 2000.

Questions:

Examine the changing face of the telecommunications supply industry as illustrated in the case and the strategic moves made by major players. Why did Siemens acquire Plessey?
Was it a case of a "categorical commercial imperative"?

Case Timing: 1989

STRADDLING CONTINENTS

Rudolf Mooshanger was deputy chairman of Siemens AG's supervisory board. By profession he was a factory mechanic working in one of the company's Munich plants. Like all his colleagues on the supervisory board, he could well be forgiven any self-satisfaction he might have felt at the results his company reported in 1988. In the circumstances they were very good indeed.

The supervisory board was charged with supervising the management of the firm's affairs on the basis of written and oral reports supplied by the board of directors. It had, therefore, the task of checking on all major aspects of the company's business situation during the previous year. Siemens' financial position, capital investment policy and restructuring programme had come in for special scrutiny by the board. On this sat representatives of the workforce, management, trade unions, shareholders and bankers. The findings were that the company had coped with all the problems of fiscal year 1988 much better than expected. The company had had a successful year with sales increasing by 15 per cent to DM 59.4 billion. There had been problems admittedly, with falling prices and exchange rate fluctuations very much to the fore, but the future looked good.

DRAM (Dynamic Random Access Memory) chips are capable of storing massive amounts of information on a single chip. Siemens were producing a 4 megabit version in their Regensburg plant. They were the largest selling single 'family' of chips and the product field where fierce worldwide chip competition was greatest.

ASICs (Application-specific Integrated Circuits) are high-value chips made to customers' specifications for specialised applications.

RISC (Reduced Instruction Set Computer) chips are known as 'intelligent chips' because of their exceptionally fast processing speeds.

ISDNs (Integrated Services Digital Networks) are internationally-standardised systems for expanded digital communications facilities - 'phone, telex, facsimile - using advanced chip technology and fibre optics. They are used in proprietary switching systems (e.g., Siemens' EWSD or Plessey's System X) for public ('ISDX') and private sector ('PBX') use. An ISDN product technology exchange deal was signed in 1988 between the US' Advanced Micro Devices and Siemens.

EXHIBIT 1 : CHIPS WITH ALMOST EVERYTHING

Source: *The Financial Times* 3/2/89

Note: A 1988 study by In-Stat, the US market research organisation, put the estimated world value of the ISDN market for chips at $600m by 1992. By the year 2000 this was expected to have risen to $3.6 billion.

The company had begun the mass production of DRAM mega-chips, of which it was the leading European supplier, and was well-placed to pioneer the further development of its range of ASIC chips. Both were critical to the manufacture of hardware and software for ISDNs. The acquisition of the ROLM Division of IBM, announced in December 1988, was planned to expand the company's PBX business in the USA and consolidate Siemens' position as one of the leading world suppliers of communication systems.

In Europe, the company was also aiming to strengthen its position and had taken steps to do so by launching, in partnership with Britain's General Electric Company (GEC), a takeover bid for one of Britain's front-edge technology firms, The Plessey Company. The battle turned out to be, in fact, a relatively short one. Plessey's defences were exposed as wholly inadequate to counter the combined Siemens-GEC campaign to increase their European power base in this way. The launch of the bid came, interestingly, only one month before the announcement that GEC and the French company Generale d'Electricité, were to merge their power station manufacturing businesses.

With annual sales ten times the level of Plessey's, Siemens alone would have been large enough to bid, with fair anticipation of success, for its prey. Especially if Siemens' famed liquidity is borne in mind. With GEC linked in with Siemens, the forces of finance, if not industrial logic, were to prove irresistible.

For GEC the process of thinking through this acquisition had been less straightforward. Its first takeover bid for Plessey, made in 1986, had failed on grounds of the safeguarding of the national interest, following strong representations from the Ministry of Defence and companies like Thorn EMI. No-one anticipated that, this time, the opposition would be less.

Indeed, the bidders launched their offer in November 1988 in the certain knowledge of likely statutory intervention. Both were wary of the power of Britain's Monopolies and Mergers Commission (MMC) and of the European Commission (EC) itself to intervene to halt the bid. Had not the last GEC bid been stopped, in the words of the MMC Report, because:

We have come to the conclusion that, in a changing technical environment, the potential benefits of the merger, claimed by GEC, in relation to the rationalisation of research in a merged group are more than balanced by the potential loss of competition in, and for, research in electronics between the two existing research organisations?

Element	Plessey		GEC		Siemens	
	1984	1988	1984	1988	1984	1988
Sales T/O [£m]	1254	1301	4800	6178	15273	19791
Pretax income on ordinary activities [£m]	176	172	671	708	774	825
Employees [000]	N/A	30	N/A	157	310	353
Total Assets [£m]	1132	1292	4674	5224	14258	19872
Equity [£m]	490	623	2239	2715	4232	5878

TABLE 1: COMPARISON OF RESULTS (1984-1988)
Source: Companies' *Annual Reports* for 1988

Note: An exchange rate of 3 DM/£ has been arbitrarily used for purposes of comparison.

COMPARATIVE ELEMENT	PLESSEY		GEC		SIEMENS	
	1987	1988	1987	1988	1987	1988
Sales T/O	1430	1301	5939	6178	17144	19791
Profit on ordinary activities:						
before tax	184	172	668	708	866	825
after tax	122	121	420	451	425	463
Order Book	1363	1739	6050	5912	16798	18247
Retained earnings for year	74	82	294	271	228	260
No of employees [000]	32	30	160	157	359	353
R&D Expenditure		291		670		2160
Total Assets	1329	1292	5436	5224	18295	19872

TABLE 2: A QUESTION OF SIZE
Sources: Company *Annual Reports*.

Note: All data £m. An exchange rate of 3 DM/£ has been arbitrarily used for comparison purposes.

In the defence field, also, the last GEC-only bid had been halted because of the assertion by the Ministry of Defence that, were the takeover to proceed, the Ministry of Defence would have been deprived of *the appreciable financial savings which might otherwise be expected to result from competition*.[1]

The caution of the bidders was by no means misplaced, if the content of one of the first speeches by Sir Leon Brittan as newly-appointed EC Competition Commissioner was anything to go by. Speaking on the 27th January 1989 at Newcastle University he declared that *it is always competition, and only competition, which provides the stimulus for efficiency, for innovation and for ensuring the widest consumer choice.*[2]

EC Telecommunications Ministers last week rejected a plan by the Commission ('The Open Network Provision Directive') to impose deregulation unilaterally on the telecommunications industry. The Commission has, therefore, to reconsider its plans to liberalise data telecommunication services in the EC. The Directive, allowed under article 90 of the Treaty of Rome, would have avoided long delays in obliging national telecommunication authorities to admit private competition for the supply of data communications, data banks, electronic mail and financial transfers. National authorities would continue to have sole control over the networks themselves, as well as telephone and telex services. The article 90 'imposition' method - none of the usual consultation with governments is required - was used last year to liberalise the telecommunications terminal markets but is now being challenged in the European Court of Justice by four EC governments.

EXHIBIT 2 : A RETHINK IS NEEDED
Source : *The Week in Europe*, European Commission, 4/5/89

OPENING GAMBITS

If GEC and Siemens felt any apprehensions about the nature of the take-over fight they were about to enter, they did not reveal them when launching their £1.7 billion bid. It was a case of building on their previous successful co-ownership deal over the GEC-Osram subsidiary and extending the three year old collaboration they had so far enjoyed. The bidders' Strategy Paper spelled out their reasoning:

With the pace of change in Europe accelerating, GEC and Siemens propose to create a significant new European partnership. The acquisition of Plessey will provide the catalyst to give effect to the common objectives and will provide a better springboard for further substantial expansion together. [3]

Such a collaborative move was well in line with the 1988 McKinsey study *Strengthening the Competitiveness of UK Electronics*, carried out for the National Economic Development Organisation (NEDO). This Report indicated that UK companies needed to develop *a critical mass* if they were to capitalise on 1992 chances. What better way for Plessey to achieve this than by being part of the two largest electronic and electrical manufacturing concerns in their respective countries? That was a key plank in the bidders' argument.

Not that everyone agreed with the findings of the Report. Sir John Clark, head of Plessey, for one. He reacted to the damning criticisms in the Report of his company and its UK competitors, GEC, Racal and Ferranti, by referring to it as *a monstrous travesty of the facts based on massive generalisations.*[4] What had particularly angered him were the criticisms that his company was among those which were *numbers-driven* rather than *issues-driven* and the generalisation that *in terms of organisational evolution, many UK electronics companies had structures and management processes which were 'state of the art' for the management of diversified portfolios in the late 1960s and early 1970s but which have worked against the development of successful international businesses.* Their divisions were not run (so the study asserted) on a highly de-centralised basis with *relatively autonomous, budget-driven profit and loss centres.*

Stephen Walls, Plessey's new Chief Executive (and ex-Financial Director of US' Cheseborough-Pond), was another. Nor did he see the takeover bid in the same glowing light as GEC and Siemens. His concern throughout the battle was to try to preserve the integrity and independence of the company he had so recently joined. His opening salvo showed his mettle. *Plessey* he declared *has consistently invested in the future. I find it irritating that two companies who are not renowned for their imagination or for their commitment to the future are now combining to bid for a group that has demonstrated so clearly a strategy for growth.*[5] His attack was also aimed at the *unfair advantages* enjoyed by US and Japanese companies because of *the sheer mass of protective legislation they enjoy at home* which inhibits *competition on an equal footing.* Was he worried, he was asked, by the likely City view of the current situation, given Plessey's recent strategy in seeking growth by buying up Ferranti's chip business and expanding by acquisition in the USA? Clearly he was not:

Plessey in 1986/7 was perceived as ex-growth. Telecommunications was fiercely competitive, defence relied too much on the MOD and microelectronics was stuck... I think far too much is made of the City's short-termism by some managements. We realise we have to balance the short-term needs of the City with the long-term needs of management. [6]

Stephen Wall's views cut very little ice with the chief executives of GEC and Siemens, Arnold Weinstock and Karl-Heinz Kaske. The latter had no doubt of the eminent logic behind the bid. *1992 is a major question for us* he said. *If we Europeans do not regard Europe as our home market, then we are going to have difficulties. There are a dozen companies in the world who do public switching (i.e. ISDNs/ ' phone exchchanges/PBXs tec.)... each company has spent £1 billion to develop a digital switch and everyone has been asking for years who will be able to afford the next generation* [7] *... There is nothing protectionist about a Single European Market. We have to form units to withstand the competition. The next generation of telecommunications will need about £2 billion for R&D. Siemens, even if we are called a bank with manufacturing interests, cannot go it alone.* Chips would be, he concluded, *the basic material of industrial companies for the next decade.* It is note-worthy that the 1988 cash reserves held by Siemens amounted to an estimated £7 billion.[8]

Japanese Company	World Sales Rank	World Chip Revenue 1988 [$b]
NEC	1	4.5
Toshiba	2	4.3
Hitachi	3	3.5

TABLE 3: WHO'S WHO IN WORLDWIDE CHIPS
Source: Dataquest

Note: Japan enjoyed more than 50 per cent of the world chip market in 1988

Of the fierce world wide competition for telephone exchanges (and particularly for the private branch exchanges set up to handle all the internal data communications of a major company) there was no question. In the US' PBX market a GEC-Siemens-Plessey link-up pooling their PBX models would have taken the combination into third place behind AT&T and Canada's Northern Telecom. The latter was already owner of 28 per cent of the UK's second-largest electronics company - STC. In the chip area alone, quite apart from the Japanese and US leaders, there was formidable European competition. Adding Plessey's production of ASIC chips to that of Siemens would take the group to third position in the European league table, behind Philips and the Italian-French company SGS-Thomson.

It is interesting to find, in this context, that both Plessey and Siemens had stated ambitions to pioneer research work into the next generation of semi-conductor technology. Their programmes were planned in the context of the European Community Joint European Sub-micron Silicon Initiative (JESSI). This was aimed at producing chips capable of storing 63 m bits of information, equivalent to 4,000 pages of typewritten text.

The Plessey defence document launched in January 1989 did not mince words. The bid, it declared, was *an unwelcome irritation for our shareholders and a frustrating distraction for this company's management.* It was based on *a poverty of imagination* and a recognition of *the competitive threat* posed by Plessey. Given some of the arguments advanced by the bidders these were words which needed justification if the bid was to be warded off.

ANOTHER DISTRACTION?

It was in January 1989 that another bidder entered the ring. But this time it was not Plessey which was the intended victim, but GEC. The bidder was Metsun, an off-the-shelf company created by City financier Sir John Cuckney, with the intention of master-minding a £7 billion takeover bid and, it was said, splitting up (and selling) GEC's assets. Arnold Weinstock, 26 years at the helm of GEC, was not impressed with preliminary reports of Metsun's bid preparations - *We will have to look at the rabbit before we shoot it* he declared.[9] Nor were others. But the more Bryan Gould, the Labour Party's Industry spokesman looked at the issue, the more concerned he became:

We are conceding control of the heartland of British manufacturing industry on the eve of.. 1992. We shall have no power to control investment, research or plant closure. Such an important move as this would not have happened abroad without the Trade Secretary (of the country in question) being intimately involved. Here the Government simply washes its hands.. You cannot leave questions about the ownership of such a company to the vagaries of boardroom dealing, share dealings and who employs the cleverest merchant bank. [10]

The same was true of engineering union leader Gavin Laird. He was, he stated, happy to see *more dynamics in GEC* but not as the victim of a takeover that would mean *plant closures, redundancies and cutbacks.* The reference to *dynamics* could be seen to relate to the range of difficulties GEC had experienced in the relatively recent past. These included the cancellation of the £1 billion Nimrod early-warning radar system for the MOD, delays in producing the Fox-hunter radar system for the RAF's Tornado aircraft and problems with the diesels for British Rail's 125 Inter-City trains. Both Bryan Gould and Gavin Laird had reason to be anxious because GEC was, in fact, Britain's largest manufacturer.

The menace of Metsun meant little to Siemens and GEC who, by mid January 1989, had extended their holdings in Plessey to the statutory level of 14.9 per cent prior to the ordering of the two anticipated enquiries into the takeover attempt. The first, recommended by the Director-General of the Office of Fair Trading, Sir Gordon Borrie, focused on the potential effects of the possible narrowing of competition in critical product areas, one of which was defence electronics. The second, instituted by EC Competition Commissioner Sir

Leon Brittan, was to deal with Plessey's charge that the bid was a prima facie breach of Article 85 (1) of the Treaty of Rome.

ELECTRONIC SYSTEMS		
Marconi defence electronics & components, GC Avionics, Yarrow shipbuilders		
Sales £2137mm	Profit £209m	Est. Value £1800m
TELECOMMUNICATIONS		
GEC has 50 per cent share with Plessey in GPT		
Sales £732m	Profit £102m	Est. Value £726m
AUTOMATION & CONTROL		
Avery weighing machines, Gilbarco & Avery Hardoll garage pumps, GEC traffic automation		
Sales £551m	Profit £46m	Est. Value £240m
MEDICAL EQUIPMENT		
Sales £367m	Profit £112m	Est. Value £112m
POWER GENERATION		
Power station turbines, Ruston gas turbines, GEC & Ruston diesels, Paxman ship diesels		
Sales £524m	Profit £56m	Est. Value £396m
ELECTRICAL EQUIPMENT		
Railway locos & signalling equipment, power cables, wire, switchgear, transformers, lifts, boilers		
Sales £734,	Profit £58m	Est. Value £418m
CONSUMER PRODUCTS		
Hotpoint, Creda, Redring, Xpelair & Osram		
Sales £582m	Profit £60m	Est. Value £507m

TABLE 4: GEC - INDUSTRIAL COLOSSUS OF THE UK
Source: *The Times* 9/1/89
Note: this is only a partial statement of GEC's Activities. 1988 financial data.

TRUMP CARDS

As if the situation were not embroiled enough, it was also in mid January that GEC announced a major joint venture deal with General Electric of the United States, and this within 24 hours of the reference of the Plessey bid to the Monopolies & Mergers Commission.

Under the terms of the deal, GE and GEC would have 50 per cent each of a new company which would be set up to run their corporate interests in a wide range of fields, notably consumer electronics and medical equipment in the European market. An interesting twist to the tale was the fact that John Welch, Chairman and Chief executive of GE, had previously been in contact with Metsun over the possibility of joining in with their bid - *seriously dancing* were the words he used,[12] but had turned them down on *seeing their cards*.

US Company	Year				
	1984	1985	1986	1987	1988
INTEL	198	2	[203]	248	453
MOTOROLA	387	72	194	308	445
TEXAS	276	[141]	63	321	366
NATIONAL	64	43	[93]	[23]	63
ADVANCED MICRO	165	[10]	[95]	[64]	19

TABLE 5: NET PROFITS IN US CHIP FIRMS: $m [11]

Lord Young, Secretary of State for Trade & Industry, decided in late March 1989 not to refer the joint venture to the MMC.

Company or Group	1987 European Sales T/O [m$]
US Companies: Texas Instruments, Motorola, National Fairchild, Intel	1603
Philips Synetics	969
Japanese Companies: Hitachi, Toshiba, NEC, Fujitsu	704
SGS-Thomson	535
Siemens	446
UK Companies: Plessey & Ferranti	157

TABLE 6: WHO'S WHO IN EUROPEAN CHIPS
Source: Dataquest data, *The Financial Times* 13/12/88 & 2/2/89

The alliance struck between GEC and GE was by no means an isolated occurrence in the world's high-technology industries. Indeed quite the reverse. The 1980s had seen a virtual mania for takeovers, mergers and (failing that) collaboration deals. GEC was involved in not a few of them. Take, for instance, the merger of the Alsthom Division (power generating and heavy engineering activities) of the major French electrical engineering and telecommunications group, CGE, with the power division of GEC which was announced in April 1989. This 50:50 deal made the combined company the second largest power engineering group in the world after ASEA BROWN BOVERI, the Swedish-Swiss group formed in late '87. Only one month before, the French space and defence Matra Group had unveiled a share exchange agreement with GEC and Daimler Benz.

Siemens also had been in the lead with the well-publicised December 1988 deal with the ROLM Division of IBM, the USA's third largest indigenous manufacturer of PBX. It had also engineered the purchase of a £32m (FF 346m), 51.7 per cent stake in the French computer group, IN2, in early 1989. The link-up between GEC and Siemens itself put them into the number two spot in Europe (behind France's Alcatel) so far as telecommunications were concerned.

GEC and Siemens clearly needed to be large and powerful to compete, in the defence market, with such giants as the German Daimler Benz corporation whose portfolio included Dornier and AEG and who, in addition, owned a sizeable slice of its technological stable-companion Messerschmidt-Blohm-Bolkow. The slice was, with the whole-hearted agreement of the German Kartellamt, to become, later in 1989, almost the entire cake.

Media commentators naturally speculated whether *a white knight* would emerge from the ranks of the European telecommunications majors - Thomson-CSF the French state-backed company, A T & T, Philips and Olivetti were the most frequently mentioned, to save Plessey from the clutches of GEC and Siemens by offering just such a link-up deal, but it was not to be. Plessey was left to inveigh against the GEC-GE joint venture:

GEC is ceding management control of one business after another. It is rapidly becoming an investment trust... GEC is putting yet more of its strategic business under the control of foreign companies. In the case of GE it is putting business in the control of a foreign company with a track record of aggressive rationalisation.[13]

Metsun was left, by contrast, bemoaning the GE-GEC deal. In a 26-line company statement entitled 'More poison pills from GEC?', a company spokesman stated *These transactions raise important issues over the valuations of shareholder assets and pre-emption arrangements which can shut out bids and more beneficial transactions for GEC shareholders from elsewhere.* The *elsewhere* being, presumably, Metsun, which was widely thought to be working in concert with Plessey.

Whether they did or not or were or not are moot points, since, at this juncture, in mid January 1989, Metsun effectively faded from the scene. Lord Weinstock wasted no sympathy: *A fortnight ago, I said we would have to see the rabbit before we could shoot it. It now looks as if it had myxomatosis.*[14] Plessey was again on its own, with only the prospect of victory in its legal move to buoy up Stephen Wall's spirits.

PROS AND CONS

One deduction about the Plessey takeover bid situation was inescapable for Rudolf Mooshanger and the other members of Siemens' supervisory board who included representatives from the Deutsche Bank and the Union Bank of Switzerland. Namely, that the systems and structures for managing both Plessey and GEC were radically different from those in Siemens. They must have been interested that an institution such as a supervisory board did not exist in the British system. They must also have been concerned by widespread media comment that the style of management in Plessey and GEC drew more on paternalism and autocracy than it did on the model of participative industrial management applied in Germany and advocated in the Social Charter. Plessey, it was widely known, had been strategically driven in recent years by Sir John Clark, the son of the company's founder. Sir John Clark's vigorous style is well revealed in Plessey's 1988 Report:

Plessey has a culture which has been developed over 70 years...Corporate character of the right quality... is often the deciding factor in winning orders... High integrity, reliability, innovation; in short, being able to do what you say you will do is still the decisive factor in business. It is an essential part of the Plessey ethos. This character is inherent in Plessey people. They respond to an environment where opportunity is matched by demanding standards of performance; where sensible discipline goes hand in hand with reward... We have a strong team extending from the top down through several echelons of management. This gives us a depth of experience and control in our businesses and has the attributes of good management.

Nor was the style of leadership of Arnold Weinstock different in some ways from that of his GE partner 'Neutron Jack' Welch, so nicknamed by the media because of his ability to turn companies around by eliminating staff surpluses whilst leaving the buildings standing. The Chairman and Chief Executive of Britain's largest manufacturing company, with a cash mountain of £1.23 billion to back his current moves, could certainly look back over a 20-year acquisition strategy which owed much as much to the ruthless as it did to the fearless. The much improved GEC position in early 1989 also made it possible to reject the scathing criticisms of GEC's international performance made in the NEDO Report 'Performance & Competitive Success' (Summer 1988).

Despite business culture differences there was every reason for Siemens' supervisory board to commend the buy-out of Plessey. Nothwithstanding the fact that 1987/1988 had been a more difficult trading year than the one before, almost half the fall in profits had been due to currency changes, there was clear evidence of a well-grounded strategic plan at work in Plessey. The year had seen not only the setting-up of GPT but also the purchase in the USA of the Sippican Group and of the Canadian Leigh organisation. Both acquisitions strengthened the company's ability to deal with North American defence markets. In microelectronics, too, there had been strong progress with the take-over of Ferranti Semiconductors. This, according to the Plessey 1998 Report, made the company *the undisputed UK leader in application specific integrated circuits (ASICs)*. It was given by Dataquest the ranking of *the fastest growing European integrated circuit supplier*.

The Report also stated that, in Plessey, *telecommunications are undergoing radical change. The transition from analog to digital technology is in its final phase; the installation of integrated services digital networks, ISDN, has begun... The use of optical fibres is opening up new dimensions in transmission services*. In all of these, the Report asserted, the company was well placed to advance. It particularly underlined the fact that, through the setting up of its new Roborough facility in May 1987, it was *well placed to secure further growth in ASICs*. Indeed the order book situation for gallium arsenide semiconductors (located managerially within Plessey's Engineering and Components Division) gave reason for *a high degree of confidence.* It was a field in which Plessey saw themselves as having *world-class capability*.

The jewel in the Plessey crown was telecommunications. GPT was on line to become the leading manufacturer and supplier of tele-communications equipment in the UK. Current tie-up moves between GPT and Telenet would add, it was felt, considerably to Plessey's position as the leading UK supplier of packet switched data products (related to the market for PBX and public 'phone exchanges). Its Stromberg-Carlson subsidiary in the USA was achieving strong and growing sales of 'phone switching equipment and digital central office equipment to the public utility Bell companies. Compared with this, Siemens' postion in the USA was relatively weak. Market penetration for System X - the technologically-advanced digital public 'phone system - and the associated Flexible Access System (FAS), employing an advanced fibre optic network, was proceeding apace. Plessey's ISDN capability had gained in both a major share of the UK market and the position as the leading supplier to the army.

Lastly, but by no means least, Orbitel - the joint venture between Plessey and its erstwhile UK telecommunications competitor Racal - had achieved success in its first year of operation as the leading UK supplier to the fast-developing mobile telecommunications market. The EC's commitment to opening up public procurement was clearly having an effect. Orbitel's stated R & D target was to develop production to meet the needs of the new pan-European digital cellular system scheduled to enter service in 1991.

C'est une alliance limitée au seul radiotéléphone cellulaire numérique de 1992. Pourtant, l'accord que Siemens vient de passer avec la SAT [Societe Anonyme des Telecommunications] est une consolation pour le groupe allemand, qui désespère de se faire une place au soleil de ce coté-ci du Rhin... Chacun a besoin de l'autre pour tenter d'obtenir une part du gâteau qui excite beaucoup l'appetit des constructeurs en ce moment: l'ouverture a l'horizon de 1992 d'un radiotéléphone européen à standard unique représentant un marché de plus de 100 milliards de france. Mais le développement du futur radiotéléphone superinformatisé coûte cher; de 600 millions de francs à 1 milliard suivant les évaluations... Le tandem Siemens-SAT est donc un peu une association de dernière minute qui vient s'installer dans les starting-blocks, aux cotés des équipes déjà constituées: Matra-Ericsson, Alcatel-AEG-Nokia, Racal-Plessey ... Paradoxe des alliances; le nouvel associé de la SAT, Siemens, avait déjà passé un accord de recherche avec Ericsson sur le projet de radiophone. Translation note 13 on page 110.

EXHIBIT 3: RAPPROCHEMENT EUROPEEN
Source: *Le Nouvel Economiste* 22/4/88

PLESSEY 0 – GEC/SIEMENS 1

The end, when it came, was quick. The legal moves made by Plessey to try to gain control of GPT having failed (as had a forthright Plessey attack on GEC's chip manufacturing record). It became evident, as the studies by the Monopolies and Mergers Commission and the EC progressed, that all would hinge on whether the deal would be found acceptable to the two authorities. Stephen Walls campaigned ferociously, stating that:

The facade of Euro-collaboration and 1992 has now been removed. Plessey will not allow itself to be bought on the cheap by two overweight conglomerates who want to carve it up for their own benefit.

But it did not seem to matter.

On the 23rd March 1989, Lord Young announced that he had decided not to refer the GE/GEC joint venture to the MMC, a major blow to Plessey. On the 19th April the European Commission gave provisional clearance for the bidders to proceed with their takeover move. On the 21st April Lord Young followed suit, having been given assurances by GEC and Siemens which more than adequately met the worries transmitted to the MMC by interested parties in respect of defence radar, military communications and avionics. Plessey shares closed at 263p as against the initial offer by GEC/Siemens pitched at 225p in December 1988. This valued the company at £2 billion. The city was pleased.

It was not quite the end of the matter, however. Plessey continued to fight by revealing a plan to sell its stake in Hoskyns, the computer services company it acquired in 1988 possibly as part of a wider-ranging demerger scheme for ts computer services group. Stephen Walls also kept insisting that, if the takeo\ er did go ahead, the bid price should reflect the full and fair value of the company, well in excess of £3 share. Considerable prominence was also given to the speculation that Plessey would build on the 2.2 per cent stake they had acquired in Ferranti in July to create a £2.4 billion electronics group.

Then, a bombshell: less than two weeks away from the closing date set for the bid, the seventh of September 1989, came news that Sir John Clark was quitting as Chairman and handing over executive power to Stephen Walls but would remain as non-executive Chairman. It was clearly a major blow to the man whose father had founded the company.

The end for the company as an independent entrepreneur came on the eighth of September 1989 when it was announced that GEC and Siemens had gained control.

* * * * * * * * * * * * * * * * * * *

APPENDIX 1 : MATTERS JAPANESE

As a response to the European Commission's ruling that chips should not just be assembled in the Community but manufactured there, Fujitsu announced in February 1989 plans to build a $100m (£57m) production plant on Wearside. At that date the only Japanese company producing, as opposed to assembling, was NEC, at Livingstone in Scotland. Assembly and testing operations were carried out by Fujitsu (Tallaght, Ireland), Hitachi (Landshut, W. Germany) and Toshiba (Braunschweig, W. Germany). The Fujitsu announcement preceded by two months the news that SGS-Thomson was to purchase the UK chip maker, Inmos from Thorn EMI.

Licensing was another interesting feature of the increasingly cosmopolitan chip business. RISC chip designs were licensed by US technology leaders MIPS, SUN Microsystems and Motorola to Siemens and NEC, Fujitsu and Hitachi respectively and Siemens' DRAM design is licensed from Japan.

Analysts were concerned at the possible effects on such technology trades of the Reciprocity Trade Bill which US Congressman Tom Campbell was about (December 1989) to introduce. The aim of this Bill was to achieve reciprocity in international investment between the USA and its trading partners. Joint ventures like that between GE and Toshiba, to share costs of research, manufacture and market development in respect of world-market lighting products (e.g., fluorescent tubes), announced in January 1989 could, it was thought, be affected by such a Bill.

Of such trade-restrictive developments in the US, *The Times* editorial of the 22nd August 1989 entitled *Rising Sun* remarked: *America's rejection could be Britain's opportunity.*

APPENDIX 2 : THE EUROPEAN PLAYING FIELD

Mrs Thatcher had never been at pains to disguise her forthright commitment to market economics, in general, and increasing Britain's competitiveness, in particular, in her relationship with her European partners. Her speech at the Newspaper Press Fund in Glasgow on the 3rd February 1989 was indicative:

Not for us Fortress Europe, closing inwards on itself against the rest of the world. We want Enterprise Europe, whose industry and commerce are efficient enough to prosper in fair competition. [17]

The CBI had, however, queried the extent to which the UK was more vulnerable than some of its mainland counterparts to cross-border acquisitions (CBAs).

The data given in Table 7 lies at the heart of such concerns.

Mainland Firms acquiring UK firms		UK firms acquiring mainland firms	
Target	Bidder	Target	Bidder
Rowntree	Nestlé [SW]	Center Parcs [D] [65%]	Scottish & Newcastle
Morgan Grenfell	Deutsche Bank [G]	Carat [F] [50%]	WCRS
Metal Box	Carnaud [F]	Banque de l'Union Européenne [F]	NatWest
RTZ Chemicals	Rhone Poulenc [F]	Elsevier [D] [15.4%]	Pearson
RTZ Oil & Gas	Elf Aquitaine [F]	Newmot Mining [G]	Clyde Petroleum
Coates Bros	Orkem [F]	Flachglas [G]	Pilkington
Total value [£m] of these trades = 5,529		Total value [£m] of these trades = 1,292	

TABLE 7: TOP SIX ACQUISITIONS IN EUROPE BY
EUROPEAN FIRMS (1988-9)

Note: Acquisition Monthly data. Letters in brackets denote nationality of bidder (SW = Switzerland, D = Holland, F = France, G = Germany). Figures in brackets denote share of ownership bought. [18]

In fact the imbalance in EC ownership flows had grown apace since 1984. The UK deficits (i.e. value of UK acquisitions in remainder of EC minus the value of their purchases of UK companies) were £m 203 (1984), 32 (1985), 866 (1986), 326 (1987), 3033 (1988) and 1656 (1989, first 11 months).[19]

The Confederation of British Industry had long expressed concern about the legislative, regulatory and cultural barriers which inhibited British acquisitions on the mainland (called, in Economist shorthand, *Economic Chauvinism*) and the openness of our capital markets and the ostensible short-termism of the City which facilitated the converse. Similarly, the British Government was seeking changes in EC Directives 5 and 13 on Company Law and Takeover Supervision to try to harmonise corporate legislation.

Among the barriers that were regarded by the CBI as particularly problematic in Germany were the extent of employees' statutory rights, limitations on the transfer of shares, restrictions on voting rights (irrespective of the per cent of shares held), the position of company directors (with statutory terms of office), cross-share-holdings (both corporate and bank) and the extent to which the banking system was involved in holding equity shares, either direct or indirect (but with proxy voting rights).   It was estimated that the three largest German banks - Deutsche, Dresdner and Kommerz - held directly no less than five per cent of all German equity shares.

APPENDIX 3 : THE HOUSE DIVIDES

This (Britain's unemployment rate of 6 per cent as opposed to the rate of the rest of the EC-9 per cent) has been achieved not by restrictions but by a policy of sweeping away unnecessary restrictions and regulations.   One lesson we have learnt in this country is that businesses create jobs.   They are not created by regulations. (Norman Fowler, Secretary of State for Employment)

Madame Papandreou (European Commissioner for Social Affairs) will go down in history as the face that launched a thousand bankruptcies. (Jonathan Aitken, Cons Thanet South)

In reality the arguments about the details of the Social Charter are a smoke screen to conceal the rejection of its central principles.   The Government is against anything 'that stands up for the rights and interests of the people in Europe against the vested interests of wealth and power'. (Tony Blair, Chief Opposition Spokesman on Employment)

The Charter is pretty anodyne and toothless... something of a non-event.. a fig-leaf to cover the competition free-for-all of 1992. (Ronald Leighton, Newham NE, Labour)

These are examples of the arguments that were deployed by the Conservative Government and the Labour Opposition in the debate on the Social Charter that took place in the House of Commons on the 29th and 30th November 1989. The Charter - containing 43 Community instruments and 17 Directives, according to Norman Fowler - relates to such issues as protection of children, equal pay, trade union representation, minimum wages, worker participation either directly or indirectly.

An Opposition amendment to accept the Charter was rejected by 273 votes to 203.   A Government motion to take note of the Charter was accepted without a division.

APPENDIX 4 : KEY SIEMENS BUSINESS AREAS

The Siemens organisation consisted of three types of divisions: product-based, geography-based and corporate. In the last were functional headquarter activities - R&D, Finance, Planning and Development, Product and Logistics and Personnel. There are two geographical divisions, Germany and International, indicative of the almost 50:50 split in Siemens' 1987/8 sales. The product-based divisions were as follows:

Energy and Automation: switchgear, drives and automation equipment for a variety of manufacturing industries, especially steel and automative. Sales in 1987/8 were 13 billion marks out of the Siemens total turnover of 59,374 billion marks. Siemens is participating strongly in international moves for standardising communication equipment to MAP (Manufacturing Automation Protocol) specifications.

Power Plants: Siemens builds power stations of every kind - fossil fuel-fired, nuclear and regenerative. Sales in 1987/8 were 12.7 billion marks.

Communication and Information Systems: Computers, lasers printers, peripheral storage units, multi-terminal graphics systems, software. Sales were 10.7 billion marks.

Telecommunications Networks and Security Systems: EWSD switching systems, ISDN's mobile radio, 'phone exchanges etc. Sales were 10.5 billion in 1987/8.

Electrical Installations and Automative Systems.

Semi-Conductors: DRAM & ASIC chips. Sales were 1.5 billion marks.

Passive components and Electronic Tubes.

It is noteworthy that, at the end of fiscal year 1988, 22 per cent of employees were graduates and equivalent and 24 per cent were unskilled or semi-skilled workers. The comparable figures for 1978 were 15 per cent and 32 per cent. Siemens spent no less than 300m marks (approx. £100m) on vocational training in 1987/8.

Source: Siemens *Annual Report* for 1988

NOTES & REFERENCES

1   City split over £1.7 billion bid, *The Times* 17/11/88
2   Brittan points the free market way ahead for EC firms, *The Guardian*, 28/1/89
3   GEC and Siemens make £1.7 billion bid for Plessey, Derek Harris, Sheila Gunn and Colin Narborough, *The Times*, 17/11/88
4   Plessey get McKinsey backing, *The Financial Times*, 6/3/89
5   A marriage made for Europe, John Jay & David Brierley, *The Sunday Times*, 20/11/88
6   The battle for Plessey, Nick Gooding, *The Sunday Times*, 20/11/88
7   As 5
8   The Siemens perspective, Nick Gooding, *The Sunday Times*, 4/12/88
9   £7 billion takeover threat to GEC, John Jay, *The Sunday Times*, 8/1/89
10 Giant GEC takeover shock, Nicholas Wapscott, *The Observer*, 8/1/89
11 Captains take charge at chip makers, Andrew Pollack, *The International Herald Tribune*, 21/7/89
12 GE forges $1.4 billion link with GEC, David Brewerton & John Bell, *The Times*, 14/1/89
13 As 12
    TRANSLATION OF EXHIBIT 3: It is an alliance limited to the only 1992 digital cellular mobile phone. However, the deal that Siemens has just made with SAT is an attractive consolation prize for the German group who despaired of finding a place in the sun this side of the Rhine. Each needs the other to be able both to get a slice of the cake, which, at the moment, is tickling manufacturers' appetites - the opening-up of the 1992 one-standard European mobile phone market, a market worth over 100 billion francs... But the development of a smart mobile 'phone is expensive: 600 million to 1 billion, according to forecasts... The Siemens-SAT tandem is, therefore, something of a last-minute starter, alongside teams which have already been chosen... Matra-Ericsson, Alcatel-AEG-Nokia, Racal-Plessey... One paradox in all these alliances is SAT's new associate. Siemens had already set up a research deal on the mobile 'phone with Ericsson
14 GEC turns the tables, John Jay and Margaret Park, *The Sunday Times*, 22/1/89
15 GEC & Siemens recast bid, Derek Harris, *Times*, 7/2/89 Siemens & GEC bid derided by Plessey, Hugo Dixon *Financial Times*, 7/2/89
16 Plessey value in excess of £3 per share, David Brewerton, *Times*, 7/8/89
17 Thatcher praises United Europe, *Independent*, 4/2/89
18 *The Sunday Times*, 3/12/89
19 As 18

SOURCES FOR APPENDIX 3: *The Times*, Parliament

THE CHANNEL TUNNEL

Abstract:

This case spans the period 1989-97 and deals especially with the financing of the Channel Tunnel. The case context is, of course, the moves made at the French and British ends of the Tunnel (to create a suitable high-speed infrastructure) and by the ferry competitors (to negate any competitive advantages that Eurotunnel might secure). The case material allows conclusions to be drawn about differences between the French and British government stances on public expenditure and the overall commercial viability of the project.

Question:

Explain why the Tunnel has provided its creators, builder, financiers and shareholders with what appears to be a non-stop migraine.

Case timing: 1989 - 1997

CROSSED LINES

Tuesday, July the fourth 1989. A sultry summer's day in London. Prime Minister's Question Time in the House of Commons.

The exchanges that took place that afternoon between Mrs Thatcher, Conservative prime minister, and Neil Kinnock, leader of the Socialist opposition, were as heated as the weather. The subject was the series of weekly national one-day rail strikes the National Union of Railwaymen (NUR) were carrying out at the time.

Would she intervene *constructively and immediately* [1] in efforts to resolve the dispute, enquired Neil Kinnock? Mrs Thatcher's answer did not go quite so far as to identify him as *the striker's friend*, a description of the Labour leader used by MP David Sumberg (Con., Bury South). It did specify, however, who Mrs Thatcher thought was to blame for the transport chaos and commuter suffering that had been caused since the start of the NUR action three weeks before.

> *I note* she declared *that he has no thought for the travelling public... This is a dispute for the unions and management to resolve. Under the 1956 agreement, before industrial action there should be recourse to the National Staff Tribunal. The NUR has broken the agreement on pay... The unions have had the opportunity to meet British Rail at any time and place to resolve out-standing issues. The NUR has set preconditions.. and this is totally contrary to the 1956 agreement.* [2]

Neil Kinnock attacked again, this time from a different quarter. *Will she at least stop being irresponsible and accept the common-sense argument put by the Daily Telegraph this morning, that to outlaw strikes in the public services would be indefensible and an attack on the employee's ability to withhold labour?* The shrift he got from Mrs Thatcher for this reference to possible Conservative thinking was even shorter:

Why does he not have a flash of responsibility and condemn the strike? [3]

The following day Mrs Thatcher followed up this sharp counter-attack with a robust defence of her Government's railway policy.[4] On investment, in real spending on electrification, she said, the Government had spent half again as much each year as had been spent under Labour. In terms of 1989-90 prices, she continued, the greatest year for investment in rail had been 1987-88 at £594m. For 1988-9 the figure was £629m and for 1989-90, £781m.

This was followed by a topical contribution from Barry Field (Con. Isle of Wight):

Even the average reader of Thomas the Tank Engine understands that it is not possible on the one hand to call upon the Government to defeat inflation, and, on the other, to give in to all railway strikers' demands without stoking up inflation. Will she propose a serious economic policy for Mr Kinnock or send Mr Controller to have a word with him.

Other Government Ministers continued to apply pressure for a settlement of the dispute. Nigel Lawson, Chancellor of the Exchequer, for example. In a statement made at a meeting with union leaders at the National Economic Development Council on the fifth of July, he said: *The real damage being done is to the future of the railway itself and to jobs in industry. Rail has a great potential future in this country, especially with the Channel Tunnel in prospect. But what case can the BR Board make out for putting still more taxpayer's money into the railways if union disruption makes them a high risk investment?.* [5]

British Rail Chairman Sir Bob Reid also shovelled more coal on a glowing fire by announcing, together with a record year's profits of £304m, a blunt challenge to the union:

We are not prepared he said *to yield to a powerful trade union which is taking it out on the public... We need to break up the negotiating machinery not the railways.* [6]

That there was a major rail transport headache facing the Government could not be denied, however. In Hyde Park alone on the fifth of July no less than 4,200 cars had been parked under the Government's Emergency Regulations by strike-hit commuters. Traffic congestion had been the stuff of which legends are made. Indeed, the whole situation was giving much useful ammunition to a Neil Kinnock already buoyed up by the Labour Party's recent gain in political stature. The combination of its successful policy review, re-aligning several of its previously left-wing policies more towards the political centre, and its convincing victory over the Conservatives in the European Parliament elections in June 1989 had given the Labour leadership, hitherto seemingly somewhat demoralised by ten years of Mrs Thatcher's administrations, a new lease of life. A considerable fillip had also been given to Labour efforts by the tabling of Commissioner Papandreou's Social Charter of Workers' Rights at the Madrid summit of Common Market leaders in July 1989. Rejected virtually out of hand by British government ministers Norman Fowler and Sir Geoffrey Howe for its stress on the desirability of Europe-wide regulation of such things as minimum income and working times and for its advocacy of the right to strike, the Charter was heavily backed by Commission President Jacques Delors.

Party	% of poll in		No of seats in	
	1984	1989	1984	1989
Conservative	40.8	34.1	45	32
Labour	36.5	40.2	32	45
SLD & SDP	19.5	6.9	0	0
SNP & Plaid Cymru	2.5	3.3	1	0
Green Party	0.5	15.0	0	0

TABLE 1: UK EUROPEAN ELECTION RESULTS 1984 & 1989

Note: The UK turnout was 40 per cent. The UK is the only country in the European Community to use the first-past-the-post electoral system.

In the ministers' view, such a document did little but run counter to job creation in the European Community. Indeed, it threatened to hold up further steps towards the implementation of the Single European Market by the end of 1992.

Subject of Contention	BR view	NUR view
Pay rise warranted [%]	7	10
Pay & changes to national bargaining should be discussed	separately	jointly
Pay should be dealt with by arbitration only at the	Railway Staffs National Tribunal	Advisory, Conciliation & Arbitration Service

TABLE 2: GROUNDS FOR ACTION

Note: The three-member RSNT had an independent chairman but no remit for discussing the national bargaining system, set up in 1956, which BR wished to do away with. In its place BR sought a trade-based system [operating staff, civil engineers etc.] with a national council and some form of arbitration for each, coupled with area and local bargaining. This would enable BR to compete better in the labour market, it was said.

Of course, the change in the make-up of the European Parliament as a result of the elections was also a strong encouragement to Neil Kinnock and his team. Out of a total of 518 MEPs, no less than 246 were left-inclined. Only an extra 14 needed wooing to give the left - in which the Socialists were the largest single grouping, control of the Strasbourg Assembly.

As Table 2 suggests, there were wide differences between the NUR and British Rail over what, it was claimed, the state-owned company could afford. In fact, BR's 1988/9 performance, the third successive annual surplus and the highest since nationalisation, had been bolstered by two non-operating elements: property sales and lettings (65 per cent of profits) and government subsidies of

£549m (down £230m on the previous year). It had achieved the highest level of passenger miles since 1960, 21.3 billion, despite having what John Prescott, Labour's Transport Spokesman, said were the highest rail fares in Europe.

The NUR strikes, and those of its partner railway union ASLEF in the form of bans on overtime and rest day working, were thus seen as potentially highly damaging to BR's future by both the Government and management. Given the possibility of the future privatisation of British Rail (very much in line with Government policy on nationalised industry), it was not surprising that ministers were showing their concern. *The Times*, however, saw the issue in more general terms in its editorial of the fourth of July:

Should it be acceptable for public sector unions with monopoly power to use it in essential services against the public interest? Ought there to be legislation against this abuse? Under this Conservative Government, the unions have been brought under more effective law by stages. Secondary strikes and picketing which intimidates by the force of numbers have been outlawed. Individual workers have been given rights against the closed shop. Strike ballots and the election of union officials have rescued union members from the unbridled power of union bosses. So, should there be now legislation to protect the public interest against the misuse of union power? [7]

ALARM BELLS

The possibility of a rail strike was an alarming prospect for Alastair Morton. He was co-Chairman of Eurotunnel - the Anglo-French consortium formed to build the Channel Tunnel. The big danger was, of course, that its results could alter the planned level of £580m of Tunnel-link related investment by BR.

Labelled by a House of Lords Select Committee *the greatest engineering project ever undertaken by the private sector*, the Tunnel was scheduled to commence operation in 1993. It would offer, for the very first time in recorded history, a land route linking Britain to mainland Europe and would be equipped to handle enormous quantities of freight and passengers.

| Forecast by: | Passenger Traffic [m] | | Freight Traffic [m tonnes] |
	1993	2003	1993
British Rail	13.4	17.4	6.1
Eurotunnel	16.5	21.4	14.8
SNCF	NA	NA	7.2

TABLE 3: 1988 CHANNEL TUNNEL TRAFFIC FORECASTS [8]

Its major advantage was stated as the speed with which the European rail traveller could move from London's city centre to other European cities. Paris would be only three hours away and London-Brussels just over two and a half hours. On top of this there was the possibility of time-saving economies for road freight and such attractions as the convenience of sending rail freight in the same container direct from, say, Scotland to far into the European heartlands. Not that everyone was quite so sanguine as Euro-tunnel at the prospects ahead, however. The Leeds' Chamber of Commerce report 'Reaching the Tunnel' stated that the 1988 BR plan to marshal northbound freight traffic in Willesden (North London) was likely to make rail transit uncompetitive with the road/ferry alternative. The report also took the view that it would take something like 8-10 years to upgrade UK freight routes to the standard needed.[9]

BR's John Welsby, Director for International Traffic and responsible for some of the negotiations with Eurotunnel, was also less than euphoric about the importance of the Channel Tunnel for some of BR's clients when he commented:

Whether we arrive at our destination point an hour or two later than is theoretically possible is a matter of indifference to some of them. You are talking about the inventory costs of holding stock for an extra two hours and that is peanuts compared to the importance of reliable transport. [10]

But such concerns could not detract from the gigantic conception and the formidable engineering work involved. Two rail tunnels, each 50 kilometres long, with a service tunnel between were under construction. Giant tunnel boring machines (TBMs), costing between £7.5 and £15m, each gnawing away at its designated 22 kilometres of chalk marl in the knowledge that Eurotunnel faced possible penalties of £1m in extra interest charges for each day the tunnel building fell behind schedule.[11] At each end, Folkestone and Coquelles, near Calais, there would be a terminal with links to each country's motorway network for the lorries, buses and cars which will be carried in the Tunnel on specially-made shuttles running at 12-minute intervals. Trains would simply run straight through the Tunnel using special new high speed rolling stock commissioned jointly by BR, SNCF and SNCB. Its theoretical maximum capacity was stated as 140 such trains per day.

Eurotunnel had already taken steps to come to terms with British Government policy when, in August 1988, they had launched a campaign to achieve private financing of the estimated £1 billion cost of building the rail link. It had been a move welcomed by Transport Minister, Michael Portillo:

It seems to me that there could be a major opening here for the private sector. If they have sufficient confidence in the high traffic forecasts, they could step in and share the risk with British Rail.. making it possible for a new line to be built earlier than otherwise. [15]

But this would also have meant some relaxation in the way in which public spending totals were computed by the Treasury; at the time all private sector spending on infrastructural projects was counted as if it were in the public sector.

The policy was also strongly endorsed at the Conservative Party's Brighton Conference in October 1988 by Paul Channon, Secretary of State for Transport. He spoke of the attractiveness of using private sector money for road building as well as railway construction:

What a revolution that would be! Why should we make the automatic assumption that bureaucrats or even politicians have some God-given right to decide what kinds of roads we need and where.. My vision is of a Britain with a first rate transport system combining public sector investment with the initiative and imagination of the private sector. [16]

The French, in the throes of preparing to celebrate the bi-centenary of their Revolution, were strong proponents of a different line of argument. They could point to their burgeoning TGV rail network as an outstanding example of a sector giving a highly profitable return on state spending. The British Government's commitment to private funding was exemplified in Section 42 of the Channel Tunnel Act 1987. No Government money would be available for spending on the link or building the associated London terminal. The potential difficulties created as a result of the NUR-ASLEF strike were simple additions to an already problematic investment situation.

The roots of this lay, firstly, in the fact that British Rail's initial view-point was that a high-speed rail link of the French 145mph TGV type was not needed. Secondly, having revised that viewpoint, BR contended that such a link, if constructed, could not be in use until 1998. Thirdly, it was the company's intention to invest only £590m on rolling stock and the Waterloo terminal compared with an SNCF outlay of some £1,200m. This included France's building of the much-welcomed Paris-Lille TGV link (with a Calais spur) in time for 1993.

It was the government's unwillingness to contemplate public sector expenditure in constructing the rail link which was the main bone of contention, however. The principle had been restated, formally, by Mrs Thatcher in the Commons on the 9th March 1989:

It is government policy that the users of the new (high-speed) line should pay the full costs, including environment costs... We do not subsidise airways or ferries to the continent. [13]

It was not a principle which Alastair Morton warmed to. Speaking at the Institute of Directors' Annual Convention, he attacked this capital spending approach as *obsolete* and contended that infrastructural investment (e.g., railways) was different in character from ordinary industrial investment and needed to be treated as such. He called, therefore, for a change in what he called *ossified Treasury attitudes* since, without urgent improvements in Britain's infrastructure, British business post-1993 would, in his view, find itself short of a level playing field.[14]

The Anglo-French Treaty which set the project in motion granted Eurotunnel a concession until 2042 under which the company was free to operate the tunnel under its own commercial policies. This meant gaining income from fares for vehicles and charges paid by the national railways. Additionally, the deal struck between Eurotunnel and the contractors actually responsible for designing and building the Tunnel, Tarmac, Taylor Woodrow, Bouygues, Spie Batignolles etc., provided for saving-sharing if the project is completed below budget, and for significant contractor penalties if not.

Britain's Trade Surplus [£m] with:		Britain's Trade Deficit [£m] with:	
USA	40	EC	13453
Oil exporting countries	3088	Other W European countries	5980
		Other developed countries	3502
		Rest of world	1382
Total	**3491**	**Total**	**24317**

TABLE 4: BRITAIN'S 1988 TRADE POSITION
(CURRENT ACCOUNT) [12]

Fortunately, geological surveys had indicated that about 90 per cent of the tunnel route is made up of chalk marl, an almost ideal tunnelling medium. In the undersea section nowhere would the thickness of tunnel cover be less than 17 metres and for the most part it would be 40 metres. Each operating tunnel would itself be 7.6 metres in diameter.

Any alarm felt in mid-July 1989 by members of the Eurotunnel board would not have been caused by the progress being made in the construction of the Tunnel. Indeed, after some early setbacks, this was thoroughly on target. The problem lay, conversely, with the creation of the requisite London-Tunnel high speed rail linkage and with any environment-reclamation work that might be needed as a consequence.

NOT IN MY BACK YARD (NIMBY)

Right from the outset of the project, it had been clear that the latter could be a very significant problem for all involved. The level of acrimony generated among those most likely to be affected by the housing destruction, environment blight and dislocation by the creation of the London-Tunnel link was amply illustrated by comment made during the Commons debates on the King's Cross Railway Bill which provided for one of the two London termini for Tunnel traffic. Tony Banks (Lab. Newham North West) was among the most outspoken:

> *British Rail have experienced great difficulty in securing the support of an MP to present the Bill to the House. Sir George would find that he had been handed the parliamentary equivalent of the black spot from Blind Pugh. If he goes through Kent, he should take bodyguards. It is outrageous that such a vital strategic matter will be decided without the proper consideration of the planning needs of London and the South East. There has been no consultation.. What confidence can MPs have in British rail when it is seeking to build a second terminal even before the first is built. The level of ineptitude in failing to understand in the first place the level of passenger demand.. is hard to describe.* [17]

The attack mounted by Robert Dunn, Conservative MP for Dartford, a constituency right in the path of the development, reflected the anger that was being felt by residents of Kent. *If British Rail wish to place a high-speed route through my constituency, they can do so on one condition: it goes underground. The battle of King's Cross today is the battle of... Kent tomorrow.*[18]

Public hostility of this nature posed an intricate problem and one that British Rail could well have done without. Their interest lay in promoting the business advantages of the Tunnel link in order to take advantage of what *The Financial Times* called *a step change in Britain's physical links with continental Europe.*[19] This involved Sir Robert Reid, as BR Chairman and President of the Community of European Railways (CER), in supporting the creation of a Euro-network of high speed rail links, a move strongly advocated by EC Transport Commissioner Karel van Miert. One stage of this was, of course, already under way in France with the massive planned extension of the TGV network.

Another was the North European Project aimed at creating a dedicated London-Brussels-Amsterdam-Cologne-Frankfurt linkage. Such was immensely important to BR since the UK had been hitherto seen by mainland operators as *a peripheral market.*[20] The CER plan put to the Commission on the 24th January 1989 was ambitious to a degree: over 18,000 miles of new track and 190 mph trains. The plan, costed out at £62 billion was based on the premise that *Europe's geography and demography favour the development of a high speed rail network capable of meeting the needs of a population of 366m unevenly distributed across the continent.*[21]

Country	Subsidy	Country	Subsidy
Luxembourg	16.06	Italy	10.52
Austria	8.88	Belgium	8.19
France	5.83	W. Germany	5.37
Holland	3.45	Denmark	3.19
Switzerland	2.39	Britain	1.95

TABLE 5: EUROPEAN RAIL SUBSIDIES

[£ PER TRAIN KILOMETRE] – 1986 [22]

BR ended the formal enquiry procedure by unveiling its proposed route plan for the Tunnel-London link on the eighth of March 1989. Even then it was certain that the public furore would continue. The plan contained environmental safeguards which had, it was said, raised the cost by £500m. The maximum train speed would be 140mph as opposed to France's 180mph; 23 of the 68 miles of track would be in tunnels and 33 per cent in cuttings. The link would be completed in 1998.

Two groups had put in bids to build the link, Trafalgar House Group and the P&O Group. Clearly BR needed to consider in their approach to them the facts that, whereas their subsidy from the Treasury had been in excess of £1 billion, by 1992/3 it would be £477m (both in 1989 prices) and that their debt stood at over £1.1 billion in 1988/9. The consortia themselves needed to consider the extra costs involved in providing the requisite environmental protection. Not for nothing did Sir Nigel Broackes, Chairman of Trafalgar House and a supporter of the BR route plan, declare on the seventh of October 1989 that, if Governmental cash were not forth-coming, *the rail link will not get built.*[23]

Nevertheless, BR was pressing ahead with its strategy as, on the 8th August 1989, it announced its 'Through Plan' for high-speed Edinburgh-Paris and Manchester-Brussels link-ups using 30 new trains costing £500m, in accordance with requirements under the 1987 Channel Tunnel Act. A start date of 1993 was foreseen for this.

A study of the current levels of congestion led Andre Bernard, co-chairman of Eurotunnel, to declare *air travel in Europe is estimated to grow at between 4-6 per cent p.a. between now and the turn of the century. Already runways are at capacity and traffic lanes are overcrowded.*[24]

Airport	Passengers Moved [m]	% rise over '86
London	55.4	13.7
Paris	37.0	10.5
Frankfurt	23.2	13.5
Rome	14.3	13.5
Amsterdam	13.6	7.5
Madrid	12.0	10.9

TABLE 6: EUROPE'S TOP 6 AIRPORTS (1987) [23]

Note: European controllers were handling 40 per cent more traffic in 1989 than in 1983. This steep growth pattern was likely to be given an extra boost when the second phase of the EC deregulation of air traffic [with attendant price competition and an end to restrictions on capacity working] was planned to come into effect in January 1991.

ROUGH WATERS

The railway unions were not the only ones to be causing summer difficulties in 1989 for the Conservative Government. On the eighth of August the Transport and General Workers' leader Ron Todd called a halt to a month-long strike of registered dock workers. Further action, he told a meeting attended by 500 of his 1,200 members at Liverpool docks, would be *futile*. From his point of view it was the saddest of all possible celebrations of the centenary of the Great Docks Strike of 1889 which had done much to lay the foundations of modern British trade unionism.

From the Government's viewpoint it was simply a welcome end to the Dock Labour Scheme, *a statutory scheme* that - in the words of Lord Brabazon of Tara, Transport Under-secretary - *has outlived its usefulness and now serves only to damage the majority of our major ports through the practices it perpetuates.* [25]

The Scheme had come into existence in 1947 as a way of doing away with a much-hated system of casual working. In its hey-day, in 1948, it had covered 79,000 dockers; in May 1989, at the start of the dispute, only 9,200 were covered. The decline of the Scheme was reflected by the growth of non-Scheme ports and a switch in containerisation technology in such ports, based on the extent of job protection in Scheme ports. Here dockers were guaranteed pay (even if there was no work) or even if their employers had ceased to exist (in this case they were placed on the National Dock Labour Scheme's Temporary Unattached Register). No company in a Scheme Port could legally use non-union labour to do the work of registered dockers. It was a job for life in some of

Britain's major ports like Southampton, Liverpool and London. And, for Mrs Thatcher's Government, an anachronism to be eliminated.

> *Pour arriver à des nouveaux gains de productivité, elle (P & O) veut allonger le temps de travail de chaque équipage et licencier 400 marins. Refus brutal signifié en janvier 1988 par le syndicat des marins (NUS) en grève depuis lors. A présent les dirigeants de P & O vont jusqu'à licencier les 700 grévistes refusant les nouvelles conditions de travail et embaucher les non-syndiqués. C'est la rupture avec la pratique du monopôle d'embauche syndicale, le 'closed shop', qui remonte à plus de quarante ans dans ce secteur.* Translation note 39 on page 134.

EXHIBIT 1: TUNNEL BATTLES
Source: *Le Nouvel Economiste* 6/5/88

Neither Felixstowe nor Dover was a Scheme Port. Between them such ports had taken an increasing share of Britain's trade, from 42 per cent in 1982 to 52 per cent in 1988.

The Government's instrument to put its policy into effect was the eight-clause Dock Work Bill which, having successfully passed all Parliamentary stages, was given the Royal Assent in July. The Government did not foresee major difficulties in abolishing the Scheme, it seemed, since the employers, Associated British Ports, has stated categorically that there would be no return to casual working and there was a high level of redundancy payment on offer to volunteers. So it was. Despite a 3:1 strike ballot and a variety of unofficial and official actions, the TGWU was defeated. A key element was the injunction granted by the Court of Appeal's Lords Justices Neill, Butler-Sloss and Stuart-Smith on the seventh of June against the dockers on *balance of convenience grounds*.

> In Europe the Government was isolated in its opposition to employment protection rights and measures to promote worker and trade union consultation rights.. A series of minimum rights to increase the dignity and security of people at work was needed, in law; rights to a safe working environment; proper protection against dismissal or unjustified redundancy; a national minimum wage; effective anti-discrimination laws and full rights for part-time workers. There must be a clear and effective right to be a trade union member and to take part in union activities without fear of victimisation.

EXHIBIT 2: EXCERPT FROM THE SPEECH BY ROY GRANTHAM
Source: Chairman, TUC Employment, Policy and Organisation Committee, TUC Conference, fifth of September 1989

Another port strike had, in fact, ended just before the dock strike started. It had taken place at Dover in response to P&O action to reduce the size of crews on their cross-channel ferries and had lasted over a year.

This move was part of a strategic response on the part of Sealink and P&O, who between them shared 80 per cent of the cross-Channel ferry traffic, to the challenge of the Tunnel. Other elements included the purchase by P&O of two 'superferries', *The Pride of Dover* and *The Pride of Calais,* and, by Sealink, of two high-capacity RO-ROs. The plan was for both companies to run hourly sailings by six super-de-luxe ferries round the clock for 364 days per year. The Dover-Calais trip would take 75 minutes. Each of the 26,000 ton superferries could carry 2,300 passengers plus a maximum of 650 cars or 100 lorries; the RO-ROs would take 1,800 passengers. Was the head of Sealink worried about the competitive situation? It did not seem so:

P & O is in a better position than we are because they are running a non-union operation but we believe the unions will see to it that we must be kept competitive... It is the policy of the Government that the ferries will survive. If the ferries were not there the Tunnel could just price itself in any way it wanted. It could take terrible advantage of the travelling public. The Government does not want to see the ferry companies go bust in a disorganised competitive environment.[27]

By the start of February 1989 only 500 of the original number of 2,300 sacked for refusing to accept new working rosters remained on strike. Their protests outside Dover docks had been to no avail.

Region	Vehicles per '000 population		
	1965	**1987**	**% rise 75/87**
Greater London	323	392	21.4
Other SE	373	473	26.8
E Anglia	411	494	20.2
S West	396	484	25.4
E Midlands	340	402	18.2
W Midlands	328	411	25.3
Yorks & Humberside	288	358	24.3
North	255	315	23.5
Great Britain	**321**	**401**	**24.9**

TABLE 7: CAR OWNERSHIP IN BRITAIN (DEPT OF TRANSPORT)

Note: David Marshall (Chairman, Commons Transport Committee) commented (*The Times* 17/8/89) that the 1989 British Road Federation Report *highlighted the mess the Government has made of the nation's transport needs over the past years. We have chaos in the air, chaos on the roads and chaos on the railways. Our roads,* said *Times* correspondent Michael Dynes, are *among the most congested in Europe.*

The relative success ostensibly achieved by the Conservative Government's trade union policies (as evidenced in part by the results of the rail and dockers' disputes) was, in late 1989, clearly strengthening the Government's resolve to do more.

What the Government had in mind was spelled out by Norman Fowler, Secretary of State for Employment, at the Conservative Party Conference in October 1989. Here he launched proposals for the final abolition of the pre-entry closed shop in Britain and for the outlawing of all types of secondary action, including wildcat strikes. He promised also that the Government's review of the possibility of banning strikes in essential services would continue.

Period	Road User Taxation [£m]	Road Expenditure [3m]
1982/3	10018	2918
1983/4	10766	3026
1984/5	11576	3127
1985/6	12414	3304
1986/7	13630	3473
1987/8	14720	3578
1988/9	17030	3817

TABLE 8: ROAD TAXATION & EXPENDITURE
(BRITISH ROAD FEDERATION)

Note: There is a record 23m vehicles in Britain. Each road user has just 56 feet of space.

Nor was there any prospect that Britain would agree to the possibility that *worker directors* would be included in the European Commission's proposals for the European Company Statute. Britain's threat of litigation over the issue (made in August 1989) was said to be 'serious'. As Mrs Thatcher declared at the 1988 Conservative Conference: *We haven't worked all these years to free Britain from the paralysis of Socialism only to see it creep in through the back door of central control and bureaucracy from Brussels.*

POKER GAMES

It was not surprising that Eurotunnel's share price should fall following the company's interim statement on the 9th October 1989, that shareholders would be facing a £400m rights issue and that a further £1.5 billion might be needed to finish the project. The size of the fall in the price that had occurred since May - from over £11 to £5.28 - was, however, quite dramatic. Even the normally ebullient Eurotunnel Chairman, Alastair Morton, moderated his optimism in stating that *cost increases will have an adverse effect but Eurotunnel will be reduced from being incredibly to very profitable.*[28]

Date	Estimated Cost of Tunnel Completion [£b]		
Nov '87	4.87		
Oct '88	5.22		
Feb '89	5.38		
Jul '89	5.73		
Oct '89	Eurotunnel	:	7.0
	TML	:	7.5
	Banks	:	8.0

TABLE 9: TUNNEL COSTS ESTIMATES
Source: Tunnelling into Turmoil, Philip Beresford, *The Times*, 8/10/89

Note: The two equity issues which produced Eurotunnel's £1 billion capital were poorly received with a sizeable number of shares left with the underwriters.

Of the variety of factors which lay behind the shareholder cash call and the forecast rise in borrowings, the most important was the dispute among Eurotunnel, the contractors Transmanche Link and the sponsoring banks over the size and nature of the cost over-run. Its cause was less in question as the issue of who should pay and who was at fault. This latter was obviously coupled with criticism of management of the project whose costs seemed to be spiralling out of control.

Three things were, in fact, causing the escalating costs: the inflation in equipment costs, the extent of the Tunnel's disaster-proofing (against terrorism, fire etc.) and last, but by no means least, the strengthening of the shuttles to meet the EC's maximum lorry load capacity of 40 tonnes, from which the UK had long been derogated.

Another problematic factor was the failure by both Trafalgar House, as the most likely to win the contract to build the Tunnel-London rail link, and by Eurotunnel itself to persuade the British Government to follow the French example and contribute public funds. Eurotunnel's Graham Corbett (Finance Director) voiced his company's deep concern when he stated *I don't see how they (the British Government) can sit back and say that what the market decides is fine.* [30] There was also the issue of the precise route for the rail link. This remained highly contentious.

Yet another element was the extent to which the full Tunnel carrying capacity could be properly employed given the mix of traffic it was going to handle. Perhaps unduly cautious, BR's Channel Tunnel Project Manager spoke of a potential 65 per cent utilisation factor and said the scheduling problems were *an operating nightmare.* [31]

Alastair Morton had been highly optimistic in July 1989 about Eurotunnel's prospects:

In the original 1987 prospectus we said we needed an average 2.5 per cent annual economic growth to meet our revenue forecasts. Because growth has been much stronger than that, we will meet out targets even if we only get 1.3 per cent annual growth between now and 1993.

EN ROUTE

The *Times* editorial on the tenth of December 1993 said it all. The Tunnel was indeed a *notable feat of civil engineering* but it had truly suffered from nothing less than *a troubled history.*[34] It was hoped by many that the difficulties would begin to disappear once the official opening had taken place on the 6th May 1994.

Sir Alastair Morton was one such. At the end of January 1994 he surveyed the scene.

We still have a claim for more than £1 billion outstanding from the contractors he said. *We have another .. £1 billion funding to do to pay for the cash flow deficit for a period after starting and we've got a big arbitration litigation outstanding against the two railways for a further £1 billion.. My workload will go down as we solve the remaining problems.* [35]

No wonder he appeared chastened by his experiences. He was speaking of the challenges still to be faced in the final stages of completion of the giant project.

All was not difficulty, however, especially as his replacement as chief executive of Eurotunnel, Georges-Christian Chazot, had already been chosen. The Tunnel was now scheduled definitely to open for business on May the sixth 1994, assuming no further problems, that is. The company would then move from being a design to an operating company, having been supported through the thick and the thin by its 630,000 long-suffering shareholders, and cash would start to flow in. By 1996 the company was confident, it said, that it would be handling 13m passengers and 13 m tonnes of freight. Also, the route for the £3 billion Tunnel-London high-speed rail link had finally been selected, on 24th January 1994, by the British government. This project was planned to be completed by 2002.

But challenges also loomed large. Like Eurotunnel's 1994 daily interest bill, £1.6m. Or the fact that, even if the link route had been successfully selected there was still considerable uncertainty over who would pay for it. In fact, the extent of public funding was said by the government itself to depend on the financial package to be put forward by the winning contractor in the tender to build the link. In early 1994, the economic situation facing the Conservative government and its attitude to increasing public expenditure, the first intractable, the second hostile, meant that the government was seeking 'partnerships in funding' for public works wherever possible. And then there was the issue of widespread objections from all living on or about the new route to the demolition of their homes and the building of tunnels. Said Labour MP Tony Banks *First there was the Nimby. Now we have got the Undie - not underneath my garden.* [36] Labour's shadow Transport Secretary, Frank Dobson, was scathing of the government's handling of the matter:

The dither and blight continue he said. *There are still doubts about the intermediate stations. Proper environmental protection (to those affected by the building of the link) has not been guaranteed. Compensation terms are still not fair to all concerned. All the blight has not been lifted. The necessary funds have not been found.* [37]

Sir Alastair Morton was clearly not exaggerating when he added that *the real job from now on is what the chief executive is going to do to make the company profitable.*[38] On the other hand, there were those who argued that the major work had already been done against, it often seemed, impossible odds.

PROGRESS REPORT

The Tunnel had made undeniably slow and expensive progress. By October 1991 the cost of building had already risen to more than £8 billion and the contractors had been up to six months behind target on the task of laying track and installing cable, pipework and signalling. Nevertheless, Eurotunnel was confident that it would meet the original opening deadline of the 15th June 1993.

It needed to be confident because the builders, Transmanche Link (TML), were then still claiming damages against Eurotunnel for extra work due to changes in the specifications required. The sum involved was £810m. The dispute had become a permanent feature and soured relations between the two parties.

As called for in the contract between Eurotunnel and TML, the dispute had been referred to the International Chamber of Commerce arbitration panel in Bruxelles. The banks and shareholders funding the project watched anxiously as the meetings of the panel and the protagonists came and went and as their moods oscillated between anger and resignation.

By September 1992 agreement had been reached on the bulk of the TML claim, which had now risen to £1.2 billion. But a gap of £150m remained, and try as they might, it seemed unbridgeable. Each side considered that the other would yield and pressed on.

The banks urged the settlement of the dispute and speeding-up of the work. Their concerns were the way in which the Tunnel's completion date had become a moveable feast and the Tunnel's voracious appetite for more and more funds.

It was announced on the eleventh of October 1993 that a 'final' cash call would be made to shareholders in mid 1994. An estimated £500m in shareholders' equity and an equal sum in loans from the Tunnel's consortium of 220 banks would be needed to cover the projected cost of delay in opening the Tunnel and the TML claim. The Eurotunnel announcement also said that late delivery of some of the rolling stock, difficulties with the supply of the Eurostar trains and very much tougher price competition from the cross-channel ferries would delay until 1998 the date when Tunnel revenues would equal interest payments on the accumulated debt. Shares closed 6p down, but at least Eurotunnel had settled the TML claim.

FIRE, FIRE

The intensely damaging fire that took place in the freight section on the Tunnel on November 18th 1996 was sadly quite symbolic of many of the difficulties that Eurotunnel was still having. It was not that the 50-kilometre tunnel had not proved an attractive alternative to ferry and plane, it had, and the Folkestone-Calais service for cars and lorries had notched up a 45 per cent slice of traffic. Overall, the company was claiming a 50 per cent share of cross-channel revenue.

The fire immediately deprived Eurotunnel of an estimated £1m per day in revenue from the cars and lorries service, exacerbating what appeared to many to be the company's impossible financial situation. Even worse, it seemed at the time that the eventual official accident report might demand a replacement of the lattice-sided rail cars, based on the consideration that they might, in fact, have contributed to the spread of the fire. If so the bill would run to £25m.

An impossible financial situation? The truth was that Eurotunnel was unable to pay the interest on the £8.5 billion it owed its backers, a consortium of 200 banks, and had unilaterally declared a repayment moratorium. Indeed, even before the fire, one estimate suggested that the losses expected for the 1996 operating year might be in the order of £650m on a revenue of £430m. The critical focus of company attention was on whether the banks would be prepared to accept a debt-equity swap (i.e., writing off approximately 50 per cent of the debt in exchange for 54.5 per cent of the equity) and, more importantly, whether Eurotunnel's 730,000 long-suffering private shareholders would accept such a dilution of their ownership. It is interesting to note that the majority of these were French.

In fact, there was a battle royal raging between two groups of shareholders with different stances on the matter. The Adacte investors group were bitter at the way in which, they claimed, they had been misled by the 1994 Eurotunnel propectus and were resolute in their opposition to any *unsatisfactory* deal with the banks and prepared to force the company into bankruptcy. By contrast, AES (Association of Eurotunnel Shareholders) was more supportive, especially as they were hoping that the French and British governments might consider extending Eurotunnel's operating licence beyond 2052 to help matters.

The British and French governments did, in the event, extend the franchise to 2086, on the basis that shareholders would back the salvage deal, but demanded in return a share in the eventual profits. Patrick Ponsolle, executive chairman of Eurotunnel, was pleased with this as he was with the support promised for the plan by Northern Cross Investments, a group that held 36.7m of the 920m shares issued. But everything hung on the extraordinary general meeting being held on the tenth of July 1997. This was the day on which the shareholders would have to accept the package. Or face the consequence that the banks would take charge of the Tunnel (the right of "substitution") and appoint an alternative operator. Whatever else, the French and British governments had made known that no public money would be available.

On the first of July 1997, Christian Cambier spoke for the Northern Cross investors. He said they were prepared to support the plan but continued, "we're playing Liar's Poker. We would lose everything if Eurotunnel went *bankrupt*."[38] This was the day on which Eurotunnel's share price hit £1. In early 1994 it had traded at £6.

* * * * * * * * * * * * * * * * * * *

APPENDIX 1 : SELECTED ECONOMIC DATA

(1)　　The 1980s, as compared with the 1970s, had seen an exceptionally high annual economic growth rate in Britain (four per cent as opposed to one per cent average). This growth had been accompanied by a major rise in home and share ownership, both heavily promoted by Conservative Governments over the period 1979-1989.

(2)　　Although Britain's per capita gross income rose by 16.5 per cent in real terms between 1976 and 1986, her performance lagged behind that of France, W. Germany and Italy based on a purchasing power parity basis. (PP irons out differences caused by exchange rate fluctuations and inflation and is a standard EC measure).　On a net disposable income basis, cash after taxes and social security payments, Britain also lagged behind these competitors.

(3)　　By 1988 the level of household debt in Britain had reached £300 billion, approximately equal to the annual flow of household disposable income. In 1988 alone the level grew by a net £54 billion.

(4)　　1988 and 1989 had seen a substantial deterioration in Britain's non-oil trade balance. This was especially marked in the manufactures and consumer goods areas. A net deficit was recorded in July 1989 of no less than £2.1 billion.

(5)　　To avoid a crash in sterling (and the concomitant "imported inflation" due to a low £ value) investment money needed to be attracted into Britain at interest rates in excess of those covering the current account deficit. Government policy was to use domestic interest rates to buttress the value of sterling. Bank base rate thus moved to 15 per cent in early October. It was hoped that this would be the culmination in the fastest and highest upward movement ever seen in Britain. Economic growth since the start of 1989 had been flat.

(6)　　On the eleventh of October 1989 the £ dipped to a two year low against the DM and the $. Speculators clearly thought that with inflation running at over eight per cent p.a. and borrowing costs extremely high, British manufacturing capabilities would be hit. This was a problematic turn of events in the light of two political factors: the wide-ranging industrial debates about Britain's competitiveness and about the desirability of Britain's joining the European Monetary System (EMS). The first was brought to even sharper focus by an Employment Institute study by Christine Greenhalgh and Mary Gregory which indicated that the 'British Disease', an inability on the part of British manufacturers to meet demand in Britain either qualitatively or quantitatively, could only now (October 1989) be eradicated by increased public spending on education, research and development. Failing this, Britain would be relegated, the study found, to the European second division of low-wage, low-quality producers after 1992. *The Chancellor* commented the Institute's Director, John Philpott, *is, of course, unlikely to accept this prescription and, even if he did, it would be anathema to the Prime Minister* (*The Times* 12/10/89).

Indeed so, given the Conservative Government's adherence to market economics. This was making its presence felt in the Government's unwillingness to join its major EC competitors in the EMS until, as Mrs Thatcher said, "*the time is right*". This system allows for the movement of a partner currency within a narrow range of relative values, with support mechanisms and stabilising devices to bring it back into line if it shifts too radically. Joining the EMS would be an essential first step, on Britain's part, to accepting the Delors Plan for European Monetary Union (EMU) with its provision for moves towards the creation of a European Central Bank, a common currency and greater approximation of EC partner's monetary and fiscal policies. As Mrs Thatcher pointed out at the Madrid summit in June 1989, this was also not going to occur without a great deal of British opposition.

APPENDIX 2 : A MATTER OF ROADS

(1) In 1989 the British Government was assailed on two sides by powerful advocates of increasing public sector infrastructural expenditure. The CBI was one, in the form of its Director General John Banham. His views were uncompromising. *I must warn you,* he told a CBI Conference on the 16th March 1989, *that the locusts will not easily be kept at bay. Last year the CBI said the priority should be investment not consumption. This was regarded at the time as politically naive and self-interested. Unfortunately (in the light of the rising balance of payments deficit), it turned out to be right.* [32]

Without going so far as inferences about "locust years", the Commons Select Committee on Transport called for more spending over and above the £6 billion earmarked by the Government for spending over the next ten years, in the light of *the seriousness of transport problems nationally.* [33]

(2) Labour's plans for dealing with the congestion crisis hinged on curbing car use through higher taxes on use and tougher treatment of the current £1.6 billion a year tax perk. This would be coupled with pledges to revitalise bus, tube and rail transport. Other possibilities enunciated by Labour's spokesman John Prescott [34] included charging motorists to enter big cities at peak times and reducing the maximum speed on busy motorways to 50mph.

(3) French policy was unashamedly ambitious: to make France the heart of the European motorway network by the turn of the century. To achieve this a National Roads Master Plan was drawn up in 1988. Not only did it take the Channel Tunnel requirements fully into consideration (as did France's extension of the TGV network) but it would also result in an eventual total in France of 37,550 kilometres of motorway and fast trunk roads. 8,550 kilometres of this will be tolled.

(4) Britain's M20, the London-Dover motorway link, was scheduled for completion in 1991.

NOTES & REFERENCES

1	Thatcher inflaming rail conflict, Kinnock tells MPs, *The Times*, 5/7/89
2	Ibid
3	Ibid
4	Railway strikers risk losing their jobs, says Thatcher, *The Times* 6/7/89
5	Beside the Lake, *The Times* 6/7/89
6	*The Guardian* 6/7/89
7	Restricting Strikes, *The Times* editorial, 4/7/89
8	**(a)** 180mph journey to Dover promised, but not before 1998, Rodney Cowton, *The Times* 15/7/88
	(b) Blockage in the Channels that lead to the Tunnel, *The Times*, 3/11/88
9	*Op cit* (8)(b)
10	BR explores Eurotunnel traffic potential, *The Financial Times* 29/9/88
11	Undersea tomb for Chunnel's giant borers, *The Times* 9/10/89
12	Europe: A gap becomes a chasm, Tony Thirlwall, *The Guardian* 24/8/89
13	*The Times* 10/3/89
14	*The Times* 1/3/89
15	*The Sunday Times* 11/9/88
16	*The Times* 12/10/88
17	Parliament 8/5/89, *The Times* 9/5/89. Sir George Young was the Bill's sponsor
18	Ibid
19	*The Financial Times* Survey 9/5/89
20	Ibid
21	(£62 billion scheme will cut hours off train travel, *The Times*, 25/1/89
22	The Railway Bazaar, *The Observer*, 2/7/89
23	*The Sunday Times* 4/12/88
24	Airlines face competition with confidence, Pierre Bary and David Black, *The Independent* 4/3/89
25	Minister pledges striking dockers will be defeated, Stephen Goodwin, *The Independent* 10/6/89
26	Dock managers roll up sleeves to defeat strike, *The Sunday Times* 16/7/89
27	Ferries prepare to ride out storm, Kevin Brown, *The Financial Times* 9/5/89
28	Quoted in *International Management*, October 1989
29	Dispute over soaring costs darkens ET gloom, John Bell, *The Times* 10/10/89
30	Cash ultimatum on channel link, Richard Caseby, *The Times* 8/10/89
31	Chunnel in crisis over train target, *The Guardian*, 5/6/89
32	Thatcher's locust years, David Walker and Derek Harris, *The Times* 17/3/89
33	MPs call for more road and rail cash, Nicholas Wood, *The Times* 23/8/89
34	'Vive La Celebration', *The Times* editorial, 10/12/93
35	'New entente cordiale links past with future', Sarah Bagnall, *The Times*, 22/1/94
36	'Missing links still blight Channel line', Tim Jones and Jonathan Prynn, *The Times*, 25/1/94

37   As 36

38   Playing Liar's Poker* with Eurotunnel, Andrew Jack, *Financial Times*, 2/7/97
     *Note: Liar's Poker is a game of bluff involving dice.

39   EXHIBIT 1: *In order to achieve new productivity gains, P & O wants to
     increase each crew's working time and sack 400 sailors. The NUS' stone-wall
     rejection of this approach in January 1988 had led to a strike since then. At
     present the company is going so far as to sack the 700 strikers who are refusing
     the new working conditions and to take on non-union labour. It's a break with
     the practice of the closed shop monopoly which, in this sector, goes back over
     40 years.*

THE BERLIN WALL

Abstract:

This case contains detailed historical data about the demise of the Soviet empire in E. Europe and the steps taken by each country there to re-establish its independence. Such steps are presented against the backcloth of the turmoil taking place in the USSR and its major constituent republics in the late 1980s and the climactic 1989 summit meeting between presidents Gorbachev and Bush. The case illustrates the interesting paradox that, whilst the Eastern part of Europe was welcoming the disintegration of one sort of hegemonic bloc, the Western part seemed to be rushing towards integration within another.

The Berlin Wall can be read in conjunction with the Ikarus case.

Question:

Review the political and economic changes resulting from the removal of the Berlin Wall. Discuss the relevance of these changes for Eastern and West European businesses. What are the downside risks if progress along the perestroika track is not made quickly in Eastern Europe?

Case Timing: 1990

SIC TRANSIT TYRANNIS

In the theatre of contemporary politics few men can have been called upon to play such a macabre final role as Nicolae Ceausescu. President of Romania and gerontocrat extrordinaire, he had been Secretary General of his country's Communist Party since 1965.

It was on the 21st November 1989 on the podium of Bucharest's Palace Hall that he entertained Party faithful, meeting for their XIVth Congress, to an inspiring and not-to-be-missed six-hour marathon monologue. During this epic performance he received no less than 67 standing ovations.

On Christmas Day of that same year he had time only for a two-hour performance, this time before a military tribunal, before he was found guilty of treason against his nation and, together with his wife Elena, shot.

The dictatorship and personality cult of this couple had long been a by-word in the West and, wherever such by-words were possible, East. Now it had wrought their deaths. What *The Times* obituarist called *grandiose schemes of social engineering* [1] had been reviled by a powerless Romanian people. These had included the policies of forcibly resettling agro-industrial sections of the population and outlawing contraception and abortion, whilst simultaneously specifying a production target of five children per couple. When allied with policies creating bread-line standards of living (partly to ensure repayment of all debts to the West), they had formed an explosive mixture which erupted ultimately in a vitriolic nation-wide revolt against the Secretary General, his ubiquitous securitate (security police) and all other aspects of his rule. His much-vaunted Scientific Socialism and national credit-worthiness were as nought against accusations of genocide, destruction of the economy and the alleged salting-away of more than £500m in foreign banks.

Other governments of Eastern Europe, to one degree or another, were bending before the storm of populist revolt against doctrinaire Communist rule and, by implication, Soviet political hegemony, that swept through their countries in 1989. Not so Ceausescu's Romania. *The ruling-out of the Capitalist system... is the leading requirement for a just society* he had told Congress delegates in his November speech.[2] Dissent of any kind had meant imprisonment, all meetings with foreigners had had to be reported and, since 1984, all typewriters had had to be registered with the police. An estimated 10,000 perished in the violence which eliminated his regime.

Nicolae Ceausescu was not the only long-serving Secretary General of an East European Communist Party to fall prey to spontaneous revolt in this turbulent year but, as the decade turned, it seemed highly unlikely that his spectacular fate would be shared. Others would be merely degraded and/or imprisoned.

The East German leader, Erich Honecker, for instance. Having resigned his office in October 1989, he suffered the indignity of being placed under house arrest. Some of his closest colleagues were accused of having caused *grave damage to the economy* and of having *enriched themselves personally through the abuse of office and corruption*.[3] Evidence of high living in Wandlitz, the protected enclave where a set of these Party leaders lived, was shown on national TV. The publication of the accusations was accompanied by the resignation en masse of the entire East German Government and with the subsequent purging of the Politburo and the Volkskammer.

The attacks on the Party leadership had begun in late September when the Party organ, Neues Deutschland, had accused Günter Mittag, erstwhile Deputy General Secretary, of *an unseemly misuse of power and a bourgeois lifestyle*.[4] This corruption, said the paper, was *all the more painful and incomprehensible in that these people had for decades handed out to others the bread of poverty*.[5] They had preached water, so it was said, but drunk wine.

By the third of December the East German Politburo had duly resigned and Erich Honecker had been stripped of his membership of the Communist Party, together with trade union leader Harry Tisch and Alexander Schalk-Golodkowski, the eminent Party apparatchik who had had responsibility for the management of the country's hard currency reserves. *The swamp* proclaimed the Party's Berliner Zeitung *must be drained dry*.

And so, perhaps, it was. With editors no longer subject to the control of the Ministry of Agitation and Propaganda, they had a field day. The Minister for State Security was arrested on corruption charges; Gunter Wendland, the Director of Public Prosecutions, resigned; Egon Krentz, replacement for Erich Honecker, proved no more than a stop-gap.

The congratulatory message that came to his successor, Gregor Gysi, from USSR President Gorbachev spoke volumes:

What has happened was bound to happen. We Soviet Communists know from our own experience that life cannot be shackled by dogma. What has been accumulating for years and could not find a way out has now burst out in a cleansing system.. Lies, double standards let alone graft and lawlessness have always been poisonous to Socialism. The strength of social justice is in overcoming the alienation of working people from poverty...and establishing democracy. [6]

It was only as recently as the seventh of October that President Gorbachev had last met Erich Honecker for a fraternal meeting, and that on the occasion of celebrating the 40th anniversary of the founding of the German Democratic Republic.

In early November Todor Zhivkov, Bulgaria's Party chief, also found himself deposed and in legal trouble. Over 70, and of an age with Ceausescu and Honecker, he must have found the charges against him hard to bear. But not as mortifying as the task that his Czechoslovakian counterpart, Gustav Husak, must have had when he had to welcome the first non-communist government in his country for 41 years before he too, on the tenth of December, resigned. Had he not been, along with his much-hated Prime Minister Milos Jakes, the architect of the suppression of the 1968 *Prague Spring* with the aid of Warsaw Pact forces? This had been an all-too-premature expression of a national wish for personal freedom and autonomy, inspired by Czechoslovakia's leader in 1968, Alexander Dubcek. Gustav Husak too, along with Vasil Bilack (the Party's ideological chief), had lost his Party ticket by Xmas 1989. Explaining the transition, the new Party chairman Ladislav Adamec stated:

The victory of Stalinism over Leninism was fatal for Czechoslovakia. We have to examine the full 70 years of our Party honestly.. We have to see why a country with our tradition of civilisation and democracy was so deformed.. This may be our last chance (as a Party) to ... remain an important political force.

In six short months in 1989 the hard-line totalitarian leaderships in 5 front-line Warsaw Pact countries had been swept away in a welter of intensely-joyful nationalistic, populist uprisings. East Germany, Hungary, Czechoslovakia, Bulgaria, Romania. In each case their Communist rulers had been weighed, found wanting and dispensed with. Each successor government had the tricky problem of what to do with its national secret police, the main-stay for so long of the previous regime. Their work, for so long unmentionable, had at last been shown up on every television screen throughout East Europe.

VERTIGO

Business folk in board rooms from Sydney to Cincinnati could well be forgiven for not understanding and appreciating the subtle intricacies of the European Community's onward progress. Keeping track of change was just as often as mystifying a procedure for their EC counterparts.

Now both had to face up to yet another imponderable of mammoth, long-run significance taking place in East Europe. This was a part of the world which had for so long suffered commercially from a sort of economic and social apartheid that many prudent Western investors had, unless forced, paid it scant regard.

Some businessmen, like Italy's Carlo de Benedetti and the USA's Jack Welch, saw in the changes exciting new commercial opportunities to be seized immediately and with both hands. The latter, for example, in late 1989 negotiated the purchase by General Electric of a 50+ per cent stake in Tungsram, the Hungarian light manufacturer, for £150m. It was the largest private investment to date in Hungary since World War II.

Others saw the auguries as good, but not unequivocally so. All the nations in question were deep in the travails of political revolution, anxious about the potential economic effects of a breach in the USSR's system of economic subsidisation and political tutelage. This, through Comecon and the Warsaw Pact, had for decades buttressed faltering Communist rule. They were up to their ears in Western debt and needing to improve their economic performance dramatically, if only to try to provide more food and basic commodities for a people which now knew better. The social strains, separatist, nationalistic and inegalitarian, this would entail, were seen as immensely dangerous. Yet moves towards some sort of market economy were being widely canvassed in each country as practically unavoidable. Some countries seemed better placed than others.

Poland had travelled fastest along the political road. It had had an earlier start with the creation of the first pluralist (Solidarity, Communist Party and minority parties) government in Eastern Europe and with the appointment of its first non-communist Prime Minister, Tadeusz Mazowiecki. By contrast, its economic situation was dire. Annual inflation running at over 600 per cent; food shortages of Gargantuan pro-portions; a six billion rouble debt outstanding to the USSR. No wonder Lech Walesa, founder of the Solidarity trade union and a tireless promoter of his country's interests, pleaded for international aid. He freely admitted the key problem in a speech to both houses of the US Congress on the 15th November 1989. *All the countries of Eastern Europe are bankrupt today* he declared. *The Communist economy has failed in every part of the world.* [7]

It was not just a question of more aid to help rebuild the Polish economy, and make sure previous debts were repaid, but of practical help with food and know-how training. The Group of 24 (the world's most industrialised nations), the EC's Foreign Ministers, the US Congress and West Germany were all sympathetic, especially with loans to underpin Poland's currency. So was the International Monetary Fund, within, that is, the guidelines it was obliged to work to.

To meet the terms of the IMF loan Poland needed, Finance Minister Lesek Balcerowicz drew up a package including the privatisation of state industry, acceptance of a massive increase in foreign in-bound investment and, for the first time in the country, laws to allow bankruptcy, unemployment and income tax.

Hungary's Prime Minister, Miklos Nemeth put forward a not dissimilar plan to try to secure a £1 billion stand-by credit from the IMF for his country and head off what he saw as the possibility of internal economic collapse. It was thought that a pre-condition for IMF help would be moves to reduce the nation's £1.5 billion hard currency deficit. His plan accented the liberalisation of ownership laws and the promotion of private enterprise, the cutting of subsidies on food and housing and the de-regulation of prices. The imposition of an increase in profit tax was intended to help pay for unemployment which would occur once the law on closing down loss-making state enterprises was enacted.

The IMF concern was also to cut back on Hungary's 1989 £18 billion debt. In per capita terms this was (at £1,800) the highest in Eastern Europe, with Poland second with £1,000. Although other help was in prospect (from W. Germany and the EC), the 50 per cent reduction in budget deficit the IMF was seeking looked a political impossibility since it was authoritatively estimated that fully 20 per cent of the population was on the bread-line. With free elections scheduled for early 1990, as was the case in E. Germany, Czechoslovakia and Romania, it was by no means certain that the Balcerowicz plan would create the proper basis for a dismantling of Poland's command economy.

> *The Council for Mutual Economic Assistance (CMEA) was a mechanism for co-operation which accomplished much for four decades but ran into negative tendencies in the 1970s. It has become old and obsolete and should be replaced by a new structure which harmonises the economic inequalities.*
> Soviet trade official, Sergei Ouganov.

EXHIBIT 1: THE TIMES THEY ARE A-CHANGING
Source: Moscow Man says Comecon is obsolete, *The Independent* 6/1/90.
CMEA is another acronym for COMECON.

In East Germany the situation was different. It was, in the words of the *Economist, the least poorly-performing economy in Eastern Europe.*[8] Here, the massive popular street demonstrations in Dresden, Leipzig and E. Berlin seemed based more on politics than economics.

The politics of the street prevailed on Egon Krenz, the replacement for Erich Honecker, to temporise by doing two things which speeded his own downfall: first, by announcing, on the 15th November, a Bill to abolish the leading role of the Communist Party in East Germany by abrogating Article 6 of the country's constitution and, second, by allowing the easing of foreign travel. With the borders of adjacent countries open to the flight of E. Germans from their homeland to W. Germany, the latter was an unavoidable action. A mass demonstration in Karl-Marx-Stadt finally brought an end to Egon Krenz's 'Wende', his promised new beginning, and a further threat to the Socialist Unity Party (i.e., Communist) or SED. Up to then the Party had always scored runaway successes in the polls. Indeed, a triumphant Egon Krenz had only just announced to the entire nation on television the results of the 1989 May elections: a 99.8 per cent vote in East Germany for the SED!

As elsewhere, there was a pattern to the events. Mass city demonstrations of the people as a whole, resisted initially by the Communist authorities and then allowed to proceed; capitulation by the government and then by the main organs of the Communist Party itself; a name change by the latter and an agreement to free elections in which the protest groups (New Forum, Civic Forum *et. al.*) would play their part; temporising changes in the Communist Party's electoral programme in an attempt to keep some power prior to, and win votes in, the free elections; a new government struggling to get the economy into a shape where foreign aid would be forthcoming; ethnic and religious unrest; finding a new social space for the secret police; weaning many people away from indoctrinated subservience. It all amounted to a difficult birth for each new East European democracy.

In Czechoslovakia, admittedly, the pattern was a little different. Here, at first, the authorities acted more brutally to suppress protests. But as the nature of these remained non-violent and as they grew and grew in volume, the Communist government lost its nerve. The symbolism of internationally-televised candlelight protests taking place at Christmas in Wenceslas Square in Prague was obvious to all. Even the Soviet News Agency was critical of the policy of suppression by using armed force. All the demonstrators had wanted on one occasion where force had been used was, it commented, *open and honest dialogue about free elections, the resignation of the government and the release of political prisoners.*[9]

Nation-wide street protests in Brno, Bratislava, Prague and Liberac, with the slogan of *Away with the Communists* and the use of the old Czech tricolour, did little for the cause of maintaining Communist rule. Milos Jakes went quickly, too, tainted with 1968 and the aftermath of non-stop repression. So did Ladislav Adamec, one of the shortest-serving Prime Ministers in Eastern Europe, once he had promised leaders of the opposition Civic Forum movement that there would be no martial law and no more police action to stop peaceful protest. No doubt a national strike that was particularly severe in Ostrava - an industrial region centred on the Klement Gottwald steel complex with its 40,000 workers - helped this decision along. It certainly had an effect on the government's decision, on the 28th November, to abrogate Article 4 of its Constitution. This had given the Communist Party a monopoly of power in the country.

> *No-one believes in Communism any more.. We have to establish a new social order. We do not want Marxism any more.*
> From a speech by Michel Sahar, a leader of the People's Party, in Wenceslas Square, 23/11/89.

EXHIBIT 2: WE KNOW WHAT WE WANT [10]

By the eighth of December, a new Government and a new Prime Minister, Marion Calfa, were in office pledged to multi-party government in future and free elections in the Spring. By the year's end, the leader of the Czech dissident movement Vaclav Havel had been sworn in as President and Alexander Dubcek, for so long a non-person in his own country, had been appointed as Speaker in the country's parliament. His *Socialism with a Human Face* seemed finally to have won through, after more than 20 years. It was the sweetest of victories.

YALTA TO MALTA

A major element affecting this display of political pyrotechnics in Eastern Europe was the nature of the changes taking place in the relationship between the world's military super-powers, the USA and the USSR. The outcome of the summit meeting held in Malta in mid-winter 1989 between the two Presidents, George Bush and Mikhail Gorbachev, was seen as critical to further developments in this area.

There was no doubt about President Bush' position. At his meeting with G7 leaders (the group of the world's richest nations) in July 1989, he declared that the USA's interest lay in the development of more market-oriented economies in Eastern Europe, not through the latter-day equivalent of post-war Marshall Aid but through economic assistance, offered on a sound commercial basis. There were attractions, like East Europe's labour supply and untapped consumer potential. But there were also threats, from potentially cheap competitive consumer products based on the scrapping of some heavy industry and a switch to new technology. There was hunger as well, not only for food but also for debt moratoria (on past debt) and new investment (using fresh debt). If the plan of US Treasury Secretary Brady was to be put into operation to reduce debt principal and interest rates on existing debt (as in Mexico), then, in the US President's view, price deregulation and the development of ownership rights would have to have priority.

A switch to consumer product manufacture and a change in technology would not come easily to, say, Poland. Here no less than 30 per cent of electronics output, 46 per cent of vehicle production and 15 per cent of ship-building in 1988 were estimated to have been ordered by the military, and, pre-dominantly the Warsaw Pact and the USSR. What would the Bumar tank factory in Gliwice or the hand-grenade plant in Niewiadov do in such a re-tooling contingency? Where would their 'peace dividend' lie?

Nevertheless, President Bush was optimistic about the future. Changes had, he said in the speech commemorating his first anniversary as President on the seventh of November 1989, *gone too far to set back the fledgling steps towards democracy. I don't think you can contain the people's aspirations for freedom by going back to totalitarianism.*[11] At least he had also President Gorbachev's assurances that force would not be used to decide matters in Eastern Europe, as had been the case under the Brezhnev doctrine.

As the Malta summit approached, President Gorbachev had more on his geo-political plate to worry about. Internally, the Soviet Union seemed at times in real danger of balkanisation. There was rising nationalism in Moldova. Azerbaijan and Armenia were at daggers drawn. Bulgaria was in torment and turmoil. There had been mining strikes in the Kuzbas and there was the threat of them in the Donbas. Over many of the most industrialised regions of the USSR hung the heavy stench of pollution produced by labour-intensive, long out-dated technologies.

The Georgian parliament's declaration on the 24th November [12] that it had been illegally annexed by the USSR and that its right to secede was *holy and inviolable*, a sentiment totally at variance with the absolutist Brezhnev doctrine, caused immense concern in the Kremlin. It amplified the threat posed by the resurgence of Islam as shown by the disturbances on Azerbaijan's borders with Iran and Turkey.

Worse. The 243-1 vote in the Lithuanian parliament to remove Article 6 from the constitution that had been imposed on them in 1976 by the USSR's President Brezhnev; its decision to accept a multi-party system of government with free elections; its Communist Party's turn-of-the-decade decision, taken by the Central Committee 866-160, to secede from the USSR by making its Communist Party independent of Moscow. All these, taken together, were seen as a critical threat to the federal government of the USSR. And where Lithuania led, Latvia and Estonia would not lag.

As if these schisms were not enough, President Gorbachev had also the economy to grapple with. In late 1989 it was causing alarm. So far as long-run reform in the perestroika programme was concerned, the new Property Law was under debate. It did not sanction the private ownership of land but gave to the farmers tenure of rented land, such that they could bequeath it to their families. It did not foresee the ownership of shares in industry by private individuals but did allow for the ownership by workers of shares in their firm, a sort of joint stock company arrangement.

> *By turns or in combinations, towels, toothpaste, toilet paper, sugar and light-bulbs have disappeared from the shelves. Now you cannot buy detergent or cheap soap.*

EXHIBIT 3: NOT FOR LOVE, NOR MONEY EITHER
Source: *Izvestia*, quoted in Now the Red Army has to pay the Reckoning, Brian Moynahan, *The Sunday Times*, 26/3/89

This was small beer compared with the revelations of the USSR's economic difficulties. Problems publicly aired included a runaway money supply (an estimated 400 billion roubles cash at bank, in circulation and under mattresses) a budget deficit between 36 billion roubles (according to Leonid Gostev, Finance Minister) and 100 billion (so said Leonid Abalkin, Deputy Prime Minister). This latter indicated a budget deficit/GNP ratio of eleven per cent, as compared to the US' four per cent. There had also been a slump in planned hard currency export earnings from oil, petrol, machinery, rolled ferrous metals resulting in a large deficit on balance of payments.

The managerial disarray was evident. On the 15th of November Leonid Abalkin made a speech in which he looked forward to the transition of the USSR to a *Socialist market* via *the middle way* of wage restraint, gradual price and tax reform, comprehensive social security and gradual reduction in state ownership. But he issued a stern warning. *If we do not manage our programme and do not stabilise the economy in the next year,* he said, *a rationing system would become inevitable and that would be an end to reform.*

To help manage the programme, Nikolai Ryzhkov made known the plans for the coming year in a speech to Congress less than two weeks later, with the law banning strikes in key industries now safely through the Soviet parliament. They were much the same as before: a continuation of centralised planning, no price reform until 1991 and no massive imports of Western consumer goods. Certainly, little evidence of *the middle way.*

The critical issue that both Presidents were naturally anxious to discuss at their Malta meeting was disarmament. The doctrine of *reasonable (defensive) sufficiency* seemed to be taking the place of that of its over-costly forebear – *global (offensive) reach.* The two men proclaimed at the end of their eight hours of meetings that *the cold war is over.* They had set *an ambitious agenda* for the three sets of arms reduction talks then being carried on. These were the Conventional Forces in Europe (CFE) discussions in Vienna, the START talks in Geneva on strategic nuclear weapons and negotiations on chemical weapons.

It was clear that there were interests at stake which were seen as more strategically significant than the military and that the talks were building on arms cut-back intentions previously announced in the USSR, the Pentagon and NATO. Indeed the West Germans alone, in a plan put forward by Defence Minister Dr Gerhard Stoltenberg on the 30th November, had spoken of reducing their armed forces, the largest in Western Europe, by 70,000 by the mid 1990s.

Such talk was not, of course, meat and drink to the USA's top 20 defence firms which included such giants as Rockwell, Grumman, General Dynamics and McDonnell Douglas. At the time they were sharing some $20 billion of annual Pentagon contracts. Nor for that matter the European defence industry with its eight majors, British Aerospace, Ferranti, GEC, Daimler-Benz, Thomson CSF, Phillips, Thorn-EMI and Racal.

MEANWHILE, BACK ON THE EC RANCH

There was not a little speculation that the changes taking place in East Europe and in the USA-USSR relationship would affect the speed at which the partners in the European Community would try to secure full implementation of the Single European Act and its social and financial derivatives - the Social Charter (SC) and Economic and Monetary Union (EMU), the first stage of which was the European Monetary System (EMS). Would they affect the stance of the UK, which, under its prime minister Mrs Margaret Thatcher, seemed resolutely opposed to anything substantive that smacked of a reduction in national sovereignty?

The pressure on the Conservative Government in respect of the EMS was heavy and it came from within the Party's own ranks and from its business supporters as well as from the EC Commission and its EC partners.

The 13th EC Directive on Company Law proposed that the national authorities regulating the conduct of takeovers should put it into a legal framework. This would act as a guarantee of transparency, ensure equality of treatment of shareholders and discourage *unacceptable* forms of leveraged buyout.

The UK position was one of a non-statutory Takeover Code and a relatively open market situation. It did not permit a situation, as in Germany, where the voting rights of shareholders did not necessarily reflect the per cent of the holding (i.e. some shareholders were not enfranchised) and there were sometimes limitations on the power of shareholders to appoint/dismiss directors. The exercise of voting (the custodian bank system leading to a bank-management nexus) by proxy without the specific authority of the shareholder was similarly not allowed.

EXHIBIT 4: THE BRITISH WAY

Particularly strong attacks on the Government's stance came from the House of Lords in their EMS debate in January 1989. This from Lord Seebohm (admittedly an Independent but also a former chairman of Barclay's bank):

Monetary union is firmly on the agenda whatever the Government does. Repeatedly it has been said that the USA and Japan have the advantage over Europe because they have a common language, no internal barriers, a common currency and common fiscal policies. Is the Government going to rule out such things? If so, the Single European Act makes no sense.[13]

Ex-Government minister, Michael Heseltine, was one of a group of Conservatives who, within the House of Commons, supported the EMS concept and were opposed to what they saw as the Government's 'minimalist' approach. Their views were paralleled by those of the Confederation of British Industry (CBI) which was particularly supportive of the Exchange Rate Mechanism (ERM) element.

Another ex-Conservative minister was also prominent in his support for the UK's entry. To be sure, Sir Leon Brittan (as the EC's Competition Commissioner) had a different perspective but he was nonetheless emphatic in stating that it was in the UK's interest to join, and speedily.

The UK Government's position did not change from the time of the Madrid summit, with its face-saving endorsement of the principle of merely studying the EMS. It was re-iterated frequently by Lord Young (in the Lords) and by the chancellor of the exchequer, Nigel Lawson, until his resignation on the 27th October.

The ERM is widely seen as operating as a counter-inflationary mechanism in which members' currency values are harnessed to that of the deutschmark and, hence, to W. ERM is a semi-fixed currency parity system which helps give greater exchange rate stability to the currencies in it by putting limits on their ability to move against each other. The maximum amount of change allowed - upwards or downwards around the value level accepted for the currency - is 4.5 per cent, i.e., the French franc can move between 3.2792 and 3.4305 to the deutschmark. If the franc looks like falling below the floor or 3.4305, the Banque de France is obliged to sell deutschmarks, even if this means borrowing them from the Bundesbank. The last re-appraisal of parities was in January 1987.

Germany's monetary policies. The Delors Report advocates ERM as a first step along the path to EMU, other steps being permanently fixed exchange rates, a single European currency, binding central rules on national budgetary policies and a European system of central banks with sole responsibility for formulating and implementing Community monetary and exchange rate policy. EMS relates to all aspects of monetary union but does not include fiscal or budgetary matters. The UK, so its Government had said, would join the ERM when the time was appropriate i.e. when EC partners had scrapped exchange controls (France, W. Germany, Italy), had allowed untrammelled running of financial services and had reduced their subsidies to state industry (France and Italy).

EXHIBIT 5: EMU FOR BEGINNERS

Thereafter it was his successor, John Major, who played the dead bat. He gave the clearest statement of the UK Government's position in the debate in the Commons on the Delors Report on the 2nd November 1989. It favoured, he declared, concentrating on developing a yet closer relationship among the sovereign states of the European Community with their separate national traditions and political structures. But, in this relationship, liberal free-market policies, parliamentary accountability and the sheer diversity of member states would continue to be valued. Supporting this view and the Government's position as indicated by its paper *An Evolutionary Approach to Economic and Monetary Union*, Mrs Thatcher herself stated:

It shows you can achieve closer economic and monetary co-operation much better and more rapidly by working with the grain of market forces than by setting up new bureaucratic and highly-centralised institutions which are not accountable to anyone. It honours the commitment we made at Madrid that we should put forward an alternative approach. This is the alternative approach. [14]

This viewpoint was again strongly presented by Mrs Thatcher at the Strasbourg summit of EC leaders in December 1989. The grounds for her opposition to the Delors Plan and to president Mitterand's advocacy of revisions to the Treaty of Rome (by 1992) to pave the way for EMU had been well-laid by stinging UK attacks on the slowness with which other EC members were implementing agreed EC policies in comparison with the UK's exemplary record. UK foreign secretary, Douglas Hurd, speaking on the 24th November, for example:

We are the ones who are pushing forward the Single Market programme.. Of the charge of being half-baked Europeans we are innocent. We plead guilty to the charge of working for a liberal and open Europe. But that isn't a crime: it's a necessity. [15]

So far as subsidies by EC governments to their manufacturing industries were concerned, he had no doubts. *It is not defensible* he said *that Italian subsidies to manufacturing industry should stay at £16 billion whereas ours are down to less than £2 billion... We don't believe in the European Super-State.* [16]

The UK prime minister resisted the clarion call for a *closer-knit'* Community contained in a letter to the *Times,* signed by 30 of the Conservatives' 32 MEPs. Nevertheless, she did yield at the summit and agreed to a date being fixed for a forthcoming inter-governmental conference on EMU.

On the central issue of wholehearted acceptance of the principles behind it, she was outvoted 11-1.

The other contentious topic at the summit (apart that is from failure to fully endorse the Schengen Plan for the abolition of internal frontiers) was that of Commissioner Papandreou's draft Social Charter of Workers' Rights. Given the proposals for curbing wild-cat strikes in the UK contained in the Green Paper put out by Norman Fowler, Employment Secretary, on the eleventh of October 1989, the UK Government's resistance to the notions involved was not surprising.

Why was it needed when, in the UK Government's view, Britain's international competitiveness was being restored? According to Commissioner Papandreou, *the need for a Community social policy arises not only from considerations of social justice, it is also essential for economic reasons. For example, it is clear that an equitable social order - accepted by the majority of the population - is a very important factor, conducive to economic development and the efficiency of production and growth.* [17]

Was the belief that the Social Charter (SC) would impose an EC-wide minimum wage well-founded? No.

Was a degree of national diversity in implementing the action programme based on the SC to be allowed? Yes

Were health and safety aspects contained in this programme to be subject to qualified majority voting in Council? Yes.

Would there be only one definition of a decent wage, irrespective of country and industry? No.

Would the mere declaration of a commitment to the principles of the SC be legally binding? No.

EXHIBIT 6: SO NOW YOU KNOW
Source: Commission evidence to the Commons Select Committee on Employment,
Euro-commission *Weekly Report*, 19/10/89

This logic was rejected root and branch by the UK Government who interpreted the Social Charter as setting the scene for *a virtually unqualified right to strike* (Norman Fowler's words). This view was echoed by the Institute of Directors who regarded the Charter as *little more than a blueprint for protecting the rights of organised labour*.[18] Even the cogent argument advanced by an All-Party Committee of peers failed to cut any ice with the Government. They had said that *the Government would accept the draft Charter as a basis for negotiation... or the other eleven states may well go ahead and sign it without any UK participation.*

On the issue of acceptance of the Social Charter, Mrs Thatcher was outvoted at the Strasbourg summit 11-1.

THE WALL COMES DOWN

Weighty as these matters were, they were dwarfed by the symbolism, and potential practical consequences, of an event that took place on the ninth of November 1989: the decision by the East German Government to begin to dismantle the Berlin Wall. It was a step of the most momentous consequence as, for the last 40 years, it had signified a clear and unbridgeable demarcation between West and East, between Capitalism and Communism. The ideological Bastille in which the peoples of East Europe had been contained was no more.

West Germany, by 1988, was already the world's biggest exporter (£323 billion vs USA's £322b v Japan's £265b), and enjoyed a trade surplus of £69 billion (vs Japan's £78b). For this country the question of the impact of the ultimate removal of the Berlin Wall was of the greatest possible economic and political significance. After all, the two Germanies had been originally *ein Volk*. As West Germany had always had a policy of accepting all refugees of German stock from the East and as German re-unification was pledged in the W. German constitution as a key aim, the issue of the re-integration of the two Germanies politically was critical.

Country	Pop [m]	GNP [b£] latest est.	Economic potential as rated by Fortune magazine [Dec '89]
E. Germany	16.6	155.4	A
Czechoslovakia	15.6	118.5	B+
Hungary	10.6	68.9	B
Poland	38.0	210.5	C
Rumania	23.0	94.7	D+
USSR	289.3	1406.0	N/A

TABLE 1: WHO'S WHO IN THE EAST

Note: the figure given for the USSR is GDP not GNP. The USSR has the largest oil and gas reserves in the world. It is the largest producer of cereals, potatoes, sugar beets, oilseeds, cotton, iron ore, asbestos, nickel and chromite.

If E. and W. Germany were combined, its population would number 80m and GNP would be £1.4 trillion, nearly double the size of the next biggest EC economy, France.

E. Germany's industry was based on 130 national Kombinate, huge vertically-integrated industrial combines. Their productivity was thought to be, on average, fully 20 per cent below comparable companies in W. Germany. This assessment proved, on closer inspection, to be wildly exaggerated.

President Gorbachev, whose policies of *democratisatsia, perestroika* and *glasnost* had contributed much to the opening-up of East Europe's Pandora's Box, was insistent that Germany's right to self-determination remain hedged about with a mass of political qualifications. So also the communiqués issued at the end of the NATO and EC summit meetings, that were urgently called in December 1989 to discuss the turn of events. The EC statement read:

We seek the strengthening of the state of peace in Europe in which the German people will regain its unity through free self-determination. This process should take place peacefully and democratically in full respect of the relevant agreements and treaties.. in the context of dialogue and East-West co-operation. It has also to be placed in the perspective of European integration. [19]

Chancellor Helmut Kohl of West Germany had made no bones about his position from hearing the news for the first time; any political re-integration of the two Germanies had to be based on true democracy in East Germany, as a first premise. But his interest was declared in a news conference on the 20th December at the end of his historic two-day visit. *The will of the people is an historic fact and to deny this fact would be an error before history. The peace in Europe will not be a lasting peace until the German people are granted self-determination.* The popular reaction on the part of many in the East was, as subsequent Leipzig street demonstrations in January 1990 showed, heavily in favour of re-unification. Even the East German Government seemed in favour of the prospect provided, so they said, that it would be accompanied by a wholesale de-militarisation of the two territories.

But lesser goals were more easily reached. The Brandenburg Gate at the heart of Berlin was re-opened at Christmas. Bilateral talks between the two Economics Ministers, Frau Christa Luft and Helmut Haussman, resulted in a draft of a treaty on extending economic and political ties which was to be signed by Helmut Kohl and Hans Modrow, the East German Prime Minister, before the free elections in May 1990. Apart from other things, this would set up a Joint Economic Commission to guide intensified trade and investment co-operation.

The French had their worries, particularly about the possibility of another *Gross Deutschland*. Would uncertainties over the Wall slow down the construction of the European Community and release nationalistic feelings that might inhibit progress? Such concerns were voiced by Prime Minister Michel Rocard who called for a radical move *to devise a new relationship between the EC, which is moving towards political union, and the countries of that other Europe which is in the midst of transforming itself.* [20] Mrs Thatcher was not so worried by re-unification specifically. Borders? *We do not discuss borders. They are not on the agenda at the moment... The main ball...the most important thing is to try to get democracy in the Soviet Union, Poland, Hungary, East Germany, Czechoslovakia, Bulgaria.. and you must do nothing that will make it more difficult.* [21]

There's a natural case for Germany. It will be the biggest beneficiary of developments in Eastern Europe... In a sense, they can be viewed as the equivalent of the small South-East Asian countries in the 1970s; and Germany will play the role of Japan. Richard Eats, GT Unit Trust Group.

EXHIBIT 7 : A WIN-WIN-WIN SITUATION?

Source: Investors see Europe as best market of the 1990s, *The Sunday Times*, 7/1/90

Note: that the Oxford Economic forecasting Group estimated that developments in E. Germany (which has no tariff barriers with W. Germany) could promote W. German exports by 0.5 per cent p.a. in the 1990s either directly or through an increase in counter-trade (barter, offsets etc.).

But borders were being discussed elsewhere.

The VEB IFA-Kombinat based at Karl-Marx-Stadt made Brabant cars (known colloquially, along with Wartburgs, as 'Steinzeitautos' or 'Stone Age cars'). It also made engines for Volkswagen cars. In the pre-war period in East Germany the Auto-Union Werk in Zwickau and the BMW factory in Eisenach had been among the technological and commercial leaders in Europe. The pedigree was there, at least.

Questioned about the possibility that Volkswagen might now target its production of Polos not (as previously planned) in the SEAT plant near Barcelona but in East Germany, the Kombinat's Director-General, Gunter Voigt, responded in a highly positive manner:

Wir bauen hier kein Polo nach Volkswagen Plänen. Wir wollen mit der Hilfe des Volkswagenkonzerns eigene neue Fahrzeuge entwickeln. [22]

The Volkswagen HQ was at Wolfsburg, just five miles distance from the East German border. Well might it have been interested in the prospects of improving collaboration. After all, the Kombinat's workforce was highly skilled, fluent in German, tired of black market living and paid, on average, less than $3 US per hour.

* * * * * * * * * * * * * * * * * * *

APPENDIX 1: STRAIGHT TALKING

It is important Americans understand the reality that power in the world, including economic power, is shifting gradually from West to East... Americans make money today by shuffling it around instead of creating and producing goods with some actual value... The American economy is an economy without substance. It must return to a real production economy... No matter how much the United States continues military expansion, if Japan stopped selling them semi-conductor chips there would be nothing they can do... The Americans say there is a US-Japan trade imbalance... The truth is there are few things in the US that the Japanese want to buy but there are a lot of things in Japan that the Americans want to buy... American corporations hire workers right and left and build new plants whenever the market is bullish in an attempt to maximise their profits... I must ask American executives if they regard workers as mere tools... Some of Japan's business leaders have long had an interest in Siberian development... Some of them are of the opinion that Japan should go neutral, revoking the US-Japan Security Treaty, if the Soviets will return the North Islands, granted that Japan would be given the right to develop Siberian resources... The time has come for Japan to tell the US that we do not need American protection. Japan will protect itself with its own power and wisdom

Source: *A Japan that can say No!*, a book of speeches by Akio Morita (chairman of Sony) and Shintaro Ishihara. Quoted in Land of the Rising Sun turns the heat on America, *The Sunday Times* 29/10/89.

Note: The Japanese Prime Minister Toshiki Kaifu began his tour of East and West Europe on the ninth of January 1990.

NOTES & REFERENCES

1   *The Times* 27/12/89
2   Romanian leader scorns reforms, Mary Dejevsky, *The Times*, 21/11/89
3   Former East German chiefs arrested, Patricia Clough, *The Independent*, 9/12/89
4   Leaders *converting luxuries to cash* as prelude to great escape, Ian Murray, *The Times*, 29/9/89
5   'Pressure grows for Krenz to quit', Peter Godwin, *The Sunday Times*, 3/12/89
6   'Gorbachev gives his full backing to East Berlin', Mary Dejevsky, *The Times*, 18/12/89
7   Walesa appeals for US aid to avoid utter *catastrophe*, Lionel Barber, *The Financial Times*, 16/11/89
8   Germany United, *The Economist*, 9/12/89
9   'Czechoslovakia under pressure', Edward Lucas, *The Sunday Times*, 19/11/89
10 'Military pledge as Party crisis grows', Richard Bassett, *The Times*, 24/11/89
11 'Bush believes East European reforms to be irreversible', Peter Riddell, *The Financial Times*, 8/11/89
12 *The Economist* 25/11/89
13 Parliament 23/1/89, *The Times* 24/1/89
14 Parliament 2/11/89, *The Times* 3/11/89
15 'Hurd says Britain is EC's pace-setter', *The Independent*, 25/11/89
16 As 15
17 *The Week in Europe*, European Commission, 19/10/89
18 'Social Charter will lead to destruction of jobs', Fowler says, Tim Jones, *The Times*, 30/10/89
19 *The Times,* 22/12/89
20 'East and West must start all over again say French', Patrick Marnham, *The Independent*, 18/11/89
21 'E. bloc democracy gets top priority', *The Times*, 24/11/89
22 *Der Spiegel*, No 50, 1989. *We are not building any Polos here in line with Volkswagen plans. What we want to do with the help of the Volkswagen concern is to develop our own new cars.*

IKARUS

Abstract:

Ikarus, the Hungarian bus company, fell on hard times when the Berlin Wall was taken down and its trading environment changed dramatically. Other E. European companies, Skoda for instance, suffered less and were able to continue to operate and even to attract inbound foreign investment. Such companies can *symbolise* the changing fortunes of the countries in which they were located, affected as they were by the G24 plan to re-invigorate Eastern Europe. Ikarus the company, with all its troubles, is taken in this case to test the extent to which the economies of Eastern Europe will fly (and stay aloft) in a new world.

Questions:

Can Ikarus, the Hungarian bus company, be saved and restored to economic health?
To what extent is the metaphor of Ikarus, the mythical unfortunate flier with the wings of wax, appropriate to describe the situation of all Eastern European countries?
Which, in your view, can be most easily re-invigorated?

Case Timing: 1990

155

A NEW MODEL FROM SKODA

At the start of the 1990s there was great excitement in car and truck plants throughout Eastern Europe at the enormous potential for the future resulting from economic developments then taking place.

In February 1990, for example, Suzuki, the Japanese car maker, announced that it planned to set up a Y20 billion Hungarian production plant at Esztergom on the Danube to begin operations by 1992. The joint venture deal with Suzuki's partners - the Hungarian Autokonszern (50 per cent), C.Itoh (10 per cent) and the World Bank's IFC (10 per cent) - had been greeted with great enthusiasm by the workforce of Ikarus, the famous Hungarian producer of buses, who were leaders in the Autokonszern consortium. Following on from the visit paid to Hungary by the Japanese Prime Minister, Toshiki Kaifu, in early 1990, the agreement was taken by them to augur well for future inbound investment for both their company and the country.

But a bare two months later it was a different story for Ikarus employees. Their euphoria waned when they were notified by the Hungarian government that, because of the unwillingness of Ikarus' main customer (the USSR) to meet its payment obligations on some of the buses shipped in 1989 to the Soviet Union and an order cancellation, it was suspending production at the company's two plants. It was a major blow to Hungary itself, as well as the company's workers, since the buses made up some ten per cent of the country's total exports to the USSR and helped pay for imported oil.

This struck a negative note in a sometimes highly positive picture, given that the wish to engineer deals like that of the Suzuki joint venture was not an isolated phenomenon in Eastern Europe in 1990. Skoda of Czechoslovakia was another example of an Eastern European firm actively seeking a Western partner.

Widely known in Western Europe for its utilitarian cars since its nationalisation in 1946, it wished to build on the recent success it had been having with its 1300cc Favorit hatchback. Styled by Bertone of Italy, this car was being produced at a rate of 600 per day on a partly robotised line in the city of Mlada Boleslav, 60 km from Prague. The 16,500 strong workforce at this Skoda plant some of whom, in former days, were prisoners supplied under contract by the Ministry of Justice to work in the Skoda foundry, were anxious to regain the high reputation that the company had enjoyed in the international market-place prior to the Second World War for its engineering excellence and design skills. To do this the company needed to move away from a situation in which domestic demand far outstripped supply and in which the company's margins were fixed by the Czech government in the export, as well as the domestic, market.

In April 1990 Skoda indicated that, with the help of its advisers, which included Price Waterhouse, it was reviewing co-operation proposals from a galaxy of interested parties including Subaru, Mitsubishi, Renault, Citroen, BMW, General Motors and Volkswagen. Renault had already made plain its wish to build an assembly plant for its Trafic utility van in Czechoslovakia and hence rated its chances of a link-up with Skoda as high. Karosa, the main Czech bus producer, by contrast, had teamed up by this time with the German manufacturer Neoplan to produce coaches.

> *Skoda is seen as a very solid car in the East. We want to improve its image, give it a bit more pep and sportiness, and get away from the image of the monopoly supplier. East German cars were the symbol of a detested regime. That is not true of Skoda.* (Volkhard Kohler, VW Planning Director)

EXHIBIT 1: A REAL PRODUCT PLUS! [1]

Taking over, creating a joint venture, or merging with an East European manufacturer was never going to be the easiest of undertakings for any Western car maker. In Skoda's case, the manufacturing technology on the assembly line was up-to-date but no less than 6,500 of the company's 22,500 workforce were estimated to work in non-productive jobs in Skoda - company-owned child-care centres, holiday homes, repair shops etc. - and needed reassurances about their future employment from potential acquirers.

In the event this did not act as a deterrent to the winner in the bidding contest: Volkswagen. Indeed, adding this acquisition to the Volkswagen new developments under way in Eastern Germany - a new, fully-integrated car plant to be built near the old Trabant factory in Zwickau - did much to substantiate the company's claim that it was re-drawing the European car-making map.

It was a deal of this sort that Ikarus was anxious to secure as it, too, asked for international bids in a tender operation.

A MATTER OF MONEY

Part of the investment interest that had led firms as large as General Electric of the USA into taking holdings in selected state-owned East European companies (like, in GE's case, Tungsram of Hungary) and into setting up joint ventures was based on the prospects of a substantial increase in the level of Western aid to East Europe.

It was thought likely at the start of 1990, on the basis of a detailed assessment by the UN Economic Commission for Europe (ECE), that the Western world would be only too keen to assist with East Europe's development needs. One of the mechanisms for so doing was grants and/ or soft loans offered under the auspices of the World Bank, the IMF, the European Bank for Reconstruction and Development. This acted on behalf of the European Commission, itself the agent of G24.

This was certainly the hope of the Czech and Hungarian governments, both struggling to come to terms with the results of their entry into the new world of democratic rule and economic market-place. Poland, too, though at the end of November 1990 still without a democratically-elected President and lower House of Parliament (Sejm), shared this hope. Not only was Poland encumbered by the highest level of official debt in East Europe but its government was still dominated by representatives who had been, until February 1990 when the Party ceased officially to exist, Communist.

Acceptance of the rule of law
Respect for human rights
Multi-party system
Free and fair elections
Economic liberalisation

TABLE 1: G24 AID CONDITIONS FOR EASTERN EUROPE

But it was going to be a major task, comparable, in the ECE view, to the post-war Marshall Aid Plan for Western Europe and involving a projected $16.7 billion of aid per year for 4 years. The Marshall Plan had, in fact, cost the USA 1.3 per cent of its GDP at the time, a figure coincidentally equal to the highly contentious level of the US budget deficit for 1989/90.

The international commitment to meet the need, as of November 1990 and in the light of the G24 Paris summit, seemed equally substantial, however. A G24 short term aid plan of $2b had been put together on top of US pledges of almost $1 billion.

In addition to this, Soviet agreement to the re-unification of Germany in mid 1990 brought in its train German help for the USSR in a variety of forms, including a DM12 billion grant and a DM3 billion trade credit. To these were added further valuable trade credits by France and Spain, negotiated during President Gorbachev's visits to West Europe in late 1990.

Hence the stage was set for momentous economic and political changes in the USSR and East Europe. Help was subject, of course, to countries' meeting the G24 criteria set for the international aid they were seeking and with the obvious proviso that the countries in question would be able to continue with their existing trading relationships, as desired. In the case of the USSR, there was also the question of the maintenance of that country's export earnings from oil and gas.

When it became clear that there had been a further breakdown in the Uruguay Round of the GATT talks in December 1990, the consequences for the disruption in the international trade system and concomitant protectionist moves also became more apparent. These could not fail but have knock-on effects on trade patterns in the East.

Naturally enough, anyway, opinion differed on the magnitude of the transformation task. Michael Gibbins of Accountants KPMG Peat Marwick McLintock was one commentator who erred on the side of caution. At a conference in October 1990 he declared *There is clear evidence of a groundswell of opinion (in Eastern Europe) in favour of the old economic order which provided security and state protection* and that the financial and political complexities facing Western investors were 'immense'. In his speech he ranged over some of the difficulties involved in brown field site operations in East Europe. These included the objective valuation of corporate assets, securing proper title to them and appraising the liability and cost of environmental damage previously and currently caused by the company in which the investor might be interested. The conclusion was a sour one. *There are very few existing businesses in Eastern Europe* he declared *which are of sufficient calibre and strength for direct investment.*[2]

On the other hand, a report issued in April 1990 by the prestigious consultants Cambridge Econometrics took a bullish view. Having analysed, and rejected as unlikely, two alternative scenarios for the development of the region ('No Future' and 'A Valley of Tears') they plumped for the third, 'An Early Take-off' as the most likely to occur. On the specific condition that countries in East Europe would speedily accept market economy principles and introduce their practices, the report argued that the switch from Communism to Capitalism would create a market for West European goods currently larger than that of the USA's.[3]

> *As country after country in the Eastern bloc forsakes planned Marxist for free markets, those of us in the automotive industry see potential for substantial growth.*
> (Hans-Jorg Hungerland, Volkswagen Sales Director, Volkswagen brand)

EXHIBIT 2: GROWTH POTENTIAL IN THE EAST [4]

The message from the USSR which gathered strength as 1990 progressed was, however, in flat contradiction. Take, for instance, the almost despairing comment of Leonid Abalkin, the USSR's Deputy Prime Minister, as he backed the introduction of the Ryzhkov Plan to move to the basics of a market economy. At the 28th Congress of the Soviet Communist Party; he declared:

> *The choice (between continuing with a command economy and switching to a market economy) has already been made. We can no longer continue balancing between two stools.. almost every sector of the economy is in a shambles. Without such a transformation the country has no future as a great power.*[5]

Among the most intractable problems to be faced in any such change were the facts that the Soviet Union, in Article 40 of its constitution, guaranteed the right to work and that the country, in the words of presidential adviser Nikolai Petrakov, had created *a human being with a non-market psychology*[6] who was being portrayed publicly as being in danger of being sold into *capitalist slavery.*[7]

THE SOVIET FACTOR

As 1990 progressed, East European governments became increasingly anxious to make progress with their reforms. Especially those contemplating the possibility of joint venture/merger/takeover deals involving previously state-owned enterprises like Ikarus.

Three particular issues were coming to be of increasing political visibility and importance and tension was plainly rising. Firstly, the political turmoil in the USSR. Secondly, the breakdown of COMECON and its elaborate network of obligatory trading relationships based on soft-currency transferable roubles. Thirdly, the problem of oil.

As if it were not enough that extraction and shipment difficulties in the USSR had drastically curtailed oil supplies to Czechoslovakia, Poland and Hungary in mid-1990, the USSR was insisting that, as from the first of January 1991, all future supplies would have to be paid for at the international market price in hard currency. The previously-used alternative (of obtaining supplies from Iraq in exchange for arms) was no longer open to these countries since the UN embargo caused by Iraq's invasion of Kuwait. Indeed, all three were owed very substantial sums of hard currency and oil supplies by Iraq for previous deliveries.

From the Ambassador of the USSR:
Sir, One cannot help feeling overwhelmed by the display of sympathy and concern for the situation in the Soviet Union on behalf of the British public. There are hardly any words that can reflect truly the depth of our appreciation and gratitude. The reasons for the dire situation with food supplies to some major Soviet cities are well-documented. I would like to point out that this is a price the Soviet Union is paying for the difficult transition to a market-orientated economy. It is important to note that the interests of those in need in Moscow and Leningrad would be best served through financial aid. This is not a situation that requires sending food parcels, warm clothing, blankets etc. I would like to inform your readers that a special charity account has been opened by the USSR Embassy at Barclays Bank. Any help would be much appreciated. Yours, L Zamyatin

---

EXHIBIT 3: LETTER TO THE TIMES

Note: On the 3rd December 1990 by a majority of 602-369 the parliament of the Russian Federation voted for a resolution supporting - with several constraints, admittedly - the principle of the private ownership of land. This is a historic break with communist principles enforced since the 1930's.

The most salient of the three issues, in December 1990, was the first. President Gorbachev's plan for a new USSR Union Treaty (to permit greater federation-republic power-sharing) and his proposed new governmental structure (giving greater say to the Federation Council) were denounced by an array of opponents, chief among whom was Boris Yeltsin, president of the largest of the Soviet republics, Russia. On top of this there was the contentious question of the president's having been granted powers to rule by decree (*ukaz*), as and where necessary. This was justified in the eyes of many by the appalling shortages of food and other staples (*defitsiny*) suffered by in Russian cities like Moscow and Leningrad. These shortages had been caused by a disastrous blend of black marketeering, inefficient distribution systems, inadequate resources and the with-holding of supply by other republics and regions.

So desperate was the problem at the onset of the 1990 winter, that President Gorbachev was delighted to accept the German government's offer of immediate and major food aid. Ironically, some of the food stocks sent on the first airlift appeared to have been taken from the strategic stockpile that had been held in Berlin against a possible repeat of the Soviet blockade of that city!

> *You thought you had built.. humane Democratic Socialism. But we have not... not even a Socialist society. If we want an affluent economy which encourages scientific and technical progress with shops filled with quality goods and an end to the disgrace of queues and speculation, then we have no choice but to switch to a market economy.*

EXHIBIT 4: LEONID ABALKIN
Speech to the 28th Congress of the Soviet Communist Party, July 1990

Even a foodstuff as basic as the simple onion was unobtainable in the Moscow state food stores. Uzbekistan and Kazakhstan had simply stopped supplying. Those maritally inclined will be interested in the fact that wedding rings had also been withdrawn from sale ever since the Russian republic had refused to enact a federal directive freeing up their price (as one of a category of non-essential goods).

It was in this context that controversy raged over the relative merits of two plans for the further advancement of President Gorbachev's New Economic Mechanism. These were the gradualist approach referred to earlier and advocated by the USSR's prime minister Nikolai Ryzhkov. The second was the 500-day 'Dash for the Market' plan put forward as an official alternative by a team headed by Stanislav Shatalin and supported by Boris Yeltsin.

That President Gorbachev himself blew hot and cold over these alternative options is not surprising. Had he not been publicly jeered at during the 1990 May Day parade in Moscow? Had he not been forced to climb down by speedily having to countermand aspects of the Ryzhkov plan to de-control prices? Not for nothing did Marshal Dmitri Yazov (USSR Defence Minister) appear on Soviet TV twice in late November 1990 to speak to an alert audience about the need for proper order and security.

HUNGARY AND FOREIGN INVESTMENT

The Hungarian government was clearly sensitive to the political image presented by such developments in the USSR and felt the need to offset any negative reactions stemming from such a picture. It therefore announced that it would guarantee all Ikarus's debts when it was privatised - by public tender - in December. The company had already been exempted from the provisions of the Bankruptcy Law passed in April 1990. The authorities certainly did not want a repeat of the adverse publicity that had been attracted when the state-owned travel and tourism group IBUSZ had been floated simultaneously on the Vienna stock exchange (50 per cent of shares) and that just set up in Budapest (40 per cent). The remaining ten per cent of the stock was kept in the hands of the employees. The flotation had been met with disinterest in Hungary (an eleven per cent take-up) and wild acclaim in Vienna. The heavy over-subscription in Austria had led, in fact, to the widespread criticism in Hungary that the nation's assets had been sold off far too cheaply to rapacious Westerners.

It was a criticism that weighed heavily with Ivan Tompe, head of the State Property Agency (SPA), who was charged with the privatisation of large slices of the 85 per cent of the economy that was still in state ownership. Naturally enough, in the light of his sizeable task, which also involved vetting joint ventures (of which 500 in the year to September 1990) and policing foreign buy-ins. This brought with it the need to advise the government on matters such as the appropriate level of hard currency profit repatriation and the tax discounts and tax holidays that should be permitted on foreign holdings.

Both these measures were successfully introduced, but the suspicion of profiteering by foreigners ('economic colonisation') had always to be set against the primary requirement, attracting foreign capital for the revitalisation of industry, in all SPA thinking. It was a concern that was clearly evident in the government's 40 billion forint 'Flagship Privatisation Plan' covering hotel groups (Hungar-hotels, Pannonia and Danubius) and 20 other major industrial concerns. This was the first, and most direct, step in a process that was eventually planned to cover 10,000 small businesses and 2,700 larger enterprises by the end of 1992. Not that there was a lack of successful precedents in 1990 to guide future SPA policy. Quite the reverse.

The French groups Paribas, Spie Batignolles and Accor had set up a Joint Venture (JV) with the Novotel Hotel and Conference Centre division of Pannonia: Machines Bull were working with the Videoton electronics group: Digital Equipment had established a partnership with Hungary's largest computer services company: Daewoo and Samsung were involved in JVs in the television field: UK media tycoon Robert Maxwell had bought a 40 per cent stake in the Budapest evening paper *Estihirlap*. Other Hungarian companies had launched themselves on the Vienna and Budapest exchanges or planned to do so. But such actual and anticipated successes could not disguise the stark nature of some of the economic difficulties faced by Hungary, of which a potential buyer of Ikarus needed to be only too aware.

High on this agenda were the country's per capita indebtedness to the West, cabinet strife (between the prime minister and his finance minister Ferenc Rabar) over a planned 25 per cent reduction in the 1991 budget deficit and the supply and price of Soviet oil. On the 28th October 1990 the government found itself giving in to striking drivers over its attempt to raise fuel prices by 80 per cent. Despite an 80 per cent plus reliance on Soviet oil supplied through the Friendship Pipeline, it found it could not use the price weapon to cut back usage. After all, the price de-regulation introduced in January, along with strict controls on wage rises, had had substantial recessionary consequences, such that what *The Economist* called *the Communist legacy of political quiescence* [8] could no longer be relied upon.

THE POLISH PUSH

Poland also was seeking Western partners and feared a slowdown in the rate of enquiries. It was being closely watched by Hungary as a competitor for inbound investment. Like Hungary, Poland had sought revitalisation of its economy, through what was labelled 'shock therapy'. Against a ten-year back-ground of political agitation against the Communist regime, the trade union Solidarity led by Lech Walesa had set up in 1989 a government charged with putting forward a bold new economic strategy. Taddeus Mazowiecki was its prime minister and Leszek Balcerowicz its finance minister. He gained fame by spearheading a programme to improve Poland's economic productivity via the use of selective deflationary mechanisms (Figure 1, page 165). To prepare for what became known as the *Big Bang* gamble of the Balcerowicz plan, the prime minister sought, in February 1990, an extra credit line of $1 billion from the IMF and the World Bank and negotiated with Poland's creditors a moratorium on debt servicing.

This was valuable because, since 1981, Poland had not repaid any borrowed capital and only part of the interest owed on its international borrowings. The new deal meant that it would pay interest on existing debt only over the period 1991-1999 and repay principal from 1999 onwards.

Company to be privatised	Industry Sector
Tonsil	Audio
Exbud	Construction
Slaska Fabryka	Cables
Kronsnienskie Huty Szkla	Glass
Prochnik	Clothing

TABLE 2: SHOW CASE PRIVATISATION

Note: $26m was expected from the privatisation of these companies. Foreign investors were to be allowed to buy up to ten per cent of the shares. As with other investments the difficulty was one of an agreed valuation of assets, most of which in an advanced state of depreciation. The Nowa Huta Steel Mill in Cracow was another candidate for privatisation. Here, in preparation for this event, a new Chief Executive had just been chosen in the normal fashion by the firm's Employees' Council.

It was on this basis that Poland had created the Council for National Estate (CNE) to oversee structural and ownership changes in its industry and, in January 1990, removed price controls. In this month alone prices shot up by 78 per cent and the real value of savings was commensurately eroded. Part of the reasons for the massive price rises to follow lay in what Sir Alan Walters, former adviser to the British Prime Minister, Margaret Thatcher, over the period 1979-1990, called the *monumental price distortions experienced under Communism.* [9] Like, for example, the price of an airline ticket from Gdansk to Warsaw (50p) or the price of coal (one sixth the international price).

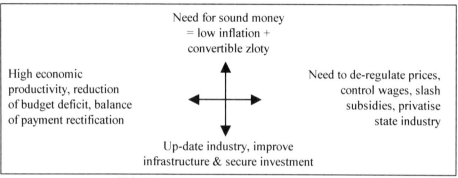

FIGURE 1: THE BALCEROWICZ PLAN

When the price of fuel oil shot up in February by 600 per cent, companies were warned that, if they sought to increase wages, they would suffer appropriate tax penalties.

The government's stated intention was to privatise 70 per cent of public sector industry (7,600 enterprises) within two years, in part using privatisation bonds, exchangeable for shares, issued to the population. As a precursor to privatisation, the number of joint ventures and the level of foreign minority investment grew, especially in the fields of telecommunications and finance, as Table 3 indicates.

Telecommunications
Here the relaxation of COCOM rules in mid 1990 gave a large boost to the technological aspirations of the two Polish monopolies that were to be split up. On top of this, cellular phone networks and fibre optic cabling looked all the more realisable because of the joint venture between the French Alcatel and the Polish Teletra, Eltra and Elektim companies.
Finance
The infrastructure here was much helped by the creation of a joint venture between the NMB-Postbank of Holland and the Bank Handlowy w Warszawie. There was also the breakthrough in government finance methods (for East Europe, that is) with the Polish National Bank's selling 30 day money certificates - short-term bills - as from September 1 1990.

TABLE 3 : FROM THE GROUND UP...

In late August 1990 the Poles scored a significant success. They secured a $65m loan from the European Investment Bank to modernise PGNGN, Poland's oil and gas utility. The loan was aimed at improving energy efficiency and freeing-up valuable coal supplies for export to the West. It could not have come at a better time since the combination of adverse changes, supply decline and price rise, in the oil market threatened to turn a Polish trade surplus of $2.48 billion for the first 7 months of 1990 (in which arms sales figured quite prominently) into a deficit in excess of $1 billion for 1991.

Such plusses had, however, to be set against some minuses. As Zbigniew Lis, one of the Gdansk shipyard Solidarity leaders, put it:

There is unemployment, a lack of direction. Black marketeers are having a field day. Scandals are erupting throughout the government. The old Communist bosses are coming back and buying up new ventures. The rich are just getting richer. As for the workers, we haven't any savings anymore.[9]

There was, indeed, ample cause for despondency. In this heavily Catholic country, where agriculture supported 40 per cent of the working population and contributed no less than 16 per cent of GDP, most farms were small and privately owned. There could not but be concern at the contrast between the unregenerated nature of the Sejm (lower House of Parliament) and the upper chamber, where, in the 1989 election, Solidarity won 99 per cent of the seats.

Nor did the election contest for the new Polish president in November/ December inspire any confidence. Stanislaw Tyminiski, a Canadian businessman (admittedly of Polish extraction), managed to out-poll Taddeus Mazowiecki and contribute to his resignation as prime minister. With living standards some 40 per cent down and output 30 per cent down on the 1989 levels and with unemployment in excess of 1m, some disillusionment was bound to be evident.

PEACE DIVIDENDS IN CZECHOSLOVAKIA?

Not surprisingly, the moves made by its erstwhile COMECON companions towards re-establishing their economic fortunes aroused keen interest in Czechoslovakia, bounded as it was in the West and South, respectively, by Germany and Austria. The re-unification of Germany and the incipient demilitarisation of parts of the country meant an immediate and welcome spurt in hard currency tourism. But, as elsewhere, there were different views on the proper speed of change. Valtr Komarek (first deputy prime minister) was publicly very much concerned with the social costs of too speedy a transition to the market, whereas finance minister Vaclav Klaus counselled a swift dose of

Capitalism as the unavoidable cure for the country's economic ills. The resultant strategy, as Table 4 indicates, looked to be what the government saw as a well-structured approach.

Timing	Content of Move
Jan 1990	Substantial devaluation of tourist korona.
April 1990	Range of laws passed covering joint ventures, joint stock companies and privatisation. Foreigners could own up to 49% of a joint venture.
June 1990	Beginning of the quest for EC membership.
July 1990	Beginning of process of reducing all state subsidies and increasing the price of public transport and fuel.
Jan 1991	All prices to be de-regulated. The korona would enjoy internal convertibility i.e. trading companies will be able to convert it into foreign currency.
Jan 1992	Full korona convertibility.

TABLE 4 : THE CZECH RE-VITALISATION STRATEGY

It had to be. Czechoslovakia was, and is, an artificial creation dating from the Trianon Treaty of 1918 which brought together the country's two ethnically-dissimilar halves. Its real democracy began only in June 1990, when Civic Forum won a convincing victory in a free election with a 95 per cent turnout at federal level and in both parts of Czechoslovakia and when President Vaclav Havel took up his post. A *Times* leader of the eleventh of June 1990 indicated what it saw as the disastrous consequences of a potential failure to adapt. There was, it declared *a cloud hovering on the nation's shoulder - as across Eastern Europe. A sort of corporatist nationalism, a mix of chauvinist xenophobia and revived central statism.*

There were some Western businessmen who preferred to probe, slowly and methodically, for opportunities. But there were others who were more interested in plunging.

Like Bell Atlantic and US West in the telecommunications field or like Thomas Bata, the largest private shoe-maker in the world, returning to his native roots to make shoes in the factory in Zlin where the family business had first started. The Czech mood was similarly up-beat as manufacturers like BAZ (buses and trucks) and SKLO-UNION (glass) looked hard for Western partners. Others were not quite so sure. The inhabitants of the Czech cities of Martin and Dubnica, for instance. The first had been the birth-place of the relatively high technology T54, T55 and T72 tanks - standard Warsaw Pact issue - and was now facing redundancy.

In the second was located the famous ZTS arms factory where mobile rocket launchers (katushas) were made. It was workers and managers in arms plants like these who had contributed no less than 46 per cent of the total value of Czech foreign trade over the past 15 years and whose products had been so eagerly bought by Iraq and other militant countries. What would their future be now that the European Conven-tional Forces Treaty had just been signed, in November 1990, in Paris?

IKARUS ALOFT?

The provisional tender contest for Ikarus was won, much to the delight of the company's 18,000-strong workforce, by CEIHC. This was a Toronto-based consortium made up of members of various Soviet transport ministries (Russia, Ukraine, Byelorussia, Uzbekistan), the Moscow City Transport Association and the Taiwanese Ching Fong Investment Co. It had, in the process defeated 14 other bids. These had included Mercedes Benz and MAN from Germany, Renault and Ikarus' main supplier of parts, the Csepel Automotive Works.

But there were difficulties and these appeared to be growing more intractable as time went by.

Poland's FSO and Fiat were planning in early 1990 to jointly produce the Fiat TIPO, firstly on the basis of imported kits and then by creating a production facility. Hitherto the Warsaw-based FSO has been producing out-dated Fiat models under licence. Indeed it is estimated that 50% of the cars produced in the Soviet Union and East Europe in the 1980s were Fiat-derived: Lada, FSO and Yugo - for instance.

Fiat was also planning to assist with the development of a huge new 900,000 cars per year plant at Yelabuga on the banks of the Kama river. The project was valued at $7 billion and aimed at almost doubling the USSR's car output. The company would be taking a 30% equity stake in one phase of the project. Sadly, the first stage of development had had to be deferred because of Soviet government financial difficulties.

Fiat also announced (in May 1991) that it had taken a 30% stake in the USSR's biggest car maker, VAZ (Volskij Avtomobilnij Zavod), which produced the Lada. A new model was to be produced at VAZ's Togliatti plant on the Volga. VAZ produces some 750,000 out of the USSR's annual car output of 1.2m units and employed 95,000 workers.

EXHIBIT 5 : FIAT LUX [10]

There was the question, for example, of the company's valuation. Ikarus had been valued by Price Waterhouse at $150m in early 1990; the State Audit Office considered it to be worth $200m, even though its results for the year to September 1990 showed a drop in output from 13,000 to 9,700 units and its revenue had fallen from $380m to $120m. In addition RABA, the Hungarian machine and Carriage Works, was heavily critical of the foreign-backed acquisition of a majority stake in Ikarus and Csepel at the tender price of $170m.

Another issue was that of future prospects. Although the auguries for a revival of real demand from the USSR seemed poor, Ikarus had received strong orders from Kuwait and Iran for buses and trolley buses in March 1991. The problem in meeting these orders was the fact that RABA had, itself, increased the prices of the parts bought from it by Ikarus by up to 400 per cent. It cited increased world competition, the dollarisation of Soviet and East European trade and the end of Comecon.

These issues were casting an increasingly long and dark shadow over the potential sale of Ikarus to CEIHC. For many, the key question was *would Ikarus ever fly again?*

* * * * * * * * * * * * * * * * * * *

NOTES & REFERENCES

1   Western cars make their marque, Kevin Done, Andrew Fisher and Leslie Colitt, *The Financial Times*, 2/4/91

2   Fear of Stampede Mentality in E. Europe, Toss Tiemen, *The Times,* 19/10/90

3   Europe 1994, Cambridge Econometrics

4   As 1

5   Gorbachev opts for free market, *The Times*, 10/4/90

6   Soviet planners forge ahead with brakes still on, William Millinship, *The Observer*, 29/4/90

7   As 4

8   *The Economist*, 6/10/90

9   After Poland's Big Bang, the fight for academic freedom, Alan Walters*, The Times,* 29/8/90

10   Fiat to take 30 per cent of Soviet carmaker, *The Financial Times,* 28/5/91

AIR EUROPE

Abstract:

Air Europe ranges widely over the economics and politics of a major European industry whose continued success was vital to the EC economy: aviation. The background to the centre-piece of the case, the collapse of International Leisure Group (ILG) in 1991, is, firstly, progress towards the de-regulation of air transport in Europe and, secondly, the impact on the economics of plane-building and airline operation of the major recession in the industry at the end of the 1980s. The case thus allows study of the three stages in the industry's value chain (plane making, airline operation and tourism) against the background of a substantial down-turn in the business cycle.

Interestingly, despite ILG's spectacular failure, its chairman, Harry Goodman, took little time to get back in business. By 1999 he was chairman and chief executive of TV Travel Shop, a highly successful package holiday sales company valued at £52.5m of which Harry owned 6.5 per cent.

Questions:

Explain the collapse of ILG. Assess the implications for the industry of major changes in the European business cycle.

Do you believe that the eventual deregulation of air transport in the European Union will necessarily benefit all players in the industry, airlines and plane makers, especially?

Do you think that it will, in fact, take place?

Case Timing: 1991

DOWN TO EARTH

On the eighth of March 1991 the UK-based International Leisure Group (ILG) collapsed with debts estimated at over £500m. The powerful shock waves of the decision to put the company into receivership reverberated widely. After all, it comprised the country's second largest travel and tourism operator which had already been alerted to a looming crisis by the death, in February, of its competitor, British Island Airways.

The key factors behind the drama were, of course, the severity of the recession in the UK and a collapse in confidence in the UK's tourist business, caused specifically by the Gulf War. ILG's demise left 25,000 holiday-makers stranded abroad, at no more than a moment's notice. The confidence-shattering period for the tourism trade had begun in January 1991 with a slump in package tour bookings and consequent forecasts that, even with a successful outcome in the Gulf War, holiday bookings for the year would be likely to be 20 per cent down on 1990.

ILG was shown to be tragically exposed to the change in demand for both holiday and scheduled air services. Its corporate divisions included a package tour operation, Intasun, and an airline, Air Europe, which serviced Intasun requirements and operated as a competitor to European national flag carriers (British Airways, Air France etc.), on scheduled routes in Europe. Intasun was second only in market share in the UK package tour business to the Thomson Organisation and traded under a range of top brands like Global, Lancaster, Skiscene and Club 18-30. It focused heavily on popular demand for destinations in Spain and North Africa.

Like ILG, the Thomson Organisation was also an integrated operator with its own airline - in this case Britannia - but the two differed in the extent to which ILG had a third operating division which was involved in the procedures for leasing aircraft to Air Europe. This consisted of such companies as AE Finance and AE Norsk Ltd.

They also differed in the way in which they had in the past developed to capitalise on the growth in cheap package tour demand. This had mushroomed from three million holidays in 1976 to 12 million in 1988, accompanying the mammoth expansion in global air travel which had occurred over this period. Whilst Britannia in 1990 had a fleet of Boeing 737s half of which were ten years old, Air Europe had updated its fleet of 37 Boeing 737s and 757s, Fokker F100s and McDonnell Douglas aircraft, ingeniously using them on scheduled services in

Europe at peak times and on package tours at other times. It was noticeable also that the ambition of Harry Goodman, head of ILG, lay very much in building up the scale of Air Europe's scheduled operations. This he had done to the point where he was known to the satirical magazine Private Eye, very uncharitably in the light of his erstwhile position as chief busker to the Variety Club of Great Britain, as 'Greedman'.

On the basis of the forecast made in 1990 by analysts SRI International that the European annual air traffic volume would rise from 267m passengers in 1988 to 740m in 2010, Harry Goodman's enthusiasm can be seen to be justified. It was certainly in line with the £100m fleet expansion move he had begun in 1987 on the basis of a mixture of plane leasing and ownership, based (in part) on debt finance. Not, of course, that all UK providers of travel and tourism services had been able to succeed in the past against this background of fluctuating demand growth. Indeed ILG's fate could be set against the collapse of even more prestigious operators like Clarkson's and Court Line (1974), Laker Airways (1982) and British Caledonian (taken over by British Airways in 1987). Adjusting to the vagaries of supply and demand, managing competition from entrenched airlines and matching oil price and currency parity realities to anticipations were key managerial tasks in this highly volatile industry. Failing to come to terms with these imperatives had taken its toll, at different times and to varying extents, of the once-famous leaders of all these companies.

So, too, was 51-year-old Harry Goodman. A self-made Croesus, he had worked his way up from humble North London origins to own at one time or another a Learjet, a Rolls Royce Silver Spur and other trappings of entrepreneurship. He had moved through the creation of a small travel agency, Sidcup Travel, to the establishment in 1966 of his first travel company (Sunair), sold subsequently to Cunard, and then his second (Intasun) in 1973. His plan to set up Air Europe in 1979, involving the acquisition of three new Boeing 737s for £18m, was initially snubbed by the banking fraternity. In the 1980s a consortium of 60 banks with Citibank (USA) and the Japanese Mitsui and Sumitomo in the lead, was to prove much more accommodating.

And now, as of the eighth of March 1991, he had been obliged to admit defeat. *We worked out butts off* he said *to make an airline that was bloody good and then we got knocked out the sky. We are back to square one... It's a sad day. It was a fabulous concept and a fabulous airline. My sorrow is for the dedicated people who worked in it and for my customers.*[1] The future of ILG was now in the hands of Tim Haywood, administrator with the multisyllabic accountancy firm KMPG Peat Marwick McClintock, who was charged with finding buyers for some or all of the business. On the tenth of March he declared that he was already talking to some potential purchasers and had some optimism.[2]

EUROPEAN AIRLINE DEREGULATION: THE STORY SO FAR

Part of the uncertainty any potential buyer of any of the saleable parts of ILG might have felt in making a bid would clearly have related to the European Commission's progress towards its stated goal of airline deregulation in Europe. The two were intimately related.

Since the mid 1980s, the two Commissioners responsible for ensuring competition within the European Community (in line with articles 85 and 86 of the Treaty of Rome) had voiced concern with the situation in the airline industry in Europe and had acted to change what they saw at best as competition avoidance. Each successive step taken by them had been anxiously studied by the major European operators for its impact on airline economics and by national government for its political ramifications.

The Americans, who decided that, if airlines were free to fend for themselves in a deregulated environment, prices would tumble and competition would increase, were proved spectacularly wrong. In practice the smaller airlines were swallowed up by their larger and richer rivals until the handful of giant airlines was able to dictate prices and timetables at will.	*Airline deregulation is working in Chicago and in most airports across the USA, says the Dept. of Transportation... Government has no business telling airlines how much they can charge and what services they can provide. The government gave up that authority in 1978. As a result most travellers enjoy better service and cheaper fares. There are fewer airlines now but most places have more flights. Deregulation works.*
Source: 3/1/90 'Airlines hoping to double 1989 total of 1.1b passengers', Harvey Elliott, *The Times*.	Source: 20/2/90. Leading article in *USA Today* - 'Let Competition fix Airline Problems'.

EXHIBIT 1 : TAKE YOUR PICK

Of course, the Commission was also taking rather more general steps to try to achieve its declared aim of *a more level playing field in Europe* for competing industrialists. Among these steps were the re-shaped 13th Company Directive, which focused attention on disparate company ownership and control practices in the EC, and measures curbing state aid to industry. There was also pressure to achieve EC-wide acceptance of the Community Charter of the Social Rights of Workers. This enshrined the principle of worker participation.

It was in 1987 that the first major indication of the Commission's airline deregulation intentions had been given. On the eighth of June, Belgium's transport minister Herman de Croo chaired a meeting of his EC colleagues to discuss the European Transport Council's response to a threat from Peter Sutherland (the-then Competition Commissioner) to bring an action in the European Court of Justice to break up the European national airlines' price-and-route-fixing cartel and to declare its practices illegal. As can well be imagined, independent European airlines in IACEC (Independent Air Carriers of the European Community) like Air Europe, Danair and Britannia strongly supported this approach.

The Council meeting broke up after two days of recrimination and with agreement on some of the major issues firmly postponed. Fare discounting up to a level of 45 per cent was to be officially permitted in future, though. The participants also struck a deal whereby two national airlines, then sharing a route between their two countries as national flag-carriers, would have their shares reduced from 50 per cent to 40 per cent by 1990, thus allowing access to that route by new and independent competitors ('Multiple Designation Rights'). But, in return for these concessions, ministers wanted airlines to be exempted in future from competition rules. Nor was any progress made on the issue of the so-called 'Fifth Freedom Right' or cabotage. Under this, airline X from country X would be allowed to fly to country Y, pick up passengers there and take them on to other airports in Y or even country Z. This latter position was, if anything, made more rigid by the restrictions on the maximum permitted level of foreign ownership of their national carriers applied by individual governments. These were W. Germany 49 per cent, France 30 per cent, Italy and Spain 25 per cent, UK, unstated as a percentage but *not a controlling interest*, US 25 per cent.

December 1987 saw a conclusion to some aspects of these long-running battles with a liberalisation agreement. Under this governments stated that they would not automatically turn down every application for a cheap fare. But the deal was a grudging one on the part of some.

The UK government's view was nothing if not bi-polar. On the one hand it was believed that cheaper *freedom of the skies* air travel would come as one of the real benefits from a true 1993 Common Market yet, on the other, there was some support for the trenchant British Airways position that cut-price tariffs would never be commercially viable. BA's Chief Executive, Sir Colin Marshall, interpreted Air Europe's reaction to the agreement - a pioneering price for the London-Munich return trip of £135 as compared to the *normal* fare of £386 - as *very high risk* with *a hard-to-predict outcome.*[2]

Sir Leon Brittan, Competition Commissioner, giving the P & G lecture at Newcastle University on the 27 January 1989, stated that air transport was a priority area. *I believe* he said *much greater liberalisation... must be achieved... Air traffic is still too expensive in Europe and this is largely due to a plethora of restrictive practices by airlines and governments.* His predecessor had once referred to civil aviation as *the most antiquated and anti-competitive industry in Europe.* According to the European Court of Justice ruling (13/4/89) that it was illegal to fix tariffs - either bilaterally or multilaterally - within an EC country or between an EC country and a third country. Community airline regulations then in force were governed by the 1987 Air Transport package and applied only to routes between EC countries.

The Commission agreed in December 1990 to exemptions from the competition rules of the Treaty of Rome in respect of planning and co-ordination of capacity, consultation on tariffs and rates, landing and take-off slot allocations at airports, computer reservation systems.

EXHIBIT 2: THREE STEPS FORWARD...
Source: European Commission

There was much criticism of the perceived 'poacher' approach of such independents as British Island Airways, Ryanair, Virgin Airways and Air Europe (all of whom were intent on fare slashing) from older-established 'game-keepers' like Air UK. Its MD, Stephen Hanscombe, attacked Air Europe in 1988 for its cut prices declaring that:

It has yet to be shown that Air Europe's product will work. Their aircraft are over-used. Any delay, for instance by a strike in Corfu, can have a cumulative effect on the machine's subsequent duties. A crew can run out of working time in Sicily and have to rest for 12 hours, leaving no back-up at Gatwick (where Air Europe was based).[3]

The same arguments over price-cutting and route sharing were still being voiced in 1990. Indeed, Michael Bishop, chairman of British Midland, was refused permission by the French government to undercut Air France by £100 on the Heathrow-Charles de Gaulle, Paris service in April of that year. This was in line with the law as it stood, which stated governments at each end of the route had to agree to the reduced fare and either could object to it (and veto it) on the grounds that the fare was uneconomic. Widespread public disquiet existed about the relative costs of flying in Europe and the USA and the diseconomies of protectionism. There was further anxiety also about anticipated EC legislation which would allow airlines to go ahead with fares approved by only one of the governments at each end of the route.

Country	Extent of state-owned public enterprises as a percentage of each industry in:			
	Telecommunications	**Coal**	**Air**	**Rail**
USA	0	0	0	25
Japan	33	0	0	25
Germany	100	50	100	100
France	100	100	75	100
UK	0	100	0	100

TABLE 1: COMPARISONS OF STATE OWNERSHIP
OF CERTAIN INDUSTRIES
Source: OECD (*The Financial Times* 12/2/91)

In fact, the 'double disapproval' system targeted for introduction after 1992 would require governments at each end of a route to each reject new lower prices in order to stop their being introduced. Said John Parr of the Air Transport Users' Committee: *Liberalisation is splendid as long as there are effective safeguards against firms using predatory tactics to get others off a route and against those with dominance on routes charging higher fares.*[4] Again, Air Europe had led in wanting to cut the London-Geneva fare by 16 per cent.

A landmark agreement was, however, reached in March 1991, after more than a year of intense debate, in the area of predatory tactics. The European Transport Council, on a majority vote basis, empowered the Commission to take action against Europe's largest airlines who competed on a particular route against small price-cutting airlines by fixing, for a short period of time, artificially low - even loss-making - fares with the intent of driving the competitor out of business. The agreement was enough to inspire the Commission to seek to move further along the path leading to full-scale liberalisation of European airways. Their hope was that, as from the first of January 1993, airlines could operate on any route and set any price they chose.

COMPETITIVE STRATEGY IN THE AIRLINE INDUSTRY

Recession commented Sir Adam Thomson, the ill-starred chairman of British Caledonian during the period of soaring oil prices at the start of the 1980s, *is when you have to tighten your belts. Depression is when you have no belt left to tighten. And when your trousers are round your ankles, you're in the airline business.*[5] In 1990 and 1991 there would have been few airline chiefs who would not have echoed this sentiment. All were in some distress, some were in deep distress, some were irretrievably lost. Over the decade 1981-1991 the global airline industry had oscillated between a loss of £6b (1981) and projected minimum loss of £2b (1991). Only as recently as 1988 the 200 members of IATA had made a combined profit of $2.5b! This sorry state of affairs forms the backdrop to Air Europe's collapse.

The most public in their grief were the American airlines. The pride of Pan Am had been humbled. As losses mounted it had had to dispose of its Pacific routes (in 1986 to United Airlines, based in Chicago) and was being forced at the start of 1991, to dispose of its London routes (also to United). TWA was in a similar state and was trying to sell its Chicago-London route to American Airlines.

Continental joined Eastern in filing for protection from creditors under Chapter 11 of the US Bankruptcy Code in December 1990. It had been suffering from the same complaint as Pan Am, TWA and Northwest, an unsuitable debt burden, but the pain was obviously much greater. Pan Am and TWA were said, in fact, to be teetering on the brink of Chapter 11 receivership and since 1985 Pan Am had indeed run up losses of over $1b.

Continental had, over time, come to symbolise airline deregulation in the USA having successively acquired Peoples Express, Frontier and New York Air to become the USA's biggest domestic carrier. It had then run a cut-price, no-frills operation tearing up union deals and providing what many regarded as indifferent service for its passengers. It lost no less than $885m in 1989.

To make ends meet, Midway had sold off its assets as Philadelphia International Airport. This was an impossibility in the UK since all airport assets were leased to airlines by the statutory owners, the British Airports Authority.

USAir and Delta had also suffered heavy losses in the third quarter of 1990, blaming increasing fuel costs, the age and rising fuel-inefficiency of their fleet and heavy competitive fare discounting.

The underlying reasons for this distress were underlined at the 46th General Assembly of IATA which took place in Geneva in October 1990. It was a case of a combination of rising costs for fuel, the cost of acquiring new aircraft and the level of interest rates that had prevailed world-wide since 1987. The dramatic rise in the price of kerosene that took place in 1974 and over the period 1979/81 was repeated on the second of August 1990 when, as a result of Iraq's action against Kuwait, it rose by 120 per cent. Note that this came on top of a situation in 1989 where the total revenues of the 200 IATA members had risen by 15.5 per cent and costs by 17.9 per cent.

But, whereas, at the start of the eighties, airlines collectively had been able to increase prices by over 40 per cent to cope with a crisis in which overall demand fell by five per cent and revenue by 35 per cent, competition among them now made this impossible. Hence their especial problems. In September and October 1990 alone, 10,000 workers lost their jobs. The run of IATA member profits over the period 1985-1989, which cumulatively had yielded almost $5b, was over.

Element	Airline					
	BA	**AF**	**LH**	**ALI**	**SAS**	**KLM**
Total revenue $m	7655	5245	6805	3555	3285	3025
Operating Profit $m	600	334	N/A	126	223	198
% of revenue from						
Home market	10	15	16	15	25	-
Europe	28	34	35	42	53	23
Mid East & Africa	2	13	3	5	1	5
North Atlantic	29	14	22	16	11	30
Other International	31	24	23	21	9	41

TABLE 2 : PATTERNS OF BUSINESS (1989-90)
Source: Shearson Lehman Hutton & Annual Reports
BA = British Airways, AF = Air France, LH = Lufthansa, AL = Alitalia, SAS = Scandinavian Airlines, KLM = Dutch National Airline.

Not that all US airlines were doing badly. By comparison, the top three, American Airlines, United & Delta, were reasonably healthy. But even the ebullient Bob Crandall, American Airlines Chairman, was pessimistic *If there is not a reasonably prompt recovery, we'll all be out of business* he said. *I've been in the business for 20 years and never seen it so bad. It's an absolute disaster.* Nevertheless he was still a strong believer in the virtue of competition: *Open skies is the only policy which makes sense for everybody. Limitation only delays the settlement day.*[6] Since 1980 he had turned around a loss-making company and more than doubled both workforce and size of his modern, fuel-efficient fleet. Even though American Airlines was seen as a strong performer, it had still posted a first quarter 1991 loss of $195m.

The reversal in the IATA trading pattern from 1989 onwards put into sharp relief the transatlantic thrusts of the world's biggest airlines, based not only on marketing ability but on the extent of their capability for linking-in domestic and international business. For Sir Colin Marshall of British Airways it was a relatively simple matter, *Size brings muscle. An air-line is a major business. The more muscle you have, the more beneficial is the bottom line.*[7] With this credo firmly in mind it had pursued the notion of an investment deal linking itself with Sabena (the Belgian state airline) and the Dutch flag carrier KLM, only to have its plan disallowed by Sir Leon Brittan. This had been aimed at permitting BA effectively greater access to the 'hub' airport of Bruxelles (from where radiated 'spokes' to other European capitals), as a supplement to 'hub' activity based on London Heathrow. It was a bitter blow to Sir Colin Marshall, whose view was that:

> *Increasing liberalisation in Europe can only lead to increasing competition which will inevitably force airlines closer together. I think the globe as a whole is too large and too developed for any one airline to secure its future by itself. The only sensible way is through alliances - we have to look at the partnership concept.*(8)

Having failed to make the KLM-Sabena-BA link-up, BA made plain its interest in a BA-Sabena link.

Other European Airlines who followed the BA logic included SAS (owner of 9.9 per cent of Texas Air and 17 per cent of Continental) and KLM which had bought ten per cent of Northwest. Swissair, faced by the intractable prospect of a hugely unfavourable change in yen-franc parity, domestic inflation, a falling load factor (per cent occupancy of aircraft) and a delay in acquiring new planes, had sought to compensate by buying five per cent of Delta. A marketing link between Air France and Lufthansa had also been forged.

Supplier	Forecast of aircraft sales [1988-2006] %		
	Narrow Body [e.g. A320]	Wide Body 3-4 engine [e.g. A340]	Wide Body 2 engine [e.g. A330]
Airbus Ind.	41	18	53
Others	59	82	47
Total %	100	100	100
Value of new air-craft sales [$ billion]	147	216	147

TABLE 3 : JAM TOMORROW? [11]

Air France and Sabena, additionally, looked to their government owners for assistance in their straightened circumstances and were, in 1991, duly given the promise (not without concern being expressed by the European Commission) of aid for restructuring and re-capitalisation. This amounted to F2.4b and BF19b, respectively. The former was, indeed, already the subject of a long-running Commission inquiry into its bid to buy a 54 per cent stake in rival French airline UTA, which itself (like Air France) owned 33 per cent of Air Inter, the internal French carrier. The comment on this takeover bid by Michael Bishop, chairman of British Midland, was very much to the point:

If this goes through, it will be a complete disaster for European aviation policy. The French are cocking a snook at the European Commission. We shall soon see if Sir Leon Brittan has any teeth ... Air France has gone so far over the top that even the man in the street can see that the move is anti-competitive. [9]

The move was, in fact, allowed by the Commission but only after an agreement, in October 1990, that the French government would disaggregate Air France's resultant 97 per cent domestic monopoly by 1992. Handing out routes to such bidders as the regional French airline TAT and the upmarket holiday company, Clubmed would be required.

The fact that EC Transport Commissioner Karel van Miert approved the Belgian governments' rescue package for Sabena in June 1991 meant that Sabena could resume its talks with potential partners, like BA or Air France. Both of these airlines had indicated their interest in acquiring a substantial stake, up to 40 per cent, in Sabena.

DOG FIGHT OVER HEATHROW

Air Europe had operated from Gatwick, an airport in the South of England which ranked second in importance to London Heathrow. It was shared with a host of smaller scheduled carriers and major package tour airlines. In addition it was home to Virgin Airways, the thrusting but comparatively small international competitor to British Airways. Virgin was owned by Richard Branson. Stansted was the smallest, and farthest from London, of the trio of airports in this region. Issues of airport and traffic control capacity were coming to be of critical importance, given the seemingly unstoppable onward flight to airspace saturation in Europe. Heathrow, because of its size, history, facilities and proximity to the capital was the preferred operational centre for all airlines – big and small, state-owned or independent, national or international. Gatwick, perhaps unwarrantably, was seen as second-best.

To use an airport, an airline needed firstly to be licensed by the UK's official airway regulator, the Civil Aviation Authority (CAA) and, secondly, to have been allotted an appropriate number of "slots" per week for take-off and landing. British Midland, for instance held 15 per cent of the total number of slots at Heathrow as against BA's 38 per cent.

Having a licence to use Heathrow and having the right number of slots at the right time of day was clearly of the greatest strategic importance to airlines. So much so that there was consistent pressure for access from those not allowed into Heathrow, like Nippon Airways, Cathay, Air New Zealand and Air Europe. This was impossible to achieve without express support from the CAA, which reported to, and advised, the British government on all aspects of aviation management. Certainly, neither licences nor slots were commercially tradeable. Indeed, such was the capacity pressure on Heathrow that the only slots not taken up in early 1991 were those which were considered virtually unusable by any of the airlines already licensed. Any change in the pattern of usage of Heathrow could, and would, clearly affect the pattern of usage of other airports.

> *Every seat on British Airways on the 23rd April 1991 is free. All you need to do is post a coupon stating your preferred destination. If you've already paid for a flight by BA, you'll get a voucher for a further flight to the same value.*

EXHIBIT 3: COME HITHER

Note: This BA advertisement was featured in 27 languages in newspapers in 62 countries. It drew five million responses and involved 50,000 free flights. It is reckoned to have cost 60 per cent of the company's annual Marketing budget.

It was, therefore, a major shock to the system when, on the fifth of March 1991, the UK's Transport Secretary Malcolm Rifkind changed the 14-year old traffic distribution rules governing access to Heathrow. It was a critical innovation. A deluge of applications from international airlines for access began immediately. Richard Branson called it *the most historic decision* in 50 years of airline history; it was to take Virgin's Heathrow slots from 28 to 40. Within days he had cut all Virgin international fares by 15 per cent. *We have worked towards this for seven years,* he said, *and are delighted that there has finally been a move to break the biggest monopoly in the UK industry.*[10] Interestingly Virgin, with its eight Boeing 747s had just been voted 'Best Airline' by Which magazine. Interestingly also, much to the consternation of British Airways, on the seventh of March 1991 Transport Secretary Malcolm Rifkind upheld a CAA decision made in January to transfer two of the UK's total allocation of 38 slots at Japan's Narita airport from BA to Virgin. BA chairman Lord King had complained bitterly that, when BA was privatised four years before, he had received assurances that there would be no such arbitrary changes but his complaint did not avail. By contrast, Richard Branson's assertion that he could not compete effectively on the London-Tokyo route unless he could operate a daily service, did.

The background to the government's decision to 'open up' Heathrow lay in the fact that, in order for United Airline's parent company to be enabled to buy Pan Am's Heathrow operations, the government needed to be able to re-assign licence and slots from one operator to another, as a matter of principle. The government's new approach meant that all existing slot holders could sell them if they wished and that a new block of 50,000 slots was available for allocation among new users by a committee on which sat all the existing users. By the 8th March no less than ten 'new' airlines had made slot applications. The changes made for an extension of 'interlining deals' whereby airlines collaborated in a marketing alliance to 'pass on' customers to each other.

Air Europe did not profit from the 'opening-up' of this airport.

The deal brought to a close the uncertainty that had existed in the transatlantic market ever since Pan Am and TWA had tried to sell their slots. They were delighted. British Airways was not; it now had to face voracious Heathrow competition from United and from American Airlines. The latter was number one in the world with 559 planes (+196 on order), as against BA's 235 (+77 on order) and United 464 (+273 on order). Both were highly efficient, highly competitive carriers and represented a major threat. Transatlantic price competition, remarked Stephen Wolf, chairman of 'Fly the Friendly Skies' United, would be matched *even if it gets to the point where you will fly for free and we will given you £100 to do so.*[12] Such was the rivalry faced by Air Europe in its segment.

It was pressure from challenges such as this and from adverse cost movements that had led BA, as the leading UK carrier, to re-appraise its operations in depth in 1990.

Lord King had been chairman since 1981. He had successfully taken the company through the turbulence of, firstly, a dramatic cut in staffing levels (59,000 down to 37,000) based partly on the justifiable fear at the start of the 1980s that the company was facing impending bankruptcy and, secondly, the acquisition of British Caledonian which had raised staffing levels in 1990 to 53,000. Among the results of this re-appraisal were decisions to cut back again on staff (eight per cent in 1991 with a possible further five per cent in 1992) and pull out of routes, like London-Dublin. He seemed to have no intention of letting the company be toppled from its position of being arguably the most profitable major airline in the world, with an operating profit in 1989-90 up 14 per cent on the previous year.[13]

OPEN SKIES: THE TRANSATLANTIC ISSUE

They had aces, but they didn't use them properly.[14] Thus Lord King on another matter of strategic importance to the European airline industry, the bilateral negotiations which took place in early March 1991 between the US and British governments on their transatlantic aviation relationship. These talks, too, formed part of the air industry background wich affected Air Europe's ability to determine a successful strategy.

What was at stake in these negotiations was the extent of access to be enjoyed in the future to the USA by UK airlines and vice versa. What both sides said they wanted overall was clear. In the words of Paul Gretch (Director of International Affairs at the American Transportation Dept.) it was *to explode the whole system and make it totally open for both sides.*[15] In practice there were, from the UK perspective, several highly contentious strands. First of these was the subject of cabotage, the right, in this case for British carriers landing in, say New York, to pick up passengers and carry them to another final US destination or third country, in other words to compete within America with American carriers. The second was the-then restricted number of destinations in the USA that UK carriers could fly to. The third was the law governing the extent of foreign ownership of US airlines.

The new British Prime Minister, John Major, and President Bush were scheduled to meet in Bermuda, the week after the negotiations, to discuss (*inter alia*) their outcome. A positive mood, reflecting the degree of agreement and concord generated between the two during the highly successful Gulf War, was expected. It was hoped that the British government's acceptance of the CAA's report on the need to open up Heathrow and transfer the 12 TWA/Pan Am routes to United and American would be highly influential.

In the event, what was conceded by chief US negotiator Samuel Skinner fell far short of BA requirements, as Table 4, page 185, indicates.

Before the event BA had felt aggrieved at the government's *authority to set up these deals to support such a fundamental restructuring of the US aviation market from which BA, as a competitor, is excluded.*[16] After the event, they felt, in Lord King's words, *sold out.*[17] The blame was laid squarely at the Malcolm Rifkind's door:

These developments will mean further redundancies. How many I do not yet know ... Government transport policy? What transport policy? [18]

(1) Britain to nominate a second carrier to the USA
(2) The two British carriers between them could fly direct to the USA from 6 continental departure points as well as from the UK.
(3) No. of countries and cities in the USA to which a UK carrier could continue after a stop-over in the USA (without picking up passengers) was increased.
(4) Britain could fly to New York, pick up passengers and fly on to Seattle and Sydney.

TABLE 4: BERMUDA 2 RE-VISITED

Note: Bermuda 2 was the name of the treaty governing the US-UK aviation relationship

AIRBUS: ANOTHER PIECE IN THE AIR INDUSTRY JIGSAW

But this was not the only transatlantic aviation matter causing heated debate in Europe and the USA and causing major market uncertainty. There was also the issue of Airbus Industrie and the case which the USA had laid before GATT that the companies' planes had been, and were being, unfairly subsidised. This was of mammoth international significance in that it was one of the items which had contributed to the failure of the most recent stage of the Uruguay Round of GATT negotiations in December 1990.

As well as being world number two in the manufacture of civil aircraft, Airbus Industrie was one of the most important symbols of European collaboration. The project had first seen the light of day in 1969 when the French and German governments had decided to develop a civil aircraft themselves as a rival to the global dominance in the sector of the USA's Boeing, McDonnell Douglas and Lockheed. From the start it was given the status not of a public corporation but of a 'Groupe d'Interêt Economique' (GIE). Under French law a GIE does not have to publish its results. The resultant organisation comprised a manufacturing and marketing relationship among the partners, British Aerospace, Messerschmidt-Blöhm-Bolkow (now part of Daimler-Benz), Casa of Spain and the French state-owned company Aerospatiale.

Airbus Industrie's first sales breach of the make-or-break US market was in 1978 when Eastern Airlines bought 20 A320s. Since then the crescendo of complaints about unfair competition had grown non-stop. And so had Airbus' Marketing success. The product range in 1991 comprised A310, 320s, 330s and 340s which offered significant competition at all levels in the aviation market, except that of the Jumbo Jet (Boeing 747) and its extension, the Boeing 777. The 'fly-by-wire' A320 was regarded as the most advanced civil airliner in the world and a stretched version was being worked on. By 1989 the company had climbed to its current position in the rankings. This was an important record since in as recently as November 1987 it was claimed that Boeing and McDonnell Douglas together had supplied 84 per cent of the commercial passenger aircraft then flying.[19] Air Europe's fleet of 37 aircraft consisted in the main of Boeing 737s and 757s; they had not contributed to Airbus Industrie's significant success.

In fact, Air Europe had been operating in an industry where there was substantial disagreement not only about *the rules of the game* but also acrimony over the types of aircraft sold.

(a) *Wettbewerbnachteile durch einen niedrigen Dollarkurs.*

(b) *Die Zusammenarbeit leidet unter Unflexibilität und wird ungenügend kontrolliert und koordiniert. Es fehlt an Geschlossenheit auch durch die organisatorische Trennung von Absatz und Produktion. Eine Balanzierung des ganzen Ergebnisses gibt es nicht.*

(c) *Ein groupement d'intérêt économique nach franzosischer Recht ist ein loser Verbund in dem keiner einen klaren Letztentscheid hat ... die Partner wissen nicht zu welchen Kosten die anderen produzieren ... Ein Unternehmen dem der Staat Kredite gewährt, die erst beim Erreichen der Gewinnschwelle zuruckgezählt werden müssen (was bei der Airbus Industrie der Fall ist), kann kaum daran interessiert sein mit aller Gewalt aus der Verlustzone herauszukommen.*

(d) *Die Entscheidungen des Direktoriums und Aufsichtrates müssen sofort nach einem Mehrheitsvotum verbindlich gemacht werden.*

Translation note 20 on page 193.

EXHIBIT 4: DER FLIEGENDE SUBVENTIONSGRAB [20]

Airbus had suffered since its inception from a barrage of criticism from within Europe and from the USA. The former related to perceptions about the inadequacy of Airbus Industrie's managerial approach and the extent of its partners' losses, accumulated as it sought to break into world markets in the '80s with highly-competitive, fixed $ prices (it is a convention that all planes, like oil, are priced in $). These losses were covered by respective governments, with the exception, that is, of those of British Aerospace which was privatised in 1985. When the $ began to decline in Autumn 1987, the problems became acute to the point that the four governments, ultimate guarantors of the project, set up an inquiry into its operations. Among the findings were the facts that Airbus had swallowed up at least $10b in public subsidies and that, as of November 1988, it was unlikely to be profitable until 1995. Whilst the discussions about required changes were still being carried on, Airbus Industrie decided that market conditions warranted what Adam Brown (VP, Strategy) called *an absolutely high expansion of output*.[21] There were those who counselled caution. Edzard Reuter, for one. As head of Daimler Benz, he was in the process of acquiring MBB when he said:

> *Only strict managerial criteria should be considered. Airbus has no chance of being profitable unless every question of national prestige is dropped ... I get the impression that nobody at Airbus can tell whether they are making or losing money. We have to know whether Airbus can become profitable on a commercial basis or whether it will always need subsidies; in which case we'll pull out.* [22]

By 1990, with the managerial re-organisation complete, DB and BAe considered that the way was clear to create a basis for the transformation of Airbus Industrie into a trading company.

Any criticism of Airbus Industrie from inside Europe was a sensitive matter. The organisation's company constituents worked with advanced technology, employed thousands in plants all over Western Europe and were politically and economically under constant scrutiny. The chairmen of its supervisory board had been highly prominent public figures, for example Franz-Josef Strauss, prime minister of the German State of Bavaria, which in 1988 owned 24 per cent of MBB. Industry ministers in Mrs Thatcher's administrations in the 1980s (especially Kenneth Clark and Lord Young) were politically involved in pressing for change, having themselves been instrumental in arranging the governmental loan to BAe of £250m for Airbus development purposes.

Criticism from the USA was different in category and in volume; passions were involved. The attacks were long standing and hinged on the extent to which Airbus Industrie represented unfair competition for Boeing and McDonnell Douglas. Arguments ranged over the legitimacy of such supports as state coverage of development expenses and operating losses and re-imbursement for the costs of adverse currency swings, like, for example, the movement in the $/£ rate from 1.30 to 1.86 over the period mid-1987 to mid-1988. The counterclaims, made frequently by Airbus' chief executive Jean Pierson, were that the US plane makers' civil developments were being funded out of advances made on the back of government-funded military R&D (in part responsible for the massive budgetary deficit in the USA in the 1980s) and that Boeing was cross-subsidising the production of 737s and 757s from the massive earnings on 747s.

The dispute reached the ultimate level of a GATT panel in early 1991. It was simply a case of pouring oil on to an already blazing fire as GATT talks were then quite acrimonious. Tensions like these could ultimately reflect themselves in rising global protectionism and were a major factor making for insecurities in the international aviation industry, from which Air Europe was to suffer so gravely.

Jean Pierson, Airbus' head, was unabashed at his rejection of the US' claim that his consortium had received direct subsidies totalling $25.9b. In a speech on the 24th April 1991 he declared *Airbus stands as the only recourse against the monopoly of the civil aviation industry by US manufacturers. It must carefully protect its hard-won position in the strictest respect of international agreements.*[23]

AIR EUROPE IN CONTEXT

To Tim Haywood, ILG's administrator, such concerns as the re-negotiation of Bermuda 2 or the success (or otherwise) of Airbus Industrie must have seemed secondary matters. Even if, in fact, they were not. His challenge was what, if anything, to do with Air Europe.

It had had a fleet of 37 mainly-leased jets employed in well-established operations from Gatwick. It had also had the anticipation of carrying 1,300,000 package holiday makers abroad on its top-brand tours of whom no less than 400,000 had made advance bookings. Harry Goodman had enjoyed the closest possible relationships with hotel chains in Spain ever since the crash of Clarkson's in 1974 which had left the hotel trade in disarray and he had personally offered to take over (at a considerable discount) the bed space thus freed up. Spanish hoteliers had rushed to accept his offer. The company had CAA licenses for European routes and slots which it could try to sell or which, in the event that there were not buyers forthcoming, would revert to the CAA to be later re-assigned to interested parties. Dan Air, a major beneficiary of the Air Europe collapse, showed their keenness by applying to the CAA for 10 of their route licences almost immediately.

Tim Haywood knew how urgent the problem of attracting offers was. The syndicate of 14 Air Europe banks, led by Citicorp, had started the re-possession of jets before the public announcement of the receivership. The company's statutory Travel Operators Study Group (TOSG) and ABTA bonds guaranteed package tour holiday-makers booked with any ILG subsidiary their money back or an alternative holiday, but it also effectively debarred the company from trading. There was also a question of whether the ILG's brand names (Intasun, Lancaster, etc.) were, in fact, saleable.

Country	1987	1988	1989	1990	1991 [forecast]
US	3.4	4.5	2.5	1.0	0.2
Japan	4.3	6.2	4.7	5.6	3.6
France	2.2	3.8	3.7	2.8	2.1
Germany	1.5	3.7	3.8	4.5	2.8
Italy	3.0	4.2	3.2	1.9	1.7
UK	4.5	4.3	1.8	0.6	[2.1]

TABLE 5: GROWTH RATES FOR G7 COUNTRIES [% p.a.]
Source: IMF *World Economic Outlook*

When the CAA finally withdrew Air Europe's operating licence on the 13th March, the matter became academic. There was little more Tim Haywood could do.

Indeed so. On the 20th April 1991, it was announced that it was likely that creditors in ILG would receive a mere 2p in the pound.[24] The once private, then public, high-flying ILG, which had again gone private under expansion-minded Harry Goodman in 1988, had well and truly crashed.

* * * * * * * * * * * * * * * * * * *

189

APPENDIX 1: THE NATURE OF THE ERM

In late 1990 the UK government agreed to join the European Community's Exchange Rate Mechanism (ERM). This is a mechanism for linking together the currencies of participating nations within a specified parity band and is a major step on the road towards Economic and Monetary Union (EMU). This latter would involve a single currency and a single banking authority ('Eurofed') for the whole of the EC.

The pound was taken into the ERM at a central rate of DM 2.95, around which level it was (June 1991) allowed to fluctuate six per cent at maximum. Thus the pound could theoretically rise in value to DM 3.13 or fall to DM 2.78. In practice, the Bank of England and other European central banks could take steps to ensure stability around the central rate, by buying and selling currency accordingly. In the event that international market pressures forced a sustained rise in the value of the pound and the banks' sale of sterling failed to halt the rise, then the UK chancellor could, quite independently (as of June 1991), cut interest rates to reduce the appeal of the pound. Any change in the UK's domestic interest rates would thus impact on the value of the pound within the ERM and vice versa.

Given that the Conservative government led by prime minister John Major no longer believed that devaluation of sterling was a viable option (John Major, as Chancellor of the Exchequer, expressed this view - as a member of Margaret Thatcher's government, on the 6/10/90), the acceptance of membership of the ERM could be seen as a method for strengthening the government's resolve to fight domestic inflation by relying to a greater extent on taxation and public spending limits. Certainly, its ability to move the pound out of its DM 2.78 - DM 3.13 range was now severely circumscribed by ERM membership.

APPENDIX 2: AIRLINE INDUSTRY BACKGROUND INFORMATION

(1) Performance indicators in the airline industry included fuel efficiency (fuel cost per seat mile), load factor (per cent of plane seats occupied). Extremely high attention was paid to these factors.

(2) The 'hub and spoke' concept is the notion of linking together an international airport in a central location (e.g. Bruxelles) with regional airports that can act as 'feeders' for it (e.g. Strasbourg) on the assumption of two airlines' 'interlining' i.e., passing their passengers to each other.

(3) In March 1990 both Boeing and Airbus made forecasts of future aircraft sales. The former reckoned that 10,000 aircraft worth some $626b (£382b) would be delivered between 1990 and 2005. Airbus' estimate was for 12,000 jets worth $700b over the next 20 years of which just under 50 per cent would be replacement sales.

(4) Both Boeing and Airbus were making strenuous efforts to increase capacity working in 1989 as their order backlogs grew apace.

(5) Airlines were increasingly moving in the late 1980s to aircraft leasing rather than ownership of planes via long-term debt finance. The effect of this was to change a long-term interest burden for short-term lease charges which, if not met, would mean repossession of the aircraft by the leasing company. Thus the leasing charges represented, in the short run, an inescapable short-term debt. Among leaders in the leasing field were Guinness Peat Aviation, International Lease Finance Corp and Ansett.

(6) Engines for aircraft were supplied to specification by individual companies (Rolls Royce, Pratt & Whitney or SMECMA, for example) or by consortia like International Aero Engines (Pratt & Whitney, Rolls Royce, Motoren und Turbinen Union, Fiat Aviazione and Japanese Aero Engines) or CFM (General Electric and SNECMA).

(7) In mid April 1990 it was announced by Boeing that up to 20 per cent of the airframe for its new 777 would be made by Mitsubishi, Kawasaki and Fuji in Japan.

(8)   Airlines which, by the end of 1990, had bought from Airbus included Northwestern, TWA, Braniff and, in Europe, Air France, Iberia, Lufthansa and Sabena.

(9)   *The era of cheap air fares is over. The shortage of airport infrastructure and integrated traffic control systems means that there is insufficient scope for the sort of economies of scale that would engender low fares* said Dan Wild of BZW on 15/4/90. European transport ministers had, in fact, agreed in July 1989 to set up a new £40m air traffic control centre in Brussels to replace 12 national systems in co-ordinating flights in 23 countries from 1993.

(10) Karel Van Miert, EC Transport Commissioner, unveiled the so-called 'Third Package' on air transport in July 1991. It comprised major, and controversial, steps to seek to deregulate price competition in the European airline industry with effect from January 1993. It built up further safeguards against predatory pricing and advocated the wholesale introduction of the double-disapproval system. Also proposed in the package was a plan for a single European licence for airlines, allowing them full cabotage possibilities.

NOTES & REFERENCES

1   Airlift helps stranded passengers, Margaret Driscoll, *The Sunday Times*. All Hands on Deck, *The Sunday Times* 10/3/91

2   Turbulent Time for Air Fares, Nicholas Bethell, *The Sunday Telegraph* 7/8/88

3   As 2

4   Foreign airfix glues UK fliers to higher fares, Ian Birrell and Christopher Ward, *The Sunday Times* 22/4/94

5   Airlines happy to double '89 total of 1.1b passengers, Harvey Elliott, *The Times* 3/1/90

6   Scourge of the world's runway, Paul Betts, *The Financial Times* 18/3/91

7   BA sizes up airline rivals for world-wide link-ups, Chris Blackhurst, *The Sunday Times* 3/9/90

8   As 7

9   AF flies into storm over UTA link, Ian Jenkins & Jonathon Todd, *The Sunday Times* 14/1/90

10 Fort Heathrow breached at last, Andrew Davison, *The Sunday Times* 10/3/91

11 BA warns new deal will cut profits, Angela Mackay, *The Times* 12/3/91

12 Americans start Heathrow airlines war, *The Times* 5/4/91

13 How BA became the world's favourite airline, Ivan Fallon & John Cassidy, *The Sunday Times* 27/5/90

14 King of Heathrow takes on the raiders, Andrew Davison, *The Sunday Times* 17/3/91

15 BA finds cloud in clearer skies over Atlantic, *The Times* 12/3/91

16 *The Times* 17/12/90

17 Britain and US agree transatlantic pact, Harvey Elliott, *The Times* 12/3/91

18 Rifkind blamed for BA crisis, Jane Renton, *The Observer* 17/3/91

19 Airline rivals vie for ground, Ian Williams, *The Sunday Times* 1/11/87

20 All quotations are from the *Frankfurter Allgemeine Zeitung*. (a) 9/9/87 Airbus to make profit by 2000. *Competitive disadvantage through a low dollar rate.* (b) 8/4/88 Experts criticise poor collaboration at Airbus. *The collaboration is suffering from inflexibility and is inadequately coordinated and controlled. There is a lack of decisiveness because of the organisational separation of production and marketing. There's no balance sheet for the entire operation.* (c) 4/5/88 The Flying Subsidy Hole. *A groupement d'interet economique is, under French law, merely an association in which no-one has the final say ... the partners do not know each others' costs ... An undertaking which receives state credit which does not have to be repaid until a profit is made, is not interested in pulling itself with all its strength out of the loss zone.* (d) 14/4/88 Decision made on Airbus re-organisation. *The decisions of the board of directors and supervisory board must immediately start to be made on the basis of majority voting*

21   Breaking the order Barrier, Ian Williams, *The Sunday Times* 29/1/89
22   Airbus Climbs, Bryan Moynahan, *The Sunday Times*. Note Article 7 provides for very stiff penalties for those breaking their contract. 9/4/89
23   Airbus chief votes to fight off GATT challenge, Paul Bells, *The Financial Times* 24/4/91
24   ILG Travel Creditors, Mary Fagan, *The Independent*

PIRELLI

Abstract:

This case documents the attempt by Pirelli, the Italian tyre maker, to acquire Continental AG, its German rival, in the early 1990s. It was an opening round in the non-stop consolidation of the global tyre industry that would occur throughout the decade. The case sets the logic of the bid in the context of power politics in the global tyre and car industries at the time and against the backcloth of moves in the European Community to determine EC rules and regulations on mergers and the social charter.

It is interesting to note that, after the failure of the bid, each protagonist pursued a different strategy to seek success. For Continental it was a case of reducing standard tyre production in favour of making high technology *intelligent tyres* and becoming an automotive industry supplier of higher value-added assemblies. Pirelli sought its future in alliances, with Michelin and with Cooper Tyre and Rubber. In early 1999, the world leaders in the tyre market were Goodyear-Sumitomo (20% share) and Michelin SCA. Continental and Pirelli ranked a distant fourth and sixth, respectively.

Questions:

How secure was Pirelli's logic in seeking to take over Continental AG?
How strong was Continental's defence?
Where does EMU fit in?
What does the case reveal about German business culture?

Case Timing: 1991

A BID TOO FAR?

In September 1990 the Italian industrial giant Pirelli launched a take-over bid for the German tyre manufacturer Continental AG (Conti). It was done with the very best of intentions, namely to allow the combined tyre company created through the bid to challenge Michelin's powerful global market position and to enable Pirelli to come to terms more efficiently and effectively with the universal slow-down then taking place in the tyre industry. In the light of Pirelli's unhappy experiences during their joint venture attempt with Dunlop in the 1970s, a similar sort of manufacturing alliance had been firmly ruled out. It was to be a take-over bid, just like Pirelli's buy-out of the US Armstrong Tyre Corp, or nothing.

From the Pirelli perspective, a victory had been scored once 51 per cent of Conti shares had been secretly and successfully acquired. In the view of Horst Urban, Conti's chief executive and chairman of the board of directors ('Vorstand'), the fact of this level of share ownership did not signify control. Nor, for that matter, did it in the eyes of Conti's supervisory board ('Aufsichtsrat'), one of whose key functions was to select the members of the board of directors and half of whose members were chosen by the workforce.

As time progressed, this divergence of view on the significance of the 51 per cent holding widened, as Morgan Grenfell and Merrill Lynch were drawn into the fray as advisers to Conti and Pirelli, respectively.

British interest in the ensuing drama was intense and heightened, if anything, by the facts that, firstly, Morgan Grenfell had been recently bought by the largest German bank, the Deutsche Bank, and that, secondly, Conti owned the National Tyre Service, the UK's second largest tyre distributor. It also had a 13 per cent holding in the biggest, Kwik-fit. Conti was a major German company with sales in 1989 of DM8381 and 47,495 employees. Its tyre brands included Continental, Semperit and Uniroyal.

To Leopoldo Pirelli, company chairman, the logic of the move was incontrovertible. A fierce price war was taking place in the world tyre market and the industry's overcapacity and capability for producing longer-life tyres was putting intense pressure on margins. On top of that, some 80 per cent of global sales were made by a handful of companies. Market leaders were the French Michelin, the Japanese Bridgestone and US' Goodyear. As of January 1991, however, Conti wanted to retain its independence and it was supported in this intention, both on principle and in terms of the nature of the bid itself, by a coterie of Germany's largest car-makers and banks. For this, as *Exhibit 1* indicates, was no ordinary bid.

> *You have chosen to characterise this battle as a nationalistic contest, with the major German car makers intervening.. to protect German control of Continental, and have ignored the compelling commercial and financial reasons for rejecting a merger. I can do no better than recall the.. comment that "Continental was supposed to gear itself up to the eyeballs to buy Pirelli Tyre on 50 times earnings, or twice the current share price, and then cede control of the combined group..". This must be the first time a company has been expected to pay a massive premium to lose rather than to acquire control of a business.. Continental's rejection is not fuelled by a "Fortress Germany" mentality but by a need to protect the company.. from a hostile proposal which would be extremely damaging...*

EXHIBIT 1: A LETTER TO THE EDITOR
Source: Letter from John Craven, chairman of Morgan Grenfell, to the editor of *The Financial Times*, 14/2/91.

The German company had been somewhat incensed, it seemed, by what they clearly regarded as Italian effrontery. Continental was operating at full capacity in early 1991 and had been profitable in the second half of 1990, a competitive feat in the tyre industry equalled only by Bridgestone: Pirelli certainly was not and had not been. Pirelli was seen to be unduly exposed in its Turkish and S. American market operations: Continental - strong in Europe, North America and the Far East - was not. In fact, Conti's bid defence document spelled out the reasons why, in their view, there was an absence of "a good business fit" between the two groups and why it was unclear how economies of scale could be achieved through the takeover. Having just finished a major rationalisation and modernisation programme, involving a co-operation deal with the ex-East German tyre kombinat Fürstenwalde, Conti was loath to see others reaping the benefits. So the initial reaction of the two boards of Conti, to reject the bid and offer instead an alliance, held firm against Pirelli's attempts to engineer success.

There remained, for the European stockbroking fraternity, the problem that Pirelli had bought 51 per cent of the shares in the company. So far as Conti was concerned, however, this did not seem to constitute a major obstacle to continued resistance, since, like many other German companies, it was covered by a provision in the German Stimmrecht law. This limited individual shareholders, irrespective of the volume of shares held, to five per cent of the voting rights.

> *Companies are just beginning to learn what nations have always known: in a complex, uncertain world filled with dangerous opponents, it is best not to go it alone. Great powers operating across broad theatres of engagement traditionally made common cause with those whose interests ran parallel with their own. No shame in that. Entente - the striking of an alliance is a responsible part of every good strategist's repertoire. In today's competitive environment, this is also true for corporate managers"*

EXHIBIT 2: MAKING FRIENDS TO INFLUENCE PEOPLE
Source: Global Logic of Strategic alliances, Kenichi Ohmae,
The Harvard Business Review, Mar-Apr 1989

It was also the case that Conti felt itself well capable of building up with the help of Volkswagen, B.M.W., Daimler Benz and shareholder banks (like the Norddeutsche Landesbank (Hannover), the Dresdner, the Berliner Handels bank and the Frankfurter Bank) a blocking minority of 25 per cent of issued shares+1. It should be noted that banks such as the Norddeutsche were themselves holding shares or acting as proxies on behalf of Conti shareholders who had deposited their shares with banks. Interestingly, Carl Hahn, the MD of Volkwagen, had once been Conti's chief executive.

As if this did not give protection enough, it was expected (again under German law) that the predatory Pirelli would not be able to achieve a sufficient majority of votes at an Emergency General Meeting of share-holders (75 per cent was the level for many German corporations; 50.1 per cent was the case with Conti) to unseat the supervisory board. The workforce at Conti was also highly supportive of the company's stand. In their view, according to the Frankfurter Allgemeine,

Eine Politik der Unabhängigkeit war richtig und möglich.. Continental dürfe nicht zum Spielball von Finanzspekulanten werden.[1]

The workforce was, it was said, as keen to avoid anything that smacked of an anti-Italian posture as they were to forestall any reduction in jobs that might ensue from a takeover and was prepared to vote as company shareholders (Belegschaftaktionäre) to this end.

The increasingly exploratory tense to-ing and fro-ing between Horst Urban and the chairman of Pirelli's German subsidiary, Gert Silber-Bonz, came to a head on the 13th March 1991. This was the day on which an Emergency General Meeting of shareholders had been called for by Conti shareholder, Alberto Vicari, to debate two motions: firstly, to overturn the five per cent voting right limit and, secondly, to vote on the Pirelli offer. Pirelli, with 32,328 employees and 1989 sales of 4294 billion lire in its tyre division, was anxious to make progress.

A TWO SPEED EMU?

A key element fuelling Pirelli's impulsion to acquire a dominant interest in Conti was the progress being made by the European Community along the 1992 road to a Single European Market and to economic and monetary union (EMU).

The Community had, in fact, dramatically increased the speed of this progress since the time when the-then British Prime Minister, Margaret Thatcher, had signalled her opposition to further E.C. integration moves. Her speech on the 21st September 1988 in Bruges spoke volumes:

We have not successfully rolled back the frontiers of the state in Britain only to see them re-imposed at a European level with a European super-state exercising a new dominance from Brussels.[2]

The British antagonism had, in fact, been still very much in evidence in the White Paper that was issued in December 1989 in response to the Delors Report. The British government in this indicated its *fundamental reservations* [3] about the Commission's EMU proposals for a common European currency (ecu) and a European central bank.

But, from the time of his EMU report in 1989, inexorable pressure from Jacques Delors, President of the European Commission, had brought the debate on European political and economic integration into greater prominence. As, for example, in his speech to the European Parliament in January of that year when he called for *a new institutional framework* in which the Commission would enjoy more power and the European parliament would have greater say - relative, that is, to national parliaments. This, and the boost given to the integration principle by Chancellor Kohl and President Mitterand at their Elysee talks on the 26th April 1990, ensured a groundswell of mainland European support for further political, economic and monetary union progress. It was thus that the topic came to be discussed at the Dublin summit two days later, much against the wishes of Margaret Thatcher, whose view was that talks on union would merely be *esoteric.*[4]

Not that anyone could take for granted wide-ranging support for all the practicalities which might emerge from an endorsement of the principle. France, indeed, in the person of Prime Minister Jacques Chirac had made it plain that *il faut conserver entre nos mains l'essentiel de la maîtrise de notre destin.*[6]

The British doctrine of parliamentary sovereignty has never been compatible with the acceptance of Community law and the rights of European judges to interpret it.. The majority in the Community intend to create a federal structure and will do so with or without British participation. It will involve a single currency, a European central bank.. It will be a United States of Europe.. The truth is that Britain's future must lie in Europe; there is no alternative.

EXHIBIT 3: THE OBSERVER'S VIEW [5]

There were also hesitations in Dublin among other EC members which resulted in a short deferment of the debate on whether to set in train preparations for series of inter-governmental conferences. But the pressure for progress was unremitting and Britain appeared to many as a by-stander rather than a leading contender.

More and more in Britain the focus of business attention centred on the so-called stage 1 of EMU, the European Monetary System (EMS) set up in 1979, whose principal component was the Exchange Rate Mechanism (ERM). This latter linked each European currency in the ERM to the German mark at a central, specified parity level. It allowed for some fluctuations around this level (but within a tightly limited band) which promised to give a considerable degree of stability to members' commercial relationships, as well as buttressing the external value of their individual currencies and that of the ecu. Each ERM member was pledged to maintain the ratio. It was the EMS which, in fact, had operationalised the ecu as the European unit of currency. Its value was based on fixed proportions of the basket of individual currencies from which it was drawn.

The fact that, in mid-1990, the Belgian government, already (like all Britain's major mainland EC partners) a member of the ERM, decided to peg the Belgian franc more closely to the German mark, hit home in Britain. Would such a move, to cut Belgium's huge budget deficit through the sort of stern monetary and fiscal discipline required to keep up the franc/mark exchange rate, work in Britain? After all, in Britain at that time, domestic demand, the money supply and the enormous balance of payments deficit were all still rising apace, despite bank base rate moves to seek to rein back inflationary pressures.

EC Commissioner Sir Leon Brittan indicated the nature of the dilemma facing the British government in a speech at the Centre for Policy Studies on the fifth of July 1990. He urged acceptance of the need for the country to join in the moves to implement EMU since, even if it did not, its interest rates would be determined ultimately by the decisions of the European Federal Bank ('Eurofed') created through the EMU process. *Is that extra quarter of an hour of crisis so precious an addition to our sovereignty* he queried *that it is worth putting British industry at a permanent competitive disadvantage?* [7]

The riposte by the British Chancellor of the Exchequer, John Major, was swift and negative. In a speech the following day to the Welsh CBI he rejected as unworkable the Delors three-stage EMU plan. This would ultimately have involved a single monetary policy based on a single interest rate as well as an independent 'Eurofed', as unworkable. His theme was that of the Prime Minister, Margaret Thatcher, as declared in a speech on the 22nd June 1990, before she left London for the second Dublin summit:

> *If you lose sovereignty over monetary and budgetary policy, you haven't got much sovereignty left. And, in any case, that is what our parliament - the oldest parliament in Europe by far - was created to protect the citizen against.* [10]

The debate in Britain, nevertheless, grew in intensity as the year progressed. On the one hand there was the argument that, under a single currency system, any participating country would not have the freedom or authority to unilaterally devalue, whatever the reason and however strong the internal political pressure or economic rationale. Certainly, France, which had entered the ERM in 1979, had since then devalued the franc five times prior to 1987, but only with the explicit agreement of its partners. Such an attack on elemental British freedoms was seen as insufferable by industry minister, Nicholas Ridley. EMU and all its works was, he claimed *a German racket to take over the whole of Europe. It has to be thwarted. We've always played the balance of power in Europe.. and never has it been more necessary than now.* [9]

Certainly, it was recognised widely in Europe that previous inter-national attempts at fixed exchange rate systems - the gold standard, Bretton Woods, the snake, the crawling peg, the Plaza Accord and the Louvre Meeting - had all ended in failure.

The counter-argument, expressed forcibly by the Paris-based Association for the Monetary Union of Europe, hinged on the power of the EMS to deliver currency stability and inflation control. Given its membership of leading European industrialists like the heads of Fiat, Philips, Total, Volkswagen and Ferruzzi, the Association had considerable clout.

> *UK economy heading for serious recession with inflation still rising.. The Gulf crisis set to deepen general slump in investment and increase recessionary pressures.. The 1980s - a frenetic import-led boom involving massive rising indebtedness (private and corporate) and a massive shortfall in investment in industrial capacity. "In 1981 there was a surplus of £4.5 billion in our trade in manufactures; now we have a deficit of £15 billion. To join the ERM with an over-valued exchange rate would be to institutionalise our lack of competitiveness".*

EXHIBIT 4 : THE GODLEY VIEW [10]

The embattled UK government in August 1990 responded to EC pressures by launching its own plan for a hard ECU as a sort of European reserve currency and an alternative to a single currency. Jacques Delors expressed great interest in the suggestion, which would, he said, be studied by the Commission as a possible contribution to full movement towards EMU.

By November of that year the pace of advance towards EMU had quickened considerably. The October Rome summit had shown Britain to be isolated on the issue; the deputy Prime Minister, Sir Geoffrey Howe had resigned over matters European; Britain had joined the ERM; staging posts for the full implementation of EMU were being actively discussed by the *open border* Schengen group of EC nations.[11]   Still the arguments raged in Britain among those who saw membership of the ERM as *a severe anti-inflationary discipline* [12] and those like the Bruges Group of MPs who saw it as the thin end of the Federalist wedge.

Six months later, they were still raging. In the meantime Margaret Thatcher had resigned as prime minister, being replaced by John Major, and Jacques Delors had rejected Britain's hard ECU proposal. Instead he had suggested in its place a neat amendment to the forth-coming draft Maastricht Treaty on Political and Monetary Union which had been under active debate by EC Finance Ministers since the Rome summit in 1990. This was that Britain should sign the treaty on the understanding that a future British parliament could either delay or veto the implementation of a single European currency. The new Chancellor of the Exchequer, Norman Lamont, was pleased. *We have always believed we can reach agreement* he said. *M. Delors has always been constructive.*[13] Even so, according to Foreign Secretary Douglas Hurd, there was need for substantial change in the treaty before it could be supported by the government.

HEAVY WEATHER IN THE CAR INDUSTRY

The commercial weather which Pirelli and Continental were experiencing in their industry at the start of 1991 was nothing if not stormy. The gales that were striking the global market for cars and tyres were themselves powerful enough, but the pressures in the market for corporate control of the companies supplying them were reaching hurricane level.

Over the period 1985-1990 there had been large-scale takeovers and mergers galore involving Europe in most business sectors, like, for example, ASEA-Brown Boveri, Siemens-Nixdorf, Metal Box-Carnaud, Fujitsu-ICL, Nestlé-Rowntree and Rhone Poulenc-RTZ Chemicals, Philip Morris-Jacob Suchard and BSN-Nabisco. These had been based on such eminently realistic economic truths as minimum efficient scale characteristics, reduction of transaction costs and the appropriate size of 'critical mass' spending on technological progress. So far as EC-based companies were concerned, takeovers and mergers were often wrapped up with the notion of Europe's avoiding being the prisoner of more advanced, and more technologically advanced economies, like Japan and the USA, and thus becoming 'a screwdriver plant' continent which simply assembled products researched, developed and possibly made elsewhere.

The business atmosphere, notwithstanding, was not gloomy for some, like the Economist writer who wrote the following cornucopian message in June 1990:

As Europe enters the 1990s the mood has changed from eurosclerosis to europhoria as economic-political developments swing in its favour. In the 1980s European economies grew by an average of barely 2 per cent pa well behind the USA's 2.8 per cent and Japan's 4.2 per cent. Economists blamed Europe's arthritic labour markets, bloated public sector, high tax rates and government meddling. Now three momentous events - the creation of the Single European Market, German re-unification and the re-building of Eastern Europe - should put Europe back in the fast lane in the 1990s.. with a super-charged engine.[14]

By 1991, though, it was a different story. Many parts of the Western industrialised world and not a few industries were in deep recession.

Some in the world car industry saw the answer in protectionism, especially against the thrusting Japanese. Lee Iacocca, chairman and CEO of Chrysler, for instance:

We have this obsession that anything built overseas is better. We're not going to let that kind of crap go unchallenged any more. Trade with Japan was wrapped in a Teflon kimono. Maybe it's time to start peeling back the kimono.. I think we've been hosed.. how can you have free trade if their market is closed.. If it's not closed on the manufacturing side or ownership, it's closed in the retail distribution system.[15]

This was, to a degree, the thinking in France where Edith Cresson, industry minister and, as from May 1991, prime minister, was strongly identified with keeping Japanese car imports into the EC (including 'transplants', i.e., those wholly or partly made in the EC by such producers as the UK-based Nissan and Honda) within the strict market quota. The level of this amounted to three per cent for France and one per cent for Italy and was still in force whilst Renault and Volvo were engineering their cross-shareholding deal and GM had taken a half share in Sweden's Saab-Scania. The Commission's viewpoint was forcibly expressed in negotiations with the Japanese government and amounted to a demand for a period of five years of restraint after 1993 on Japanese car imports.

The UK, having attracted the lion's share of Japanese in-bound investment in this field, strongly favoured open access. This attitude was not shared by Jacques Calvet, president of the French PSA group (Peugeot and Citroen). He, like Iacocca, was vociferously opposed to allowing increasing penetration by Japanese car makers such as Toyota, Honda, Mitsubishi, Nissan and Mazda who, with their compatriots, had achieved a staggering 11.7 per cent sales share of the European market in 1990 at a time when the market overall fell in volume by 1.1 per cent. *They call me* he declared proudly in February 1991 *Mr No. Mr Veto. I've even heard the flattering suggestion that I'm the French Mrs Thatcher.*[16]

The car market negotiations between the European Commission and Japan which took place in June 1991 were thought to be premised on permitting a Japanese Euromarket slice in the late nineties not exceeding 16 per cent.

There was great concern in the $45 billion p.a. world tyre industry. This commodity industry had recovered in the mid 1980s from heavy financial losses based on intense competition (especially in the OEM market) and over-capacity, only to suffer from a recurrence of the illness at the start of the 1990s. One special worry was the level of new entrants into the low profile, high performance (and high margin) segment which the high technology performers had pioneered in the mid 1980s. Pirelli, despite its high level of product innovation and factory automation (the Bollate plant), was exposed insofar as, in 1989, 51 per cent of its sales were of car tyres and 20 per cent of its sales revenue was made in Brazil.

The industry had recently completed, as a result of pressures to improve economies of scale and (as in other global industries), another round of concentration, to the point where Michelin enjoyed a world market share of 22 per cent, compared with Goodyear Tyre and Rubber's 20 per cent, Bridge-stone's 17 per cent, Conti's eight per cent, Pirelli's seven per cent and Sumitomo-Dunlop's six per cent.[17]

In 1989 Michelin had acquired the US' Uniroyal Goodrich for $1.5 billion and Bridgestone had taken over the US' Firestone Tyre and Rubber for $2.6 billion, having outbid Pirelli in this latter contest. The US General Tyre group belonged to Conti, which also had links with Yokohama Rubber and Toyo Tyres of Japan. According to Tom Barrett, the Goodyear chairman, the extent of concentration in the world market had gone from eleven players in 1985 with a market share of 80 per cent to five with the same share by 1990.[18] Only 5 years before, five US companies had been the biggest in the world. In spite of all the pressures he still claimed that Goodyear was in *a better position* to make the *shift to globalisation* that the motor industry was making, with *the big tyre makers close behind*.[19] Nevertheless, the company plunged into losses in 1990 of $38m after a 1989 profit of $207 m on sales of $11.3 billion and $10.8 billion respectively.

It was clearly the concept of size which lay behind the Pirelli bid for Conti. Its bid arguments rested on pooled R & D spending, transfer of Pirelli's advanced production technology to Conti and brand and market segment rationalisation. The company claimed that a merger would not lead to a wave of job losses.

WORKER PARTICIPATION: CULTURE POOLING

The Pirelli bid was taking place against a fascinating scenario of EC Commission moves to try to involve workers in European industry to a greater extent in the dynamic of European Community development. To a degree, these moves were a continuation of a past strategy which had spawned in the past such creations as the Vredeling directive, aimed at giving workers a greater say in the running of industry through processes of information and consultation.

The appointment of Mrs Vasso Papandreou as Commissioner gave an enormous impetus to many new plans in this area, however. Take, for example, the pressure for the enactment of the European Company Statute (derived ultimately from the Vredeling directive) specifying that every EC firm with over 1000 employees should set up a supervisory board (or more popularly 'Works Council') for the purpose of involving the workforce in some of the decisions affecting them. Where a company worked in more than one European country it indicated the need for 'group councils' to be set up with pan-European workforce representation. France, Germany ('Mitbestimmung') and Holland already had domestic legislation for such processes and bodies and the French multinationals

Bull, Thomson and BSN were regarded as role models for their work in setting up group councils. Such councils in France had, by law, to be consulted prior to major company moves and in Germany representatives of employees and trade unions had a statutory right ('Mitbestimmung') to 50 per cent of the seats on supervisory boards of public stock companies with more than 2,000 employees. The Fifth Company directive covered worker representation on such boards.

The British Institute of Directors was hostile to such thinking. Sir John Hoskyns, its president and former head of Margaret Thatcher's Policy Unit, indicated as much in his 1989 Conference speech. He declared that EC plans for *Social Europe* would result in *a collectivised, protectionist, over-regulated utopia* redolent of outdated *social engineering*. This was also the thinking of former Industry Secretary Lord Young who labelled planned moves to implement Social Europe as *corporate and dirigiste*.[20]

A second elemental strand in the Social Europe thrust was the Social Charter of Fundamental Rights for Workers. When Vasso Papendreou spoke of this and the wide range of social provisions it would entail (like European codes of practice on pregnancy and maternity leave and better child care facilities) at the Blackpool Women's TUC conference in March 1989, she received rapturous applause. The TUC Congress had given Jacques Delors himself exactly the same sort of welcome in 1988. The Social Charter was adopted by all EC members except the UK at the Madrid summit in summer 1989.

The German Handwerkkammer or craft guild system predates Bismarck. Employers in 450 trade groups pay to be members of the national association which allows them, through the right to employ apprentices, a key statutory role in regulating training and employment in these trades. It is considered that the system ensures quality of output for the consumer and stabilises the labour market, by helping to reduce the threat of teenage unemployment. Participating companies must hold a Vollversammlung (five-year assembly) at which employees' representatives have one third of the votes.

EXHIBIT 5: HANDWERKKAMMER SYSTEM [21]

In mid 1990 three more draft directives derived from the Social Charter were presented by Vasso Papandreou to the Commission for formal endorsement. The first covered such issues as giving part-time employees the same state/ company benefit entitlements as full-timers, compelling employers to justify recruiting part-timers for new vacancies and forbidding temporary employment contracts lasting more than three years. The Commission asked her to redraft it and find a stronger rationale for her proposal to have it decided upon in the European Council by qualified majority vote, as opposed to unanimity. Other directive elements under discussion related to the strengthening of the EC health and safety laws related to nightworkers etc. In all there were planned to be 46 measures based on the Social Charter.

All of these draft proposals were regarded as manna from heaven by a British Trade union movement which had been systematically marginalised under the three Thatcher administrations over the period 1979-1984. Under the slogan 'Catching up with Europe', the TUC launched a major initiative in September 1990 to secure Charter implementation. *Britain* said the TUC statement *is at the bottom of the league table in child care, in state pensions, in the right of workers to have a say in how their company is run.. Its record on training is one of the worst in Europe.. Consultation and concensus have worked in countries like Germany. There is no reason why they cannot work here.*[22]

The British government remained opposed to the Charter, on the one hand, and to the notion of statutory representation of the workforce's interests through Works Councils, on the other. But they clearly recognised the extent of support among mainland countries for the principle involved in the works Council proposal and sought to find a solution to their dilemma which they could present with confidence at the meeting of Social Affairs Ministers in May 1991.

The plan that was presented by Employment Secretary Michael Howard was said to offer *a practical, flexible, alternative approach to that of the legislative straitjacket which would be imposed by the binding directive.*[23] His thrust was one of maximising employee involvement but with an approach *based on flexibility and respect for the diversity of approaches adopted in the different member states.*[24] It was an implicit rejection of (in the words of the Institute of Directors) *a model of employee involvement, from outside, which could damage and undermine employee relations in businesses which already have their own arrangements.*[25]

By the middle of May 1991, there were strong indications that Britain found itself at considerable odds with the other members of the EC on this issue.

EUROPEAN TAKEOVERS

One of the key pre-occupations of the EC's Competition Commissioner at the turn of the 1990s was the subject of mergers and acquisitions (M&A). This was a subject of great interest to Conti and Pirelli. The passing of the Single Market legislation had provoked a spate of activity in this field in Europe as individual firms built up their ability to compete at the expense of the competition.

The interest of the European Commission as a whole obviously lay in the improvement such changes would bring about in the ability of the Community to compete as a trading bloc in world markets, as well as to improve internal prosperity. It also lay in the conditions that applied to the market for corporate ownership, which like all other product and service markets, it was empowered to police, using articles 85 and 86 of the Treaty of Rome to do this.

This duty brought into sharp relief, in many M&A situations, the clear differences between Anglo-Saxon and continental practices in respect, for instance, of ownership instruments and rights, the role of banks, cross-ownerships etc. A relatively transparent public company ownership system in the UK contrasted with ones on the mainland which contained entrenched technical barriers to hostile takeover, as Exhibit 6 indicates.

Level of obligatory shareholder disclosure in mainland EC often less than in UK.

Tendency for a narrower spread of share ownership than in UK. Greater level of family ownership of medium-sized firms than is usual in the UK.

Phenomenon of a multi-tier share structure with tightly controlled voting rights exists. Ownership and control do not necessarily co-align.

Cross-holdings between industrial partners more common than in UK.

Banks play a larger role in industrial management as owners of shares in their own right and as representatives of the shareholders who lodge their shares with them (proxy votes). This is especially the case in Germany where banks are represented on supervisory boards and where there is a two-tier board structure.

Power of boards to issue more shares to existing shareholders to frustrate a predatory bid (e.g., Holland).

Public access to share register may be less than in UK. Bearer shares, lodged with banks, amplifies the difficulty of tracking down owners.

EXHIBIT 6: FEATURES OF THE CORPORATE CONTROL MARKET
IN MAINLAND EUROPE

Note: the 1989 Coopers & Lybrand Report *Barriers to Take-overs in the European Community,* commissioned by the DTI.

The Commission saw itself as inextricably involved in regulating this particular market and in the fields of legislation that were involved like company law competition policy and labour law.

It was in 1990 that new rules for the scrutiny of large European take-overs were agreed and introduced by the Commission. The Brussels-based Mergers

Task force was empowered to examine all takeovers that met three sales volume- and size-related criteria. The directive covering the policy of takeovers, the 13th Company Law Directive, related *inter alia* to equal treatment of all shareholders, prohibition of the issue of new shares to frustrate bids and the obligation, once a company had acquired 30 per cent of a target, to make a full bid. It also included provisions allowing for the dismissal of directors by shareholders and to prevent a company from buying up its own shares (to stop a hostile bid), unless authorised by share-holders at a full share-holders meeting.

The UK was naturally resistant to what was perceived as intrusion in this field. Given the proportion of M & A activity in Europe which involved the UK, the primacy of London as the European finance nerve centre and the effective UK M&A control machinery (Office of Fair Trading & Monopolies and Mergers Commission) this was not surprising. UK resistance to outside control grew even stronger at the end of the eighties because of the economic down-turn, with its penal interest rates, and as recession reduced the M & A flow.

It grew even more when the volume of proposed takeover bids for privately-owned UK firms by French firms, owned in part or whole by the state, became significant. To the point where, in July 1990, Peter Lilley, the UK Trade and Industry Secretary, issued the Lilley doctrine: *Britain's policy of privatisation and competition would not be allowed to be undermined by changes introduced by the EC through the 'back door'.*

> *When a company outside the EC wants to acquire a base.. the relative openness of the UK means that it has only one port of call - Britain. It is extremely difficult to carry through a contested bid in the Community.. We need a level playing field.*

EXHIBIT 7: ONE-STOP SHOPPING
Source: John Banham at the CBI National Conference 1988. [26]

One of the most powerful statements of British hostility towards the whole of the Commission's regulatory approach came with the speech by Sir James Goldsmith at the Institute of Directors dinner on 12th June 1990. *We do not want* he declared *a European superstate which is centralised, monolithic, dirigiste and seeks to impose uniformity. We do not want an all-powerful super-parliament nor a super-bureaucracy and an extra layer of super-laws which compete with national laws.* [27]

FINIS

The EC Mergers Task Force was not involved in the Pirelli bid for Conti. Nor were the Italian or German governments, who could have sought, had they seen fit and had the regulations regarding the values of mergers applied, to seek to block the bid by invoking article 9 of the EC Merger Rules. This allows member states to object to a merger if there is a distinct *market problem*. Article 21 - not relevant in the Pirelli case - also allows for merger scrutiny by national governments on grounds of public interest in the fields of banking, media and public security.

> *L'Allemagne et le Japon conduisent parallèlement des politiques micro-économiques nourries d'un dialogue permanent entre les pouvoirs publics et les responsables industriels. C'est ce qu'il faut faire ici et vite..Il ne faut perdre de vue l'essentiel, qui est la force industrielle.*
>
> Translation note 28 on page 213.

EXHIBIT 8: THE FIRST GOSPEL ACCORDING TO EDITH CRESSON
Source: Industrialistes contre libéraux, Eric le Boucher, *le Monde*, 17/5/91

Here the proposed takeover was, indeed, the subject of intense debate. But it chiefly involved Conti shareholders and their representatives at the Emergency General Meeting held on the 13th March 1991. The vote on the proposed reverse takeover bid by Pirelli went heavily against the Italians. Pirelli itself abstained from voting on grounds of a desire to agree mutually a friendly formula for uniting the two companies in its $1.27 billion plan.

What was significant, though, was the 66 per cent vote by shareholders in favour of dropping the five per cent limit on their voting rights as individuals. This represented, it was widely argued, a possible historic turning point in German corporate history as well as a major breach in Conti's defences.

At the meeting in Hannover's Congress-Centrum Stadtpark Conti shareholders had been regaled with over nine hours of boisterous debate on the pros and cons of the bid argument and the procedures involved. During this, chief executive Horst Urban had played a prominent and hawkish role in spelling out the need to protect Conti's independence. Within two months, however, he had been asked by Conti's supervisory board to step down as chief executive. March 13th had been for him a Pyrrhic victory; May the ninth the day of defeat.

Europe cannot be just a large market. The Europeans cannot depend on the outside world for certain products which are essential for their technological future or their defence. An urgent effort is needed to ensure a common future in key sectors like cars and electronics: let us be bold and inventive.. Forty years ago the founding fathers created a European Coal and Steel Community. Today it is a true Electronics Community we need.

EXHIBIT 9: THE SECOND GOSPEL ACCORDING TO EDITH CRESSON
Source: Cresson demands EC industry pact, Ian Davidson,
The Financial Times, 23/5/91

The changed position arose out of the subsequent attempts Pirelli had made to negotiate further on bringing the two tyre giants together. Ulrich Weiss, chairman of Conti's supervisory board and board member of Deusche Bank, played a key role in this second round of the drama. It was clear that opposition to some sort of merger was weakening. After all, Pirelli was said to be losing heavily in the European OEM tyre sector, in which its share was so high that it could not afford to quit, and Conti was suffering substantial losses in the USA, a fact which had clearly contributed to the fall in its share price from a 1991 high of 250DM to 204DM. It was noteworthy that not only was Conti's US General Tyre subsidiary suffering the combination of cut-throat competition and a slump in the car industry, but that the DM value of US sales had fallen 14 per cent in the first quarter of the year. Michelin, too, was in deep financial distress, to the point of announcing, on the tenth of April 1991, the sacking of 13 per cent of its entire French workforce. It blamed the ruinous price war in the tyre market for its difficulties. Mr Akira Yeira, Bridgestone president, had maintained when his company took over Firestone (*a whale swallowing another whale*, he said) that, in the global market, only the big companies would survive. *In this industry size is important.*

By the 16th May, Continental had appointed Guiseppe Vita as a member of its 20-strong supervisory board, as a Pirelli representative. Hans Detlev von Garnier, one of Deutsche Bank's directors, had left to make way for him. The negotiations were set to continue...

* * * * * * * * * * * * * * * * * * *

NOTES & REFERENCES

1   Auch die Beschäftigten lehnen eine Fusion mit Pirelli ab (Even the employees reject a merger with Pirelli), *Frankfurter Allgemeine Zeitung*, 22/2/91. *A policy of independence was both possible and correct.. Continental should not become a plaything for financial speculators.*

2   Charter for economic Liberty, *The Guardian*, 21/9/88.

3   December 1989 White Paper 'Developments in the European Community', Andrew McEwen, *The Times*, 4/4/90

4   Thatcher resists talks on EC political union, Richard Ford and Jamie Dettmar, *The Times*, 21/4/90

5   Britain's lost sovereignty, *The Observer* editorial, 24/6/90

6   Europe - L'heure des clivages, Henri Paillard and Olivier Pognon, *Le Figaro*, 11/4/90. *We must keep control in our own hands of the essential factors governing our destiny.*

7   Sovereignty for 15 minutes, *The Times*, 6/7/90

8   *The Times* 23/6/90

9   Ridley's future in cabinet put in doubt, Philip Webster, *The Times,* 13/7/90

10   Recession deep, inflation high, Wynne Godley, *The Observer*, 19/8/90

11   Schengen Group.   The Schengen Accord, to which the UK is not a party, scrapped border formalities and eased the movement of people and goods among the Netherlands, Belgium, Luxembourg, France and Germany.

12   Why devaluation is wrong, *The Independent* editorial, 5/1/91

13   EMU dispute ended by Delors concession, Wolfgang Munchau, *The Times,* 13/5/91

14   Europe's Horn of Plenty, *The Economist*, 2/6/90

15   Iacocca declares war on foreign cars, Barbara Reynolds, *USA Today*, 20/2/90

16   Calvet's campaign to freeze Japanese auto imports rankles EC competitors, E. S. Browning, *The Wall St. Journal*, 21/2/91

17   Tyre showdown marks a watershed, Andrew Fisher, *The Financial Times*, 12/3/91

18   Demotion fails to deflate the Goodyear gusto, John Griffiths, *The Financial Times,* 10/5/90

19   As 18

20   As 2

21   *The medieval organisation of craft guilds survived all over Europe.. In Britain they became moribund.. but elsewhere they had substantial legal powers.. In a French or German town no artisan could practise his trade unless he belonged to the appropriate craft guild and he was bound by a complicated code of regulations. Originally, the guilds performed useful social functions. They had protected the interests of the consumer and secured a fair reward for the producer. But by the 18th century they had degenerated into close oligarchical bodies*, A Birnie, *Economic History of Europe*, Methuen 1957, page 7.

22 Crying need for a Social Charter, Nicholas Comfort, *The European,* 25/8/90

23 Lessons on winning the workers' trust, Michael Dixon, *The Financial Times* 20/2/91

24 Howard carries his worker involvement plan to EC ministers, Philip Bassett, *The Times*, 6/5/91. Note that John Major's plan for a hard ecu curried little favour in EC circles, either. The government's plan was intended as a counter to a single Eurocurrency (which could well have meant the demise of the pound sterling) and foresaw a system in which national currencies would co-exist alongside the ecu.

25 As 24

26 As 24

27 Mergers not takeovers are the key to Europe, Iain Jenkins, *The Sunday Times*, 6/5/90

28 Goldsmith gives vision of Europe, Derek Harris, *The Times*, 13/6/90

EXHIBIT 8: *Germany and Japan are carrying out similar microeconomic policies which feed off a permanent dialogue between private sector management and public authorities. That's what we must have here, and quickly.. We should not lose track of the most important thing - industrial strength.*

29 Pressure is on for Firestone, Stefan Wagstyl, *The Financial Times*, 6/6/90.

Note that Bridgestone bought Firestone for $2.6 billion in 1988. Firestone's losses in 1989/90 dragged Bridgestone's consolidated earnings down by 75 per cent to Y9.6 billion ($63.5m). Net return on sales fell from 3.4 per cent to 0.6 per cent

GROUPE BULL

Abstract:

Groupe Bull, long a headache for the French government, was privatised in April 1997, with the government retaining a 17.4 per cent stake and France Telecom enjoying a blocking minority of 17.7 per cent. It was, despite its comparative lack of profitability and its need for strategic alliance, one of France's industrial *crown jewels*.

This case deals with one of the dilemmas preoccupying the French government at the start of the 1990s: the best way of handling the future development of the nation's high technology industries. Groupe Bull is a superb example of the tensions involved in this dilemma. It is an ailing company seeking to compete in an increasingly-demanding and highly-turbulent market place. Allowing strategic participations in its ownership to competitors was the chosen course of action.

Questions:

Why did Groupe Bull offer stakeholdings to NEC and IBM?
Why did they accept?
Would you agree, on the basis of case data, that the industry is going through "a holocaust"?

Case Timing: 1992

RISING STORM

In the early 1990s clear evidence emerged that many of the major players in the global computer industry, who had enjoyed great success in the 1980s, were facing a rising business storm. The increasing pace of technological change in the industry was a key cause of this and the Thomson-CEA link was just a by-product of the changes in the area of the key raw materials (chips) used by the industry.

In the very eye of the storm was to be found 'Big Blue' - the global computer giant, IBM. It had been hit hard, having suffered its first decline in sales for 13 years. Among other major casualties was Groupe Bull, whose post-tax losses in 1990 amounted to no less than a staggering 6.8 billion francs. Olivetti, also, moved into loss in fiscal 1991, for the first time in 13 years. Its losses amounted to almost F8B against a turn-over of F236.5B.

> In 1991 Groupe Bull was seeking another supplier of RISC (reduced instruction set computing) technology. This used advanced chip design and complex software to create powerful, low-cost computer systems. It was invented by IBM and was the technology of choice for midrange and personal computers. It was available only from US suppliers - Hewlett Packard, IBM, Acorn, Digital Equipment, Sun and MIPS.

EXHIBIT 1: HELP NEEDED

No part of the economics of producing and marketing the industry's hardware, software and services was left untouched by the imperatives of technological change. As computing had developed in the higher value-added areas of industrial and commercial management in firms in the USA and Europe (in, for instance, computer-integrated manufacturing (CIM)), users' pressure on manufacturers like IBM and Groupe Bull to meet their changing demands had grown more and more insistent. Such requirements related especially to 'open systems' hardware/software which, unlike previous proprietary products (branded products from Apple, Digital, Nixdorf etc), was totally compatible with other manufacturers' products and which could be sold, as a commodity, on a price competition basis.

Perhaps the most striking evidence of change was the marked switch in customer preferences for many applications away from the traditional mainframe computer to new smaller, superfast microcomputers. The desk-top PC, the personal micro-computer, had, in fact, by the early 1990s, become a commodity item, capable of more and more processing work as more and more power was packed into it. Organising sets of PCs into interlinked 'open system' networks brought with it a huge increase in computing power and sophistication, particularly in the case of the larger, workstation PCs.

This revolution had been a possibility ever since IBM's launch of the PC (in 1983, in Britain). The company had, in the process of creating success for itself, spawned a whole host of companies manufacturing IBM clones. One indication of this was that the price of the original IBM PC at launch was F35,000; in November 1991 a similar system could be purchased for F7,275.[1]

Lap-top computers were the latest entrant to the micro-computer range; some of these, too, could be networked. And, as if that were not enough, hugely powerful 'notebook-size' computers were beginning to come on stream. Like Apple's Macintosh 'Powerbooks', 9in by 11in fold-up versions of popular desk-top PCs. These appeared in late 1991.

Stock Exchange and Company	12 month share price High	Low	Capitalisation
New York:	**$**	**$**	**$m**
IBM	139.5	94.4	56,284
AT & T	39.9	29.2	42,507
Hewlett Packard	56.5	25.1	12,493
Intel	58.5	34.5	8,485
Motorola	71.2	45.9	8,164
Digital Equipment	81.7	47.5	7,559
Apple Computer	72.7	33.2	6,083
Tokyo:	**Yen**	**Yen**	**Yen B**
Hitachi	1,340	990	3,275
NEC	1,700	1,190	1,985
Fujitsu	1,280	901	1,710

TABLE 1: SELECTED LEADERS IN THE COMPUTING INDUSTRY
F 9.7 = 1£ = $1.81 = 234 Yen. 1 Billion = 1,000m (12) F = French francs

The small size of such hardware resulted from the development of increasingly narrow circuits, which allowed makers to pack more functions on chips, and by the creation of innovatory higher-duty memory chips themselves. In late 1991, Texas Instruments and Hitachi announced a deal, for example, to cooperate on the development of the 64 MByte D-Ram chip. The agreement extended a previous information-sharing accord which had existed for 10 years into the sphere of joint design and manufacture. Early in 1991 NEC and AT & T Microelectronics had also signed a co-operation deal on D-Ram development, the cost of which was put by AT&T at F2.7B.[2]

In software, more and more commercial organisations were seeking 'open' industry-standard material which could be used by any and all of their computers. Again this was a field in which proprietory suppliers had long led.

FIRM FOUNDATIONS?

Industrial Meccano. That was one way an editorial in the French business magazine *L'Expansion* put it.[3]

For Pasquale Pistorio, president of SGS-Thomson, one of the few European computer chip makers still in existence, it was, however, more a case of *the third-world economic degeneration* that Europe would face if it had *no more home-grown semiconductor companies.* The subject under debate was, in fact, the plan put forward by French Prime Minister Edith Cresson - to create a European computer chip giant.

It had long been Pistorio's view that his French-Italian company, owned jointly by state-owned Thomson-CSF and IRI-Finmeccanica, had no other option but growth. *We, who today have a 2.7 per cent world market share, do not have the size to sustain investment in R&D and we are too big to be a specialist.* For him, this meant effectively a thrust to increase sales from the current level of F8.1B to F54B by the turn of the century. It also carried with it inescapable short-term decisions, notably to come to terms with the F518M loss incurred by the company in 1990 and the uncertainties of the recession in the global computer industry which, in mid 1991, showed few signs of abating. Announcing redundancies of 3800, he declared at the end of October 1991 that the company intended to fight to become a volume producer and escape from the *instability zone* in which he thought competitors like Philips and Siemens were finding themselves.

The stage was set for the implementation of the Cresson plan by the 1991 deal struck by Philips and SGS-Thomson, whereby Philips gave to its partner the job of meeting its needs for the next generation of chips. This would be developed at SGS-Thomson's new Crolles factory in Grenoble from late 1993.

	M. Fr. Rounded	
	1990	**1989**
Assets		
Current assets	17,793	19,931
Other assets	2,498	2,142
Fixed assets	8,273	8,992
Total	**28,565**	**31,066**
Liabilities		
Current liabilities	15,079	13,340
Long & medium term debt &		
long term provisions	11,961	10,047
Advances by French state	1,541	41
Equity	(16)	7,636
Total	**28,565**	**31,066**

TABLE 2: GROUPE BULL – BALANCE SHEETS AS AT 31/12
Source: Company Financial Reports (B = 1,000M)

This was very much in line with Philips' decision to reduce substantially its contribution to the European Community's major chip research project, JESSI (Joint European Submicron Silicon Initiative). It was also bound up with the agreement between Siemens and IBM to co-operate in the development of advanced Dynamic Random Access memory or D-Ram chips. These chips were capable of massive memory storage. Indeed, a 64 MByte version could store no less than 16,000 pages of text. Their deal, announced on the fourth of July 1991, was to work together in expanding the IBM France plant at Corbeil Essonnes.

The Cresson plan was unveiled in December 1991 and brought together the chip-making interests of France's profitable national nuclear agency (CEA) and those of Thomson-SGS in a new organisation called Thomson-CEA. It was an intricate, incestuous marriage, since Thomson-CSF owned 17 per cent of France Telecom and 13.9 per cent of Groupe Bull and the state-owned France Telecom was itself a stakeholder in Bull, to the tune of 17 per cent. *This set-up* said Edith Cresson *resembles exactly what has been done by some of our major competitors. I am thinking particularly of Toshiba which brings together the nuclear and electronics industries.*[7]

For *Le Monde* commentators Pierre Gay and Caroline Monnot [8] the plan represented a curious return to former policies of industrial restructuring such as had been experienced under Charles de Gaulle. It was his influence which had brought together elements of French industry in 1966 to form the substantial CII (Compagnie International pour l' Informatique) as a way of combatting at the time the much-resented and much-feared American domination of the computer industry. CII, interestingly, was later absorbed into the state-owned Groupe Bull, along with Bull's integration of the US Honeywell company.

Country	Government aid per employee in the manufacturing sector over the period 1985-8	
	Ecu	$
Italy	3077	4000
EC Average	1439	1870

TABLE 3: HELPING MANUFACTURING INDUSTRY [9]

Le jeu de Meccano que l'on croyait demodé avec le néoliberalisme socialiste refait surface wrote Pierre Gay and Caroline Monnot *Les temps changent.. L'ennemi aussi - hier, c'était l'Amerique imperiale. Aujourd'hui ce sont les 'fourmis japonais'.*[10]

To the French government the task was clearly straight-forward. Was it not faced with incontrovertible proof of the threat from US and Japanese manufacturers? According to Dataquest, seven of the top world memory chip producers were Japanese and only three (Texas, Motorola and Samsung) were not, a critical fact in a bitterly fought global chip trade battle that had been going on since the start of the 1980s. The US-Japan semiconductor trade agreement signed in 1991 had been aimed at reducing the bitterness by ensuring that Japan would give greater access to foreign producers to its domestic semiconductor market. A market share 'allowance' of 20 per cent by the end of 1991 had been specified, but not reached. Nor was it likely to be in 1992 either, given the progress being made, with foreign market penetration in the last quarter of 1991 having reached only 14.3 per cent.[11]

GROUPE BULL: PARTNERS SOUGHT

It looked as if, in January 1992, Groupe Bull was on the point of making a new, and very important, business alliance. On the 13th, Francis Lorentz, its

President and Director General, announced that the negotiations that the Groupe had been carrying on with two prospective American partners, IBM and Hewlett Packard, had entered their final stage. One was to be selected. The alliance would, given Groupe Bull's public ownership, have to be ratified by the French government. Much hung on the choice, not least potential access to the lucrative French government computer market. IBM was seen as the front runner, with a five per cent stake discussed as a firm possibility.

Bull had worked very hard to increase its attractions after the 1990 débâcle of losing some F6.8B. It had reduced its number of key plants from 13 to five and cut its workforce by 20 per cent (9,000 jobs) since November of that year. But it was fearful of a repetition of the same hesitations that the French government had had, when agreeing to the 4.7 per cent stake that had been taken in Groupe Bull by the Japanese company NEC.

Through its membership of the MIPS group of RISC technology producers/users (which included Microsoft, Compaq, NEC, Siemens) Groupe Bull already had a stake in developing and using RISC technology. But here again, Lorentz felt that MIPS was not sufficiently broad-based to guarantee the success of its particular choice of RISC technology and that it might not adequately reflect the company's high quality product needs.

For the French government such technicalities were not the main issue. It had announced in April 1991, much against the grain of the European Commission's policy of increasing competition in the Community, that it was going to inject some F6.6 billion into the company. Now, at the start of 1992, in order to protect the interests of its 'national champion', it was paradoxically being obliged to consider the possiblity of sanctioning further foreign ownership. And this against a background of an 1991/2 EC computer trade deficit of some F54B.

Groupe Bull was practising what it preached in terms of creating larger competitive groupings in Europe, also. It had entered with Olivetti and Siemens-Nixdorf into a consortium to bid for EC contracts in the advanced software technology field. One special target in this was the tender for ENS, a $ billion programme to forge computer links between governments. The companies' joint approach was premised on a situation where, in the USA and Japan, at least 90 per cent of all domestic contracts went to domestic suppliers, whereas, in Europe, the figure was only 30 per cent.[12]

Groupe Bull thinking also followed some of the lines advocated in the report produced by the French government's Commissariat du Plan, published on the 27th June 1991. It proposed an urgent strategy for the European electronics industry resting on three key elements, a 'Buy European' law, compensatory payments for firms undertaking industrial restructuring and high level of computer education in the EC.

The danger with this lay in the fact that state aid to companies might run counter to articles 92 and 93 of the Treaty of Rome, which EC Competition Commissioner Sir Leon Brittan was charged with upholding. It was a tense subject in France in 1991 as the second largest computer maker SMT-Goupil was on the point of expiry.

> *Tordons le cou de deux idées recues: la première voudrait que la Communauté Européene et la Commission en particulier exercise un préjugé défavorable à l'entreprise publique. La seconde voudrait que l'entreprise publique et concurrence soient deux concepts antinomiques. L'aspect essentiel.. est celui des aides d'état. A cet égard la préoccupation de la Commission est d'organiser une égalite de traitement entre les entreprises publiques et les sociétés privées autour de règles communes.. Il est essentiel que les interventions financières des états soient transparentes.* Translation note 13 on page 230.

EXHIBIT 2 : SIR LEON SPEAKS [13]

French government permission to NEC to purchase a 4.7 per cent stake in Groupe Bull had also done nothing to reduce the tension. Edith Cresson who, in Caroline Monnot's words, *allait mettre le holà à l'invasion japonaise,*[14] had had to eat the humblest of pies.

Were there any European alternatives to an American alliance for Groupe Bull?

Philips were, in fact, in the process of selling their computer division to DEC, so they were out of the running. Their deal involved Philips' annual sales of F5.5B and 7,000 employees in Holland, Germany and Sweden. DEC, by contrast, had a European sales turnover in 1989/90 of almost F29B (40 per cent of global sales) and 35,000 staff (29 per cent of total).

Olivetti was also a questionnable proposition at the time, despite the fact that Carlo de Benedetti was once more back in personal charge of a company 42 per cent owned by CIR, a company personally controlled by him. He had turned Olivetti round before in 1978 and it was hoped in November 1991 that he would do it again. But the task was formidable. The standard route of cutting costs by large-scale redundancies was not easy in Socialist Italy; increasing sales by building on the attractive PC marketing agreement Olivetti had struck with DEC was, given the market situation, not easy either. Nor was Carlo de Benedetti interested solely in the bottom line. *I have* he said *a sense of pride and commitment to this company... In life it's not always a question of money.*[15]

There were, however, two plus factors. Firstly, the company's strong balance sheet and, secondly, the costs then being achieved in Olivetti's electric typewriter plant in Singapore. These were estimated as being in 1991 a seventh of those in Italy. This is highly significant when it is borne in mind that Italy's labour costs increased over the period 1986-91 at almost twice the rate of the UK's and that Italy's employers contributed substantially more in social security cost per unit of pay than their UK, German and French counterparts.[16]

In the event, redundancies were negotiated with the workforce which was scheduled to be reduced by 5,000 to 44,500 by the end of 1992.

	Fr. Million	
Profit & Loss Account	**1990**	**1989**
Sales Turnover	34,579	32,721
Cost of Sales	22,474	18,624
R & D	2,989	2,933
Overheads	11,466	10,512
Net Financial Expenses	1,119	696
Provision for Re-structuring	3,952	
Other losses (net)	45	130
Loss before taxes	7,466	174

TABLE 4 : BULL FINANCIAL DATA
Source: Company information. All figures rounded.

Siemens-Nixdorf Informationssysteme did not look all that attractive from an alliance standpoint, either. Since Nixdorf's forced bailout by Siemens, the turnaround of the company had been slow. Its loss for 1991 was F2.9B, including restructuring costs. It was taking longer than anticipated to return it to profit. This, according to Supervisory Board chairman Hermann Fanz, looked likely in 1992/3.[17]

It was Sir Leon Brittan who was pre-occupying the French government most, however. On the tenth of July his office began to probe the plan to give F6.6B francs to Groupe Bull, F4B for capital and some F2.2B for R & D spending. Were the spending to have been given as an *operating aid to a company in difficulty,* it would have been outlawed, with payment forbidden or restitution required. On the 24th July it was further announced by his office that all state-owned enterprises with annual turnovers over 250m ECU would in future have to send their financial statements to Brussels for scrutiny. It was then, on the 16th September, the turn of those companies infringing anti-cartel regulations to have their knuckles rapped. A new system of high fines was to be installed.

France had had previous experience of the approach of this particular Competition Commissioner. In 1990, he had ordered Renault to repay F6B of state aid. This was done, although Renault actually obtained the funding later as an equity injection. This was similar to a rights issue and something of which the Commission could not complain.

There were those in France who were fundamentally opposed to the spirit shown by Sir Leon in exercising his role. Jaques Fournier, President of the European Centre for Public Enterprise, for one. He declared:

Les entreprises publiques..commencent à trouver obsessionelle et, pour tout dire, franchement dangereuse, la recherche à tout prix de la concurrence et le liberalysme de type britannique, défendu par un des Commissionaires Europeens... L'Europe n'est pas seulement un marché. [18]

The position taken by Dominique Strauss-Kahn, French Industry Minister, in late 1991 was to push hard at the Commission for help to be given by the state to nationalised industry where *profitability is not an immediate issue*.[19]

Groupe Bull did not want Commission antagonism to spoil the company's re-structuring chances. For an anxious Francis Lorentz, quoted in Le Nouvel Economiste, there was enough *péril en la demeure* [20] as a result of the situation facing the company in its industry.

IBM RESURGENS?

Groupe Bull's seemingly most favoured choice as partner, IBM, was itself not in the best of financial health. The fact of its first loss in company history, equivalent to over F15B, in 1991 was banner-headlined across Europe. *It had been*, said chief executive John Akers, *a disappointing year.*[21] Certainly compared with 1989, when IBM had made profits equal to F20B. Not only had the company had to make a further reduction of 30,000 in its workforce but it had also to cope with a massive F18.4B restructuring charge. All this on top of the moves started by John Akers in 1991 to make IBM *more competitive and efficient* in *an industry in turmoil.*[22]

Of its 1990 total revenues of F362B, mainframes and PC/work-stations were each responsible for approximately 16 per cent. Mainframes had brought in no less than 29 per cent of sales in 1985 by themselves.

In the old days of proprietory systems, each computer company had developed a separate system. It was like having to change your telephone system every time you wanted to call abroad. Sun Microsystems is one of the manufacturers that manufactures "open systems" computers that enable systems from different manufacturers to work together. This make for open hardware, software, applications interfaces, graphics, networks...(23)

EXHIBIT 3: SUNSHINE FROM SUN

The warning signals had been there from the start of 1991. The launch of an advanced IBM desktop computer did not create overmuch sensation; Compaq were thought likely by the trade to be able to make it at a lower price. IBM cut prices; competitors followed suit. More and more customers were deferring purchase of mainframes as global economic conditions worsened. Akers' conclusion was simple – *We need to run a smarter race by reducing our costs faster than technology and other factors are reducing prices. We must keep driving to make IBM more agile.* Not so easy when you are dealing with a company that had, at the start of 1991, 373,000 employees world-wide.[24]

The challenge was biggest in the personal computer (PC) area, where IBM's world market share had been squeezed from 35 per cent in 1983 to 22 per cent in 1990. This made the chief executive, he said, *goddam mad.* Everyone in the company seemed far too *comfortable* at a time when the business was *in crisis.* The personnel had a *mind-set problem.*[25] This was not surprising. The company had prided itself on its product excellence, its closely-knit and centralised organisation and its job-for-life policy. Its personnel had followed, as directed by the company's founder, the same sartorial regime throughout the company's 70 year history.

What Akers was seeking to power through, therefore, amounted to a cultural revolution. Company independence, goal-related performance, changed reported relationships, flatter hierarchies were all involved. Task-based work groups were created to deal with business opportunities in the PCs and workstation fields. The company was going to go into the service-provision as well as the product supply business in a much bigger way.

We are going through a holocaust. The distribution and dealer channels are going bankrupt. This year alone prices have fallen by some 25-40 per cent. Customers recognise that there's not too much difference between an IBM PC from a dealer and a mail order Dell.

EXHIBIT 4: THE SQUEEZE IS ON [26]

The size of Akers' task is shown by comparing IBM with Fujitsu. In 1965 IBM sales had been 40x those of Fujitsu. By 1991, they were 4x. The chairman of Fujitsu, Takuma Yamamoto, had pledged to overtake IBM in size by the early 21st century.

Fujitsu had grown strongly by acquisition in the 1980s. The companies in question were the US mainframe maker Amdahl Corp (a 44 per cent stake) and the UK's ICL, with a combined annual turnover of almost F27B. The trend was continued with ICL's acquiring Nokia Data of Finland in May 1991.

The battle plan followed by the company was, in the chairman's words, *to go global by going local. We are* he said *doing business in a borderless economy but there is a rising tide of nationalism and you have to find ways of avoiding conflict. That is one reason why we give our partners autonomy.*[27]

So entrenched were many in their views, that a technology alliance between IBM and Apple, hitherto deadly rivals particularly in the PC field, would have seemed quite preposterous. And yet that is precisely what took place in July 1991. It was indeed a breath-taking move, what with IBM having a 12.9 per cent share of world PC sales and Apple 7.2 per cent. As recently as 1984 Apple had spent a million $ on a TV commercial that portrayed 'Big Blue' as *Big Brother*! Apple had been the archetypal Silicon Valley innovator, the company that solved problems.

But Apple was now entering, according to its new chief executive John Sculley, a new era in which alliances were of the greatest importance. He had started with a deal with the Japanese disk-drive maker Sony, called the ASAHI project, to make an IBM-compatible super-portable computer notebook, the Macintosh Powerbook.

We had to cut the company in half. We have gone from 17,700 to 8,500 and cut manufacturing facilities from 5m to 2m sq ft. Five years ago we had a proprietory product line that was as good as any in the business, but the company was not focussed on the market. From now on it's open systems, off-the-shelf RISC chips and industry standard software.[28]

EXHIBIT 5: DESPERATE REMEDIES FOR DATA GENERAL

Similarly, IBM had just concluded another alliance before the deal with Apple. Under this, the office equipment supplier Wang arranged an OEM agreement to sell IBM's mid-range computers, workstations and PCs and to convert its image-processing software to run on IBM desktops.

The Apple-IBM alliance moved Apple, in Scully's words, from a position as a *niche player in a high growth segment of the industry* into *the mainstream of corporate computing.*[29] As a former president of Coca Cola, he had realised, he said, that Apple would not be able to shape the industry in the 1990s as it had in the 1980s. Without change, it would become irrelevant. Moving away from the company's creative roots and product differentiation was for many executives, he remarked, *like walking into the Vatican and renouncing Catholicism.*[30]

Norsk Data was brought into the IBM-Apple partnership in August 1991 as, in part, a way of further extending IBM's and Apple's 26 per cent penetration of the Norwegian market. All were clearly intent on offsetting any loss of position in the branded product domain. This further extended the European possibilities for IBM which (according to Datamation) held 54 per cent of the market for mainframes, 23 per cent of that for midrange systems and 17.6 per cent of that for PC/work-stations.

MATTERS JAPANESE

NEC - allowed by the French Socialist government to take a 4.7 per cent share, clearly had had a lot to offer to Groupe Bull. Almost a 100 years old and with more than 105,000 employees, the Nippon Electric Company was one of the top ten electronic product makers in the world. An investor par excellence in product and process innovation, in the previous twenty years, NEC had also followed a consistent strategy of decentralisation. In 1988, for example, it created a new R&D laboratory in New Jersey. It had also put much effort into shifting production overseas. This had started in 1958 when it created manufacturing facilities in Taiwan. By 1992 it had no less than 71 subsidiaries abroad, constituting a complex array of overseas manufacturing and assembly points. One of the most interesting of the linkages was that which sent chips from the plant of origin in the USA to the finishing plant in Singapore and then back to the USA (among other markets) for final sale.

Intriguingly, NEC started life as a subsidiary of Western Electric in 1899. Now, capitalised at F7.3B and with a turnover of F143B, it was, among other things, a leading global producer of chips.

> *The Japanese economy is now being seen not as a friendly locomotive of trade, but as a hostile steamroller* declared Sir Leon Brittan in a speech to the Keidanren. *It is a simple fact that Japan retains a business culture and elements of economic regulation which have the effect of discouraging imports.* Bilateral deals in the chip field between the USA and Japan had aroused *great suspicion* and *grave concern* in the EC, especially as Japanese investment in Europe was still 17 times European investment in Japan.[31]

EXHIBIT 6: JAPAN AS STEAMROLLER

Despite its strong position in the market, the chip industry had been, since 1984 when prices were at their height, in considerable turmoil and a major problem for the company. To the point where AT & T had struck a technological collaboration deal with NEC as one way of standing up to the competitive threat posed by the alliances arrived at by Toshiba with Motorola and Hitachi with Texas Instruments.

The EC's Utilities Directive (90/531/EEC) will come into force in the UK on January 1 1993. It applies to water, energy, transport and tele-communications and covers all contracts for the procurement of supplies and works above certain thresholds (400,000 Ecu for supply contracts, for example). All contracts above this threshold have to be opened-up for Community-wide tendering and have to be publicly notified in the Journal Officiel. Strict rules will govern the awarding of contracts.

EXHIBIT 7: OPEN COMPETITION IN EUROPE

NEC had entered the link-up business for its mainframe computer products quite early. Its 1985 deal with Honeywell was aimed at securing, through Honeywell, greater market access through wider distribution for NEC brands. This continued when Honeywell was absorbed into Groupe Bull and Bull became responsible for distributing its large systems - DPS 9,000 - throughout Europe. NEC had over this period been able to take good advantage of Groupe Bull's exceptional strength in its own domestic market. This position had been argued as being wholly reasonable by the French government on grounds of national sovereignty. It regarded the *hyperindustrial* nature of electronics (the extent to which high tech knowhow and capabilities - as in electronics - lie at the heart of many advanced industries) as a key feature in its logic of maintaining an individual and enduring French manufacturing capability.

* * * * * * * * * * * * * * * * * * * *

APPENDIX 1: INDUSTRIAL DEVELOPMENT IN FRANCE

France began its industrialisation before Germany. The initial pattern of state backing for industry and commerce under Jean Baptiste Colbert, Minister of Finance under Louis XIV, was entrenched within the over-arching ideology of mercantilism: the notion that the business of the state was to amass wealth. This pattern fitted in well with a hierarchical social system, family ownership and a legacy of guild discipline until the revolutionary changes of the late 18th century. It was the case, however, that France lost out in its mercantilist rivalry, maritime and colonial, with England.

The system's ability to adapt and meet the requirements of war was tested to the limit under Napoleon 1 who produced for his European empire the formula of external protection, through the Continental System, and internal industrial revitalisation to meet the needs of war. This latter took place through, for example, the setting up of chambers of commerce (1801) as an aid to commerce and conciliation boards (Conseils de Prud'hommes) to deal with labour problems. Such institutions helped carry forward the notion of the need for commercial and industrial training, a notion which had been supported by guilds until they were abolished in 1774. Napoleon's reforms also included the creation of a powerful, skilled and meritocratic state bureaucracy (based on the grandes écoles) which has endured ever since as a bastion of French élitism.

The need for French banks to assist in industrial development as a matter of principle was well established under Napoleon II who set up Crédit Foncier and Crédit Mobilier specifically for this purpose. Conversely, the French state's involvement in industrial and commercial ownership and management is very much a post-1945 phenomenon. The tenth National Plan covered the period 1989-1992 and laid down indicative targets and broad policy thrusts. But, here too, policy has oscillated, depending on economic circumstances. The prevailing mood of the socialist government in France in the early 1990's was for a retrenchment of the ownership and control which had been painstakingly built up, through the policy of developing 'national champion' firms, in the late 1980s. For this the services of nationalised banks had been used in no small measure. The 'Ni Ni' approach of President Mitterand (No more nationalisation, no more privatisation) seemed to be at an end.

Worker consultation, through the 'comité d'enterprise' (works' committee) is carried out in all firm employing 50 people or more.

NOTES & REFERENCES

1   Will computer makers end the cold war?, David Guest, *The Times*, 4/11/91

2   Hitachi and Texas agree joint chip venture, Steven Butler, Robert Thomson and Michael Skapinker, *The Financial Times*, 21/11/91

3   Le Meccano Industriel: strategie ou bricolage, Gerard Moatti, *L'Expansion*, 23/2-25/2/92

4   SGS Thomson looks for a partner, Michael Skapinker, *The Financial Times*, 25/10/91

5   As 4

6   As 4

7   France plans giant electronics conglomerate, William Dawkins, *The Financial Times*, 19/12/91

8   La tentation du Meccano Industriel, Pierre-Angel Gay and Caroline Monnot, *Le Monde*, 21/1/92.
        The game of industrial Meccano that we thought had become anachronistic, given the rise of socialist neo-liberalism, hasn't. It's resurfaced. The Times have changed. Yesterday the enemy was imperial America, now it's the Japanese 'ants'.

9   European state subsidies brought to book, Lucy Walker, *The European'* 5-7/7/91

10   As 4

11   Fresh cracks in US-Japan chip pact, Louise Kehoe, *The Financial Times*, 6/2/92

12   Datastream shares report, *Computing*, 7/11/91

13   Entreprise Publique et Concurrence, Sir Leon Brittan, *Le Monde*, 3/7/91 *Let's here and now knock two received ideas on the head. One, that the European Community and the Commission, in particular, are prejudiced against public enterprise. Two, that the notions of public enterprise and competition are incompatible. What is really important.. is the question of state aid. Here the Commission is concerned with ensuring equality of treatment for the public and private sectors with rules common to both...It's vital that any state involvement is transparent.*

14   Un groupe japonaise dans le capital de Bull, Caroline Monnot, *Le Monde*, 10/7/91. *Edith Cresson was going to put a stop to the Japanese invasion.*

15   De Benedetti returns to Olivetti helm, Haig Simonian, *The Financial Times*, 15/11/91

16   Olivetti looks East, John Perrotta, *The European*, 28-30/6/91

17   Computer Hopes, *The European*, 8-10/11/91

18   Les entreprises publiques contre-attaquent a Bruxelles, Alian Faujas, *Le Monde*, 22/11/91.
        Public enterprises... are getting to the stage of finding that one of the European commissioners is pursuing an obsessive and frankly dangerous approach to

competition matters. It smacks of liberalism of the British type.. Europe, you know, isn't simply a market.

19   France twists EC electronics accord, Tom Walker, *The Times*, 19/11/91

20   Informatique - Alliances en rafale, Pierre-Antoine Merlin, *Le Nouvel Economiste*, 22/11/91. *There's perils ahead at home.*

21   IBM swings to major loss, Larry Black & Mary Fagan, *The Independent*, 18/1/92

22   As 21

23   Company literature

24   As 21

25   IBM's war with Apple ends in a surprise deal, David Brierley & Andrew Davison, *The Sunday Times*, 7/7/91

26   Excessive input creates overload, Ian Cane, *The Financial Times*, 4/7/91

27   Now Fujitsu will tackle the giants, *Fortune*, Brenton Schlender, 1/7/91

28   Signs of daylight emerge after eclipse, Louise Kehoe, *The Financial Times*, 18/10/91

29   The odd couple of the computer world, Louise Kehoe, *The Financial Times*, 30/7/91

30   IBM intensifies product push into European market, Alan Cane, *The Financial Times*, 10/10/91

31   Japan as Steamroller, *The European*, 20-26/2/92

ERM

Abstract:

This case documents aspects of the British government's decision to leave the European Union's Exchange Rate Mechanism in September 1992 and allows the decision to be appraised against the background of continuing steps towards further European economic integration as foreseen by the Maastricht Treaty. The ERM and GATT cases deal with the macro business environment within which European business was working. The Europe plc case forms an introduction to both of these. EMU can be read as a sequel to this case.

Questions:

What is ERM?
Why is it important to major European businesses?
Was "Black Wednesday" all that black for Britain?

Case Timing: 1992

E.R.M. MATTERS

British businessmen could easily be forgiven for any feelings of bewilderment. At the time, the Major government and its Labour opposition seemed, at best, puzzled and, at worst, powerless in knowing how to deal with the financial hurricane which struck Britain on the so-called *Black Wednesday*, 16th September, 1992. Not only did this event blow John Major's Cabinet totally off its European policy track, but it led to a large-scale, unplanned and highly controversial devaluation of the pound. How could the British business community come to terms with an instant switch from a fixed sterling parity rate within the European Community's Exchange Rate Mechanism (ERM) to a shifting £ value? Especially if the government itself appeared (to many money market observers) foxed by the extent of such a massive policy reversal? Had not any devaluation of the £ been flatly ruled out as even a remote eventuality by John Major himself only days before, in principle and in practice, as an unthinkable 'quack doctor' remedy for Britain's economic ills? Had not Chancellor Norman Lamont had also borrowed massively and, ultimately, to no avail in Britain's fight-back against the currency markets to defend the pound?

The problems facing John Major's government, it must be admitted, resembled nothing seen before. The government's reaction to attack from the massed ranks of foreign exchange speculators, quitting the ERM, was interpreted at the time as, either an economic defeat of major magnitude (by the opposition) or as dragging a kind of victory from the jaws of defeat (by the government). The speculators' defence was, of course, that what they were doing wasn't speculation and, even if it were, its effects could well be argued to be wholly salutary in exposing the ERM's fraught underlying realities. British managers in the export business who, anyway, were wholly unconvinced of the virtue of a high-value, fixed rate £, must have welcomed what was interpreted as a substantial economic and political reverse by others. The proclaimed mainstay of Conservative government economics, its fixed exchange rate within the ERM, had been removed at a stroke.

It is clearly of critical importance for managers involved in EC operations to disentangle and to understand the issues surrounding, and possibly explaining, the British government policy change. In doing this from a non-partisan perspective, it is necessary to examine a whole series of paradoxes which lurk at the heart of Britain's

European equation. These, it can be argued, well-nigh inhibit any speedy and logical solution to the challenges facing any British government.

* To be eligible for Economic and Monetary Union (EMU) within the Maastricht treaty framework, a country must be a member of the Exchange Rate Mechanism system which fixes its parity relative to the Deutschmark within a prescribed band. The band can be narrow or broad, depending on the freedom of movement allowed.
* Its inflation rate must not exceed 1.5% above the average of the 3 best performing countries and its long term interest rates no more than 2% higher.
* Its currency must have been comfortable within the narrow ERM band for 2 years at least.
* Its PSBR must not exceed 3% of GDP and its national debt/GDP ratio must be less than 60%.

TABLE 1: CONVERGENCE CRITERIA FOR ELIGIBILITY FOR EMU

The ERM system of fixed-parity exchange rates was, to begin with, seen by EC members as a necessary springboard for the Community's on-going build-up towards potential economic and monetary union, as called for in the Maastricht Treaty of 1991. The fact of a government's fully-paid-up membership of the ERM allowed it to belong to the select group of those with 'total EC commitment'. The system itself ranked in political importance alongside the creation of a unified European Community market-place (by the first of January 1993), as laid down by the Single European Act, 1986.

In late September 1992, after Britain's sterling devaluation, the other members of the ERM were giving every sign that they were not prepared to allow the British government to change the rules of membership, i.e. to repair what John Major had called the "fault lines" which helped the speculators' achieve their British victory, nor to re-enter the ERM on terms other than those of their setting. This, despite the British Prime Minister's insistence on the need for future ERM reform and also despite Britain's temporary position as President of the European Council over the period July to December 1992. '

The ERM and the Maastricht Treaty were seen by leading mainland EC protagonists as essential bases for any future development of European political and economic union. Given that fact, Britain's action in being forced, either temporarily or permanently, to quit the Mechanism raised not a few doubts as to the country's level of commitment to further EC development à la Maastricht. Was the British government, in fact, still wholeheartedly EC-supportive, faced as it was by an increasing number of querulous Eurosceptics, Baroness Thatcher and Lord Tebbit included? Was the Labour opposition, after the resignation of Brian Gould from the Shadow Cabinet over the issue, still rock-solidly for Maastricht and the ERM? Highly pertinent questions, particularly as John Major had pointedly made known on the 24th September that Britain would not take further steps towards the ratification by parliament of the Maastricht Treaty until the position of the Danes on their negative referendum verdict had been satisfactorily clarified. Nor was there to be, he had declared, any possibility of a British Maastricht referendum, along the lines of the two previous referenda (both on EC membership), even in the teeth of the opposition's clamour for one.

*	The Treaty commits the 12 European members to forge an even closer union among the Peoples of Europe. This will eventually involve a commitment to common foreign and security policies, with decisions being made on a consensus basis.
*	The treaty will eventually give the Community a bigger say in European education, public health, consumer protection, industrial R & D by replacing unanimity with majority voting at EC meetings. There will be an inter-governmental framework for justice and home affairs.
*	The EC will set up a "European Monetary Institute" by 1/1/94. This will become by 1999 at the latest the European Central Bank and will issue a single EC currency. The European economic and monetary union will cover only those nations which meet convergence criteria.
*	Britain can opt out of monetary union and European council decisions on social affairs.
*	Modest increase in powers for European Parliament
*	Cohesion fund to help poorer countries

TABLE 2: ELEMENTS IN THE MAASTRICHT TREATY

Of course, were Britain economically unable, rather than just unwilling, to rejoin the Exchange Rate Mechanism within a realistic period of time, then this would itself hold up the process towards further EC integration. Unless, that is, the other main-line supporters of forward progress took steps to get round the problems. One such possible move might be the creation of an alternative to a 12-member EC: a two-speed Europe, for example, centred around a central mainland politico-economic axis and involving members such as Britain only on a peripheral basis. Membership of such a 100 per cent Eurocentric inner sanctum would depend on the speed and extent of acceptance of new convergence rules (as set by the new member grouping) or speeded-up conformity with the old Maastricht rules for mainlanders or special dispensations (such as the Danes were requiring) for codicils to the Maastricht Treaty.

It is noteworthy that the German government strongly supported the French franc, when it, too, came under speculative attack at the end of September 1992. This was shortly after the markets' successful onslaught of the £. The aid was stronger (it was alleged by the British) than that given, as required by Maastricht rules, to the British pound during its death throes. The Bundesbank's support for the franc was interpreted by some as giving credence to the view that, officially and unofficially, the German government and the Bundesbank had thought the £ over-valued within the ERM anyway and were not over-saddened at its devaluation. It was also suggested by some that the German and French government regarded their existing rapprochement as a key to further European federalisation, whatever its character, and, therefore, were bound to be mutually supportive in financial terms.

Whatever the specifics of the debate, the fact remained that the prime movers in the push for EC political and economic union were the French and German governments and they were not brooking any delay. Their supporters included such EC members as Ireland, whose population voted strongly for Maastricht. It cannot be established whether they did this out of ideological conviction or, with one eye fixed on the cohesion funds the Treaty would provide, out of pure self-interest. All those integrators who wanted to progress the matter to what they saw as a satisfactory conclusion, the due ratification of the Maastricht Treaty unanimously by all EC members, as required by the Treaty of Rome, were certainly agitating for positive action. Even if, in strict legal terms, the Danish referendum "No" had, of itself, destroyed the Maastricht Treaty. The agitation would, it was thought, certainly continue up to the special EC Council meeting on the 16th October 1992 called to discuss the crisis.

The British were, therefore, in the dock. They are clearly seen by Maastricht fast-trackers as economically suspect (because they had moved out of the ERM) and politically backward (because they were seemingly not prepared to outpace the Danes by pushing the Maastricht ratification bill through the Commons). In economic terms, their position was shared by the Italians, similarly overwhelmed by unsustainable foreign exchange pressures in September 1992 and forced to leave the Mechanism. So far as politics was concerned, however, it seemed to many outside observers that Italy's support for integration was inversely proportional to the extent of her undeniable economic woes. As of October 1992, these were formidable, far more extensive and intractable than those of a Britain in the midst of its deepest recession since the 1930s.

The British recession, so critics alleged, had been powerfully sustained by the deflationary impact of the high level of interest rates which Britain, in order to sustain sterling at the right level within the ERM, had been obliged to maintain. Indeed, it had been keen to apply these since it began ERM membership 17 months before under Mrs Thatcher's leadership. Critics argued further that the ERM had simply aggravated Britain's main economic problem, the anti-Keynesian emphasis given by the Conservatives to inflation control rather than employment creation. Interestingly, the Labour party voted at its October Conference in 1992 in support of Maastricht and ERM, whilst simultaneously endorsing a substantial public sector works programme to reduce the growth in unemployment.

To such an accusation the government's defence was that, firstly, membership of the ERM was valuable not only in itself, as a mark of Britain's interest in being (in John Major's words) *at the heart of Europe*, but also as an essential tool of anti-inflation policy. In this latter, they argued, there is nothing if not a clear continuity of policy. In other words, the ERM was helping Britain to do something it would have done anyway.

A second defence of government policy lay in the commonly-held British view that the comparatively high level of German interest rates maintained by the Bundesbank was a function of purely domestic German concerns. German investment to rebuild East Germany and assist with industrial development in other parts of Central Europe had little to do precisely - it was argued - with the underlying macro-economic position of the rest of the EC. German reliance on monetary rather than fiscal policy to provide the necessary funds was also alleged to be a policy which had forced other EC countries to pay a heavier-than-anticipated price for assisting with Germany's unification. In this, the very independence of the Bundesbank deflected any potential criticism of the German government for inadequate use of taxation for build-up purposes. In other words, the level of interest rates which Britain had been paying since ERM membership was higher than would have been warranted for strict control of the UK money supply under UK macro-economic conditions, alone.

MAASTRICHT PARADOXES

The problems faced by Britain seemed intractable and no grand strategy solution looked to be on the cards to cope with the Maastricht and post-ERM trauma. Even Sir Robin Leigh-Pemberton, Chairman of the Bank of England, counselled the government against using its new-found interest-rate freedom to expand the economy and break out of the UK's deflationary impasse.

The problems took the form of a set of paradoxes for policy makers. The first of these was that, whilst France was a leader in the push for Maastricht and a strong believer in all forms of Franco-German rapprochement, President

Mitterand himself had just received a wafer-thin vote of confidence for his EMU plans in the French referendum. Almost half of the 70 per cent of those who voted said *Non* to the ratification of the Treaty. And, as if that were not enough, opinion polls in Germany were signalling less than total support for Chancellor Kohl's position. Among the chief worries of the Germans was the extent to which their particular bulwark against inflation, the Bundesbank's strength as an independent political institution, might be weakened by the Maastricht changes. Hence, the paradox that the French and German peoples could not be assumed to be wholly for Maastricht, even if their governments could be. The notion of an *EC House Divided Against Itself* also extended to the Danes, who, with their referendum, rejected the Treaty.

The second paradox related to the nature and extent of the foreign exchange speculation which so gravely damaged the position of the Italian and British governments as they fought to maintain their currencies within the ERM. To have the possibility of overt, and unregulated, speculation attacking at will any currency within the ERM, and forcing its revaluation, arguably strips the nation concerned of any real-time economic sovereignty. All the more so, if the attack has little apparent reference to the economic fundamentals which may be said, rightly or wrongly, to underpin the currency's value. The paradox is, on the one hand, that the ERM was (in principle) incompatible with 1992-style unregulated, speculative foreign exchange dealing and, on the other, that the British government was firmly wedded to the principle of free trade. This covered not only the freedoms of the Single Market but also the unrestricted workings of the forex system itself. Perhaps not surprisingly, given the volume of forex trade in London, the UK's currency was particularly susceptible to speculative movements. Hence, a major conflict of principle which the British had at some time to confront was again looming large. Certainly, the Germans, the French and the Americans were all showing signs that they would like to help in, if not lead, the process of curbing excesses in the international trade in money. It is thought highly improbable that any Conservative British government would accept such a volte-face in its policy.

Domestic British politics, as previously mentioned, gave rise to the third paradox. Here, the curious phenomenon existed that, whilst the opposition attacked the government for their economic management during Britain's membership of the ERM, they firmly supported Britain's membership of the ERM and the associated anti-inflationary posture.

Nicholas Brady, US Treasury Secretary, on 23rd September 1992 called for an examination of world-wide capital flows and their effects on the stability of the international monetary system. Issues to be considered included the number of market participants, the range of new derivative products, the spread of international transactions and the sheer volume of daily transactions which, at $1000B per day, were roughly double the total reserves of the major industrialised countries. A similar idea, aimed at stemming government's growing loss of power to control capital, was generated by his predecessor James Baker at the 1986 Tokyo leaders' summit and at the annual IMF World Bank meeting in 1987.

EXHIBIT 1: FOREX TRADING UNDER STRAIN?

Their pre-devaluation argument for more flexibility within the system may have been unattainable, since the ERM was not intended to be a member-friendly Currency Reform Club. It was aimed at institutionalising as Near Zero Inflation as was realistic, under Bundesbank leadership.

The fourth paradox concerned the Treaty of Maastricht itself. Quite apart from the areas of technical drafting which critics said left much to be desired, there was the issue of the convergence criteria for EMU. Naturally, these needed to be set at the level which would allow centralised EC macro-economic management to be efficient and effective. However, setting debt/GDP and deficit/GDP ratios that satisfied a Bundesbank-equivalent 'Eurofed' on macro-economic performance would be meaningless if (i) the majority of members of the EC were far from reaching the criteria even before the 1992 currency turmoil (which they were), (ii) they were now, as of October 1992, much further from that goal (iii) the criteria themselves had an element of inbuilt deflation (which they did) and (iv) the topic was being discussed in the 1992 context of an Alice-in-Wonderland global economic climate and at the very bottom of the global business cycle (which it was). In short, Maastricht was now, arguably, a flawed instrument. The purposes for which it was devised may have been sound, argued it opponents, but it could not be applied, as European Commission President Jacques Delors and the French and German governments were specifically requiring, without further ado.

The fifth paradox related also to the Treaty and was highly salient to UK's EC strategy as a whole. It is that there were, in fact, two versions of the Maastricht Treaty, not just one. The first was for the mainlanders and Ireland and the other, with its opt-out clauses, was for Britain. Because of the amount of political acrimony that went into the creation of these two treaties, none of the main parties involved would concede to any changes whatsoever. Hence, no renegotiation was said to be, or even thought, possible. The danger for Britain, if Maastricht were renegotiated, was that it might lose the only two elements, the escape clauses on the single currency and the social chapter, that, in the British government's view, made the Treaty not just palatable to parliament but a first-order negotiating triumph and justifiable source of governmental pride! The paradox here is, therefore, that the British could not afford to seek renegotiation, even if the other members would allow it (which they wouldn't, so they said), however difficult acceptance by the House of Commons of the package was going to be. And, as the October 1992 Conservative Party conference showed, even a three line whip would not allow the Maastricht Bill an easy passage through the Commons in the 1992 Session.

---

* London is the world's leading financial market. It's the largest forex trading centre [£300B daily] and the largest share trading centre, too [£300B + daily].

* It's Britain's No.1 wealth earner and the UK financial sector accounts for a larger GDP % than in other industrialised countries.

* Its gilt-edged market funds the government's budget deficit [£4.4B daily turnover], handling the £125B stocks outstanding.

* Unlike Frankfurt and Paris, it is largely unregulated by government. Barriers to trade are few.

EXHIBIT 2: NO SHACKLES PLEASE, WE'RE BRITISH [1]

The sixth policy paradox, was the most intractable and placed the Maastricht and ERM supporters in the British government and opposition in the most exposed political position. It lay in the necessity for them to claim that the fact of Britain's being ousted from the ERM and pushed off the Maastricht highroad was not a politico-economic reverse for Britain, but somehow a victory. If it were seen as a defeat, then Britain might be regarded by EC rivals as having moved even further along the de-industrialisation trackway towards a weaker economy. This view might cause the markets to sell sterling even more and, ultimately, increase the level of import-cost led inflation in Britain.

The seventh, and final, paradox related to the matter of EC subsidiarity: taking decisions at the best possible level of governmental decentralisation. In order to preserve whatever vestiges of sovereignty were possible in the supranational, federal world that Maastricht was thought by British opponents to be leading to, the British government needed to trumpet the need for subsidiarity. Yet it is undeniable that the Thatcher and Major governments had been among the most centralising British governments this century, in their curtailment of the scope and authority of local government. What would happen if Britain's EC partners conceived of subsidiarity in the context of Welsh and Scottish assemblies, alongside German Länder and French provinces, and not purely at the Westminster level?

CHALLENGES AHEAD

The Birmingham EC summit on the 16th October 1992 took place against a background of mounting interest, if not anxiety, in Britain about what the government intended to do in terms of its European and domestic policies. There was no shortage of advice from ex-leaders, such as Baroness Thatcher, the former British prime minister. (See Exhibit 3.)

This Conservative government, like its predecessors, should have as its main priority the maintenance of our constitutional freedoms, our democratic institutions, and the accountability of Parliament to the people.... Because I believe in these principles so deeply, I cannot support the ratification of the Maastricht treaty, and I welcome sterling's departure from the exchange-rate mechanism. The ERM and Maastricht are inextricably linked. The first is a prerequisite to the fulfilment of the second. We found the confines of the first unbearable - the straitjacket of the second would be ruinous.... Thanks to the decision to float the pound, we now have a chance to follow an economic policy that puts British needs first. Like the Maastricht treaty, the ERM in no way represents what is best for British interests....We now need an economic strategy which works with markets, not against them, is realistic and sustainable, and provides a framework for growth....We must return to the policy of domestic monetary control that worked throughout most of the 1980's, cutting inflation from over 20 per cent to under 4 per cent while the economy expanded....Our political debate on the Maastricht treaty and the future development of Europe has been conducted in, if possible, even less rational terms than our discussion of exchange rates....We are warned, from home and abroad, that it would be a national humiliation if Britain were left in the 'slow lane' while others sped towards economic and monetary union....But, as Lord Salisbury once pointed out, half the errors in politics come from taking metaphors literally.

EXHIBIT 3: THE BARONESS SPEAKS [2]

Chancellor Lamont faced a tough task at the beginning of October. A speech at the Conservative party conference and a grilling from the Commons Treasury and Civil Services Committee, not to mention the statutory Mansion House Speech, lay ahead. Each would be critically analysed by the money markets for signs of new policy developments. Clearly he was determined not to give any hostages to fortune in his various media appearances in early October, since his message was plain and repetitive. It focused on the rationale behind Britain's ERM membership, beating inflation and the need for policy continuity. In his Party Conference speech he elaborated on some of the tools that could be used to continue his ex-ERM policy. They included a new target for inflation (<4 per cent for the remainder of this parliament and a long term aim of two per cent or less), a growth range for MO (notes and coins in circulation) of 0-4 per cent but no formal target for broad money or the exchange rate. Was it likely that conditions for resumed ERM membership would exist shortly? *Unlikely* was his answer.

We have beaten inflation before with a floating pound and, with the same determination, we will do it again. So let there be no doubt about Britain's economic policy...Outside the ERM, there is even more reason to keep a firm grip on public spending...In the past the annual public spending round has simply encouraged ministers to make higher and higher bids for more public money that was not there. Starting this year there will be a ceiling for the total increase in public spending... This applies above all to public sector pay...Inside or outside the ERM, our policy objective must remain the same, to bring our underlying inflation rate down to the levels enjoyed by our major world competitors. No magic wand exists.

EXHIBIT 4: CHANCELLOR LAMONT'S CONFERENCE SPEECH [3]

It was obvious that the issue of containing public expenditure was his main preoccupation. The Treasury's original forecast for the Public Sector Borrowing Requirement (PSBR) for 1992/3 and 1993/4 had been £28B and £40B respectively, this latter equalling 6 per cent of GDP. The government's view was that such a rise in borrowing was in itself inflationary (since it expanded the money supply) and conducive to higher interest rates (because it competed for funds). Not that this was necessarily correct. Britain, in 1989, had had interest rates of 15 per cent (real nine per cent) and had had a budgetary surplus.

> *This house congratulates Her Majesty's Government on its leadership in foreign affairs, especially during the UK presidency of the EC and urges the Government to continue to build an open and outward-looking community.*

EXHIBIT 5: MOTION FOR DEBATE AT
THE CONSERVATIVE PARTY CONFERENCE

Thus, the government made it plain to the media that the deliberations in chancellor Lamont's own public expenditure committee (EDX) were firmly focused on spending containment. Interest rates would not be cut, chancellor Lamont told the Commons Treasury Committee on the 12th October, since to do so would cause the pound to fall and thereby stoke inflation. There would be no 'artificial stimulus' to the economy and public sector pay would be restrained. Certainly the National Institute of Economic and Social Research forecast that a ten per cent devaluation would bring a per cent points increase in retail price inflation of 3.8 in 1993, 3.7 in 1994, 2.0 in 1995 and 1.1 in 1996.[4]

Go Ahead, as now	Change
Activate the Urban Regeneration Agency and network of 82 Training and Enterprise Councils to aid the unemployed.	Switch aim & toolkit from inflation-containment to aiding recovery.
Stonewall on anti-inflation policy and public expenditure control.	Apply for cohesion fund money as UK per capita GNP now appears to meet EC criteria (90% of average).
Press ahead with Maastricht bill and rejoin ERM at earliest opportunity.	Rapid and deep cut in interest rates.
Do not lower interest rates if this threatens to unleash inflation.	Pump-prime capital spending on infrastructure.
Seek to become *the low cost, high productivity Hong Kong of Northern Europe* (5)	Boost money supply by deliberately underfunding the PSBR and thereby *monetising* the deficit.
	Take advantage of the ERM exit.
	Do not press ahead with the Maastricht bill
Tolerate political unpopularity.	Tolerate political unpopularity.

EXHIBIT 6: 1992 STRATEGY OPTIONS
FOR THE BRITISH GOVERNMENT

So far as public expenditure was concerned, the total for the year, £244.5B, was, he said, sacrosanct. There might well be cutbacks in capital spending on transport, schools, hospitals and prison buildings, a reduction in the planned NHS budget and a public sector pay freeze as a result of this stance, claimed some commentators.[6]   No wonder Social Security secretary Peter Lilley was worried about possible curbs in his department's £71B p.a. budget. The benefits which were at risk here were not pensions and unemployment (which were uprated for inflation) but family credit, housing benefit, income support and one parent benefit (which were not). Demands on his departments were increasing all the time as a function of demographic changes and unemployment growth alone.[7]

The markets did not much warm to the sound of this and on the 5th October the UK stock market suffered its biggest fall for five years, with £20B wiped off share values. Sterling fell to DM 2.37, a far cry from its erstwhile central ERM rate of DM 2.95. CBI Director General, Howard Davies asked:

Would it not assist the process if the government to develop a policy for economic growth...? Without such a policy the government is dancing in the dark.

This was followed by a highly critical comment from Neil Johnson, Director General of the Engineers Employers Federation about the 265,000 UK engineering jobs that had 'evaporated' in the previous three years. *The decline in the economy* he stated *seems to have been accompanied by ministerial paralysis...we need, and we need urgently, a clear vision of the priority actions necessary to bring about lasting economic recovery.*[8] This last statement came in a week which saw two announcements of major substance to British industry: the closure of the British Aerospace plant at Hatfield (where the world's first jet airliner, the Comet, had been made), and the loss by Vickers of a prestigious £1B order for a new battle tank for Kuwait to the US' General Dynamics.

The Times editorial was unprecedentedly harsh in its judgement. *To maintain tight fiscal and monetary policy in the depths of a recession is not just politically suicidal but sadistic* [9] it stated, drawing attention yet again to Britain's dependence on its mainland Europe partners for 60 per cent of its trade.

A NEW DAY DAWNS

The 16th October 1992, the day of the Birmingham EC summit meeting, was witness to a nationwide eruption of political hostility towards the government on the part of the British media. It was a reaction to events that was fully equal in magnitude to the ERM economic débâcle of the month before. The trigger had been the specific declaration that 31 coal mines were to be closed with the direct loss of 30,000 miners' jobs. They were no longer, in the governments' view, economic to operate. John Major's hope for a substantial start at Birmingham on the path to defining and implementing the 'subsidiarity' sub-text in the European Community's approach was also not met, save in the blandest of terms. The ERM did not seem to have been discussed at the summit.

Media attention, by contrast, was focused on the elemental fact that the British economy was, at that time, showing no signs of recovery. Although all OECD countries were undergoing prolonged recessions, the UK's was worse. Its unusual severity was based, firstly, on a strong and continued, anti-spending reaction by consumers and companies to their personal and corporate indebtedness. The high levels of this resulted, in no small measure, from the boom under Chancellor Nigel Lawson which had peaked in 1988. Since then debt repayment had caused consumption and house purchasing to fall off sharply. The debt to income ratio for householders was then without precedent; it was equal to one years' flow of total disposable income. The second cause of the lack of recovery had to do with the government's anti-inflationary stance which, as previously mentioned, was clearly deflationary in impact. Not the least significant of its effects was falling house prices, to the point where householders who had bought over the past 3 years were suffering from 'negative equity', a situation where the mortgage debt on the house was higher than the house value. The third element was the weakness of world demand and the seriousness of this for Britain's exports. One of the government's defences of its position was the fact that the recession was not just a UK affair: it was a global phenomenon.

The widespread conclusion from commentators was that Britain would suffer yet another year of recession and that the one per cent fall in interest rates announced on the 16th October 1992 was a necessary, but by no means sufficient, move towards what all government critics perceived to be required - a massive economic policy switch.

Attention was drawn by such critics to the UK's massive 1991 and 1992 balance of payments deficits, in which the overvaluation of sterling was held to have been a big factor in causing uncompetitiveness, and the revisions over the period 1986-92 in the official estimate of Britain's net overseas wealth. This, according to the latest Pink Book had declined from £100B to almost nothing.

If the Treasury were to fill old bottles with bank-notes, bury them at suitable depths in disused coal-mines which are then filled up to the surface with town rubbish, and leave it to private enterprise on well-tried principles of laissez faire to dig the notes up again, there need be no more unemployment and, with the help of the repercussions, the real income of the community, and its capital wealth also, would probably become a good deal greater than it actually is. It would, indeed, be more sensible to build houses and the like; but if there are political and practical difficulties in the way of this, the above would be better than nothing.

EXHIBIT 7: JOHN MAYNARD KEYNES' VIEW [10]

Parliament was, therefore, beginning its 1992-3 session against the backdrop of a media litany advocating the swiftest of all possible switches from *laissez faire* to moderate Keynesian economics. As, apparently, little could be done to alter the French protectionist stance on agriculture, which had resulted in yet another collapse of GATT talks, the leader writers advocated policies heavily in support of purely British interests. Even Howard Davies, Director General of the CBI and strong supporter of Maastricht ratification, was strongly in favour of a public spending round strongly weighted towards backing capital projects (with no pay rises for public sector employees) and a new White Paper on enterprise. This, he said:

must include longer-term priorities for public spending to correct our competitive weaknesses in infrastructure skills. There should be action on investment allowances and corporation tax. And it should flesh out Mr. Heseltine's welcome commitment to provide business support services comparative with the rest of the world.

But it was the growth in unemployment that was most responsible for the political outcry. With John Major only six months into his new administration (after a fourth consecutive Conservative poll victory), the condition of the UK job market was causing great anxiety. At current rates of progress and with UK unemployment at its highest level in October 1992 for five years, it was expected to top three million at the turn of the year.

Output and expenditure		
	1991 £bn at 1985 Prices	**91-92 % change**
Personal consumption	269.0	-0.9
Government consumption	81.9	1.4
Fixed capital	72.5	-3.6
Stockbuilding	-3.5	-0.1
Exports of non-oil goods and services	110.7	3.8
Imports of non-oil goods and services	123.8	6.5
GDP	408.6	-1.9

TABLE 3: UK ECONOMY PERFORMANCE COMPARISON
(Source C.S.O.)

The key question was, therefore, what the Major government could, would or should do to deal with these issues, as it began, on the 19th October 1992, its new parliamentary session. Minds were certainly going to be concentrated by the hostile mine closure motion that the Labour opposition had laid down for debate on the 21st October. The government, it seemed, could no longer count on the wholehearted support of its thin majority in the Commons to win the motion.

* * * * * * * * * * * * * * * * * * *

APPENDIX 1 : A NOTE ON ECONOMIC POLICY

The 1989-92 UK recession was the longest, by far, since the Second World War. It bore many resemblances to the slump of 1929-33. The key problem then had been a long-lasting, high fixed exchange rate coupled with an anti-inflationary government approach which drove down consumer prices by 15 per cent over the period 1925-34. But instead of making industry more competitive, the fact of the £'s being over-valued (by virtue of its being tied to the gold standard) exacerbated the effects of a world-wide economic downturn, especially in Britain. By the end of 1930 unemployment here had soared to the level of 2.5m and, because of the increasing pay-out of unemployment benefit, the government's budget had gone into deficit.

The Labour government of Ramsey Macdonald had been loath to leave the gold standard and negotiated large-scale credits to support the £. It, too, was assailed by a flood of speculation against the £. The National government that succeeded it in August 1931 attempted to shore up the tottering edifice by seeking to balance the budget via a ten per cent public pay cut. Neither stratagem succeeded and, despite further £ support operations, sterling was forced off the gold standard on September 20, 1931. Recovery eventually came in the mid 1930s but had more to do with the rearmament boom than it did with the lower exchange rate, the government's cheaper money policy and an end (after 85 years) to free trade through the imposition of a general tariff. This depression signposted the end, until the 1980's, of laissez faire economics. It heralded protectionism and interventionism throughout Europe.

One of the key elements in the recovery from the slump, in the 1930s was the 'monetising' of the budget deficit. Instead of financing the borrowing requirement £ for £ by selling gilts and savings certificates, the government financed a part of it by simply increasing the money supply. This it did by borrowing directly from the banks. This did not, however, since the banks could *create credit themselves,* siphon off investment funds that otherwise would have gone to industry.

So far as the UK situation in 1992 was concerned, the already well-extended and long-running debate between the NeoKeynesian school (led by Wynne Godley) and the NeoMonetarist school (with Professor Patrick Minford and Sir Alan Walters in the lead) became much more animated, but its particular contours led to considerable blurring of doctrinal positions.

The classical Keynes' approach is laid out in John Maynard Keynes' General Theory of Employment, Interest and Money (1936) which held that, contrary to previous popular belief, there are no natural tendencies (1) for an economy to reach equilibrium at full employment, nor (2) for markets to automatically stabilise themselves. Indeed, given that equilibrium could be reached at less than full employment and given the need on social and economic grounds to reduce unemployment, he advocated (a) a reduction in bank interest rates (to stimulate investment), (b) progressive taxation (to make incomes more equal and increase the per cent of income people spent on consumption) and (c) public works investment.

The Monetarist approach, by contrast, harks essentially back to the classical quantity theory of money which is expressed through the identities.

$$MV = PQ$$

Where M is the quantity of money, V is its velocity of circulation, P is the average price of goods and services and Q is the quantity of goods and services. It is oriented as an economic policy approach to the problem of dealing not so much with unemployment, as with that of inflation. Monetarists argue that changes in the money supply are the chief determinants of price levels and of production, employment and spending. They do not accept that fiscal policy is necessarily an effective stabilising device (as do the Keynesians) and object to the notion of 'fine tuning' the economy. The chief protagonist of Monetarism has been Professor Milton Friedman of Chicago. His belief is that changes in the money supply are, in fact, responsible for causing changes in the business cycle.

APPENDIX 2: SELECTED E.C. DATA

EC Country	Population M	GDP M ECU	GDP Per Capita [ECU]
UK	57.3	776,052	13,531
Belgium	9.9	149,985	15,087
Holland	14.9	218,092	14,602
Denmark	5.1	97,419	18,964
Germany	79.3	1,190,158	15,008
Ireland	3.5	29,606	8,396
Luxembourg	.3	9,289	24,613
France	56.4	931,850	16,509
Portugal	9.8	46,654	4,749
Spain	38.7	383,830	9,901
Italy	57.6	844,834	14,653
Greece	10.0	52,514	5,234

Source : OFFICIAL DATA, 1991

NOTES & REFERENCES

1   Setting the Pace of Finance from One Square Mile, Iain McKelerie, *The European,* 1-4/10/92

2   *The European* 8/10/92

3   Defiant Chancellor warns of clamp on public spending, Nicholas Wood and Ray Clancy, *The Times,* 9/10/92

4   Economic Policy in a Floating World, *The Financial Times,* 5/10/92

5   *The Sunday Times,* 18/10/92

6   Major to postpone debate on ERM reform. Philip Stevens and Alison Smith, *The Financial Times*, 5/10/92

7   Lucas, the British automotive and aerospace manufacturer declared 4,000 redundancies on the 12/10/92

8   13/10/92 Engineers hurt by Whitehall "paralysis" and lack of strategy, Patricia Tehan, *The Times*

9   *The Times* Editorial, 13/10/92

10   Quoted in Energy Strategy Burnt Out, *The Sunday Times,* 18/10/92

CANARY WHARF

Abstract:

The Reichmanns built prestigious city centre office blocs in the best locations - Toronto, New York and London. This case study deals predominately with the reasons for the collapse of their empire in 1992, despite what looked to be an excellent strategy, and its apparent recovery later.

Questions:

Explain the Reichmann family's strategy. What was their risk-return orientation?
Why did the Canary Wharf project fail at first and then later succeed?
Would you buy shares in Canary Wharf in September 1999?

Case Timing: 1992-1999

THE RISE AND FALL OF EMPIRE?

On the 15th May 1992 the world's largest property company, Olympia and York (O&Y), filed for bankruptcy protection in Toronto. What looked to be possibly the biggest private company collapse in recorded corporate history was an ignominious end to the dreams of the company's owners, the Reichmann family, once reputed to be the fifth richest family in the world.[1] It left in limbo the fate of the company's giant Canary Wharf development, Europe's biggest office complex, half-completed in London's Docklands.

Gerald Greenwald, installed as company president in place of Paul Reichmann, was at pains to reassure his Toronto press conference. *This is not*, he declared, *a bankruptcy. This is not a liquidation. This is not the end of O&Y. This is a restructuring.*[2] To which Steve Miller, the man chosen by the Reichmann family to lead the negotiations with the creditor banks, added forcefully *this is a strong, on-going company that will continue as the world's premier real estate development company.*[3]

It was indeed true that the Canadian Companies Creditors Arrangements Act and Chapter 11 of the US' Bankruptcy Code did allow a company's existing managers breathing space to seek a re-structuring. In Britain the UK equivalent of administration also allowed the same respite against the demands of creditors. This facility notwithstanding, it was a time of nightmare for the banks, credit institutions and world-wide investors who had for so long backed the company. O&Y's indebtedness amounted to no less than $12 billion.

The size of the difficulty was amply expressed by the reaction of the international stock markets to the news. The Canadian dollar sank to a two year low, the Nikkei fell 730 points to 18,074, fuelling further world-wide speculation of the imminence of a further cut-back in Japanese lending, and British banks and property companies were heavily marked down. The FTSE itself closed 12 points down, a tale of misery for all concerned.

It had not always been thus. The original fortunes of Paul Reichmann (ex-company president) and his two brothers had been made in the company they founded, Olympia Tile. This company had since expanded to become North America's biggest tile and carpet distributor. From the proceeds from its sale they were able in the 1960s to branch out into real estate. The Reichmanns began well in Toronto, their first *office city* came in 1975, and they built up steadily away from their home base. In the process, Paul Reichmann personally became one of the richest men in the world.

> The application of advanced communications technology means that knowledge-intensive businesses are becoming more flexible, with more services possibly contracted out to private companies - possibly 'spun-off' from within themselves. It also means that more employees can work more from home. At a time of increasing pressure to cut costs, this process will 'inexorably extend' to most of the service sector and to manufacturing also. The content of work will change, with some types of job becoming 'de-skilled' and some demanding higher levels of qualification. Companies will be come increasingly flexible in their employment patterns and there will be more 'freelancers' - independent professionals - selling their own 'work portfolios'.

EXHIBIT 1: THE HANDY VIEW [4]

O&Y's decision to buy the so-called Uris package of commercial buildings in Manhattan, precisely at the trough of the 1976 New York property slump, turned out to have been a spectacularly successful break-through. The value of this single portfolio item was to increase by a factor of ten over the next decade. It provided the basis for a swelling cash flow stream which enabled the company to both expand even more its commercial property interests and to diversify its industrial share-holdings. The bigger the company became, the more audacious were the Reichmanns' exploits - to the point where their supporters credited them with a degree of invincibility well-suited to the company's name.

By the mid 1980s O&York had become New York's biggest commercial landlord with 14 skyscrapers, all of high quality. The company was well on its way to creating its massive inventory of commercial property in Canada, USA and Britain.

> On the 19th May 1992 O&Y representatives told holders of $548m of notes, secured against the world's largest office building, that they stood to make huge losses on their investment. Predictions on the basis of the current slump in the Manhattan property market showed that the anticipated cash flow from rent in 1994 ($5.2m) would be insufficient to cover the interest payments on the notes ($35.9m)

EXHIBIT 2: THE TALE OF 55, WATER STREET, NEW YORK [5]

Not that there had not been mistakes in the past. In 1989 the company had lost heavily in its attempt to seek to rescue the Canadian real estate owner, Campeau Corporation, which had overstretched itself in acquiring two US retail groups. Furthermore, the changes which had taken place in the London property market since the purchase of a nine per cent Reichmann stake in Rosehaugh, the London developers, had also been wholly adverse and had made for a heavy loss on the deal.

But, until this most recent crisis, the company had been universally seen as inspired in its choice of property sites to develop and blessed with financiers and private partners. Each was selected, like the Hong Kong magnate Li Ka Shing, to help with specific building projects. O&Y had also been safely protected by its diffuse and complex legal structure which separated all assets from each other in such a way that creditor banks could not seize still-valuable properties to recoup their investment in others that had lost value. Thus, when O&Y's Canadian holding company (and its 28 subsidiaries) filed for bankruptcy protection, the move included neither its profitable Manhattan real estate nor Canary Wharf.

Nationality of Banks	Name of Bank	O&Y Debt Outstanding at 14th May 1992 [$]
Canadian	Imperial Bank of Commerce	1000
	Royal Bank	1000
	Nova Scotia	400
	Montreal	300
US	Citibank	400
	Chemical Bank	200
	Citicorp	500
Hong Kong	Hong King & Shanghai	800
European	Commerzbank	350
	Credit Lyonnais	350
	Barclays Plc	200
Japanese	Tokai, Fuji, Daiwa, Mitsubishi etc.	225

TABLE 1: OLYMPIA & YORK PARTIAL BANK DEBT
AT 14TH MAY 1992 (figures rounded) [7]

As a privately-owned company, O&Y had also enjoyed the obvious privilege of not having to give detailed financial information about itself, either to the financial community or, for that matter, to specific backers. It came as a considerable shock to many, therefore, when the value of O&Y's corporate investment portfolio was revealed on the 15th May 1992 as $3.1 billion (as against $4 billion in January), having fallen by 26 per cent since 1991.[6] Not only that, but the net worth of the company had dropped to $4.6 billion from its January 1991 level of $6.8 billion.

In spite of past prestige, the dramatic slide of the company was triggered very quickly in early 1992 by three newsworthy events. Firstly, the fact that, once the Dominion Bond Rating Service of Toronto had put O&Y's Canadian bond rating on 'alert', due to what was called *an unprecedented lack of investor confidence*, on February 13th, the company had been obliged to halt its attempt to roll over its $800m commercial paper programme. This was itself connected with the down-grading of two of O&Y Developments' Eurobond issues by Standard & Poor's (triple B minus down to B) and Moody's (Ba-1 down to B-1). These bonds had a face value of $548m and had been sold, as Exhibit 2 indicates, to help finance the 53-storey skyscraper at 55 Water Street, Manhattan. At the end of May 1992 they were trading at less than half face value and were classed by analysts as *very low grade speculative stock*, in short, *junk*.[7]

The second event was a lawsuit. It seems that the prime mover in squeezing company cash flow beyond the critical point was its British legal run-in with Morgan Stanley. In mid-May the High Court upheld its specific performance judgement whereby O&Y was ordered to pay an outstanding $240m claim by Morgan Stanley over a dispute concerning the bank's new HQ building at Canary Wharf. Clearly, it could not do so.

Then there was the fact that O&Y found itself unable to make due interest payments on its own Canadian flagship, a 72-storey marble sky-scraper in down-town Toronto, called First Canadian Place. This was the final straw.

THE GATHERING STORM

The 1992 crisis at O&Y had been building up over the last three years. The major difficulty, so far as Canada and the USA were concerned, was the extent of the company's investment in two sectors which were economically very exposed to the formidable economic recession of the early 1990's. The first was commercial property. In this sector, according to Brooking Institute's Anthony Downs, *the disaster is already so widespread that this (the O&Y collapse) doesn't hurt much anymore*.[9] By common consent it was certainly worse than the oil-induced 1974/5 property crash.

The range of building projects in which O&Y had invested was massive. In theory, the positive cash flow arising from these developments should have been so large as to enable the company to funds its debts without difficulty. In practice, in this recession, the amount of vacant office space in individual financial centres and overall, couples with the inevitable downward pressures on rents, had sharply reduced corporate income. One of the first hints of trouble for O&Y had, in fact, been its approach to Lazard Frères in November 1990 to try to get buyers for 20 per cent of its US property portfolio. Other evidence was not far to seek; the company's prestigious ITT building in New York was 100 per cent vacant.

Country	City	Key Developments	Space m sq ft	Vacant Space %
Canada	Calgary	Esso Plaza Shell Centre Amoco Building	2.84	8.6
	Toronto	First Canadian Place Scotia Plaza Aetna Building Exchange Tower	5.12	17.0
USA	New York	World Financial Centre Park Ave, Ave of the Americas Broad St. Water St. Liberty Plaza Broadway	23.0	18.0

TABLE 2: O&Y PROPERTY EMPIRE (N. AMERICAN MAJOR CITIES) [10]
Only properties above 0.65 m sq ft listed in these cities. O&Y owned about
40 m sq ft of office space in N. America in total.

The formula behind O&Y's market development strategy for commercial property had always been the same: move to new cities which were not being exploited - select prime commercial office locations which were under-valued, buy/build high-quality, architecturally-distinctive properties - take advantage of any special municipal grants and/or tax breaks, proceed speedily with debt finance secured. Combined in situations of strong economic growth, these elements were enough to make for a secure corporate asset base and strong cash flow. It was a formula that had been used over and over again to grow the company to its 1992 size and which succeeded best when the economic cycle was in O&Y's favour.

But the 1992 New York property market, for example, was in a highly depressed condition. Not only were rent values 30-40 per cent below the peak reached at the height of the business boom in 1987, meaning increasingly intense if not desperate competition for tenants, but there was a prevailing view among investors and bankers in 1992 that values would not rise again for three more years. Hence, prices for large (and even prestigious) downtown office blocks were heavily depressed.

O&Y's method of financing the developments, by placing considerable reliance on bank debt and bonds, was problematic for all parties only in the event of a serious down-turn in company cash flow. Not that the N. American bank lenders showed themselves interested in playing up the O&Y crisis. *The market realises that the world is not going to come to an end and that life goes on* declared a philosophical Reid Farrell, adviser to the Canadian Imperial Bank of Commerce.[11] Indeed, it was argued by Helen Sinclair of the Canadian Bankers Association that, not only was the Canadian banking system very well capitalised (*probably the best in the world*) but that O&Y 's problems would not result in a credit crunch.[12]   The estimated 3.3$ billion owed by the company to the Canadian banks indeed represented only 13 per cent of the banks' equity.

It was rumoured, however, that the Bank of England had stepped in on June 15th to support the Canadian dollar and there were strong worries in the property community about the ripple effect that might arise if O&Y property were sold into an already depressed market. Dan Mazankowski, Canadian Finance minister was especially concerned at this.

Company	Range of Activities & current results	Holding [%]
Gulf Canada Resources	Energy company. Net loss in 1991 C63$	74.0
Abitibi-Price	World's largest newsprint producer Loss in 1991 C76$m	82.0
Trizee Corp.	N. America's largest real estate corporation	35.0
Trilon	Financial corporation	10.0
Santa Fe Energy	Oil & Gas Producer	15.2
Santa Fe Pacific	Railways & Mining of the Aitcheson, Topeka and Santa Fe line	15.4
Home Oil of Calgary	Energy Producer	47.0

TABLE 3: O&Y CORPORATE INVESTMENT IN N. AMERICAN PUBLICLY-TRADED COMPANIES [13]

The second sector in which the Reichmanns had invested heavily was a mixture of industrial companies. As Table 3 indicates, energy pre-dominated. The problem here was the value of these companies as assets with which O&Y could satisfy creditors' claims. The fall of almost a third in the market value of these securities since 1990 was little short of a catastrophe for the company. As can be seen from Table 3, the portfolio was heavily oriented to energy and commodity stocks. The prices for the raw materials processed by the companies in question had slumped since the onset of the recession.

The extent of O&Y's difficulties in these two areas could not be hidden despite the vigour of the O&Y fightback. This involved, to begin with, the hiring of top-notch 'financial engineers' Gerald Greenwald and Steve Miller as turnaround specialists. As the very first high-ranking 'outsider executives' in this highly secretive company, it was they who, presented the initial restructuring plan to banks on the 18th April. It sought more short-term capital and a debt moratorium and made a commitment to 'no asset sales'. They pointed out that, despite the O&Y debt of $12 billion, the alternative to acceptance was *a Doomsday scenario*. Paul Reichmann would not be a member of the committee to implement the restructuring plan, it was stated.

By the 7th May, and after defaults on payments on mortgages on the World Financial Centre (New York) and Scotia Plaza (Toronto), the company's message was different. This time equity shares in the company were being proposed as a trade for a selective debt write-off and, as Gerald Greenwald pointed out, this included participation in *the crown jewel*, the Canary Wharf project. For this plan to succeed, $700m extra would be needed immediately. *Neither the company nor the banks can win without the other* he said and with these funds *we plan to finish Canary Wharf and.the Jubilee Line... in 1996.*[14]

This too did not avail and JP Morgan, the US investment bank, went ahead with foreclosure proceedings on the 13th May.

CAPITAL IN CRISIS

It was in London that the fall in property values had been felt most keenly. Here the slump was already three years old and, in the words of Gerald Ronson of property magnate Heron International, *this property recession is deeper than anyone in business today can remember. We have seen nothing like it before.*[15] The city centre office market was especially hard hit with vacancy rates already at 18 per cent and rents on new lettings down by a third on 1991 levels.[16] Obviously, under such circumstances, buildings under construction or recently-completed represented a pure and open invitation to developers and banks to, ultimately, squander money.

As can be imagined, builders, valuers and auditors had, since 1989, stalwartly and consistently under-rated the impact of the rising recession, optimism being clearly part of their professional duty. Now, at the start of 1992, there was simply no escape from the harsh task of fully revaluing assets.

And it was not only the property developers who faced problems in this regard. A reduction in the value of the assets of a highly-geared property company posed as much a difficulty for its banks as it did for the company itself.

In fact it was the case, as Stephen Mansell, Midland bank economist, pointed out, that *the market is so thin, it is hard to ascertain what the real market value of property is.*[17]

The City had borne the brunt of the downward slide in values. There was, in April 1992, already a stock of unlet office space in London equivalent to the entire office supply of Birmingham and Manchester combined.[18] And, as if that were not problem enough, according to Allied Property Research, permission had already been granted for another 100m sq. ft., enough to increase London office space by a staggering 50 per cent.

The top five UK property companies, Land Securities, MEPC, Hammerson, Slough Estates and British Land, had, between them, suffered a fall in market capitalisation from £7299m on the first of September 1989 to £4441 on the fourth of April 1992.[19]

Positive Factors	Negative Factors
London's air links Telecommunications system	Lack of co-ordinated transport/housing policy
Self-regulatory environment	Poor road & rail links
Skilled workforce	Quality of life

TABLE 4: THE FOREIGN BANKERS' VIEW OF LONDON [20]

The ultimate reason behind the dramatic expansion in the supply of office space in London was plain. Mrs Thatcher's Conservative government had created a set of expansionary conditions in the UK economy in the second half of the 1980s through a powerful relaxation of monetary policy. This strategy was paralleled by a similar growth in money supply in the USA and Japan where it had led to problems with the Savings & Loan débâcle and the after-effects of the ending of the bubble economy, respectively.

So far as Britain was concerned, it had led to an uplift in the extent of the service economy, especially in the South East of the country. Coupled with the prospects arising from Big Bang (financial deregulation) in 1986, the start of this strategy for regeneration conjured up a commonly-held view of virtually never-ending demand for City office space. Developers hastened to enter into the spirit of the thing with an explosive building spree.

At the start of the 1980s the office stock was growing (in 1990 prices) by £1 billion per year; by 1990 this figure was over £5 billion. It became, ultimately, a matter of hubris.

For London firms, rising office availability was of clear benefit. Yet, for some of them, it also posed severe decision problems, as between staying in London or moving out to cheaper accommodation and other attractions in the provinces. For those who needed to stay, the fall in rental values and a possible change in the conditions of the lease, typically from 25 years with five-yearly price reviews (and upward only reviews at that) to on-going leases with break clauses, was a life line. And, given the impact of the recession overall on services employment in the South East, it was a life-line they were only to eager to seize.

What of the exposure of UK banks to loans secured against property? Certainly, banking supervision had improved dramatically since the 1973/5 property crash and moves to adopt the European Community Capital Adequacy Directive offered safeguards but, even so, longer memories harked back to the admonition that the Governor of the Bank of England had given in May 1987 to the banks. Then he had warned against property overlending in view of the fact that bank loan books had risen by 70 per cent since 1985. By 1992 it had, in fact, reached a staggering £40 billion.[21] UK banks and insurance companies were reacting to the economic crisis and the new technology opportunities now available (e.g., Automatic Teller Machines) by initiating their redundancy programmes. These began to roll in early 1992.

Bank	Loans [£b] April 5, 1992	Loans as % of Shareholder's Equity	1991 Return on Equity
Barclays	5.4	94	8.0
Lloyds	2.5	101	22.3
Natwest	2.5	42	1.8
Midland	1.8	78	1.4

TABLE 5: UK MAJOR CLEARING BANK DATA (1991 and 1992)
Note: The combined bad debt provision of these banks
on March the sixth 1992 was £4416m. [22]

Another major additional challenge was faced by London's office developers in 1992. It was the impact of Britain's membership of the Exchange Rate Mechanism on the country's trading capability, as it fed through into the balance of payments on current and capital account. The fact that Britain had entered, irrevocably it seemed, a fixed parity system eliminated the government's ability to alter the parity of the currency and reduced to a minimum the government's independent control over interest rates. In fact, the level of interest rates in the UK over the period 1991 and 1992 was said by critics to owe more to the requirements of German unification - high rates can stimulate international lending as well as curbing inflationary pressures - than it did to UK domestic economic policy.

Indeed, although the British government was justifiably proud of the extent to which the ERM-induced rates had slowed down price rises in the UK economy, the deflationary effects on output and employment were obvious. So much so, that the USA broke ranks with other G7 members at the start of July 1992 by reducing its base interest rate to three per cent to try to stimulate its flagging economy.

Centre	Total Occupation cost. £/sq. metre [1]	Capital Value ECU/sq. metre [2]
London West End	761	10,860
City	718	9,600
Paris	650	12,700
Frankfurt	449	12,170
Milan	412	8,579
Manchester	308	3,860
Brussels	220	3,860
Amsterdam	162	3,170

TABLE 6: FIGHTING HARD [23]

Note (1) Rental values relate to a sample of typical prime office properties
(2) Notional typical prime site capital value based on typical rents and yields

CAPITAL COLLAPSE

It was the £1.6 billion Canary Wharf development which epitomised all these problems. Not only was it Europe's biggest commercial development and, as such, aimed at maintaining London's primacy as the leading European financial capital, but it was also a prime symbol of the 1980s brand of economic liberalism that came to be known in Britain as 'Thatcherism'.

The Conservative government led by Mrs Thatcher had set up the Docklands Development Corporation (LDDC) in 1981 as an agency to utterly rejuvenate this major and derelict part of the city of London. So bad were conditions that, at the time, the land was held to have negative value.

British Telecom are carrying out a one-year experiment into 'Tele-working'. This allows some jobs to be done from home, using E Mail and videophones. The new technology available allows all homeworkers to remain in contact with colleagues and supervisors. The company estimates that, by 1995, some two million Britons could be working three days a week at home in this way.

EXHIBIT 3: THE FUTURE OF WORK? [24]

Despite being the focus of political attention, Mrs Thatcher herself turned the first sod on the site - Canary Wharf made little progress under the LDDC until 1987 when, at the height of the commercial property boom, O&Y bought 72 acres at a 'give-away' price of £400,000 per acre and began building their 'crown jewel' complex. It was scheduled to consist of 13 buildings in all, each of the highest quality, in a parkland setting with mature trees (imported from Germany), statues and fountains. Only the first two building phases had been completed, creating 4.5m sq. ft. of office space as opposed to the planned 10m. and costing £1.6 billion. This included the stunning and prestigious Canary Wharf Tower, justly described as the only 'world-class skyscraper' in London.[25]

By May 31st 1992 only 2500 people were working at Canary Wharf (out of the potential 25,000), it was only 14 per cent let. It was said that, with rent holidays and fitting allowances, the return per sq. ft. actually being achieved was considerably below the original asking price of £30 per sq. ft. Even so, few companies had been attracted to a site which, however desirable, offered few amenities (shops, cafes etc.) which were open. Even less so, once Enterprise Zone tax breaks ended in April 1992 and the burden of the Uniform Business Rate (payable even on empty office space) was included in the equation.

Perhaps the main cause of difficulty in signing up tenants was accessibility. Canary Wharf was three miles from the City and poorly served by the much over-loaded Docklands Light Railway and the River Bus. O&Y contributed financially to the Railway as part of the agreement whereby the company developed Canary Wharf as a private sector operation and the Department of the Environment, through the LDDC deal, bore the main responsibility for creating the infrastructure. So far, an estimated £3.5 billion of public money had been spent on this and on direct and indirect subsidies to the developers.

London's status as a world financial centre and Europe's business capital is undoubted.. I welcome the decision of the Lord Mayor of London and the Corporation of London to undertake a campaign to ensure that any European Central Bank (as called for in the Treaty of Maastricht) is located in London.
Edmund Dell, President, London Chamber of Commerce & Industry.

EXHIBIT 4: STATEMENT OF REAL INTENT [26]

It was estimated that completing the Canary Wharf infrastructure would cost the Treasury a further inescapable £1.5 billion, since the transport element that remained to be built, the extension to the under-ground Jubilee Line to link Canary Wharf in to the City, was the key to the success of the entire venture. It is this project that O&Y had pledged to pay £400 million towards. The first tranche of £40m had fallen due in early 1992 and O&Y had been unable to meet its obligations.

Apparently, Paul Reichmann had foreseen none of this as he was appraising the risks involved in the project. Comparing it with the World Financial Centre he had built in Manhattan's Battery Park, he had stated in 1990 that *doing one building here (at Canary Wharf) would be risky; doing nearly a dozen is not. On a scale of one to ten, if you say the risk with Battery Park was nine, here it would be one.*[27]

The attitude of the Major government to tight public spending control during the recessionary period in the early 1990s lay behind the heavy stress it placed on the need for a contribution by the property developers of Canary Wharf to the Jubilee Line cost. This commitment, it made abundantly clear, was to be met by any future owners.

For almost two years, the government's counter-inflationary strategy has been based on sterling's membership of the exchange rate mechanism. The ERM is not an optional extra, an add-on to be jettisoned at the first hint of trouble. It is and will remain at the very centre of our macro-economics strategy. Retail price inflation has fallen from nearly eleven per cent at the time of entry to less than four per cent today. As inflation has come down, we have been able to cut interest rates nine times from 15 per cent to ten per cent today - below the average of the last 10 years. Both Management and unions are getting the message that it we want to compete with the rest of Europe, we must not award ourselves pay increases far in excess of their levels. Britain's trade performance has confounded the pessimists. Exports are at a record level. I cannot believe we could have achieved all this outside the ERM. But despite these achievements, and the progress we are making towards our medium-term objectives, there are those who try to blame the present difficult economic situation on our membership of the ERM. As soon as the going gets rough, the quest begins for the easy way out. They cast around for a painless, cost-free route to higher growth with low inflation. I would be the last person to say that, to coin a phrase, there is no alternative to our present policy. Plenty of alternatives are suggested. But in my view, they are all illusory or destined to fail. They would not deliver low inflation. The cut-and-run option? Cut interest rates and (you get) a run on the pound. As the Russians say, only mousetraps have free cheese....

EXHIBIT 5: THE CHANCELLOR SPEAKS [29]

Given the apparently poor commercial viability of the operation, it is not surprising that the banks funding the London development were gloomy about this particular burden. They themselves had finally lost patience with providing bridging finance and speculating on the attractiveness of debt-for-equity swaps. They called in the administrator, Ernst and Young, on the 28th May to try to unravel the problem. He had one bare month to find a route out of O&Y bankruptcy. They had lent O&Y over £500m and the most realistic value that could be placed on the Canary Wharf development was £600m.[28]

The tenants, too, could not have been content with the turn of events. The interest that KPMG Peat Marwick, Manufacturers Hanover Trust (MHT) and the *Daily Telegraph* had in moving to Canary Wharf had been partly determined by the fact that O&Y had been prepared to buy the leases on some or all of their previous London offices. In the case of MHT it was 40,000 sq. ft. of office accommodation at 7 Princes St. that was 'taken back'. This made at least for some commitment to stay. However, a group of the most concerned tenants, including Texaco, Ogilvy & Mather, Morgan Stanley and Maersk met on the 29th May to form a pressure group to ensure that the administrators would honour all O&Y promises on the project - maintenance of the estate, development of the retail facilities and transport - especially the loss-making River Boat owned by O&Y.

Other potential tenants whom O&Y had wooed intensively, with inducements such as (it was rumoured) initial rent holidays, included American Express, Texaco and several government departments (Environment, Transport & Trade). The government said that it would only consider a move if Canary Wharf offered *good value for money... on a strictly commercial basis*.[30] The two American companies were, so it was said,[31] on the point of refusing to go ahead with the deal unless they too had all undertakings honoured.

If all prospective tenants did in fact relocate the occupancy rate would rise from the existing minuscule level to 40 per cent. Clearly, the administrators needed this to help them with marketing the rest of the £1.6 billion project.

What the administrators did not need was the enormous negative impact on business confidence that resulted initially from the UK government's forced decision, on the 16th September 1992 to suspend its membership of the ERM. This had been caused by an unprecedented weight of international speculation against what was regarded as an artificially high £ value. The governments' move was in flat contradiction of all its previous policy statements and its apparent wish to meet some of the elementary monetary criteria set for Economic Monetary Union within the EC.

As for Paul Reichmann himself, he had been, it seemed, transformed from the "Einstein of Real Estate" into "The Man Who Blew $10 Billion." [32]

THE PHOENIX RISES

It did not take long, however, before Paul Reichmann bounced back. In late summer 1992 he helped put together a consortium of investors to buy Canary Wharf from the creditors who had halted O&Y's London operation in its tracks. The attempt failed but was repeated successfully in 1995 when the banks indicated they were only delighted to sell the complex for £800m. With a five per cent stake in a consortium which included the Tisch family and the Saudi prince Alwaleed bin Tala bin Abdulaziz Algaud, Paul Reichmann was again at home in Canary Wharf. Perhaps he needed to be, because it was estimated by the British media that his family had lost at least a billion dollars over Canary Wharf.

But not just at home, however. On the 25th March 1999 Canary Wharf PLC went to market with an initial public offering of 27 per cent of its stock. Paul Reichmann, executive chairman, held a stake of eleven per cent in the company which was capitalised at approximately $4 billion, alongside other members of the lending team that had bailed out the project in 1995. Canary Wharf was on its way, rents were $58 per sq ft, lower than in the City but acceptably high, and looking smart. It was thought that, whilst the complex had lost $2.5 billion in the two fiscal years to 1999, it would make profit by 2001.[33] Certainly, by September 1999 its rental income was said to be *surging*.[34]

Investors could also reckon with three additional attractive features. Firstly, the 81-acre office development still benefitted from the massive tax allowances made available by Mrs Thatcher's Conservative government to the developers. Secondly, the company had hundreds of millions of pounds in tax losses (available, that is, to offset against future profits) as a result of the 1992 collapse. Thirdly, the Jubilee Line was up and running.

So, the question was how would investors react to the sale of a further slice of the company's equity announced on the 27th September 1999? The price was 391p and it was intended to raise £200m. After all, Canary Wharf still had 6.5m sq ft potentially available for development.

* * * * * * * * * * * * * * * * * * *

NOTES & REFERENCES

1   Recession and energy prices trip Reichmanns, *The Independent,* 16/5/92
2   O&Y's leaning tower of debt, Lorana Sullivan, *The Observer*, 17/5/92
3   As 2
4   Walking the Tightrope, London Business School Professor Charles Handy, Conference, 3/7/92
5   (a) O&Y tells Water street investors they face big loss, Bernard Simon & Robert Peston, *The Financial Times*, 20/5/92
     (b) Water Street cash dries up for Olympia bondholders, Mattew Bond, *The Times*, 20/5/92
6   As 2
8   (a) Debt shakes a $20 billion edifice to its foundations, Vanessa Houlder, Robert Peston, Bernard Simon and Allan Friedman, *The Financial Times*, 30/3/92
     (b) O&Y sends tremors around the world, Clyde Farnsworth, *International Herald Tribune*, 16-17/5/92
     O&Y bonds ranked as junk, Philip Robinson, *The Times*, 1/5/92
9   Worrying but no panic on bankruptcy filing, Lawrence Malkin, *The International Herald Tribune*, 16-17/5/92
10   As 8a
11   As 9
12   As 9
13   As 8a
14   O&Y invites bankers to become shareholders, Matthew Bond, *The Times*, 8/5/92
15   Property men find there is no hiding place from the slump, Matthew Bond, *The Times*, 3/4/92
16   As 15
17   London to let, Rufus Olins and Matthew Lynn, *The Sunday Times*, 5/4/92
18   As 17
19   As 17
20   London Chamber of Commerce & Industry *Annual Review*, 1991-2
21   Property's £40 billion debt crisis, Nick Goodey & Stella Shamoon, *The Observer*, 5/4/92
22   (a) *The Economist* 9/3/92 and (b) 17
23   *The European* 14-17/5/92
24   BT pilot scheme allows operators to work at home, Diane Summers, *The Financial Times*, 2/7/92
25   Docklands merits our commitment, *The Sunday Times* Business comment, 29/3/92
26   as 20
27   Nightmare in Docklands, *The Observer*, 31/5/92

28   Canary Wharf valued at £600m, 12/6/92

29   Extracts from a speech by UK Chancellor Norman Lamont to the European
        Policy Forum on 10/7/92

30   Ministers stall on O&Y, Rufus Olins, *The Observer*, 24/2/92

31   Top three Canary Wharf residents threaten to quit, Angela Mackay, *The Times*,
        26/6/92

32   Anthony Bianco, *Family, Faith, Fortune and the Empire of Olympia and York*,
        Times Books, 1997

33   Canary Wharf has something to sing about, Kerry Cappell, *Business Week*,
        15/3/99

34   Canary Wharf cuts loss for year, *The International Herald Tribune*, 18-19/9/99

35   as 34

GATT

Abstract:

The GATT case study deals in a wide-ranging fashion with a variety of issues all central to the conclusion of its Uruguay Round of GATT. For instance, questions of protectionism, NAFTA-EU trade bloc rivalries (and, in that context, the creation of APEC) and the implications for economic prospects in China, Japan and the UK. All of these carry immense connotations of future uncertainties for the European business community. This case can be read as part of the sequential stages in EU development covered by the European PLC, ERM and EMU cases.

Question:

Was John Major entitled to be so enthusiastic about the GATT result so far as Britain is concerned?

Case Timing: 1993

WINNERS, ALL?

Superb. That was how British prime minister John Major described the deal that successfully ended the Uruguay round of the General Agreement of Tariffs and Trade (GATT). After an inordinate period of international wrangling a deal had finally been struck at the eleventh hour of the deadline day, the 15th December 1993. In a statement to the House of Commons [1] John Major said:

After seven years of long, hard and often fraught negotiations.. it removes the threat of collapse in the world trade system.

Britain was the world's fifth-largest exporter of goods and commercial services. Indeed, it ranked higher in the global league table for exports per capita than either the USA or Japan. Hence the importance of the agreement as *a platform for recovery, growth and jobs* to a country which already had some of the most open markets in the world. Britain would, continued the statement, *be one of the biggest gainers from cuts in worldwide tariffs, quotas and other restrictions.* According to an independent estimate, the deal would add as much as four per cent to its national product and 400,000 extra jobs would be created in Britain over the coming decade.

Trade Group	1967	1992	2013 (forecast)
OECD	65.6	55.0	35.0
Asia-Pacific	11.2	19.8	36.0
Others	23.2	25.2	29.0

TABLE 1: WHO'S WHO IN WORLD GDP (%) RANKINGS
Source: OECD Data

This was welcome news. In the 1993 European Union (EU) annual award of regional aid, based on comparative unemployment rates, Britain had scored highest. The European Commission had indicated in its report that the country continued to suffer the worst industrial decline in the Union by awarding it £1.69 billion in aid, the largest award made. For the very first time parts of London were selected for aid as unemployment blackspots.

Among the UK's chief expected GATT beneficiaries were Scotch whisky producers. They exported products worth over £2 billion per year and would gain substantially from lower prices brought about by the tariff cuts negotiated. In Japan and Singapore whisky prices would fall by between 25 per cent and 30 per cent, for instance. Chemicals and pharmaceutical manufacturers stood to gain heavily, also. The latter now faced a zero tariff in respect of their sales to the USA and Japan.

ICI was one such company. It foresaw a bright future in post-GATT times, even in a congested and highly competitive market-place, arising from new forms of strategic alliances among producers. In a speech to the Society of the Chemical Industry at its European annual meeting in Rome on the fourth of October 1993, chairman Sir Denys Henderson stated that such alliances were an 'imaginative', as well as a logical, answer to the challenges of meeting the massive capital needs of high-risk, long-term businesses in this sector. Old-style outright mergers and large-scale, all-purpose conglomeracy were not now necessarily appropriate to achieving scale economies in a more open world trading system.

Element	Canada	Mexico	USA
Population (m)	27	81.2	254.7
GDP ($ billion)	582	283	5611
GDP/capita ($)	21,537	3,485	22,204

TABLE 2: NORTH AMERICAN MARKET (1991 DATA)
Source : OECD, IMF.

Note that the NAFTA 1993 pact eliminates tariffs between the three countries over the next 20 years. It creates the world's largest trading bloc with a combined output of $7 trillion and a population of 370m. By way of comparison the European Economic Area has a population of 354m.

Eduard Balladur, the French prime minister, shared the euphoria of his EU colleague, John Major - but for different reasons. He had succeeded in winning last-minute compromises in the heated negotiations for the French position in two areas which were seen by his government as crucial: the continuation of acceptable levels of EU financial support for French farmers and the exclusion of the audio-visual sector from the GATT deal. Both were referred to in the statement he made to the Assemblée Nationale on the 15th December [2] when he declared:

We have obtained more than we dared hope even a month ago. The Blair House pre-agreement (on permissible world levels of agricultural subsidies) was re-negotiated. Our European partners supported us in the negotiations. We have managed to preserve the future of French culture (by refusal to accept US demands for greater market openness to American films etc.). The agreement we have reached is in the long-term interest of France.

It was a statement which drew wide-spread acclaim in France, not least because of how the Prime Minister was seen as having successfully resisted American 'cultural imperialism' pressures. The threat to French indigenous culture posed by the overweening power of Hollywood had, indeed, been averted and the danger of further rural decline reduced. No wonder Alain Carignon, French communications minister, was inspired to call it *a beautiful victory.*[3]

The European Union unanimously endorsed the deal on the 15th December. It was expected that US President Bill Clinton, having just steered the North American Free Trade Agreement (NAFTA) successfully through Congress, would face no real difficulty in achieving ratification of the GATT agreement in 1994. Similar hopes existed that all other members of the 116-nation GATT organisation would do likewise by the deadline of end 1994. The popular view was that all had been winners.

A QUESTION OF RICE

There were high hopes that, whatever else it achieved, the GATT deal would be instrumental in opening up protected markets, such as that for agriculture, in so-called 'protectionist' countries. US farmers were especially keen, for instance, that the Japanese rice market should be opened up. This had long been a major stumbling block in bilateral US-Japan negotiations, strangely enough since Japan was the world's biggest food importer.

Since the 1930s, in fact, the Japanese government had strictly controlled the output and distribution of rice as a staple food. Price-setting, too, had remained a government prerogative, the level current in December 1993 being about six times the world market price. In the event that rice had to be imported, due to a Japanese crop failure, for example, the government profited by selling, as a monopoly supplier and at internal prices, the supplies it had obtained at low world prices. In 1992 when the Japanese harvest was badly affected by adverse weather, imports amounting to eight per cent of domestic consumption were the order of the day.

The policy of support for the rice farmers had seemingly contributed to the electoral supremacy of the Liberal Democratic Party over the period 1955-93. It was said by bitter critics to have *bought the votes of farmers.*[4] Whilst such aid had clearly given stability in terms of the country's food supply, it had also clearly institutionalised the inefficient use of land. The average rice-growing plot size was less than a hectare. Notably, also, the majority of rice farmers were aged over 60 and the agricultural population was a distinctly ageing one.

The GATT talks swayed Japan's view on rice. It agreed to allow four per cent of Japanese rice requirements to be imported, over a six-year period of grace. After this, the volume would rise to eight per cent, but there would be negotiations about 'tariffication', involving duties possibly as high as 700 per cent. The final agreement was accepted by the Japanese Prime Minister Morihiro Hosokawa with a hesitant statement that *the day will come when this decision will be judged positively by history.*

The GATT talks also affected Japan's views on other trade matters. With widespread anxiety being expressed in Japan at the seeming fall in the country's international competitiveness, and the effect of the post-GATT market openness, the appeal of further offshore investment grew apace.

The problem was, according to Mineko Sasaki-Smith of Morgan Stanley, that Japan was suffering from a form of 'structural gridlock',[5] shaped by a set of inter-related factors. These were, first, the impact of the 1989-93 global recession in Japan. An exceptional fall in domestic demand and declining exports, especially, were now causing a steep drop in corporate profits, asset values (like the shares listed on the Nikkei index or property) and real wages. These, in their turn, were exacerbating the recession.

Second, systemic rigidities in the Japanese politico-economic system were bolstering operating inefficiencies and slowing down productivity growth. Important among these were 'the job for life' policy still practised by many Japanese firms, the corporatist nature of the banking-industry complex and the statutory protection of certain sectors of the country's retail trade.

The third factor in the circular equation was the rising value of the yen. This had been driven relentlessly upwards by Japan's massive trade surplus with the USA and the EU. The surplus on trade with the former was anticipated to be $55 billion for 1993, no less. By the start of December 1993, the yen had reached the level of 105 yen/dollar and, to the immense worry of politicians like trade minister, Hiroshi Kumagai, was clearly undermining the future for exports from Japan.

The last significant factor was the potential bad debt problem facing Japanese banks. The fact was that Japanese banks, partly as a product of the tight banking-industry relationship mentioned above, were carrying some 50 trillion yen of commercial debt. Some 60 per cent of the debt was considered doubtful since it was collateralised against property whose value had fallen since 1989 by 50 per cent as a result of recession.

The conventional answer to Japan's problem of declining internal competitiveness was taken to be yet another 'bold program of fiscal stimulus' to get the economy moving ahead, say, through government-financed public works programmes.[6] There had been no shortage of reflationary moves of this nature since 1991.

By contrast, the unconventional answer was said to be for Japan to tear down even more of the trade barriers than called for within the GATT deal and expose the protected Japanese market-place itself to greater international competition in order to regain more of its competitive edge.

This latter would, if applied, pose an unusual challenge to the newly-elected government of Morihiro Hosakawa: how to deal with any potential politically-damaging increase in Japan's official 2.8 per cent unemployment rate and/or in the number of the 'hidden unemployed'. These were employees who were typically surplus to company requirements but retained on the payroll - a major convention in Japanese business culture. Their number was put by the Sumitomo Life Research Institute at 2.5m.[7]

A meeting of the USA's leading Japanologists was held in Santa Fe in late 1993 to discuss the issue. Entitled Japan as a Techno-Economic Superpower, it debated whether Japan could or would change its nature as a corporatist, 'state-led' economy. This was an economy based on a business culture bedrock of subsidised capital for industry, huge highly-integrated and powerful conglomerates, mutually beneficial government-industry links and high import resistance. It is noteworthy that this was a form of business culture copied by many of Japan's trade partners on the Asian seaboard.

Would Japan move towards a US-style, laissez-faire capitalism and a firm belief in free trade? The Japanologists' response was unequivocally *No*.[8]

And yet Japan had signed up to the GATT accord and had recently shown real signs of opening up its car and semiconductor market to American companies. What was its real intent on free trade? The USA had long been pre-occupied with this. Given that the triad of the USA, Japan and the European Union were responsible for producing almost two thirds of global GNP and almost 60 per cent of world trade, its interest was not surprising. Rice was, therefore, seen as one touchstone of whether or not GATT could open up the Japanese market for manufactured goods. In 1963 Japan imported 2.5 per cent of its manufactured goods; in 1993 it was still importing just three per cent, as against the US level of eight per cent.

Were Japanese industrialists happy about the GATT outcome for their country? Not if the Nikkei index was any guide. Whereas in Britain, the FTSE index was hitting all-time record levels by the end of 1993, helped not a little by the government's expansionary policy of low inflation and low interest rates, the Nikkei finished the year at 17,417. Of this total, 597 points alone had been added, with heavy governmental support, in the last three days of the year. This was a far cry from the halcyon days of 1988/9 when it had hit the 40,000 mark.

Opinion in the USA was also divided on the ability of the Japanese manufacturers to take full advantage of the market-opening opportunities that the GATT deal would offer. There were those who believed the thesis that the USA was suffering from 'imperial overstretch' and inescapable decline, much to the benefit of Japan. The highly credible theory advanced by Yale historian Paul Kennedy in his Rise and Fall of the Great Powers indicated that all empires eventually began to suffer from impotence. They simply cost too much to maintain. The USA, on this basis, would, he asserted, travel the self-same path that the British Empire had travelled before.

Supporters of this theory of historical inevitability saw Japan as the natural inheritor of the US' mantle of economic power. They focused attention on Japan's undeniable and enduring strengths, a well-educated, highly-skilled and strongly-disciplined workforce; consistently out-standing levels of spending on high-technology R&D; powerful manufacturing capabilities, especially in miniaturisation and automation; negligible government budget deficit; low consumer debt and a consumer savings rate of 15 per cent; a staggering $120 billion annual trade surplus.

Others were not so sure of Japan's potential. The USA, they argued, had regained its pre-eminent position as the leading world maker of cars and semi-conductors and was pulling strongly out of recession when the Japanese economy and polity were still heavily affected by slump conditions. For them Japanese weaknesses were all-too-visible, a comparative Japanese technology-lag in certain strategic industries like software, systems integration and information highways, when compared to the USA; the strategic impact of low-priced imports such as Compaq and Dell PCs; grave political uncertainties about the future; the growing lack of competitiveness in terms of wage costs and yen parity.

APEC

In the 25 years to 1992 Asia's newly-industrialising countries (NICs) – Korea, Hong Kong, Singapore and Taiwan – had averaged eight per cent p.a. growth in real incomes. In fact, it had been reliably estimated in 1992 that, if current rates of development were to continue, South Korea's real GDP would exceed Britain's in less than two decades.[9] Manufacturing investment funds from around the globe were continuing to pour into the region to take advantage of the competitive advantages the NICs had on offer.[10]

These statistics point to four widely-discussed hypotheses which are of significance to the GATT global trade debate. Firstly, that the later countries industrialise, the faster they do it and the more modern the technology they employ. Japan and Germany both began their large-scale primary industrialisation drives in earnest only in the 1870s, for example. Their re-industrialisation, after the ravages of the Second World War, involved the creation of innovative and new-technology production methods not applied at the same speed or to the same extent by the victors.

The second hypothesis is that labour-intensive, low/intermediate technology industries will increasingly be located in low-wage or even poor regions, such as the NICs listed above, provided, of course, that their workforces can be educated/trained to required world standards of productivity, flexibility and quality.

The European Community has failed to foresee, or even to recognise, the massive shift of wealth and power from Europe to the Pacific Asia or the equally great shift.. in North America from the Atlantic to the Pacific coasts.. In global terms, Europe has been outpaced by Asian economic performance. It is fashionable to point to the problems of China - inflation, agrarian discontent, the imbalance between the industrial and peasant populations, widespread corruption.. Yet the growth of the Chinese economy continues to be spectacular.. By 2000, the real size of the Chinese economy is likely to be equal to that of the present EC.

EXHIBIT 1: THE CHINA FACTOR
Source: What the bloc-heads miss, William Rees-Mogg, *The Times*, 25/11/93

Thirdly, that global investment will increasingly be channelled to regions which meet such fast development criteria. It is quite possible, of course, that incremental units of high technology investment will produce relatively few new jobs per unit. Indeed, if made such investment is made in industries where the productivity (i.e., output/worker) is low, then the new technology could displace workers through a shift in the man-machine balance. Naturally, account must also be taken in reviewing investment outcomes of supply-side rigidities in the workings of economies. An example of this occurred over the period 1971-1990 in Europe. Here, only 10 million extra jobs were created, as opposed to the 30m in the USA. In Europe the high wage levels required, the high start-up costs for small new businesses and the trade union restrictions applied militated against the creation of new high-value jobs. In the USA, none of these elements applied. In short, one of the results of global restructuring could well be, therefore, 'jobless growth' in some of the world's advanced economies.

> *Clinton grandly proposes that members of an obscure grouping called APEC should become a free trade zone. But.. reconciling the structural mercantilism of the Asian development model with the general openness of the US will not be accomplished by generic appeals to free trade.. The one concrete step taken at Seattle was a joint pledge to cut tariffs.. The serious barriers are, of course, non tariff ones.*

EXHIBIT 2: THE VOICE OF DISBELIEF [11]

The last hypothesis is, that, if the first three premises are valid, the world's economic centre of gravity will ultimately shift from today's rich countries to today's poor ones.[12] Of course, as the poor nations become richer, their competitive capability will be expected to decline, if only because of the appreciation of their currency and the expectations of rising living standards among their populations.

The APEC (Asia-Pacific Economic Co-operation) forum was set up in 1989 to try to increase multi-lateral trade co-operation among Pacific regions and to spur forward economic endeavour on the basis of growing NIC success. Its members are Australia, New Zealand, Canada, USA, Japan and the six members of the ASEAN trade bloc, Brunei, Indonesia, Malaysia, Philippines, Singapore and Thailand. China, Hong Kong and Taiwan were admitted in 1991.

It was partly to harness the formidable economic potential of the NICs that the USA first collaborated in building up the APEC platform. The growth rates of the NICs had increasingly revealed the need for US involvement in the steering process. In fact, only two days after Congress had agreed his plan to establish the North American Free Trade Area (NAFTA), President Bill Clinton met with 14 political leaders from Pacific Rim countries at the 1993 APEC Conference in Seattle.

Group/Country	Exports $ bill	GDP $ trill	GNP/capita $
East Asia & Pacific	251.4	96	650
Japan	314.4	3.36	26,930
USA	397.7	5.61	22,204

TABLE 3 : APEC ECONOMIES COMPARED (1991 DATA)
Source : World Bank & GATT. Trillion = '000 billion

The APEC meeting on the 19th November was seen by the USA as fundamental. As the first APEC meeting called to discuss trade liberalisation, US trade secretary Warren Christopher indicated his government's view that it represented *an important, but first, step towards a more open and liberal trading regime* in the region. Japan was still, so far as the USA was concerned, *the cornerstone of the US' Asia-Pacific policy* even though the current bilateral trade imbalance was *unacceptable*.[13] The APEC programme of simplification and harmonisation of customs regulations under discussion at the meeting would, however, be very helpful, he reckoned, as an additional step towards cementing further collaboration.

The political support given by the Clinton administration to APEC was taken by some commentators as proof that America understood the extent to which comparative manufacturing advantage was being globally re-orientated to the Far East.[14]

CENTRE STAGE

The main focus of world attention was, however, on the cliff-hanging talks that successfully resulted in a GATT deal on the 15th December. GATT estimates indicated the likely global pay-off over the coming decade: an increase in world trade of up to $300 billion and up to two million extra jobs. The delight among the key GATT negotiators, Mickey Kantor (USA) and Sir Leon Brittan (EU), and the 116 signatories was palpable. Furthermore, a new organisation was created, the World Trade Organisation, to police the treaty.

The deal was certainly wide-ranging, as Appendix 1, page 290, indicates. But it was nothing like as definitive as some GATT members had hoped and there were clearly some sticking points left to iron out.

One critical area which GATT did not progress, as certain GATT members wished, was the services sector, particularly financial services. The City of

London was highly disappointed at the way in which anti-discriminatory GATT rules would apply in future. The USA would no longer insist on complete discretion on how to treat foreign financial institutions operating in the USA, but it would extend 'most favoured nation' treatment only to those countries which offered reciprocal access to US institutions within six months of the treaty's application in 1995.

Trade Partnership	Trade value	% of total
Europe exports to Asia	129.3	3.7
Asia exports to Europe	184.8	5.3
Europe exports to Americas	152.7	4.4
Americas exports to Europe	174.7	4.9
Asia exports to Americas	236.4	6.7
Americas exports to Asia	153.6	4.4
Intra-Europe trade	1241.4	35.4
Intra-Asia trade	413.5	11.8
Intra-Americas trade	270.4	7.7

TABLE 4: WORLD TRADING PATTERNS - 1991
Source : GATT, OECD

The textile agreement was also the subject of enormous contention, involving, especially, third-world countries. A feeling of this is conveyed by the *Financial Times* leader on the 16th December 1993 which stated, somewhat wearily, that:

In textiles, gradual phasing out of the protectionist Multifibre Arrangement will eventually allow greater international competition and force overdue restructuring of textile industries in the developed world.

It would be ten years before the full effects of this would be felt. Certainly, traditionally-closed markets like the USA would be more open to product from lower-cost producers like Greece, Portugal and Italy.

Textiles was, in fact, a great bone of contention between the USA and China. Clothing accounted for 17.4 per cent of Chinese 1992 exports to the USA but it was known that there had been massive circumvention of quotas through trans-shipment. This was the practice of attaching false country-of-origin labels (Vietnam, Jamaica etc.) to Chinese goods.

Commodity producers in the developing world were also not so content as they could have been. A possible danger they faced was that the prices of their exports would be driven lower, whilst they would not be able to keep the prices of imported foods down through subsidies. Nor would they be able to erect barriers against imported manufactured goods. Some studies revealed, in fact, that Africa could be a net loser from the GATT deal.[15]

Average % pa growth rates (1980-91)		
Group or Country	**Export Volume**	**GNP/capita**
East Asia & Pacific	10.2	6.1
Japan	3.9	3.6
USA	4.0	1.7

TABLE 5: APEC ECONOMIES COMPARED
Source: World Bank & GATT

Nor was America fully content with the GATT pay-off. The country's second largest exporter was the film industry. In 1992 it exported no less than $3.6 billion of entertainment products to Europe. It, above all, was seeking a major liberalisation in audio-visual trade and was highly discomforted by the French GATT success in being able to maintain, against the odds, its tax on cinema-goers to American films and its use of that money specifically to subsidise French film production! So frustrated was Mickey Kantor with the EU stance that he pulled the audio-visual elements out of the GATT deal altogether. Said Jack Valenti, president of the Motion Pictures Association of America:

I'm outraged. The failure of the EC to negotiate seriously was a deliberate act of protectionism.. The negotiation has nothing to do with culture unless European soap operas and game shows are the equivalent of Moliere. This is all about the hard business of money. [16]

CHINA - THE NEWEST GATT MEMBER?

In order to advance its case to become the newest member of the GATT family, China announced on the 30th December 1993 that it was going to unify its two-tier exchange rate system. This was, according to its Ministry of Trade & Economic Co-operation, *a key for further reform of the foreign trade system* which would have *a profound effect on the development of China's foreign trade.*[17] The two-tier system had meant that tourists used one rate of exchange (5.8 yuan/$) whilst commerce was effectively obliged to employ another (8.7 yuan/$). This had led to frequent US' accusations that China had been able to manipulate the system against the interests of overseas trade partners. The move was made on the first of January 1994. In terms of International Monetary Fund calculations, it amounted to a 33 per cent devaluation of the yuan.

The unification of the rates, at least, was welcomed by the USA whose 1993 trade deficit with China was running at a level of $23 billion. Chinese Trade minister Wu Yi also announced that his country would undertake to create a convertible currency within five years.

The move was part of what could only be called China's 'Big Bang'. Alongside this was the planned introduction of a new central bank system, a domestic money market and liberalised trading exchanges (gold, capital etc.) as well as a reformed tax structure. Shanghai would resume the role of hub of China's trading network that it had enjoyed between 1919-38 under Kuomintang rule when it had dominated the whole of Asian trade and finance.

Country	Exports		Imports	
	$b	% of total	$b	% of total
USA	447	12.1	552	14.4
Germany	429	11.6	408	10.7
Japan	340	9.2	223	6.1
France	236	6.4	240	6.3
Britain	191	5.2	222	5.8
Italy	175	4.7	185	4.8
Netherlands	140	3.8	134	3.5
Canada	135	3.6	130	3.4
Belgium-Lux	123	3.3	126	3.3
Hong Kong (a)	118	3.2	122	3.2
China	85	2.3	81	2.1
Taiwan	81	2.2	72	1.9
S Korea	77	2.1	82	2.1

TABLE 6: WORLD'S TOP EXPORTERS (1992)   Source: GATT
Note **(a)** Exports include re-exports. Imports include many goods imported for re-export.

The city's stock market was already the largest in China; it traded copper and petroleum, oilseeds and grains more heavily than any other. The future, given further financial deregulation, looked good. As Zhu Zhenhua, head of research at the People's Bank of China (Shanghai branch) stated:

Shanghai's influence will spread out like a Chinese fan... Under the old system, the People's Bank of China sliced up credit like a cake and all the banks in Peking tried to grab a bigger slice. In a market economy, what role will the bank headquarters have? You'll see a lot of new banks opening in Shanghai. [18]

East Asia Country	Investable capital held by governments and corporations including foreign exchange reserves (US$ billions) (a)		Rise in Country stock market value (b)
	1990	**1993**	
Hong Kong	110	235	109.5
Taiwan	140	215	67.2
China	N/A	38	-
Singapore	25	76	74.1
Malaysia	33	46	105.6
Indonesia	18	36	73.5
Thailand	32	45	103.4
Total *(excl China)*	**358**	**653**	

TABLE 7: ECONOMIC GROWTH IN THE TIGER MARKETS OF EAST ASIA
Source: (a) Citibank Global Asset Management (b) Datastream.
Figures relate to 1992/93.
Note (i) By comparison percentage stock market value increases in UK: 20.5, Germany: 32.3, France: 23.9 and USA: 7.0
(ii) The main stock exchanges in the Tiger markets are the Nikkei (Japan) and the Hang Seng (Hong Kong). The two market indicators are closing relentlessly.

The prospects emerging from China's 'Big Bang' and potential GATT membership were so good in the view of Germany's industrial flagship, Daimler Benz, that it was planning to be the first non-Chinese company to be listed on the Shanghai bourse. It had already obtained main-board listing in November 1993 on the New York stock exchange, so the Shanghai listing would be a complementary move in the company's globalisation strategy. Daimler Benz was already very active in China, building buses in Peking and Shanghai, as well as being heavily engaged in discussion with First Automobile Works about engine manufacture. It was the intention of Chancellor Kohl to build on this and other German company relationships with Chinese industrialists through his visit in November 1993. It was a great success.

It needed to be. 1993 had not been a good year for the German economy. The country had suffered heavily from the first real recession in living memory and a breach in the permanent economic growth psychosis the Germans had come to accept as a reality. Output had fallen, both as a result of the effect of the recession on spending and of the additional costs of integrating the two Germanies, by 3.8 per cent. Wages, already high by British standards (themselves more than 6x the level in Malaysia), rose by 6.8 per cent. Unemployment was nearing four million. The trade unions were still a force to be reckoned with. Social costs were difficult to reduce, so entrenched was the German view of the superiority of their Sozialmarktwirtschaft (social market economy) over the mere market economy approach, such as was practised in Britain.

But the prospects for British firms in China at the end of 1993 did not look anything like so attractive as for their German competitors. On the 18th December, a mere three days after the GATT deal, China announced that British firms would be banned from winning more than a ten per cent share of the Guangzhou's city's underground railway scheme, valued at $1.7 billion. GEC and BTR were the two British firms most affected by this particular decision but other companies, like Rolls Royce, were fearful that the punitive attitude would extend to them.

The Commission's analysis of the challenges facing Europe provides the clearest evidence to date that the balance of argument in the EU is indeed, as Mr Major loves to claim, swinging his way.. The paper firmly identifies government-erected barriers to hiring as a main reason for Europe's poor record in creating jobs. It argues that regulation has priced unskilled labour out of world markets and that non-wage costs must be overhauled - even if that means lower wages and less job security for many...Some plans.. bear the old hallmarks of 'social economy' engineering.. But the Commission's dismissal of systematic job-sharing to cut dole queues is realistic. And its robust defence of open markets, worldwide as well as within the EU, should be music to British ears.. Above all, the paper challenges European governments to face up to the inevitability of a continued steep decline in the share of manufacturing in total employment.

EXHIBIT 3: SIGN OF THE TIMES - THE EU WHITE PAPER ON JOBS AND ECONOMIC GROWTH (DECEMBER 1993) [19]

What was annoying the Chinese was the democratisation process that Britain was seeking to implement in its Hong Kong colony. This was due to be handed over to China in 1997 and the British administration was most anxious that, prior to leaving, it would leave in place a sustainable form of democratic government. Totalitarian China, equally, was adamant that it should not. It did not want a deviant legislature in Hong Kong or indeed any aspect of political control outside the hands of the Communist party.

The two were, however, wholly inter-dependent in economic terms. China's investments in Hong Kong were worth a minimum of HK 120$bn; 25 per cent of the colony's GDP was dependent on links with the mainland: 44 per cent of all China's exports and 25 per cent of her imports in 1992 passed through Hong Kong.

What had brought the problem to a head - after two years of abortive and acrimonious debate, that is - was Governor's Patten's tabling the first part of the democracy legislation in mid December 1993. The Chinese foreign ministry declared that the British had *sabotaged* the talks and spoke ominously on the likely effects on Sino-British trade relations. Li Ziliu, mayor of Guangzhou, was more to the point when he stated his city council's viewpoint:

Tricks played by Britain in the talks over Hong Kong will affect business opportunities for British firms in China. There are still a couple of contracts for the project available for bids but British companies will have no chance. [20]

Britain's difficulty in this was the fear that others might be able to capitalise on the huge level of further economic growth anticipated in China and the consequent rise in the demand for high technology goods such as Britain could supply. The rate of expansion in this mighty economy over the first five months of 1993 had been dramatic and, even though measures were being taken by Vice-Premier Zhu Rongji to curb over-heating, the expectation still was for annual growth in excess of ten per cent. China, according to the British Machine Tool Technologies Association, was already the third largest export market for their members. What would happen if British industrialists were cut out of this potential trade bonanza? Many suppliers did not, however, fear the worst. Were China, as a GATT member, to be bound by the terms of the GATT deal of the 15th December 1993, such targeting of British companies as was happening at Guangzhou would, in fact, be unlawful.

A NEW AGE DAWNS?

Two questions faced the British government over the GATT deal. The first was whether British industry could, and would, rise to the occasion and take full advantage of developing trade opportunity, or would others do better.

The government had no doubt about the strength of the new economic base for British industry that it was creating through its policies. These, at least, should give industry the springboard it needed. As Anthony Nelson, Economic Secretary to the Treasury indicated:

The sharp fall in business failures shows that the economic recovery is well under way. The fall has occurred earlier and more rapidly than in previous economic cycles, reflecting a revival of confidence associated with low inflation and a reduction in interest rates which that has made possible. [21]

His colleague Stephen Dorrell, Financial Secretary to the Treasury, backed this up by saying that government policy was to create a less cyclical future. *What we don't want* he declared *is a consumer recovery which gets out of control, which leads to an inflationary boom and balance of payments difficulties of the kind we have seen in the past.* [22]

Equally important were other strands of policy, such as the greatest possible reining-back of rises in government expenditure, in health, education, personal social services and social security, and a high level of fiscal tightening. Both of these were to ensure the tax burden of operating the public sector was reduced as far as practicable.

Country	Rate of increase (%) in real GDP		
	1993	1994	1995
USA	2.8	3.1	2.7
Japan	(0.5)	.5	2.3
Germany	(1.5)	.8	2.2
France	(0.9)	1.1	2.7
Italy	(0.1)	1.7	2.3
Britain	2.0	2.9	2.9
Canada	2.5	3.7	4.1
Remaining 17	.4	1.7	2.8
Total OECD	1.1	2.1	2.7

TABLE 8: OECD FORECAST - MUCH JAM TOMORROW
Source: OECD

The president of the Board of Trade, Michael Heseltine, was very enthusiastic at the 1994 prospects for the combination of successful government policies and the GATT breakthrough. The gloom engendered by the key finding of the government's own early 1993 study of Britain's industrial competitiveness, that the country was about 25 per cent less competitive than Germany, Japan and the USA in terms of overall output, productivity and growth, was a thing of the past. Nevertheless, he said, trying to reverse Britain's long-term competitive decline was not easy. *After 40 years (of decline), there is (still) a gap. Trying to reverse that is about a cultural shift.*[23] He was confident that the government's liberal economic policies would bring about the shift required.

After all, at the end of 1993 inflation in Britain was at its lowest for 25 years; interest rates were at levels not seen since 1977; strikes were almost non-existent; exports were at record levels.

There was, of course, a contrary view. This argued that the runaway rise in share prices in London had more to do with the availability of international money and the unattractiveness of fixed interest stock at times of rising share prices. However, critics had to agree the foundation for British success did look better. As the *Guardian* leader writer grudgingly put it on the 30th December 1993:

On an optimistic scenario, the hugely deflationary effects (£40 billion) of two 1993 budgets could be offset by a revival of world trade, low interest rates, stock building, the effects of (the 1992) devaluation and (falling) oil prices.. and the successful conclusion of three initiatives for freer trade (GATT, NAFTA and the European Single Market).

The second question facing the British government was whether it could persuade its EU partners of the correctness of its approach to raising industrial competitiveness. Britain's Foreign Secretary, Douglas Hurd indicated the difficulties that had been overcome in a *Sunday Times* article on the second of January 1994:

In 1993 the European Community was.. no longer moving towards becoming a superstate. By agreeing to the GATT international trade settlement, it also moved away from the idea of a protectionist Fortress Europe.. Together, the GATT settlement, the European single market and the Maastricht treaty offer a real prospect of something better. [24]

He reviewed the challenges that lay ahead - especially the 1.5m increase in the EU unemployment level in the year to end December 1993 and that fact that most of continental Europe, unlike Britain, was still deep in recession. His prescription was simple and straightforward:

We need to apply rigorously the principle of subsidiarity. The Community should concentrate on those things that lie beyond the reach of individual members states.. Decentralisation, openness, sound economics and respect for popular feeling - that is the way the European debate is turning... The last Brussels summit agreed the need for deregulation, flexible labour markets and reductions in social costs - the formula which is helping to shrink Britain's dole queues. It is a pity that parts of the Commission plus the Labour and Liberal democratic parties here still hanker after centralising measures (e.g. the European Social Charter and economic and Monetary Union) that would put fresh burdens on employers and costs jobs... [25]

TO THE BREACH, DEAR FRIENDS...

On the 14th February 1994, the Nikkei again fell by more than 500 points. The cause was the collapse of the trade discussions between President Clinton and Morihiro Hosokawa. No agreement had been reached on a new agenda, sought by the USA, to correct the massive Japan-US trade imbalance. High on this agenda was the topic of 'managed trade'.

The Americans had demanded that the Japanese establish benchmarks for opening-up markets such as cars, vehicle ports, telecommunication, medical equipment and insurance. These would involve numerical import targets. The Japanese refusal to accept American arguments had been backed at home, but heavily attacked in the USA, on the grounds that a damaging trade war could result from the negotiating impasse.

The mood in America about the talks breakdown was nothing if not sour. Mickey Kantor referred not just to this but also to an alleged violation of the 1989 USA-Japan Semiconductor agreement (by which companies such as Motorola should have been given access to the Tokyo market) when he said:

This is a classic case of the determination of Japan to keep its markets closed, particularly to leading edge US products. [28]

There was, in fact, total absence of the GATT, or even the APEC spirit, in the Clinton administration which was claimed to be on the point of reviving a draconian trade provision known as super 301. This piece of legislation was passed by Congress in 1988 and had lapsed in 1990. It provided for the identification of countries which had erected barriers against US imports, laid down a timetable for their elimination or, if they were not removed, US retaliation.

Japan clearly had other problems in coping with the talks breakdown. Not least of these was the rise in the yen to the highest level in five months. This, according to the Bank of Japan was not justified by 'the economic fundamentals'. However, more trouble was to follow. The Ministry of International Trade and Industry (MITI) had been instrumental in framing the Japanese strategy to counter the USA's proposals. It had argued that they would involve undue bureaucratic meddling in the private business of Japanese companies. Imagine the embarrassment to MITI when it was disclosed that it had sent out an 'administrative guidance' letter to leading Japanese business organisations recommending that they publicly support the government's economic policies. On the 14th February, Hideaki Kumano, MITI vice-minister withdrew the offending document and apologised for what he called the *misunderstanding*.[27]

* * * * * * * * * * * * * * * * * * * *

APPENDIX 1: KEY FEATURES OF GATT DEAL

Item	Main Action Taken
Industry	36 per cent ave cuts in the tariffs for industrial products. This brings the ave. imposition to 3 per cent.
Agriculture	36 per cent ave. cuts in the tariffs by developed countries and 24 per cent by the developing world. Phase-in periods are 6 and 10 years, respectively. Direct income support to farmers still permitted but producers and exporters will get less subsidies.
Textiles	Phase-out of the Multi-Fibre Arrangement and introduction of a new multilateral trade framework.
Intellectual Property	Introduction of comprehensive and binding rules on patents, copyright, trademarks etc. Persistent Chinese infringement of rules - a major source of US irritation.
Dumping	Rules tightened.
Public Procurement	Access to international tenders widened.
Services	The trade agreement creates a foundation for future liberalisation of national telecommuni-cations and financial services.

Notes

(a) Agriculture accounts for eleven per cent of total world trade

(b) World trade gains ($b 1991 prices in 2002) for European Union, Japan and USA put by the OECD at 71.3, 42 and 27.6, respectively

(c) The GATT round could produce an extra 460,000 jobs in the EU by 2005.

(d) Transport - air and shipping - was to be handled outside the GATT [26]

(e) China's population was 1.2 billion at the end of 1992.

NOTES & REFERENCES

1   GATT deal 'superb outcome' for UK, Jill Sherman, *The Times*, 17/12/93
2   Balladur's GATT triumph, Anne-Elisabeth Moutet & Lucy Walker, *The European*, 17-23/12/93
3   France proclaims 'beautiful victory' after GATT agreement, Charles Bremner & George Brock, *The Times*, 15/12/93
4   Japan lifts the lid on rice imports, Kevin Rafferty, *The Guardian*, 13/12/93
5   Japanese exporters shape up to 100 yen era, Hugh Lewinson, *The Times*, 18/8/93
6   What Japan needs to do is buy some prosperity, Rudi Dornbusch, *Business Week*, 6/12/93
7   Japan is sailing towards an unemployment iceberg, Joanna Pitman, *The Times*, 22/10/93
8   The Pacific Rim: Why Clinton is at Sea, *Business Week*, 13/12/93
9   Abandon the EC slow boat to nowhere, Brian Reading, *The Sunday Times*, 5/9/93
10   US reassures Japan & China on Asia policy, Jurek Martin, *The Financial Times*, 16/11/93
11   As 8
12   From Third World to World Class, DeAnne Julius and Richard Brown, *The Observer*, 21/11/93
13   As 10
14   As 11
15   Europe will gain while Africa gets little help, Wolfgang Munchau, *The Times*, 16/12/93
16   US and EC clear way for trade free-for-all, George Brock, Times, 15/12/93. Failure on services sells America short, Irwin Stelzer, *The Sunday Times*, 19/12/93.
17   China untangles currency system, *The Guardian*, 30/12/93
18   China's 'big bang' promises boom for Shanghai, Andrew Browne, *The Times*, 31/12/93
19   Jacques' other ideas, *The Times'* Leader, 10/12/93
20   China chops British trade, John Kohut, *The Sunday Times*, 19/12/93
21   Optimism up as fewer firms collapse, Ross Tieman & Philip Bassett, *The Times*, 31/12/93
22   Britain looks to 1994 with new optimism, Philip Bassett & Edward Gorman, *The Times*, 29/12/93
23   Heseltine hails competitive future for UK, Philip Bassett, *The Times*, 28/12/93
24   Enough of building Europe - now it must do something, Douglas Hurd, *The Sunday Times*, 2/1/93
25   As 24

26   Deal promises $300 billion boost, Colin Narbrough, *The Times*, 16/12/93.
      Doing good, despite themselves, Martin Wolf, *The Financial Times*, 16/12/93
27   MITI issues apology over pro-government memo, Michiyo Nakamoto, *The Financial Times*, 15/2/94
28   Phone Skirmish heralds US-Japan trade war, Martin Fletcher, *The Times*, 16/2/94

EUROPEAN STEEL: THE KLÖCKNER QUESTION

Abstract:

The Klöckner case focusses upon the European steel industry as it passed through a dark period in the early 1990s. Issues such as the nature and structure of the industry and the extent of political control over it are reviewed in the context of shifts in the pattern of supply and demand among East and West Europe and the USA. Many of the problems of the industry are reflected in the challenges facing the German steel maker, Klöckner.

This case can be read in conjunction with Thyssen Krupp AG

Questions:

Analyse the changing dynamics of the European steel industry in the period covered by the case. What is the nature of the steel trading relationship between the USA, Eastern Europe and the EU and how does it affect these dynamics?

In this context what are the key success factors for a major player in the industry?

Would you buy a stake in Klöckner's Bremen plant for 1DM?

Case Timing: 1993

RUNNING FOR COVER

It was the cumulative effect of depressed industry prices and the slump in orders from German car makers that finally tipped the balance for Klöckner-Werke, Germany's fourth largest producer of steel. On the eleventh of December 1992 it applied to the German courts for protection from its creditors and permission to begin writing off debts. It owed no less than DM2.7 billion (£1.08 billion). With gearing in excess of 200 per cent, it had been a hair's-breadth away from bankruptcy and the first German company of size to be placed in this invidious position in ten years.

The debts had been run up by the company's parent (Klöckner AG) and by Klöckner-Werke's two steel divisions. By contrast, the newly-established subsidiary which handled plastics was trading profitably. Fortunately, Deutsche Bank was Klöckner's main creditor and, as it had promised rescue aid, it was assumed that all the composition proceedings would be successfully out-of-the-way by mid-1993 at the latest, as required by law.

The company had long been distressed. Not only had it not paid any dividends for years, but it had been obliged to offset the weakness it inherited from the slump in steel demand at the turn of the 1980s by diversifying away from an over-focused position on low value-added steel products. One move had been comparatively successful. The acquisition of companies that manufactured plastic products required by the motor industry had yielded profits. But, it was to be years, 1999 to be precise, before the company managed to secure the freedom of action that came with settling all its debts.

The move that had caused the biggest problem, in its timing at least, had been in the steel sector. The DM 400m hot steel galvanising mill that Klöckner had been building in Bremen with Finnish and Japanese partners was not scheduled to come on stream until 1993 and the investment had heavily undermined Klöckner's already-overstretched corporate liquidity. The problem was that the comparative success in one move had been substantially offset by failure in the other.

Product sector	1989/90	1989/90	1990/91	1991/92
Steel	292	204	(35)	(200)
Machinery & Materials	139	115	83	60

TABLE 1: KLÖCKNER OPERATING PROFIT (DM MILLION)
Source: *Wirtschaftswoche* 18/12/92

Furthermore, the underlying weaknesses of Klöckner, as a firm which was relatively under-capitalised and lacking economies of scale, had become clearly visible in the context of a slump in European steel demand. The European Union (EU) steel industry was going through a crisis at the start of the 1990s which was every bit as bad as the previous one at the start of the 1980s. Indeed, according to Klöckner chief executive Hans-Christoph von Rohr, the prices it was getting for its steel in late 1992 were DM150 tonne lower than those obtained in 1990.

Could Klöckner's 3.4m tonne steel-making capacity be taken over as a safe-guarding move by the leading German steel manufacturers Thyssen and Krupp-Hoesch? That was one option. The danger there was the likelihood that such a move would be likely to be opposed by the German Kartel-Amt. On the other hand, would the discussions under way between Klöckner and the Dutch company Hoogovens bear fruit? Or would British Steel do a repeat version of the deal by which it had bought Klöckner's Mannstaedt mill in Troisdorf in 1990? Or would one of the thrusting German ship-builders, Bremer Vulkan, for example, consider the possibility of backward integration by buying the Bremen mill. Each of these were seen as strong possibilities by the media at the time.

Given that Klöckner was almost on the point of starting up the most modern European flat-rolled steel sheet plant in Bremen, there were certainly some plusses to be considered by potential partners. On the other hand, with spare capacity in steel-making in the European Union amounting, in Hoogoven's view, to 40m tonnes,[1] out of a total available capacity of 140m, there were reasons to think that closure of Klöckner's capacity might be a more logical outcome.

Certainly, other EU manufacturers who were also in difficulties would benefit immediately from such a move. Not for nothing did commentator Wolfgang Monchau refer to the troubles of Klöckner as *the latest, and seemingly most daunting, symbol of the decline of an industry.*[2]

By the end of December 1992 the news from Klöckner was more hopeful, however. The company, with Deutsche's Bank aid, had reached a deal with its creditors to carry on operating, as before, until February 1993.

Then a commercial court would decide what to do about Klöckner's petition for 'Vergleich', the equivalent of Chapter 11 protection in the USA. It was a sort of stay of execution. The question was whether Klöckner could use the time that had been bought to amend its fortunes.

THE BIG PICTURE

The word 'crisis' was applied in 1992 and 1993 by many in the European steel industry to the situation that was faced by all producers. Steel consultant Dr Rod

Beddows was even more forthright when he declared, in the light of a review of industry prospects by MEPS, a leading consultancy based in Sheffield, England:

The industry is feeling very shell-shocked. People are saying it's the end of the world.[3]

The cause of the problem was not far to seek: almost all Europe's steel-makers were running at a loss. The reasons were many. Prices had been spiralling downwards since the start of recession in 1989. As demand fell and output dropped, manufacturers could no longer cover the full costs of production. As this happened, they had to decide whether to cut prices further in order to keep market share. As of mid 1992, incentives to buy on the basis of already 'incredibly low' selling prices abounded. To keep in business in a situation of high unused capacity meant cost-cutting by 'big steel', especially by laying off labour. This did nothing to shorten the recession.

---

* All imported raw materials have internationally-denominated costs. The relative value of a nation's currency affects both costs and selling prices.

Economies of scale in terms of raw material purchases are significant. So are those in production and marketing. But, under certain conditions, minimills (i.e. small, dedicated production units) can, in fact, achieve larger scale economies than big, highly-integrated mills. Particularly if they (a) employ non-unionised and highly flexible labour (b) use electric furnaces and (c) manufacture from scrap.

* Specifications on grades of steel are increasingly standardised. This makes homogenisation of production, R & D etc. much easier. It fosters globalisation.

* Capacity working is vital since a substantial proportion of costs is fixed due to the high level of machine intensity involved in say, continuous casting or electric arc furnace working.

EXHIBIT 1: SOME CHARACTERISTICS OF THE STEEL INDUSTRY

It was only in 1988 that the industry could really begin to congratulate itself for having at last emerged from its previous difficulties. It had taken a full eight years for the Davignon Plan, introduced at the height of the recession in 1980, to work to the full by reducing EU capacity for hot-rolled products by almost 30m tonnes and employment by 263,000. The Plan itself had been introduced by Commissioner Davignon under the 'manifest crisis' clause in article 58 of the 1951 European Coal and Steel Community Treaty to try to regularise conditions in an industry which was, due to falling demand and excessive price competition, almost destroying itself.

Self-congratulations had been premature, however, as recessionary conditions struck the industry again in 1989. All the big players were equally affected.

* Germany

The picture in Germany involved the leading steel-makers Thyssen and Krupp-Hoesch. For the former what was needed, in the view of chairman of the board Ekkehard Schulz, if the industry were to be put back on an even keel, was a *Strukturkrisenkartell*.[4] This was a temporary volume-sharing agreement involving the major market players.

As the results in Table 2 indicate, the company's experiences had been traumatic. In the last quarter of 1992, Thyssen's output of steel had been 25 per cent down and in the first quarter of 1993 no less than 57,000 of its workers were affected by short time working. By unifying the management of the raw steel and stainless steel divisions of the company, almost 19,000 jobs were scheduled to go by the end of 1994 in a company that had, until now, avoided redundancies.

Financial Results	Steel		Stainless Steel	
	1990/1	**1991/2**	**1990/1**	**1991/2**
Turnover (DM m)	10439	9903	3322	3071
Exports (DM m)	38	39	45	47
Profit before Tax (DM m)	651	125	(79)	(354)
Steel Production:				
Raw (k tonne)	10319	9907		
Rolled (k tonne)	9775	9236	973	965
Workers (ave)	45688	45125	14486	13496

TABLE 2: THYSSEN RESULTS 1990-1992 [5]

By the end of January 1993 Thyssen's results had worsened to such a degree that chief executive Heinz Kriwet was hinting that the company might not be able to maintain its dividend for the coming year. At a press conference in Duisburg on the 28th January 1993 he spoke ominously of a possible *eiserne Rationalisierung im Kern des Stahlgeschäftes* [6] By the end of March 1993 he was obliged to report an even greater worsening of market conditions and difficult, but not dangerous, times ahead as a result of the increasing *Wettbewerb der Ministahlwerke mit ihren viel günstigeren Kostenstrukturen*.[7]

For the firm of Hoesch AG of Dortmund, the trauma was even greater. They were already part of the rationalisation Kriwet spoke of. In 1992 the company lost its existence as an independent producer and was incorporated in a union with its old rival Krupp AG.

And not without considerable shareholder opposition and some acrimony, either. The fusion of the two companies was designed to maximise the synergistic potential in the two production fields of raw and stainless steel and was not only seen as feasible but highly desirable. But to achieve the link-up, Krupp was obliged to give dividend guarantees and adopt a Hoesch share valuation. This caused some dissension. The merger was planned to be finalised by the end of 1993 and would save DM 300m annually, it was thought.

In the meantime, the combined group had also to announce, on the ninth of March 1993, that it was to close down its entire Rheinhausen complex in the Ruhr in order to make a further annual saving of DM 240m.

Further urgent action was needed, it declared, in view of likely losses of DM500m in 1992/3 and its plan was to reduce crude steel-making capacity from the current 725,000 tonnes to 540,000. A total of 2400 jobs would thus disappear at its other main steel making site in Dortmund by 1995.[8]

*   France

State-owned Usinor Sacilor (U-S) was the leading French producer. Led by President and Director-General Francis Mer it, too, was heavily embroiled in difficulties. For example, in December 1992 he had to contend with large-scale worker demonstrations, orchestrated by a group of trade unions (CFDT, CGTC and Sidestam CGC) in Lorraine. These protests were against what was seen as a further stage in the company's decision to close down steel-making totally in Lorraine.[9] This was, however, a minor irritant compared with the big problem - the continued losses at its German subsidiary, DHS, in which it had a 70 per cent ownership stake. DHS controlled Saarstahl (a maker of rod, bar and wire) and Dillinger Hütte (a sheet steel producer). Almost all the remaining shares were in the hands of the regional state of Saarland. So bad were the anticipated losses for 1993 for the U-S group as a whole, FFr. 1.5 billion in the view of finance director Robert Hubry, that the French parent decided on May 18th 1993 to follow the Klöckner example and seek court protection from its creditors (déposer son bilan) for DHS.[10] From whichever angle it was a major management challenge. Saarstahl had received DM 3 billion in German state aid in the ten-year period to 1988 as well as a loan of FFr. 1.4 billion from U-S.

Francis Mer was not only the chief executive of U-S but also the chairman of Eurofer, the Association of European Steel Producers, one of whose roles was to seek fairness of competition in its market-place. To compound the difficulty, Oskar Lafontaine, Saarland's Social Democrat prime minister, had publicly pledged to aid Saarstahl to maintain its production of 2.2m tonnes by whatever means possible.[11]

U-S had, in fact, bought out the Saarstahl group as recently as 1989. It had previously been owned by the Luxembourg steel group, Arbed SA. The resultant Franco-German link-up had been backed, as indicated, by large subsidies from the Saarland government, but to little avail. Not only was the subsidiary suffering, but the parent U-S declared a loss of FFr. 2.4 billion for 1992, as well.

* Britain

The main British producer British Steel, widely recognised as one of the EU's most efficient, was also very unhappy with its market-place position. On the 29th June 1992 Sir Bob Scholey made his final presentation, as company chairman, of the company's annual results. The loss in the year to end March 1992 amounted to £55m, due (he said) in no small part to low prices. These had been pressured downwards by intense industry rivalry, producers' unwillingness to curtail capacity, economic stagnation in Europe and the weakness of export markets, like the USA.

Under such circumstances, the strategy of this private sector steel maker had been aimed at higher productivity (cost-quality improvements), further moves downstream into higher-value steel production areas (coating etc.) and better management of distribution relationships.[12]   But, as the Times Business Comment columnist pointed out:

> *During a decade of heavy investment, British Steel cut its cost base and re-inforced its technical skills. But is this enough to win a battle with state-sponsored rivals (like state-owned Usinor-Sacilor)? The company's cash pile has now gone. Capital spending is cut to the bone. More cost savings will be found, but less easily. Henceforth British Steel should husband resources. State-owned competitors have deep pockets.*[13]

The situation did not improve as the year progressed. Indeed, on October 28th 1992 the company announced that it was cutting production by 20 per cent, whereupon the value of its shares fell again, this time to 56p. At privatisation in 1988 they had stood at 125p.

THUNDER AND LIGHTNING

The storm in international trade had been gathering strength ever since the major breakdown in the Uruguay Round of GATT talks in 1990, and the subsequent failure to patch up differences among key participants, finally broke, so far as the global steel industry, was concerned, in June 1992. It was then that American producers filed in the USA a range of cases alleging that subsidised steel products had been unfairly dumped in the USA.

At the start of July, as news came of the possibility of punitive 150 per cent duties on half the US imports of European steel, the EU warned its major trading partner of the consequences of 'firing the first shot' in a potential transatlantic trade war.[14] This was serious stuff: at least 2.5m tonnes of steel, worth at least $2.5 billion was affected. European steel had an overall six per cent share of the American market.

The US International Trade Commission (ITC) had 45 days in which to investigate the complaints by 12 producers led by US Steel and Bethlehem Steel.

If the complaints of unfair subsidy and dumping at *far below market value and often below cost of production* [15] were upheld, it would report this to the Commerce Department which would then take action.

This was by no means the first time that the ITC had been involved in such deliberations. Indeed, similar action by US producers at the start of the 1980s had led to a deal, known as 'The Voluntary Restraint Agreement' (VRA), by which EU producers undertook to limit their exports to the USA. This was based on a global Multilateral Steel Agreement which itself was due to expire on the 31st March 1993. The VRA itself lapsed as a result of failure of US-EU talks in Geneva to agree new terms.

OECD Countries	m tonnes		
	1990	**1991**	**1992**
Consumption	325.7	308.3	304.2
Production	382.5	367.2	362.7
Capacity Used (%)	79	76	76

TABLE 3: OECD STEEL OUTPUT AND USAGE DATA

The ITC had a lot of work ahead of it: 84 official complaints involving 21 countries, of whom seven were EU members. The allegations cited global over-capacity, decline in market demand and *massive foreign subsidies* [16] as reasons for the crisis. Despite its privatisation, British Steel was singled out as a firm which had benefited from British government subsidy in the 1970s.

The EU reaction was to accuse the USA of trade 'harassment'. It argued that the EU had not, in fact, increased its exports to the USA and that, in many cases, the prices its producers charged were above domestic prices, especially those of non-unionised US minimills operated by such firms as Nucor. But Bethlehem Steel, having sustained a 1992 third-quarter loss of 92 cents/share on sales of $1.01 billion was in no mood to listen. Nor was the US government.

On the basis of prima facie evidence, the administration unilaterally imposed temporary import duties on steel plate from Britain, France, Germany, Italy and Spain at the start of December 1992. The duties ranged, according to the gravity of the supposed offence, from one per cent to 59 per cent. The US Commerce Dept would, it said, make a full ruling in April 1993 and in the meantime duties levied would be held 'in escrow' (i.e., kept on deposit).

Naturally enough, imports into the USA began to moderate as the duties started to bite. EU suspicions of US producers' intentions were further heightened when they announced, on January 1 1993, a price hike of up to $20 per tonne in flat rolled steel, used in car and appliance manufacture.

The Europeans fumed. Richard Needham, British trade minister, asserted that Washington was trying to protect its *uncompetitive and inefficient* steel industry; His French counterpart, Domenique Strauss-Kahn, declared that *the Americans push for a GATT accord and, elsewhere, do exactly the opposite.* For Ruprecht Vondran, president of the German Iron & Steel Association, *the world's biggest economy has delivered a serious blow to the principles of the international division of labour.* François Mer said simply that the moves were *unfair and dishonest* since the Europeans had only used an average of 70 per cent of their steel import quota.[17]

Characterising the US move as the first protectionist act of the new Clinton administration, commentator Serge Marti, in Le Monde, declared portentously *La guerre d'acier est relancé.* [18]

OPEN HOUSE?

At least some of the causes of Klöckner's weaknesses were rooted in problems nearer to home.

On the first of January 1992 the European Community had taken the bold step of abolishing import quotas for the producers in the Vishegrad countries, Poland, the Czech and Slovak Republics and Hungary. Major steel makers like Slovakia's Vychodoslovenske Zelezarny (VSZ), Hungary's Csepel and Poland's Sedzimir had literally raced to take advantage of the new exporting freedom. The move offered new hope to the economies of the countries in question and a life-line to such depressed industrial centres as Vitkovice, Ostrava, Chomutov, Krakow and Katowice which specialised in the production of crude and rolled steel.

Firms in these areas had already been following a variety of strategies to modernise their facilities and improve their output. VSZ had set up joint ventures with Austria's Voest-Alpine and was discussing plans with Hoogovens to modernise its tin sheet production. It had carried through a managerial revolution involving de-layering and the establishment of a profit centre mentality.

The company, audited by Ernst & Young, claimed levels of manning, automation and quality fully equal to those of Western European competitors.[19]

The Polish government had approved a $4.5 billion plan to reduce the country's steel-making capacity from 15m tonnes (at the end of 1992) to 11.7m by 2002, whilst raising the level of technology used, by switching to continuous casting for example. Polish producers were intent on taking full advantage of Poland's Association agreement with the EU which removed all barriers to their sale of their steel in the Union by 1998.

European Union	1980	1992
Crude steel production (m tonnes)	138	132
Steel industry employees ('000s)	600	380

TABLE 4: EU STEEL OUTPUT AND EMPLOYMENT DATA
Source: Wirtschaftswoche 19/2/93

The logic of the sales push by the Eastern Europeans was beyond reproach. It was based on the irrefutable fact that steel, as well as agriculture and textiles, was one area where the countries of Eastern Europe enjoyed competitive advantage. This resulted from a cocktail of plusses like under-valued currencies, cheap labour rates, low energy prices, cheap raw materials from Russia and direct as well as indirect state subsidies. It was also the case that, according to the Frankfurter Allgemeine's leader writer, *Kapitalkosten und Kosten für den Umweltschutz wurden nicht einkalkuliert.* [20] Perhaps the most critical element in the entire rationale, though, was the EU's wish to ensure success for the serious and difficult politico-economic reforms the Vishegrad countries were undertaking. Whatever else, these demanded the maximum level of EU support.

The problem faced by Klöckner and all other competitors within the EU was the absolute level of steel imports from Eastern Europe, coupled with the rate of increase that had occurred since the start of 1992.

For example, imports into Germany, France and Italy in the 1st quarter of 1991 had amounted to 80,000 tonnes. In the corresponding period of 1992, the volume was 213,000 tonnes [21] By November 1992, Eastern Europe was running an annual 3m tonne surplus, as opposed to a 1989 deficit of 1m tonnes.[22] German steel makers were especially angry about what they saw as *Unfaire Konkurrenz.*[23] In particular, they cited the Czech Republic.

According to Paul-Helmut Hay, president of the German Raw Steel Federation, *die Preise basieren auf dem Willen Beschäftigung zu schaffen und Devisen zu erhalten.*[24]

Producer	Country	Output	1991 T/O	Employees
Usinor-Sacilor	F	22.8	28.0	98
British Steel	GB	12.9	13.4	49
Ilva	I	11.3	11.0	40
Thyssen	G	11.1	13.7	60
Krupp-Hoesch	G	8.7	7.9	30
Arbed	L	7.6	5.3	16
Hoogovens	NL	4.9	4.5	15
Cockerill-Sambre	B	4.4	4.0	12
Preussag	G	4.2	3.1	10.5
Voest-Alpine	A	4.1	6.0*	33*
Ensidesa	S	3.9	3.1	15
Riva	I	3.7	2.7	5
Klöckner	G	3.4	2.5	8

TABLE 5: THE EU'S BIGGEST STEEL PRODUCERS
Source: International Iron & Steel Institute

Output - m tonnes crude steel ; T/O - billion DM;
Employees - '000s. F = France, GB = Great Britain, I = Italy, L = Luxembourg, NL = Netherlands, B = Belgium, S = Spain, A = Austria, * = includes steel trading.

The solution put forward by Germany was direct and simple: a reverse of the EU's 'open door' policy. Initial discussions between Eurofer and the European Commission in June 1992 elicited a promise from the Commission that it would use conciliation procedures to try to solve the dispute. These did not avail and, by the end of 1992, it was British Steel that was taking the lead in demanding further action to stem what it labelled *the surge in unfair imports* from state-owned Eastern European producers.

The company's chief executive contrasted the speed with which Britain's EU partners Germany, France and Italy had already imposed tight import controls with British *feet-dragging* on the issue.[25]

But not everyone in Britain was in favour of protectionism. Jim Rollo of the Royal Institute of International Affairs, for instance. He declared that:

Eight months after the EU signed association agreements with the Czechs, Slovaks, Hungary and Poland which apparently liberalise the steel trade we see the Community being bloody-minded at the first hurdle. If they do this for steel, what will they do for electronics? [26]

The Times also weighed in on the side of the free traders. In its editorial of the 24th February 1993, evocatively entitled *Steel Curtain* as opposed to 'Iron Curtain', it declared that the erection of barriers to steel imports would be wrong. *A more short-sighted approach could hardly be imagined.*[27] Whilst the individual country barriers did take effect, there was agreement that the solution could only be found ultimately at the EU level.[28] Ruprecht Vondran, president of the German Steel Federation, led with the suggestion of what he called *ein unorthodoxer Vorschlag.*

This would involve the EU's taking over part of the social costs of closing surplus capacity in East Europe. With about 350,000 steel workers in the entire region receiving an average annual income of some 5000 DM, such a DM 200m Social Plan would help create an *Abfindung für jeden*, he said.[29]

A BRACE OF PLANS

The predicament of the European steel industry in 1992 and 1993 was, in fact, so serious that the European Commission, as stakeholder for the destinies of industry players, had once more to become involved. It was in many ways a repeat of the 'manifest crisis regime' that had been installed at the start of the 1980s. During this period surplus capacity had had to be shut down to avoid the worst excesses of 'dog-eat-dog' competition and try to stabilise prices. And, after all, it was only in 1988 that the industry began again to compete on an open basis after spending eight years under the follow-on from this regime.

In late October 1992, Eurofer put forward a voluntary capacity-cutting plan to the Commission which they thought would achieve their aims. It covered output and consumption guidelines and financial help in respect of redundancies.

At stake was a key industry strategy issue: how best to handle the relative decline of an old industry sector whose importance had waned just as, under the impetus of technological change, the importance of other new industry sectors had increased. The plan was necessary because of the dire consequences of failure to agree common action in the EU forum. The danger was that individual countries would apply 'unilateral financial measures' (state subsidies) to help their individual industries, almost ignoring the extent to which these were, and were seen as, illegal under EU law. (Appendix 1, page 311).

Element	France	UK	Germany	Japan
Labour cost/hour ($)	17.3	14.2	26.2	18.7
Paid holidays (days/year)	25	27	30	11
Hours Worked/week	39	38.8	37.6	41.5
Taxes/GDP %	43.8	33.3	43.7	29.6

TABLE 6: THE COST OF DOING BUSINESS IN THE EU
Source: Institute of the German Economy in Cologne.
Latest Comparative Data - October 1993

The EU response was the Bangemann Plan of November 1992, aimed at an emergency restructuring of EU steel making. Redundancy payments would take the lion's share of the money made available but the Plan also covered in outline the action needed to combat the alleged dumping of Eastern European steel which had helped cause the 30 per cent slump in EU steel prices since 1990. Such a Plan was of clear potential benefit to Klöckner who, it will be recalled, had until February 1993 before a commercial court would make a decision on its Vergleich petition. Such a 'Krisenkartell' was fully supported by the German market leader, Thyssen Stahl.

The outline Bangemann plan was followed by the steel-makers' own Braun plan, which took into consideration detailed evidence from some 80 EU producers on how to deal with the estimated 15 per cent over-capacity level.

Issued in February 1993 and named after the EU's special envoy for steel, Fernand Braun, this put forward the view that the Community as a whole should bear the restructuring cost of bringing demand and supply back into line by 1996. The steel makers put the cost of shedding jobs (50,000 proposed) and reducing their steel-making capacity, by 8.5m tonnes in crude steel and 6.6m tonnes in rolled products, at £4.8 billion.[30] There were two immediate problems with this and both were aired at a meeting between Martin Bangemann (EC Industry Commissioner), Karel van Miert (EC Competition Commissioner) and steel chiefs on the 9th February, 1993. Firstly, the EU was only prepared to offer £700m for restructuring. Secondly, the amount by which capacity needed to be reduced, in the Commissioners' view, was 26m tonnes of crude steel and 18m tonnes of rolled product, a volume far in excess of what the producers were prepared to give up under their own Braun plan. The meeting itself took place against the background of an OECD forecast that EU steel production would fall by 2.6 per cent in 1993 after its 3.6 per cent drop in 1992.

Let's wrap up the GATT round but abandon the premise that the only good recipe is perfectly free trade. Most other capitalist nations want a managed brand of capitalism, not laissez-faire. They use development and technology subsidies, business-government partnerships and a degree of managed agriculture to protect farmers from periodic bankruptcy. If a mixed economy is so toxic, why did it work so brilliantly after World War II? The need is for common rules, but not necessarily those of Adam Smith. [31]

EXHIBIT 2: A PROPER CONCLUSION TO THE GATT ROUND?

As a result of the obvious differences between the two plans and disarray among the producers, the newly-formed Krupp-Hoesch concern added its voice to Thyssen's calls for an immediate 'Strukturkrisenkartell' to deal with the problem.

The key difficulty over the plans for the cut-backs was, of course, who would carry the burden of job losses. This had been the cause of immense dissension among the European steel makers, and their government backers, at the time of the 1979-82 recession. So it was to prove again.

As industry ministers met in Brussels at the end of February 1993 to consider their version of a rescue package, German steel producers issued a powerful attack on Italy and Spain for continuing to support their allegedly bankrupt, state-controlled manufacturers. The 1992 losses at the Italian Ilva and the Spanish CSI group amounted, in fact, to no less than 20 per cent and 30 per cent of turnover, respectively. Yet Klöckner had been forced to seek protection as a result of losses totalling only nine per cent of turnover. Britain, similarly, attacked the Italians and the Spanish but made plain its interest in the fact that, as of the first quarter of 1993, Krupp-Hoesch was losing DM 1m/day whilst Thyssen was haemorrhaging money at the rate of DM 3m/day. The Italians counter-claimed that Klöckner, despite its difficulties, was still operating and that Ekostahl, the East German steel producer that the German federal government was pledged to protect, was economically not viable and should be closed forthwith.

GRIDLOCK

On the face of it, dealing with Klöckner had seemed a simple matter. By the end of May 1993, The European Commission had decided, after considerable debate, to approve a suggested 40 per cent debt write-off at Klöckner. This was a solution that satisfied Klöckner creditors and enabled the company to carry on working. The offer was based on the expectation of cast-iron guarantees of capacity reduction at Klöckner.

> *Effective action (against E. European steel imports) would go a long way to create a climate which would preserve a competitive environment.[32] Unless subsidies are eliminated by the Commission and member states, there is a danger that efficient private-sector companies such as British Steel will be forced to cut capacity further while weaker, but state-supported enterprises are sustained.[33] The Council of Ministers must now bring matters to a head in order to prevent insolvent state-owned companies forcing some private sector producers out of the market.. Prices are still at a level which cause efficient producers in Europe to incur considerable losses.[34]*

EXHIBIT 3: THE VIEWS OF BRITISH STEEL CHIEF EXECUTIVE, BRIAN MOFFAT

Not only did the deal fall foul of purely German rules affecting debt re-scheduling deals, however, but there was an increasing crescendo of opposition to the rescue attempt from Rome and Madrid. The head of Ilva, Hayao Nakamura (ex-representative of Nippon Steel in Italy), expressed his unwillingness to accept any 'orders' from either the Commission or the Germans for a 'voluntary' cutback in capacity under circumstances where others were aided. *I don't want to talk to these people about reduction of my plants* he declared. *In Japan, if the steel market goes down too much, the big five steelmakers meet, agree on acceptable price levels and send inspectors to check on each other 24 hours a day.[35]* By the same token, Spanish Socialist PM Felipe Gonzalez had been obliged to support all the steel plants (including a new minimill) that were located in the Basque region.

Had he not just failed to win an overall majority in the June 1993 general election and were his coalition hopes not dependent on Basque nationalists? Especially in view of the highly-publicised 'March on Madrid' that the Basque and Asturian steel workers had carried out in October 1992 in defence of their jobs. This had led to a Madrid demonstration involving 40,000 people.

It was a case of impasse. No-one would compromise enough to allow a voluntary cut-back agreement to be achieved. The impasse ultimately involved gridlock among Ilva, CSI and Ekostahl, and their respective governments.

The loss-making Ilva had been created in 1988 when the Italian steel industry had been restructured following the liquidation of Finsider by its owner, the state holding conglomerate Instituto per la Riconstruzione Industriale (IRI).

It could not be floated on the market - to raise more money - since, under Italian law, to qualify for this, companies had to have recorded three consecutive years of profits.

Hence, to help with recapitalisation, the Italian government effectively made available to it an extra £160m (L 350 billion) in September 1992. If such a subsidy were found to distort European steel competition, the money, declared the European Commission, would have to be repaid.[36] Naturally, Italy was opposed to German state aid if, thereby, Italy were to lose. In November 1993, Britain, firmly backed by private steel maker British Steel, refused to give any concessions on state aid to Ilva. This was problematic in view of the political consequences of further cutbacks in the Italian steel industry, especially in terms of unemployment in the Mezzogiorno.

The crisis at CSI was caused by the EU ruling in September 1993 that the Spanish government should cut back its aid to the state industry and slash production. This followed a warning from British, German and French steel makers that they could not possibly accept the Brussels plan to cut steel capacity, if Spanish and Italian subsidies continued unabated.

Ekostahl was a steelworks located in the Brandenburg region of Germany, almost on the border with Poland.

The premier of Brandenburg, Manfred Stolpe, was seeking from the EU Commission not only recognition of the special status of the region but also tangible aid. Specifically, he wanted an endorsement of the DM 200m aid package for the plant which had been promised by the government's Treuhandanstalt. This was tantamount to creating a 'new steel-making facility'.[37]

In November 1993, Britain, again firmly backed by British Steel, rejected outright the compromise deal struck on Ekostahl between Bonn and Brussels. This, according to the Germans, was a mistake since it could force the Commission to abort its plan to cut capacity.

The situation became even more complex when, on the 19th January 1994, a deal was struck between the Italian Riva Group and the Treuhandanstalt which transferred 60 per cent of Ekostahl ownership to the Italians. The Italians planned to build up the capacity in Eisenhüttenstadt by adding a hot rolling mill.[39]

In the centre of this Europe-wide storm Klöckner had its own challenges. It had finally decided to come out of steel and, as of October 1993, it was seeking to sell off its steel-making businesses. Bremen, keen to preserve the company as the city's second-biggest employer, was now a possible bidder. So were Arbed and Hoogovens. Krupp-Hoesch were also in the running.

Their interest was of particular concern to the European steel community since it was reported, at the end of November 1993, that Thyssen and Krupp-

Hoesch were exploring a scheme to pool part of their steel-making operations to form what the media called *Deutsche Stahl*.[38] Set against the background of a possible end to the long-running Uruguay Round of GATT on the final cut-off date of the 15th December, this was momentous news.

The finalised Klöckner plan posed a considerable conundrum for other producers and for the European Commission. What Eurofer wanted was to pay Klöckner £300m for the Bremen facility and close down its hot-rolled mill. The European Commission, by contrast, was prepared to allow Klöckner debt write-offs in return for a cut-back in its Bremen steel-making capacity. What Klöckner itself proposed was the sale of 75 per cent of the facility to four local companies in a consortium led by the city of Bremen. The cost? A symbolic one Deutschmark each! [40]

SHADES OF MACHIAVELLI'S PRINCE

British Steel was further embroiled in the political and economic row over European steel when it was accused, on the 16th February 1994, of joining in a price-fixing cartel in the 1980s. Along with 15 others, it had allegedly broken European competition law though 'a clear-cut and systematic' cartel which had shared markets and information as well as rigged prices in steel beams. Klöckner was not among them, although such leading producers as Krupp-Hoesch, Thyssen, Arbed and Saarstahl were. British Steel's £24.3m fine was almost three times the size of the next largest as the company was regarded by the EU commissioner Karel van Mierk as the ringleader. *This* he declared, *is a case where everything which could be infringed has been... and we needed to be tough.*[41] He added that infringements of the law which took place over the period 1980-8 had been disregarded because of the conditions that applied at the time. The fines would be imposed by the Commissioner under article 65 of the European Coal and Steel Community Treaty.

There was the clearest possible indication that the plan put forward by the Commission in December 1993 to restructure the industry was not at first seen by producers as relevant to their needs. This plan did achieve the agreement of the German, Italian and Spanish state-owned producers to capacity cuts of 5.5m tonnes but only in exchange for final, one-off state grants amounting to £5.2 billion. A further element in the plan was the anticipated 'quid pro quo' whereby the private producers would reduce capacity voluntarily by 10.5m tonnes or, failing that, contribute to a compensation fund for those that did.

The problem was that the private producers had simply not accepted their prescribed role, arguing in fact that the subsidies allowed amounted to unfair market distortion. British Steel was the most outspoken in its complaints. It had itself received no state aid since 1985 and had been privatised in 1988.

So far as the alleged cartel was concerned, the company argued that it had not been possible to move swiftly away from the 'legal cartel' the Commission had acquiesced in towards acceptable 'open market competition' after 1988. The over-supply conditions in the industry made it impossible. Whether or not this argument would succeed at appeal was not clear.

Certain it was, however, that British Steel's shareholders felt aggrieved. Since privatisation the share value had risen by only 16 per cent and now the EU was threatening to remove what amounted to almost the whole of the company's profits for the first half of 1993. Nor would the company's managers by overjoyed at such an outcome. They had worked hard to reduce working capital only to find that the company was in a much better position to pay the fine than ever before.

The British press also took a dim view of the move. Thus one of the more incisive comments;

It is a stunt of which Machiavelli would have been proud. A governing body (the European Commission), anxious to cook up a deal of which it should be ashamed, counter-attacks... its most vociferous opponent, accusing it of crimes that are curiously similar to those it is itself contemplating... The EU dislikes price-fixing, except when it is done officially to prevent economic reality overtaking inefficient producers or national champions... British Steel has warned that it will opt out of the (capacity-reducing plan) charade unless there are signs of common sense at the EU. Yesterday's fines show that our European masters have other ways of forcing us into line. [42]

* * * * * * * * * * * * * * *

APPENDIX 1

Policy of the Community : Rules of Competition
Treaty of Rome, 25th March 1957

Article 85

1. *The following practices shall be prohibited as incompatible with the common market : all agreements between undertakings, all decisions by associations of undertakings and all concerted practices which may affect trade between Member States and the object or effect of which is to prevent, restrict or distort competition within the common market...*

Article 86

1. *It shall be incompatible with the common market and prohibited, in so far as trade between Member States is liable to be affected by it, for one or more undertakings to exploit in an improper manner a dominant position within the common market or within a substantial part of it...*

Article 92

1. *Save in the case of exceptions specified in this Treaty any aid granted by a Member state or through State resources in any form whatsoever which distorts or threatens to distort competition by favouring certain undertakings or the production of certain goods shall, in so far as it affects trade between Member States, be incompatible with the common market...*

3. *The following may be considered to be compatible..*
    (a) aid intended to promote the economic development of regions where... there is serious unemployment.
    (d) such other categories of aid as may be specified by the Council by qualified majority decision on a proposal from the Commission.

Article 93

1. *The commission shall in conjunction with Member States submit to constant examination all systems of aids existing in those States. It shall propose to the latter any appropriate measures required by the progressive development or by the functioning of the common market...*

APPENDIX 2: INDUSTRIAL DEVELOPMENT IN GERMANY

The Industrial Revolution came late to Germany. Only after 1860 did it become a marked feature, and then with quickly increasing clarity. Before, the country had had a history of localised manufacture, innumerable tariff barriers, bad roads and little capital - all expressive of the political fragmentation that existed among the innumerable German states prior to Bismarck and the (predominantly European and land-based) German Empire in the 19th century.

Limited partnerships in, and family ownership of, manufacturing firms were commonplace whereas limited companies, unlike in England, were a comparative rarity until the latter part of the century. A major additional impetus to industrialisation within the authoritarian Empire under Bismarck came in 1870, with Germany's devastating victory over the French. To assist with improving the manufacturing base, the Deutsche and Dresdner banks were set up in 1870 and 1872 respectively, the previous banking structure under the farming-co-operative Raffeisen banks and small private banks being wholly inadequate to the task of promoting industrial growth.

From this date, it was co-operation (through loans) between German banking and industry systems and then, increasingly, bank co-ownership (through equity holdings) which can be seen to have contributed to Germany's success as an 'Industriestaat'. Over a period in excess of a century, interrupted by defeats in two world wars and by Hitler's totalitarian dictatorship, this form of banking-industry complex has safeguarded German industrial ownership. This latter has itself been strengthened by the possibility of applying the Stimmrecht law (shareholder voting rights do not depend on share ownership level), as well as promoting its development. State ownership of industry in Germany is, by contrast, not a particularly prominent feature: aid for R&D is.

One by-product of the need to develop and protect was the early creation in Germany of giant enterprises, spanning a huge range of activities within a particular industry, like the early Kartells (19th century) and the Konzerne (like Krupp and IG Farben), in the 20th. Present-day examples are Siemens and Daimler Benz, in which Deutsche Bank has a 28 per cent stake, which could well be called Kombinate. With cross-ownerships and the safeguard of the Mitbestimmung principle, (worker co-determination via worker membership of supervisory boards) such firms are well-nigh impregnable to predatory attack. Workers in them enjoy substantial statutory employment rights (working time, representation, training, maternity leave, job protection etc.), a factor which makes for a high level of commitment to maintenance of the status quo, as well as very high labour costs. Some of these rights date from the legal framework of social protection laws introduced in Germany in the 1880s.

Interestingly, some of the features of the current Gewerkkammer statutory training and employment regulations date back to the medieval guild system, which was, in fact, never abolished in Germany. Indeed, in the 19th century, several of its institutions became instruments for state insurance as well as training.

NOTES & REFERENCES

1   Dutch, German steel groups in co-operation talks, Christopher Parkes, *The Financial Times*, 12/11/92

2   Germany's powerhouse says farewell to steel, Wolfgang Munchau, *The Times*, 12/12/92

3   Europe's steel industry peers into the abyss, Andrew Baxter, *The Financial Times*, 16/10/92

4   'Structural crisis cartel' Thyssen Stahl fordert Marktbereinigung durch ein Krisenkartell, *Frankfurter Allgemeine Zeitung*, 20/1/93

5   As 4

6   'Iron Rationalisation at the heart of the steel business' Thyssen ist zu einem harten Preiskampf bereit, *Frankfurter Allgemeine Zeitung*, 29/1/93

7   'Competition of the mini mills with their much more favourable cost structures'. Thyssen ist auf ein sehr schwieriges Geschäftsjahr eingestellt, *Frankfurter Allgemeine Zeitung*, 20/3/93

8   Ruhr Steel complex to close, Colin Narbrough, *The Times*, 10/3/93

9   Manifestation contre la 'liquidation' de la sidérurgie en Lorraine, *Le Monde,* 13-14/12/92

10   Le sidérurgiste allemand Saarstahl depose son bilan, Caroline Monnot, *Le Monde*, 20/5/93

11   French shut German steel works, Colin Narbrough, *The Times*, 20/5/93

12   Tighter margins behind £55m deficit at British Steel, Andrew Baxter, *The Financial Times,* 30/6/92

13   *The Times*, 30/6/92

14   US takes hard line over steel dispute, Tom Walker, *The Times*, 2/7/92

15   US Steel's dumping complaints sound familiar, Nancy Dunne, *The Financial Times,* 22/7/92

16   as 15

17   France issues warning over US duties on steel, Colin Narbrough and Tom Walker, *The Times*, 29/1/93.

18   'The steel war is relaunched'. Washington rélève les droits de douane sur les importations d'acier en provenance de dix neuf pays, *Le Monde*, 29/1/93

19   Slovak Steelmakers find success has a price, Alan Robinson, *The Financial Times,* 16/6/92

20   'Capital costs and costs for protecting the environment were not included'. Klage wegen billiger Importe im Gespräch, *Frankfurter Allgemeine Zeitung*, 2/2/93

21   Emergency talks on East steel flood, *The Times*, 18/5/92

22   Imports threaten British Steel jobs, Christopher Huhne, *The Independent*, 17/11/92

23   'Unfair competition' *Frankfurter Allgemeine Zeitung*, 2/2/93

24   'Prices are based on the wish to create employment and obtain foreign exchange'. Aufs Blut Gereizt, *Wirtschaftswoche*, 4/12/92

25   Steel dumping threat to jobs, Simon Beavis, *The Guardian*, 17/11/92

26   Steel dumping duties upset E. Europe, Vincent Boland, Christopher Bobinski, Nicholas Denton & Anthony Robinson, *The Financial Times*, 20/11/92

27   *The Times*, 24/2/93

28   As 25

29   'An unorthodox plan creating a job opening for everyone' , EG Beihilfe fur Osteuropäische Stahlarbeiter, *Frankfurter Allgemeine Zeitung*, 18/6/93

30   EU opposes quotas to prop up steel, Tom Walker & Colin Narbrough, *The Times*, 10/2/93

31   Clinton has to zero in on the global economy, Robert Kuttner, *Business Week* 21/12/92. **Note** that the final deadline date for the Uruguay GATT round was the 15th December 1993

32   British steel themselves against market distortion, *The Guardian*, 17/11/92

33   BS cuts payout after losses reach £149m, Philip Bassett, *The Times*, 22/6/93

34   British Steel back in black, Susan Gilchrist, *The Times*, 16/11/93

35   Japanese Chief of Italy's Ilva Rejects European steel Plan, Maureen Kline, *The Wall Street Journal*, 21-22/5/93

36   Italian steel faces EU curb, Andrew Hill, *The Financial Times*, 7/7/93

37   EU to close the door on a lifeline for steel jobs, Lucy Walker, *The European*, 8-11/4/93

38   German steel giants in talks on alliance, Colin Narbrough, *The Times*, 1/12/93

39   Übertragung der Ekostahl AG an Riva, *Neve Zürcher Zeitung*, 20/1/94

40   British Steel chief says EU pact in danger, Andrew Baxter, *The Financial Times*, 11/1/94. **Note** that Klöckner had already disposed of its stainless steel division by this time.

41   EU Plan to revamp steel industry in ruins, James Landole, *The Times*, 16/2/94

42   Brussels needs to stop this metal bashing, City Comment, *Daily Telegraph*, 17/2/94

EUROFIGHTER

Abstract:

The project for the European Fighter Aircraft was established during the Cold War and was enthusiastically supported by the four European countries who decided it was vital to their defences. In changing times, however, the viability of the project has not been seen in quite the same light by the participants. The case thus deals with the issue of cross-border collaboration between governments and businesses in the design and construction of what was re-named as the Eurofighter. Getting European partners to collaborate in building "a political aircraft" in a changing world is shown to be a stern management test.

Questions:

Do you share the view that the Eurofighter is an aircraft that no-one wants, that can't be afforded, but which must be built?
Why?
Why not?

Case Timing: 1993-2000

SHOCK WAVES

On the 30th June 1992 the German government announced that it was no longer prepared to proceed with the purchase of the original version of the European Fighter Aircraft (EFA), on grounds of excessive cost. Instead, the government declared, it wished to go ahead with a smaller, slimmer alternative, called the Eurofighter 2000. It was an announcement that threw into turmoil the future of the £22 billion, four-nation programme to build an aircraft designed to meet Europe's defence needs in the 21st century.

EFA had been billed as a leap-forward in aircraft technology and deserving of comparison with the USA's finest fighters, the F22 Stealth and its F16C. A Luftwaffe study had, in fact, commended its most attractive combination of combat effectiveness and operating costs. Conceived before the ending of the Cold War in Europe, EFA had been planned to have the operational role of dealing with the anticipated stream of Warsaw Pact Mig 29s and Sukhoi SU 27s escorting Backfire bombers on their missions over Western Europe.

Date	Event
13/8/61	Berlin Wall built. East Europe is sealed off. Cold War hots up.
10/3/66	France quits the North Atlantic Treaty Organisation (NATO)
21/8/68	USSR invades Czechoslovakia
Dec 1979	USSR invades Afghanistan
9/11/89	Berlin Wall falls
1/7/90	Warsaw Pact is dissolved
July 1990	NATO offers East diplomatic relations
Feb 1991	Vishegrad countries seek NATO integration.
Jan 1994	US' 'Partnership for Peace' plan launched. Involves possible NATO-Vishegrad countries security association.

TABLE 1: KEY DATES IN NATO HISTORY

Bill Jordan, head of AEEU, Britain's largest manufacturing union, called the German decision *disastrous.* For him and his members the project amounted to simply *the single most important military development in the world.*[1] No less than 32,000 British jobs were said to depend, directly and indirectly, on the successful completion of the programme.

When the original memorandum of understanding to commence EFA development had been signed in 1988, the plan was for the four partners to buy 765 planes. Germany and Britain were to purchase 250 each, with break-even put at 400.[2] Clearly, a German pull-out now, with all development work not completed, would seriously jeopardise EFA's future.

The EFA project had been launched with high hopes in the mid-eighties by a consortium of countries. All were concerned with European defence and were anxious to maintain their countries at the leading edge of space technology. Britain and Germany led the collaboration with a 33 per cent stake each, followed by Italy (21 per cent) and Spain (13 per cent). The French were no longer involved with the venture, having decided at an early stage to proceed with the design and manufacture of their own state-of-the-art fighter aircraft, the Rafale.

> *How can you make long-term plans when you have got to cope with exchange rate volatility, interest rate volatility, price volatility? We have had stop-go since the end of the Second World War... We cannot keep losing capacity and capabilities under the recessionary hammer... Modern manufacturing capabilities, once abandoned, cannot easily be revived in the subsequent upturns. As the UK's oil surplus becomes smaller, the performance of our manufacturing sector will play a major role in determining the UK's sustainable rate of growth in the 1990s.*

EXHIBIT 1: THE IMPORTANCE OF MANUFACTURE
Source: Pen Kent, Associate Director of the Bank of England, *Government failure blamed for decline of British industry,* Ross Tieman, *The Times,* 21/10/93.

British Aerospace was the leading British contractor, with 2,500 employees directly involved in development work and in building the first EFA prototype at its factory in Lancashire. It was very worried, having always considered EFA as *the most cost-effective means of meeting the operational requirements of the four air forces.*[3] So too was its German counterpart, Deutsche Aerospace (DASA), a key subsidiary of Daimler-Benz. Furthermore, according to the German Space Industry Federation (BDLI), some 20,000 direct and indirect jobs in a large number of German suppliers depended on EFA.

But the German government had gone out of its way to stress that it did not want to abandon the project. It stated that it would, in fact, continue to meet the development costs but wanted a lower-cost version of the plane – a requirement initially labelled by Britain's defence procurement minister as *an extravagant piece of nonsense.*[4]

Differences in the viewpoints of the British and the German governments emerging from this initial clash resulted in an, at times, acrimonious debate which lasted well into 1994.

Germany had, in fact, found itself in a major dilemma over EFA.

On the one hand, the country had made a contractual commitment to help develop EFA. Failure to meet its pledges would result in compensation claims from partner countries and leading contractors. And, were it to want to proceed, it had to accept the BDLI calculation that the net cost of EFA to the government, after allowing for all sources of taxation income, would be less than the cost of buying realistic alternatives, such as Mig 29s or the Swedish Gripen. On the other hand, the German government considered that the military threat from former Warsaw Pact forces no longer existed and, hence, that the rationale for wanting EFA had lessened, if not disappeared. In fact, the USSR had ceased to exist and the Russian army had been culled by over 1m men.

Britain did not appear to suffer from such qualms. Defence Secretary Malcolm Rifkind answered project criticisms by his German colleague, Volker Rühe, by citing the political and military instability existing in former member countries of the USSR. They still controlled, he contended a formidable arsenal of Mig 29s and SU 27s, as did a number of problematic countries like Iraq, Iran and North Korea.

Britain rejected outright the German plan for a smaller aircraft. Not only would it have lower endurance (via less fuel load), but it would also suffer from a lack of agility in sub- and super-sonic flight, as well as a shortage of fire-power. With development costs having already reached the £8 billion mark, it made little sense to scrap the seven prototypes now in their final assembly stage nor to backtrack on the new EJ 200 engine that had been specially engineered by Rolls Royce, MTU, Fiat and ITP. For good measure, the British added the fact that changing EFA's tailor-made radar, flight control and electronic warfare systems would put the scheduled 1999 completion date for the project back by at least five years.

During this time, each country would, of course, have to maintain its increasingly ageing fighter fleet. For Italy and Britain, this meant F104 Starfighters and a mix including Phantoms and Tornados, respectively.

The British riposte to Volker Rühe's proposal was buttressed by a report from the House of Commons' Defence Select Committee issued in March 1992. This declared, after a searching evaluation of the economics of the project, that *there is currently no sign of any suitable alternative to EFA which could begin to offer the same level of performance at an acceptable cost, with anything approaching comparable technological benefits.*

This view was shared by Casa, Spain's state-owned aerospace company and the country's leading EFA contractor. Eighteen Spanish companies and over 2,000 skilled engineers had been involved in the development phase. If successful, it was authoritatively estimated that EFA would earn some 31 billion pesetas annually over 16 years for Spanish industry.[5]

Element	Country			
	UK	Germany	Italy	Spain
Workshare (%)	33	33	21	13
Commitment to July 1992 (£b)	2.7	2.0	1.35	.67
Total no of jobs involved ('000)	32	20	15	17
Main building contractor	BAe	DASA	Alenia	Casa
Main engine contractor	GEC	MTU	Fiat	ITP

TABLE 2: WHO'S WHO IN EFA [6]

However, the British media were not as sure of the viability of the project as was the defence minister. One leading paper, *The Sunday Times*, referred to the project as *absurd* and said that the British government was trying *to persuade us to buy an aircraft we do not need, at a price we cannot afford.* What the Germans had done in making their announcement was said to be *a disguised blessing.*[7] Its attack continued with barbed references to other 'political' aircraft, like the Nimrod, which had been ultimately scrapped by previous British governments after very substantial development expense.

Another paper, the Evening Standard, was also highly critical. Its editor wrote:

It is always tempting for Britain, with a long and proud history of intervention in world affairs, to cling to outdated notions of what a small and economically weakened nation can achieve. yet it is time to dispel the pipedreams.. Defence creates fewer jobs per £ spent than any other activity.. Britain in the 21st century will need real jobs, not the phoney jobs that come from redundant defence projects. And does the world really need more than two major producers of fighting aircraft?[8]

Such criticisms helped impel the British Chancellor to do again what his German counterpart had just finished, carry out another review of the economics of the EFA project.

Of course, it was not just this project that would be subject to Treasury scrutiny: Britain's entire annual defence budget of £9 billion was re-appraised in 1992 and again in the run-up to Kenneth Clarke's November 1993 budget and wide-ranging economies made wherever possible. It was again under re-appraisal in April 1994.

It was known that the Italians and Spanish were also seeking, by every means possible, to curb government expenditures and restore their economies to health after the ravages of recession. The problem for the British, according to John Townend, chairman of the Conservative backbench finance committee, was that, if Italy and Spain were to withdraw from EFA in order to save money, Britain, too, might be forced to end the project.

ROUND TWO

It was also on the first of July 1992 that GEC first made an approach to the British ministry of defence to enquire about the possibility of a link-up between itself and British Aerospace. The aim was, of course, to strengthen Britain's position as a European defence supply leader, in general, and to improve the BAe-GEC ability to cope with the German EFA announcement, possibly by becoming a single contractor, in particular. It was expected by Lord Weinstock, GEC chairman, that substantial improvements in scale economies and management streamlining would result from such a link-up.

> *We now live in a world where there is.. no direct threat against the British Isles.. We are not locked into an arms race. The threats are different and more complex.. serious insurgency.. potential nuclear proliferation.. terrorism.. religious fundamentalism.. nationalism. Britain alone cannot assume responsibility for world stability.. The time has now come to ask whether we need to maintain our robust national air defence capability.*

EXHIBIT 2: SHOULD THE UK CHANGE ITS TACK?
Source: Former British Defence Minister Tristan Garel-Jones,
The Sunday Times, 11/7/93.

GEC was in a strong position to make a suggestion of this nature. Its pre-tax profit for the year to end March 1992 was £829m (£818m for the previous year) on sales of £9,430m (£9,438m). Its cash surplus amounted to a sizeable £876m (£528m) and its spending on R & D had been £1,040m.

BAe was, by contrast, much weakened. Its market capitalisation had fallen by no less than £400m since May 1992 and it was now having to think of making provisions of over £1,000m to deal with the severe consequences of the recessionary downturn in its aircraft businesses, Airbus, regional jets and military aircraft. The share price was languishing at 243p, having hit a high earlier in the year of 379p. Its ability to fund long-term R&D from its own resources was becoming increasingly problematic.

On the other hand, GEC also had much to lose if EFA was cancelled. The company had spent £270m in acquiring Ferranti's radar business (and thus the EFA contract) and it was thought that, ultimately, £2,000m of business would be placed with GEC and its subsidiaries as a result.

The BAe posture, and that of the ministry of defence, was negative. BAe was much more concerned with keeping the Germans involved. Its chief executive, Dick Evans, stated bluntly:

We can't allow the Germans to walk away from the European aerospace industry. Europe has collectively to get its act together in military aerospace, as it has with Airbus in commercial aircraft, to compete head-to-head with the Americans in world export markets. The EFA has huge export potential.[9]

For Kumar Bhattacharyya, professor of manufacturing systems at Warwick University, it was impossible to understate the importance of EFA and co-operation on developments in software development, materials (e.g., carbon fibre-reinforced plastics) and control systems. *The economics* he declared *might look quite straightforward, but there's a lot more to this project than just the cost of an aircraft.*[10]

The worries facing the two companies, whether separate or combined, were greater than just the problem of EFA. They were rooted in the extent of world competition in the defence market at a time of severe recession. The talks that took place in London on the sixth of July 1992 between the British and German governments to try, if possible, to smooth over differences showed that German manufacturers were just as preoccupied.

But the talks did not succeed. At first Volker Rühe remained committed to his position. No new money was to be ploughed into aircraft production unless it was a new and cheaper version, the Eurofighter 2000. The British offered major cost cuts in EFA, but no redesign. To do this, said Malcolm Rifkind, meant throwing the £5 billion spent so far down the drain. *You've heard of the film 'Top Gun'...* said his colleague Jonathan Aitken scathingly *...Eurofighter 2000 would be Bottom Gun.*[11]

The next set of partner talks took place at the start of August. Volker Rühe's opening gambit was to state categorically that *EFA is dead.*[12] The Spanish were not in any better mood. They disclosed that, to curb their budget deficit by the equivalent of £1.7 billion, they were hoisting tax rates across the board and slashing non-essential public expenditure. Their budget deficit in the first half of 1992 had been 40 per cent above target. This led Defence Minister Julian Garcia

Vargas to claim that the economic situation in Spain would not allow the production of the aircraft *as it stands*.[13]

Malcolm Rifkind was obliged to give ground. By September, not just cost savings but also the scaling-down of the fighter aircraft was under discussion. Factors such as switching to one EJ 200 engine (instead of two), altering the airframe, using an alternative radar system and buying some parts off the shelf were among the topics addressed.

The attention of the partners to the need to get the right sort of *quality bang per taxpayer's buck* was clear. It was, in fact, further raised by the acclaim that the Russians won at the 1992 Farnborough International Airshow for their low-priced products. State-of-the-art Backfire bombers, the swing-wing Su 24 MR attack plane and the Yak 141 -the world's first vertical take-off supersonic aircraft- were on sale to all who wished to purchase, for hard currency that is. China had already purchased 24 SU 27s for $1.2 billion cash and barter goods and Iran was known to be buying TU 22 M3 bombers and Mig 29s and 31s in a deal worth $2.2 billion. It is also noteworthy that the cost of a Mig 29 was $25m as opposed to the $40m a buyer would have to pay for an F/A 18. [14] The Russians were desperate to sell one of the few manufactured product types in which they had claimed global competitive advantage.

> *When I am told that the world is transformed into a quiet and tranquil place, I say that we cannot assume what the world will be like in ten years' time.. One goes back to 1931. Who was then anticipating that in two year's time Hitler would be in power and eight years later the world would be at war. To make the Spitfire took long enough, but to produce EFA takes a damn sight longer.* Defence Secretary Malcolm Rifkind.

EXHIBIT 3: WARS AND RUMOURS THEREOF
Source : Eurofighter, *The Sunday Times*, 13/9/92

But it was still a fraught issue. Commentator Conrad de Aenlle called Eurofighter 2000 *an expensive flying camel*, a reference to the perverse way in which committees are said to tend to work.[15] Daimler Benz spokesman Christain Poppe cut to the heart of the challenge when he asked *How much can you shrink the aircraft.. and maintain.. sufficient performance for doing the task it must do? First, it is a political question.*[16]

Would it be feasible for the Germans to add to the stock of Mig 29s they had inherited when the Berlin Wall was dismantled? Not according to Daiwa's Aerospace Institute analyst, Howard Wheeldon. In his view *the Mig 29 was an excellent aircraft*. But would the European Community *risk killing off its aerospace industry*, he asked? [17]

Mark Lambert, editor in chief of Jane's *All the World's Aircraft*, spoke for many in the industry when he stated:

> *My feeling is that they will come to an agreement.. at reduced prices. The chances are 50:50 because Kohl and his party are in such trouble. Germany is so pacifist and they are worried about the cost of German re-unification.. If you have a fully-rounded airforce, then you must have an airplane like EFA. None of the countries involved has anything like it.* [18]

To try to remove the project from its state of being in *a limbo between reality and fiction*,[19] the four partners finally agreed on two sets of EFA re-appraisal studies to be completed by mid-October. This delay raised all sorts of speculations. Rome was said to have approached McDonnell Douglas to enquire about the F/A 18 fighter already used by Madrid. There was talk of buying the Swedish Gripen or the French Rafale off-the-shelf.

However, DASA injected some reliability into the debate when it announced job losses totalling 7500 over the coming two years. Defence, the company said, would not be affected by the cutbacks. The Jäger 90 (the original German name for the Eurofighter) was, according to DASA's Defence division, *paradoxerweise eines der sichersten Planungselemente.* [20]

Country	Defence spending in constant 1985 prices as % of national GDP	
	1988	**1992**
USA	6.1	5.4
UK	4.1	4.9
France	3.8	3.4
Germany	2.7	2.2
Italy	2.2	2.0
Spain	2.1	1.6

TABLE 3: CHANGING PATTERNS IN DEFENCE SPENDING
Source: NATO data.

The required reports, from defence ministries and the manufacturers, were ready on time and decisions were duly made. Would there be any significant re-design? No. Would a 30 per cent cost reduction target now be set and strictly adhered to? Yes. It was finally agreed that the plane would be called 'Eurofighter 2000' and that the cost reductions would be achieved through changed work-sharing deals, cutting the logistical support and down-grading some of the equipment. The bottom line, so it was said, was a five per cent loss in performance and a delay in bringing the plane into service in exchange for major economies. Eurofighter would not now be ready until 2005.

Volker Rühe was very pleased. At a NATO defence ministers' meeting in Gleneagles, he said that he had not felt able to justify the project to the people of Dresden and was sure that the streets of Birmingham were *not paved with gold*.[21] On his return to Germany, he acclaimed Eurofighter as *Der Einfach Jäger- Ein neues Jagdflugzeug fur eine neue Zeit*.[22]

The final agreement was signed in December. British defence minister Malcolm Rifkind was delighted. *The operational requirement for the RAF will be fully satisfied* he said. *Our taxpayers should also be pleased*.[23] Volker Rühe agreed that a brand new plane had been impossible since well over half of the earmarked development money, £8 billion, had already been spent. He too was pleased with the deal. It made possible a number of German opt-outs on the use of British equipment, if required, the ECR 90 radar, for instance; Germany did not have to commit any extra funds to the project before the next elections in 1994; it would not be obliged to make any decision about its production requirements until 1995. Given the tense party-political situation facing Chancellor Kohl as a deep recession deepened further in late 1992 in Germany, this agreement offered much comfort.

For different reasons, British industry shared this view. As Howard Wheldon said:

> If EFA had gone, the British aerospace industry would have collapsed. The aircraft is that important. [24]

MATTERS CONTEXTUAL

Nevertheless, so strong were the adverse economic and political pressures on the German government in 1993 that, by the end of the year, the country's Bundesrechnungshof (National Audit Office) was urging it *to buy Mig 29s instead of the Eurofighter*. It said that the development of the plane had reached *an extremely critical stage*.[25] By this time DASA's defence sales, in 1991 50 per cent of its turnover, had slumped to a low of 27 per cent.

Gunter Rexrodt, Germany's economics minister diagnosed the problem thus:

> We are in a cyclical downturn, the end of which cannot be foreseen. A downturn is also a recession... We must devote our entire resources to preventing it from becoming the deepest since the war.[26]

His annual report, delivered to the Bundesrat in March 1993, spoke of a shrinking economy with falling output, orders and investment. The only expected rise was in unemployment. The problems of dealing with the economic and social dereliction in East Germany were certainly taking their toll, he said, but the situation was not a catastrophe. In fact, the best case scenario indicated that the further weakening of the economy would be lessened if stringent economies were made in public spending. And that was the proposal.

Volker Rühe announced a £364m reduction in defence spending in February. In March, the German finance ministry called for an extension of the timing of the Eurofighter programme to make it easier to finance.

Restructuring :
US defence companies were speeding up their plans as Pentagon budget cuts bit deep in 1993. The government's target for spending was $53 billion, 6 per cent down on 1992. Lockheed was acquiring General Dynamic Corp's military plane business. Martin Marietta was taking over GE's defence electronics work. In the process these two might come to dominate the industry.

Cutting Capacity :
Excess capacity in defence products was rising and needed drastic pruning. McKinsey data indicated that there was long-term work only for 3 of the 7 US airframe makers.

Diversification :
Conversion to civilian products was a strategy of choice for such major producers as Hughes and TRW Inc.

Exporting :
A strategy pursued aggressively by all players capable of it.

EXHIBIT 4: US DEFENCE COMPANY STRATEGIES
Source : Nowhere to run, nowhere to hide,
Eric Schine and Amy Borrus, *Business Week*, 11/1/93

A similar note, in terms of defence spending, was struck in the 1993 report by the French Commission of Defence to the Assemblée Nationale. It noted that the country's defence sector had lost jobs at a much higher rate than other sectors, to the point that direct employment in defence manufacture was likely to fall below 200,000 by 1995. The Paris RPR depute, Rene Galy-Dejean called it u*ne crise sans précédent.*[27] The causes of the problem were threefold. Firstly, the fall in domestic orders for new equipment. Here, government cut-backs had had severe impact. Secondly, the fall in exports over the period 1977-90. Table 2, on page 319, illustrates further details of this massive fall. The third factor was the extent of the *guerre économique*, economic war, that the USA was said to be fighting to win defence business on a global scale.

The British government, too, was hard at work in 1993 analysing defence spending. Its National Audit Office was similarly involved in appraising the Eurofighter project, yet again, in the light of public concern over continued cost escalation.

On the fifth of July 1993 the ministry of defence published its review. It forecast more job losses in a sector where some 130,000 jobs had disappeared since the end of the Cold War. Given that, in the UK, approximately 1m jobs were connected with the defence sector,[28] there were worries that two of its policy orientations might spell further losses. These were a likely change in the policy of not agreeing to mergers among defence contractors (of the BAe-GEC variety) and a change in the government's willingness to source abroad.

The White Paper revised dramatically the demand requirements set out in the previous Options for Change study on the basis that *a major external threat* of cold war proportions was now unlikely to emerge. Table 3 gives details of the alterations involved.

Country	Year	
	1986	**1991**
USSR	14,731	3,930 (a)
USA	10,304	11,195
France	4,096	804
UK	1,500	999
Germany	1,120	2,015
China	1,463	1,127

TABLE 4: EXPORT SHIPMENTS OF MILITARY PRODUCTS ($M).

Source: Institute of Stockholm Note: (a) = Russia only.

The key questions continuously arising in the Eurofighter debate were its viability as an attack aircraft in a Warsaw Pact attack scenario and its cost. At a possible £50m per aircraft, it would be the most expensive weapons system of its type ever bought by the British government.

Aircraft Type	In use 1990	No of aircraft needed in the mid '90s by RAF	
		Plan A	Plan B
Tornado F3	92	122	100
Phantoms	65	0	0
Hawks	72	52	50
Tornado GR 1s	148	112	112
Harriers	76	52	52
Jaguars	40	40	40
Buccaneers	30	0	0

TABLE 5: UK AIR DEFENCE REQUIREMENTS FOR EXISTING PLANES
Source: *The Times* 6/7/93
Note: Plan A is the 1990 'Options for Change' projection. Plan B is the revised July 1993 projection.

A MEETING OF MINDS?

Given these pressures for economy, it was inevitable that the issue of a possible link-up of some form between GEC and BAe would again come under consideration. And so it did, with substantial media support. *The Sunday Times* expressed its view in forthright terms:

There is no question that, if Britain is to remain a serious player in the defence industry, merger there must be. The rationale is overpowering... France is poised for consolidation. Germany's defence equipment industry is now concentrated in Daimler-Benz. Reasons? ... First, the technological driver.. Second, marketing muscle around the world. [29]

But the talks were soon again called off. In July 1993 there was clearly no meeting of minds between the two chairmen, GEC's Lord Weinstock and BAe's John Cahill.

There were difficulties also in the Eurofighter project itself. EFA's maiden flight had been due to take place in 1991. The UK-German project negotiations had meant re-scheduling this to Autumn 1993. Technical difficulties in the computerised flight control system, the mix of fly-by-wire (DASA) and software (GEC-Marconi), were causing anxiety. After all, the first production model of Sweden's Gripen had crashed in August, ostensibly over difficulties in this area. In fact, such planes as Eurofighter are deliberately designed to be aerodynamically unstable. This improves their dog-fighting capability but means they must be driven by computer. The plane was now set to fly for the first time in March 1994.

On 9th January 1994 Friedrich Bohl, Chancellery minister, endorsed a proposal by members of the Bavarian Christian Social Union (minority party members of Chancellor Kohl's coalition government) that Germany's 1982 statutory restrictions on arms exports should be relaxed. These prohibited arms sales to any conflict zone or area of tension. They backed up regulations which banned the use of German troops in military engagements outside the Nato area.

EXHIBIT 5: THE WAY AHEAD?
Source: Bonn Urged to ease arms rules, Ariane Genillard,
The Financial Times, 10/1/94

There was also political tension in the air as US president Bill Clinton arrived in Brussels for the start of the 1994 NATO conference. He brought with him a US proposal, entitled 'Partnership for Peace', which was aimed at gradually building up the security linkages between Nato and the Vishegrad countries of central Europe (Poland, Hungary and the Czech republic). Manfred Wörner, Nato secretary-general, was at great pains to support the plan and indicate that it posed no threat whatsoever to Russia.

One who disagreed was Vladimir Zhirinovsky, leader of the Liberal Democratic party, which had emerged victorious in the Russian 1993 elections. Not noted for Delphic utterance, he did not mince words in reacting to the Nato proposal:

It would be a huge mistake and tragedy for NATO, Europe and the whole world if they move to take in our neighbours... We will not allow a single foreign division near Russia's borders. Any military unit which receives orders to move towards Russia will be exterminated.[30]

In view of this, his attitude towards NATO's ultimatum to the Bosnian Serbs to use air strikes against their gun emplacements in Sarajevo if the guns were not removed by Sunday 20th February 1994, can be imagined. As can the irritation of Russia's president Boris Yeltsin at not having been contacted by NATO before the decision. He, too, was blunt in his comment on the fraught situation:

Some people, he declared, *are trying to resolve the Bosnian question without the participation of Russia.* ***We will not*** *allow this.*[31]

MOVING ON

By late 1996 Germany was still dragging its feet on what had now become known as Eurofighter. The pressure on its government of meeting the still-outstanding bill for German re-unification and the Maastricht EMU criteria in the middle of a recession seemed too great for it to sign the production go-ahead and it adopted a series of stalling tactics. As a consequence, the British, in particular, increased the pressure on the Germans. The result was a series of mutually unsatisfactory meetings resulting in sometimes imperfectly understood "understandings".

It was said that a "breakthrough" meeting took place on the fifth of January 1997. This certainly resulted in a new group agreement on funding for what was by now a \$60 billion project, and on workshare arrangements. The Germans would buy 180 and the British 232.

But, by mid-1997, firm orders had still not yet been placed. This was despite the facts that Britain's new ambassador, Christopher Meyer, had, since taking up office at the start of the year, consistently worn a gold Eurofighter lapel badge and that Tony Blair and George Robertson, prime minister and defence secretary in Britain's new Labour government respectively, were pressing hard. In an interview with the German Bild magazine, the latter indicated his concern:

The concept of European defence makes little sense if we have to buy all our fighters from the United States. An exit by Germany would seriously damage the credibility of European co-operation.[32]

The problem, as ever, was the state of public finances in Germany. On the 26th June 1997 Volker Rühe and Theo Waigel, Germany's Finance Minister, met for yet another parley on Eurofighter finance. The point at issue was not the need for the fighter, Volker Rühe said it was "absolutely necessary", but the need to balance the contribution to be made by the government for production investment costs with that made by DASA, the main contractor. It had agreed provisionally to pay back to the government the £357m (DM1 billion) aid it had received for launching another project (Airbus) before schedule to enable the government to assist it with Eurofighter. It was almost too much for an exasperated British defence secretary who declared:

Without the Eurofighter we run the risk of losing the European aerospace industry.[33]

Exasperated he might have been at the time, but worse was to follow for George Robertson. Hopes that the first contract for the Eurofighter would be won were dashed in May 1998 when the United Arab Emirates, faced with, on the one hand, a virtuoso flying display from the American F16 and, on the other, by a plastic mock-up of the Eurofighter, chose the former. Their order was for 75 planes. Commentator Christopher Booker pulled no punches:

As the bill for Britain's share of the four-nation Eurofighter project soars to £15 billion, the plane -at £60m a-piece – is fast becoming the most expensive single item the British taxpayers have ever had to fork out for – and the biggest white elephant.[34]

And not only was George Robertson faced with the Treasury's insistence that the British defence budget be further cut back, by £628m in 1999, but the same pressures were evident in Germany. Here, the defence cut back sought by Hans Eichel (treasury minister) from defence minister Rudolf Scharping over the four years from 1999 were of the order of £6 billion, newly-installed members of the SPD-Green government having never been keen on the Eurofighter. Indeed, the SPD's Deputy Bundestag leader, Gernot Erler, dismissed it as "a burden from the Kohl era".[35]

A millennial contribution from DASA's CEO, Manfred Bischoff, did not make government economics any easier, either. He insisted in a speech on the 3rd January 2000 that the armaments for the Eurofighter should also be made in Europe. He wanted an assurance that the British would not wish to buy Raytheon's Amraam missiles, heavily promoted by president Clinton, in preference to the more expensive Meteor. This latter missile was produced by Matra BAe Dynamics with the participation of subsidiaries of DASA, CASA and Alenia. It was seen as a vital symbol of European cooperation, a major step towards the creation of the planned European Aeronautic Defence and Space Company, and key to its becoming one of the three world leaders in its field.[36]

In a world which, in 2000, was still suffering from war (Chechnya), potential for war (India and Pakistan) and massive civil disruption (Kosovo and Indonesia), such a creation was, in his view, a necessity. He received the assurance he needed. By providing Raytheon with orders for a new airborne stand-off radar and ordering the Meteor -whose price, incidentally had been cut by half to secure the £1 billion order- the government managed to balance the equation. As The Guardian's David Gow declared:

The move has enabled the British prime minister to prove his commitment to developing a pan-European defence capability, while remaining loyally transatlantic in outlook.[37]

* * * * * * * * * * * * * * * * * *

NOTES & REFERENCES

1   Unions condemn disastrous EFA vote, Ross Tieman and Wolfgang Munchau, *The Times*, 1/7/92

2   Partners assess the viability of a three-way split, Paul Betts, *The Financial Times*, 2/7/92

3   Bonn fails to back the EFA, Quentin Peel & Paul Betts, *The Financial Times*, 1/7/92

4   As 1

5   Casa says alternative fighter not acceptable, Ian Burns, *The Financial Times*, 2/7/92

6   *The Financial Times*, 2/7/92

7   Leading article, *The Sunday Times*, 5/7/92

8   Eurofighter is redundant, *The Evening Standard* leader, 3/7/92

9   *The Sunday Times*, 5/7/92

10   As 9

11   As 9

12   Freeze on Eurofighter contracts agreed, Peter Bruce, *The Financial Times*, 5/8/92

13   As 12

14   Get your red-hot bombers, tanks, missiles, Richard Melcher & Deborah Stead, *Business Week*, 21/9/92

15   Eurofighter will be meaner, if not leaner, Conrad de Aenlle, *The International Herald Tribune*, 7/9/92

16   As 15

17   As 15

18   As 15

19   EFA - that queasy feeling, David White, *The Financial Times*, 16/9/92

20   'paradoxically one of the safest planning items', Der Jäger 90 war nicht der Grund fur den Stellenabbau, *Frankfurter Allgemeine Zeitung*, 9/10/92

21   Germany spurns EFA at any price, David Fairhall, *The Guardian*, 21/10/92

22   'The Simple Fighter - A New Fighter for a New Age', Rühe lehnt den Jäger 90 weiter ab, *Frankfurter Allgemeine Zeitung*, 2/11/92

23   European Fighter aircraft to go ahead as Rühe surrenders, Michael Evans, *The Times*, 11/12/92

24   How Eurofighter came back from the dead, Andrew Lorenz, *The Sunday Times*, 13/12/92

25   Eurofighter flies into turbulence, Michael Evans, *The Times*, 26/11/93

26   Rühe's break on Eurofighter threatens jobs, Ian Verchere, *The European* 11-14/3/93

27   'An unprecedented crisis'. Une industrie militaire en faillite, Jacques Isnard, *Le Monde*, 11/10/93

DAF

Abstract:

DAF, the European truck maker enjoyed a boom and then went bust. The case charts the reasons for its success, failure and attempted re-construction (as separate companies in Holland and Britain) in the context of competitive developments in the European truck industry.

Question:

Why did DAF go under? Can the phoenix rise again? How can it be kept aloft?

Case Timing: 1993

DANGER AVERTED?

On the eleventh of June 1993, the 700 workers at the Leyland Trucks Manufacturing (LTM) plant in Leyland, Lancashire were in festive mood. They had a major victory to celebrate, namely the successful management buy-out of their firm from the receivers, accountants Arthur Andersen. This factory, *as modern and efficient as any in Europe*,[1] had previously been a major production division of Leyland DAF, the UK arm of the Eindhoven-based DAF NV. Now, so far as ownership was concerned, it was on its own. It would continue to manufacture its competitive range of light-duty trucks.

It was only months since the parent DAF NV and its Leyland DAF subsidiary had both been forced into administrative receivership. Since that fateful day in February 1993, every effort had been made to salvage and turn around a major European company whose products were highly respected in the market place. This had now succeeded in terms of Dutch-Belgian operations. Son of DAF NV was alive, supposedly well and called DAF Trucks NV.

The break-up and sell-off of Leyland DAF was also well-advanced. LTM and the old Leyland DAF van plant at Washwood Heath, Birmingham, whose product line was, in the words of industry analyst Kevin Done, rather *out-of-date*,[2] had been the first management buy-outs.

Unemployment level in Birmingham districts	Nov 1989	Feb 1993
Washwood Heath	13.1%	22.1%
Aston	22.1%	31%

TABLE 1: CHANGES IN UNEMPLOYMENT LEVELS [3]

The salvage process had necessarily involved the break-up of the ownership of what had been a previously highly-integrated European manufacturer of lorries and vans, but not some of the key supply linkages. LTM in Britain, for example, was to carry on assembling its existing product range. Separately-owned subsidiaries of DAF Trucks NV would then, by agreement, sell these trucks in the British and continental markets.

To ensure successful continuity, it was vital to all concerned to maintain the operational cohesiveness of what now were independent firms. It was especially important to retain the loyalty of dealers who, in the highly competitive European market for trucks, were nothing if not fickle.

The receivers had had a complicated task in selling-off the other now-discrete elements of the former British DAF Leyland operation. These comprised the modern, automated spares, storage and distribution operation based at Chorley, Lancs (not planned to be included in the new DAF Trucks NV system), and the Albion axles factory (Glasgow). Each of these had supplied components to, or worked with, other parts of the organisation including the Dutch and Belgian factories at Eindhoven and Westerlo, respectively.

DAF NV, by comparison with other truck makers, had been noteworthy for being a relatively integrated producer, making a large part of its components in-house. This included truck engines, although those for the 45 Series of small trucks were supplied by Cummins (US-owned) and Peugeot-Talbot also made those for DAF vans. Except, that is, for the 200 Series which were obtained from Perkins of Peterborough.

To:	Hirozaku Nakamura, company president, Mitsubishi.
From:	Chorley Borough Council.
Re:	Possible re-use of Leyland DAF plant in Chorley as European base for Mitsubishi's truck operations.

We think that the present situation presents a unique opportunity for an ambitious player in the world commercial vehicle market to make a significant intervention here.

EXHIBIT 1: A HEARTFELT INVITATION [4]

The LTM management buy-out was particularly interesting from three standpoints. Firstly, the receivers did not disclose the payoff to DAF NV creditors that was realised through the sale. Secondly, the 230-acre LTM factory site was purchased not by LTM but by Lancashire Enterprises, a development agency sponsored by the Lancashire regional authority (i.e., the County Council), who leased it to LTM. Thirdly, the fact that the Leyland plant was known to have enough capacity to meet the truck needs, in its class, of the entire UK market.

John Gilchrist, Managing Director of LTM, was clearly delighted with the management buy-out (m.b.o.) and confident about the expected future turnover of £140m in the first year of working. So was the remaining workforce at the plant. Here the workforce had been 28,000 in the 1960s and was now 2,500.

So was Allen Amey, managing director of the van plant. Regional development funds for his team's m.b.o, under the Industrial Development Act 1982, were being channelled through the Birmingham Heartlands Development Corporation, one of eleven bodies charged by the British government with the task of urban economic regeneration. The receivers had also been delighted with the backing the m.b.o. plan had received from investors, including 3i.

The plan valued the plant at some £40m, despite the fact that production was running at below 50 per cent capacity when the deal was struck on the 25th April.

This is a landmark day for Leyland and DAF vans declared Allen Amey. *The long-term future of the plant is secured.*[5]

TWO STEPS BACK

The situation is rather grim as far as finances are concerned. The question is, how long can DAF NV hang in there.. This is a classic case where you have a company in financial difficulties.. It isn't a company that has bad products. They need money.

Thus analyst Dagmar Bottenbruch of Credit Suisse First Boston on the worrying situation facing DAF NV at the start of December 1992.[6]

By the first quarter of 1993 the situation had got much grimmer and not just for this truck maker. In 1993 both Renault-Volvo and IVECO were losing money.

So bad had DAF NV's cash-flow problems become at the start of the year that it was forced into prolonged and intense negotiations with bankers, the Dutch Government and the Flemish regional authority on a Fl. 1.8 billion ($978m) refinancing package. These broke down amid mutual recriminations and, on the 2nd February 1993, DAF NV decided to seek court protection from its creditors. This was a major blow to its owners, who included British Aerospace Plc (10.9 per cent) and its bankers who were owed an estimated Fl. 3-3.5 billion. To its management, who had tried desperately to stem the company's cumulative Fl. 800m losses over the previous three years, it meant bitter defeat.

Some competitors thought that court protection, the equivalent to Chapter 11 of the US Bankruptcy Code, might well, in fact, turn out to be the first step toward bankruptcy. Unless, that is, an accommodation with creditors could speedily be found. Until then, the fear was that DAF's credit lines with suppliers might be frozen and DAF NV's entire 12,650-strong European workforce could not be paid.

There was another consideration overhanging the discussion: that DAF NV had been *continuously under-capitalised.*[7] This was a view not disproved by the confidential study by Coopers & Lybrand on which the restructuring plan was eventually based.[8] For DAF NV to have been the smallest of the full-line truck makers in the EC and to have had such a comparatively broad product range, requiring an onerous investment programme, was a problematic combination. Indeed, DAF NV was the only non-car manufacturer to produce vans.

As can be easily imagined, the uncertainty initially plunged all DAF's operations into something resembling panic. Within hours, the company's integrated just-in-time supply system came under threat as anxious suppliers pondered the situation. This placed assembly operations in DAF plants as far apart as Leyland (Lancs) and Eindhoven in considerable jeopardy. Calm, of a sort, did return soon, however.

But, it must be said, in early February 1993 a deal with creditors looked unlikely. The banks and the two Governments to whom DAF NV had looked for a life-line were at loggerheads. Each laid the blame for the failure of the rescue bid firmly on the others. Both of them effectively wanted to limit their financial exposure and, if new loans had to be given, to ensure for themselves the best possible security.

The banking consortium, led by the ABN-Amro Bank of the Netherlands, seemed the more pliable of the two; they were prepared to loan a further Fl. 50m short-term. The governments were not prepared, however, to stump up the extra Fl. 100m short-term loan which the banks were insisting they contribute, especially under the tight conditions set for any long-term bail out by the banks.

Although ABN-Amro had the biggest exposure, other prominent consortium members were the ING Bank and Rabobank (Netherlands); National Westminster, Lloyds and Barclays (Britain) and Banque Générale (Belgium). No wonder they were anxious. DAF NV's gearing (its total debt as a proportion of shareholders' equity) was estimated to exceed 300 per cent, with total indebtedness put at Fl. 3 billion.[9]

What appeared to be the most likely outcome of the receivership was the break-up of DAF into its constituent parts, with the fate of each being considered on its discrete commercial merits.[10] Under such circumstances, DAF's heavy truck manufacturing operations would be disassociated from the manufacture of light vans and from DAF NV's financial subsidiaries, whose debts were thought to exceed Fl. 2 billion alone. The elements that were incapable of being saved would, it was thought, remain within DAF NV which would be allowed to go bankrupt. Unfortunately, shareholders in DAF NV would lose their entire investment. By contrast, the rescuable elements would (according to this scenario) be incorporated into a new DAF company, which could be privately sold or floated on the stock market. The secured creditors of the old DAF would have their debt swapped into equity stakes in the new company.

At all events it looked likely that the Leyland DAF subsidiary would be de-merged from its parents and, as we have seen, this is precisely what occurred.

As the month of February progressed, all concerned -shareholders, workforce and creditors increasingly needed a speedy resolution to the company's difficulties. By the end of the month the DAF NV weekly average share price had hit a new low of Fl. 5, having been Fl. 25 only one year before. This indicated clearly the depth of the crisis facing DAF NV. Shareholders like VADO (the founding Van Doorne family, 10.3 per cent), ABN-AMRO (10.3 per cent) and Dutch insurance groups AEGON and ING (together 17 per cent) were right to be worried.

DAF NV's bankers found themselves, after all, able to respond positively and quickly to the company's plight. Although their aid was small-scale and temporary, amounting to a Fl. 60m short term loan, it did allow the company to keep on paying wages and meeting trading expenses for the rest of February. The Dutch Government agreed that it, too, would help with short-term financing [11] in order to give the receivers time to review long-term prospects for the company.

The appointment of two sets of administrative receivers, Louis Detering and Friso Meeter for the Netherlands and John Talbot and Murdoch McKillop for the UK, confirmed the view that a split-up of DAF NV was to take place on geographical lines. This involved the UK administrators, both partners in Arthur Andersen, in trying to ensure a continuation of Leyland DAF trading and the development of a strategy which would ensure the sale of Leyland DAF's three principal British subsidiaries as going concerns. This they clearly achieved, at least in respect of the manufacturing arms of what had been Leyland DAF, the truck and van plants.

DUTCH RESCUE

DAF NV could well have taken considerable comfort from the fact that, in its original turnaround negotiations, the Dutch government and the Belgian authorities had shown every sign of willingness to help. Offers of convertible loans of Fl.100m and Fl.110m respectively were heart-warming. With the Dutch government's already owning two per cent and the strong DAF brand loyalty in Belgium and the Netherlands, DAF NV could, of course, feel doubly assured of aid.

But there was also the issues of regional employment and contribution to export earnings for governments to consider. So far as the first was concerned, DAF NV employed 6,000 in the Netherlands and 2,000 in Belgium. By comparison 5,500 had jobs in Leyland DAF. Additionally, an estimated 15,000 additional jobs in the UK hung on the latter and the cost to Britain's economy of the closure of Leyland DAF operations in Britain was put at £1 billion.[12]

Of course, any possibility of a bail-out exclusively funded by the governments involved would have been well-nigh impossible. Objections from the EC's Competition Commissioner, citing articles 92 and 93 of the Treaty of Rome (1957), would have stopped such a plan in its tracks.

The re-started rescue attempt began with the comments of the Dutch economic affairs minister, Koos Andriessen, to the effect that it was the three British banks, National Westminster, Barclays and Lloyds, who had provoked the collapse of the original rescue package and impelled DAF NV into receivership by refusing to lend any more money. It ended, as has been noted, with the parcelling-up of ownership of the parts of DAF NV between the continent and Britain and a plan for the creation of the new company, DAF Trucks NV. This owed as much to the inspiration of the Dutch and Belgian governments as it did to their aid. Financial details of the re-financing package are contained in Table 2.

*	A total of Fl 467m to be raised in fresh equity
*	Of this the Dutch government is to put up Fl 195m and the Flanders regional government Fl 75m
*	The two governments together will own about 57 per cent of DAF Trucks NV
*	Banks and Insurance Companies will provide FL 110m extra equity, institutional investors Fl 50m and the company's suppliers, dealers and importers a further Fl 37m
*	Dutch Banks (ABN Amro, Rabobank, ING Bank and the Dutch Investment Bank) and the Dutch subsidiary of Credit Lyonnais to provide loans of Fl 400m

TABLE 2: THE REFINANCING PACKAGE FOR DAF TRUCKS NV

The new company, DAF Trucks NV, would retain control of the Dutch and Belgian medium and heavy truck activities and employ 3,500 people. All branches of DAF NV Finance, the wholly owned subsidiary hitherto responsible for advancing purchase loans to buyers and referred to by company creditors as *a black hole*,[13] would close.

Leyland DAF would be de-merged but formal supply agreements would be signed between DAF Trucks NV and some of the British component manufacturers who had once been part of the Leyland DAF.

1970s	Millions of £s of public money spent on the state-owned Leyland plant - show-piece of nationalised industry. Given state-of-the-art assembly equipment. Policy of active industrial investment followed by Britain's Conservative and Labour governments.
1987	DAF took over Leyland Vehicles when it was privatised. In the process it became the largest UK truck manufacturer. This company had been part of British Leyland, which also owned the Rover group. British Aerospace which took over Rover obtained a 40 per cent stake in DAF NV in this way. The British government wrote off £750m of the company's debts when it was sold to DAF NV.
1988	Leyland Bus, another part of British Leyland, having been bought in an m.b.o. led by Ian McKinnon in 1987, sold to Volvo.
1991	British Aerospace did not subscribe to the DAF NV rights issue. Its stake had fallen previously to 16 per cent

TABLE 3: MATTERS HISTORICAL

Throughout the process of restoring the companies to health, all four receivers laid a considerable amount of emphasis, despite necessary differences in ownership, on the way in which former DAF NV subsidiaries could and would continue to offer an integrated product range to DAF NV's 1300-strong dealer network across Europe. As Murdoch McKillop pointed out *The key concept is to keep that integrated product range together... The sum of the whole is worth much more than the sum of the parts.*[14]

The final rescue deal was struck only days before the 26th February, the date on which the short-term credit availability period previously agreed with the banks was due to expire. It is to be noted that aid by the Dutch and Belgian authorities was aimed at safeguarding the jobs involved at Eindhoven and Westerlo. Indeed, the Belgian financing was conditional on the maintenance of around 750 Belgian production jobs in Flanders (hitherto some 1,400 people had worked in the Westerlo cab and axle plant) and 400 in the Eindhoven HQ.

DAF Trucks NV was not the first company in recent times that the Dutch government had felt it necessary to support. Philips, the electronics group, and plane maker Fokker had similarly found themselves in trouble at the start of the 1990s and turned to foreign companies as well as their own authorities for help.

Apparently, such help as was given was provided more for pragmatic reasons than out of a sense of ideological commitment to the virtues of interventionism. Whatever the precise rationale, DAF Trucks NV was now a major case of Dutch government investment in industry, a 42 per cent equity stake no less. But not only was there no political controversy in the Netherlands over the move, there was also a groundswell of popular public support. The trade unions and the DAF works council mobilised this in the form of obtaining pledges from some 70,000 people to a special Fl.12.5m bond under the campaign motto of *Keep DAF on the Road*.[15] Ruud Lubbers, the Dutch prime minister, and the members of the PSV Eindhoven football club were early subscribers.

Were the company to fail again, the embarrassment would not only be financial, as it had been for all the shareholders who took part in DAF NV's 1989 flotation, but political.

The revelations which were made at the shareholders' meeting in Eindhoven on the 15th April 1993 did not inspire overmuch confidence. The new company was known to be facing serious challenges from shareholders' and creditors' claims against the old DAF NV. Already the value of DAF NV bonds had dropped from Fl.1000 to Fl.30 and shares were now trading at seven cents.

Imagine the furore when it was announced at the meeting that shareholders and unsecured creditors would actually get nothing from DAF NV's liquidation. This, in spite of an actual improvement in DAF NV's net losses over the period 1991-2 from Fl. 395m to Fl. 257m, inclusive of all extraordinary charges.

BRITISH RESERVE

The attitude of the British government towards the possibility of turn-around aid for Leyland DAF, the former UK subsidiary of DAF NV, was wholly different from that of its continental counterparts. Michael Heseltine, trade and industry secretary, spelled out the position in a statement to the House of Commons immediately after DAF NV's announcement of administrative receivership. Whilst he supported any move to turn Leyland DAF around, he said, there was to be no public money made available for any rescue other than that available from statutory regional development funds. This was a viewpoint that his Labour shadow, Robin Cook, rejected totally. He stated that a collapse of Leyland DAF would inflict yet another blow to what he said was Britain's shrinking industrial base.

The Times supported the Government's stance on the grounds that *if one company is to be shored up by public money, others with no access to public funds will be disadvantaged*, adding that:

Leyland DAF's efficient plant in Lancashire.. is just the sort of operation that should take advantage of sterling's devaluation. It would make a fine base for a Japanese manufacturer whom continental rivals might be keen to keep out.[16]

This position was endorsed by IVECO Ford's chief executive in a letter to Michael Heseltine. It stated:

Surely there can be no further government support for a company with such a track record. We think it right that you do not intend to bail out Leyland DAF because clearly there is too much manufacturing capacity available even for an annual market of 50,000 trucks... Should there be any change in policy, then IVECO Ford would look to receive an equal benefit.[17]

Michael Heseltine stuck consistently in the months to come to his belief in what he called *a market solution* for the Leyland DAF problem. *I don't believe that intervening with (government) money produces long-term solutions*, he declared. His opposite number, Robin Cook, equally resolutely clung to his argument about the company's situation. There could, he claimed, be no clearer example of how *Britain is losing out to countries with an industrial strategy because we have a government with none.*[18]

Throughout the period immediately after the declaration of receivership, the main union involved, the Amalgamated Engineering & Electrical Union, kept up the pressure for governmental intervention. According to John Allen, chief union negotiator, a massive 18,000 jobs could be lost in Britain if the company were liquidated, without taking into account the dealer network which itself employed 5,000 people.

Location	Leyland DAF Division Activities	No of jobs
Glasgow	Truck and van axle production	550
Leyland	Truck assembly. Engine and components assembly. Truck engineering	2,200
Chorley	Parts, warehouse and distribution	400
Birmingham	Van production. Components production. Van engineering	2,000
Thame	Sales & marketing	330

TABLE 4: LEYLAND DAF JOBS AT RISK

Governmental reserve on the need to intervene with aid remained unchanged as receivers fought manfully in early February to save the companies involved against such threats as a halting of supplies to the van and truck plants and a threatened strike.

With the agreement of the receivers, limited production at the Leyland DAF truck factory had begun again on the fourth of February and at the van plant in Washwood Heath, Birmingham on the fifth. But both were soon in trouble.

In-bound and out-bound material supplies were a problem. Leyland DAF, for example, was a major supplier of body panels to Rover group's Range Rover and Land Rover factories and immediate worries were raised about the possibility of serious disruption, at least until the panel tooling used by Leyland DAF, but owned by Rover group, could be moved.

Though a major headache for those involved, this was a comparatively small problem, however, compared with the potential challenge facing the estimated 500 British suppliers who provided Leyland DAF with parts worth some £250m p.a. GKN, one of the leaders, embargoed deliveries of axles and prop shafts on the tenth of February and said that the suspension would remain in force until the situation became clearer.[19] Cummins, which made the engines for Leyland DAF's best-selling truck, the 45 series, followed suit. Within a week, however, the receivers had been able to issue the necessary guarantees.

The strike threat was averted on the eleventh of February by strong action on the part of the administrative receiver. It had started with mass protest meetings held at the Leyland plant and with what convenor Derek Bullen called a strike 'mandate' backed by an estimated 70 per cent of the workforce. It ended the same day with a letter from Murdoch McKillop which said:

If there is strike action, then all 5,500 jobs with Leyland DAF will be lost, with a knock-on effect on suppliers.. I don't know whether we can succeed, but without your help we cannot.[20]

As it was, the receivers announced more than 1,600 job losses at Leyland DAF that very night. Worse, the receivership situation was such that the company was wholly unable to meet its obligations to pay contractual redundancy. The government-operated statutory redundancy scheme provided significantly less compensation. This compared unfavourably with the terms offered to those made redundant in Holland: they each received up to 70 per cent of their final earnings for the previous 4 years. [21] There was massive disbelief and consternation among workers made redundant, but no disruption.

A week later, however, things were looking better for those left in employment. The receivers had been given a clear statement of intent that a team of managers, headed by Allan Amey, managing director of the Birmingham van plant, wished to proceed with a management buy-out of that factory. They hoped that, among other things, this would head off a potential problem with its mature product line, concerning Renault. Sadly, it was a case of misplaced confidence.

Renault had, in fact, had a product innovation alliance with Leyland DAF for a new van called the Excel, whose development had been scheduled to take place at Birmingham. They cancelled this agreement in mid-February in favour of a new partnership, thought to be with car-maker Volkswagen.

Nevertheless, Allen Amey exuded confidence about the m.b.o. He declared:

We believe that many of the elements needed to underpin a successful business are already in place. We have experienced managers backed by a loyal workforce. The events of recent weeks have clearly demonstrated that we have the support of customers who want to go on buying our vehicles.[22]

Similarly, hopes rose for the future of the Leyland truck plant, once a supply agreement had been struck with DAF Trucks NV. It was also rumoured that Paccar, one of the USA's leading truck makers with 1992 sales of £2.5 billion might also be interested in a bid for the Leyland plant. It already owned Foden, the specialist British lorry producer, and had in fact tried to buy Leyland when it was de-nationalised in 1987, only to be beaten to the punch by DAF.

Both these factors gave considerable impetus to the management buy-out that John Gilchrist was seeking to mount for this part of Leyland DAF. This, as we have seen, was successfully steered through by June 1993.

Negotiations by a management team to buy the Chorley parts operations took longer to gestate. But here, as elsewhere in the old Leyland DAF, there was a mood of optimism. It was certainly shared by Ian McKinnon, a former Leyland DAF director, who persistently, but unsuccessfully, sought to buy both the Chorley and the Leyland operations from the administrators.

ROUGH WATERS

DAF NV's collapse in early 1993 was certainly brought on by cash flow problems. But it is also rooted in the competitive conditions that existed in the west European truck market in the late 1980s and in the strategies that key players sought to pursue in that context. The number of truck makers in Western Europe had already dwindled from 25 in 1975 to ten in 1992 and there appeared on paper to be very strong reasons why the number should decline even further.

The costs of doing business, developing new products, meeting the new EC environmental regulations, financing a strong dealer network for example, had risen to such a degree as to favour only those manufacturers enjoying powerful economies of scale.

The European Single Market certainly offered immense growth opportunities for road transport. Some 65 per cent of all goods traded in the EC were transported by road in 1991. But it also threatened, through the EC's planned deregulation of road transport, a major increase in competition among hauliers who would have their ability to protect themselves in their own home markets removed. On top of this, it posed an associated problem in terms of the numbers of trucks that would be bought in future by the larger haulage groups. The US experience of de-regulation was that lorries had been used to much greater capacity (for out-bound and in-bound haulage without cabotage restriction) and that trucking profit margins had shrunk as competition intensified. This combination of de-regulation and economic conditions resulted in the US truck making industry's working to 55 per cent capacity in 1992.

But it was market conditions, above all, which had the biggest effect. Table 5 indicates the size of the changes in the market demand over the period 1990-1992. It illustrates only two years of a critical recession that had begun to take effect in Britain in 1989 and had now (in 1992/3) started to hit France and Germany.

As Table 5 shows, total sales of the smaller trucks in 1990 were down by 11.6 per cent on 1989; the fall in sales for the larger trucks was 5.9 per cent. Additionally, DRI predictions for 1992 had previously indicated that demand for the larger trucks in the above countries would be down by a further ten per cent. Their report, issued in November 1992, stated bluntly:

Turmoil in European currency markets, deteriorating national economies and increasing uncertainties over the prospects of any economic recovery have added to the mood of gloom.. in the truck industry. German unification and the boom it injected into the market are fast fading away as the market faces re-adjustment to lower levels of demand.[23]

Britain had borne the brunt of the 1989-93 recession in terms of truck sales. Not since the early 1950s had sales levels been so low. Conversely, the need for replacement of trucks maintained beyond their normal life created theoretically at least, the potential for rising demand.

Country	Up to 6 tonnes		Over 6 tonnes	
	1990	1991	1990	1991
Germany	103.6	129.7	68.3	105.5
France	370.6	328.0	49.4	43.9
UK	230.1	163.4	44.7	29.8
Italy	147.8	147.8	32.0	25.3
Spain	191.1	158.7	24.9	20.4
Total	**1341.3**	**1186.6**	**278.4**	**275.2**

TABLE 5: ACTUAL TRUCK SALES
('000 UNITS) 1990-2 [DRI European Trucks Forecast Report]

Against this background, the moves made by major truck makers who competed with DAF in Western Europe make interesting reading:

*   Mercedes Benz

Mercedes Benz of Germany was the largest European truck maker, with a 31 per cent share in 1992. It was the main subsidiary of Daimler Benz, which was itself over 20 per cent owned by the Deutsche Bank. It had experienced the full weight of the cyclical downturn in its home market place, having moved from record output levels in early 1992 to short-time working in mid-1993. This had obliged it to shelve plans for a DM 1 billion plant at Ahrensdorf in Eastern Germany. Mercedes was holding fire on its original plan to buy stakes in the Czech Republic's AVIA (31 per cent) and LIAZ (20 per cent).

*   Volvo & Renault Vehicules Industriels (RVI)

The Swedish Volvo company announced in 1990 an emergency package to cut its operating costs by $255m by end 1992. This involved the loss of 1,150 jobs, bringing its global workforce down to 18,100. In 1992, it followed this up with another cost-cutting move. A saving of a further $425m was envisaged by 1995 and a further 1,980 jobs were to go.

State-owned RVI, which had a 45 per cent cross share-holding agreement with Volvo, was similarly cutting costs. In December 1992 it closed its Dunstable plant, once one of the leading truck building centres in Europe. In its day it had been home to marques like Bedford, Commer, Karrier and Dodge. It had had a chequered ownership: Rootes Group (1950s) and Chrysler (1960s). In 1978 Peugeot had bought it. They had sold it, in 1981, to Renault.

RVI, having been frustrated in attempts to win a Czech partner (IVECO was outbid by Mercedes Benz in the bid for an alliance with LIAZ), was working with the STAR group in Starachowice in Poland.

*   IVECO

IVECO was the commercial vehicles subsidiary of the Italian giant Fiat. It had been originally put together as a collection of Italian, French and German truck makers. It was in the process of digesting two major operations - joint management of the IVECO-Ford UK truck business and the recently-acquired Spanish truck maker Enasa, formerly the state-owned Pegaso Trucks, which DAF NV had also tried to buy. It too was seeking to bring costs under control. In 1991 its losses amounted to £40m. The proposal for a link-up between IVECO and Tatra, the Czech maker of heavy off-the-road vehicles, was still under consideration. This complemented the agreement that IVECO already had with Uralmash of Russia to produce joint venture products at the Uralaz plant at Miass.

The key concerns underlying these moves relate to the extent of over-capacity in the industry, as evidence of a long run structural imbalance of supply and demand, and the price war that has been running for over a year, particularly in Germany. The British market, the key sales area for Leyland DAF with over a 25 per cent market share, had been hugely problematic.

Although the Japanese were major players in world markets, Isuzu, Hino (part of Toyota), Mitsubishi and Nissan were numbers 2,3,4 and 5 in world size rankings, they had as yet no major presence in the European market place. In 1993 Mitsubishi showed no sign of wanting to take up the Chorley Borough offer, shown in Exhibit 1 on page 335.

DEGREES OF FIT

Against such well-heeled and sizeable competitors DAF NV had evidently found it difficult to navigate in the European market-place of the early '90s. Table 6 indicates its relative achievement in 1991 and 1992.

Truck Maker	1991	1992
Mercedes Benz	31.0	32.5
Iveco	18.6	17.9
Volvo-RVI	18.4	16.4
MAN	12.1	13.1
DAF	7.2	7.8
Scania	6.1	6.0
Others	5.9	6.3

TABLE 6: WEST EUROPE TRUCK MARKET SHARES (%, Jan-Aug)
Source : DRI data

Nevertheless, it had tried to work miracles.

Before its collapse it had been negotiating with Mercedes Benz over a possible strategic alliance, only to be finally and definitively rebuffed. Not only that, it had the comment of Helmut Werner, Mercedes-Benz chief executive elect, to chew over. He had said, that, so far as trucks were concerned, *By the end of the 1990s we will have three supranational strategic alliances in Europe, each with one major company at its core.*[24] As if that were not enough, the Daimler Benz finance director, Gerhard Liener, had indicated:

The more our (Mercedes Benz trucks') European market share grows, the more we are exposed to risks. We don't want more than 32 per cent.. We do not have any intention of becoming a (DAF) shareholder. They would be very happy.. but we are not going to do that.[25]

347

So far as marketing was concerned, DAF NV had cut its prices to the bone, so much so that some rivals asserted that DAF NV had been *giving trucks away*.[26] It had also, and at great cost, expanded its dealer network.

Country	Up to 6 tonnes			Over 6 tonnes		
	1992	1993	1994	1992	1993	1994
Germany	179.1	149.6	143.1	97.0	74.5	63.8
France	301.2	317.4	337.1	36.3	37.1	42.6
UK	152.0	168.5	184.3	29.0	32.7	37.4
Italy	144.8	143.7	150.2	20.1	18.0	22.8
Spain	178.2	186.9	192.6	18.2	18.6	20.7

TABLE 7: FORECAST TRUCK SALES (DRI data)

DAF NV had clearly tried to get larger by bidding for Enasa and the Austrian manufacturer Steyr, but had been twice rejected. This could have been a re-run of the successful late 1980s strategy it had pursued in respect of Leyland. In this, DAF's heavy trucks had been well complemented by Leyland's light and medium trucks and the two dealer networks - in the UK and on the continent - had created synergistic and substantial sales possibilities.

> *The UK has experienced a recession similar in nature but far worse in degree than in other major industrialised countries. The origin of recession was essentially domestic, a reaction to the previous debt-financed boom. By mid-1992 the UK's economic performance was clearly out of line with the other major industrial countries and with its EC partners, and yet the country had tied its hands in terms of monetary and exchange rate policy independence [27]... The UK recovery is still fragile, with just 1.5 per cent growth this year and 2.5 per cent next (compared with a fall in total EC GDP of .5 per cent this year and modest growth of 1.25 per cent next)... Employment in the EC is forecast to fall by more than 1.75 per cent in 1993, the worst performance in the history of the EC... 20 million people out of work.[28]*

EXHIBIT 2: FINANCE COMMISSIONER CHRISTOPHERSON SPEAKS

DAF NV appeared, in 1987, to have found the answer to its problems through the creation of Leyland DAF. Admittedly, the merger led to 2,600 job losses in Britain and difficulties had been experienced with profit margins in Britain (the thinnest in Europe).

But for the next three years the company rode the boom in the European truck market. Indeed, it still had, in 1993, the newest range of trucks in Europe (after IVECO), although this advantage was set to be eroded. DAF NV profits had soared from Fl. 63m to Fl. 172m and its £370m stock market flotation in June 1989 was hugely successful. Its shares, priced at Fl 45 had carried a Fl. 10 premium.

And then there was the collapse in February 1993. For all concerned the question now was *Would the phoenix that had been DAF NV rise again?*

* * * * * * * * * * * * * * * * * * *

NOTES & REFERENCES

1   Business Comment, *The Sunday Times*, 7/2/93
2   Leyland may offer low-cost production base, Kevin Done, *The Financial Times*, 4/3/93
3   Birmingham's engine room is slowing down, Paul Cheeseright, *The Financial Times*, 13/2/93
4   DAF receiver denies Leyland closure plan, Celia Weston and Mark Milner, *The Guardian*, 6/2/93
5   Leyland van buy-out is completed, *The Times*, 26/4/93
6   DAF in talks with banks, Dutch Government on bail-out, Martin Du Bois, *The Wall Street Journal*, 7/12/92
7   Double Dutch dealing, *The Times* editorial, 4/2/93
8   DAF plan excludes UK plants, Robert Peston & Kevin Done, *The Financial Times*, 5/2/93
9   DAF sinks under Fl 3 billion debt, Kevin Done, Ivor Owen, Andrew Baxter & David Brown, *The Financial Times*, 3/2/93
10   DAF, a victim of Europe's truck shake-out, seeks shield from creditors as aid talks fail, Martin du Bois and Timothy Appel, *The Wall Street Journal*, 3/1/93
11   DAF wins a £22m temporary lifeline from bank creditors, Kevin Done, Robert Peston & Andrew Hill, *The Financial Times*, 4/2/93
12   As 7
13   As 10
14   Receivers predict DAF break-up, Kevin Done, *The Financial Times*, 10/2/93
15   Dutch rescue keeps DAF on the road, Ronald van de Krol, *The Financial Times*, 22/2/93
16   Double Dutch Dealing, *The Times* editorial, 4/2/93
17   Iveco Ford urges no bail-out for DAF, Kevin Done, *The Financial Times*, 6/2/93
18   Heseltine defends no cash stance on Leyland DAF, Ronald van de Krol, Richard Donkin & Ralph Atkins, *The Financial Times*, 22/2/93
19   Parts ban at Leyland, Ross Tieman, *The Times*, 11/2/93
20   Strike threat puts all Leyland jobs at risk, Ross Tieman, *The Times*, 12/2/93.
21   No cash left for redundancy pay, Kevin Maguire, *The Daily Telegraph*, 13/2/93
22   Buyout bid for Leyland DAF to go ahead, Mary Fagan, *The Independent*, 1/3/93
23   Outlook remains gloomy, Kevin Done, *The Financial Times*, 23/11/93
24   Squeeze tightens as sales plummet, Kevin Done, *The Financial Times*, 23/11/93.
25   Daimler Benz rules out share stake in DAF, Kevin Done, *The Financial Times*, 20/11/92
26   European Price War drove Leyland DAF over the edge, Mathew Lynn, *The Sunday Times*, 7/2/93

27   EC issues gloomy forecast on economic prospects, Tom Walker, *The Times*, 4/2/93
28   EC admits to worst recession for 40 years, Tom Walker, *The Times*, 17/6/93

THE PORT OF ST PETERSBURG

Abstract:

This complex case deals with aspects of the situation facing the port of St Petersburg - as ship-building and transportation centre - in the light of the decision by Bremer Vulkan, the German ship-builder, to take a sizeable ownership stake in the Severnaya Verf company. This strategic decision can be reviewed in the light of the major focuses of the case: firstly, the changing face of global shipbuilding and transport and the pattern of investments being made by Western companies in shipyards round the Baltic littoral and secondly the political situation in Russia at the time.
This case can be read in conjunction with Perestroika and Russia at the Crossroads

Question:

Examine the changes taking place in international shipping (shipbuilding and transportation) that were taking place at the time and seem likely for the future. Examine the shipbuilders' strategies. Indicate whether or not you think Bremer Vulkan's strategy was sound. What sort of problems do you think the company would encounter if and when it sought to change "the world of work" in the Severnaya Verf?

Case timing: 1993-4

THE BEST OF TIMES, THE WORST OF TIMES

On the third of December 1992, President Yeltsin at long last signed the decree intended to revitalise Russia's merchant navy. This must have come as welcome news to Oleg Terekhov, general manager of the port of St Petersburg, since, as Exhibit 1 shows, the Yeltsin plan was very ambitious and had major implications for the size and scope of his port's activity. It augured well for St Petersburg's falling competitiveness as Russia's only remaining major port in the Baltic.

There could be no doubt that, for Terekhov and his team, the long-awaited decision was a rare opportunity to restore the port to the greatness it had historically enjoyed since its founding by Peter the Great at the start of the 18th century. Specifically, it would mean new facilities, moorings, hydraulic installations and larger container-handling capacity, as well as an improved infrastructure. These would substantially increase St Petersburg's trans-shipment capability and restore some of the prominence it was beginning to lose to its Baltic neighbours.

The wide-ranging Yeltsin plan for the revival of Russia's mercantile marine covered, firstly, the creation of 14 new ports and the development and modernisation of the 40 existing ones. Secondly, it aimed at a renovation and extension of Russia's fleet. To complement these two aims, it also planned to create a new and highly-efficient marine transport infrastructure (covering port, road and railway facilities and communication systems) and to improve education and training facilities at naval academies and colleges.

The purpose was to increase, by the year 2000, the handling capacity of Russian seaports by 150m tonnes and raise the size of the fleet by 8.4m deadweight tonnes. By contrast, in 1993 its ports could only handle 166m of the current 260m tonnes of external trade.[2] Depending on the particular element, the cost of the plan was to be be met by the specifically-constituted government Revival Fund, by shipping companies' own internal cash flow and by loans from Russian and foreign sources.

EXHIBIT 1: MEASURES TO REVIVE THE RUSSIAN MERCHANT NAVY –
PRESIDENTIAL DECREE SIGNED 3/12/1992 [1]

While the planned expansion would take effect over the longer term, port management hoped that simply publishing the outlines of the plan would help immediately in dealing with many of the physical and personnel problems the port had suffered since the break-up of the former Soviet Union. In 1991 and

1992 such difficulties had come thick and fast and had caused senior port managers many headaches.

All those involved recognised the harm that the USSR's disintegration had done to Russia's position as controller (within the former USSR) of a huge and integrated sea transport machine. Now, whereas Russia's need for transportation capacity was put at 200m tonnes p.a., its current fleet capacity did not exceed 100m tonnes p.a. This meant that Russian manufacturers and traders had to spend much of their difficult-to-earn hard currency on buying shipping services from foreign suppliers. This was a costly situation for a country which – as leader of the USSR – had been one of the world's largest fleet operators.

Now, only so far as the Baltic was concerned, Russia had given up docks and terminals, refrigerator ships, ferries, bulk carriers, tankers and gas carriers. It had also relinquished control over major shipping facilities in what had become sovereign Estonian, Latvian and Lithuanian soil. The loss of such ports as Riga and Ventspils was much bewailed, especially as Kaliningrad and St Petersburg were now in direct commercial competition with them.[3]

Even nearer to home had been the financial effects of these and associated changes on St Petersburg's Russian customers. Two port users in particular had found things very difficult – Sovcomflot and the Baltic Shipping Co.

SOVCOMFLOT AND THE BALTIC SHIPPING CO

Sovcomflot was a major owner and operator of a massive fleet of ships. As its name (Soviet Commercial Fleet) indicates, it had managed the operations of the bulk of the former Soviet mercantile marine. In 1993 it operated one of the most modern fleets in the world as a state-aided, profit-driven enterprise. The wide range of ships used included crude oil and product tankers (the largest of which are called Suezmaxes), gas and chemical carriers, container ships and so on. The aim was to self-operate and/or hire out ships to independent shippers at highly competitive rates.

Sovcomflot's problems were partly connected with the fact that, in 1991–92, worldwide shipping rates had plummeted. The resulting fall in cash flow could not have happened at a worse time since the company had just taken delivery of no less than 28 new vessels from Korea. Especially badly hit were the returns from the ten Suezmax tankers being used in the spot market to transport oil.

In January 1993 Francois Lachèvre, director of the Sovcomflot division responsible for commercial tanker operations (Geneva-based Sovchart) did not, however, seem unduly concerned:

If you know an owner today who has good cash flow, tell me. It is correct that we have a very good balance sheet (US$ 1 billion) and we have been facing, as any shipowner in the world, some pressure on our cash flow. The problem is when you have a huge fleet, which every day costs a lot of money, that it is more and more difficult to pay demurrage.[4]

Demurrage is the cost of failure to load or discharge a ship within the time stipulated in the shipping contract. It is paid, as a daily rate, by the ship-owners to those chartering the ship and reclaimed, wherever possible, by the ship-owner from the port which has been inefficient. In 1992 Sovcomflot paid out $5m in demurrage. It was a big problem in the port of St Petersburg.

By the end of April 1993, Sovcomflot's other problem was causing even more distress. Ex-Sovcomflot subsidiaries which had been spun off under the 1991-3 restructuring of the company had already received assets (ships, yard facilities etc.) worth $500m, free of charge. Under the restructuring legislation the company had been empowered to ask these former subsidiaries to pay for the shares they had been allotted in Sovcomflot. Among the most prominent who had refused to pay for such shares were the Baltic Shipping Co (owing about $4m), Latvian Shipping ($5m) and Estonian Shipping ($4m). As Vadim Kornilov, Sovcomflot chairman, pointed out:

All of this money is considered to be bad debt. They seem to have no intention of paying and, if this is really the case, we will have to take legal action.[5]

Indeed, the company had already had two Latvian ships arrested.

To cover losses arising from these cash flow difficulties Sovcomflot had, in fact, switched its strategy in the first half of 1993. It had stopped acquiring ships and started selling them, describing the move as an attempt at *streamlining operations*. In April 1993 it was, in fact, seeking to sell three new gas carriers and two Suezmax tankers. The chairman was not exaggerating when he said:

Generally speaking, we are suffering now from the consequences of the dissolution of the Soviet Union. This (1992) was not a very good year for us.[6]

While some of Sovcomflot's difficulties were of indirect relevance to port manager Oleg Terekhov, those of the Baltic Shipping Co (BSC) were of immediate concern. BSC was a major user of the port and was based in the city. Not only did the company owe a claimed $4m to Sovcomflot but their vessel, Kapitan Kanevsky, had been impounded by the Dutch authorities in March 1993 for the non-payment of debts amounting to $4.4m. To cap it all, company president Viktor Kharchenko was also under arrest.[7]

It was an inglorious situation for the company which, having been set up in 1922, had once controlled the port itself. Indeed, BSC could trace its venerable commercial history back to 1830 and the foundation of the St Petersburg-Lübeck Steamship Co.

THE BALTIC SEABOARD

Oleg Terekhov and the chief executives of St Petersburg's two major civil shipyards, The Baltic Factory and the Severnaya Verf (Northern Wharf), must have welcomed President Yeltsin's decree for yet another reason. This was the sheer pace of change in ports along the Baltic coast, literally from Lübeck to Gdansk. These were now directly rivaling St Petersburg, as never before in the last 60 years, in both trade and shipbuilding.

Commentators with an historical turn of mind may compare aspects of the economic developments taking place along the Baltic coast in the 1990s to elements in the formation and rise to economic power of the medieval Hanse (see Exhibit 2, page 358). Whatever else, present-day *free market* reformers can see in the investment of capital by foreign owners the necessary means to restore the fortunes of east Baltic ports and yards. Under Communist rule these had undeniably suffered economic decline and technological obsolescence. Others, more critical of the current trend, view in-bound investment as being reminiscent of nothing more than colonialism.

The former East Germany in the early 1990s was a case in point.

The change which gained most publicity was the purchase by West German shipbuilders Bremer Vulkan of the Neptun Werft (shipyard) in Rostock, against stiff competition. The takeover took place in May 1993 with the agreement and assistance of Germany's Treuhandanstalt – the state agency charged with handling the successful disposal of former E. German companies. Two of the conditions of the deal were that Vulkan would carry out a \$226m modernisation programme and that none of Neptun's workforce would lose their jobs.[8] Some of Neptun's own managers were participating in the new ownership structure.

One of the reasons why Bremer was highly popular with its new East German workforce was the fact that it had already agreed a 26 per cent pay rise to workers at its other East German yard in Wismar, MTW Schiffswerft, in response to the trade unions' claim for this amount.

The pay claim was, in fact, quite legitimately based on an agreement made among the government, employers and unions when the two halves of Germany were reunited, namely that East German wages would be brought up to

From 1150 onwards the Hanseatic League came to political and economic prominence. It was at heart a guild of German merchants, who, having established themselves throughout the Baltic seaboard, became a highly successful and integrated European trading network. Through conquest and negotiation (Treaty of Stralsund 1370) they gained more and more control of trade in the Baltic. Their branches in towns like Koenigsberg (Kaliningrad), Rostock, Danzig (Gdansk), Riga and Novgorod were run as a cohesive business undertaking from the central headquarters in Lübeck by a tightly controlled hierarchy of members who used commonly-accepted financial systems (e.g. discounting bills of exchange). Members of the Hanse fraternity lived apart from other town-dwellers, initially under a sort of monastic discipline. Ultimately, and as a by-product of the Hundred Years War which disrupted all Mediterranean and Danube-based trade, the league came to enjoy a trading monopoly in the Baltic. Members exercised their dominion with edict-issuing diets which took place every three years in Lübeck. The league held sway until the end of the 15th century.

EXHIBIT 2: THE HANSEATIC LEAGUE

West German levels within an agreed schedule. The increase for 1993 was stipulated at the time to be 26 per cent. The pay equalisation is scheduled to be completed by the end of 1995. Bremer was acting in an exemplary fashion.

In the event, the view of most German employers in early 1993 was that the pay rise could not be paid to workers in Germany because of the weakness of the economy. The eventual refusal to meet the claim sparked off a serious national strike involving members of the IG Metall union.

It was in Poland, however, that the potential competition for St Petersburg was most clearly visible. The Polish yards fully recognised the importance of the ship replacement cycle and foresaw that another cycle was about to start – on a global basis.

Here the collapse of Communism in 1989 had led to dramatic and highly visible changes in the shipbuilding and port activities of two key centres – Gdansk and Szczecin. The latter, in particular, had made huge strides, with aid being provided liberally by the province of West Pommerania. According to Szczepan Olesinski, Director of Economic Policy for the region:

Our contribution was significant. Over the past two years the governor has held a protective umbrella over that company. This allowed the shipyard, employing nearly 5000 workers, to survive. [11]

Some 40 per cent of world shipbuilding capacity has disappeared since the start of the 1970s. The world's shipping fleets were growing old. These two facts were said to augur well for remaining competitors. Since 1989, Erik Tonseth, the chief executive of the $3 billion/year Norwegian machinery combine Kvaerner had, like Bremer Vulkan, been following an aggressive strategy of acquiring shipyards. By the end of 1991 it had four per cent of world capacity and seven per cent of world orders. By 1992 shipbuilding was accounting for half the group's profits. The Finnish Wartsila and the Polish Gdynia yards were acquired at the start of the 1990s.

The Vulkan deal was untroubled by strikes of former East German ship-builders. Not so the neighbouring Kvaerner Warnow yard, nor the Volkswerft and the Peenewerft in Stralsund and Wolgast, respectively. Now under West German ownership, they had offered only a nine per cent wage rise and found this to be unacceptable to their workers.[9]

EXHIBIT 3: THE KVAERNER STRATEGY [10]

The umbrella comprised a write-off of one third of the yard's accumulated debt and re-negotiated terms for the balance.

The second element in Szczecin's success was its growing ship sales. On the basis of its much-improved productivity and worker flexibility, it had won several large container ship orders over the period 1991-3 from German owners (see Table 1, page 360). With three months allowed for building from keel laying to launch and a further three months from launch to delivery, cash in the Szczecin yard was also being rapidly turned around. Regular and reliable stage payments by customers further reduced the need for short-term debt and raised the yard's financial performance.

Such changes in technology and operating systems were high on the *wish-list* of St Petersburg yards, like Severnaya. But here a *workers' collective* (*rabochoe sobraniye*) mentality still existed. This meant that many strategic decisions were still being made by the workforce, as opposed to directors appointed by shareholders. Such a mindset still endured even in many newly-privatised companies where the old meeting of the workers' collective had become the new shareholders' meeting. Indeed, under the most popular form of privatisation in Russia, 51 per cent of the shares of the privatised company were given to the workforce.

The third element was the planned privatisation of the Szczecin yard in May 1993. This, it was thought, would further increase the workforce's commitment and productivity. Certainly no mass labour layoffs were on the cards as part of the privatisation, the unions would not accept them. Hence, more productivity gains were essential to achieve the required growth in profitability. Exhibit 4 indicates some of the types of improvements being sought by leading yards, worldwide.

Manufacturing Country	Number of container-ships ordered by West Germany	Order Value (DM Million)
Poland	46	1,926
S. Korea	27	2,156
Mexico	6	310
Singapore	2	60
Argentina	2	40
Total	**87**	**4,492**

TABLE 1: WEST GERMAN CONTAINER SHIPS ORDERED (1990–4) [12]

To carry out the flotation a joint stock company had been set up by the Privatisation Ministry. As of May 1993, all the shares were to be sold, at symbolic prices, to the yard's employees, four Polish banks and a management holding company. The Polish government itself was to retain a holding.

Whilst some shipyards are able to concentrate on such high value-added ships as Liquid Natural Gas carriers (LNGs) and super-large containerships (*post panamax boxships*) others are concentrating on more basic improvements like computer-aided design and real-time monitoring systems. These systems had monitors showing production operations and bar code scanners for scanning work into and out of work stations. Real-time computerised systems were also used to maintain control over shipments of cargo at all stages as it moves from the point of origination through to its final destination. New, modular methods of ship construction also needed to be explored as they have been found highly successful in Japanese yards.

EXHIBIT 4: SEEKING PRODUCTIVITY GAINS

Gdynia was another Polish shipbuilding centre where considerable progress was being made. The acquisition of the yard by Kvaerner – at a dramatically low price due to its heavy indebtedness – brought it to a new sense of reality. *In Poland in the past*, commented the yard's commercial manager, Antoni Bialous, *ships came to us – we didn't have to go looking for them.* [13] Now it was recognisably different.

So, too, for the port of Gdynia. Here the port's marketing team scored a significant breakthrough in 1992. It succeeded in attracting to Gdynia the high-volume West Europe-Russia cargo business of London-based United Baltic Corporation (UBC). Previously all UBC cargo had been shipped into St Petersburg, with the Baltic Shipping Co as partner. According to Michael Finn, Baltic trades manager of UBC, there had been an excessive rise in trans-shipment delays in St Petersburg in 1992 and great difficulties in maintaining control of shipments once they were off-loaded. These problems were further compounded by the Baltic Shipping Company's inability to settle its obligations.

The Gdynia marketeers had clearly capitalised on St Petersburg's immense management difficulties. They were also, in Finn's view, making efficient and effective use of their relatively limited marketing budget to win over new clients to the port. To do this they targeted direct mail sales campaigns to ship charterers and shipping offices, to owners and to other possible partnership-ports.

This alertness to client need helped ensure that both they and the managers running the Gdynia port jointly provided a high level of service to port users. UBC said they were delighted with the speed and efficiency of the Gdynia operation.

Furthermore, the Gdynia marketing team claimed that transport logistics, by road and rail, from Gdynia to Central Europe and Russia were better than those from St Petersburg, even with its access to the giant Russian October Railway network. Their system of freight tracking certainly allowed users like United Baltic to keep control even of FOB shipments right through to their final destination.

MATTERS ECONOMIC

It was one thing to plan for change and quite another to implement it. So Oleg Terekhov must have thought when he considered the political and economic developments taking place around him in Russia in early 1993.

There were, undeniably, plus factors.

President Yeltsin had had his personal authority as president re-affirmed in the referendum on the 25th April. His Constitutional Convention had created a new draft Constitution, to be approved by the 88 regional assemblies specially created for the purpose, before being ratified by the Congress of Peoples' Deputies.

The Central Bank had agreed to pressure from the government to tighten its credit policy. The resultant slow-down in the printing of new money and the raising of interest rates led to a fall in the level of month-on-month inflation and a rouble-dollar stabilisation around the 1000R/$ rate. The IMF had reacted to this news by releasing $1.5 billion from its transformation facility. Natural gas prices rose by 700 per cent in July.

The privatisation of Russian businesses, both large and small (i.e. shops and restaurants), was beginning to make greater progress. So far as the first is concerned, each Russian citizen had received a voucher worth R10,000 which entitled the bearer to buy shares in privatised firms (at 1991 prices). As well as being used for the intended purpose at auction sales, they came rapidly to be traded in the open market where their price in late 1992 fell to R4000. Now they were back to almost face value. Employees could, of course, buy shares in their own companies on privatisation. Small-scale privatisation was also proceeding apace. Almost 50 per cent of shops and restaurants were said to be in private ownership.

The minus factors were equally significant.

There was almost total discord between President Yeltsin's government and the revanchist representatives in the Congress of Peoples' Deputies. The previous organisation linkage between the Central Bank and the Congress had allowed it to go on printing huge quantities of paper money to prop up chronically-ill state firms (like the Baltic Shipping Co) and the bank could not be relied on totally by the Yeltsin government to comply with government anti-inflation policy. Perhaps even worse, in July 1993, Congress moved to suspend the workings of Yeltsin's *speeding-up privatisation* decree, No. 640, which had only been issued two months before. This was sure to slow down the sales of shares in privatised companies at auction. The new Chernomyrdin administration and the reorganisation of government in late 1993 showed signs of bringing some extra stability, but things were still extremely difficult in mid-1994:

Roads needing substantial repair
Several port bridges too low and narrow for appropriate access
No direct rail access to all parts of the port
Congestion in work areas
Lack of suitable power and water supplies
Cranage effectiveness limited

TABLE 2: CONDITIONS IN ST PETERSBURG MERCHANT PORT

The weakness in the governmental machine exacerbated greatly two other internal problems. Firstly, Russia's almost total absence of foreign currency and gold reserves. Secondly, the growing political insecurity within Russia itself, resulting from separatist tendencies, and between Russia and its now independent neighbours. Two potential flashpoints were the Ukraine and the Crimea. The dispute in the Ukraine was, in part, over the ownership of the former Red Banner Black Sea Fleet.

The G7 members had the task of balancing these factors when they met in Tokyo in July 1993. They decided to provide Russia with a $3 billion Stabilisation Fund, a strong vote of confidence in President Yeltsin and his plans for change. The first tranche of this – $1.5 billion – was handed over in 1994.

LEVEL PLAYING FIELDS?

A clear fact of business life for Oleg Terekhov and his colleagues emerges from this discussion of change factors: the need for St Petersburg, as port and shipbuilder, to compete effectively for the first time with its rivals. This is not, of course, to suggest that it had been unsuccessful in the past. Indeed, the October Factory and the Severnaya Verf both enjoyed international reputations for their shipbuilding achievements. The former had specialised in state purchases (*goszakazi*) of massive ice-breakers (like the famous series which included the *Arctica*, *Siberia*, and *Russia*) whilst the latter had focused its attentions more on tankers and cargo ships.

As for the port, it had made as much progress as possible in moving from being just a traditional bulk handler of grain/ore/coal towards becoming a modern container port as well. Its investment strategy, within the Yeltsin plan framework, called for a virtual tripling of container-handling capacity, with all the infrastructure and machinery this required, by 1997. The logic for this had been determined by the port itself separately, on the basis of Interport International data. These data suggested a highly positive international growth in the level of global container traffic by the year 2000. The need to increase Russia's port facilities to aid Russia's economic turn-around was obvious.

However, discussions with major St Petersburg port users, Maersk, Sealand and ITS, for example, had proved highly revealing. They had helped to pin-point for senior port managers the management system changes that would be needed to ensure future customer satisfaction. It was clear that ship turnaround times, the need for secure storage of containers and the availability of accurate information about cargo movements into Russia (by road and on the October Rail network) were causes of major anxiety to Western shippers. At the heart of all the complaints seemed to lie a lack of management foresight, planning, motivation and control on the part of port management. The hope was that the physical revitalisation of the port would bring much needed improvements in this area.

The port's own expansion plan was, in the light of such factors, a prudent one. Anatoly Bilichenko, head of the commercial division of the port, was one of the directors who had rejected an earlier plan put forward by the Baltic Shipping Co.

This company had wanted a $19 billion super-port involving a huge extension of the docks and terminals along the Gulf of Finland. It had been, declared Bilichenko, *a typical example of our old way of thinking... Communist-style gigantism.* Any new money, he went on, should come from *improving the capacity of the present port.*[14]

Nevertheless, further analysis of the world shipping scene suggests that attempts at improving the port's competitiveness, based just on an increase in the port's size and efficiency, would not be as easy as might be thought. For one thing, there was the issue of how nations subsidised their shipbuilding industries. The Organisation for Economic Co-operation and Development had tried to deal with this by issuing in 1991 a draft agreement on stopping subsidies.[15] They were prompted in this by the USA which had stopped subsidising its industry in the early 1980s.

Privately, however, many countries continued to subsidise. Large European shipbuilding nations like Denmark and Germany were accused in the early 1990s of persistently offering yards *soft financing arrangements* and/or direct state subsidies to enable them to attract orders. Such charges affected leading builders like the giant Danish A.P. Moller company (owners of the Maersk Line) and Danish shipbuilders Burmeister and Wain. It was claimed that they and others were actually receiving twice the amount of shipbuilding subsidy allowed for under European Community rules in the early 1990s.[16]

On the other hand, it was a fact that Europe's share (by value) of world new ship orders had fallen from 27 per cent in 1988 to 18 per cent in 1992 and that, in the field of tankers and dry bulk carriers, 40 per cent of current world output, European prices were typically 20 per cent higher than the Japanese or Korean level. The latter's technology expertise was such that, according to experienced commentator Dan White of London investment house County Natwest, they could turn out VLCCs and box ships *like sausages.*[17] Of course, it was counter-claimed by the Europeans that their Far Eastern competitors were similarly aided by their governments, as in the case of the rescue by the Korean government of Daewoo in 1989.

> *Der Weltschiffbestand ist überaltert. Ersatzinvestitionen lassen sich vielleicht ein, zwei Jahre hinausschieben aber das Rosten der Schiffe kann niemand aufhalten.*(18) *Doch, trotz dieser hervorragender Zukunftsaussichten wird das Wettbewerb im Weltschiffbau gegenwärtig... unzureichende Neubaunachfrage, erhebliche Überkapazitäten... Zur fortgesetzt ruinösen Preispolitik fernostlicher Werften ist seit dem vergangenen Jahr verstärkt der Preisdruck auch von osteuropäischen Werften hinzugekommen.*
>
> Translation, note 19 on page 369.

EXHIBIT 5: THE STATE OF PLAY IN WORLD SHIPBUILDING 1993

The third factor of importance was clearly an element in St Petersburg's favour: the extent to which a comparatively low currency parity would enable a shipbuilding nation to be competitive in its pricing. An example of this was the order received in April 1993 by Finland's MASA yard (part of the Kvaerner Group) for four LNG carriers. The deal was worth 5.5 billion Finnish markka ($1 billion) and was the largest order ever placed with a Finnish business. The customer was the Abu Dhabi National Oil Co. Part of MASA's attractiveness was that, since 1991, the markka had fallen in value against the yen by over 50 per cent. By comparison, the rouble was still falling in value month by month.

It was, therefore, an enormous breakthrough in turnaround possibilities for St Petersburg, as port and shipbuilder, when it was announced, in October 1993, that the German Bremer Vulkan organisation was acquiring a 15 per cent stake in the Severnaya Verft.

It was increasingly clear in 1994 and 1995 that such a move was absolutely necessary for any revitalisation of the port's shipbuilding capability to take place. In 1994, for example, there had been a reduction of 13 per cent in the size of the Russian component of what had been the Soviet fleet on top of the depletion that had taken place before. The net result was that, by late 1994, more than 85 per cent of Ruusian export goods were being carried in non-Russian ships.

The outlook, as reported by the UK's Ocean Shipping Consultants, was also poor. This body assesses the trade prospects for the oil, dry bulk and container sectors. Notwithstanding the difficult problems for Russia in the oil sector and iron ore sectors (potentially declining demand), the chief problem area for Russia was the under-development of containerisation.

Whilst world container trade expanded by almost 200 per cent during the period from 1980–93, the expansion in the former Comecon bloc was 76 per cent. Clearly an opportunity for any yard that could capitalise on it.

However, the general problem posed by the size of the world's ageing transport fleet (on the one hand) and Russia's particular situation (on the other) was so severe that, in the words of the executive director of Russia's Maritime Transportation Department, Boris Grishin, an order for 75 ships would be *a painkiller and not a cure for the Russian shipping malaise.*[20]

* * * * * * * * * * * * * * * * * *

APPENDIX I : OFFICIAL ECONOMIC DATA FOR 1994

☐ Ministry of Economy's 1994 Report spoke of Russia's 'imbalanced economic situation'.

☐ Privatized companies accounted for 62 per cent of GDP in 1994, as against 53 per cent in 1993. Of these privately owned businesses accounted for 25 per cent (21 per cent in 1993).

☐ Service industries accounted for 50 per cent of 1994 GDP as against 42 per cent in 1993. Comparative figures for manufacturing were 43.5 per cent (49 per cent in 1993). But bottlenecks in wholesale distribution, banking and financial services grew.

☐ The monthly consumer price index fell to 3.2 per cent in 1994 from 9.4 per cent in 1993 and 26.1 per cent in 1992. Fixed prices covered some 25 per cent of 1994 production. But the accumulated inflation backlog remains high.

☐ The 1994 budget deficit exceeded 10 per cent of GDP and money supply was 'excessive'.

☐ Industrial production fell in 1994 by 21 per cent, the fifth year in succession this has occurred. High technology manufacturing was the worst affected; fuel the least. In fact, as per cent of total output, fuel and energy accounted for 31 per cent in 1994 (26.7 per cent in 1993) whilst engineering fell over the period from 20 per cent to 15.7 per cent.

☐ Market-led reforms in agriculture resulted in a drop in output in big farms but improvement elsewhere. Overall crop output volume declined in 1994 by 9 per cent.

☐ Investment in fixed assets fell over the period by 27 per cent. Russian banks invested their funds predominantly in foreign currency in 1994.

APPENDIX 2: COMPARISON OF BALTIC PORT FACILITIES

CHARACTERISTIC	ST PETERSBURG	GDYNIA, POLAND
Largest Vessel	Max. length 260m draft 11m	Max. length 247m, draft 11.35m
Accommodation	Port consists of several basins with depths in principle cargo handling areas ranging from 6.5m to 11.5m. Numerous berths-timer-handling areas, fishing port and passenger terminal. Several canal systems connect the port with the vast interior of Russia.	Massive artificial port protected by concrete breakwaters 2.5km long. Water area of 244 hectares. Total wharfage 17km of which almost 11km is of commercial use.
Storage	Warehouse and concreted open storage area are available. There are also coal stores.	Total warehousing and shed space of 204,497 sq metres. Open storage space of 327,865 sq metres.
Floating Cranes	From 15-300 tonnes	Of 65 and 100 tonnes capacity.
Container and Ro Ro (Roll-on Roll-off)	Only 2 container terminals are in operation but there are berths for handling Ro Ro traffic. Equipment includes four container gantry cranes, 2 of 40 tonnes capacity. There is a large capacity container repair facility. A new container terminal is being built in the coal harbour.	Baltic Container Terminal at Helski Quay covers 40 hectares of this 10 hectares are used for handling storage. 20,000 sq m shedded areas. Equipment includes 3 35-40 tonne cap gantry cranes and 2 multi-purpose mobile cranes of 15 tonnes. Two adjustable ramps of 24m width for Ro Ro vessels. Ro Ro berths at Danish Quay and Rotterdam Quay.
Ore and Bulk Cargo facilities	Bulk cargo including coal, grain and minerals. Building materials are handled in special areas of the port with mechanised equipment. Coal terminal can accommodate vessels up to 18,000 cwt and 9.5m depth.	30 shore-based grab cranes of 80-240 tonnes/hour capacity and four floating elevators up to 250 tonnes/hour capacity.
Weather	Year round navigation is possible with ice-breaker assistance in winter	Ice-free port

Source: Lloyds *Register of Ports*

NOTES & REFERENCES

1   'Russia's sea transport', Gennadi Gerasimchuk, *The Baltic*, July 1993
2   *Tradewinds* 8/4/93
3   As 1
4   'Only direction to go is up', *Tradewinds*, 22/1/93
5   'Sovcomflot sales are part of streamlining', *Tradewinds*, 30/4/93
6   As 5
7   *Tradewinds*, 19/3/93
8   *Fair Play*, 20/5/93
9   'E. German yards face strikes', *Tradewinds*, 2/4/93
10 'Norway's Kvaerner and the turnaround in shipbuilding', Sharon Reier, *The Financial World*, Issue 7, 31/3/92
11 'Poland looks at privatisation', Richard Clayton, *Fairplay*, 27/5/93
12 *Wirtschaftswoche*, 4/12/93
13 *The Financial Times*, 9/9/92
14 As 13
15 *Far Eastern Economic Review*, Louise Do Rosario & John Gittelsohn, 12/7/90
16 'Have our shipyards been left all at sea?', Oliver Scott, *The European*, 17-20/6/93
17 As 13
18 Diederik Schnittler, Kvaerner board member, *Wirtschaftswoche*, 18/9/92. 'World shipping is in a state of super-annuation. Investment in replacement vessels can be put off for one year, maybe two. But no one can stop ships from rusting away.'
19 *Frankfurter Allgemeine Zeitung*, 7/6/93. 'But in spite of these tremendous vistas of the future, competition in world shipping today is a matter of inadequate demand and excessive capacity. In the past 12 months, price pressure from yards in Eastern Europe has added considerably to the problem.'
20 Russian fleet is aged and shrinking fast, Nick Savvides, *The European* 5-11/5/95

BANESTO

Abstract:

Banesto is a Spanish bank that was apparently brought to ruin by the activities of one man - like Barings. The case examines the particular features of Spanish banking which may have helped this to occur and the context in which the decline took place.

This is one of a suite of banking cases that illustrate key features of the world of banking in the 1990s. It can be read in conjunction with Barings, Credit Lyonnais and The World of Deutsche Bank.

Questions:

Chart the Banesto débâcle and the Banco Santander rescue. Was it a good move to bale out the bank - or just a necessary one?

Who, or what, was to blame for Banesto's difficulties?

How strong is Spain's bank-industry infrastructure?

How important is the bank-industry complex to the Spanish economy?

Case Timing: 1994-8

THE BIG ISSUE

In early May 1994 the key question facing the board of directors of the Royal Bank of Scotland (RBS) was whether it should go ahead and pay £46m for a two per cent stake in the Spanish bank, Banco Espanol de Credito (Banesto). RBS had been offered the stake by its European partner, Banco Santander, one of Spain's most dynamic banks. The plus factor for RBS would be a further extension of the European banking network it was successfully building as well as, of course, the support it would give to Banco Santander. On the other hand, however, the Bank of Spain had been obliged, a mere six months before, to step in to save Banesto in what had turned out to be Spain's worst-ever banking crisis.

The short-fall in Banesto's loan-loss reserves was, at first, estimated to amount to some £1.7 billion (350 billion pesetas) or 15 per cent of its entire deposits. In fact, in the three days before the ruling body of the Spanish stock exchange suspended the shares on the 28th December 1993, account holders had withdrawn the equivalent of £580m and the resultant gap in Banesto's accounts was put at £2.5 billion by the Bank of Spain. An urgent stabilisation plan was unavoidable. Once this had been carried out, the Bank of Spain put Banesto up for sale. Banco Santander won control of Banesto in this auction, outbidding other leading Spanish banks who were keen to aquire such a turnaround prize.

It was in October 1988 that RBS and Banco Santander had created their strategic, cross-holding alliance. This involved RBS' holding a 1.4 per cent stake in Banco Santander, and the latter's owning a 9.9 per cent slice of RBS. Each bank regarded the deal as highly satisfactory for three reasons: first, the enormous difficulties each would have had if they had sought to develop direct operations in each other's market, either through direct acquisition or through setting up their own subsidiaries; second, the extent to which such a cross-holding gave each partner a good defence against a hostile take-over bid: third, the way in which the alliance had allowed them to set up their cross-border banking network. This was called the Inter-Bank-On-Line-System or IBOS and other Spanish, French and Portuguese banks were partners in it.

From RBS, Banco Santander had taken several innovatory product models, cheap mortgages, high-interest deposit and current accounts, for example, and developed them within the Spanish market. Santander itself was a leader in the investment fund sector and had a wide portfolio of owned companies.

Economic and Finance Ministers (ECOFIN) gave final approval to two Directives which go a long way to completing the Single Market in financial services. The Capital Adequacy Directive sets minimum Community-wide levels of capital needed by investment firms to offer certain financial services... Ministers also approved the Investment Services Directive which enables share dealers to operate throughout the Community with a single licence issued by their home country regulatory authority... Both Directives are due to enter into force on 1 January 1996, giving Member States time to establish a common system for monitoring risks incurred by the investment firms.

EXHIBIT 1: TOWARDS A FINANCIAL COMMON MARKET
Source: *The Week in Europe*, Commission of European Communities, 18/3/93

A key element in considering RBS' purchase of Banesto shares was the fact that there were many differences between UK and continental banking. Whilst RBS might know, for near certain, was what had gone wrong with Banesto, there were still conjectural factors to weigh up such as the relatively uncertain state of the Spanish economy and the rate of change in European financial services.

DISASTER

The disaster which struck Banesto, Spain's third-largest bank, in December 1993 was as humbling to its directors as it was devastating to its shareholders and its 22,500 employees. In the first nine months of 1993 the bank had been forced to increase its provisions on losses likely to arise on bad loans or investments by a large margin.[1]

As it subsequently emerged, however large the re-capitalisation had been at the time, it was wholly inadequate.

Banesto had still made profits during this period but, at £48m, they were 76 per cent down on the same period in 1992, a fact which forced Banesto to shelve a planned $400m bond issue which was part of the re-capitalisation plan. Pulling this issue helped precipitate a further 140 peseta fall in the bank's share price to 1995 pesetas.

Banesto's chairman, Mario Conde, and his board were ousted. They were replaced by a provisional administration, under the direct supervision of the Bank of Spain, headed by Alfredo Saenz Abad, deputy chairman of the Banco Bilbao Vizcaya. This meant, incidentally, further shame for Mario Conde since he personally had foiled a take-over bid for Banesto in 1988 mounted by Sanchez Asiain when he had been CEO of the Banco de Bilbao. Luis Angel Rojo, the governor of the Bank of Spain, and Pedro Solbes, Spain's finance minister, sought jointly to reassure anxious depositors in Banesto that their worries were now over.

Banesto had, in fact, been suffering for some time from over-exposure and, in early 1993, Mario Conde had enlisted the help of J.P. Morgan, the New York investment bank, as advisers and to assist Banesto with re-financing. They planned two fund-raising schemes. The first, a $1.2 billion (94 billion pesetas) equity offering, took place in August 1993. It was the most ambitious in Spain's banking history, with Morgan's own Corsair Partnerships Fund purchasing a $175m stake. The inflow of funds helped reduce the pressure already being exerted by the Central Bank on Banesto to improve its solvency.

The second was a failure. The idea was to make the convertible bond issue in October 1993 to raise a further $400m but it had to be shelved when Moody's downgraded Banesto's short- and long-term bond ratings. By December, Standard & Poor's and the London bond-rating agency IBCA had followed suit. Moody's action caused considerable upset in the Banesto-Morgan partnership. The Morgan executive in charge of the relationship, Violy de Harper, resigned and Banesto's share price accelerated on its downward track.

In 1992 J.P. Morgan, the US investment bank, created a $1 billion investment fund called Corsair Partnerships. Participants included George Soros and the General Electric Pension Fund. The idea was for Corsair to invest in American banks that were suffering from a shortage of equity capital. Investors in Corsair were told to assume an annual 30 per cent return on their investment. Up to the end of 1993 Banesto was the Fund's only investment. It had taken a nine per cent stake in Banesto in February 1993.

EXHIBIT 2: THE CORSAIR PARTNERSHIPS FUND [2]

On the 28th December 1993, it fell by a further seven per cent. This meant that Banesto's equity had dropped by a third in value since August. Spain's National Securities Market Commission stepped in to halt trading in Banesto shares.

The worries for the Association of Customers of Spanish Banks (ADICAE) were substantial since Banesto was the second biggest Spanish High Street bank (2268 branches), the third biggest in deposits and, with assets at end 1993 of £16.4 billion, fourth in the size league. The Spanish government's Deposit Guarantee Fund covered individual depositors, but only for a miniscule £5,000.

The stock market's worries did not only affect Banesto. Shares in the industrial companies, mining company Asturiana de Zinc and Agroman, a major construction company, in which Banesto had big direct holdings also fell, and by 15 per cent. Indeed, the combined effect was to produce a drop of 5 per cent in Madrid's IBEX 35 share index.

To try to balance its books, Banesto had already started to sell off some of the industrial assets owned by its subsidiary, La Corporacion Industrial y Financiera, in which it had a 96 per cent stake. This, at one time, had controlled some one per cent of Spain's manufacturing GDP.

Among early disposals were Acerinox (a steel firm) and shares in the insurance company El Fenix. After the collapse, it was also thought likely that Banesto would have to sell off its stakes in the Spanish banks Baendesco and Banco de Vitoria, as well as its major 55 per cent holding in the Portuguese bank Totta e Açores. This would be a bitter end to Mario Conde's strategy of building an Iberian banking network.

It was later discovered that El Fenix, in which Banesto held a 45 per cent stake, had suffered major losses over the period 1992–4 due in no small part to the practice of auto-cartera (self ownership of shares). In July 1994, Assurances Generales de France, already owning 25 per cent of El Fenix, was seeking to buy the allegedly value-less Banesto stake.

ALL CHANGE

The Banesto débâcle took place against a highly dynamic European background. Major changes were taking place upsetting virtually all aspects of the financial services industry.

The first element of significance was European Union legislation governing the pan-European activities of banks and insurance companies. Critical in this was the second Banking Directive which allowed licensed banks to operate across Europe with a wide product range. Possibilities included leasing, factoring, credit cards, bond and options trading and mortgage lending, as well as traditional products like retail deposit taking and corporate banking.

Similarly, the first and second Insurance Directives permitted insurers to work across frontiers. When these directives are seen in the context of Directives on solvency ratios, common accounting procedures and the handling of securities (Undertakings for Collective Investments in Transferable Securities or UCITS), a clear picture emerges of a platform for the future development of a new, and standardised, financial services industry in Europe. This platform was further extended in 1995 by the third Insurance Directive.

Single Currency Convergence Factor	GERMANY		UK		SPAIN	
	1994	1995	1994	1995	1994	1995
(1) Gross Debt/GDP %	51	59	53	55	64	68
(2) Budget Deficit/GDP %	5.6	3.6	4.8	2.5	7.0	6.5
(3) Inflation %	3.0	2.3	2.4	2.9	4.6	4.4
(4) Long-term interest rates	6.9	6.9	8.2	7.4	9.8	10.5

TABLE 1: MEETING MAASTRICHT CONVERGENCE CRITERIA
Source: *The European,* 27/1/95–2/2/95

Note: To comply with the Maastricht Treaty's criteria for single currency convergence an EU member's (1) must not exceed 60 per cent, (2) must not exceed 3 per cent, [3] must not be more than 1.5 per cent above the average rate in the three EU countries with the best record (4) must not exceed by more than 2 per cent the average rate on 10-year government bonds in the three EU countries with the lowest inflation rates.

The second element was changes in information technology and automation. These were being embraced particularly warmly in Britain which was deriving significant efficiency improvements from branch-cutting, organisational de-layering and automation. The British Banking, Insurance and Finance trade union (BIFU) calculated that over the period 1989–93 some 74,000 jobs had disappeared as a result of these changes. The model of the bank as a *paper-factory*, processing cheques and bank-notes, seemed increasingly anachronistic in Britain as plastic cards, tele-banking and automatic teller machines increased in importance.

The combination of these two pressures for change resulted in a major change in the make-up of the European financial services sector. A spate of finance sector re-alignments, mergers, take-overs and strategic alliances, took place. Increasingly, these occurred within particular sectors as, for instance, in the cases of the strategic alliance between the Banque National de Paris and the Dresdner Bank. Other major examples were Assurances Generales de France's large stake in Aachener & Münchener Beteiligungs (AMB), Royal Assurance's links with AMB or Deutsche Bank's purchase of Banco de Madrid from Banesto in 1993 and Commercial Union's acquisition of Groupe Victoire's insurance subsidiaries, Abeille Vie and Abeille Assurance, in 1994.

Such moves to build up market power rested, in many cases, on the cross-ownership of shares by financial institutions in different sectors (e.g., banking and insurance) that had long been in evidence in mainland Europe. In Germany, for example, Allianz (Germany's largest insurer) owned over 25 per cent of the Dresdner Bank and was the largest shareholder in the Deutsche Bank.

Germany was especially keen on building up what it called the *Allfinanz* model, the integrated, *one-stop* financial services company, in what was called *Finanzplatz Deutschland*. This last was a reference to the potential of Germany as the financial nerve centre of post-Maastricht Europe.

It is noteworthy, also, that the large continental bank and quoted company could enjoy a typical relationship unknown in Britain. The Anglo-Saxon model of capital finance for companies did not usually provide for High Street banks to invest in companies to whom they lend money. Indeed, in the USA they were prohibited from so doing. Instead, under this system, banks function principally as lenders and help, if need be, to arrange for companies' capital needs to be met, through the stock or bond markets. Thus, there is no such thing in Britain as the German *Hausbank* which typically holds investments in a major German company as well as supplying it with debt finance. This is, however, also the case in France and, as we have seen, in the case of Banesto, in Spain.

SUPERMARIO

Spain's Stock Exchange Commission (Comision Nacional del Mercado de Valores or CNMV) opened its investigation into the Banesto collapse as a matter of routine in early 1994. One of their findings was of particular interest: Mario Conde had borrowed £34m from the Banco Central Hispanico to help increase his personal stake in Banesto from 1.5 per cent to 4.5 per cent as recently as July 1993. The loan, secured against Banesto shares, was due to be repaid in July 1995.

This exuberance was typical of the man who had been given the title of *Spanish Entrepreneur of the Year* in 1993, along with an honorary doctorate from Madrid University. Yet he had been a newcomer to banking when he took over as chief executive of Banesto on the 17th December 1987.

Nothing about Mario Conde was reminiscent of the old banking families of Spain, the *banqueros* such as the Botins (Banco Santander), Ybarros (Banco Bilbao Vizcaya), Marches (Banco March) or the Basagoitis or the Urquijos. They had all known at least a century of grandeur and opulence in developing the tight-knit Spanish banking system. Among these families ruled *enchufismo*, a sense of identification with an old-established network. Mario Conde was, by contrast, a *bancario*, one of a new breed of self-made bankers who did things differently. He had once booked the Real Madrid stadium for a Banesto annual shareholders' meeting, for example. Even his arrival at Banesto, after pulling off the biggest private sector corporate sale in Spanish history (the sale of Antibioticos, where he was CEO, to Montedison), was spectacular. It coincided exactly with the boom resulting from Spain's entry into the Common Market in 1986 and the consequent surge in the demand for credit. As one commentator put it:

> *Conde was as generous at lending the bank's money as he might have been at lending his own... He had a risk-taking style that tempted him into lending far more than the bank could afford.*[4]

With his extensive media interests and high society profile, Mario Conde had been a larger-than-life figure, a sort of 20th century *hidalgo*, or, as Le Monde put it, another *Great Gatsby*.[5] Now, after the Banesto collapse, he was accused of *pelotazo*, sharing, and indeed promoting, the *cult of easy money* that had taken possession of Spain in the late 1980s. No longer would he attend the meetings of the *Seis Grandes*, the big six Spanish banks.

More importantly, questions were being asked about how Banesto's share price had managed to halve over the period January 1988 to December 1993 without arousing over-much government interest.

TURNAROUND

Banesto, and several of the companies it had invested in, was a casualty of the European recession which was still biting deep in late 1993 in Spain. The critical trigger for the Bank of Spain's move had been the stock market collapse and the growing realisation that Banesto's loss-loan reserves were inadequate. By the end of January 1994, in fact, the Bank of Spain had again revised this figure – to £3.1 billion.[6]

More worrisome data had also begun to emerge from the stricken bank, as Alfredo Saenz Abad's interim period of management took effect. One issue was the manner in which Banesto had managed to control so much of its own share capital. The CNMV had been informed by Banesto that the bank controlled directly only 3.85 per cent, whereas, by a variety of proxies, the control was nearer 16 per cent, as against a legal limit of five per cent. For example, a Panama-based company called Namrof owned a two per cent stake in Banesto and El Fenix held 2.5 per cent, at exactly the same time as both of them were wholly owned by Banesto.

Media Organisation	Level of Banesto holding in 1993 (%)
El Mundo (Spain's leading opposition paper)	<4
Antena Tres (Spain's leading private TV channel)	25
Grupo Zeta, large-scale publisher	12.5

TABLE 2: BANESTO'S MEDIA INVESTMENTS

Progress was being made in pulling Banesto round, however, with the Bank of Spain's Deposit Guarantee Fund and the Spanish banks supplying the capital required to make up the Banesto deficit. By mid-February 1994 the bank was up for sale and the Bank of Spain was opening investigative proceedings against Mario Conde.

Among the leading bidders in the auction had been Banesto's main competitors, BBV and Banco Santander. Adding Banesto to either would have created Spain's largest bank, with over $90 billion of total assets. Banco Santander, as we have seen, was successful in its bid and took control of its erstwhile rival in late April 1994. Happily paying the sale price of $2.2 billion, Emilio Botin declared that it was *a historic opportunity for which we have prepared and saved, peseta by peseta.*[7] Santander was now Spain's largest, and Europe's 22nd-largest, bank and well positioned to implement its turnaround strategy for Banesto.

On 23rd July 1995 Miguel Indurain rode his way into the record books as the greatest champion ever in the Tour de France cycle race. He was wearing the Banesto jersey. Aged only 31, he had not only won the race five times, but five times in a row, an achievement that marked him out from other heroic performers such as Eddie Merckx and Jaques Anquetil.

His victory was also Banesto's victory since the bank was his main sponsor. It was a fitting end to the turnaround strategy that Banco Santander had been following. This had involved, as we have noted, the sale of packets of Banesto shares to banks and insurers such as the Royal Bank of Scotland (two per cent),

Metropolitan Life (one per cent). Santander's stated long-term aim was being a 50 per cent holding only. The strategy had also comprised further sales of companies held by the Corporacion Financiera y Industrial, an almost wholly-owned subsidiary of Banesto and in its day one of Spain's biggest industrial holding companies. The residue of shares in loss makers like Agroman and Soc Asturiana de Zinc was finally disposed of by Alfredo Saenz, as was the wine producer and distributor Bodegas and 57 per cent of Tudor, the battery producer. The transfer of Banesto's holding in El Fenix, the long-established Spanish insurer, was eventually effected to Assurances Generales de France (AGF). SG Warburg estimated that it would cost AGF $183m to sort El Fenix out after the finanial mess Banesto had left it in.[8]

OUT BUT NOT DOWN?

Despite the turnaround in Banesto's fortunes, the questions about the reasons for its collapse remained as intriguing as ever. Was Mario Conde himself responsible for the Banesto's debacle? That was the key issue preoccupying the public prosecutor, the tax authorities as well as the financial press in late 1994. The answer came in the form of his arrest on fraud charges on the 23rd December 1994.

Among specific elements that would be investigated were the 605 billion peseta capital deficit in Banesto accounts, caused mainly by artificial inflation of assets, that the Bank of Spain had now uncovered and possible irregularities in Banesto's purchase of the Portuguese bank Totta y Acores. Imposing a prison order whilst the authorities' inquiries were carried out, the Madrid judge Manuel Garcia Castellon said that Conde had represented a very serious economic threat to Banesto and its shareholders.[9]

Was this how Mario Conde himself saw things? Not if his book *The System: My Experience of Power* is anything to go by. In this he asserted that Spain's political and banking system had cheated him, *an upstart and non-conformist hero*.[10] Moreover, he claimed that he was capable of leading Spain forward into a brighter political future than could be offered by the-then government under prime minister Felipe Gonzalez. He took no pains to disguise his hostility towards the former Spanish finance minister, Carlos Solchaga, and former governor of the Bank of Spain, Mariano Rubio.

Others took a different view. Commentator Julian Webster, for instance, attacked Mario Conde's book for its *cara dura*, its bare-faced cheek.[11] Jesus Cacho in his book on Mario Conde stated eloquently that Conde was *an intruder in the labyrinth of the chosen*.[12] Certainly, the self-proclaimed high flyer was brought down to earth by the sentence of six years in prison for embezzlement and forgery he received in 1997 and by his re-trial in 1998 for malversation. His glory days were well and truly over.

As for Banesto, the bank continued its recovery over the period 1995-1998. With a turnaround 180 billion peseta capital injection, the purchase of 285 billion of non-performing assets by the Deposit Guarantee Fund and a zero interest loan of 315 billion pesetas, it is perhaps not surprising that it should. However, it all amounted, as *The Financial Times* put it, *by far the largest lifeboat operation ever mounted for a Spanish bank.*[13] Banco Santander's initial purchase of stock added the necessary resuscitation factor. Indeed, by early 1998, Banesto's operations had again become so successful that Banco Santander was planning to make an offer for the 52 per cent of the shares it did not own. If carried through, the move would increase the degree of consolidation in the Spanish banking industry and cement Santander's position as the country's biggest bank in terms of capitalisation and profit.

* * * * * * * * * * * * * * * * * * *

NOTES & REFERENCES

1   Bank of Spain intervenes in running of Banesto, *The Times*, 29/12/93
2   Banesto fall-out hits New York, Philip Robinson and Colin Narbrough, *The Times*, 31/12/93
3   Fate of Banesto uncertain, John Parry, *The European*, 7–13/1/94
4   Symbol of Spanish success crashes out of high society, Georgina Power, *The European*, 7–13/1/94
5   Mario Conde, Le Gatsby Espagnol, Michel Bole-Richard, *Le Monde*, 11/1/94
6   Banesto shortfall is 35 per cent higher, Colin Narbrough, *The Times*, 18/1/94
7   Santander to offload Banesto media stakes, John Parry, *The European*, 29/4/94–5/5/94
8   Spanish awake to world of insurance, John Parry, *The European*, 13–19/1/95
9   Mario Conde faces fraud charges, John Parry, *The European*, 29/12/94–4/1/95
10   Conde's cheek, Julian Webster, *Eurobusiness*, Oct 1994
11   As 10
12   Mario Conde, *Temas de Hoy*, Madrid, 1994
13   Unravelling the Banesto tangle, Tom Burns, *The Financial Times*, 4/10/94

RENAULT

Abstract:

The thrust in the European car industry in the 1980s was towards concentration and economies of scale. Hence, some of the logic for a tie-up between Renault and Volvo. As we all know, cross-border marriages are not all that simple to arrange, whatever the justification for them. This case deals with the impediments to union faced by these two major car producers.

Questions:

Review the history of Renault and the light it throws on French business culture. Chronicle the attempted merger with Volvo and consider its rationale. Why did it fail?
On the basis of case evidence, do Renault and Volvo need partners? Would the partnerships be easy to handle?

Case Timing: 1994

"THE GAME, THE GAME'S THE THING"

On the sixth of September 1993, after a three-year business partnership in design and production, Renault SA and AB Volvo announced that they were to merge. The joint operating company was to be called Renault-Volvo RVA and it would be directed by RVC, a holding company in which Volvo was to have a 49 per cent share and the French government, as the majority owner of Renault SA, 51 per cent. The balance of holdings in RVA was agreed as 47.15 per cent for Renault, 35 per cent for RVC and 17.85 per cent for AB Volvo, an arrangement regarded by the French as wholly equitable. The deal was struck in the context of the Balladur plan, named after the French prime minister, to privatise large slices of French nationalised industry.

Renault SA was, in fact, high on the French prime minister's list for speedy disposal for other reasons. The company had in the past been regarded critically by its competitors in the European car industry because of the subsidies it had received from the French government, especially in the 1970s and early 1980s. It had now been without state aid for seven years, however, and was Europe's most profitable car maker, after BMW. It was, therefore, a saleable item for a beleaguered French government, trying to fund rising public expenditure in a climate hostile to tighter fiscal policy.

The president of the highly-profitable Volvo, Pehr Gyllenhammer, was designated head of the supervisory board (*conseil de surveillance*) of RVA, whilst Louis Schweitzer, Renault president, would chair the board of directors (*directoire*). Both companies would be headquartered in Paris. The triumphant merger announcement was made by the two executives and the French industry minister, Gerard Longuet.

The aim of the merger was to create an impressive world-wide array of plants manufacturing cars, trucks and other industrial vehicles and to bring about much more powerful market access for the group's products. The new company would rank as a giant among giants in the European car and truck industry. In terms of size, it would be number three, above the PSA (Peugeot) group. The attractive economies of scale, in design, maufacture and funding, which had merely been hinted at in the previous period of Renault-Volvo co-operation, would be made both real and permanent. RVA's turnover would amount to Fr. 245 billion and its European market share to 12 per cent. So far as heavy trucks were concerned, it would be second only to Mercedes in world rankings.

The car and truck industries in Europe were already highly-oligopolised and under immense financial strain from the twin impacts of higher competition and increased technology investment requirements. This sort of merger was, thus, seen by both presidents as both desirable and inevitable. The French, in particular, supported the merger plan which had already been approved twice by the AB Volvo board. They saw it as being *industrially and economically justified.*[1]

A MARRIAGE NOT MADE IN HEAVEN

Imagine, however, the consternation caused in transport industry circles when the shareholders of AB Volvo refused, less than three months after the merger announcement, to sanction the deal.

In fact, the alarm bells had first begun ringing for Pehr Gyllenhammer on November the first, 1993.

That was the date on which the Volvo board decided to put off the extraordinary shareholders' meeting, called for the ninth of November to agree the merger, until the seventh of December. This was to give time for the merger plan to be more fully explained and debated.

Selling the notion of a Renault-Volvo union was already recognised as a difficult task. The Swedish insurance company Trygg Hansa, which had a six per cent stake and which was, after Renault itself, Volvo's largest current shareholder, had already announced that it would vote against.

There is no longer any place in the world motor industry for the medium-sized manufacturer... Designing and manufacturing cars has become an expensive business... Even the cheapest model costing a likely £1 billion. There is little alternative for either side...Volvo has increasingly found itself alone in a cut-throat market-place where the biggest are proving to be the strongest...Renault, five years ago, may have been almost an icon in France, but to the rest of the motor industry world, it was a by-word for financial losses and inefficiency. Today the story could not be more different, with the company making money and producing some of the most interesting and innovative cars...But even Renault has had to face up to the problem of how to become one of the big players for the future.

EXHIBIT 1: MATCHMAKING CONCERNS
Source: Kevin Eason, *The Times*, 7/9/93

What were the Swedish objections? There were two difficulties. Firstly, the fear amongst Volvo shareholders and managers that the privatisation of Renault would not take place, despite the French government's many assurances to the contrary. Secondly, the potential problem of the retention by the French government of a *noyau dur* or *golden share*. This could conceivably be used to keep Volvo's voting rights in RVA and the holding company below 20 per cent even in a situation where (after Renault privatisation) Volvo's stake could rise considerably through further stock purchases. Key Volvo shareholders were not amused at the prospect.

Nonetheless, Pehr Gyllenhammer himself was not depressed. *We wanted to avoid the risk of a "No"*, he declared, explaining the delay in the holding of the extraordinary shareholders' meeting. *Now we want to achieve a clear and massive "Yes" response. We still believe in the project and the board is absolutely unanimous on this.*[2]

Would the French accelerate the privatisation of Renault to accommodate the Swedish view? There was press speculation on this but, in the event, Gerard Longuet himself ruled it out as politically impossible as well as impractical before the second half of 1994 at the earliest. Nor was there any likelihood of a shift in stance of the French government on the golden share issue. This, it had now become clear, would keep Volvo's existing voting rights in RVA below 20 per cent in spite of its 35 per cent share stake.[3] Whilst French officials were initially keen to play down the possibility of the government's actually taking advantage of their golden share, the Swedes remained anxious.

By the end of November 1993, however, the French had made their position plain. The golden share was, according to Gerard Longuet, not to be used against the interests of Volvo but to safeguard the merged group from any hostile third-party takeover.

The dirigiste thrust behind this did not please the Swedish insurance company, Skandia, which owned 3.6 per cent of Volvo. Its chief executive, Bjorni Wolrath, stated *it's not enough to make such a statement regarding the golden share. We want a written assurance that Renault will be privatised by autumn next year.*[4] For Wolrath, decisions were better based on business logic than politics.

Even personal assurances from Eduard Balladur himself and a positive promise by the French government on both issues failed to carry weight. After all, many Volvo shareholders could recall the sell-off plan that a previous Conservative French government had begun to implement in 1986, only to lose office two years afterwards. Even so, at this time, there was a majority of Volvo's institutional shareholders in favour of the merger.[5]

The dreams of Pehr Gyllenhammer ended abruptly, however, on the second of December 1993. In the face of an upsurge in shareholder and management hostility, he met with chief executive Soren Gyll in a mood of crisis. Gyll had no compunction in recommending the immediate abandonment of the merger plan. The Volvo board had turned negative.

Worse was to follow for Gyllenhammer. For 22 years the autocratic chairman of Volvo, he felt obliged to resign from the company and to sell off his shareholding.

The opposition to the merger had, in fact, grown to unstoppable proportions. The Swedish media were opposed and highly negative. The public did not appreciate the irony of Socialist Sweden's handing over control of one of its leading private companies to a joint company controlled by a Conservative French government, itself led by a Socialist president. Nor, for that matter, did the public seem, at that time, particularly enamoured of the Swedish government's plans for the integration of Sweden within the European Union (EU).

The government's idea, of course, was to join the European Union in 1995, to try to take even greater economic advantage of this huge open market place for companies just like AB Volvo. This was a key imperative because of the capital costs of remaining a serious player in the European car league.

Some Volvo shareholders had especially disliked what they saw when they came to read the small print of the second merger prospectus. This promised savings of $7.4 billion that to many looked unattainable. Other points were problematic, too. As Lars-Erik Forsgardh, chief executive of the Swedish Shareholders Association, said:

We don't like... the cross-ownership which gives Renault ten per cent of Volvo. We don't also like the poison pill which will explode if someone outside takes control of Volvo which would force the company to sell its shares in RVA.[6]

Volvo shares were on a slide. In the first week of December its market capitalisation fell substantially.

The post-mortem carried out after Gyllenhammer's departure revealed other aspects of the opponents' case against the merger. One was Gyllenhammer's own abrasive management style, for which there was ample evidence and which was especially disliked by opponents. Yet another was the opposition to the move from Volvo engineers and middle managers. When Soren Gyll met his chairman he was in possession of a letter signed by no less than 25 senior managers from Volvo's bus, truck and car divisions calling for the hook-up with Renault to be dropped. They were fearful of a loss of influence.

Nevertheless, and in spite of everything, there was still the internal logic of the merger to consider. Pehr Gyllenhammer put in thus: *in this period of restructuring in the automotive industry, I think we need a stronger structure than Volvo can provide on a stand-alone basis.* The end of the merger plan would lead, in his view, to *the end of the alliance with the French.*[7] Even more problematic was the fact that Volvo and Renault were known to be in need of some $2 billion of extra capital for investment in new technology and for product development. In the event of no consummation of the marriage, these funds would have to be raised separately by Volvo, a major burden to the company.

In this way failed a deal between two major stakeholders in the global automotive market. Had it worked, it would have created the world's sixth largest truck and car maker with sales of $40 billion. It would have fitted neatly into the pattern of mergers and acquisitions that had characterised the development of the global car industry since the 1960s.

The critical question for both Renault and Volvo now, separately as opposed to together, was *What to do next?*

Volvo were, it must be admitted, in a more exposed position than Renault. In 1992 they had produced about 300,000 units, a smaller number than Britain's Rover Group and less than a fifth of Renault's output. All were sold in the upper-medium segment of demand, where the impact of recession in the USA and Europe had been greatest. Had the two been able in future to share the costs of the most expensive part of the production process, designing and developing the floorpan (on to which the engine, suspension, steeing and gears are fixed), the savings would have enabled Volvo to price more aggressively in its markets and, some critics asserted, stay in the race through the achievement of critical mass. Now, this was an impossibility.

RENAULT RESURGENT

To Edouard Balladur, the French prime minister, the problem with Renault was always going to be its privatisation. By mid 1994, passions were already running high as the date for de-nationalisation approached.

The difficulty was that Renault was seen by many as not just a car maker. Since its acquisition by the state in 1945 the company had become a sort of national symbol for the nature and quality of its labour relations, a social widow (*vitrine sociale*) on France. So much so that the main plant, Billancourt, was known in the 1960s and 1970s as a *workers' castle* (forteresse ouvrière) and as *the social capital of France*. Hence, a critical feature of the privatisation was the way in which the previous labour relations benefits obtained under state ownership, the so-called *acquis sociaux*, would automatically be carried forward into the regime of private ownership. Not for nothing did the Confédération

Générale de Travail (CGT) trade union claim that it made the cars: Renault merely sold them. It was the only trade union not to sign the *Accord à Vivre* (Agreement to Live) in 1989 which injected an even greater, but still much-needed, degree of flexibility into the company's workings.[8] And it was still a force to be reckoned with.

Renault has been a success story since near-bankruptcy ten years ago... It has been in the black for the last seven successive years. It is currently the most profitable car maker in Europe after BMW, having produced a net profit of Fr 1.07 billion on a turnover of almost Fr170 billion in 1993. It has forecast a doubling of net profits in 1994 and a further doubling in 1995. This has been made possible by a decade-long reduction in the workforce (200,000 to 140,000) and a programme of cutting costs and tightening controls. The search for quality and an innovative product range have added to success. Renault is now freed from the Volvo cross-holding entanglement; indeed as the poorer performer of the two Volvo must pay Renault F.r 1 billion and, in the light of any privatisation of Renault by the 30th November 1994, sell off all or part of its 20 per cent holding.

EXHIBIT 2: PLUSSES AT RENAULT
Source: Renault on a fast track to early privatisation,
Colin Narbrough, *The Times*, 31/8/94

Together with the two political parties the Socialists (PS) and the Communists (PC), the CGT was pledged to resist the privatisation. Large-scale demonstrations had been mobilised at Billancourt to make the point. One such, organised by the CGT took place on the 20th September 1994 but it was attended by less than ten per cent of the workforce and was of short duration.

Others were, however, equally keen to see de-nationalisation succeed. Louis Schweitzer, chairman and chief executive of Renault, for instance. As Exhibit 2 shows, there were a lot of plusses for him to consider. His mood was highly optimistic:

Since 1985 Renault has had an uninterrupted strategy of becoming the most prosperous car builder in Europe..Because Renault had an image problem we have had to run faster... to improve our quality and productivity... Renault has also striven to be different from other car manufacturers, for example with our model range, particularly... the Espace and the Twingo.[9]

Was he worried about the recent front-page headline in *L'Expansion* referring to the failure to consummate the marriage with Volvo? This had read *Renault, too little, too alone, too late. Not at all*, he declared, when

Edouard Balladur says that he believes a grand alliance with another manufacturer is necessary to guarantee Renault's future... I do not agree. But it could be necessary to ensure its global development.[10] Had he turned down the possibility of a marriage with the Italian car maker, Fiat or anyone else? *We are always talking to everyone* was the response.

What was clearly attracting Louis Schweitzer himself to privatisation was the increased commercial freedom it might bring. As he said:

It will reinforce the autonomy of the company and ... help to clear up some of the misconceptions... I sometimes find... that people think that Renault is not a normal company, that it gets state aid, that it is not run as a commercial business. The opening of Renault's capital will give it a clearer image.[11]

The government of Edouard Balladur was itself also looking forward eagerly to receiving the proceeds from the sale of shares in Renault. On the one hand, there was, in mid-1994, a French budget deficit of Fr 300 billion to fill and only meagre receipts from current disposals of state-owned companies (e.g., Union des Assurances de Paris) and prospective sales of other state enterprises (e.g., Assurances Générales de France) to help fill it.

On top of this there was all the aid the government was then being obliged to hand over to prop up the state-owned loss makers Bull, Air France and Credit Lyonnais. On the other, there was the planned sale of Renault, valued at Fr. 45 billion and with a first share tranche expected to bring in Fr. 14 billion to the French Treasury. A further political advantage was to be gained, in Gerard Longuet's view. Not only would the sell-off improve Renault's brand image but it would also signal a significant political shift away from the traditional French state legacy of dirigisme.

FULL SPEED AHEAD

The go-ahead decision was announced at the start of September 1994. The French government would sell off 28 per cent of its 79 per cent stake in Renault. A rights issue of Fr 2 billion would accompany the flotation. As a further step in unravelling the Volvo-Renault relationship, Volvo would reduce its 20 per cent stake to 12 per cent with immediate effect.

The package amounted, in fact, to something of a compromise decision. The government had clearly been apprehensive of the potential trade union backlash to the sell-off and possible moves by the newly-privatised company to hoist productivity still further. After all, French unemployment at the time was running at over 12 per cent and both parliamentary and presidential elections were looming. It was also thought likely that the government would follow previous policy and establish a core of institutional shareholders as well as ensuring the maximum buy-in by the French public. Some ten per cent of the offer was likely to be set aside for Renault employees, anyway. Incidentally, the French government rejected the criticism that it was necessarily seeking to keep French control (*franciser*) the company.

Element	Renault			PSA (Peugeot)		
	1992	1993	1994	1992	1993	1994
No of employees ('000 rounded)	146.6	139.7	138.3	150.8	143.9	139.8
Turnover (Fr B)	184.2	169.8	175.8	155.4	145.4	166.2
Net Profits (Fr B)	5.68	1.07	3.63	3.4	(1.4)	3.1

TABLE 1: COMPARATIVE DATA – RENAULT & PSA
Source: Company Records

To begin the sell-off, an advertising campaign was launched by the economy minister, Edmond Alphondery, on the 17th October 1994. The recommended price range for bids to be tendered by institutional investors was between Fr. 163 and Fr. 178 per share. He called the company *the flower of French industry* and praised the fact that it had been profitable in 1993 unlike Europe's largest car maker, VW (a record loss of DM 2 billion) and Fiat (a record loss of L1.7 trillion). Previous policy was, in fact, followed, with eight per cent being earmarked for institutional investors and a private auction to be held for so-called *investor partners* who would buy five per cent. The newly-privatised oil group, Elf Aquitaine, had already signed up as a potential partner. Even so, this would allow space, according to the minister, for another car manufacturer to make a *major industrial investment* in Renault. The state's holding would be reduced to 51 per cent and it would certainly represent a transformation in a company that had once been *a bastion of trade union activism*.[13]

The share sale began on October 17th 1994 with 37m-42m on offer to the public; 25-28m available to institutions; 12m to partners; 6m (on preferential terms 20 per cent less than other shareholders) to Renault employees. Expectations of receipts placed the sell-off value at between Fr. 39 billion and Fr. 42.5 billion. The advertising slogan stated *Renault is opening up its capital. You can become a shareholder.*

Success was immediate so far as the institutional segment of the share offer was concerned. It was known to be 15.5 times oversubscribed. However, the offer to private investors and shareholders was less well received. Here, oversubscription was 1.4 times and 1.5 times respectively. Perhaps the forthright comment by Edmond Alphondery, made as he welcomed the remarkable results of the sell-off, dampened some of the interest. He declared:

The (full-scale) privatisation of Renault is not on the agenda. Renault is a state company and will remain a state company. The privatisation of Renault is not among the government's objectives.[14]

REALITY

Renault's share price at the end of March 1995 was trading at under the eventual privatisation price of 165 francs. This was despite the tripling of annual profits in 1994, and increase in Renault's European market share (10.6 per cent to 11.0 per cent) and a substantial clean-up in its balance sheet. The Paris bourse had clearly paid attention to the reduction in the 1994 contribution from the passenger car division, blamed by Renault on the increased unit sales of low-margin cars and the French government's franc fort policy. This latter was particularly damaging to export sales.

The Paris stock market was also paying attention to a bitter pay dispute in which the company was then embroiled. The CGT and the Force Ouvrière (FO) were adamant that their pay claim was justified. Thus Daniel Sanchez, the Secretary-General of CGT:

For years we have been pulling in our belts without saying anything. Now that the up-turn is here, we want to profit from it as well. To make up for the way in which our purchasing power has lagged behind since 1984, we want a salary increase of 1500 francs for everyone ie an average pay rise of 20 per cent.[15]

The initial Renault counter-offer was 2.5 per cent maximum, made up of slight changes to the general salary base, the individual component and the seniority premium. It was rejected by the CGT-CFDT-FO-CFTC-CGC trade union alliance out of hand.

The company had also to consider that it was not only the *col bleus* (blue collar workers) who were causing stoppages but it was also the supervisory *cols blancs* (white collar workers). They were certainly concerned with pay but were taking full advantage of the opportunity to voice grievances about the changing regime of work (productivity rises, relocation, multi-skilling) at Renault. Another source of aggravation to all the protesting workers was the fact that the annual pay settlement reached at PGA and Citroen was higher than that proposed by Renault.

Car maker	1993	1994
Volkswagen	16.3	16.0
GM	13.2	13.1
PSA (Peugeot Group)	12.4	12.8
Japanese	12.3	10.9
Ford	11.6	11.8
Renault	10.6	11.0
Fiat	10.4	10.8
BMW	6.5	6.5
Mercedes	3.2	3.5
Volvo	1.5	1.7
Others	2.0	1.9

TABLE 2: EUROPEAN CAR MAKERS' MARKET SHARES (per cent)
Source: ACEA

The month-long disruption was only brought to an end by a pay offer which worked out on average at around five per cent. It had been a salutory reminder to the shareholders in Renault of the power of the French trade union movement.

French car company	1993	1994	1995
PSA (Peugeot)	2.9	2.7	3.7
Citroen	3.0	2.8	3.7
Renault	3.7	4.0	2.5*

TABLE 3: COMPARATIVE PAY INCREASES
Source: Company Records
Note: * = first 6 months of the year

On the other hand, there were highly positive aspects to think about. For instance, Renault's 1994 earnings per share and dividends were both rising, up to Fr. 11 and Fr. 2.4 respectively, and there was the company's early introduction to the index of leading shares on the Paris bourse, the CAC 40, to consider.

Alliances were also clearly on the cards to strengthen its manufacturing capability in Europe, where it was the third largest producer, and to build on the product sales success of the Renault 19, the Laguna and, so far as Britain at least was concerned, the Clio. Here, the riveting advertising story of the epic exploits of Nicole and her Papa had helped push Renault's share of the British market to six per cent.

Perhaps, more confidence in the share price would be created if and when the French government decided, as Renault executives confidently predicted it would, to move to a full privatisation of the company by the end of 1995.

* * * * * * * * * * * * * * * * * * * *

NOTES & REFERENCES

1   Volvo halts Renault merger after revolt, Colin Narbrough and George Sivell, *The Times*, 3/12/93

2   L'assemblee generale des actionnaires de Volvo est repoussee d'un mois, Annie Kahn, *Le Monde*, 3/11/93

3   Volvo shareholder revolt grows over Renault merger, Mark Milner, *The Guardian*, 12/11/93

4   Volvo denies retreat from Renault merger, David Bartal, *The European*, 19-25/11/93

5   Fresh threat by Volvo rebels to merger deal, Colin Narbrough, *The Times*, 30/11/93

6   Volvo's suitor driven out of town, Mary Brasier, *The Daily Telegraph*, 4/12/93

7   As 1

8   Renault, *symbole national* malgre lui, Jean Michel Normand, *Le Monde*, 20/8/94

9   Renault still alone as sell-off approaches, Ian Harding, *The European*, 7-13/10/94

10   As 9

11   As 9

12   Sell-off value Renault at £6 billion, Alix Christie, *The Guardian*, 18/10/94

13   French government puts foot on accelerator for Renault sell-off, Alix Christie and Simon Beavis, *The Guardian*, 14/9/94

14   Small investors drive Renault to £95m gain, *The Times*, 17/11/94

15   Chez Renault, la CGT et la CFDT exploitent la deception des grevistes, Virginie Malingre, *Le Monde*, 12–13/3/95

BARINGS

Abstract:

The Barings case chronicles the nature and rationale of the collapse of an historic and illustrious British bank and its subsequent purchase by the Dutch bank ING for £1.

Questions:

What caused the bank's collapse?
What light does the case throw on Barings' corporate culture and Britain's merchant banking ethos?
How should derivatives trading be managed?

Case Timing: 1995-9

A NEGATIVE TURNAROUND

On the 26th February 1995, Barings, one of Britain's most prestigious securities houses and merchant bankers to the Queen, was forced into administration by the Bank of England. The company had been London's oldest merchant banking business and was founded in 1762. It had symbolised much of Britain's commercial history. Indeed, so important had Barings been in financing Britain's war with Napoleon at the start of the nineteenth century, that it had been given the title of Europe's *sixth great power.*

The bank's collapse in 1995 was nothing if not spectacular but, unlike the disaster that had overtaken Barings a century before, this time there was no Bank of England safety net. In 1890, when Barings had suffered major defaults on speculative loans made to Argentine clients, the Bank of England had been quick to demonstrate to the whole of the waiting world that all the bank's commitments would be met, without question. The City had, thus, stood four-square behind Barings and, within a period of just four years, Barings had repaid the £17.1m that had made up the rescue fund. It thus regained its former position as one of the most important banking houses in the whole of Europe and the British Empire. Now the situation was different.

The implications of the Barings disaster become worse the more one knows about it - for the bank's management, the City of London's reputation, the Bank of England's supervisory authority and the country's claims to financial probity... Barings went under in a whirlpool of corporate arrogance, a mistaken belief in easy money, a refusal to heed the dangers of speculative success.

EXHIBIT 1: BARINGS IN THE WHIRLPOOL
Source: *The Sunday Times* editorial, 5/3/95

What made the 1995 crisis all the more interesting was the speed and suddenness with which the calamity struck. Barings' directors had only just met, on the 22nd February, to decide on the level of bonuses that would be given to its 4000 staff as a result of the bank's excellent performance in the previous year's trading. The planned bonuses amounted to £105m or 25 per cent of the entire issued capital of the bank. The board was then reconvened, only a mere three days later, to hear the distressing news that the bank had just lost at least £600m in derivatives trading on the Tokyo, Osaka and Singapore stock markets and that it was faced with a stark choice: either to find a buyer to save the bank or declare itself insolvent.

In fact, the situation was even worse than that. In view of the particular nature of the contracts on which the bank had lost money, the bank had precious little time, virtually until the Far East exchanges again opened fully for business, in which to secure its future.

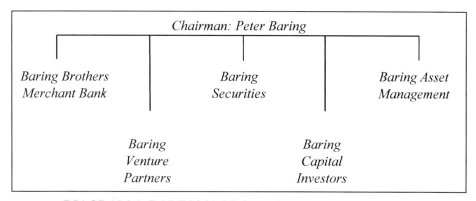

DIAGRAM 1: BARINGS' ORGANISATION STRUCTURE
Note: Barings was a private bank, owned by the charity, the Baring Foundation

The turnaround in the bank's fortunes was also marked by the fact that, in October 1994, Barings had issued against-the-trend interim figures indicating a 54 per cent rise in profits to £54.8m. Of this chairman Peter Baring had said "I think we chose the right things to do and avoided the wrong things".[1] He was also bullish at the time about the propects for the bank's operations in developing markets declaring that:

"We are seeing the markets where we were active in the 19th century coming back on screen with a speed and a size which is hard to exaggerate".[2]

Naturally, the Bank of England and the government itself were involved in handling the current débâcle. Press speculation had ran rife that the Bank would be duty-bound to cover Barings losses in the event of insolvency, given the possibility of a knock-on effect. As Labour's shadow Treasury minister, Andrew Darling, indicated:

With banks there is always a risk of a domino effect - that when one bank fails, other follow.[3]

Eddie George, governor of the Bank of England, did indeed return early from a holiday to spearhead a task force to organise emergency funding. This was duly arranged but it did not prevent Barings from being placed in adminstration to save it from its creditors. The *Times'* commentator, Anthony Harris, was alarmed at the apparent unwillingness of the government to bail out such a prominent private firm and worried about the potential impact of the crash on London's position as the financial capital of Europe. He declared:

The Bank of England behaves not like the City's protector, but like the public spending department of the Treasury... So out goes the baby with the bathwater and out goes the City's reputation and influence.[4]

TRADING IN DERIVATIVES

Barings was not the only organisation to lose substantial sums of money on derivatives trading in the frenetic conditions of the mid-1990s. On the 6th December 1994, Orange County became the largest municipal bankrupt in the history of the USA after it declared a loss on its derivative trading of no less than $1.7 billion. Previously, the major German firm Metalgesellschäft had needed bailing out by its German bank backers after it, too, had run up major losses of $1.5 billion on its trading.

Exchange Rate	Lowest traded value on given date in March 1995 on international exchanges			
	4th	7th	8th	9th
yen/$	93.75	89.2	88.75	91.20
mark/$	1.44	1.37	1.34	1.36

TABLE 1: THE US $ - A WEEK OF EXCHANGE RATE TURBULENCE

Underlying such conditions were a variety of financial and economic problems of global dimensions which, in 1994 and 1995, were throwing currency and stock markets into turmoil around the world. The 29 per cent devaluation of the Mexican peso in December 1994 and the seven per cent devaluation of the Spanish peso in early March 1995 are evidence of this. Global changes of this nature were clearly also wrapped up, as Table 1 indicates, with the level of depreciation in the $ relative to the German mark and the Japanese yen.

Adding to current uncertainties were reappraisals by the media of comparative economic fundamentals in the world's major trading nations, the imminent possibility of a trade dispute erupting between the USA and China (over intellectual property rights) and the 1994/5 trade spat between the USA and Japan (over the US' access to the Japanese market and the possible implementation of the US' trade law 'Super 301'). So did the US domestic political conflict over budgetary cutbacks between the democrat US president Clinton and the newly-elected Republican Senate leader Newt Gingrich that was then taking place. Indeed, the very size of the Republican majority in Congress had just become a significant challenge to the authority of the Clinton administration.

All of these pressures served only to increase global financial tensions and change the timing, speed and extent of speculative flows of hot money into *quality* investments and *quality* currencies.

Had the Japanese stock market gone up, the British merchant bank Barings might have reported a $900m *gain on securities transactions*. The bank's head of derivatives in Singapore, Nick Leeson, would have secured himself another very fat bonus on top of his annual basic salary of $300,000... What European taxpayers will wonder is how so much money could be *earned* from producing nothing but paper profits... When one man's actions all but wipe out his firm's capital... we are once again reminded that, in today's world, financial speculation is a zero-sum game... Your gain being someone else's loss, you are only redistibuting existing money... This scandal has shown the lunacy of big banking institutions' employing whizz-kid *punters* to trade on their own account.

EXHIBIT 2 : A LESSON FROM LEESON
Source : *The European* editorial, 3-9/3/95

And, on top of this, we need to consider the likely effect of the catastrophic Kobe earthquake on Japan's (and the world's) economy. This took place on the 17th January 1995 and was of devastating proportions. Would it lead to substantial extra investment to repair the country's damaged infrastructure? If so, would this bring improvements in the profitability of Japan's leading companies and, thereby, an uplift in the level of the Nikkei index? These were key questions. Another line of thinking led to different questions. Would the eartquake disrupt trade extensively? If so, would the current large-scale slide in the Nikkei simply continue, despite Japan's towering trade surplus, and, indeed, becom worse as a result of the Kobe factor. Associated with each set of questions was a third: what would now happen to the value of the yen? Would it continue its steep rise?

As Table 2 shows, these issues were adding considerably to stock market uncertainties for the Nikkei index.

Stock Exchange Index	Level on given date in March 1995. O=Opening C=Closing	
	5th : O	10th : C
Nikkei 225	17,040	16,358

TABLE 2: TURBULENCE ON THE EXCHANGE

In this context, trading in derivatives added much to the riskiness that was inherently involved in buying, selling and speculative trading in the physical objects with which the world had long been familiar, currencies, commodities and stock/bond prices. Derivatives were one stage removed, both as hedging and gambling instruments, from such physical investments.

Commentators Andrew Lorenz and Frank Kane[5], indicated that *derivatives are the generic name for the highly-leveraged financial instruments that feed off the international markets in currencies, equities and bonds. In their simplest form, as futures and options, they give the investor the right to deal in a security at a specific price on a given date.*

Derivatives had one over-riding attraction, namely that the investor needed to put up only a fraction of the value of the underlying security (e.g. currency, equity) in order to play the market and back whatever hunches -or reasoned judgements, depending one one's personal view- were held about future prices and market movements. Thus, if the decision proved wrong, then the investor's exposure to losses would be limited. Under normal conditions, that is.

Two major problems can arise with derivatives, however. Both are concerned with compounding the risk involved in the trades that are struck. The first is where the investor, sensing that a decision has, in fact, become more likely to be profitable, increases the number of linked contracts involved in order to maximise the pay-off. The second is where the investor begins to have some doubts about the short-term payoff from the decision (but none about the longer term), and takes out further long-term contracts to try to balance the risk in terms of the timing of the pay-off. In both cases, if the investment works out as anticipated, the result can be highly positive. But, in both cases, if the investor's assumptions prove wrong, the losses can become catastrophically large because of the compounding effect of the contracts.

So far as *Business Week* was concerned,[6] there was one background element that linked many aspects of the 1994/5 currency and equity market turbulence and the speculation in derivatives. As Exhibit 3 indicates, it was a matter of the *moving wall of money* that G7 countries had created in the early 1990s, through their low interest rate policies, in an attempt to revitalise their economies after the depression of the early 1990s.

> *In the global liquidity boom of the early 1990s, when more than $1.5 trillion in US mutual-fund money flooded the globe, money was so available, markets so ebullient and profits so rich that simple safeguards and controls went by the board..In the easy money boom, too many securities executives lost the ability or will to scrutinize high energy traders... too many bankers... neglected to ask whether they understood the complexity - or the downside - of the highly leveraged derivatives they were using to hedge financial risks. And as an influx of some $300 billion in foreign portfolio money sent stock and bond markets soaring in developing countries, too many investors and fund managers stopped asking basic questions about disclosure, accounting, value and risk.*

EXHIBIT 3: A COMMON THREAD
Source : *Business Week*, 13/3/95

WHAT SEEMED TO BE THE PROBLEM AT BARINGS?

What seemed to have gone wrong was that a single Barings employee, Nick Leeson, head of futures trading in the bank's Singapore office, managed to pile up massive losses on derivative deals in Osaka and Singapore that turned sour and that, in the attempt to cover these losses, Barings' capital evaporated. Leeson had worked for Barings since 1989. He was aged 28 and could not be said to be mathematically well-qualified. Whatever else, his business culture mind-set was hardly that of the cautious banking fraternity that Barings was thought by the City and by international partners to possess.

In fact, in the three-week period up to the so-called *meltdown*, Nick Leeson had, in fact, put together the equivalent of a £14 billion bet, based on a mixture of options and futures contracts, that the downward trend in the Nikkei index would be reversed within a specific time period. Even the Kobe earthquake had not caused him to make any change in the direction of his speculation.

The extent of Barings' exposure in this situation was highly abnormal, as was its level. Previously, Nick Leeson had confined himself to acting as an arbitrageur taking advantage of small price differentials in share prices on contracts traded on the Singapore and Osaka exchanges. This had involved the bank in taking what were, in fact, large positions in stock exchange prices but with a relatively low level of risk.

Quite suddenly, it appeared, he had exchanged the role of arbitrageur for that of speculator when, in 1994, he began to convert his contracts to *buys* and started to sell *put and call* options to raise cash. He also changed his funding strategy by using client and Baring funds, and with a considerable amount of subterfuge.

> *My concern is that, once again, we are in danger of setting up a structure (in Singapore) which will subsequently prove disastrous and with which we will succeed in losing either a lot of money, or client goodwill or both.*

EXHIBIT 4: JAMES BAX (Head of Barings, Singapore)
Reports to London on Nick Leeson's Appointment [7]

When his losses began to rise dramatically at the start of 1995, he contacted Barings in London with a request for extra funds to cover Barings needs' on the basis of the claimed requirements of a corporate client. No less than £580m was transferred from London to Singapore in the first two months of 1995. One supposition behind the transfer was that, at the time, Barings HQ was unaware of the precise extent of the bank's Singapore difficulties. Another is that were pleased to transfer the money. This notion is based on the fact that Nick Leeson's team in Singapore seemed to have developed a *Midas touch*. He was credited with having made around £19m profit in the first half of 1994, a sum which was a very large component in Baring's total profit for the half-year of £54.8m.

Whichever of these two suppositions is correct it is indisputable that Barings had traditionally been, in capital terms, only a small operator in the Singapore International Monetary Exchange (SIMEX) in contrast to dominant banks like Swiss Bank, Barclays and the Hong Kong and Shanghai.

The level of risk that Nick Leeson was running should not have been unappreciated by Barings, even if tolerated. It knew, in appointing the 25-year-old Nick Leeson to his position in Singapore, that he had been refused a licence to act as a trader in the London market. Barings HQ had previously received two negative reports, from James Bax, Barings Singapore M.D. (see Exhibit 4) and from an internal audit team sent out expressly to Singapore in August 1994, about the riskiness of its position. This latter had warned that Leeson's role allowed him *an excessive concentration of power* which could lead to *error and fraud*.[8] The bank had condoned Nick Leeson's acting as head not only of the trading operation, striking the deals on the trading floor (the *front* office), but also of the administration section where the deals were duly processed (the *back* office). Furthermore, despite his comparative lack of experience, he had been made reponsible at the outset directly to Ron Baker, head of Barings derivatives business based in London, as opposed to James Bax, the Singapore M.D.

Unusually, Barings operations in Singapore, and Tokyo and New York, were not integrated in the bank's risk-management computer system. The system, called BORIS (Barings Order Routing and Information System), was operational in London and was scheduled to be linked up with Singapore in late 1995. Had it been so at the time of the collapse, it could have alerted London to Singapore's difficulties. Among other things it might have uncovered was the use by Nick Leeson of a hidden trading account, **88888**, which enabled him to hide the losses he made.

> *Almost from the day he arrived in Singapore in 1992, Mr Leeson gained a reputation as a brilliant but risky trader. He was always standing in the Nikkei futures pit... making large trades when many of his competitors did not dare... Simex is not a big market..and does not rate in the top ten. Everybody knows everybody and everybody knew that Nick Leeson was a wild man. Mr Leeson did not fit the description of an arbitrage dealer in any respect. His behaviour and his team's huge profits make it clear that he was taking large positions in the market all along... Huge profits in this market can only mean high risk... Mr Leeson was, literally, betting the bank.*

EXHIBIT 5: A ROGUE TRADER IN THE MAKING? [9]

There was also the question, as Exhibit 5 points out, of the personality of Nick Leeson himself. Certainly, when he began to recognise that the disaster could no longer be concealed, he fled - firstly to Kota Kinabalu in Borneo and then to Frankfurt where he was taken into custody by the German police on accusations of fraud.

The SIMEX authorities and the Serious Fraud Office in London were each running enquiries on Barings' collapse, but the specific request for extradition made by the Singapore's Commercial Affairs Department related to a charge that a document, used as collateral to obtain a £45m loan from Citibank, had, in fact, been forged by Nick Leeson. It was to be July 1999 before he was released from jail in Singapore.

SAVED BY THE ING

It was in November 1994 that ING, Internationale Nederlanden Groep, decided upon a new and vigorous expansionist strategy for investment banking, asset management and, above all, emerging markets.

Consideration of Barings world-wide mainstream presence in merchant banking (Hong Kong, Singapore, Germany and France etc.) and in asset management led ING to believe at the time that Barings would make an ideal partner. Barings did not, however, share this view and responded coldly to ING's approach.

Under the entirely different circumstances of the Barings collapse, another approach began on the first of March 1995. This time, the really eager partner was Barings itself, sponsored by the Bank of England.

Detailed talks continued between Ernst and Young (the administrators), Barings and ING directors until, on the fifth of March, ING announced that they had, in principle, agreed to buy Barings for a nominal £1. The go-ahead for the deal was given by the Bank of England, the Bank of the Netherlands and Britain's High Court on the following day. Another possible partner, the Dutch bank ABN-AMRO, had withdrawn from discussions at an early stage.

> *Cross-border mergers are full of promise but rarely deliver the anticipated reward... some great exceptions to this fact of commercial life happen to be Anglo-Dutch... Why this should be so is partly explained by Dutch fluency in English, the common thread of the Protestant religion, historical wariness of peoples Teutonic and the legacy of imperial trade.*

EXHIBIT 6: WINNING CROSS-BORDER MERGERS [11]

The purchase was applauded by Dutch analysts as *a bright strategic move* and the match labelled *perfect*.[10] Above all, ING's chairman, Aad Jacobs, said that searching enquiries had been carried out by the ING team into Barings' information technology and control systems, with the conclusion that *the Singapore disaster was a one-off incident*.[11] So far as the detail of the take-over was concerned, Aad Jacobs said that the strategic fit between ING Group and Barings was *compelling*.[12]

The statement made at the end of negotiations indicated that ING was acquiring all the businesses, assets and liabilities of the Barings group and that it would make £660m in cash immediately available to ensure normal trading could be re-started.

would make £660m in cash immediately available to ensure normal trading could be re-started.

This had been facilitated by the actions taken by SIMEX to close all Barings loss-making futures contracts more than a week before their deadline for expiry. They had also sold all the Nikkei futures positions built up by Nick Leeson. All losses had been covered by the margin payments received from Barings.

> *Whoever gets the final blame, the main lesson is all too clear. Although London may remain Europe's financial capital, Britain's financial industry could easily become dominated by foreign-owned companies that are better managed, better financed and staffed by better employees than their British rivals. The smugness and mismanagement that ruined the British-owned car industry in the 1970s and undermined Lloyd's in the 1980s could also undo Britain's banks.*

EXHIBIT 7: VALLEY OF DEBT
Source: *The Times* editorial, 4/3/95

Not only had ING agreed to *seek to preserve* the jobs of Barings 4,000 employees, but it was prepared to pay bonuses of £90m to staff. This apparently had been a key issue for Barings in the take-over negotiations. The most visible losers were the Barings creditors who had invested £100m in a bond issue in January 1995! The amount they would receive in compensation was unlikely to be more than 25p in the £ and they were very unhappy.

Peter Baring, the bank's chairman, welcomed the takeover declaring that:
We give it our full support and will work with ING to develop the businesses... ING will be well-suited to help Barings achieve a rapid recovery from its present position... The fundamental strength and quality of the Barings business will enable it to become fully effective again within a short time.[13]

THE COLD LIGHT OF DAY

The July 1995 report of the Board of Banking Supervision into the Baring collapse confirmed many of the widespread suspicions ·of the causes of the collapse.

Of course, Nick Leeson himself carried the prime responsibility for having broken the Bank. In a statement to the House of Commons on the 18th July 1995, the Chancellor of the Exchequer, Kenneth Clarke, spoke of his *complex and systematic process of deception and false reporting* which had been compounded by *catastrophic errors* and had led to *staggering losses* totalling was publicly declared, he had made losses. These he had carefully concealed in secret accounts **88888** and **92000**. The £28.5m profits he reported to HQ in 1994, which chairman Peter Baring found *pleasantly surprising* and which formed the basis of the bonus proposed for Nick Leeson himself of £450,000, were fictitious.[15]

Year	Price £m	British Investment Bank	Total Assets £m	Profit 1994/5 £m	Employees	Bought by
1989	950	Morgan Grenfell	9680	80	2229	Deutsche Bank
1995	850	S.G Warburg	22,584	297	4472	Swiss Banking Corp
1995	1000	Kleinwort Benson	12,539	112	2799	Dresdner

TABLE 3: UNDER NEW OWNERSHIP
Source: *The Guardian,* 13/7/95 and *Frankfurter Allgemeine Zeitung,* 14/7/95

What had occurred was, firstly, that he had moved away from his original range of activity in Singapore. This was essentially exploiting price differentials between the Singapore, Tokyo and Osaka stock markets, an activity which Barings considered to be profitable and essentially risk-free. Secondly, the steadily accumulating losses made once he moved into futures were both concealed and then financed in a clandestine manner. How had this been possible? One of Nick Leeson's colleagues, Fernando Gueler, put it in a nutshell. *He was regarded as almost a miracle worker*, he said.[16] What had allowed it to happen? Commentators Neil Collins and Christopher Fildes claimed they knew. How did stuffy old Barings, established in 1762, more pleased with themselves every year and a model of blue-blooded banking, let themselves be turned into such a house of cards? The short answer is greed. *Mr Leeson appeared to be an alchemist...*[17]

What in fact caused the collapse was, in the words of the *Financial Times*, not the complex nature of the risks being run in new-fangled instruments but *a failure of old-fashioned internal control*.[18] The report spelled these out for Barings.

For three years, Account 88888 purportedly escaped the notice of the entire Baring Group management. They either knew or should have known about the existence of Account 88888 and of the losses. Managers with responsibility for the overseeing of Nick Leeson's deals were *grossly negligent or wilfully blind and reckless to the truth.* Senior management suffered from *institutional incompetence.*

EXHIBIT 8: INVESTIGATING THE BLACK HOLE
Source: *Report* by Price Waterhouse auditors Nickey Tan and Michael Lim to the Singapore Government into the collapse of Barings Bank., Issued October 1995

Its organisational shortcomings had allowed Nick Leeson virtual autonomy of control of his operations in Singapore since he was in charge of both the front and back offices; the reporting lines were unclear and far from realistic; the bank had no *proper system of internal controls to enforce accountability for all profits, risks and operations and adequately to follow up a number of warning signals over a prolonged period;*[19] some of the job descriptions for senior bank executives, like Ron Baker, were poorly defined.

The Bank has been slow to recognise that its approach to supervision needed to be overhauled to cope with financial conglomeration...It was there that the watchdogs of Threadneedle Street failed most conspicuously. The rapidly rising profits in Barings' far eastern operations failed to prompt the right questions about risk.

EXHIBIT 9: WHERE THE BANK OF ENGLAND WENT WRONG
Source: *The Financial Times* editorial, 19/7/95

The report also focussed attention on the alleged lapses of other players. The Bank of England, for example. The Financial Times commented sharply on the report's findings, as Exhibit 8 points out. But Eddie George, the Governor of the Bank, rejected the notion that the Bank had, in fact, acted complacently in respect of Barings as the regulatory authority. Nor did he regard the report as the result of an *old boy nod-and-wink* approach to condoning inadequacies in the City. He further rejected the notion advanced by the Commons Treasury Select Committee, that regulation should be tightened up. That would, he said, involve a *witch-hunt* approach which would be counter-productive.[20] Certainly, there was no possiblity of stopping the making of the film, Rogue Trader, which features the exploits of Nick Leeson.

* * * * * * * * * * * * * * * * * * *

NOTES & REFERENCES

1   The rise and fall of Barings, Patricia Tehan, *The Times*, 27/2/95
2   Queen's bank near collapse in £400m loss, Andrew Lorenz and David Smith, *The Sunday Times*, 26th February, 1995
3   As 2
4   Not with a bang but a whimper, Anthony Harris, *The Times*, 1/3/95
5   Barings on brink of collapse, Andrew Lorenz and Frank Kane, *The Sunday Times*, 26/2/95
6   The Lesson from Barings' Straits, Paula Dwyer, William Glasgall, Dean Foust and Greg Burns, *Business Week*, 13/3/95
7   Barings board ignored all warnings signs, Insight, *The Sunday Times*, 5/3/95. James Bax' fax to Barings head of equities in London, Andrew Fraser, was dated 25th March 1992.
8   As 7
9   The week Barings reaped its own seeds of disaster, Neil Bennett, *The Times*, 4/3/95
10   ING reassures investors over rushed Barings buy, Barbara Snit and Tony Patey, *The European*, 10/3-16/3/95
11   Barings Dutch master, Lindsay Vincent, *The Observer*, 12/3/95
12   As 10
13   Dutch Group wins battle for Barings, Patricia Tehan, Philip Webster and Neil Bennett, *The Times*, 6/3/95
14   Barings' Chief shares the blame, Richard Northedge, *The Daily Telegraph*, 19/7/95
15   The *pleasant* profits that broke Britain's blue-blooded bank, Helen Dunne, *The Daily Telegraph*, 19/7/95
16   Brown savages the *old boys' network*, Patrick Donovan, Dan Atkinson, *The Guardian*, 19/7/95
17   How could it happen? The answer is greed, Neil Collins and Christopher Fildes, *The Daily Telegraph*, 19/7/95
18   Barings and the Bank, *The Financial Times*, 19/7/95
19   Catalogue of failed controls and missed danger signals, *The Daily Telegraph*, 19/7/95
20   Bank chief attacks *witchhunt*, Patrick Donavan, *The Guardian*, 20/7/95

CRÉDIT LYONNAIS

Abstract:

This case examines aspects of the relationship among the French government, industry and the state-owned Crédit Lyonnais bank, one of the largest in the world, at a time of crisis for the bank in 1995 and during its rehabilitation and privatisation.

Questions:

To what extent were Crédit Lyonnais' strategic misfortunes of its own making?

What were its managerial problems?

What are the plusses and minuses of France's corporatist culture?

Should the European Commission rules on aid to state industry be tightened?

How secure is Crédit Lyonnais now ?

Case Timing: 1995-9

"CRAZY LYONNAIS"

Crazy Lyonnais was Eric Leser's view of the matter. This, and not *Crédit Lyonnais* as you might have expected, was the sub-title he gave to his book about the evolution of Europe's largest bank over the period 1974-1994. Critics of the bank's performance thought that this was not an unreasonable description, given that, in this time, the bank had had no less than six chairmen and chief executives (présidents directeur-generaux) and had changed its strategic direction at each successive French general election, namely 1981, 1986, 1988 and 1993. Moreover, having made a substantial profits during the so-called age of *easy money* in the 1980s and still been profitable to the tune of FFr 10 billion in the period 1989–1991, it had become, in Leser's words, *one of the European champions in banking profitability*.[1] Nevertheless, it had still managed to lose at least FFr 20 billion in the heavy recession from 1992–1994, and this, despite numerous checks and audits by the Court of Accounts (Cour des Comptes), the Stock Market Commission (COB) and the French Treasury.

By March 1995 the crisis caused by Crédit Lyonnais' losses was clear for all to see. Interviewed on French television on 15th March 1995, the economics minister, Alphonse Alphandéry, said that there might even have been some criminality involved in the bank's downfall. At the very least there appeared to be a hole in the accounts of Crédit Lyonnais amounting to some FFr 50 billion.[2] Its estimated losses for 1994 had mounted to FFr. 12 billion after provisions of FFr. 18 billion.

Crédit Lyonnais and its majority share-owner, the French government, were, however, faced with an even greater humiliation resulting from this misfortune: having to obtain the agreement of the European Union's Competition Commissioner, Karel van Miert, to a full-scale rescue package for the bank. The challenge faced was thought to be some 13 times larger than the size of the catastrophe that had brought down Barings, the British merchant bank in 1994.

The decision as to whether or not France would be allowed to restore what was its flagship bank to health was due to be made by the European Commission on the 26th July 1995. There were signs that those involved had, in fact, met the conditions set by Karel van Miert and that the go-ahead for rescue would be given. But there were still anxieties and shareholders in Crédit Lyonnais, like the state-owned industrial giant Thomson-CSF (19 per cent), had reason to be worried.[3]

OFF THE RAILS

This was not, in reality, the first bale-out that Crédit Lyonnais had been involved in. As recently as March 24th 1994 the French government, with European Commission approval, had injected FFr. 4.9 billion in cash into its balance sheet and arranged for FFr. 43 billion of bad loans to be removed from its books. State guarantees were made for FFr. 18.4 billion of this sum. Forced disposals of assets resulting from this bail-out included the sale of major shareholdings in Adidas shoes, Meridien hotels and the Les Halles shopping complex in Paris. The list also included cinemas in the Netherlands, Denmark and Britain and banks in South America. On the 18th May 1994 the governor of the Bank of France, Jean-Claude Trichet, had reassured an anxious world that there were *no more unpleasant surprises.*[4] But there were.

What had gone wrong to cause this present difficulty?

Alphonse Alphandery listed three causes in an interview on the 15th March 1995: alleged fraud and embezzlement, poor management and the steep decline in French property values that had greatly reduced the security for bank loans advanced against them that had occurred in the 1990s. Despite this, he reckoned that Crédit Lyonnais was *a bank with a future,* once *it had taken in sail,*[5] i.e., increased its productivity. *The Wall Street Journal,* in a celebrated editorial entitled *The Lyonnais Hot Potato,* stated wryly that the French Economics Minister deserved a *thespian award* for his acting performance.

In the Journal's view there were two problems with the rescue plan: first, it would be *anti-competitive,* second, and contrary to the pronouncements of the French government, the taxpayer would foot some, if not all, of the bill. It continued:

> *Despite clear European Union rules against state aid and a directorate in charge of assuring fair competition, Brussels cannot be counted upon to lift a little pinky finger against France... Karel van Miert has already approved the plan as "a good approach".*[6]

This was a view shared by Marc Vienot, chairman and chief executive of Crédit Lyonnais' big rival, Societé Générale, who had publicly protested that the plan disadvantaged Crédit Lyonnais' rivals.

Behind the immediate causes of the 1994/5 crisis, other more strategic factors had, it seemed, also played a role. Difficulties had first begun with the appointment of Jean-Yves Haberer as chairman and chief executive in 1988 by the French Socialist President, Francois Mitterand. He was to become widely known as the *Napoleon of French banking*. As commentator Tony Allen-Mills pointed out:

Egged on by Mitterand, who saw the bank as a powerful vehicle for enhancing French influence in world financial markets, Haberer plunged into a dizzying succession of questionable deals, throwing money at the imminently moribund Parisian property market... notably financing a controversial take-over of MGM studios... It lavished never-to-be-recovered loans on ill-fated tycoons such as Robert Maxwell and the bankrupt Bernard Tapie, former boss of Marseille football club and former Urban Affairs Minister. [7]

France's business culture was also to be blame in Allen-Mills' view. More specifically, perhaps, what has been called *The 2000 Club*. This was the group of *Ivy League* French technocrats, virtually inter-changeable politicians, businessmen and civil servants, who were the product of an élite education in the grande école system, in which the Ecole Nationale d'Administration (ENA) and its graduates (*Enarques*) ranked supreme. Effectively, these were the people who could be said to run France and, as he saw it, it was the *political cronyism* resulting from the system which, if not responsible for Crédit Lyonnais' failings, was the cause of the cover-ups which were alleged to have taken place.[8] The left-wing daily *La Libération* was also particularly critical of the close ties between the French government and companies and what it saw as *the impunity of the bosses.*[9]

It was also evident that the French government itself was implicated. On the 28th March 1995 Alphonse Alphandéry himself endured an unpleasant two-hour session, defending the roles played by the Bank of France and the Treasury, before the Finance Commission of the French parliament. The temperature of the debate had been raised, not only by the imminence of the French presidential election, but also by the charge made by MP François d'Aubert that testimony given on the 18th May 1993 to the parliamentary Commission of Inquiry into the problems of Crédit Lyonnais by Jean-Claude Trichet, governor of the Bank of France, was *implausible.*[10] There were now calls for legal proceedings in respect of the allegation that the bank had falsified its accounts.

Two points are significant in this. Firstly, that before Jean-Claude Trichet became governor of the Bank of France, he had been director of the French Treasury and was *the best placed of the country's civil servants to judge the true extent of the Crédit Lyonnais débâcle.*[11] Secondly, that of the testimony of Albert Pavie, Commissaire aux Comptes (head of the Audit Commission) to the Finance Commission on the second of June 1994. He asserted that an appeal had been made to his office by the public watchdog for the French banking system, the Commission Bancaire (presided over by Jean Claude Trichet), to certify Crédit Lyonnais accounts *prematurely,* in the interest of Crédit Lyonnais... and the Paris financial world.[12]

> *The banking crisis has been grossly under-estimated in France, according to Scott Bugie... of Standard & Poor's... There are too many banks in France, often barely profitable... Property speculation illustrates it marvellously. The banks rushed at the end of the 1980s into a market they considered, wrongly, to be risk-free as well as lucrative. The cost of this error is nowadays put at FFr 150 billion. On top of this, the business environment since then has been particularly unfavourable – high interest rates, company failures and the rising cost of risk-adjusted capital... plus the potential impact of new technology and growth in competition... The number of employees in French banking, according to the Association Française de Banques (AFB), has already fallen over the period 1986-93 from 254,409 to 226,847... The profitability of France's banking sector is also badly affected by the relatively high number of inhabitants/counter (guichet) compared with other countries, e.g., France 179, Britain 269, Germany 1564, USA 2221 and Japan 3794.*

EXHIBIT 1: THE FRENCH BANKING CRISIS OF THE MID-1990s
Source: Les banques françaises sont de plus en plus fragiles,
Eric Leser, *Le Monde,* 31/5/95

The matter was given even greater point as Crédit Lyonnais announced its final results for 1994 on the fifth of April 1995. Its losses were, as forecast, at FFr. 12 billion, the largest ever suffered by any French company. Of this, provisions for bad debt came to FFr. 18 billion and an extraordinary write-down on goodwill amounted to FFr. 3.9 billion. There was an additional charge of FFr. 1.5 billion for restructuring. Jean Peyrevelade, chairman and chief executive, was philosophical:

> *Personally, the past does not interest me.. Yes Crédit Lyonnais must shrink. The re-focus we're now putting in place will bring just that... We must become bankers again, and exclusively bankers.*[13]

THE CASE OF WORMS

The aristocracy of the *mandarinate*, the rule of the civil service technocrats who monopolised the government and the biggest French firms,[14] was also obliquely criticised by the Vienot committee. This committee had been set up by the Confederation of French Industry (CNPF) and the French Association of Private Sector Companies (AFEP) to produce the Gallic equivalent of the UK's 1992 Cadbury report, an investigation into key aspects of corporate governance. It reported in mid-1995.

Its timing was impeccable, as the French media, in 1994 and 1995, was reciting a wholesale catalogue of allegations of high level managerial misdemeanors (by Bernard Tapie and Pierre Suard, president of Alcatel Alsthom, for instance) and strategic inadequacies. Gerard Worms fell into the latter category. As chairman and chief executive of Suez, France's largest financial and industrial conglomerate from 1990 onwards, he was deemed by his board to have performed poorly and was forced to resign on the 31st July 1995, with much adverse publicity. He had inherited on appointment a major portfolio expansion drive, which he had subsequently re-oriented by selling off FFr. 34 billion of Suez assets. This had been partially successful as a realistic strategy but he was held responsible for Suez' 1994 loss of FFr. 4.6 billion. Suez shareholders, like the Banque Nationale de Paris (five per cent), had not been pleased with what appeared to them as a somewhat frenzied search for partners to aid Suez in its difficulties in 1993 and 1994 and had removed their support for the chief executive. This was not a traditional way of working in French business.

Thus, the Vienot Committee could not help but pay attention to the new turbulence in French boardrooms that was epitomised by the case of Worms. Its remit was, after all, to analyse the functioning of boards of directors of listed French companies. General results of the inquiry are given in Table 1.

---

1. Every board of directors (conseil d'administration) should periodically review its structure, methods of working and its membership
2. The practice of combining the roles of chairman and chief executive is endorsed
3. Independent directors would be a welcome addition to the governance system
4. There is a need for ad hoc committees to deal with matters such as remuneration and auditing.

TABLE 1: CONCLUSIONS OF THE VIENOT COMMITTEE

A key committee recommendation was for putting an end to the practice of inter-locking directorships and for placing a limitation on the number of directorships that could be held by individuals. This had led, in the committee's view, to a *reciprocal complaisance* that was damaging.[15] It was also a practice which had allowed Edouard Balladur, French prime minister until President Chirac's victory in 1995, to secure *political and national control over France's largest industrial and financial groups.*[16] Another recommendation was the need to increase the accountability, and transparency of operation, of boards. The reason for this is suggested by Exhibit 1, page 415.

Overall, the end product of the Vienot investigation was an attempt to re-structure the French system in favour of the shareholder. It was to provide, as Alain Faujas put it *a guarantee that the company's system of governance will have effective control mechanisms to head off the mistakes of the megalomaniac and avoid going up blind alleys.*[17]

> *Capitalism in France is not nearly raw enough... Corporate culture is about to be sent to Madame Guillotine... The reason is simple... The Paris bourse depends disproportionately on foreign investors because of a lack of domestic pension funds... France has to woo the foreigner... French fear of foreign investors' gaining control of the country's major groups prompted the establishment of the "noyau dur" or core group of domestic shareholders. These defensive structures left the state in a powerful position with cross holdings.*

EXHIBIT 2: THE NOYAU DUR
Source: Colin Narbrough, *The Times*, 21/7/95

Whether or not the Crédit Lyonnais affair had its roots in megalomania or blind alleys or elsewhere, it was beyond dispute that here was an instance of the failing of not just a bank, but a system. The system in question was labelled by the French the *complexe banque-industrie* (BI). It was one in which the government, through its majority ownership, was in a position to ensure the bank's long-term support to successful entrepreneurs and dynamic growth companies, on the one hand, and, if need be, static or failing state enterprises, on the other. The support could come in the form of share ownership or secured loans or both. In the late 1980s the relationship had been used purposefully to ensure that the strategic international expansion of major state-owned French firms, such as that of Rhone Poulenc in buying the American Rohrer chemical firm, was assisted to the full. The *closed club* nature of the BI complex is hinted at in Table 2 on page 418.

A study by Ian Harding and John Chalmers in late March 1995 showed that 34 senior businessmen each sat on the boards of at least six of France's leading companies and occupied no less than 279 seats between them. The net result of this BI complex has been the near-absolute lack of hostile take-over bids for companies at the commanding heights of the French economy.[18]

Name of president	Company	Also sits on the boards of banks (b) and insurers (i)
Pierre Suard	Alcatel Alsthom	Crédit Commercial de France (b), Societe Generale (b)
Didier Pineau-Valencienne	Schneider	Paribas (b), AXA (i)
Jean-Louis Beffa	Saint Gobain	BNP (b), Suez (b), UAP (i)
Jerome Monod	Lyonnaise des Eaux	Suez (b)
Jacques Friedmann	UAP	Suez (b), Parisbas (b)

Note:
(i)   Each of these executives, except for Jacques Friedmann, was at the time under judicial investigation
(ii) Jacques Friedmann also sat on the boards of Alcatel Alsthom, Generale des Eaux, Lyonnaise des Eaux and Elf Aquitaine.

TABLE 2: ELEMENTS OF A COMPLEXE BANQUE-INDUSTRIE
Source: How the Lyonnais limousine skidded off the German road,
Thierry Naudin, *The European*, 24–30/3/95.

Jean-Yves Haberer was a typical example of the genre of executives educated in the Ecole National mode and who spent their careers in industry/commerce as well as state administration. As his evidence to the 1993 parliamentary inquiry suggests, he was very proud of this. Criticising the man who became his successor after he was ousted in 1993, he said:

What Peyrelevade lacks in his culture is to have not gone through ENA and to know how the public sector works.[19]

Peyrelevade, for his part, considered that a key issue in Crédit Lyonnais' difficulties had been the weight of the personality of the chairman in what he saw as *a totally monarchic system*. A trenchant report by Equinoxe, the French think-tank, underlined this point. It spoke of *big business' relentless defence of their own assets in which the power of shareholders is absent... The time has perhaps come* it added *when allowing this state nobility to be all-powerful puts French democracy in danger.*[20]

THE RESCUE PLAN

It was, it must be admitted, a little difficult for Crédit Lyonnais to return to its shareholders for another injection of support so soon after it had been granted the last *one time only* aid in 1993. But the fact was that the bank had simply continued to haemorrhage money and it needed surgery. For a bank that was 132 years old and one of the world's largest, this was ignominy writ large. Tony Allen-Mills called it *the biggest financial fiasco in European banking history.*[21]

The plan was unveiled by Jean Peyrevelade and Alphonse Alphandery on the 17th March 1995. With it came recognition that the last rehabilitation attempt had failed. It began, as we have seen, with a bland statement that it would not cost the taxpayer anything and that it was anticipated that it would be approved by the EU's Competition Commissioner without difficulty. It then continued with a twofold scheme to deal with the bank's problems.

The first element was to spin off FFr. 140 billion (£17.6 billion) of un- or under-performing assets (i.e., loans that had turned bad and profitable/ unprofitable investments which could be, and needed to be, liquidated) into a new company, where they would be sold off as market conditions permitted. As these were not part of Crédit Lyonnais' core banking business, they typically did not require large provisions. The new company was to be called the Consortium de Réalisation (CDR) and would be run by five state appointees and five members chosen by the French financial sector. It would be state-supported and financed at a minimal rate of interest.

Estimates indicated that Crédit Lyonnais would, as a result, be disposing of 90 per cent of its industrial share portfolio which had been painstakingly built up as part of France's industrial strategy in the past. Not for nothing was the bank owner of 20 per cent of the steel giant Usinor Sacilor, 17.8 per cent of Aerospatiale and ten per cent of Framatome, all, as of mid 1995, themselves state-owned. Karel van Miert was highly supportive of this element because it did *not rely on re-capitalising Crédit Lyonnais with taxpayers' money but through stripping it of important assets.*[22]

The Financial Times put a very positive gloss on Crédit Lyonnais' misfortunes. It declared:

It looks like the sale of the century. More than 1000 industrial holdings..are being put up for sale..Foreign investment banks are already slavering at the mouth at the prospect of a slice of one of the lucrative streams of business likely to emerge from France over the next five years.[23]

The second feature was for the bank to divert part of its future profit stream to make up for losses incurred as a result of asset disposals. It was thought likely that this might depress earnings for 20 years.

The Competition Commissioner was anxious to reassure everybody that his scrutiny of the plan would be exacting. *We are going to open up the state aid procedure to look very carefully at the plan* he said.[24] The chief criteria he would be using were the extent to which the plan distorted competition and the extent of taxpayer involvement (*participation du contribuable*).

On the 26th July 1995 and, as expected, the European Commission gave its assent to the revised rescue plan put forward by the French government. For Karel Van Miert it was *a landmark decision... the first time that Brussels had ruled on a state aid payment involving the sensitive banking sector.* His support was based on the fact that the aid would not exceed FFr. 45 billion. For the French government, Alain Madelin, the new economics and finance minister, declared *this will permit Crédit Lyonnais to turn the page. But*, he added ominously, *I cannot guarantee that taxpayers will not have to put their hands in their pockets.*[25]

There was another sting in the tail, in the form of additional Commission conditions. The changes demanded by the Commission involved forcing the bank to sell off 50 per cent of its banking assets outside France by the end of 1998 (on top of existing planned industrial asset disposals through CDR). It had also to agree, in principle, to the privatisation of the bank within the next five years. Another element was that the bank would not be allowed to write off its last three years of losses against future profits. Any breach in these conditions would cause Brussels to immediately re-open the case, it was said.

Such a reduction in the size of Crédit Lyonnais' assets outside France would automatically mean the ending of the bank's claim to be the broadest-based in Europe, with 900 offices and branches in a dozen countries. It would also signify a wholesale reversal of its growth-by-acquisition strategy. This had resulted in a 50 per cent stake in the now profitable German BfG bank in Frankfurt, by far the largest-ever foreign purchase by any French bank and carried out in 1993. It had also resulted in the acquisition of a 58 per cent stake in the Italian Crédit Bergamasco. This also had contributed profit in 1994, unlike the bank's subsidiaries in Spain (CL Spain and Banca Jover) and Portugal (CL Portugal). As can be imagined, the loss of BfG was being heavily resisted by Jean Peyrelevade.

TURNAROUND

That said, there was considerable relief in government and within Crédit Lyonnais that, in the words of Philippe Lemâitre of *Le Monde* that *l'entreprise n'a pas le couteau sur la gorge*, the bank no longer had a knife at its throat.[26] It begin to downsize heavily outside France as its turnaround plan clicked in, with a workforce reduction from 68,000 in 1994 to 46,000 in 1998. So far as France was concerned the fall over this period was from 38,000 to 30,000. By 1995 it had broken even and from then onwards its net profit growth was small but steady. The loss of 1994, FFr. 12 billion, came thus to be replaced with a 1998 profit of 1.08 billion.

The climate was right for the acceptance of the other European Commission condition, the privatisation of the bank.. After 50 years of state ownership, it would be a difficult operation.. Nevertheless, the government decided to grasp the nettle and made the announcement on the 29th October 1998 that trading in Crédit Lyonnais shares would start on the eighth of July 1999. But it was not to be a total privatisation, as ten per cent of shares would remain in government hands. Intriguingly, the government also arranged for 33 per cent of shares to be bought by a hard core of institutional shareholders led by Crédit Agricole, Allianz (the German insurance group) and Axa. Their stake would amount to 21 per cent and would constitute a blocking minority sufficient to stop the bank from falling into hostile hands. The remainder of the shares, 57 per cent, would be sold to bank staff and private investors.

In the event it was the second most popular privatisation offer in France after France Télécom, possibly because the private investor stake was offered at a 70 per cent discount. With a stock market capitalisation of £6.5 billion, Crédit Lyonnais had raised £3.7 billion for the government. An ebullient Dominique Strauss-Kahn declared:

We have minimised the losses and maximised the value.

Shares soared to a 20 per cent premium when trading began and there was a perceptible sense of relief in government ranks. Not surprising, perhaps, after 12 years of such turbulence and drama.

* * * * * * * * * * * * * * * * * * *

NOTES & REFERENCES

1 Crazy Lyonnais – La morale d'une infortune, Eric Leser, Calman-Levy, 1994. The French reads *l'un des champions Européens de la rentabilité bancaire*
2 Le gouvernment veut sanctionner les responsables des malversations dans l'affaire du Crédit Lyonnais, Babette Stern, 16/3/95. The French reads *un trou*
3 L'etat organise le sauvetage de Crédit Lyonnais, *Le Monde*, 20/3/95
4 Crédit Lyonnais losses were hidden for a year, Ian Harding, *The European*, 24–30/3/95
5 France sees a future for troubled Crédit Lyonnais, Barry James, *The International Herald Tribune*, 16/3/95 and as [2]. Alphandery's comment was that customers should *avoir confiance dans le CL qui est une banque qui a un avenir*
6 The Lyonnais Hot Potato, *The Wall Street Journal*, 17–18/3/95
7 French élite blamed for bank fiasco, Tony Allen-Mills, *The Sunday Times*, 19/3/95
7 As 7
9 Crash of France's biggest bank hits Balladur hopes, Charles Bremner, *The Times*, 17/3/95
10-12 As 4
13 France sees a future for troubled Crédit Lyonnais, *The Times*, 16/3/95
14 French aim to clear up the boardroom, Colin Narbrough, *The Times*, 21/7/95
15 As 14
16 Corporate broom to sweep through French boardrooms, Thierry Naudin, *The European*, 14–20/7/95
17 M. Vienot propose une réforme prudente des conseils d'administration, Alain Faujas, *Le Monde* 12/7/95. The French reads elegantly *éviter les dérapages d'un mégalomane et les divagations d'une direction aveugle*
18 Time runs out for France's elite network, Ian Harding and John Chalmers, *The European*, 24–30/3/95
19 As 18
20 As 18
21 As 18
22 As 7
23 *The Financial Times*, quoted in France's darker side, Bernard Levin, *The Times*, 25/4/95.
24 Crash of France's biggest bank hits Balladur hopes, Charles Bremner, *The Times*, 17/3/95
25 Green light for Crédit Lyonnais rescue, Emma Tucker and Andrew Jack, *The Financial Times*, 27/7/95
26 Le Crédit Lyonnais devra ceder la moitié de ses actifs bancaires Européennes, Philippe Lemâitre, *Le Monde*, 21/7/95

FRANCE TELECOM

Abstract:

This case is about a major decision which the French government deferred. It was anticipated by some that, because of the changes taking place in the world telecommunications industry structure (cross-bloc and intra-bloc strategic alliances), in the European market-place (de-regulation) and in the volume of competition (from new and vibrant technologies), France Télécom might have to lose its state-owned status in 1995. If so, it would be treading the path towards privatisation and increasing flexibility in its operations that BT and Deutsche Telekom had already gone down. But it was not to be. The case examines this strategic decision in the context of a highly dynamic formative period for European telecommunications.

It is noteworthy that France Télécom's share value only took off once the company said it was prepared, in March 2000, to consider listing its mobile telephony units. Up to then, its stock price had languished, as a result of the market's perception of unexciting results and difficulties within ATLAS. Thus it moved to a year high close on the second of March 2000 of 219 €, up from a year's low of 63 €.
This case can be read in conjunction with Plessey and Cable and Wireless.

Case Questions:

What is happening in European telecommunications ?
Was the French government decision in July 1995 correct?
Is privatisation unavoidable ?
What light does the case shed on French corporatist culture?

Case Timing: 1995

THE BIG EVENT

On the eleventh of July 1995 last-minute discussions were taking place at the heart of French government about a key decision for the country's future industry strategy: the privatisation of France Télécom. Or, more properly, an alteration in the status of France Télécom which would prepare the ground for the sale of a 49 per cent stake in the company. At the time this major company, the second largest telecomms company in Europe, with 1994 sales of $28.6 billion, was state-owned and had the status of *an autonomous operator under public law without a capital*. Under French law, in order for it to be privatised in full (or, as anticipated, for a minority stake to be sold perhaps in 1998), its status had to be altered to that of *a normal company with a capital*.[1]

After 14 years under Mitterrand, France has lost its way. It is tormented by political and business scandals. State deficits have soared. Worst of all, an economy that in many ways is Europe's strongest cannot create enough jobs. Unemployment is 12.3 per cent. The crisis encompasses both left and right... Mitterrand put France through a Marxist experiment, playing out the nation's ancient socialist yearning. He nationalised banks and industrial companies and sharply boosted social benefits... Conversely, there have been eight years of hard-won monetary stability and high interest rates that have lowered inflation to under 2 per cent. But France's budgetary deficit last year reached 5.6 per cent of GDP, about twice the German level and above the 3 per cent limit required for Europe's economic and monetary union (EMU) by the end of the decade. A French failure to qualify for monetary union could kill a single currency and be a major reverse for tighter European Union in general.

EXHIBIT 1: AN AMERICAN VIEW OF FRANCE
Source: Can anyone fix France? Stewart Toy, Gail Edmonson, Mia Tripheni
and John Templeton, *Business Week*, 8/5/95

The dilemma for the government and for Marcel Roulet, chairman of France Télécom, was whether to yield to the forces of change – which seemed to demand an urgent thrust towards transforming France Télécom into a conventional company with shareholders – or to tread more softly. Whatever else, all parties involved were aware of the massive trade union strike that had taken place when there had been previous discussions in 1987 about such a change in status. This day of action *against privatisation and in support of the public services*,[2] had been supported by 75 per cent of France Télécom's workforce. Now the government had just lived through a re-run – a second strike at the start of May 1995, backed by 64 per cent of the workforce. This had demonstrated *very strong hostility towards the notion of a change in the company's status... It was the equivalent of a cold shower for the*

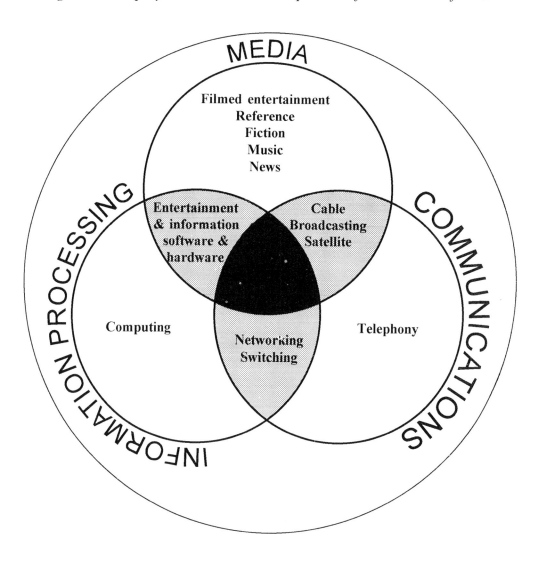

FIGURE 1: TECHNOLOGY SHIFTS –
HOW THE MULTIMEDIA INDUSTRY IS COMING TOGETHER
Source: *The Sunday Times* 17/10/93

company's board, which, until then had been convinced that the workforce would play ball. [3] Of course, the thing that was worrying France Télécom's workers, 90 per cent of whom were civil servants, was the possibility of loss of their personal status and the guarantee it carried of a virtual job-for-life.

Equally, those concerned knew only too well of the European Union (EU) timetable for the de-regulation of the telecommunications industry and the consequent dismantling of monopolies in all the EU countries that still had them. Nor was anyone ignorant of the changes that the industry itself was then facing as a consequence of massive shifts in technology (see Figure 1 on page 425), international trade developments and major re-alignments in the competitive line-up. Furthermore, there was now a new French president in the Elysee palace, Jacques Chirac. As his 1995 election campaign had shown, he was anxious to show his mettle in dealing with not only further revitalisation of French industry but also the country's severe unemployment problem. His prime minister, Alain Juppé, had publicly pledged to reduce France's 12 per cent unemployment rate by creating 700,000 new jobs by the end of the decade.

The privatisation of France Télécom had long been a thorny issue for the French government. In 1993 the Dandelot report, prepared for the-then Industry Minister, Gerard Longuet, had indeed spoken of the need to open up 49 per cent of France Télécom's ownership to non-state shareholders but it had also echoed the prevailing wisdom of the time. This was that the sale of minority holdings in the company to strong commercial partners was preferable to a wholesale sell-off to private investors. The French telecomms equipment supplier Alcatel-Alsthom might have been such a partner. So also might Deutsche Telekom, with whom France Télécom had already an important relationship. So far as a link with the leading British telecomms firm BT was concerned French union leader Eric Hayat thought this *unthinkable... even in ten years' time.*[4] Like all his colleagues he had been studying intently the downsizing and productivity changes which had been introduced by BT in the context of its privatisation. Indeed, by March 1995, these had resulted in the loss of nearly 90,000 jobs.

The Economist's view was that France Télécom's unions would probably *burn telephones in the streets rather than accept such cuts... The proposal to turn the company into a conventional company for most of its five trade unions would mean war.*[5]

THE DEREGULATION OF EUROPEAN TELECOMMUNICATIONS

The differences of opinion in France over the privatisation of its PTT (state-owned telecomms company) had long been mirrored in long debates at the EU

Council level on the speed of deregulation of the industry and the creation of openness in a 1994 market worth $230 billion, as against a world market worth $500 billion.[6]

Two countries only, Ireland and Spain, had been given five-year derogations from the liberalisation of the vocal telecomms sector that had been agreed for 1998 by the 1994 EU Directive. This Directive followed on from the Open Network Provision Directive and the Leased Lines Directive, issued in 1990, both of which had blazed a liberalisation trail on the basis of the 1987 EU Green Paper on telecommunications strategy. Opening up the European market-place to competition was seen as the best route forward by the European Council. Even so, seen from the Washington and London perspective, the *race* to a free market in Europe often looked, in the Economist's view, more like a *shuffle*.

Technology Development	What is involved in this technology	Services provided with the technology		
		Traditional	Available	Developing
Multimedia	Addition of computer hardware & software to digital technology creates interactive services, live home banking, video on demand	X	✓ (partially)	Information super-highway Services (I-Way) of all forms based on total interactivity
Digital	Range of methods of transmitting data including digital voice telephony, digitised TV, Cable TV, Mobile telephones, satellite links	X	Cable TV, Satellite Broadcasting Mobile phones etc.	✓
Analogue	Use of copper wire for transmission of voice telephony, telex, fax, cable, etc. TV transmission	Traditional phone & TV service	✓	✕

✓ Available   ✓ Partially available   ✕ Available but being phased out   X Not available

TABLE 1: THE DEVELOPMENT OF THE I-WAY

The demand projections for the size of the EU telecomms market in 1995 that had been made ten years before had indicated that sales would double to at least $100 billion. As we have seen, that was a gross under-estimate. Future predictions were that the rate of growth in a liberalised market would be twice that of a regulated market.[8] Indeed, by the year 2000, it was predicted that the industry would make up 4.5 per cent of Europe's GDP. All operators were eager to enjoy such success.

However, the euphoria arising from such forecasts had to be coupled with two stark elements from the reality of political life. Firstly, the EU had made known to the USA that, even if full-scale market liberalisation were achieved in Europe, US companies would only secure better access to the European market if Washington reciprocated. This position was communicated to the USA in October 1993 and effectively equalled the position that the Americans had been adopting in respect of European access to their market. The wariness was nothing if not mutual. Secondly, the privatisation of state-owned industry was politically problematic in many European countries. Not only was the issue in some cases an ideological one, a sheer political preference for social as opposed to private ownership or the converse, but in others it was wrapped up in a complex web of structural and regulatory matters. For example, maintenance of full employment, retention of preferential public procurement systems (even in the face of EU legislation) and anti-inflation policy were all involved in the discussion. In each country of the European Union, except for Britain that is, state monopoly control of the traditional telecomms flagship firm had been, or was still, a hot potato. So much so, that the European Commission had declared that it was *agnostic* as to whether a country's state-owned company was privatised or not, provided that the country in question opened its market by the 1998 deadline.

On the other hand, there was a practical matter at stake. In order for any state-owned telecomms company to remain competitive in a rapidly-changing, capital-intensive high-technology industry, it needed to have access to a huge volume of public capital at favourable rates. A 1985 EU forecast spoke, for example, of expenditure needs amounting to 440 billion ecus by the millenium. For those European countries which were working with heavy budgetary deficits or which were, at least, anxious to curb their public sector borrowing requirements, such extra outlays would be, to say the least, unwelcome. Indeed, it could be argued that they would tend to favour a strategy where they avoided spending more on building public ownership of assets.

Value added chain position	Task	Organisations involved
Originators of material	e.g. writing, filming	Film studios, publishers, writers
Transmitters of material	e.g. by wire, satellite	Telecommunications networks
Equipment suppliers	hardware, software	Computer companies, phone makers
Service providers	all forms	Advertising agencies
Consumers	users of the material	Private households and businesses

Note: This chain is based on commercial material not generated by businesses and private households. They, of course, generate business– or family–specific communications material which is fed into the chain also.

TABLE 2: A FIVE-LEVEL VALUE-ADDED CHAIN
FOR THE NEW INFO-AGE
Source: adapted from *Beyond the telephone, TV and PC*, Don Cruikshank,
Oftel consultative document, August 1995

This latter was, in fact, the case. In early 1993 Morgan Stanley claimed that European governments would be seeking to raise, over the coming five years, a total of $100 billion through state sell-offs and that telecomms companies would have pride of place in this.

Interestingly, France was one of the chief potential disposers of state assets mentioned in this claim and it had been, in fact, strongly pursuing such a sell-off strategy since 1993.[9] Morgan Stanley further underlined the dilemma for the French government and for France Télécom's board by stating, somewhat diplomatically:

Governments, understandably, are coming to accept that..financial and organisational challenges are best handled within the private sector. Expediency dictates that market disciplines not only promise greater efficiencies on the part of the telephone company, but also "depoliticise" the often uncomfortable transition process, particularly where employment practices and levels have to be modified.[10]

Conversely, the view in some quarters in France, where there was already competition in the mobile telephone and satellite sectors, was that privatisation was *an ideological philosophy rather than axiomatic to competition and greater efficiency.*[11]

The pace of top-down political change in the EU telecomms industry since the 1987 Green Paper had clearly been dictated by technology shifts. But it had also been dictated by the impact on the global market-place of the deregulation of the US market for telecommunications. This had been seen to confer on major US companies a tremendous competitive advantage which they had evidently used to good effect.

The most critical de-regulatory development in the USA had been the partial dismantling in 1984 of the giant AT&T company (called *Ma Bell* by the Americans) into seven *Baby Bell* telecommunications companies (called RBOCs or Regional Bell Operating companies). Each RBOC retained a local telephone monopoly but long-distance calls were strictly subject to price competition. The 1984 development took place as a result of an action brought by MCI, at the time a small competitor to AT&T in the long distance market. It is noteworthy that a 1934 US law forbids *aliens* from acquiring more than a 20 per cent stake in any US network that uses the radio spectrum.

As a result of the 1984 change, there was massive competition in the USA in the long-distance market (among AT&T, MCI and Sprint) and in the local markets (among Ameritech, Bell Atlantic, Bellsouth, Nynex, Pacific Telesis, Southwestern Bell and US West). Even more significant were the developments that had taken place in the competition at the junction between long distance and local calls in the USA; the freedom each player had to branch out into new technology, with or without new networks, alliances and subsidiaries; and the ability each had to explore new relationships overseas. In the early 1990s, for most of these US industry giants in the USA, this amounted to what has been called *a frenzy of change.*[12] Part of this was due to the decision facing Congress in March 1995 as to whether to further deregulate the US telecomms market. It was being lobbied hard to suppress the legal barriers currently separating US operators, cable from phone and short-distance from long-distance.

THE CHANGING PATTERN OF WORLD TRADE MANAGEMENT

World trade was also being deregulated. From the endorsement of the GATT Uruguay Round trade deal at Marrakech in 1994 to the agreement of the international accord on liberalising trade in financial services in 1995 there was evidence of a commitment by leading nations to the principle of freer trade and the opening-up of markets.

The first trade agreement brought in average cuts of 36 per cent in the tariffs for industrial products in all signatory countries and made for the introduction of binding rules on intellectual property. The second, albeit an interim deal, guaranteed a measure of foreign access to banking, securities and insurance markets in some 90 countries. For some, the agreement simply underlined the extent to which their markets were already open. For others, such as Japan, allowing a new level of access to previously protected markets was foreseen. In the case of the USA, the watchword (within the framework of the accord) was to be *reciprocity* of market access and terms of trade. The GATT deal dealt also with the key features of the global trade management system, the patterns of *purely or mostly most-favoured nation treatment*, unilateral free trade (A offers B unlimited access), managed trade (A and B agree on trading equality) and full economic integration.

Renato Ruggieri, director-general of the World Trade Organisation (WTO), described the GATT accord as *a victory for multilateralism.*[13]

Britain had lobbied strongly for both agreements which it saw as vital to maintain the growing momentum of world trade. It is self-evident that the City of London thought it would prosper from an expansion in global finance activity (the provision of investment capital and forex dealing, for example) due to its extraordinarily high concentration of banking and insurance capability. As Renato Ruggieri pointed out:

Financial services are, in commercial terms, the most important of all internationally traded services and are the backbone of virtually every other economic activity.[14]

London's position as the commercial centre of Europe was indeed unassailable. Given the contribution of financial services to Britain's invisible trade balance and the nation's competitiveness, the British government was less worried than some of its continental neighbours in the EU about the possible job-displacement aspects of the trade accords in, especially, the field of manufacturing. Added to which, Britain had substantially deregulated its financial services sector from 1986 onwards so that its competitive capability in this sector could be maximised.

On the other hand, there were other countervailing forces at work. One was called *Open Regionalism*. The notion was that, whilst the trade opportunity presented within the WTO structure was potentially very attractive, it also made abundant sense for regions of the world to try to stimulate trade development in their own back-yards first. In a word, to sharpen their teeth at home.

In this way, successful intra-region trade could act as a means of building the sort of scale and scope economies that were required before a regional player could attain the critical mass level of competitive capability it needed to rival existing global players. Not only, of course, would this possibility of world market access be improved, but the corollary was that the position of regional players in their own market-places would ipso facto be strengthened. Especially, that is, if a region could build up/retain appropriate elements of protectionism at the same time.

Such countervailing forces were moving strongly forwards in the mid-1990s to create stronger regional groupings. The European Union, for example, was considering the terms and conditions which would apply to membership requests from the Vishegrad countries, Poland, the Czech and Slovak republics and Hungary, having just ingested the rump of EFTA (minus Norway). ASEAN (Singapore, Brunei, Malaysia, Thailand, Philippines, Indonesia) had welcomed its most recent member, Vietnam, on the 26th July 1995 and was considering accepting applications from Burma, Laos and Cambodia. The USA, the leading member of the North American Free Trade Area (NAFTA), was pressing ahead strongly at exactly this time with an initiative it had first explored at the Miami summit meeting of American countries in December 1994. This involved trying to arrange a hemispheric free trade region involving South as well as North America, nothing if not *thinking big*.

To complete the picture of the developing pattern of world trade management of which France Télécom needed to be aware we now need to add in another dimension. This is one where each member of the triad of major WTO trade partners, EU, NAFTA and Asia Pacific (Japan and other countries on the Asia Pacific seaboard), had already begun to consider the advantages to be derived from bilateral deals with the others as well as from trading multilaterally.

The USA led with way in participating in the construction of APEC (the Asia-Pacific Economic Co-operation forum). This body was established in Bogor, Indonesia in November 1994 through a declaration signed by NAFTA and ASEAN members, Japan, S.Korea, Taiwan and Australia. Their economies then accounted for a half of world output. Its stated purpose was to remove regional barriers to trade and investment within APEC by 2020, thus helping to speed up the process of global liberalisation. The declaration was, however, long on generalities and short on the specifics of how to achieve free-and-open trade and how to extend cuts in tariff and other barriers to non-members of APEC. Given the almost non-stop trade disputes between Japan and the USA since the start of the 1980s (Structural Impediments Initiative talks, for example) to the 1995 spat over reciprocal market access for cars, this lack of detail is hardly surprising. Japan and the USA were, of course, extremely anxious to settle their differences in 1995 because of the increased destabilisation that this was causing in the already nervous world money markets.

> *The spectre of Louis XIV's interventionist finance minister, Jean-Baptiste Colbert, may seem a stange thing to summon to a feast of bytes and binary codes. But Western Europe's industrial history has long been a struggle between Colbert and another philosophical fellow, Adam Smith, champion of the free market.*

EXHIBIT 2: WORLDS AT WAR
Source: *The Economist*, 13/8/94

The EU's Trade Commissioner, Sir Leon Brittan, was following a similar tack when he called for the creation of a new *transatlantic economic area* linking the USA with the European Union. The historic ties between the blocs constituted perhaps the most important global relationship but current political issues, trade disputes, environmentalism, crime, demanded urgent consideration. This call built on an earlier initiative dating from November 1990, called the Transatlantic Declaration, which had set up a high-level forum for such debate. Of special importance to current discussions were the consequences of the demise of NATO's common enemy (USSR) and the EU's thrust towards an independent defence capability.

As if to complete the third leg of the Open Regionalism relationships, the ASEAN group at their meeting in Brunei in mid-August 1995 called for an East Asia-European Union summit to be held in 1996. The proposed venue was Thailand and the month March.

All involved in these accords stressed the extent to which they contributed to the creation of a free and growing world trading system. It is highly noteworthy, however, that neither the GATT trade deal nor the Financial Services Accord dealt with the key issue held over from previous negotiations because of major international disgreement, the future pattern of trade in telecommunications. Freeing up world trade in this strategic sector was so contentious an issue that it was to be negotiated on separately at a later date.

METASTRATEGY

The fact that there had been no WTO agreement governing the operation of the international telecommunication market-place was not a worry to some of the major players in the industry. Indeed, judging by their behaviour, it might instead have been an inspiration.

In terms of take-overs and mergers, the period of the mid-1990s has rightly been described as *an old-fashioned feeding frenzy* in which companies, caught up in *Darwinian struggle for survival in a world of international competition, deregulation and technological upheaval* were *snatching up competitors at home and abroad to expand their global market share and improve earnings.*[15] Among factors contributing to this were the weakness of the $ (relative to the mark and the franc), the increasing availability of low-cost debt, the strong balance sheets of some acquirers (particularly the Europeans). There was also a strong perception that companies in the USA and the EU needed to *buy* access (i.e., via strategic acquisitions or alliances) to future-critical markets they would otherwise find impossible to penetrate, whether for economic or, perhaps more significantly, political reasons. This last was especially significant in determining moves made in the early 1990s by US and European players.

We could extend the list by including the justifiable fear that some telecomms companies had of being technologically isolated (because they could not individually spend enough on R&D to keep up with their rivals, for example) or of losing position in the value chain (perhaps becoming the subcontractor in a previous relationship of equals or of being treated as a tied producer). These motivations also led straight to moves made by companies to network and ally with previous competitors, customer and suppliers, either in discrete business areas or across the board. Deals could involve something as simple as verbal agreement or something as complicated as cross-holdings in each other shares. Naturally, it is important to recognise the extent to which, on the one hand, they stopped short of creating a cartel and, on the other, implicitly or explicitly served to oligopolise the industry. (See Figure 2 on page 436.)

The more exposed the position of the company, the more it might feel obliged to build itself a web of contingent global relationships which would stabilise (at worst) and enhance (at best) its risk-return position. To create such a web in the global telecommunications industry at this time of technological change goes well beyond the basic definitions of standard business strategy into a new world of business power politics – the world of what could be called *metastrategy*. (Gk meta, over; strategein, to lead an army).

France Télécom was confronted in the period 1992–1995 with a range of meta-strategic link-ups among actual and potential multimedia competitors resulting from the world-wide changes in the technology, politics and economics of the industry. Indeed, as we shall see, it was a player in one itself.

All show the inter-activity and dynamism of what was becoming the world's most mobile industry. In a world where its competitors were building world-wide *power webs*, isolationism for any large player would be disastrous.

Perhaps the European prototype for the building of such a power web was the June 1993 Anglo-American deal between BT and MCI. This took place on the eve of the sell-off of the British government's last remaining stake in the company. The deal was announced as *an historic alliance*, worth £3.5 billion. It involved BT's purchasing 20 per cent of MCI for $2.8 billion (almost a tenth of its market value) and was said to be earnings un-dilutive. MCI had been founded some 30 years before and had risen to become Number Two in the long distance phone market in the USA, after AT&T. BT was also to contribute £750m to set up a joint venture to be called CONCERT. This would handle both partners' business in the international telecomms field, where the two companies were globally ranked fourth (BT) and sixth (MCI). CONCERT would also develop new joint multimedia services thus avoiding duplicate investment.

The agreement was given speedy approval by the US Justice Department but took a time to win clearance from the US Federal Communications Commission. The combined sales of the partners was $25.6 billion.

The BT-MCI deal acted, as can be imagined, as a powerful stimulus to BT's European rivals. Almost within a year, France Télécom, Deutsche Telekom and the number three American long distance phone operator, Sprint, had concluded a similar alliance. The Europeans, too, were to buy a 20 per cent equity stake for $4.2 billion (£2.8 billion) and would seek through their relationship to build the basis for a truly global network. This would necessarily involve bringing in other partners in the Asia Pacific region. Sprint, whilst only having ten per cent of the US market, was well-advanced in the provision of local and cellular services and had a strong clientèle of multinationals. The joint venture that would be created by the partners would build and operate a fibre optic network to form part of the *one-shop, seamless world-wide service* which was their intention. The resultant joint venture was to be called PHOENIX. The combined sales revenue of the three partners was $72.1 billion.[16]

What MCI got	What BT got
A 24.9 per cent stake in a joint net-working company to market communications.	20 per cent of MCI's equity. BT agreed not to raise its stake for 10 years.
Services to multinational firms, plus rights to market in North and South of America and the Caribbean.	A 75.1 per cent stake in the new joint global networking company. BT would market to all Europe, Asia, Africa & the South Pacific.
A $4.3 billion cash infusion so that it could move into new markets, e.g. wireless communications. The right to buy all BT's US assets.	MCI's help in turning round its loss-making Syncordia subsidiary in the USA.

TABLE 3: CARVING UP THE WORLD Source: *Business Week*, 14/6/93

FRANCE TELECOM

Disney + Capital Cities, ABC TV (1)

Turner Broadcasting + CBS (2)

ORIGINATORS OF MATERIAL
MEDIA

Viacom ⟶ Paramount

Microsoft + Turner Broadcasting (9)

Sony ⟶ Columbia

Time Warner + US West

Newscorp + MCI (3)

INFORMATION
PROCESSORS

TRANSMITTERS OF MATERIAL
- COMMUNICATIONS -

IBM ⟶ Lotus (7)

Microsoft ⟶ Latuit (8)

Bell Atlantic + Telecommunications Inc (

AT&T ⟶ McCaw Cellular (

BT + Electronic Data Systems (6)

Notes:
(1) 1995
(2) Under discussion August 1995
(3) 1995
(4) 1993 A $12b deal, the biggest merger in US history
creating a company with $60b in assets. Ray Smith was chairman
of TCI, US largest cable TV company. He said "Bell Atlantic, TCI &
Liberty media combine leading telephone, wireless and cable
networks in the USA & overseas with the new multimedia
technologies together we will make the information superhighway
a reality."

(5) 1993, A $12.6b takeover
(6) Refused by the US Justice Dept...in 1993
(7) 1995
(8) Refused by the justice Dept
(9) Under discussion August 1995

+ = Alliance

⟶ = Takeover or acquisition of

⟹ = Links-up occurred in this
 sector of industry

☐ = Example of links

FIGURE 2: EXAMPLES OF 1990s MEGADEALS IN
THE MULTIMEDIA INDUSTRY

436

The American market leader, AT&T, was not amused at the presumption of the Europeans. Its protest was strongly-phrased:

We urge the United States government to condition approval of the proposed equity investment in Sprint on the French and German governments' opening the telecomms markets on the same terms as the US market is open to France Télécom and Deutsche Telekom. We do not believe that monopoly profits should be used to enter the US market when similar markets in Europe are closed to US operators. We are not content to wait for the European Union's planned telecomms deregulation in 1998.[17]

Helmut Ricke, chairman of Deutsche Telekom, rejected any notion that the German market was a *closed shop* and claimed that almost 30 per cent of the company's equipment purchases came from international companies. Marcel Roulet, France Télécom's president, stated that *French and German markets are certainly more open than many other European markets.*[18]

Notwithstanding its feeling of unfairness over this link-up, AT&T lost no time at all time in further securing its place aboard the globalisation bandwagon by pushing through a deal with Unisource, a consortium formed from the Swedish, Swiss and Dutch telecommunications utilities. This took place on the 23rd June 1994. The company was already in the position of having a major alliance with Japan's KDD, Singapore Télécom and other Asia Pacific telecomms companies, called WORLD-SOURCE. This deal thus extended the range of AT&T's global coverage considerably. Telefonica, the Spanish telecomms utility applied to join the Unisource consortium in September 1994.

The Unisource-AT&T joint venture, in which Unisource had a 60 per cent stake, was named UNIWORLD. The sales revenue of AT&T alone amounted, in 1994, to $39.9 billion.

As Figure 3 on page 438 indicates, the tie-ups which can be referred to most easily by their joint venture titles, CONCERT, PHOENIX and UNIWORLD, were not unusual in scale or in direction in the mid-1990s. These Euro-American relationships merely brought together similar types of operators and allowed them to build a reciprocal market access unobtainable by other means. Additionally, they did allow possibilities for product line and technological diversification.

What they did not do, as several of the examples in Figures 2 and 3 illustrate, was to create *value chain partnerships* of companies performing wholly different functions, using wholly distinct technologies, which often spanned trade blocs. The risk involved in striking many of the deals shown in Figure 2, page 436, was greater but the frenzy to proceed with them no less in the turbulent multi-media market-place of the 1990s. It was another aspect of

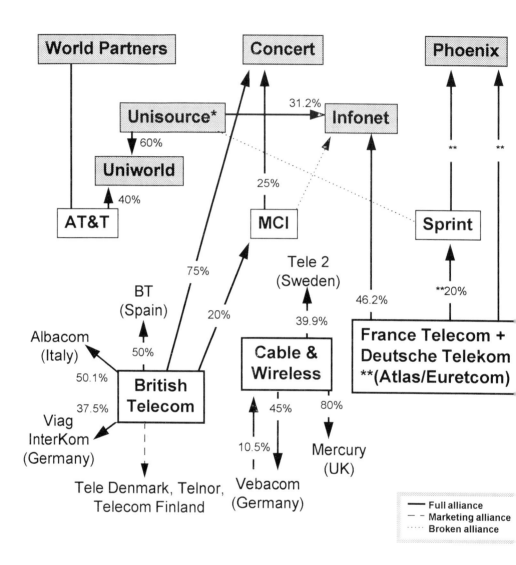

* Unisource is owned equally by PTT Telecom (Netherlands), Swiss PTT, Telefonica Spain, and Telia (Sweden)
** Subject to regulatory approval in US/EU

FIGURE 3: THE ALLIANCE WEB
Source: Unisource aims to dial up a borderless Télécom service, Barbara Smit,
The European, 21–27/04/95

market development to which the alert competitor needed to pay substantial attention.

DOMESTIC MATTERS – DEUTSCHE TELEKOM

The pattern of changing global telecomms technology, industrial deregulation and the creation of international power webs also impacted on the domestic strategies followed by Europe's leading utilities, the market leader Deutsche Telekom and the number three player, BT, in the early 1990s.

Deutsche Telekom faced the largest array of problems. Paradoxically, one of its biggest was the fact that the company was one of the German finance ministry's best investments!

Finance was, in many ways, the most stressful issue. Extra capital, one authoritative 1992 estimate spoke of half a trillion dollars over the coming five years,[19] was needed by Germany to continue to rebuild the East and to reduce budget deficits. This latter was important in view of the up-coming 1996 Inter-Governmental Conference which would (it was thought) seek to endorse the EU's stringent Economic and Monetary Union (EMU) criteria which had been agreed in the Maasstricht Treaty.

Maastricht is a road to ruin. It promises to impoverish Europe. The convergence criteria in the Treaty were invented by central bankers, designed simply to combat the menace of inflation... The criteria set targets for inflation, government bond rates, nominal exchange rate stability, public sector deficits and debts. No mention is made of economic growth or unemployment. Indeed, governments are congratulated as good Europeans if, as France is still doing, they sacrifice jobs and prosperity for Maastricht's sake (by maintaining a "franc fort" within the EU's Exchange Rate Mechanism). We live in a recessionary world where competitive exchange rate depreciation and trade protection are coming back into fashion... To survive and succeed Europe needs flexible labour markets, low taxes and social security contributions, high profits to finance up-market moves to higher technology products... Maaastricht offers the opposite.

EXHIBIT 3: A BRITISH VIEW OF MAASTRICHT
Source: Major is wrong, Maastricht is not good for Britain,
Brian Reading, *The Sunday Times*, 6/6/93

Deutsche Telekom similarly needed extra capital to continue its modernisation drive and to expand. $13 billion was the sum Helmut Ricke reckoned he needed to beef up its balance sheet.[20] The difficulty was the extent to which Germany's high rates of interest, themselves in part caused by the surge in demand for debt since the collapse of the Berlin Wall, made servicing extra debt not just a headache, but a migraine. The company's long-term debt at the end of 1994 already amounted to $75 billion, in part the result of modernising the antiquated East German telecomms network.

Squaring the circle, for the German government and Deutsche Telekom management, meant raising equity investment by selling off a stake in the state-owned company. This would entail, as we saw in the case of France Télécom, a change in its constitution. Such was the force of the privatisation argument that even the Social Democatic Party (SPD) agreed that such a change was unavoidable. But three key questions then arose.

First, related to the level of privatisation. Just how much would be sold off? Second, related to the manner in which Deutsche Telekom, partially privatised yet still enjoying an unrivalled power position in its German market-place, would be regulated by the government to ensure it did not abuse its position, e.g., by over-pricing its services or extending its dominance into new areas of activity. The promise of too heavy a control hand would inevitably reduce the value of the shares that would be offered for sale. The third question related to productivity. More than half of Deutsche Telekom staff had civil service status and would be extremely difficult to lay off in any post-privatisation strategy to drive up efficiency. Indeed, seniority alone guaranteed the jobs of 20 per cent.

Clearly, handling these changes in the world's third largest telecomms company, with a 1992 turnover of $32 billion and a staff of over 230,000, would not be easy. Hence, the German parliament took its time in setting about the privatisation legislation, once a cross party consensus on the principle had been reached in May 1993.

But Helmut Ricke was impatient. In 1990 Deutsche Telekom had been transformed from a department of the Bundespost into a market-led enterprise. This was necessary in the light of the growth of actual competition in the German market from new technology products, like cellular phones (for example, from such companies as Mannesmann and Thyssen who were taking full advantage of the new free market), and lower-priced competition for international business 'phone services (BT, for instance). Complete deregulation of the EU market by 1998 meant that Deutsche Telekom had no choice but to press forward. As executive director of telephone services for business customers, Hans Huber knew the challenge only too well. *The market is changing so quickly* he declared *if we don't move fast we will be killed.*[21] By 1998, it will be recalled, the company would lose its monopoly on basic telephone services and control over the network infrastructure. Digital mobile phones in Germany had already been liberalised and, in 1995, there were three competitors in the market.

Company	Number of Employees	
	1992	1994
Deutsche Telekom	231,000	225,000
France Télécom	155,285	167,882

TABLE 4: WHO EMPLOYS WHOM
Source: *Frankfurter Allgemeine Zeitung*, 28/6/94 & 24/6/95

And there was yet another difficulty for a company that had been called *a lumbering giant.*[22] At least the word *giant* is not unrealistic when it is considered that Deutsche Telekom was Europe's largest telecomms company in terms of size of network and number of phone lines and that it already owned the world's largest cable TV network connected to 14.5m homes. This constituted excessive market muscle in the eyes of the European Commission who had stepped in to quash some of the company's planned link-ups in Germany (a joint multi-media venture with Bertelsmann and Kirch and the acquisition of Debis from Daimler Benz, for example.)

In May 1995 the Commission was also dragging its feet in accepting the Deutsche Telekom-France Télécom link (ATLAS) on grounds that it might be anti-competitive. Nor was it especially enthusiastic about PHOENIX.

The government's decision to proceed with the privatisation concluded with the announcement, at the end of November 1994, that the lead bankers for the sell-off of the two available tranches of Deutsche Telekom shares (25 per cent in mid-1996 and 24 per cent in 1998) would be Deutsche Bank, Dresdner Bank and Goldman Sachs. This was welcomed by the markets. What was not, was the unexpected announcement that chairman Helmut Ricke was stepping down from his post, for *personal reasons*. The news broke on the 9th December 1994, less than three weeks before the conversion of Deutsche Telekom from a state-run company into a joint stock company, in preparation for its privatisation, was due to take place.

The first step in the process of dismantling Deutsche Telekom's monopoly status unleashed a flood of new link-ups among players anxious to stake out their positions in the large and lucrative standard phone market-place. An important strategic alliance, for example, was struck between Britain's Cable & Wireless (CW) and Veba, the diversified energy group. A new joint venture, called Viag

InterKom, was also formed between BT and the Bavarian utility Viag. Thyssen announced in early 1995 the formation of a consortium with BellSouth International. RWE was linking up with Mannesmann and Deutsche Bank in a new venture. But at least Deutsche Telekom could console itself with the fact of the alliance it had forged with France Télécom, Eunetcom, when it had turned down BT's invitation to join in with a link-up in BT's US operation, Syncordia. Some of these link-ups are shown in Figure 3 on page 438.

The enthusiasm of the potential new entrants was increased at the time of the CW-Veba link by the thought that German telecommunications minister Wolfgang Botsch might allow new entrants into the market in 1997 (and not 1998), even though this would need ratification by parliament with a two thirds majority. But this was not to be and, when the liberalisation process was spelled out at the end of March 1995, the German government kept to the EU timetable. No restrictions on the number of competitors would exist, however, and, by the time of the announcement, the government had already received 7 licence applications.

The new chairman, Ron Sommer, previously head of Sony's European operations, took over in early 1995. It was, he said, *the biggest challenge in German industry.*[23] After all, the 540,000-strong German Postal Union had pledged to do all possible to head off redundancies and Deutsche Telekom, on the best estimates, needed to lose at least 60,000 of its employees by the year 2000 to raise its competitiveness.

Furthermore, the company had been in a state of suspended animation since 1994. Then it had made a profit of over £3 billion but had been obliged to pay over a levy to the German treasury of £5.2 billion.

But Deutsche Telekom's new strategy was revealed in an up-beat mood in Berlin in March 1995. It comprised a wide range of moves to upgrade line services, carry out a host of pilot programmes in interactive TV and multimedia, which, incidentally, BT was legally prevented from doing, and finish the digitising of the network. R&D spending would also rise by 2000 from 1.6 per cent of sales revenue to two per cent. Clearly, the announcement by Telecomms minister Wolgang Botsch that no direct competition with Deutsche Telekom in the standard phone sector would be allowed before 1998 was also helpful.

DOMESTIC MATTERS – BT

BT was in an entirely different league so far as its modus operandi and market-place was concerned. For one thing, the legislative framework it was working within did not allow a monopoly of lines. Other operators, AT&T for instance, could, if they chose, lease lines from BT and use them to offer a full range of international services to their clients, predominantly international businesses. The practice of buying private circuits from a telephone operator and then selling services to users, called *resale,* was encouraged in Britain as being conducive to competition. By mid-1993 some 13 companies had applied for a UK telecommunications licence for this purpose. They included AT&T and Swedish Télécom. Each was keen to target UK subsidiaries of their big domestic customers and to undercut or out-compete their British rivals.

Another key factor was that, in the UK market, unlike in France or Germany, there was already a direct rival in the standard telephone market. The actual legislation which set up British Télécom as a privatised company in 1984 (49 per cent government stake) and which allowed for the sale of the first tranche of shares had also institutionalised competition in the form of Mercury, a subsidiary of Cable and Wireless, thereby creating a basic duopoly. The last tranche of BT's state-owned shares (the name was changed in 1991), 22 per cent, was sold by the British government in July 1993. The company became wholly privately owned at this time.

A third difference was the extent of management's acceptance of the need for pro-active change as perhaps the over-riding parameter of future business success. As Iain Vallance, BT's chairman pointed out:

The PTTs (state-owned national operators) cannot survive indefinitely. We reckon that, ultimately, there will be only a handful of global players, including a couple from the US, a Japanese group and maybe two from Europe. We aim to be among them... AT&T feels that our move (in linking up with MCI) is the thin end of the wedge. So far, it has faced small, under-capitalised competitors. BT is the first member of the big league that has chosen to play (link-up) game... You can be a very big shark in your market place, but it is the piranhas which will tear you apart... You have to organise youself to resist the piranhas.[24]

The reference to *sharks* is important because Iain Vallance was strongly against the PHOENIX link-up. He called it *grotesque* and said that it would create *the largest monopoly in the world.*[25]

What had BT done domestically to fight off the *piranhas*? First, it had altered the structure of its communication divisions to more specifically meet customer requirements (business and personal divisions) and had clearly separated the management of the network from the customer-facing elements (production and marketing). It had used the opportunity of privatisation to ensure its development had occurred with negligible debt. Second, it had undertaken over the period 1990–93 what Andrew Lorenz referred to as the *largest and fastest streamlining drive ever implemented by a British company*. This was called Project Sovereign.[26]

	1983/4	**1993/4**
Turnover (£ billion)	6.9	13.6
Pretax profit (£m)	.99	2.7
Fibre in network (km million)	<.5	2.6
Employees ('000)	241	151.6

TABLE 5: COMPARATIVE RESULTS FOR BT

Notes:
(i)   In the 1970s annual spending per user on refurbishment of the network was £18 compared with France's £51. France's system became the most advanced in Europe
(ii) Since privatisation Bt's customers have enjoyed a real reduction in their tariffs of 40 per cent
(iii) According to *The Sunday Times'* commentator Roger Eglin (4/12/94) the regulatory regime placed on BT – as compared with that placed on its EU rivals – was *impossible*.

By 1993, BT had achieved a major reduction in its workforce with the aim of reaching a core of 100,000 by 1995. So far as the improvement in productivity was concerned, Bruce Bond, BT's director of products and services, reckoned in 1993 that *it must be the best in the world. In absolute efficiency terms, we are now in the top 25 per cent of telecomms companies world wide.*[27] BT had also used its CONCERT joint venture with MCI to enter data services, a far less regulated market than voice services. Trials had been run with Thorn EMI, among others, with a view to beginning virtual voice services on a UK-USA-Australia network in 1995.

It is important to stress also what BT had not been able to do, given its position under the Telecommunication Act 1984. It could not raise prices on a *basket* of services, including inland phone calls and domestic line rentals, by more than the limit stipulated by the control limit placed on it by Oftel, the body set up by the government to regulate the industry. The guide line for price rises in 1994 and 1995 was that the rise for the *basket* should not exceed the UK Retail Price Index (RPI) minus 7.5 per cent. BT was also, by statute, unable to carry entertainment in any form on its phone lines before 1997. Nor could it apply for a licence for a personal communications network where Vodafone was the market leader. Nor, for that matter, could it enter, as Deutsche Telekom had done, the cable TV market. Little wonder that, in the words of Michael Smith and George Parker-Jarvis, *the path for BT lies in growing businesses outside Oftel's remit, not least by developing overseas networks for major corporate customers worldwide.*[28] One of these, as we have noted was the link-up with Viag in Germany. Of the thinking behind this move, Iain Vallance said:

> *We are looking at the main countries in Europe... We are putting together a jigsaw and we want the right pieces in place. It is worthwhile hastening relatively slowly to ensure we get it right... The important thing is to get a position in the main countries. In Europe, quite clearly, there is going to be a pan-European market at some stage.*[29]

The focus for the future of BT, *now a lean, mean fighting machine* in the words of Alfred Mockett, MD of BT's Global Communications, would be to offer global service to the top 2000 multinationals. The task? To provide them with a total, global, desk-top to desk-top communications package for data, voice or vision, responding to the prime customer request that was coming up time and time again, *Give me a single point of contact and single billing in one currency. I want you to simplify my business for me.*[30]

CRUNCH TIME

This, then, was the context in which the French government and the management of France Télécom were facing up to the decision of how to proceed with the first stage in the company's privatisation: the change in its status. In the event, the French government decided, on the 12th July 1995, not to proceed.

Q *What form of new status do you want France Télécom to have?*

A It's up to the government. But there are two priorities in my view. The state must manage France Télécom in such a way as to prepare it for the shock to come. Second, it must provide France Télécom with a capital structure to allow it to be opened up to partners. This will allow cross-ownerships, between ourselves and Deutsche Telekom, for example.

Q *Do you foresee a privatisation in the longer term?*

A If, by privatisation, you mean handing over a majority of shares to private shareholders, I don't think that would be desirable. I think the state should keep strategic control of the company... For me... the fundamental point is that the state keeps majority control. And that's the way our German partners see it.

EXHIBIT 4: FROM THE HORSE'S MOUTH
Source: A conversation with the president of France Télécom,
Caroline Monnot, *Le Monde*, 6/7/93

The previous government had been firmly committed to the fast-track advance. So had Alain Madelin, economics minister in the new government of Alain Juppé. But the counsel of Francois Fillon, minister for information technology, had apparently prevailed. He was concerned at the fact that France Télécom's workforce had refused to accept the change of status. It was a major victory for the two unions, SUD and CGT, that had campaigned against privatisation. Would this deprive France of the chance to develop some of the competitive capabilities (*les armes semblables* as *Le Monde* called them) of its major international rivals? Whatever else, the trade unions were delighted. A CGT statement declared:

If this decision is confirmed, it will mean the halting of the strategy of France Télécom and the French government over the past 10 years as a result of the mobilisation of workers, managers and users. It is a tremendous encouragement to widen the movement against the strategy, since its essentials are still in place. These relate to the European Commission's decision to open all the infrastructure and services, now under a public monopoly, to competition.[31]

Within two short weeks of the decision Alain Madelin had been dismissed and Marcel Roulet had resigned.

* * * * * * * * * * * * * * * * * * * *

NOTES & REFERENCES

1   French Télécom chief in row over sell-off delay, Colin Narbrough, *The Times*, 13/7/95

2   France Télécom est victime de son propre changement, Caroline Monnot, *Le Monde*, 13/7/95

3   As 2

4   France puts in call to all operators, Ian Harding, *The European*, 29/7-1/8/93

5   *Economist,* 11/3/95

6   Phoenix flies over first hurdle, Allen Lane, *The Financial Times*, 15-16/7/95

7   Last one to the draw, *The Economist*, 13/8/94

8   Privatisation dogma marches hand-in-hand with financial need, Mark Milner, *The Guardian*, 12/10/93

9   As 8

10 Global trade deal agreed over financial services, Frances Williams, Lionel Barber and Nacy Dunne, *The Financial Times*, 27/7/95

11 Sell-off boom revitalises telecomms sector, Dawn Hayes, *The European*, 2–5/7/92

12 An old fashioned feeding frenzy, Christopher Farrel et al., *Business Week*, 1/5/95

13 As 10

14 Brittan hails new transatlantic era, Michael Dynes, *The Times*, 31/7/95

15 As 12

16 *Le Monde* 12/1/95

17 AT&T threatens to block three-way telecomms link, Tim Castle, *The European*, 17–23/6/94

18 As 17

19 Germany's Telekom is calling to investors, Igor Reichlin and Leak Nathan Spiro, *Business Week*, 26/10/92

20 As 19

21 We're making a 180-degree turn, *Business Week*, 21/11/94

22 As 19

23 Big Challenges for Deutsche Telekom chief, Michael Lindemann, *The Financial Times*, 31/3/95

24 BT versus the world, Anrew Lorenz, *The Sunday Times*, 16/5/93

25 Differences emerge over EU growth, 16/11/93

26 As 24

27 As 24

28 Down the wire for BT3, *The Observer*, 16/5/93

29 Why BT is aiming to breach the walls of fortress Europe, Andrew Lorenz, *The Sunday Times*, 8/1/95

30 The battle to be a global player, Roger Eglin, *The Sunday Times*, 4/12/94

31 As 2

MAD COW DISEASE

Abstract:

The onset of BSE ("Mad Cow Disease") in Britain caused a series of interlinked public health, economic and political crises in the European Union which will not end until well into the first decade of the twenty-first century. Within Britain itself, the government was attacked by the public, the media and the farmers themselves for its alleged mishandling of the issue and the Commission of Inquiry's report is still anxiously awaited. Within Europe, Britain's government and farming industry were subject to a major political onslaught, the culmination of which was a total ban on British beef exports. Though lifted since, France and Germany were still refusing access in early 2000. Throughout the case there is a leitmotif of the farming lobby demanding CAP compensation for their sufferings as well as that of the embroiled difficulties of the CAP itself.

This case study thus epitomises many of the business and political tensions that still *divided* the European Union's members at the start of the new millenium.

Question:

Analyse the British government approach to BSE over the period 1985-97. What did it do and why did it act as it did? Do you regard the strategy, as you see it, as an effective one?

Case Timing: 1985-98

A LOAD OF TOSH

"Tosh". That was the slang word used by Downing Street to reject the highly critical draft report of the committee of inquiry by Members of the European Parliament (MEPs) into the BSE (or "mad cow disease") epidemic. The word means "total rubbish" and, although the remark was made by a civil servant rather than a politician, it clearly carried the sign of British government approval. Such undiplomatic language was a measure of the heat that had been generated throughout Europe over a tragic cattle disease – Bovine Spongiform Encephalopathy (BSE) or "mad cow disease"– that had affected consumers, producers and politicians throughout Europe in quite disastrous ways since the start of the 1990s.

Year	No of UK cows contracting BSE
1988	92
1989	7137
1990	14181
1991	25032
1992	36682
1993	34370
1994	23944
1995	14298
1996	7751

TABLE 1: INCIDENCE OF BSE IN BRITAIN
Source: EU states "hiding" scale of crisis, *The Guardian*, 20/3/97

The reason for the British government's outburst was not far to seek. The draft report, drawn up after a six month period of inquiry and published in February 1997, called for action to be brought against Douglas Hogg, Britain's Minister of Agriculture, Food and Fisheries (MAFF). It alleged that the BSE crisis had been mishandled in Britain and called on the country to pay back the £500m aid it had already received from its European Union partners as compensation for the slaughter of the cattle that had taken place. The report also hinted that some British scientists could not be trusted to be impartial in their assessments and criticised the way that the British government had "manipulated" the EU's scientific committees. This, it reckoned, had kept the BSE disease quite improperly off the top of the public policy agenda for years. Furthermore, one prominent committee member, Labour MEP Pauline Green, head of the majority Socialist group in the European parliament, laid the blame for the BSE problem squarely on the British government's "single-minded, ideological commitment to deregulation" in the agricultural market-place.[1]

There was also a question of political protocol involved in the MEPs' inquiry. When the committee visited London in December 1996 to gather evidence for their report, they had invited the British Minister of Agriculture to meet them. A refusal had been given on the grounds that Ministers of the Crown were answerable only to the House of Commons and not to the European Parliament. As a result, one Conservative Eurosceptic MP, David Heathcoat Amory, was moved to remark that the MEPs' approach smacked of "arrogance ..and their own self-importance in Brussels" in actually expecting such a thing to happen.[2]

> *"It would be better to minimise BSE (problems) by practising dis-information. It would be better to say the press have a tendency to exaggerate" (memo from Gilbert Castille, Commission official, October 1990).... "All discussion of BSE inevitably causes problems in the meat market. In order to maintain public confidence it is essential not to provoke a re-opening of the debate. It would be prudent to avoid a discussion in the scientific committees" (letter from Guy Legras, head of the Commission's Agriculture Directorate, to Ricardo Perissich, head of the Internal Market Directorate, March 1993)... At no time did markets take priority over health but we needed to avoid panic which was not supported by scientifically-based information. We were trying to manage uncertainty...but with a pretty laughable level of staffing".* (Evidence by Guy Legras to the MEPs' committee of enquiry.)

EXHIBIT 1: KEEPING THE LID ON THE PROBLEM
Sources: EC hushed up the BSE scandal for 5 years, Stephen Bates,
The Guardian, 3/9/96 and BSE "badly monitored" by EU,
Caroline Southey, *The Financial Times*, 2/10/96

The MEPs' report did not only find Britain guilty. It also heavily censured the European Commission for its "incompetence" and "negligence". Pauline Green, in fact, called the Commission's civil service procedures on public health "shambolic".[3] However, Jacques Santer, Commission President, rejected the criticisms contained in the report. He was also obviously relieved, in the light of the emotion the report had generated, that it contained no reference to a vote of "no confidence" in either him or the Agricultural Commissioner, Franz Fischler. In view of Exhibit 1, page 452, this may be somewhat surprising.

Others were not so sure of where the blame, if any, should lie. Lord Plumb, a British MEP who sat on the inquiry committee, said the outcome bore "all the hallmarks of a witch hunt".[4] For Sir Stephen Wall, Britain's Permanent Representative in Brussels, it was "absurd and insulting" that the committee, chaired by German MEP Reimer Böge, should have accused British scientists of being involved in some sort of conspiracy, given that Britain had spent some £60m on research into BSE and related diseases since 1986.

Heated though the exchanges were, and whatever their specific rationales, there was no disguising that they related to an extremely serious, Europe-wide problem of public health in general, and food safety regulation in particular. As the *European* newspaper's editorial writer claimed:

With multinational companies operating throughout the single European market, customers have to be certain that the food from any member state is safe. The European is always wary about governments being stripped of their powers and authority being transferred to Brussels. But one area in which this is clearly justified is where there is a threat that crosses frontiers. Public health...falls into this category.[5]

The way the paper recommended this should be dealt with was by establishing an independent European Consumer Agency to check on food quality across the EU, even though this would mean a substantial extension of the European Commission's authority in this field.

The European newspaper also thought that Jacques Santer had been right to reject the MEPs' proposal to withhold funds promised to Britain for BSE eradication, until it put its house in order. It felt as well that the committee was wholly correct in recommending to the European Parliament that the Commission be given just nine months in which to take "urgent and effective action" to transform food and agriculture policy in the EU.

The matter was indeed serious. For one thing, the European Parliament was scheduled to debate the MEPs' report, one of the most politically high profile and controversial documents that the EU Parliament had ever produced, at the end of February 1997. In so doing, it would consider specifically the censures on the British government. Not only that, but there was an additional concern contained in the evidence that Jacques Santer had himself submitted to the committee. He reckoned that Britain had tried to pursue a policy of non-co-operation over European business in order to try to force a premature lifting of the European Union's global export ban, before there was proper evidence that British beef was safe. This showed that, Britain had been, in effect, guilty of putting "political considerations" first. He declared:

I had a lot of difficulties with the British government. I was threatened often but never did I cede. I refused to let myself be influenced by political pressure. I refused to give in to blackmail.[6]

It was also at this time, as we shall see later, that Britain's Labour opposition was laying down their parliamentary vote of censure on the Conservative government over the BSE issue. So, not surprisingly, there was considerable tension in the air at Westminster for those government ministers most involved. After all, it was now a minority government and the forthcoming British general election was, at that time, only months way.

THE BACKGROUND TO BSE

In specific terms, the draft MEP's report accused Britain of failing to put into proper effect a ban on meat and bone meal used as cattle feed, and of not including key BSE controls in veterinary inspections at the height of the epidemic between 1990 and 1994.[7] In more general terms, the report was a means of drawing attention to the crisis that had affected British farming since November 1986, when the first case of BSE had been reported in Kent.

BSE was a fatal disease, affecting cattle. It caused massive disruption in the functioning of the central nervous system in cows, ultimately rendering them, in effect, senseless and incapable of co-ordinated movement. It was analogous to a disease in sheep called scrapie or "staggers". Note that by far the greatest proportion of cases registered in the EU had occurred in Britain.

In short, four things had happened since 1986 to cause a crisis. Firstly, a connection had begun to be suspected between the onset of BSE and a new, low cost feed that farmers had just begun, with official support, to give to their cows. This feed was called Specified Bovine Offal (SBO) and was made with protein from slaughtered cattle and sheep. It was obviously unusual to use this for cattle feed, as cows are by nature ruminants and herbivores. To some critics of the government's approach it was also highly immoral. But it was, nonetheless, a profitable way for renderers (disposers of the parts of animals that are not put immediately into the human food chain) to use up parts of animals that otherwise would have to be destroyed and for farmers to give their herds a high protein diet. Dairy farmers were especially keen to use it and raising productivity in milk and beef production was the key reason why the British government sanctioned it.

The suspicion that SBO might tend, in some way and on occasion, to be contaminated, and thus the direct or indirect cause of BSE, led to the second link in the chain: a ban on the use of this feed. So far as UK cattle were concerned, the this measure was put in place in July 1988. Those ingredients in the feed thought to be most infectious (brain, spinal cord, tonsils, thymus etc) were also banned from human food in the UK in November 1989. No action was, however, taken by the British government to ban SBO from pig and poultry feed until March 1996. This was despite two fact that the 100,000th case of BSE had already been recorded in Britain by July 1993. The net result was the widely agreed estimate that, by December 1995, over 700,000 BSE-infected cattle could have been consumed by humans.

Years	Exports of meat and bone meal, for use in feed for cows and poultry, from UK to European mainland (tonnes)
average 1985-8	10,000
1989	30,000
1990	17,000
1991	22,000

TABLE 2: EXPORTS OF MEAT AND BONE MEAL FROM UK
Source: *Nature*, 13/6/96

Note: The NFU were quoted as saying that the lack of a ban on UK exports of meat and bone meal, despite the ban on its use in the UK for cattle and sheep, did not cause them to question exports. The EU ban on SBO imports into the mainland was imposed in 1990.

The third feature was the rising belief in scientific circles that a virulent and fatal illness then attacking humans, a new form of Creutzfeld-Jakob disease (CJD), had close similarities with BSE. This belief was based on work that had been done by an international research team led by Professor Roy Anderson, Director of the UK Centre for the Epidemiology of Infectious Disease, into 12 cases of a new strain of CJD that had been recorded by the end of August 1996. There was, however, no proof of a causal link even though, when the news of the isolation of the new form of CJD broke on March 20th 1996, there was a wave of Europe-wide alarm at the likelihood of a connection. Indeed, it was the British government's announcement on March 27th 1996 that a BSE-CJD link was possible that provoked the EU into imposing a total ban on UK beef exports. Up to this point British government ministers and agricultural experts had maintained that "British beef was safe".[8]

454

The fourth element was the way in the mid 1990s in which British scientific opinion about the possibility of the maternal transmission of the disease from cow to calf was changing from flat rejection ("it cannot happen") to possibility ("it might be happening"). Cases of BSE were still occurring at the rate of almost 200 per week in mid-1996. It was then argued that this could only have taken place if contaminated SBO was still being used or if maternal transmission was occurring. The release of information by Douglas Hogg, on August the first 1996, to the effect that the risk of transmission was, "after adjustment", only one per cent did not, in fact, seem to remove any public worries. Quite the contrary result was achieved, with *The Times* commenting acidly:

> *In 1988 the government maintained that BSE could not be passed from cattle to humans. In 1989 the government's scientists said the disease could not be passed from cow to calf. Both confident assertions have now been contradicted. The government's record suggests that today's settled scientific opinion can become tomorrow's discredited bromide. The Ministry may be right, but playing down risks and hoping for the best is not the right way to restore confidence.*[9]

The worries of Professor Anderson's research team were more than amply expressed by one member, Christopher Donnelly. He indicated in late August 1996 that, in order to substantially reduce the number of cases of BSE that were expected, the issue of maternal targetting, the slaughtering of the offspring of cows with BSE, should be urgently addressed.

Giving evidence to the MEPs' committee of inquiry, Keith Meldrum, the British government's Chief Veterinary Officer, had been obliged to concede that there had been "failings in animal health controls" and the service could well "have done better".[11] This led the editor of *Country Life*, Clive Aslet, to label the Agriculture Ministry as the "Ministry of Madness" and lambast it for incompetence.[12] Another critic, Charles Clover of *The Daily Telegraph*, placed the blame somewhat differently when he said:

> *Farmers argue that they are the innocent buyers of a cattle feed which is thought to have caused the disease. Yet farmers are still taking our subsidy money instead of pursuing the feed manufacturers through the courts. The real difference between farmers and everyone else is £3 billion a year in subsidies. It is amazing that after 17 years of Conservative government we still have centrally planned agriculture, a system of support prices and quotas for some commodities, such as milk. Yet agriculture is now so efficient and global markets so accessible that subsidies are no longer necessary. This is a nannied culture which enables farmers to blame the government or Brussels whenever*

anything goes wrong. The truth is that mad subsidies probably caused mad cow disease.[13]

There was, of course, another, but now distant, possibility for the continuation of the cases of BSE, namely that farmers were managing to continue somehow to sell diseased cattle as healthy. After all, they had been able to do this between 1988 and 1990 and had had a good incentive to do so at the time: the amount of compensation paid by the government for cattle with BSE was put at 50 per cent of the value.

A HOT AUTUMN IN 1996

Farmers all over Europe were angry at the way in which the incidence of BSE and the official responses to it were depressing the demand for their beef. As prices fell, and as politicians argued over what should be done, their livelihoods came under attack. One such British farmer was Fraser Macleod, leader of Farming Collaboration (FC), a lobby group set up to represent the interests of some 20,000 beef farmers in Scotland and northern England.

Their first contention was that the National Farmers' Union (NFU), the traditional voice of the British farm lobby, was incapable of forcefully representing the concerns of its members. They were, in fact, the "first link in the food chain",[14] spending their time producing suckling calves which were then sold on for fattening by large-scale farms and then slaughter. According to Fraser Macleod, many of the beef suckler farms were located in "extremely marginal areas where there is no alternative to livestock farming". Given that the price they were getting for the calves in autumn 1996 was 88p/kg, as compared to 132p/kg one year before, they were seeking a government "top-up" of £150 per calf and reform of the European Union's Common Agricultural Policy (see Exhibit 2 on page 457) to give them more support.

The CAP, in the FC's view, did not contain a beef meat regime which met their specific concerns properly. Certainly, in the view of Alistair Davy, a breeder of Limousin cows in Swaledale, the economics of the beef industry were now punitive. His price had fallen from 1995 to 1996 to below break-even point and the government support deal announced in July 1996, partly funded by the EU, was, he felt, wholly inadequate.

FC's second claim was even more serious. Fraser Macleod reckoned that:

The single industry policy adopted by the Government and NFU has worked against our interest. Mainstream dairy farmers have been pampered by it and many beef farmers feel they have been asked to "carry the can" for dairy farmers who they see as mainly responsible for creating the BSE problem by the intense use of meat and bonemeal as animal feed. In herds that have had a case of BSE in animals born on the farm, the option of slaughtering the whole herd should be considered.[15]

The statement was given even greater point by the fact that, although 90% of all Britain's BSE cases had occurred on dairy farms, their owners had not suffered financially to anything like the degree of the beef farmers as they had been able to continue to sell milk without restriction. It is noteworthy that the key focus of the government's Over Thirty Months Scheme (see Exhibit 3, page 459) was on such farms.

The key feature of the Common Agricultural Policy (CAP) is the fact that it gives financial support to EU farmers on the basis of contribution made by the EU governments. In short, it has the form of a fiscal transfer giving farmers insurance against the rigours of operating in a competitive price-driven market-place. The financial support or subsidy is given on the basis of farmers' meeting bureaucratic rules and regulations in respect of prices and quantities produced and is intended to guarantee the adequacy of farmers' incomes, the value of their land and Europe's food self sufficiency. The problem is that the cost of the CAP, met by the taxpayer (via taxes) as opposed to the consumer (via prices), is still seen as excessive. This is despite a major reform which was carried out in 1992 to curb spending.

The conclusion of the GATT Uruguay Round in Marrakech in 1994 brought an EU commitment to reduce export aid on farm produce by 38 per cent and the pegging of the CAP and regional support budgets for 1997 at 1996 levels, i.e. approx $50 billion and $30 billion respectively. Some 30 per cent of the CAP budget is earmarked for meat and milk products. Increasing pressure in international trade is increasingly forcing the EU to think of de-coupling the CAP from specific levels of food production – which are interpreted as highly protectionist – and spend the aid funds on regional policy and so-called structural funding of the agricultural community. In other words,. to pay farmers to stay at home and not produce food on a larger scale than allowed for, within the current set-aside formula

---

EXHIBIT 2: A BRIEF OVERVIEW OF THE CAP

Big money was at stake here. Some estimates suggested that, by September 1996, the value of the EU's 85m cattle had been reduced by over £6 billion.[16] It was also politically problematic for the government, given the extent to which a disproportionately high number of Conservative MPs had rural constituencies and their Labour counterparts had predominantly urban electorates.

Germany was one of the European Union countries that was opposed to any relaxation of restrictions on the export of British beef. Its farmers, too, were angry at the slump in their revenues. Their highly intractable stance was such as to draw the comment from Michael Forsyth, the government's Scottish Secretary, that some EU countries (i.e., Germany) were, in fact, seeking "the cynical elimination of a formidable competitor (i.e., Britain) in the European beef market".[17]

In August 1996, after the announcement that BSE could possibly be transmitted from cow to calf, the concern in Germany was with avoiding any further collapse in the market for beef meat, milk and milk products and with tightening controls on British cattle to the maximum. One German farmer, Jann Dirks, a breeder of red-whites in Schleswig-Holstein, was forthright in his condemnation:

The British government is to blame. They have failed to get a grip on the problem. Through their inattention and sloppy pursuit of selfish economic interests, they have ignored the fears of consumers. I accuse Britain of being selfish.[18]

Many French farmers, as can be supposed, supported direct action to vent their anger. Ageing agriculturalists such as Rene Courteix, mayor of the aptly-named village of St Merd-les-Oussines near Limoges, for whom the arrival of *vache folle* had been truly *catastrophique*, were more philosphical. In the small towns and villages of rural France, the threat of an increase in the pace of *desertification* or emigration to the towns through the economic consequences of BSE represented for them a psychological as well as a political crisis. Perhaps it was just as well for French farmers that Jacques Chirac, President of France had been raised in Brive-La-Gaillarde in Corrèze and was reputed to be the only President in France's fifth Republic able to milk a cow.

Other French farmers acted differently. Veronique Bichou, for instance, who brought her herd of cows to the Champ de Mars in central Paris to lobby the government for compensation. Or Arnold Puech-Dalissac. He it was who helped mount "Night Operation" in August 1996 and "Operation Dead Massif Central" in October of that year. Both were openly recognised as illegal schemes aimed at stopping and searching British lorries carrying agricultural or farm produce. The organisations responsible were France's two biggest farmers' unions, the FNSEA and the Young Farmers, and their complaint was that the British approach to BSE had caused the collapse of the French beef market, consumption having fallen by no less than one third since March 1996.

For the French farmers it was simply a case of using near-terror tactics against British drivers. "They (the drivers) always look frightened when they see a hundred French farmers waiting for them on the dock" said one incensed agriculturalist.[19] Such tactics were aimed, it was said, at reassuring French consumers that British beef was not slipping through the continental blockade.

The Irish farmers shared the sense of outrage at what was happening, and showed it. They were in a more difficult position than some others since 90 per cent of the beef cattle reared in Ireland on farms averaging 12 cattle were sold abroad. Any move on the part of the Germans, French or Italians, Ireland's three best export markets, to substitute home-grown for imported beef necessarily meant a major reduction in BSE-free Irish exports. Even if demand fell (as it did) in these three countries in 1996, it did not mean that local producers would suffer to the same degree as the Irish exporters. And, of course, there was the extent of the dependence of a whole range of ancillary Irish jobs on livestock production in what is a heavily agricultural country.

The reason why the British government wished to reduce the amount of compensation paid to dairy farmers under the Over Thirty Months Scheme (OTMS) was because, since its introduction in May 1996, the scheme was being overwhelmed. The scheme compensated farmers for not selling for food dairy cattle aged over 30 months. These would normally have entered the food chain (e.g. dairy cattle at the end of their working lives sold for beefburgers etc.). The trouble was that too many cattle were being brought to slaughter and that some farmers were pre-empting others in the queue. What was in effect being provided was, in the words of NFU's Policy Director, an attractive, if not highly profitable, "market for cull cows".[20] As of the 14th October 1996 when the cut in compensation took effect, there was a huge backlog of cattle awaiting slaughter.

EXHIBIT 3: A SCHEME THAT WAS JUST TOO SUCCESSFUL...

The mass demonstrations that took place outside the EU Agriculture Ministers' meeting in Killarney in September 1996 were, therefore, not unexpected. What was unexpected was their tone. The farmers were extremely bitter about the fact that, firstly, the European Union had acceded to the UK's request to cut the compensation paid to its dairy farmers by ten per cent, because of the way in which the OTMS plan was working. It set an undesirable precedent. Secondly, they rejected the need for the CAP budget to be constrained. The Irish farmers' anger at their financial losses was reduced only by the news that a more positive final compensation package was to be agreed by EU ministers in Luxembourg in October.

As can be imagined, the reaction of British farmers to the government's ten per cent cut-back was vitriolic. When Douglas Hogg, the minister of agriculture, attended the South West Dairy Show at Shepton Mallet on the 2nd October 1996, he was jostled and manhandled by farmers shouting "Hoggy, Hoggy, Hoggy, Out, Out, Out".[21] One week later, at the Conservative Party Conference, he was said by *The Financial Times* to have "faced a roasting from furious farmers".[22]

THE FLORENCE ACCORD

In theory, all these disputes among EU members and their farmers over BSE should have been solved by the EU agreement that was struck at Florence on the 21st June 1996. The deal had been a long time a-coming and it was Jacques Santer, Commission president, who was acclaimed by virtually all sides for having engineered it. The hope was that, with the BSE problem dealt with, the UK would begin to give its assent to all the 100 EU Council decisions that it had been deliberately holding up to try to win support for its stance on BSE ie a total removal of the export ban.

It is also of interest to note that Britain had further upset its EU partners by refusing to advance the negotiations on European Union development, the inter-governmental conference (IGC), since their launch in March 1996 in Turin, through its resolute opposition to any dilution of its national veto in Council decision-making.

Any position on BSE and on lifting the UK export ban needs to be seen in the context of considerable misgivings about the effectiveness of past actions taken by the UK. Britain is too lax in implementing the controls" (EU Commission's paper tabled at the Florence summit)..."BSE was treated as a dangerous disease...but not as a national emergency and I would not exempt the NFU from that criticism. In retrospect we should have done more bullying".(Ian Gardiner, policy director, NFU)..."Changes in rendering practices at the time may have permitted sufficient infectivity to get into the meat and bone meal fed to dairy cattle. In the early 1980s farmers were increasing this in the hope of raising milk yields and securing a higher EU milk quota". (Chris Bostock, head of molecular biology at Britain's Institute of Animal Health)...

EXHIBIT 4: WORRIES ABOUT BSE
Source: New measures haunted by past mistakes, Deborah Hargreaves,
The Financial Times, 21/6/96

What had indeed been agreed at Florence was the principle of a stage-by-stage lifting of the EU's global ban on the export of British beef, but without any timetable. The removal was to be staged progressively as Britain implemented BSE eradication measures. These included a cull of beef, as opposed to dairy, cattle which was far larger than the British government had anticipated but 70 per cent of whose cost was to be met by the EU.

Had the British government capitulated to its EU partners' demands? No, said Prime Minister John Major. He declared:

Some of the stories in the last 24 hours are from Alice in Wonderland. There is no question of a climb-down. That's absolute nonsense. This has been a squabble. We had something to sort out.[23]

It was certainly true that the British government had already secured the removal of the EU's ban on the export of beef by-products on the 3rd June 1996, but the aim of getting the global ban on beef exports lifted within a specified time frame had definitely not been reached. Indeed, quite the opposite. It was agreed that the final EU decision for this would rest with the European Commission and would depend on the assent of the European Standing Veterinary Committee (ESVC), made up of national officials from all the European member countries.

It was, of course, the ESVC committee, which had, until June the third, consistently refused to lift the ban on beef by-products. Now, at least, Britain could export semen and tallow. Should Britain now wish to export beef outside the European Union, it could do so, but subject to European Commission permission.

Had Britain's strategy of holding-up decisions, instituted eight weeks after the EU ban on exports was brought in, actually worked? Chancellor Kenneth Clarke thought so. The summit had, after all, also conceded that the ban on embryos would be progressively lifted. But other elements in the deal were less clear-cut. Britain, after all, had had to accept the European Commission's insistence on an identification programme for all UK cattle, the destruction of all animal-based feed and the proper policing of all actions taken, with control to be in the hands of a special super-committee of experts. This it should be noted, set up in Britain a more vigorous system than applied in many mainland EU countries.

British farmers were not as pleased with the outcome as might have been expected. So far as Britain was concerned, the NFU was glad the bickering was over but said to be "devastated" over the increased cull requirement. On top of this was the fact that the EU agriculture council meeting after the Florence summit had allocated only a further £26.7m towards helping UK beef producers who were selling beef at depressed prices, 17 per cent of the total available for the whole EU. But when he learned of the Florence decision that 147,000 beef cattle would now be slaughtered instead of 80,000, Francis Anthony, BSE expert at the British Veterinary Association said "It's just not science. It's more like burning witches to placate the gods".[24]

French farmers, true to form, mounted a blockading exercise in Toulouse, appropriately named "Operation Escargot", and burned an effigy of John Major in Strasbourg. They claimed that the Florence deal would do little to compensate them for losses arising from the further erosion of public confidence. Exhibit 4, page 460 appears to illustrate that their concerns were well-grounded.

The Times editorial pulled no punches either. In its view:

The plan was probably the best that John Major could have expected..The beef crisis was Britain's fault in the first place...Every week that passes before the ban is lifted causes lost jobs in the beef industry...A better deal would be unlikely to be offered...the more conciliatory such a package is to Britain the harder it will be to sell it to the parliaments of other states...The other EU member states were determined to ensure that Britain would not be seen to benefit from...blackmail.[25]

In the event, John Major went out of his way to underline his gratitude to Douglas Hogg for the way in which he and his department had handled the "multiple challenges of an issue with huge agricultural, trade and political ramifications". Despite the total absence of dates in the Florence accord, he was confident about Britain's ability to get most of the beef ban lifted by November 1996 (i.e., on animals under 30 months old from herds certified to be BSE-free). This would open the path to a resumption of British exports worth £350m a year to the EU. The cost of eradicating BSE in the UK would be £2.5 billion over the coming three years, it was said. The Labour opposition, reflecting on the Florence experience, simply wanted the minister of agriculture sacked. For shadow minister, Brian Wilson, Douglas Hogg was the political equivalent of "a clapped-out old milker".[26] The government had indeed, in his view, been forced into "a massive climbdown".[27]

WINTER WORRIES

The disclosure on August the first 1996 that maternal transmission of BSE from cow to calf was possible after all amounted to most observers as yet another major blow against the £4 billion per annum British beef industry. It came at a time when the main industry organisation, the Meat and Livestock Commission, was claiming that beef consumption was 24 per cent down from the previous year. At an emergency meeting of the ESVC, Keith Meldrum, the government's chief veterinary officer, faced another barrage of questions from his European colleagues. The chief point at issue was the possible need to extend the planned selective slaughter of 147,000 beef cattle, as agreed at Florence, even further. This was, of course, in addition to the one million dairy cattle being handled under the OTMS scheme. The NFU was appalled at this. There was no scientific justification for any further culling, they declared. It would be "mere political expediency".[28]

1. British government's blackmailing tactics over Council decision-making
2. British refusal to hand over to the French government research data on BSE and CJD
3. EU's inadequate control on beef exports
4. Lack of co-ordination in France of inspection of British imports and a shortfall in sanitary controls
5. Fraudulent British exports of contaminated BSO feedstock - labelled as of Irish origin.

TABLE 3: THE FRENCH PARLIAMENTARY COMMISSION REPORT ON THE MISMANAGEMENT OF THE BSE CRISIS
Source: French MPs attack beef "deception",
Paul Webster, *The Guardian*, 22/1/97

The upshot of the ESVC meeting was that the European Commission made it clear that there would simply be no phased ending of the beef export ban. Britain's MAFF tried to play down the significance of the new maternal transfer findings but the German government, in the form of Werner Zwingmann, Keith Meldrum's opposite number, was in no mood to compromise. It wanted the selective culling programme to now include the last-born calves of BSE-infected cattle.

The debate became even more confusing with the announcement by an Oxford University research team that, according to their findings, BSE would virtually disappear by 2001 without any cull.[29] Certainly, reliable data indicated that the incidence of BSE was falling rapidly in Britain (see Table 1 on page 450).

The matter came to a head with a statement by Downing Street that Britain would not go ahead with a selective cull of 147,000 cattle, as required by the Florence agreement, unless the EU lifted the export ban on herds that were certified BSE-free. Minister Douglas Hogg, in fact, fared very badly when he put his demand (together with the British government's view of the evidence and the conclusion that there was nothing to fear) to his EU partners. Conversely, members of Britain's Conservative government rallied round the cabinet, reckoning that the Florence agreement and the constraints it had imposed on Britain were now redundant. The German reaction, on the other hand, was one of total incomprehension of the British stance. For his part, Franz Fischler, the Agriculture Commissioner, declared :

As long as the UK do not meet the preconditions, then an end to the export ban is simply not a possibility.[30]

Marc Roche, writing in *Le Monde*, attributed John Major's decision to backtrack on the Florence plan to British domestic politics ("considérations de politique intérieure"). Specifically, he argued that the policy was causing great divisions within the Conservative government and that the government itself was a minority one and was facing a general election within a year.[31]

Meanwhile, the OTMS scheme was proceeding apace but, paradoxically, not quickly enough. Not only was it too successful, as Exhibit 3 shows on page 459, but Britain's abattoirs actually could not cope with the demand.. In August the government had put the backlog of dairy cattle over 30 months old to be destroyed at 150,000 and rising rapidly. Hence, the highly unpopular decision by the government to cut the compensation can at least be understood. The Ministry was being overwhelmed. So much so, that it was considering hiring freezer ships and more cold-storage warehouses to deal with the problem.

There was another paradox to consider also and that was the extent to which demand for British beef had now risen, to 85 per cent of pre-BSE scare levels, its shop price had fallen to levels some found attractive. As an aside, Kevin Taylor, Keith Meldrum's deputy, proudly announced to the Festival of British Beef Conference run by the Meat and Livestock Commission on the 24th October that his wife caused chaos in restaurants by insisting on British beef "on grounds of safety".[32]

Then, in what seemed a surprising about-turn, the British government decided to retract its decision to backtrack on the Florence plan. The change of mind was announced on the 12th December 1996. The government still maintained that there was no firm evidence to justify proceeding with the agreed cull but progress, it said, had to be made. It was clearly a relief to have the chance of at least reducing the pressure emanating from Brussels. The government had certainly had a rough ride whilst trying to change its EU partners' minds.

The Conservative government had also faced an all-party attack in the Commons on its handling of the BSE crisis, surviving what had amounted to a vote of no confidence by 303 votes to 302. And it was still heavily pre-occupied with the massive challenge of how to dispose of all the animal carcasses in the OTMS that had not yet been incinerated. Ministers were even considering the possibility of burning them in power stations.

The statement that Britain, after all, would press ahead with a cull of cattle that were most at risk was welcomed by Franz Fischler. Nevertheless, it was made plain that there would be no easing, despite Britain's high hopes, of the export ban. The consequence was that Douglas Hogg was attacked anew. He had already received a vote of no confidence from the NFU, in October 1996 that is, and was again savaged by its president, Sir David Naish, at the NFU's annual meeting he said that parts of the government's approach to BSE amounted to "an utter disgrace".[33]

The Labour opposition dutifully put down its new motion of censure against the government on the 17th February 1997 and Douglas Hogg, and his former ministerial colleage, Douglas Hurd, dutifully rebutted Labour charges. The Labour call that the agriculture minister's pay be docked by £1,000 was said by Douglas Hogg to be "a cheap political stunt". So far as the damage to consumer confidence was concerned, what was causing the most difficulty was, he contended, Labour's repetition of the "alarmist headlines of the tabloid press".[34] But there still remained an undeniable problem, since government figures suggested that the cost of the BSE crisis to date was £3.3 billion and there were now 230,000 corpses of cattle held in cold storage awaiting incineration.. The government won the censure debate this time by a better majority than last time, 13 votes.

THE PLOT THICKENS

When the news leaked out that that a report into Britain's meat industry commissioned by the Meat Hygiene Service (MHS) and intended for publication in March 1996 had been delayed (or suppressed), there was a huge outcry. Professor Richard Lacey, a microbiologist who had been heavily involved in the BSE affair declared :

We are seeing the same pattern of government behaviour. Commission advice from the experts, but then ignore it if you don't like the conclusions or they might work out to be too expensive.[35]

The £1m report was written by six members of the MHS' Hygiene Advice Team, under the leadership of veterinary officer Bill Swann, and was based on an audit carried out over the period 1994-5. The MHS itself had been created in 1995 as an agency of the Ministry of Agriculture, Fisheries and Food (MAFF) to oversee health regulations.

Just why the MHS report had not been published was the subject of considerable political mudslinging based on intelligent conjecture, but it is evident that its timing, from the British government's viewpoint, could have been much better. Worse still, it amounted to a damning indictment of major public health shortcomings in the operation of Britain's abattoirs. Some of these were, in Bill Swann's words, "absolutely dreadful", which certainly could have contributed to the spread of BSE. *The Times* remarked gravely that "the failure to publicise the report was incompatible with a proper concern for public health".[36] It took Douglas Hogg to task for claiming not to have read the report - an "astounding" and "inexcusable" situation and considered that:

no reform or reassurance from the Ministry of Agriculture ("More Awful Food Failings") can now pass muster. It cannot be made sufficiently distant from the producer interests that it is intended to regulate.[37]

It was also no defence against the industry's failures, said *The Times*, that the government had set up the centralised Meat Hygiene Service to take over from un-systematised local authority inspectorates two years before.

The Labour opposition could hardly rejoice at the government's discomforture. The problem was, in the words of Labour Spokesman Nigel Griffiths, "why on earth things were allowed to deteriorate this far. If this report had not been suppressed, there is a high possibility that lives may have been saved".[38]

As a background to this furore, three things are noteworthy. Firstly, according to a study carried out by researcher Jean Shaoul of Manchester University, 160 out of 402 British abattoirs had been exempted from EU regulations on layout and hygiene standards, on grounds of derogations, until December 1996. Secondly, slaughterhouse profitability, already high in early 1996, was now rising. Since the cattle cull organised by the Intervention Board, another government agency, started in May 1996, abattoirs had been receiving £87.50 per animal as opposed to the sum that had been suggested to government in a report by accountants Coopers and Lybrand as "more realistic" – £40. The 60 abattoirs involved, of which six were responsible for most of the cull, had in fact received £12m from the government over the period March-June of that year. No competitive tendering process had been involved. Thirdly, negotiations led by the Intervention Board to try to reduce the fee did not start until mid-August 1996.

> *"It appears from the very many phone calls from members that, far from improving, standards of hygiene are steadily decreasing...There is no need to tell you that this is a potential timebomb...It now appears that, far from being encouraged to enforce stricter hygiene standards, MHS inspectors are being actively encouraged to ignore breaches of regulations and in some cases threatened if they try to take action by slowing down the line speed"..."Our levels of enforcement in hygiene leave much to be desired. We repeat our concern, particularly with the faecal contamination of carcases and would urge you to take immediate action to alleviate this" (Peter Comrie, general secretary of the Association of Meat Inspectors).*

EXHIBIT 6: THE HYGIENE TIMEBOMB
Sources: "Timebomb" in abattoirs sparks new hygiene row, Ewen MacAskill, *The Guardian*, 12/3/97. Tighter rules promised by Minister for meat hygiene, Polly Newton, *The Times*, 12/3/97

There was more. A leaked letter from Peter Comrie, general secretary of the Association of Meat Inspectors, to the chief executive of the MHS, Johnston McNeil and to government Minister Angela Browning, spoke volumes (see Exhibit 6). The outcry drew an agreement from John Major that the government would now proceed to publish a hygiene league table of slaughterhouses. It had, it said, already disciplined 45 MHS inspectors and sacked three for not maintaining proper standards in their work.

Thus, yet again, on the 12th March 1997, Douglas Hogg found himself forced back to the despatch box in the House of Commons to defend the government's record. Mathew Parris, *The Times'* political sketch-writer, conjured up well the air of political unreality :

Let us hope that the next government keeps what has become a Commons tradition: the weekly Westminster Hogg-fight...a fiesta similar to a modern Spanish bull-fight...Douglas Hogg is dragged to the chamber, where he snorts and stamps his feet and is then forced to read an incomprehensible statement...Whatever MPs declare, the Hogg maintains an air of jaunty and bellicose confidence, charging around the ring, bellowing and butting people.[39]

A more trenchant attack was mounted two days later from a different quarter, *The Express* newspaper, traditionally a staunch supporter of the government. Indeed, it went a long way to reflect the view of the leader of the Labour opposition Tony Blair, that "people know the Government has made the most almighty cock-up of the whole thing".[40] Under the banner headline "The Scandal of our Meat" the paper cited the comments of Mark Lee, one of the inspectors sacked from the Meat Hygiene Service, for inadequate inspection of meat in abattoirs.[41] His specific offence, in fact, had been the "premature stamping" of meat.

Mark Lee's list of criticisms was long and wide-ranging. The change in the procedures for feeding cattle before slaughter on animal rights grounds, they now had to be fed 12 hours before slaughter whereas five years before it was 48 hours, meant that cattle arriving at the slaughterhouses were dirtier. The labour used in the slaughterhouses was often unskilled, sometimes even "youngsters straight off the dole queue who cut through the intestines and cause contamination". This was a problem, he said, that the industry giants with large plants "don't want to discuss and don't want highlighted". Perhaps the most significant comment he made, however, was that:

I think the public should know that the meat inspector has just 36 seconds to examine the carcass (on visits made randomly by the MHS to slaughterhouses) while the slaughterman is working opposite him removing the spine. You are not allowed to stop the line. You must thus protect the public in the 36 seconds dictated by commerce.

It was in the light of this that Paul Tyler, Lib-Dem agriculture spokesman commented:

This confirms our suspicions that it was in an effort to cut corners that the Government nationalised meat hygiene in 1995.[42]

THE WAY AHEAD

Whatever the hopes of the UK government and the European Commission, the political heat from the BSE crisis in early 1997 was simply refusing to die down.

True, the European Commission president had survived the February 1997 censure motion by MEPs. It had called for the resignation of the Commission, but it had been voted down by 326 to 118. Nevertheless, as we have seen, the Commision was given a relatively short space of time to effect the reforms demand by the inquiry team. So extensive were the committee's recommendations (see Table 2 on page 454), that Paola Buonadonna, writing in The *European*, referred to the newly-established duties speedily added to the role of Health Commissioner, Emma Bonino, as "a sweeping change" and a "poisoned chalice".[43]

The Commissioner herself was now to be responsible for public health on top of fisheries, humanitarian affairs and consumer rights. She lost no time in issuing three new plans for her enlarged Directorate. One: in future, all seven scientific committees which previously reported to the Agriculture Directorate would now answer to her. Two: her team would investigate, and seek to confirm, the relevance to the EU of the politically-independent Food and Drug Agency model used in the United States. Three: she would seek more vigorously to include public health in the EU framework of competences.

1. A total ban on the use of SBO as an animal feedstock
2. The setting up within the Commission of a Public Health Protection Unit and a European Agency for Veterinary Inspection
3. The introduction of an independent EU research programme
4. The UK to introduce animal and herd identification
5. New legal powers for the Commission to overrule "subsidiarity" i.e. to intervene in conflict situations where EU member's individual interests may be at variance with those of the EU.

TABLE 4: FINAL RECOMMENDATIONS OF
THE MEPs' BSE INQUIRY COMMITTEE
Source: *EP News*, February, 1997

This last plan was, in fact, already incorporated in proposals to be discussed at the EU intergovernmental conference in Amsterdam in mid 1997. If agreed by EU heads of state, the result would be that public health matters in individual states would, in future, be subject to qualified majority voting and European parliament involvement. Emma Bonino reckoned that this would be "the moment of truth" since it would mean that public health could begin to be managed on a pan-European basis and would be the way to "find out whether health protection and consumer protection are becoming a priority or just something to be looked at in emergencies".[44] More specifically, however, her first task on assuming the enlarged role in early March 1997 was to lobby for more funds.

The substantial victory gained by Labour in the British general election held on May Day 1997, 419 seats as against the Conservatives' 165 and the Social Democrats' 46, made possible a shift in the Britain-EU relationship over BSE.

Tony Blair, the new Prime Minister, indicated quickly that he would pursue the same strategic goal as his predecessor, namely the total lifting of the world-wide beef export ban on British beef, but in a much more flexible manner. There would be much more co-operation with partners on matters of EU concern, for example, in respect of Britain's willingness to sign the Social Chapter. So far as public health was concerned, there would be a thorough overhaul of Britain's approach in all respects at home and abroad. As the country's new Agriculture Minister, Dr Jack Cunningham, pointed out:

We are looking at a new BSE agenda. Quite clearly we believe a more constructive, open dialogue is going to be helpful. We have inherited a difficult and complex situation and I am not going to set dates or deadlines for when this can end.[45]

Optimism aside, in mid-1997, Dr Cunningham faced a full and daunting in tray. Three issues were paramount. First, the abattoirs were now simply unable to cope with the demand from farmers seeking to have their cows slaughtered before the deadline (4/8/97), on which the OTMS compensation rules were to change. Second, on the second of July the European Commission claimed that the UK was breaking the world-wide ban on beef exports. They had, they said, hard evidence that British beef was being exported to EU and non-EU countries using falsified documents. Initial evidence indicated that the claims were wholly justified and that beef had been illegally exported to Belgium, the Netherlands, Egypt and Russia. Third, the Treasury, on the 26th June1997, put the cost to the UK of dealing with the BSE crisis, over the period 1988-1997, at £4 billion.

On the 23rd November 1998 European Union farm ministers, acting on expert advice, lifted the ban on the export of British beef, once a trade worth £700m to Britain. It was a victory for the British government, but a Pyrrhic one, as the French were prepared to break EU law to stop imports and the German Länder prevaricated.

* * * * * * * * * * * * * *

NOTES AND REFERENCES

1   Tosh jibe enrages MEPs, Stephen Bates, G, *The Guardian*, 19/2/97

2   European MPs direct anger at Britain over BSE crisis, Charles Bremner and Andrew Pierce, *The Times*, 19/2/97

3   As 2

4   As 2

5   Thoughts for food safety, editorial, *The European*, 20-26/2/97

6   Britain accused on blackmail on beef, Neil Buckley, David Wighton and Robert Preston, *The Financial Times*, 16/1/97

7   Mad cow "pardon" riles parliament, Paola Buonnadonna, *The European*, 16-22/1/97

8   700,000 BSE cattle "fed to humans", Tim Radford, *The Guardian*, 29/8/96

9   A crisis of confidence, *The Times* editorial, 2/8/96

10   As 8

11   Why the beef industry has led itself to slaughter, Charles Leadbeater, *The Observer*, 22/12/96

12   So the ministry of madness strikes again, Clive Aslet, *The Times*, 2/8/96

13   Mad Cows and Ministry Men, Charles Clover, *The Daily Telegraph*, 3/5/96

14   Beef farmers set to break ranks with NFU, Deborah Hargreaves, *The Financial Times*, 5/8/96

15   Beef farmers call for cull of all herds with BSE, Michael Hornsby, *The Times*, 6/8/96

16   EU politicians edge away from the brink on beef, Caroline Southey, *The Financial Times*, 10/5/96

17   As 16

18   Britain blamed in German fury, Peter Bild, *The Times*, 6/8/96

19   Farmers in France stage night raids to block British beef, Ben McIntyre, *The Times*, 30/8/96

20   Hogg jostled by angry farmers at Dairy Show, Michael Hornsby, *The Times*, 3/10/96

21   As 21

22   Hogg faces roasting from furious farmers, Maggy Urry, *The Financial Times*, 8/10/96

23   (a) Who blinked first, Andrew Grice, Michael Prescott and Peter Conradi, *The Sunday Times*, 23/6/96 and
(b) Major claims victory in beef war, Philip Webster and Charles Bremner, *The Times*, 22/6/96

24   As 23a

25   Best for Beef, *The Times* editorial, 21/6/96

26   Major tells Hogg well done and your job is secure, Arthur Leathley, *The Times*, 28/6/96

27   UK offers concessions over beef, Robert Preston, Neil Buckley and Lionel Barber, *The Financial Times*,20/6/96

28   New scare wrecks beef truce, Stephen Bates, Paul Brown and Michael White, *The Guardian*, 2/8/96

29   Major faces new Tory strife on beef ban, Caroline Southey, George Parker and Alison Maitland, *The Financial Times*, 29/8/96

30   Brussels sees no prospect of beef ban being lifted, Andrew Pierce and Charles Bremner, *The Times*, 21/9/96

31   "Vache folle": M. Major n'a pas convaincu sa majorité en suspendant son plan d'abattage des bovins, Marc Roche, *le Monde* 22-23/9/96

32   Conference message falls on empty seats, Robin Young, *The Times*, 25/10/96

33   Hogg warns beef progress slow, Maggie Urry, *The Financial Times*, 6/2/97

34   Hogg's blunders cost thousands of jobs, says Labour, Polly Newton and James Landale, *The Times*, 18/2/97

35   Families of E Coli victims line up to sue ministries, Martin Wainwright, *The Guardian*, 3/3/97

36   *The Times* editorial, 7/3/97

37   as 36

38   Meat industry hygiene report was suppressed, Polly Newton, *The Times*, 6/3/97

39   It's fiesta time as Commons lives high off the Hogg, Mathew Parris, *The Times*, 13/3/97

40   Beef–Think of the Future, *Country Life*, 19/9/96

41   The scandal of our meat, Alun Rees and Paul Crosby, *The Express*, 14/3/97

42   as 41

43   Bonino grasps poisoned chalice, Paola Buonadonna, *The European*, 27/2-5/3/97

44   As 43

45   Minister gives no sign of new move on BSE, Stephen Bates, *The Guardian*, 13/5/97

CABLE AND WIRELESS

Abstract:

This complex case study illustrates several aspects of the formation of business alliances in the multi-media industry – telecommunications, internet and television – at a time of substantial global, political and economic change in the late 1990s. The analysis of case data allows conclusions to be drawn about the rationale and nature of key business alliances affecting major players in European telecommunications, as well as the nature of C&W's strategy.

Questions:

Using case data, indicate which are the key drivers affecting the multi-media industry in the late 1990s. Which do you regard as the most significant of these key drivers?

Analyse the way in which key players are using business alliances as a strategic response to the competitive demands placed upon them.

Indicate the nature of Cable and Wireless' strategy over the period of the case. How would you describe it?

What are your overall conclusions about the way the industry is developing?

Comment on the leadership styles of C&W Chief Executive Officers.

Case timing: 1996-2000

THE C&W – VEBA LINKAGE

In early February 1997 media rumours began to circulate that Cable and Wireless (C&W), Britain's second largest telecomms company, was about to abandon its membership of Vebacom, the European business alliance it had created with the diversified German energy group, Veba. If true, such rumours would have signified a large and surprising switch in the company's strategy literally only months after it had persuaded another important German utility, RWE, to join Vebacom.

C&W had bought a 45 per cent stake in Vebacom in 1996 for £712m with the express intention of using the alliance to bid for one of the lucrative mobile telephony licenses that the German government was awarding. Given the strategic importance of mobile telephony to C&W as well as the expanding opportunities in the German market, the company appeared very pleased with the move. So much so, that Veba itself had no hesitation in rejecting the rumours as being without foundation. Following the inclusion of RWE in the Vebacom alliance the C&W stake had indeed fallen to 22.5 per cent, but Veba still regarded its British partner's contribution as very important, if not critical, to its bidding capability.

Vebacom had, in fact, been one of the leading bidders for the German licences, along with Deutsche Telekom, Viag Interkom, an alliance between British Telecom (BT) and the German VIAG organisation, and another wholly domestic and very powerful consortium called Mannesmann Arcor. Of these the biggest contender was, of course, Deutsche Telekom, the newly privatised market leader in the German telecommunications field, which enjoyed a privileged position in the cable sector, as well as in the fixed wire and mobile telephony fields. It was rich, powerful and, unlike its British counterpart, BT, established in all sectors of the telecommunications business. (See Table 1 on page 475.) BT, by contrast, had been privatised in 1984 but had had severe restrictions placed on its ability to go into the cable and entertainment fields. Selected comparative financial data are given for BT and C&W in Table 2 on page 478.

Two further elements of C&W's approach to competing in the German mobile market did not seem to square with the rumour, either. The first was that C&W's action in persuading RWE to quit its relationship with Viag Interkom had been interpreted by Veba as a real coup for Vebacom. The second was that any move by C&W to leave Vebacom would, in fact, have amounted to a reversal of what was thought to be the company's previously robust strategy. And, at exactly the time when arch-competitor Viag Interkom was doing exactly the opposite, building up its bidding base by including the Norwegian state-owned telephone operator, Telenor, in its consortium.

Telenor for all its small size, compared that is with Deutsche Telekom, BT and C&W, was a technology leader in mobile telephony and gave Viag Telekom the capability of exploiting the growing convergence between fixed wire and mobile telephony. The deal involved Telenor's carrying its full share of the £2.6 billion investment that Viag Interkom was planning for the next decade, namely building a combined fixed wire-cellular 'phone network covering eight major German cities.

Existing, but ageing technology	Existing, but innovative technology
Fixed wire telephony	Mobile telephony
Limited interactive services	Digital, interactive services based on cable technology ('phone, Internet, Video-on-demand)
Free-to-air Analogue TV (Direct broadcasting by e.g. BBC)	Satellite Digital TV
Satellite Analogue TV (provided by e.g., BSkyB)	Terrestrial Digital Cable TV

TABLE 1: TECHNOLOGY CATEGORIES IN THE MULTI-MEDIA SCENE

Note: The critical breakthrough in the multi-media scene is the extent to which new technologies (cable and satellite) can be used in conjunction to transmit digitised material, thus powerfully expanding the range of services that can be provided e.g., 'phone, personal banking, video on demand, pay-per-view TV etc.

Vebacom was, of course, facing a similarly massive scale of investment in the German market but, unlike Deutsche Telekom, Viag Interkom and Mannesmann Accor, it had not yet succeeded in winning one of the first mobile telephone licences to be granted by the German government. C&W had also to reckon with the strong likelihood that Deutsche Telekom would continue to remain the dominant player in the highly competitive German market-place in all aspects of telecommunications, despite both its privatisation and the deregulation of the whole European Union market-place that was planned for January the first 1998. This was chiefly because of the power position that Deutsche Telekom had enjoyed as a state-owned utility. Yet another difficulty C&W had also to recognise in considering any pull-out was that that Veba owned 10.4 per cent of C&W.

A NEW FACE ON THE BLOCK

Nevertheless, the rumours were true, after all. C&W announced on the fourth of February 1997 that it was pulling out of Vebacom. This was, as can be imagined, much to the consternation of RWE and Veba. They believed, according to commentators Alan Cane and Fred Studemann of the *The Financial Times*, that the Vebacom alliance had been "one of the strongest in a volatile and unpredictable market".[1]

Nevertheless, C&W shareholders looked content at the news, the share price rose by 15p to 479p, whilst pointed questions were asked by a quizzical media about the company's future strategy focus under its newly-appointed chief executive, Dick Brown. He was an American and had been vice chairman of Ameritech Corp, the Chicago-based "Baby Bell". This was one of the local 'phone companies in the USA that had been created when the giant monopoly AT&T had been broken up.

Commentators were especially interested in the paradox that one of the first things that had been done after Dick Brown took over on July 16th 1996, with the C&W share price standing at 399p, had been to bring RWE into the Vebacom alliance. Now, within months, he was taking C&W out of it.

But the Vebacom decision had not been the only surprise move that had been made as a result of the strategic review that Dick Brown had undertaken on joining C&W. In November 1996 it was disclosed that NYNEX, the Baby Bell based on New York, was to take a 20 per cent stake in C&W's planned $500m transatlantic fibre optic cable link, a joint venture between C&W and MFS Communication. Given that 40 per cent of US multinationals were based in New York, the two-way access to large-scale international 'phone traffic that the link would give to all those involved was very welcome.

The next move had proved much bigger than the first. It involved the creation of a brand-new joint venture company called C&W Communications (CWC). This was 52.5 per cent owned by C&W. It would operate from Britain and bring together the company's fixed wire telephony interests in Britain, represented by its Mercury subsidiary and C&W holdings in cable TV companies. These were Videotron Holdings, Bell Cablemedia and NYNEX Cablecomms. The logic behind the venture lay in the potential ability of the partners to access Britain's homes and businesses directly by cable to sell 'phone, entertainment and information services and to pool the large-scale investment costs involved.

Mercury, the fixed wire competitor established by C&W in the period after the privatisation of BT, had suffered to a great extent because BT had been allowed by the UK privatisation legislation to maintain its control over those landlines it owned. These constituted a large proportion of the British long-distance phone network and also of the local interconnections. Thus, BT's sole and much smaller fixed-wire competitor in the British market since the privatisation of BT had had to lease lines from BT itself. It followed, therefore, that if CWC could raise its competitiveness by by-passing BT through direct cabling at the local interconnection level, this would reduce BT's "gatekeeping" role. But it would not be beneficial at the long-distance, inter-city level, unless nation-wide cable networks were built by the CWC consortium to replace BT's long distance fixed-wire system, or obtained from the other operators who were beginning to make their presence felt in this field. Particularly those who had discovered that the economics of operating call-back services internationally could be highly attractive.

However, it certainly did appear that all that would be needed now to make C&W a full service, "one stop shop" telecomms operator now would be to include in this alliance C&W's other subsidiary, British mobile 'phone operator, One-2-One.[2] As it was, the CWC alliance could already provide one stop shopping for everything in the range from Internet access through to TV entertainment to cable phones.

Early in 1996 the US government agreed to deregulate the US telecommunications market. As part of this it permitted the Baby Bells (the local 'phone companies) to enter the long-distance market where AT&T, MCI and Sprint had held sway. Within weeks amalgamation plans had been made such as that linking NYNEX and Bell Atlantic. But the converse – the long distance operator accessing the local market – was thought to be extremely expensive. Thus, Bryan van Dusen, director of telecomms research at the Yankee Group in Boston, was moved to remark that BT's investment did not, in his view, amount to "a coherent strategy" that made sense to the stock market. "I struggle" he said "to understand the strategic value of MCI's linkage with BT"

EXHIBIT 1: A CRITICAL VIEW OF THE BT-MCI LINK

Source: Will BT bring more to the Concert party than MCI ?,
Richard Thomson, *The Times*, 7/11/96

	British Telecommunications PLC (BT)			Cable & Wireless PLC (C&W)		
	1994	1995	1996	1994	1995	1996
Turnover (£Billion)	13.67	13.89	14.44	4.69	5.13	5.51
Total Assets (£Billion)	22.56	21.459	23.53	7.46	7.94	9.02
Profit Margin (%)	20.1	19.1	20.9	23.1	16.4	24.3
Return on Shareholders' Funds (%)	21.1	22.1	23.8	33.1	24.7	41.1
Return on Capital Employed (%)	16.1	16.2	17.3	18.8	13.6	19.8
Liquidity Ratio	0.99	0.81	0.95	1.28	1.25	1.02
Gearing (%)	36.0	38.2	40.3	87.8	92.2	128.2
No. of Employees ('000)	156.0	148.9	130	41.3	44.1	39.6

TABLE 2 : FINANCIAL DATA - UK TELECOMS GIANTS

Source : Company Financial reports. Note = Each company reporting year ends on 31 March.

BT's own strategic approach was alliance-based. To ensure that it maintained parity in world rankings, BT had made a take-over bid for MCI, the US' second largest long-distance 'phone company. It is noteworthy that MCI owned a 13.5 per cent stake in Rupert Murdoch's News Corporation and it also had a substantial stake in News Corporation's US satellite broadcasting operation, ASkyB. As Exhibit 1 shows not everyone appreciated the logic of this move, which cleared the EU regulatory hurdles in May 1997. It had previously been heavily endorsed by company shareholders.

WORLD-WIDE CHANGE

Interestingly, the C&W-NYNEX deal and the planned $20 billion BT-MCI deal both followed swiftly on the introduction of the deregulatory Telecommunications Act in February 1996 in the US. This Act allowed foreign companies greater access to the American market, in service and ownership terms, but on a basis of strict market openness reciprocity. The US regulator in such matters was the Federal Communications Commission. It was empowered to exempt 100 per cent fusion deals (such as BT's extension of its ownership of MCI from the previously-allowed 20 per cent to 100 per cent) from the standard level of 25 per cent permitted by the new Act, if the deal could be shown to be in the public interest. Naturally, the European Commission and the US government were actively investigating both these transatlantic landmark deals, just as they had done previously with Global One, the link-up between Sprint (the third-largest US long-distance 'phone operator), Deutsche Telekom and France Telecom.

Such a deregulatory framework owed much to the changes that were taking place at the time on the world stage. Indeed, it was on the 16th February 1996 that the historic World Trade Organisation agreement to liberalise telecommunication markets in nearly 70 countries had been signed in Geneva. The expectation of all signatories was that it would boost sales and investment in this global $600 billion p.a. business, which was then growing by ten per cent per year, and slash costs for consumers. The agreement had been difficult to reach, partly because of the complexity of the subject and partly because of the concessions that leading players were obliged to make.

There was no mistaking, however, the pleasure and excitement the deal aroused. For Charlene Barchefsky, the acting US trade representative, it was "one of the most important trade agreements for the 21st century" [3] whilst Sir Leon Brittan, EU trade commissioner, regarded the accord as "a major step in the creation of the information society". It would, he said, act as a "catalyst" for the European economy.[4]

The feast of statistical forecasts that lay behind the deal inspired awe. It would, it was said, treble the value of the world telecommunications business over the coming decade: create one million jobs in the USA: generate an extra $20 billion-worth of telecomms revenue over the next 15 years in the UK: ensure 100 per cent access to the world's biggest telecomms markets, compared with under 20 per cent today, for giants such as BT, C&W and AT&T.

It went almost without saying that it would also accelerate the rush towards global alliances. This had already resulted in such groupings as Concert (BT+MCI), Global One (Deutsche Telekom+France Telecom+Sprint) and Unisource (AT&T and the telecomms companies of Spain, Portugal, Netherlands etc). What else might the combination of European telecomms deregulation (from the first of January 1998), the 1996 US Telecomms Act and now the WTO agreement, bring in their train? Perhaps a link-up agreement between the Japanese NTT, the world's largest non-allianced telecomms company with sales in 1996 of $84 trillion, and Concert? If so, the result would be truly a global behemoth since it would have annual global sales of $122 trillion, equal almost exactly to the 1996 total of those of AT&T ($47 trillion), Deutsche Telekom ($46 trillion) and France Telecom ($29 trillion).

Countries	% Share of Total Revenue	% Share of International Traffic Revenue
US	29.7	25.3
EU	28.3	35.2
Japan	15.6	2.7
Total	73.6	63.2

TABLE 3: WORLD TELECOMMUNICATIONS MARKET SHARE
Source: World Trade Organisation data.

What was most significant about the WTO accord was that, firstly, the three markets responsible for 75 per cent of world telecom revenues, the US, EU and Japan, would be completely open to foreign competition from 1998. Secondly, that Japan itself was allowing further foreign equity ownership, admittedly with a maximum equity stake of 20 per cent, in its two most important carriers. As Table 3 shows, Japan almost certainly would want to make a global push in the lucrative international business sector, but clearly it did not want to give the store away, domestically.

The critical feature for the business community in all of this was "one-stop shopping": companies would increasingly want a single bill for a seamless service covering all their global telecommunications needs. Given that, according to Salomon Brothers' estimates, the world's top 5,000 corporations accounted for some 20 per cent of global revenues and that over 750 of the leading corporations were headquartered in only five countries, it is not surprising that the key providers should all target the leading multinationals. What this strategy entailed was the need to deliver low cost and highly flexible services round the world through global assets. Only in the Asia Pacific, Eastern Europe and Latin American regions was there scope for substantial *greenfield* growth, as penetration was poor and the infrastructure under-developed. Here, prospects for the cable industry as a whole were seen as favourable.

BRAVE NEW WORLD

Optimists in the industry were hoping that CWC would be able to do something about the rate of take-up of cable in Britain, as well. The ten per cent market penetration achieved by cable by the end of 1996 was labelled by Wall St Journal commentator, Janet Guyon, as "dismal" [5] by comparison with results in the US and German market. Indeed, it had only advanced to this level because of a British government decision in 1991 to allow cable companies to offer phone services in addition to TV entertainment, on top, that is, of keeping BT out of cable activity. This latter had been specifically laid down within the privatisation legislation governing the company's sell-off.

Now, however, in early 1997, growth in the use of cable for phone and Internet purposes was beginning to rise at a faster rate than for TV entertainment. Even so, there was still the problem of the control of the network. This meant that, although a cable company could own the "local loop" (the final connection access to the home or business), the local and long distance fixed wire network in Britain had remained, since privatisation, in the hands of BT. And, of course, other lesser long-distance network owners who had entered the market. These included Energis, a newly-formed subsidiary of Britain's National Grid. All cable operators would, thus, have to use BT's and others' networks, and pay the rates set, just as was done in the fixed wire phone market, if they did not own their own. Naturally, CWC's cable strategy was to extend its own long distance links (e.g., its transatlantic cable) as fast as possible.

In fact, there was no denying the up-beat mood in the market. In 1996, the UK cable industry had had its best year to date. The number of residential 'phone customers had gone up from 1.1m to 1.8m and business connections had risen from 1.22m to 2.02m. The number of cable TV customers had also moved strongly up from 1.16 to 1.65. The chief executive of the Cable Communication Association, Bob Frost, was delighted with progress:

This is further evidence that the cable industry is developing at a faster pace and that the quality, range and cost-effectiveness of services are being more widely recognised. [6]

He was particularly pleased with the creation of CWC which, he felt, would become the "new undisputed champion" of the cable industry. With the sort of central marketing of cable services that his organisation was now undertaking (things like TV entertainment, 'phone, home banking, video on demand and potentially, at least, betting), he foresaw a brighter future. Others were not quite so sure. Barbara Donoghue, for example. As MD of the media and telecomms investment unit at Natwest, she thought that the "underlying fundamentals" for cable were "quite strong", but the critical success area was not the 'phone or the interactive services side but the TV entertainment. "People "she declared "are going to be watching quite closely over the next 12 months to see how the TV side of the cable industry develops".[7] And that was where the cable industry's key competitor, satellite television, came in.

So far as the British and German markets were concerned, satellite television really meant BSkyB. It was the biggest, most athletic and aggressive player. So far as Britain alone was concerned, it was, in mid 1997, well on its way to being the dominant market player, if not the monopoly operator. In mid-1996 it was 40 per cent owned by News Corporation. Its relevance to the telecommunications industry lay in the way in which interactive services could develop in future. For example, in the case of home shopping the consumer would see the advertisement on satellite or cable TV and then use the phone (digital cable, analogue fixed wire or mobile) to order the goods.

Three things were at stake for BSkyB. The first was control of the television programmes (films, sport etc). In late 1996 BSkyB was engaged in what commentator Emily Bell called "a vicious war" with UK cable operators like NYNEX over the exclusive rights to screen pay-per-view movies from the media owners.[8] Not only was BSkyB likely to be able to outbid its cable competitors but it had apparently also threatened to take away some of the premium services it currently supplied to them if it didn't get what it wanted. These included premium movie channels and key sports events which cable companies could simply not afford to lose. Indeed, cable TV companies were so dependent for delivery on satellite broadcasters that they had even to accept the timing of programmes set by them. As the Fox studio was owned by News Corporation, it was thought likely that BSkyB would get the exclusive film rights it wanted. But there was a question mark over Paramount and Warner Bros.

The second was the issue of decoders. The decoder was the device that was needed in every business and household to obtain access to the new digital TV system. It represented virtually the gateway to the new technology. And BSkyB was bidding to control it, too.

The chosen instrument in the British market was the £600m company that BSkyB had helped to set up to produce them. Called the Interactive Services Co or ISCO it had been established in early 1997 by BT (the largest shareholder), BSkyB and Midland Bank. However, at a meeting of the British government's House of Commons National Heritage Select Committee on the 12th December 1996, BSkyB's representatives rejected the accusation that the company would deny its rivals access to vital technology at the launch of digital TV. It spoke of the "hysterical, subjective and ill-informed debate" that had been aired on the matter and stated that it did not intend "to create a digital TV monopoly".[9]

In his evidence, Sir Christopher Bland, BBC chairman, said that the BBC had throughout sought to maintain its traditional importance as Britain's main supplier of free-to-air analogue TV and wanted to share in the potential for digital TV, but, faced by all BSkyB's moves, was now having to recognise defeat. Effectively throwing in the towel, Sir Christopher declared stiffly "In the US you would not be allowed to own the digital satellite technology when you are a substantial provider of programmes". Britain's only defence now, he argued, was the regulator, Don Cruikshank, director general of Oftel, the telecommunications regulator. He would have the task of ensuring that all who wished to compete in the satellite TV market as service providers would have access on "fair, reasonable and non-discriminatory terms"[12] when the service was launched in Autumn 1997, assuming, of course, that BSkyB's market launch plan could be realised. Interestingly, satellite TV did not enjoy the same popularity in Germany as cable, whereas the converse was true of Britain.

So far as the USA was concerned, News Corporation, BSkyB's parent, and BT were actively seeking to get the best possible advantage out of the fact that, through MCI's ownership of a 20 per cent stake in News Corp, it would effectively have a ten per cent share of the newly-formed American News Corp subsidiary, ASkyB. The intention was that MCI would help to distribute ASkyB's digital satellite television service to MCI's 20 million-strong customer base and that this would pave the way for a package that also included Internet services.

Clearly, BT were acting quickly on their £12 billion link-up with MCI to exploit the entertainment sector in a way and to an extent impossible, because of the restrictive 1984 legislation, in Britain. The British government reaction to this took the form of a Trade and Industry Select Committee paper issued in mid-March 1997. This recommended that Oftel, the UK industry watchdog should force MCI to sell its stake in News Corporation as a precondition for regulatory approval for any BT-MCI merger. Naturally enough, BT executives wished to avoid this and were confident of the outcome. They should not have been, however, as, in 1998, MCI linked up with Worldcom in an earth-shattering merger, and C&W acquired the whole of MCI's Internet business interests.

BACK TO C&W

Veba accepted C&W's decision to leave Vebacom with regret, according to chairman Ulrich Hartmann. But it would nonetheless retain its ownership stake of 10.4 per cent in C&W, the value of which had gone up by $473m in the previous two years. It then reconstituted its telecom relationship with RWE into a joint venture called "o.tell.o" and declared that it would keep the 22.5 per cent ownership stake that had been C&W's "on ice" in order to sell it to a prospective new partner when the occasion arose. Despite widespread media speculation he did not think that BT would want to buy the stake. On the news that Vebacom was in no rush to sign up a new partner, shares in Veba eased very slightly whereas RWE's fell by three per cent.[13]

One reason why C&W had pulled out of Vebacom seemed to have been the highly costly extra investment that the company might have been obliged to make in the German market. Credit Lyonnais Laing's Steve Scruton indicated that Vebacom could turn out to be a "bottomless pit".[14] There was no doubt that Veba and RWE were prepared to spend heavily to achieve the ambition of getting to the number two spot for mobile telephony in Germany. As Ulrich Hartmann himself pointed out :

For our aggressive market strategy in Germany we need partners who can maintain our tempo. With RWE we have found a team-mate who will work with the same strength towards our demanding goals.[15]

Whatever else, C&W had added £800m cash to their war chest, or their investment capital, depending on how you view it, by the sale of their Veba stake. The question the company faced, of course, was what to do with it in such a fast-globalising $700 billion industry. It was an intriguing problem, partly because of the abundance of choice and partly because, in the view of veteran analyst Raymond Snoddy:

Distinctions between broadcast, telecomms and multimedia industries blur...former competitors are forging new partnerships to exploiit the new technologies...The world's most ambitious media tycoons are trying to create a new world of digital communications.[16]

THE CHINA GAME

Then there was, of course, Asia Pacific. As majority owner of Hong Kong Telecommunications (HKTel) with a 59 per cent stake, C&W were well placed to take advantage of opportunities, even if, in June 1997, the imminent hand-over of Hong Kong by Britain to China was causing disquiet in some circles. HKTel was C&W's biggest profit earner and technological flagship. Indeed, it was said in 1996 to have produced a highly disproportionate 65 per cent of C&W's total profits for the year[17] and to account for 60 per cent of C&W's market worth The company also had, without doubt, the opportunity of privileged access to a Chinese market where less than 6 per cent of homes had a telephone. But the Chinese government would obviously want its slice of the action, in return. Whether this was control of the company or simply a bigger share of the profits was one significant point at issue.

Hong Kong's new Chinese masters seemed, however, favourably disposed to the company and, even if HKTel were to lose the monopoly on international direct dialling business from Hong Kong as was now likely given the WTO Telecomms Pact, it was still powerfully placed. Said Alex Arena, Hong Kong's director-general of telecommunications :

This is such a dynamic part of the world, with the prospect of a rapid expansion of telecomms. If Hong Kong is going to remain relevant into the next century then it has to be a major services centre. And the lifeblood of a services centre is telecommunications.[18]

The projections of likely telecomms demand in China were, by any standards, huge. Firstly, there was the plan by the Communist government in Peking to spend $60 billion (£37.5 billion) before the turn of the millennium in expanding its telecomms network. Secondly, a doubling of the present level of mobile-phone subscribers by this date was highly likely.

In fact, many believed that the abortive attempt by BT to merge with C&W in 1996, had been partly based on BT's need to gain access to such an attractive Asian market. The fact that C&W had pulled the plug on these negotiations had led to the departure of C&W's chairman (Lord Young) and CEO (James Ross), a fall in the share price to less than 400p and the recruitment of Dick Brown.

The first move by the Chinese came on the ninth of May 1997. It involved the purchase by China Telecom (operating arm of the Ministry of Telecommunications) of a 5.5 per cent stake in Hong Kong Telecom for $1.2 billion. This was in addition to the 7.7 per cent stake already owned by China Everbright, a Beijing based conglomerate. The advantage available to C&W was that it would now have the ability to invest in China Telecom (Hong Kong), a subsidiary of China Telecom, set up to develop activities in Hong Kong and China itself. In other words, to give C&W preferential access to the Chinese market. Clearly this was a major coup for Richard Brown.

BACK AT BASE

But some commentators still had doubts about C&W's sense of direction. One was the Wall Street Journal's Janet Guyon. She argued that Cable and Wireless had yet to join what she called "the global club of telecom heavyweights" and questioned what might happen to the crown jewel, HKTel, in this scenario But the big problem for her was C&W's home base, the UK. Not only did BT still command an 87 per cent share of the fixed wire market but the number of operators licensed to handle international traffic had gone up from two to 49 in the last six months of 1996. Against this background, C&W's Mercury subsidiary was, she said, simply "stagnating" in the long distance 'phone market.[19]

The question, of course, was whether C&W was piloting its own way into the future. After all, France Télécom had revealed in March 1997 that it was in talks over a stake in the company, to make it into "the British relay station" of Global One in the words of FT chairman Michel Bon.[20] Moreover, it was known that Deutsche Telekom was investigating the purchase of a slice of CWC. Such purchases were, by this time, becoming much more feasible as the American government was exerting pressure on its British counterpart to drop its protection of C&W, exercised through the so-called golden share and the condition that no one shareholder could own more than 15 per cent. Now, it was said, C&W could face a hostile bid. A 12 per cent rise in 1996-7 company pre-tax profits announced on the 15th May 1997 (to £1.42 billion) only made speculation about the possibility of C&W's joining Global One more intense.

Telewest and NTL, Britain's second and third largest cable companies behind market leader CWC, have confirmed they are in merger talks. Nobody can doubt the potential of the industry in Britain - it can give the consumer access to hundreds of channels for home shopping, banking, Internet and TV entertainment - but it seems that, to date, it has promised more than it has delivered. The industry has a poor negotiating and marketing record and these two merger prospects both have deep debts. It's one thing to cable homes up, it's quite another to get them to buy services. Indeed, because of their slow and capital-intensive build-up in Britain, some players in the cable sector have acquired pariah-like status in the City, Indeed, over the four years of its existence, during which Telewest has built its infrastructure and expanded its sales revenue 36-fold, its share price has nose-dived from 182p to 82p. Credit Lyonnais Laing are forecasting that Telewest losses will last until 2005.

EXHIBIT 2: THE WORST EXECUTED GOOD IDEA IN BRITISH
BUSINESS IN YEARS.
Source based on: Ailing cable firms tune in to mergers,
Kirstie Hamilton, *The Sunday Times*, 10/8/97

The news at the beginning of June 1997 certainly seemed to indicate that Cable and Wireless was truly on track for long term success. On the sixth of June, Richard Brown and Wu Jichuan, Chinese minister of post and telecommunications, made a deal which showed the company to be China's preferred international partner. The company sold a 5.5 per cent stake in HKTel for $1.2 billion in exchange for the opportunity to invest in China Telecom (Hong Kong), a company jointly by the Chinese and C&W on a non-exclusive basis.

The notion that BT had now embarked for certain on a winning global strategy was, however, somewhat dented by the portentous announcement by Sir Peter Bonfield, BT's chief executive, that the whole of BT's relationship with MCI, including the purchase contract, would be subject to re-examination. This news, coming on 31st July 1997, was based on the fact that MCI's earnings in the USA for the previous year had been so unexpectedly low that there had been widespread questioning of the Concert deal in the City and on Wall Street. The reason for the low earnings was now evident; the very heavy cost to a long distance operator of breaking into the local phone market in the USA. Leading BT investors, such as Prudential, Standard Life and PDFM, were said to regard even a cut of 15 per cent in the £12.3 billion price that BT offered to pay for MCI was inadequate to offset the extra risk that BT was now running in this relationship.[21] As we have seen, the deal actually came to naught with the merger between MCI and Worldcom in 1998.

BOMBSHELL

C&W, like all the other giant players in the telecommunications field, were thus jockeying for position in an increasingly frenetic market-place. As the pace of technology mounted, so did the thrust towards T.M.T. (technology, media and telecommunications) and M&A (mergers and alliances), the *megamergers* between America on Line (AOL) and Time Warner and between Time Warner Music and EMI taking place in January 2000. So far as growth opportunities were concerned, it was a question, firstly, of betting on which countries, which technologies (e.g., cable, satellite, fixed wire, mobile telephony) and which market sectors (entertainment, Internet services) would prosper most and, secondly, which allies promised the best relationships. Then there was the need to consider the issue of whether software or hardware was to be preferred, as well as the end-of-the-1990s stock-market phenomenon of the massive growth in the value of *any* Internet-related stock. Critical also for any individual player was the war-chest factor – having access to the development funds that were needed for the *next* exciting venture.

In this, C&W's Dick Brown was seen as a world class mover and shaker. But, in October 1998, after only 27 months in the job, he quit. According to commentator Alan Kane, he had been an *indefatigable* chief executive.[22] Under his leadership, C&W had shaken off its heritage as an *unloved and disparate telecomms holding company,*[23] and transformed itself into an impressive operator with global reach. It had amply met the dictates of Dick Brown's business credo, the need to reposition the company in growth sectors, to control relationships and meet objectives. This meant, in his words, p*erformance, performance, performance.*[24] Hence, the departure of a leader who was widely perceived as having created in C&W *a good European management story* [25] was much lamented.

The question was whether his strategic thrust would continue. He had indeed accomplished much, having
- masterminded 21 deals, valued at over $20 billion, and sold off over $1 billion of assets in relationships where the company lacked influence
- achieved the complex merger of Mercury with three US cable television groups to create the British market leader in cable
- re-focussed C&W as an inter-continental communications giant and
- bought growth opportunity in the Chinese mainland.

But shareholders marked C&W shares down as they perceived that no obvious successor had been lined up and they stayed anxious until February 1999 when Graham Wallace, the architect of the CWC merger, was give the job. He at once gave an intimation of the direction he would take the company in: the accent would be on the booming data and Internet markets. Here, as we have noted, C&W had acquired the operations of MCI in 1998. Certainly, in the words of analyst James Dodd

> *Cable & Wireless is a seemingly fabulous collection of telecomms assets but it is still an enigma. The question is..how to make sense of that collection of assets. Graham Wallace faces three or four big decisions, such as what to do with One-to-One (a difficult 50-50 joint mobile phone venture in the UK with MediaOne, the US cable company), China and the possibility of C&W's changing the CWC set-up. The challenge will be getting the big decisions right.* [26]

FINIS

Graham Wallace set an equally fast pace to that of his predecessor. Within a month, he had made a bid to increase the C&W stake in International Digital Communications, the second largest Japanese international phone operator, from 17.7 per cent to 66 per cent. The bid was eventually, after an acrimonious battle in Japan with other shareholders, won in June 1999.

Then it was made known that, as a result of the giant merger between cable TV company Comcast (eleven per cent owned by Microsoft) and MediaOne announced in March 1999, C&W would either partially sell off or float its interests in One-to-One, the British mobile operator. This effectively took place in June, with the resultant finance available for expansion of its data and Internet services activities. Perhaps the company needed to move with this speed since, also in March, Veba sold off its holding in C&W, and the stockmarket was asking quite vociferously what the Wallace focus would be. As an offset, the June sale of C&W's stake in Bouygues, the third biggest mobile operator in France, made a $525m profit that was very welcome.

News that there was the strong possibility of a merger between C&W and Telewest, Britain's two largest cable television companies, broke in April. This would have created a group which would have rivalled BT in the telephony market and have access to 2.6m customers. Certainly, the ultimate configuration was not known but there were indications that what C&W was principally interested in was the business telephony side of the operation.

In fact, what transpired was a bidding contest for CWC. In this, the UK's third cable television company, NTL with the backing of Microsoft (with a 15 per cent stakeholding) and France Telecom, outbid Telewest to win control in July. Effectively, this meant the start of a sell-off of C&W's company's residential cable TV interests.

But the stockmarket was still not totally convinced that, in the words of analyst Doug Morrison, that after *years of being a ragbag, C&W has direction* (27) and the shares languished. Investors were further displeased with the statement of operating results given by the company on the tenth of November 1999. This warned of a drop in profits for the full year 1999-2000. It was met with a further drop in C&W's share value, worrisome in view of the share performance over the previous 12 months, a fall from 994p to 665p. What could now be done to transform the shares from a *sell* to a *buy?*

As if by magic, the value of C&W shares soared in December 1999 to over 1050p. Why? What seemed to have attracted the investors was said to be the groups' declared new strategy and the novelty value of C&W shares to US first-time buyers. What was the new strategy? It was one of C&W's *re-inventing itself as a high-quality global platform for the booming market in business data and Internet Protocol-based services (IP), these being the only infrastructure that can handle online services, from web-hosting to internet service provision.*[28]

One basis for the new strategy was a combination of ownership of MCI's Internet business and a $500m alliance between C&W and Compaq, the world's largest PC maker, to sell Internet services to smaller businesses around the world. This accord was struck in November 1999. The strategy was also based on C&W' announcement that it was to invest no less £6 billion in business data and IP services in the first two years of the new millennium. The £4 billion that the company had netted from its eventual sale of half of One-to-One to Deutsche Telecom would come in handy. So also the planned disposal of the company's remaining stake in Hong Kong Telecom, scheduled for 2000. As analyst Mary Fagan indicated, these amounted to *steps in the stripping-down of the C&W empire...on the way to its becoming a purer IP services company serving the corporate market.*[28]

A secure basis for the strategy was the sale of C&W's Hong Kong Telecom unit to Richard Li's Pacific Century Cyberworks Ltd for $38.1 billion in March 2000. The move brought a further rise in C&W's share value, up a total of 74 per cent in the year to date. analyst Gautam Naik's view on all these developments was, however, intriguing.

At a time when many European corporate brands are trying to hire US-style CEO's with a knack for wheeling and dealing, Mr Wallace's example shows that a quiet, understated style can work just as well. Starting with the premise that C&W is too small to survive in a world of telecom titans, Mr Wallace appears to have gotten it ready for sale.[29]

* * * * * * * * * * * * * ** * * * *

NOTES AND REFERENCES

1   C&W fail to reach deal, Alan Cane and Fred Studemann, *The Financial Times*, 5/2/97

2   Cable telephony, Alan Cane, *The Financial Times*, 11/12/96

3   World telecomms pact set to slash cost of calls, Frances Williams and Alan Cane, *The Financial Times*, 17/2/97

4   As 3

5   C&W makes come-back but much remains to be done, Janet Guyon, *The Wall Street Journal Europe*, 17-18/1/97

6   Unfilled Potential, Raymond Snoddy, *The Financial Times*, 11/12/96

7   As 6

8   Murdoch fights cable for pay-per-view films, Emily Bell, *The Observer*, 17/11/96

9   BSkyB promises its rivals access to digital TV, Alexandra Frean, *The Times*, 13/12/96

10 German deal puts Murdoch in the picture, Frederick Studemann, *The European*, 14-20/3/97

11 As 9

12 BBC concedes that Murdoch will control digital TV, Andrew Culf, *The Times*, 29/11/96

13 Veba sanguine about partner, Andrew Fisher, *The Financial Times*, 20/2/97

14 C&W sells its stake in Vebacom for £800m, Oliver August, *The Times*, 8/2/97

15 As 14

16 Aim for alliances for a digital future, Raymond Snoddy, *The Financial Times*, 11/12/96

17 As 5

18 Looking East for a telecomms accord, John Ridding, *The Financial Times*, 8/11/96

19 As 5

20 Pressure mounts for BT to call off merger, Christine Buckley, *The Times*, 11/8/97

21 As 20

22 The man who switched on C&W, Alan Cane, *The Financial Times*, 3-4/10/98

23 C&W loses chief executive to EDS, IHT, 12-13/12/98

24 As 22

25 As 22

26 Corporate profile, Raymond Snoddy, *The Times*, 1/3/99

27 Take a Global View of C&W, Doug Morrison, *The Sunday Telegraph*, 3/10/99

28 C&W speeds up sale of Hong Kong holding, Mary Fagan, *The Sunday Telegraph*, 12/12/99

29 C&W quiets its critics, Gautam Naik, *The Wall Street Journal, Europe*, 3-4/3/2000

EMU

Abstract:

EMU deals with the steps being taken by Germany and France in 1997 to prepare themselves to meet the criteria laid down for European Monetary Union. Investigation of their tactics during this formative EMU period allows us to appreciate the logic of the Single Currency and the nature of key drivers behind it, as they appeared at the time.

Interestingly, the relative strength of the US economy caused a major appreciation of the dollar over the period to 2000. The performance of the UK economy and its business culture affinity with the US caused Britain's currency to rise in value also. On May 4th 2000 the euro was worth a mere 58p.

Question:

Does the case evidence suggest that EMU will fly?
Why are the British so hesitant about the EMU opportunity?

Case Timing: 1995-7

A TWO-SPEED EUROPE

A single currency was meant to be the jewel in the crown of European integration. Instead it is proving to be the spikiest problem in a crown of thorns.[1]

Despite its purple prose, this statement rang true in September 1995 as European Union (EU) leaders met to discuss the next move in preparing for the 1996 Intergovernmental Conference. This would, it was supposed, pave the way for the smooth implementation of European economic and monetary union or EMU. It had previously been a matter of unanimity at the summit which set the seal on the Maastricht Treaty, except, of course, for the British and Danish who had negotiated an opt-out from this element of the treaty. But EMU was now a topic of political disagreement among those chiefly concerned. In Britain, public discussion focused not only on the timetable for monetary union and other mechanical features, such as the name for the new pan-European currency, but on the very principle.

- *The constitution combines a post-war preference for co-operation over confrontation to make wage-setting a process almost guaranteed to produce a steady rise in labour costs.*
- *Because of the concentration of ownership of shares in the hands of conservative banks, and the relatively minor role of open-market share trading, hostile take-overs are unheard of. Bloated corprocrats are secure in their jobs; profits are not maximised.*
- *Pretending an East German mark was equal in value to a West German mark has made a large segment of German industry massively uncompetitive.*
- *German firms rely on collateral-based borrowing rather than equity capital. This makes it difficult for companies based on intellectual property to obtain financing, stifling the growth of high-technology industries. Germany had only 11 new stock issues in 1994.*
- *Rigid rules govern everything from apprenticeship training to the hours when bread may be baked. These rules are unlikely to be changed significantly.*

TABLE 1: GERMANY TODAY
Source: Irwin Stelzer, 'Germany to cost us dear', *The Sunday Times*, 1/10/95

There was also some disarray in France over the issue. This sort of thing would have been unthinkable only two years before when Jacques Delors and François Mitterrand were presidents of the European Commission and France, respectively. Now the players had been changed – the rightwing Jacques Chirac was the French president – and a different political tune was being played in Paris. Paradoxically, in spite of this, France claimed, as before, that it was still heavily in favour of EMU and was proving it by maintaining its *franc fort* policy, i.e. gearing the franc rigidly to the value of the Deutschmark. Germany, too, despite its difficulties was highly supportive. Britain had even softened its line slightly to admit of the more definite possibility of EMU and was joining in the technical preparations for it.

The tense public debate centred not so much on the proclaimed political intention of France, Germany and Britain but on the reality of their domestic political situations and the implications of proceeding with the EMU plan for their economies. Aspects of Germany's position are illustrated in Table 1 on page 494.

Germany, and chancellor Kohl in particular, would be facing a general election in 1998 at the height of the final preparations for the introduction of EMU. This could result in the replacement of the German mark, a widely-revered symbol of the economic power and financial rectitude of the nation, and a more uncertain future for the country. This would be so even though the European Monetary Institute running European monetary policy was under tight German influence and located in Frankfurt. The disinflationary conditions in the Maastricht treaty (see Table 2 on page 497) which countries had to meet to qualify for EMU were, in any event, inspired by the way in which the Bundesbank had traditionally controlled German monetary policy.

The other key problem for the German government was that few EU members were looking as if they would achieve these rigid conditions in time for the Maastricht timetable to work. What might happen if only a few leading members, not including Italy and Belgium, went ahead and others could not? Even worse, perhaps, was what might occur if those outside EMU were free to practise competitive devaluations, such as the one which had contributed so well to Britain's economic recovery after the 1989-92 recession, whilst those inside were locked into a high value EMU currency whose value was maintained by strict monetary policy criteria. These were key matters of contention.

In this situation the German Government's position in late 1995 was an interesting one. Chancellor Kohl called for the strict maintenance of the strict Maastricht criteria. His economics minister Theo Waigel commented publicly on the fact that two of the most ardent supporters of EMU, Italy and Belgium, would not qualify at the time for membership. Their economies were simply too weak for them to hit the Maastricht targets.

Monetary policy refers to situations where:

1. *Governments or central banks use interest rates to either stimulate or rein back economic activity. Low rates encourage borrowing and spending and, hence economic growth. The danger is that inflation rises.*
2. *Governments increase their spending typically in a recession to try to cut the rise in unemployment and borrow extra to do so since tax revenue in a recession is low.*
3. *In inflationary times governments seek to curb rising prices. Disinflation means cutting government spending and raising interest rates. The cumulative effect of this is to cut the money supply and, hence, the country's economic activity drops as its spending capability falls. Inevitably, economic activity and employment will fall, unless the resulting drop in the country's currency value raises exports. How? By reducing the prices charged for goods that are shipped abroad, foreign sales will increase.*

EXHIBIT 1: ELEMENTARY ECONOMICS

France's economy in the mid-1990s, like Germany's, was being clearly held back by the rising value of its currency. The French franc, as a member of the fixed parity Exchange Rate Mechanism (ERM), was tied in with the German mark. This was itself strengthening relative to the US dollar and causing French as well as German industrialists substantial worries about the future of their export earnings. The French social security fabric was like Germany's, heavily welfarist and dependent on high social security contributions from employees and companies in order to disburse large benefits to claimants. Therefore, the cost pressures were not dissimilar. In late 1995 France was thus in a difficult and tense position with a new president, elected to reduce France's 12.3 per cent unemployment level, (Britain's was 8.5 per cent), who was faced with a double whammy: growing uncompetitiveness and a still-rising public expenditure deficit. This, as Table 2 on page 497 shows, also did not meet strict Maastricht rules.

Britain had been able to profit hugely from the devaluation of the £ sterling that took place when it quit the ERM in September 1992 by increasing its export sales. In late 1995, however, it still found itself outside the Maastricht budget deficit target.

EU member's performance (%) in September 1995	Two Key Maastricht criteria for EMU membership are (i) Budget deficit as % of GDP< 3% (ii) Gross public debt as % of GDP not to exceed a target of 60%	
	Budget Deficit (%)	**Debt (%)**
Germany	2.3	58
France	5.0	51.2
Britain	4.2	54.3
Belgium	4.3	134.5
Italy	7.8	124.9

TABLE 2: MEETING MAASTRICHT CONVERGENCE CRITERIA
(SEPTEMBER 1995)

Furthermore, the country had just lived through a re-election for the Conservative party leadership. This unsettling event had been brought about by a challenge on prime minister from John Redwood, a fearsome opponent of Britain's membership of anything but the most neo-liberal of European Free Trade Areas. He had been supported by one third of the MPs in the Conservative party. This is not to suggest that prime minister John Major himself welcomed the prospect of EMU, although his chancellor, Kenneth Clarke did seem to discuss the features of it with considerable enthusiasm at the ministerial summit in Spain in September 1995.

Would EMU go ahead? Would the French, fighting to raise employment and output, actually seek to disinflate the economy to meet the EMU target? Would Britain rejoin the fixed parity Exchange Rate Mechanism as a precursor to joining EMU and turn its back on the value of competitive devaluation? Would Germany risk going ahead with EMU in comparative isolation? As of late September 1995, these were significant issues. One cynical view expressed by leading political analyst Thomas Kielinger was that Germany was now insisting on the letter of the Maastricht law to ensure that EMU did *not* go ahead as timetabled, i.e., to ensure that a substantial number of EU members could not be considered as fulfilling the criteria.

EMU: ROUND TWO

The Financial Times reckoned that 1997 would turn out to be the "crunch year" for EMU. It made this prediction in its New Year editorial on the second of January and cited the two factors that would help propel EMU to such prominence. Not only, it stated, would there be a general election in Britain which could alter the country's approach to both the Social Chapter and possibly affect the chances for EMU itself, but 1997 was the year in which it was planned that the members of the single currency zone would be pre-selected on the basis of their performances against the Maastricht criteria. In fact, by mid-year, the prediction was well on its way to fulfilment, but for reasons other than the ones cited.

The year in question began with continued expression of anxieties about the concept and practicalities of EMU. As always it was the British who were the leading sceptics. Peter Kellner of *The Observer* wrote that, in his view, the European Union was not "an optimal currency area" since economies "at the edge of the Eurozone" (e.g., Greece) which were losing competitiveness (because of EMU) would not be able either to devalue their currency nor reduce their interest rates to get themselves out of difficulty.[2] The popularity of governments so caught up would plummet and, if unemployment rose as a result, rioting might occur. In such a context, help from the Euro-centre would have to be made available and that would mean fiscal transfers i.e., aid packages paid out of the tax revenues collected for the European Union budget. For this, Kellner said, a much more strongly built democratic mandate was needed. In fact, he asserted that Europe required a public with a shared sense of identity and loyalty, *a demos*, which did not now exist.

The Times analyst Anatole Kaletsky took this argument one stage further by asserting that "the creation of a common currency to make war impossible in Europe will, ironically, break up the Common Market and precipitate an economic war".[3] It would do this, he continued, by replacing the normal swings in a country's un-pegged exchange rate, which allowed the country to adjust its economy to change, with highly unmanageable swings in wages and employment.

No lesser EMU observer than Wilhelm Nölling, ex-director of the Bundesbank, bewailed what he called "the present nightmare of a rush towards EMU".[4] He cited three facts in support of his arguments. First, German unemployment was at a post-Hitler high (4.66m), in part the consequence of a budget squeeze that had already lasted three years. Second, a poll published in *Der Spiegel* magazine on the 24th February showed that 77 per cent of Germans wanted EMU postponed. The third fact was the most telling of all. Was it not paradoxical, he argued, that since the signing of the Maastricht Treaty in 1991 the government debt of EU countries had gone up from 56 per cent of GDP to 74 per cent and that EU unemployment had risen from 14m to 18m?

Supporting the development of a common EU foreign and security policy
Possible movement towards a European defence policy by merging the EU and the Western European Union
Close EU cooperation on justice and home affairs
Movement towards common policies on immigration and asylum
Flexibility for some countries to move at faster integration speeds than others.

TABLE 3: SOME PROPOSED HEADS OF DISCUSSION AT THE
AMSTERDAM SUMMIT IN MID-JUNE 1997

Would unemployment rise still further in the EU if a strong Euro were created? Fred Bergsten, director of the US Institute for International Economic thought so. His argument was short but far from sweet. The European Central Bank would wish to exert its authority to make the Euro credible; its monetary discipline measures would force EU members, in the face of tight interest rates, to think of adopting loose fiscal policies to stimulate their economies; this, both *de jure* and *de facto*, would not be possible and the currency would strengthen and become the world's key second currency. The conclusion? "If a company operates within an EMU zone it will lose business" and, hence, it should logically "operate outside and sell into the EMU zone."[5]

By the end of February 1997 the chorus of criticism was beginning to annoy EMU's chief protagonists. Wim Kok, the Dutch prime minister with the responsibility of creating agreement at the Amsterdam summit in June on the new European Treaty, played down any thoughts that there would be a delay in the EMU process. So did Yves-Thibault de Silguy, the Monetary Commissioner. In his view there would be neither fiscal transfers nor "fudging" and the Europlan was certain to start exactly on time. The word "fudging" was a reference to the possibility that, somehow, some governments who were unable to meet the Maastricht criteria honestly might resort to creative bookkeeping on their national accounts. German foreign minister Klaus Kinkel labelled EMU critics as "irresponsible" and said that their commentaries amounted to "unaffordable parochialisation" of the issues involved.[6]

But there was no doubt that the shadow of EMU was lengthening. In France, as well as Germany, unemployment was at an all-time post-war high, 12.7 per cent in the first week of January in France, and the French 1996 growth rate of two per cent had been below that predicted by president Chirac at the start of the year and widely spoken of as inadequate. At this rate of GDP growth, France's attempt to maintain the franc fort within the Exchange Rate Mechanism (as it was pledged to do) required almost certainly a higher level of fiscal tightness than was reasonable in the light of the unemployment data. This, and the over-valued franc, was seen by most French businessmen as the reason for the low growth in the first place. And, of course, low growth meant low tax receipts and either further reductions in public spending or an inability to meet the Maastricht criterion on PSBR. It was a dangerously circular problem.

It would eliminate almost entirely the possibility of war in Europe in the next century, the chief anxiety of German chancellor Kohl
It would eliminate foreign exchange speculation against the franc. At the G7 summit in Halifax in 1996, French president Chirac called speculation "the AIDS disease of our economies"
It would promote economic growth in Europe by eliminating transaction costs
It would politically transform Europe from a collection of individual countries into an economic and political super-power which was part of a new G3 organisation and which rivalled the USA.

TABLE 4: FOUR POWERFUL REASONS FOR BACKING EMU

Conversely, on the plus side, France enjoyed the world's number three ranking for its current account balance of trade surplus, considerably boosted, of course, by the so-called "green oil" contribution or trade surplus on agriculture. Also, counterbalancing the strong franc, French prime interest rates at the start of the year were 3.15 per cent as opposed to Britain's six per cent.

In fact, the French government sorely needed such positive indicators as these to offset the bad publicity it received when it capitulated, admittedly after heavy strike action, to the combined forces of France's six transport unions, led by the CGT and CFDT, in late 1996 and early 1997. By applying severe pressure, they had managed to secure retirement age at 55 for France's civil service train drivers and for its private sector truck drivers.

Somewhat ironically, Britain's problem was a rise in the value of sterling. This was being caused by the economic difficulties of continental neighbours and by the improvement in Britain's performance, alike. In the 1990s a recession had brought a growth in unemployment, productivity had risen in firms as a result of substantial voluntary (and not a little involuntary) redundancy and foreign direct investment flows had been considerable. The net result had been a combination of solid economic growth and a lack of wage-push inflationary pressures. So sterling had risen in value.

Rising prices would come, said political commentator Will Hutton. Up to now they had been held back by negative equity in the housing market and the fear of job loss but, as the labour market tightened in the late 1990s, the bankers would again suffer from "the old Pavlovian reactions and inevitably relax credit."[7] By far and away the chief reason for Britain's comparatively good showing, however, had been the 20 per cent devaluation of sterling that had taken place when the country quit the ERM in 1992. The relevance of this to the EMU debate was amply illustrated by simulations run on the National Institute and Treasury models of the UK economy. Indications were that a five per cent rise in sterling's average value typically resulted, after a one year lag, in a 0.5 per cent fall in GDP and a two percentage points fall in prices.

If anything could cheer the spirits of beleaguered EMU supporters in continental Europe, it was a Labour victory in the British general election that took place in early 1997. The British electorate duly obliged and returned a New Labour with an unassailable majority. The main cause of tacit German and French government pleasure was obviously the ending of the period of much-derided Thatcher-Major negativism over all aspects of EU development except for the Single Market. EMU had evidently been the crown of thorns.

Whilst the Conservative government's posture had been studiously non-commital, it had opened itself up to attacks from virtually all quarters. That its approach to EMU was the result of the internal political dynamics of British politics as much as of anxiety about potential EMU difficulties did not matter. The British government had been perceived by EMU adherents in continental Europe as aggressively negative. And now, a new, and welcome, hand was on the tiller, that of Britain's first Socialist prime minister in 18 years, Tony Blair. His government was not expected to follow its predecessor's strategy.

The European Commission and the French and German governments were, therefore, delighted with one of the first policy moves made by Gordon Brown, the new government's chancellor of the exchequer. It was to break some of the political linkages between the Bank of England and the government, which made the former's set-up different from the Franco-German independent state bank model. Countries that wanted to belong to EMU had, of course, to accept that central banks, and not governments, would set interest rates prior to the full-scale establishment of the European Central Bank. Now, in May 1997, the British government had taken this step. Naturally enough, another EMU club condition was prior membership of the ERM, but nothing was said on this score at the time.

ROUND THREE

If the discord created among EMU members over EMU so far can be likened to distant thunder, what happened in mid-1997 was, in fact, the arrival of a major whirlwind. The countries in its very eye were France and Germany and the violent tempest was caused by revelations that, according to the best economic projections that could be made at the time, neither seemed to be sure of qualifying for EMU. For these two countries not to qualify, after all that had been said and done, would have been regarded by both governments as an intolerable catastrophe.

France took the first step to ensure it would make the EMU club. In April the right-wing French president, Jacques Chirac, announced a dissolution of parliament in order to seek more popular support for the government. The intention was that the right-wing government under prime minister Alain Juppé would seek and obtain a larger popular mandate for the changes that France needed to push through to meet the Maastricht criteria and, as Table 4, page 500, suggests, there was still a long way to go. It was, in fact, a big mistake.

In the French government view, the election began well. Its Maastricht-oriented plan to take over the pension fund liabilities of France Télécom (FT), in exchange for cash held in FT's balance sheet, had been accepted by the European Commission. As the sum in question was equivalent to 0.5 per cent of France's GDP, it was a major contributor to meeting the single currency criteria. The manifesto issued by the Socialists, under the leadership of Lionel Jospin, proclaimed anti-unemployment goals which were considered as archaic (the creation of 700,000 new jobs, half in the public sector) and uneconomic (the reduction in the working week from 39 to 35 hours) as they were laudable. The government, at this rate, would certainly get its new mandate.

Country	Effective Convergence Criteria					
	Budget Deficit as % of GDP			Debt as % of GDP		
	1996	**1997**	**1998**	**1996**	**1997**	**1998**
Germany	3.8	3.0	3.0	60.4	62.0	62.5
France	4.1	3.1	2.9	56.0	58.0	58.5
Italy	6.8	3.1	2.9	124.8	124.3	121.5
UK	4.1	2.9	1.9	54.8	54.2	52.9

TABLE 5: MEETING MAASTRICHT CONVERGENCE CRITERIA
(FORECASTS MADE IN APRIL 1997 FOR 1997 AND 1998)
Source: Deutsche Morgan Grenfell

So it came as a great shock to Alain Juppé's government to find that, after the first round of the elections, it was trailing very badly. In fact, it was not the appeal (or lack of it, depending where you stood) of the Socialists that seemed to be at stake, so much as the fact that the Chirac administration had simply not lived up to the promises that had been made during the previous presidential and the government elections.

The solution adopted by president Chirac to cope with the adverse situation after the first round was to promise that the term of office of prime minister Juppé would end immediately after the second round of elections, whatever happened. This unorthodox move was based on the fact that the prime minister's personal popularity ranking in the polls was rock bottom. But it did not inspire confidence in the voters and, in the event, president Chirac need not have bothered since the Socialists were swept to victory. An epitaph for the outgoing government is given in Exhibit 2, below.

What was significant for the EMU process was, of course, the extent to which the new French government might follow the same approach as the former one. It was problematic since the Socialists had inherited a budget deficit which, without any further spending cuts or tax increases, would be likely to be in the region of 3.5 per cent of GDP. France itself had fallen back to the position of number 23 in the World Economic Forum's global competitiveness league table. The country's tax burden had risen from 43.2 per cent of GDP to 45.7 per cent over the period 1992-6 and, under the Juppé government, the inexorable rise in unemployment had continued. Whereas, in 1988 under the Rocard government, it had stood at 2.5m, it was now, according to ANPE figures, 3.5m.

> *President Chirac, who made absurd promises to cut dole queues, reduce taxes and increase public spending in his 1995 election campaign, has now paid the inevitable price for failing to deliver on any of them. He faces the daunting prospect of having to co-habit with a Socialist prime minister for the rest of his presidency, weakened and devalued.*[8]

EXHIBIT 2: A HARSH JUDGEMENT

The first critical question the new premier had to address in this context was the extent to which the new government could work effectively with the old president. There would be no difficulties, said Lionel Jospin, provided that the president, with all the foreign policy authority granted to him under the French constitution, would not turn into an *ultra-maastrichtien*. The second issue revolved around the extent to which the economic growth pact, which had been the central plank in the Socialists' manifesto, chimed with the stability pact which the French and German governments had adopted at the EU summit in Dublin. This latter aimed at ensuring that, once a country was accepted as a candidate for the single currency, exactly the same criteria which had been used for it to gain entry (e.g., three per cent PSBR) would be applied to it afterwards, this to ensure rectitude in the management of its public finances. Lionel Jospin's conclusion was intriguing:

It is true that the stability pact adds conditions which were not in the Maastricht Treaty...It is Super-Maastricht and it is an absurd concession that the French government made to Germany or certain German groups. So I don't feel myself bound by it. There are more than three million people out of work in France and no inflation.... So let's not proceed with economic policies made for the past.[9]

The third issue was that of the potential first-wave membership of EMU. Should Italy and Spain be allowed in? Yes, said the prime minister, pronouncing himself delighted with the convergence on Socialist positions that he thought was beginning to emerge in the EU, around the need for a job-promoting growth pact, and what he called "un gouvernement économique."[10] This last reference reflected a demand put forward by the previous government for a political mechanism which would exercise some degree of control over the independence of the European Central Bank (ECB), obviously a contradiction in terms and clearly at variance with a central feature of the Maastricht Treaty.

"It is unclear what the government is doing. If it is not overt trickery, then why bother at all, because it will have only a limited impact on the deficit and has been a public relations disaster." "The gold plan makes it more likely that monetary union will be delayed. The Germans can't even meet the criteria they insisted on at Maastricht. France got away with fiddling its figures, but this is even worse. People do silly things when they try to meet silly criteria"

EXHIBIT 3: WHY BOTHER?
Sources: Mark shaken as gold row adds to EMU worries, Alasdair Murray, *The Times*, 30/6/97 quoting Julian Callow, Dresdner Kleinwort Benson. Germans fall out over gold revaluation, Oliver August, *The Times*, 29/5/97 quoting Chris Allsop, editor of *The Oxford Review of Economic Policy.*

Why Maastricht had been heavily preoccupied with the ECB's status was because of the German experience of the success of its independent Bundesbank in controlling inflation and maintaining the value of the German mark. Given

Germany's monetary history in the twentieth century, it is not surprising that Germans should insist that, if they were to exchange their beloved marks for euros, exactly the same standards would be applied by the ECB to guarantee the stability and worth of the euro. Nor should it surprise that this custodianship role should be enshrined within the constitution under the 1957 Bundesbank Act.

Imagine the furore created, therefore, when Germany's finance minister, Theo Waigel, announced that Germany planned to revalue the Bundesbank's gold reserves and transfer the surplus to the current year's public accounts. The pupose was, of course, to reduce the level of public debt and, hence, albeit indirectly, improve Germany's chances of meeting the Maastricht criteria. Instantly, the German government was accused on all sides of financial trickery and backtracking on the *sound money-stable euro* position that Chancellor Kohl himself had so persistently and forcefully advocated since 1991. Reiner Flassbach of the Berlin Institute for Economic Research put it in a nutshell when he said "Theo Waigel has made himself out to be the high priest of correctness. Now the truth is out. He is preaching water and drinking wine."[11] In an editorial entitled "The Curse of Maastricht" *The Times* called it "chicanery."[12] A former Italian foreign minister, Antonio Martino, was even more scathing. Not only did the German action indicate the need for delay in implementing EMU, if such Italian-type "book-keeping tricks" were to be avoided, that is. Even worse, he declared:

Virtue isn't contagious. On the contrary. We aren't becoming Germans. It's the Germans who are becoming Italian.[13]

The German government would have none of this. The plan was to revalue the reserves of nearly 3000 tonnes from $95 an ounce (the price when purchased) to the current market price of $345 and thus boost the exchequer by up to Dm 40 billion. It was a "cautious" plan which would completely "protect the financial solidity of the Bundesbank". Added to which, it was only what Britain itself had done in 1979.[14] Admittedly, a change in the law would be required, but the Bundesbank's independence would not be diminished. Furthermore, it was clear that, if there were no revaluation of the reserves, there would be a $10.6 b (Dm18 b) gap in the 1997 budget which could only be plugged by taxes. As in France, the problem was poor economic performance which had placed pressure on tax revenues and, the worse the performance, the higher the budget overrun.

The Bundesbank thought differently from the government. Firstly, its central council declared that the plan was indeed "an attack on the Bundesbank's independence" and that it ran counter to the planned rules of the future ECB. A gold revaluation would detract substantially from "the credibility and stability" of the euro, itself, and moreover it went completely go against the government's claim that Germany should establish EMU credibly and sustainably on solid foundations.

Many agreed with *The Wall Street Journal* when it asked "Whatever was Kohl thinking?" [15]

ROUND FOUR

The Bundesbank did not hesitate to take action on what a leading council member, Otmar Issing, called a "more creative" move than than undertaken by other governments,[16] and what many media commentators called the "Rhinegold affair,"a highly literary reference to an episode in Wagner's opera Götterdammerung. It stonewalled to the point where it was clear that there would be a showdown with the government if it did not budge. This was expected to take place on the 5th June, the day on which the legislation was to be introduced, and when Bundesbank president, Hans Tietmayer, was scheduled to give his views on the plan to the Bundestag's finance committee.

It was not the first time under the Kohl administration that there had been war between the Bundesbank and the Government. The last outbreak had been in 1990 when the chancellor had ignored the reservations of the-then Bundesbank governor, Karl Otto Pohl, about the wisdom of the government's monetary strategy for East Germany. According to Pohl, the terms for converting the weak Ostmark into the strong Deutschmark were over-generous. Kohl won, Pohl lost and resigned.

Now, the battlefield was different and the climate had changed. Now there was comment in Germany's leading tabloid, *Bild*, that the spat was "a classic conflict between the independent minded protectors of the currency and the politicians who want to fill the empty state coffers."[17] Now there was criticism that Germany had descended to the level of the "fiscally-lax Italians"[18] and that, far from ending up with a mature Parmesan type of common currency, the version it would get would be a camembert if not a dolcelatte.(see Exhibit 4). As such the new euro would be inflation-prone and, thus, the very antithesis of the mark.

Mature Parmesan	Hard to get into, pungent and classic, but not to everyone's taste.
Dolcelatte	Tasty and exciting but with a pronounced tendency to spread uncontrollably after opening.

EXHIBIT 4: TWO CLASSIC TYPES OF EURO CHEESE
Note: Criteria for the Euro involve a hardness/softness preference and a view on whether club membership should be narrow or wide.

In early June there were rumours that Hans Tietmayer was about to resign over the issue. After all, Theo Waigel had maintained ever since the initial announcement that the plan would go through, in spite of all the market turbulence which caused investors to move out of marks and francs into perceived "safe haven currencies" such as the pound, the dollar and the Swiss franc, (see Exhibit 4 on page 506) and all the political flak. In the event, however, such a move was unnecessary, even if contemplated, since, on the third of June, the German government abruptly dropped its gold plan. The reason given was the level of opposition from the Christian Social Union party (CSU). As strategic partners in chancellor Kohl's CDU-CSU-Free Democrat coalition government they could not be ignored.

And so it was that on the eleventh of June the parliamentary censure motion put down against Theo Waigel for his mishandling of the gold plan was defeated. The Kohl government, with its small ten-seat majority, had at least retrieved the situation, but not without major loss of face. "A herd of dancing elephants in a porcelain shop" said Joschka Fischer, the Green party leader "would have caused less damage than you and your government."[19] The consequence was that the Kohl government now planned to revalue Germany's dollar reserves. This did not involve any potential conflict with the Bundesbank.

But, in the EMU context, the problems loomed just as large, if not larger. Balancing the German budget meant cutting spending or raising taxes. The first would be blocked in the Bundesrat by the Social Democrats who enjoyed a large majority. The second would almost certainly mean the defection from the Kohl government of the Free Democrats. The Kohl government seemed to have reached an impasse on this issue. But it still had the possibility of revaluing its dollar reserves.

The French, too, were restless. The spokesman for the new government, François Hollande, underlined the support of the new government for EMU. He also indicated that France needed to be sure that "sanctions will not be applied if, under the stability pact, the main objectives (i.e. of economic restraint) will not be reached. We want to have assurances that the stability pact does not mean more austerity for France."[20]

At the time, at least one Briton, so it seemed, had had quite enough of EMU. Martin Taylor, chief executive of Barclays Bank stated categorically that he now required currency speculators, of whom London had no shortage, to "blow apart" any premature move to set up a common currency. His reasoning was based on the "fantasy agenda" of the French left and "increasing distrust" of EMU in Germany. He concluded a speech to fellow European bankers in St. Gallen in Switzerland by stating that "a confident, strong, statesmanlike postponement early will give a good chance of a healthy EMU in three, four or five years' time."[21]

The Blair view...	The Jospin view...
Sometimes over the last decade we looked like defenders of a fading industrial past. The proper role of government is not old-style intervention or heaping regulations on employers. The new way...is equipping people to survive in a completely different set of economic conditions. That means flexible labour markets and developing the type of welfare state that is compatible with economic conditions today. We either modernise - or die".	*Now we have a situation of high unemployment, low growth and increasing impoverishment, we can no longer just concentrate on the economy to the detriment of people and their social concerns. Europe will only get back to growth only if we can make short-term, non-profitable investments now... I am very attached to the idea that public services remain central. Market forces – if there is no attempt to control them – will threaten the very idea of civilization".*

EXHIBIT 5: TWO FACES OF EUROPEAN SOCIALISM

Sources: Speeches by Tony Blair and Lionel Jospin at the Social Deomocratic Congress in Malmo, 6/6/97. Blair and Jospin map out their fraternal gulf, Charles Bremner, *The Times*, 7/6/97. Blair tells Europeans, Warren Hoge, *The International Herald Tribune*, 7-8/6/97.

The EU summit meeting in Amsterdam would clearly have a full agenda. As if to concentrate minds on the difficulties that lay ahead, the new French government announced that it would like the issue of the stability pact to be re-discussed – even though it had been formally agreed between the French and German governments at the previous Dublin summit. And then there was the economists' letter. Signed by more than 330 of Europe's leading left-wing economists, this open letter had been sent to newspapers through the EU on the eleventh of June. It stated:

Under the current conditions, EMU offers no perspective of an adequate response to environmental problems, of improvement in the lot of Europe's 20m unemployed and 50m poor, or for the defence and extension of the welfare state...The proposal is governed by timeless criteria and dogmas and institutionalises the dismantling of the public sector. The stability pact rules have no economic basis.[22]

Nevertheless, the German, French and European Commission viewpoint remained that EMU would go ahead as planned with the choice of participants to be made in early 1998. It contined to be strongly endorsed throughout the period May to July 1997 as the Deutschmark fell progressively in value relative to the £ sterling, from 2.75DM to 3.07DM, and as it slumped from $1.70 to $1.60 in the course of July alone.

* * * * * * * * * * * * * * * * * * *

NOTES AND REFERENCES

1   EU united in dissension, Larry Elliott, Mark Milner and John Palmer, *The Guardian*, 26/9/95

2   Peter Kellner, *The Observer*, 26/1/97

3   Businesses need not fear if Britain rejects EMU, Anatole Kaletsky, *The Times*, 31/1/97

4   Wilhelm Nolling, *The Mail on Sunday*, 23/2/97

5   And what if EMU were to turn out to be a flightless bird, Ben Laurance, *The Observer*, 2/2/97

6   Germany clings to deadline for EMU launch, *The Times*, 3/3/97

7   New dawn of inflation, Will Hutton, *The Observer*, 5/1/97

8   France and Germany are Europe's sick men, editorial, *The European*, 29/5-4/6/97

9   Lionel Jospin inscrit son programme dans la durée d'une legislature, Patrick Jarreau et Michel Noblecourt, *Le Monde*, 21/5/97

10   As 9

11   The men who preach water and drink wine, editorial, *The European*, 5/6-11/6/97

12   The Curse of Maastricht, *The Times,* 5/6/97

13   Bundesbank foresees Gold-Plan Retirement, Silvia Ascarelli, Robert Bonte-Friedheim, Matt Marshall and Brian Coleman, *The Wall Street Journal, Europe*, 30-31/5/97

14   Germans fall out over gold revaluation, Oliver August, *The Times*, 29/5/97

15   What was Kohl thinking, editorial, *The Wall Street Journal Europe*, 30-31/5/97

16   As 15

17   Will EMU rise from the ashes?, Mark Atkinson, *The Sunday Telegraph*, 1/6/97

18   As 17

19   Chancellor is left badly bruised in battle over gold, Roger Boyes, *The Times* 5/6/97

20   Socialists' call for new talks on euro pact opens rift with Kohl, Ben Macintyre, *The Times*, 4/6/97

21   Taylor urges speculators to destroy early EMU, Martin Waller, *The Times*, 28/5/97

22   330 European economists savage Euro, Larry Elliott, *The Guardian* 12/6/97

THYSSEN KRUPP AG

Abstract:

This case study focuses on the hostile take-over bid, launched on the 18th March 1997 by Krupp AG for its rival, Thyssen AG, and withdrawn shortly afterwards in the teeth of ferocious opposition from Thyssen and the German trade union movement. The case contains an array of data on the circumstances of the bid and the manner in which the subsequent link-up between the two companies was made, in the context of the state of the European steel industry at the time. On the basis of these data, an outline strategic analysis can be made to gauge the need for Krupp's link-up strategy, an appraisal which can then be used as part of a larger enquiry into the nature of German business culture. Subsequent strategic moves, to reorganise and float the Thyssen Krupp steel subsidiary, can then be appraised.

Questions:

(1) Does the Krupp-Thyssen link-up seem to make good strategic sense to you?

(2) Why did the hostile take-over bid mounted by Krupp effectively fail and why was a merger more acceptable?

(3) What light does Krupp's approach shed on German business culture?

Case Timing: 1998-2000

SUCCESS, AT LAST?

At the time there was widespread relief in Germany at the manner, if not the fact, of the link-up that had finally been forged between Krupp AG and Thyssen AG, the two giants of German steel-making. But there were still those who remained sceptical. One such was Jorg Plutar, chairman of the German Union for the Protection of Shareholders[1]. At the special assembly of Thyssen shareholders held in Duisburg on the 28th March 1998 called to give final approval to the deal, he had declared ominously that "the shadow of a merger with Krupp lies over this meeting"[2]. He had then sought to block the merger on the grounds of the lack of benefits that he thought it would bring for smaller investors in the company.

Plutar's views did not win the day, however. Most of those present were swayed by the logic of the improved situation as they saw it and by the positive views presented by Heinz Kriwet, chairman of Thyssen's supervisory board.[3] He reckoned that linking the two companies was sound in principle and likely to be highly beneficial in practice. Indeed, he paid great tribute to the role played in the merger negotiations by Thyssen's chief executive, Dieter Vogel. This highly satisfactory deal, he said, had crowned Vogel's 12 successful years with the company and, whatever views there were to the contrary, it was undeniable that Thyssen management[4] had always placed the interests of company shareholders at the top of the list.[5]

Nonetheless, there was no gainsaying that the link-up had been a matter of considerable anxiety for all concerned when it was announced on the fourth of November 1997. After all, the deal created a giant of a company with diversified steel, engineering and services interests which had annual sales of DM 65 billion (£22 billion) and employed 190,000 people. This made it, by far and away, the largest such group in Germany. The range of its activities was illustrated by the fact that Thyssen alone had, at the outset, set up no less than 19 working groups to analyse the implications of a merger for their individual operating areas.

On the other hand the two companies had already had substantial experience of close working with each other through jointly-owned subsidiaries, Thyssen-Krupp Stahl (TKS), in respect of flat steel, and Krupp-Thyssen Nirosta for stainless. Thyssen held 60 per cent of the shares in the first and Krupp the same amount in the second.

ON YOUR MARKS, GET SET, GO...

The origin of all the anxiety over the link-up can be traced directly to a bolt from the blue in the form of a hostile DM 13.6 billion (£5.1 billion) take-over bid mounted by Krupp, Thyssen's most powerful rival, on the 18th March 1997. Krupp had offered DM 435 for each Thyssen share, a premium of 25 per cent on the previous day's closing price, and had had the bid thrown back in its face. Immediately the offer was launched, official trading in the two stocks had ceased but, in unofficial trading, Thyssen shares rose to a year's high of DM. 410, whilst those of Krupp slipped back to DM. 270.

One unusual feature of the bid, apart, of course, from the extreme rarity of such a form of corporate aggression in Germany as a hostile take-over bid, was the fact of German bank involvement. Backing the Krupp move were Deutsche Morgan Grenfell, Deutsche Bank's UK-based merchant bank arm, Dresdner Bank and the US investment bank, Goldman Sachs. To defend its interests, Thyssen chose the equally prestigious quartet of CS First Boston, Morgan Stanley, JP Morgan and SBC Warburg.

Thus, leading UK and American investment banks had become involved in what would, in times past, have been a predominantly, if not exclusively, German affair. Nor did it go unnoticed that Germany itself seemed to lack domestically the requisite high value-added investment banking skills to handle such a take-over bid.

Element	Thyssen		Krupp	
	1994/5	1995/6	1994/5	1995/6
Total turnover (DMb)	33.1	38.6	24.2	27.6
Steel business turnover (DMb)	11.9	10.6	7.4	9.6
Total assets (DMb)	25.1	25.4	16.7	17.4
Total profit before tax (DMm)	1026	654	89	644
Steel profits before tax (DMm)	705	384	(217)	560

TABLE 1: COMPARATIVE COMPANY DATA
Source: company reports

Another mould-breaking feature of the bid that caught the public imagination was the fact that Krupp intended to finance it, not out of its own financial reserves, but out of debt. The company claimed that, not only could savings of DM 1 billion be made through linking and streamlining corporate activities, but that the borrowing it required for the bid could be repaid speedily later by selling off unnecessary assets, in Krupp, but more predominantly in Thyssen.

So far as the bid itself was concerned, Krupp was confident of the credit lines it needed. In the event of a Thyssen poison pill defence, it would seek, it said, to raise extra equity finance. Thyssen responded by calling the overall Krupp approach mere *asset stripping*.

The chairman-elect of Deutsche Bank, Rolf Breuer, was convinced of the wisdom of the move. He admitted that it was "extraordinary"[6] but reckoned that it was just the sort of industrial concentration that Germany needed in advance of the arrival of European Monetary Union (EMU) on January 1, 2002. On this date, the use of one single currency (*euro*) throughout the eleven EU countries (*euroland*) pledged to introduce it would bring total transparency across this region, in terms of prices, costs and taxation regimes. This fact would make competition in the European steel industry even keener.

BACK TO THE DRAWING BOARD?

There was immediate and widespread hostility towards the takeover bid in governmental and trade union circles in Germany. The unions were particularly vocal in their opposition. Writing of the massive 30,000 strong demonstration called by the unions to protest against the takeover bid, analyst Rainer Hank indicated the extent of German workers' disbelief about what their major companies were doing. How could it be, the trade unions were asking, that major German companies could be so affected by globalisation that "steel should be a matter of money and that miners should leave the Ruhr"[7]. Not for nothing did the workers consider themselves, and not finance, to be the real capital of these industries.

What *Business Week* called the *Ruhr Rust Belt*, a region of Germany which had been for a century and a half the country's industrial heartland, was in fact, now fighting back against the strategy of the Krupp CEO, Gerhard Cromme. In the process he was to acquire the nickname of *job killer Cromme*.[8]

But union leaders knew they were up against it this time. In 1991 Gerhard Cromme had skilfully engineered the take-over of Hoesch, a big rival to Krupp. He had rationalised steel production in the resulting company (Krupp-Hoesch) by eliminating 25,000 jobs and had raised performance substantially. Prominent industry analysts like Rod Beddows were now indicating that a concerted Krupp-Thyssen steel operation could achieve "significant cost advantages", possibly through the shedding of 20,000 workers. The saving might enable the company to overcome what amounted to a $30/tonne cost handicap resulting from the company's comparative lack of economies of scale in Germany.

As Germany was in reasonably good economic shape overall in 1997, the takeover bid could not be said to be the product of an emergency situation. "We have an export boom, profits are high, costs are falling and inflation is low" said Nele Loew, a spokeswoman for the leading industry union, I G Metall.[9]

Country	Number of hours taken to produce a tonne of steel	DM production cost per tonne
Germany	3	52
France	3.5	44
Britain	3.9	30

TABLE 2: COMPARATIVE ECONOMICS IN EUROPEAN STEEL
Source: Protesters in Germany add Krupp to target,
Roger Boyes, *The Times* 19/3/1997

But what mattered to the demonstrating steelworkers were jobs. The Krupp workers were in the van. Not only did they remember the effects of the Hoesch takeover but, only two months before the bid, Krupp had laid off a further 2,200 workers. Unemployment in Dortmund, declared the leader of the Krupp works council, Jürgen Hafner, would jump to 20 per cent. Georg Bongen, his counterpart at Thyssen, stated baldly:

"We believe that, if Thyssen is bought by Krupp, it will be broken up. We will not just sit back and let this happen. This is undiluted capitalism, pure Wild West (Wildwestmanieren) methods".[10]

Bongen had suffered very much the same experience, in fact. In the five months before the Krupp takeover bid Thyssen had reduced its labour force by ten per cent, partly in response to the halving of its profits that had occurred in 1996/7.

Any further job losses would simply raise the current level of unemployment in North Rhein Westphalia. At the time this stood at 12.7 per cent or nearly 920,000 out of the German unemployment total of 4.67m. In fact, in Duisburg, home of Thyssen's main steel plant, the level in March 1997 was 17.9 per cent, close to that of East Germany.

The result of the workers' hostility to Krupp's plan was the biggest post-war protest march the Ruhr had ever experienced. It was even more vocal than the mass coal miners' demonstrations that had occurred only two weeks before in response to a threat by government to reduce the increasingly onerous subsidies (*Kohlpfennig*) paid to the coal industry. The steelworkers also knew that the government had backed down as a result.

BIG BAD BANKERS ?

The banks were another target for trade union wrath. Thyssen had simply stoked the fire with its initial claim that :

"It is unacceptable to destroy a strong, healthy company that is well prepared for the future to solve the problems of another company or to satisfy the short-term profit interests of capital providers".[10]

The main protests were mounted in Frankfurt and took place outside the Deutsche Bank's twin towers HQ on Mainzer Strasse. Here marching workers chanted in unison "We will not be cheated out of our jobs"[10] and urged any passers-by who were still within earshot to cancel their accounts with the Deutsche and the Dresdner. Klaus Zwickel, CEO of IG Metall addressed them with a fierce denunciation of what he called the *casino capitalism* of the banks. This, he declared to loud applause, was "destroying the political culture of Germany". Behind the backs of the unions and workers, a move had been prepared "with secret general staff-like planning" which was aimed at destroying jobs. For Klaus Zwickel the key issue was who ruled German industry. "We are tired," he concluded" of being governed by the financial power of the banks"[11].

"The episode is the latest example of the trench warfare between would-be modernizers of Germany's clubby corporate governance and guardians of the old system. Hostile takeovers run counter to a tradition of tacit understandings between industry and banks who influence corporate policy through their shareholdings, proxy voting and lending".

EXHIBIT 1: AN AMERICAN VIEW
Source: *The Wall Street Journal, Europe*, editorial, 21-22/3/1997

It was certainly true that German banks were heavily involved with German steel. Commerzbank, for instance, together with the giant Allianz insurance company had an 11.5 per cent stake in Thyssen. It was even the case that

Deutsche Bank had shares in both Thyssen and Krupp with main board director, Ulrich Cartellieri, being in fact a member of Thyssen's supervisory board.

Intriguingly, this feature put Deutsche Bank into the strategically-exposed position of being lender, shareholder and stockbroker to both Thyssen and Krupp at the same time, an awkward political position by any standards. As was necessary, a statement was made by Ulrich Cartellieri absolutely rejecting any accusation of impropriety. Coming from Deutsche Bank, this was accepted by the German commercial establishment without demur, but not without incredulity on the part of leading politicians. An official statement from the North Rhein Westphalia's Finance Ministry told of the "incomprehensibility" of the bank's position on this issue.

Deutsche Bank mounted a spirited defence of its actions. In its statements it spoke of the need for both companies to re-establish a collective comparative advantage, if Germany's heavy industry base were not to be further eroded. It also stated that, when all was said and done, they did work together already. The Bank was not engaged in any sort of "industry politics", it said, and its actions were rooted solely in the commercial logic of industrial development in Rhein and Ruhr[12]. Indeed, it argued, the question was not whether a corporate transformation was necessary, but whether it should be handled by "outsiders", i.e. foreign bankers.[13] Its verdict was that "talk by some politicians and trade unionists of conspiracy theory and Wild West behaviour… bears no relation to the truth".[14] For Deutsche Bank's outgoing CEO, Hilmar Kopper, the matter was even simpler:

"We assessed, advised and provided the financing. With Thyssen this elicited only a strange mixture of misunderstanding and mistrust".[15]

MATTERS POLITICAL

And not just with Thyssen, either. In fact, the bid stirred up a veritable hornet's nest in the German government system, both at Federal and State level. The politicians of North-Rhein Westphalia could not mistake the threat posed by the massed ranks of steelworkers with their chants of *Kein Sozialabbau, Die Hütte muss bleiben* and *Wir sind das Kapital.*[16] As with the trade unions, it was more job losses that governments feared, and specifically in the very region of Germany where the post-war *Wirtschaftswunder* had been wrought. The notion of Thyssen employees staging overnight vigils at seven Ruhr steelplants rang alarm bells.

Others, it must be admitted, did not share their concern. Hans-Olaf Henkel, for one. As president of the trade group of the Federation of German Industry and former boss of IBM Germany, he focussed more on Germany's demonstrably high wages and inflexible regulations. The way these were affecting work practices and social security benefits, for example, explained, in his view, why Germany was suffering its highest level of unemployment since 1933. "Social consensus" he claimed "has cost us millions of jobs. Germany is a champion in exporting only one thing, jobs. Don't the longest vacations and highest number of holidays in Europe just make us sicker than anyone else?"[17]

Others saw things very differently. Chancellor Kohl called on Krupp and Thyssen to show "social responsibility" and come to a "sensible settlement".[18] For their part Johannes Rau and Wolfgang Klement, prime minister and economics minister in the North Rhein Westphalia government respectively, worked hard behind the scenes to get the two sides to talk. They were mindful in doing this of the blunt statement by IG Metall that it was not prepared to accept any redundancies, as they were of the forecast that a Krupp-Thyssen link-up would wipe out 8,000 jobs.

And talk the two sides did.

That there was great urgency in arranging negotiations was beyond dispute. Krupp, in making its hostile bid, had added yet another unorthodox condition, unorthodox, that is, for Germany, namely that there was an 8-day deadline for all negotiations on the bid.

THE WIDER PICTURE: EUROPEAN STEEL

Several additional issues of a broader nature were of significance in making a judgement of the take-over bid.

Perhaps the most important was the nature of competition in the global steel industry in the late 1990s. By any standards European steel was a mature, but highly cyclical, low value-added industry with a low level of annual growth. The standard product sector was still losing ground to aluminium in the construction, packaging and transport sector and wise operators were seeking to add value by improving their economics, their technical performance and the quality of their specialist products.

The pattern of rising imports from the aspiring members of the European Union, Poland and the Czech Republic in particular, was helping to further de-stabilise a market which had not yet recovered from its high level of over-capacity in the recession at the start of the 1990s. Indeed, Nick Judge, analyst at

Natwest Securities, reckoned that, at the time of the Krupp bid, there was still a 40 per cent surplus availability of steel in the EU market place.[19]

The pattern of productivity change since the mid-1970s was also clear. According to International Iron and Steel Industry (IISI) data, in 1975 there had been some 780,000 people working in European steel; in 1997 there were 312,000. In 1990 output per man was 334 tonnes; by 1996 this had risen to 471 tonnes. Technological change had led to the widespread adoption of innovations such as electric arc furnaces and hot (even liquid) steel rolling. There was considerable praise for the economics of high-technology mini-mills, using scrap, as against the type of plant that had been state-of-the-art at the start of the 1980s, the massive, highly integrated, port-side steel facility.

Perhaps the most marked of all the features of industrial change was the way in which the ownership pattern in the European steel industry had altered. In 1988 the state/private sector/mixed ownership split, according to commentator Olivier Collot, was heavily weighted towards the state. By 1997 this had changed dramatically towards private ownership. The shift was accounted for, in part, by political dogma and by the enormous capital requirements of steel making.

Increasingly, as the Maastricht criteria for EMU convergence began to bite, all EU governments had to ensure that funding was, wherever possible, private sector-based and not out of the government's pocket. Naturally enough, individual state aid to industry had long been officially restricted by the operation of articles 92-94 of the Treaty of Rome.

In this change process, France was typical. After years of socialistic experimentation and high subsidies for the steel industry as a whole, Usinor-Sacilor, merged only in 1986, was privatised in 1995. Leading European producers in 1997 are listed in Table 3, on page 520.

If the present looked stressful, the industry employment forecasts made by the IISI were hardly any different. They indicated that there might be a further 200,000 jobs lost in the EU over the period 1997-2005, as a result of technology improvement. For the editorial writer in Belgium's *Le Soir* this amounted to *un cataclysme social*. It was, in fact, even worse because deals that had recently been made within the World Trade Organisation (WTO) meant there could be no longer the certainty of more institutional EU help with the steel industry's transformation.[20]

On the plus side, however, IISI considered that world consumption of steel over this period would grow from the 1990 level of 648.7m tonnes to 796m tonnes. Within this total, whilst the EU volume would go up from 121.6m to 124m tonnes, Asia Pacific's share would power up from 223.9 to 390m tonnes as a result of an expected shift in the location of much heavy industry from

Europe to Asia Pacific.[21] It should be noted that this forecast was made before the nature of the 1997-8 economic turndown in Asia Pacific was appreciated in full.

Company	Country	Annual Output (m tonnes)
British Steel	Britain	15.7
Usinor Sacilor	France	15.5
Riva	Italy	14.4
Arbed	Luxembourg	11.5
Thyssen	Germany	10.4
Krupp	Germany	7.5
Cockerill Sambre	Belgium	6.3
Hoogovens	Netherlands	6.1

TABLE 3: LEADING EU STEEL PRODUCERS
Source: *Franfurter Allgemeine Zeitung,* 19/3/1997.

Note: that in mid-July 1997 Arbed merged with the Spanish producer CSI to become the leading EU producer with an annual output of 17.7m tonnes.

Against this overall background, an attempt by a major European producer to actually rationalise capacity and improve efficiency by effectively removing a competitor, as was the case with the proposed Krupp take-over strategy here, would clearly be welcomed by other players who were not involved directly. It was also virtually certain to be greeted by the markets.

And so it was with British Steel, considered by BZW to be Europe's most competitive producer. Its shares rose in value by four per cent after the Krupp bid was announced. It had been privatised ten years before and had massively reduced its level of employment, shedding 166,000 jobs, whilst substantially improving its financial performance. This had meant not only better rewards for investors but also much higher levels of investment than has been previously possible. In a world where, in the words of *Le Monde's* Philippe Ricard,[22] "the state of the stock market now matters just as much as the state of the steel company's order book", this was an excellent achievement. Notably, British Steel's strategy had involved relatively low unit wage costs, very tight control of wage increases and diversification into higher value added steels.

So far as the possibility of a Krupp-Thyssen linkage itself was concerned, to most analysts it was simply all part of a necessary consolidation process. As Credit Lyonnais' Hans-Peter Wodniak remarked:

"You have to ask yourself, do we really need a Thyssen, a Krupp and all the others, all in Germany? It doesn't make sense any more in a country with such high labour costs".[23]

A QUESTION OF CULTURE

Apart from the potential for job loss, the thing that caused the greatest anxiety in Germany was the way in which Krupp had launched a hostile takeover *(feindliche Übernahme)* for its main rival. Admittedly, it was a bold strike,[24] patterned on Krupps' bid for Hoesch and executed with aplomb by Gerhard Cromme, holder of a Harvard MBA.

But it wasn't the done thing, at least in Germany. For *The Financial Times'* Andrew Fisher it was "an extremely Anglo-Saxon take-over bid" in that it offered the same terms to all shareholders and did not allow for separate so-called "packet deals" or even equity swaps. It also rested on the fact that, as we have seen, Krupp would have had to have geared itself up massively with debt. According to the *Frankfurter Rundschau*, this was "a game of Monopoly of a size and consequence never before played out in German industrial history".[25]

The Times' commentator Oliver August reckoned that a takeover in Britain involving two companies which were "notoriously overstaffed and inefficient" would be welcomed. In contrast, the German business community, with its "cosy corporatism", would find take-overs of this form would be "anathema to the business culture".[26] Certainly, in his view, the so-called *Rhine model* of capitalism accented the social market economy in which shareholders, in the eyes of many, ranked after lenders, workers and customers in their importance as corporate stakeholders.

The German management system also allowed heavy worker participation *(Mitbestimmung)* in decision-making and endorsed liberal strike rights, he reckoned. On top of this, pension funds were not major market players in Germany and not, therefore, a strong influence on the M&A market-place as in the UK, since relatively few people belonged to UK forms of private pension scheme. Additionally, in Germany, American features that were commonplace, such as aggressive bargaining and undisputed "winner-takes-all" success thinking, were almost wholly absent.

It must also be recognised that Krupp and Thyssen were highly unusual and renowned firms. They both had played a key part in the historical development of the German Reich, and, as large-scale coal-steel-weapons conglomerates, had had major roles in all the subsequent significant political and military developments in the first half of the twentieth century. They had been, and still were, a mirror of German industrial history. On top of this, of course, the firm of Friedrich Krupp (founded in 1826) epitomised many of the most important German social advances, providing workers' housing and hospitals and establishing accident and pensions insurance, Kassen from 1861 onwards, as well as being a synonym for German militarism. The name of Krupp will always be associated, for instance, with the *Stahlkanone* of the Franco-Prussian War of 1870 and the *Dicke Bertha* siegegun of World War 1 fame.

THE WRITING ON THE WALL

On the 24th March 1997 Krupp saw the light, gave up its unprecedented hostile takeover bid and agreed with Thyssen to merge their operations. The German stock market recognised the wisdom of the move and both companies' shares rose five per cent at the news. The joint statement indicated high satisfaction with the outcome and, most especially, that it would confirm Germany's future as a major steel producer (*Überlebensfähigkeit des Stahlstandorts Deutschland*), a vital goal. Wolfgang Klement, North-Rhein Westphalia's economics minister, was a party to the agreement that had been reached. Strengthening the region's manufacturing base and minimising job losses had been his interest.

Among the factors that seemed to have swung the deal was the further intervention of chancellor Kohl. There was also urgent consideration of the statement issued by Thyssen to the effect that, if the take-over bid were allowed to succeed, the resultant corporation would have had a "very risky financial structure," with an equity base of DM 3 billion and debts of DM 48 billion.[27] That the Federal and Land governments had also been actively involved in the negotiations behind the scenes was clear. The CEO of Mercedes Benz, whose parent company (Daimler Benz) was one quarter owned by Deutsche Bank, had certainly chaired the negotiations, but it was the political leaders of North-Rhein Westphalia, a State dominated by the Social Democratic party, who had helped to steer, if not propel, the agreement through.

Gerhard Cromme thought it a good deal. He reckoned it would bring about 75 per cent of the much-needed DM 1 billion synergy savings that the full takeover bid would have achieved. Even so, Thyssen, the larger of the two companies, would dominate the merged company. Ironically, in 1988, the-then-CEO, Dieter Spethmann, had suggested to Krupp that it sell out to Thyssen!

Krupp						
Turn-over (DM.B)	1993	1994	1995	1996	1997	1998 (Jan-Sept)
Employees (000's)	24.2	24.2	27.6	27.9	27.6	17.6
	78.4	66.1	66.4	69.6	57.9	58.3

Thyssen						
	1993	1994	1995	1996	1997	1998
Turn-over (DM.B)	33.5	33.1	38.6	38.7	40.8	43.5
Employees (000's)	141.0	131.9	127.0	123.7	120.3	122.3

TABLE 4: Comparative Company Data
Source: Company Reports

The conclusion drawn by *The Financial Times* was that Krupp had "met its match," and that its chief executive, and by implication Deutsche Morgan Grenfell, had been taught a lesson in German-style business *Realpolitik* at the hands of politicians and trade union leaders. Its editorial declared grandly:

"The lesson of this episode is that Germany is not yet ready to embrace confrontational change. Despite a generational shift in German business and Helmut Kohl's rhetoric about the need to unleash entrepreneurial energies, there is a deep need for consensus and compromise".[28]

NECESSARY AND SUFFICIENT ?

Thyssen-Krupp shares were first traded on the 25th March 1999. With an annual turnover of DM70 billion and a workforce of 173,000 it was Germany's leading steel producer. It was widely seen as having created a more competitive base.

Such a base was undoubtedly needed, as only three months later, British Steel and Hoogovens announced a full merger. It would be Europe's biggest steel group, worth more than £4 billion, and would enjoy a single class of share (quoted in London, New York and Amsterdam) and a single board of directors. Its annual sales would exceed £10 billion and its workforce totalled 70,000 (of which British Steel comprised 45,000). This move took place in the context of Usinor's absorption of Cockerill-Sambre and Arbed's 35 per cent stake in the Spanish producer, Aceralia. Analyst Mary Fagan had no doubts about what was at stake:

"I think this deal is very positive. Not only does it get British Steel more sites and technology but it also gets it better distribution in Europe. This is a development that is more about structure and competitive presence than cost cutting... The steel restructuring is driven partly by consolidation in the automotive business, which is an increasingly important customer. Combinations such as Daimler Benz with Chrysler and Ford with Volvo create groups with massive buying power and a demand for seamless global supply agreements." [29]

Merrill Lynch's engineering analyst, Paul Compton, also reckoned it was a good deal. For him, it was a good geographical fit and, along with the other changes in the industry, would reduce *steel tourism* in Europe as more steel would be produced locally for local markets. It would also bring a big fall in steel-price volatility. More specifically, the culture fit between Hoogovens and British Steel was good. [30]

The Thyssen Krupp response was to set ambitious turnover targets for the group, a rise from the 1998/9 level of DM 67 billion to DM 90 billion within 5 years with more than commensurate increases in cash flow, and to re-structure the company. In May 1999, against a background of a falling share price, there was disappointment that market conditions had not improved as expected. By November, however, the mood had changed and the group decision to float the group's steel subsidiary, TKS, on the stock market in 2000 was widely welcomed. The group would continue to treat TKS, the fourth biggest European producer, as a subsidiary, provided external holdings in it did not exceed 35 per cent. As for rest of the group, the joint board chairmen, Gerhard Cromme and Ekkehard Schulz, felt that their decision to reduce the remaining 23 business areas to seven strategic business units brought the required degree of concentration and strength.

* * * * * * * * * * * * * * * * * * *

NOTES AND REFERENCES

1   Deutsche Schutzverein fur Wertbesitz

2   Aktionäre wollen die Fusion Thyssen-Krupp blockieren, *Frankfurter Allgemeine Zeitung,* 21/3/98

3   Aufsichtsrat. The supervisory board of major German companies has shareholder and workforce representatives who discuss and approve the decisions made by the board of directors. Where banks have stakeholdings in firms, they habitually serve as members of the supervisory board. The workforce is also consulted on strategic matters via the firm's works council.

4   Vorstand. The company's board of directors

5   "Von Niemandem in der Welt Übertroffen", as 2

6   Krupp bids £5 billion for rival, Ian Traynor and Chris Barrie, *The Guardian,* 19/3/97

7   " Der Stahl geht zum Gelt und die Kumpel haben das Ruhrgebiet verlassen", in Wir sind das Kapital, rufen die Stahlarbeiter, Rainer Hank, *Frankfurter Allgemeine Zeitung,* 26/3/97

8   The long arms of Krupp, David Woodruff, *Business Week*, 31/3/97

9   One Man Crusade, Greg Steinmetz, *The Wall Street Journal, Europe,* 21-22/3/97

10   Protesters in Germany add Krupp to targets, Roger Boyes, *The Times,* 19/3/97

11   As 10

12   As 10

13   Bank defends role in steel merger row, Jeremy Gray, *The European,* 27/3-2/4/97

14   As 13

15   Nur die Ausländer bei Krupp-Thyssen?, *FrankfurterAllgemeine Zeitung,* 27/3/97

16   German steelworkers turn heat on banks, Andrew Fischer, *The Financial Times*, 25/3/97

17   As 13

18   "There will be no dismantling of social benefit systems", "The factories must stay", "We are the capital" in *op. cit.*

19   Adapted from Hans-Olaf Henkel takes no prisoners in fight to save jobs, Greg Steinmetz, *The Wall Street Journal, Europe,* 21-22/3/97

20   Steel deal wipes out 8000 jobs, Mark Milner, *The Guardian*, 27/3/97

21   Steel to shed 70,000 jobs, Richard Halstead, *The Independent on Sunday*, 23/3/97

22   Un cataclysme social prédit a la sidérurgie européene, *Le Soir*, 27/2/98

23   As 22

24   "Aujourd'hui, le cours du bourse compte autant que les carnets de

commandes" in L'offensive de Krupp bouscule le capitalisme allemand, Philippe Ricard, *Le Monde*, 20/3/97

25   Krupp forges Germany's future, Jeremy Gray and David Brierley, *The European*, 20-26/3/97

26   Cromme's Zweiter Husarenstreich, Werner Sturbeck, *Frankfurter Allgemeine Zeitung,* 19/3/97

27   Bid battle with Clausewitzian echoes, Oliver August, *The Times*, 20/3/97

28   As 27

29   Krupp drops its bid for Thyssen, Peter Norman, *The Financial Times*, 25/3/97

30   Krupp meets its match, *The Financial Times* editorial, 25/3/97

31   Steel in the Melting Pot, Mary Fagan, *The Daily Telegraph*, 6/6/99

32   Steel men go Dutch for growth in Europe, Andrew Lorenz, *The Sunday Times*, 6/6/99

AIR FRANCE

Abstract:

The Air France case deals with a strike that was unusual even by French standards. The problems it illustrates are strategic in nature and concern a company which is simultaneously trying to embrace change and to improve its profitability in a challenging European and world context.

Questions:

(1) Investigate the strategic cost-cutting dilemma facing Air France. What is at stake?

(2) Was its action plan realistic and justifiable in the circumstances? How sensible was the trade union reaction?

(3) What is your view of the government's privatisation approach?

(4) Which aspects of French business culture are evident in the case?

Case Timing: 1998-9

THE 1998 FOOTBALL WORLD CUP - A GOOD KICK-OFF?

The £5m opening ceremony for *Le Mondiale*, the 1998 Football World Cup, took place in Paris on the ninth of June with four giant, colourful and exotic processions, symbolising the world's four continents, converging on the Arc de Triomphe. The French nation, host to the sixteenth contest in the series, the 32 participant teams and their supporters, could have felt justifiably proud of the spectacular way in which the tournament had started. It was a mammoth event. There were to be 64 matches played in ten stadiums in six nation-wide locations and the television audience world-wide was expected to be no less than 37 billion people. The atmosphere in the centre of Paris on the ninth of June was positively *électrique.*

Not so in the headquarters of Air France, however. Senior managers here were still trying to cope with a strike of the company's pilots, an industrial action which was as embarrassing in its timing as it was harmful in its effects. It had started on the first of June and still had not been resolved despite the ten hours of company-union negotiation that had already taken place. The results had been dire. On the third of June, for example, the company had had to cancel 80 per cent of its long haul flights and about two-thirds of its domestic operations. *Le Mondiale* was at risk.

Nevertheless, there was now some guarded optimism on the part of Jean-Cyril Spinetta, president director-general (PDG) of Air France, and his opposite number, Jean-Charles Corbet of the SNPL trade union, that better progress would soon be made. The French government was also mindful of the need to solve the issue quickly, with prime minister Lionel Jospin having already declared, "If the government can be of use, whilst naturally respecting the managerial authority of Air France, we will play a role."[1] This was interpreted as giving a large vote of confidence to the company.

It was, in spite of this, a very tense situation, with support from Air France ground staff for the pilots divided and, as can be easily imagined, considerable antagonism against the strike action being voiced by the World Cup organisers. It was also the case that Air France itself was at this time critically exposed on the international stage, with its managers wrestling with the dilemmas posed by the European Union's *Open Skies* policy. The strike could not have come at a worse time.

On top of this, and irrespective of its timing, the strike was a big issue in French domestic politics. Part of the background was a series of major transport strikes by lorry and train drivers in 1996 and 1997, to secure a lower retirement age for drivers. Typical of these was the Metro strike on the fourth of June 1998, although the trade union focus here was more pay and improved working conditions. Indeed, it was not surprising that French president Jacques Chirac himself called for "a spirit of responsibility" to be shown at this time by striking pilots. As for former conservative prime minister Raymond Barre, he denounced the pilots approach as "absolutely scandalous".[2]

On the other hand, Robert Hué, leader of the Parti Communiste and key member of the left wing coalition government of Lionel Jospin, regarded the strike as no more than "a legitimate labour dispute". As for Louis Viannet, head of the Communist-dominated CGT union, he was certainly not concerned simply with the fact of the World Cup. "Don't be surprised" he declared, "that, if the problems remain, the strikes continue".[3] In the light of such comments, France's minister of the interior spoke for many when he described his shame at seeing Air France being taken hostage ("pris en otage") at precisely the time of the World Cup [4]

To complicate matters still further, the pilots' action was taking place in the immediate aftermath of the passing of the Aubry Act (*la loi Aubry*) which specified that the French working week would be reduced from 39 hours to 35 hours with no loss of pay. This was a government move which the French employers (*patronat*) had calculated would add over ten per cent to French unit labour costs.

It was thought that, if the pilots' strike were to continue until the 10th June, it would cause grave problems for the World Cup, the very first game to be affected being the high-profile Brazil-Scotland match. Optimists reckoned that it might not be a catastrophe after all, however, since it was estimated that, for the 100,000 supporters who would travel by air within France during the competition, the railway system (SNCF) would carry one million. Not only that, the actual flights which would carry the teams would be exempted from the effects of the strike action.

Nevertheless, Michel Platini, star of France's last World Cup squad and co-president of the organising committee for the event, said that all he wanted was an end to the pilots' strike. It was, he said, *illogique et absurde.*[5] At this point he had not learned of two opportunistic strikes called by the leading rail trade unions in support of their claims for higher pay: by CGT (Paris' Metro and RER services) on fourth of June and by FGAAC (covering 30 per cent of all SNCF drivers) on 9-11 June.

Clearly, no one wanted the World Cup to be disrupted. But for Air France's pilots, and the SNPL union which represented some 60 per cent of them, there was a big problem to deal with.

> "In France, industrial anarchy, not football, is the favourite national pastime. Pilots are but the most visible manifestation of a chronic labour relations problem. Electricity and gas workers, baggage handlers, train conductors and drivers and metro staff are all threatening World Cup chaos… This is a pattern of disruption that damages France's reputation abroad, yet seems to be numbly accepted as inevitable at home. Strikes happen in France with frustrating regularity for a simple reason: they still work. The country and the government have yet to face the defining moment, confronted by Mrs Thatcher's British government in 1984-5 when she…clipped trade unions' barons' wings and, overnight, ended Britain's role as Europe's strike capital"

EXHIBIT 1: WANTED – A FRENCH MRS THATCHER?
Source: *The European,* "French own goal" editorial, 8-14 June, 1998.

This was the seemingly draconian proposal by Air France's management that, in order to improve the company's operating efficiency, pilots' salaries should, in future, be effectively *reduced* by 15 per cent in exchange for shares in the soon-to-be-privatised company. The union had pledged it would fight this proposal, designed to achieve FFr.3 billion in savings, for "as long as necessary",[6] as it would involve no salary increases for pilots over an undetermined period.

AIR FRANCE : THE EUROPEAN CONTEXT

In 1997-8 Air France made its first profit in eight years, a meagre FFr.1.8 billion.

The change-around in its fortunes was due, in part, to the inspired leadership of its CEO, Christian Blanc. He it was, who, having inherited a loss of FFr. 7.8 billion when he joined the company four years before, had successfully slashed its debt by a third, increased passenger numbers over the period 1993-7 by 17 per cent and cut staff by ten per cent. The improvement was also due, it must be said, to the FFr. 20 billion of French government subsidy paid to the airline over this period.

Christian Blanc quit Air France in 1997, however, over a draft plan for dealing with the airline's difficulties, issued by Jean-Claude Gayssot, communist transport minister in the new Jospin government. The final version of this particular plan was unveiled in February 1998 and involved Air France's privatisation. The manner in which this was to be handled was a plan for only 20 per cent of the shares to be distributed to private and institutional shareholders, including, as stated, a share to be given to pilots and other senior managers in lieu of salary increases.

City	Airport	Passengers (m) 1997	Growth 1996-7 (%)
London	Heathrow	58	3.8
Frankfurt	Frankfurt-a-M	40.3	3.9
Paris	Charles de Gaulle	35.3	10.9
Amsterdam	Schipol	31.6	13.6
London	Gatwick	27	10.8
Paris	Orly	25.1	(8.4)
Rome	Fiumicino	25	8.5

TABLE 1: EUROPEAN AIRPORTS CARRYING OVER 25M
PASSENGERS IN 1997.
Source: *The European* 20-26/7/98

It is noteworthy, as an aside, that a different form of ESOP (employee stock owning plan) had already been tried by the US Northwest Airline Inc when, in 1993, it had tried to stave off bankruptcy by selling off one third of the company to employees. Whilst the plan had allowed the pilots to capitalise on the deal in 1994 when Northwest went public, they were not so happy with the performance of their stock over the period March to September, when the price fell from $60 to $28. Perhaps this was only to be expected given the huge gyrations in world stock market prices as a result of the economic 1997-8 crisis in Asia Pacific.

The problem with the Air France plan was the fact that, at the time, the company was still not seen as a particularly good prospect in a world where most major airlines were actively seeking profitable, aggressive-defensive partnerships with others of similar mind. A potential partner for Air France would not, therefore, be so keen if it were known that its pilots were restive.

Alitalia, for instance, was trying to link up with the *Transatlantic Excellence* partnership and the *Star Alliance* (Lufthansa-Scandinavian Airlines-United Airlines etc.) had been set up in February 1997 to counter the intended merger between British Airways and American Airlines. A listing of alliances, as at the end of 1998, is given in Appendix 1 on page 541.

Sceptics reckoned that, if it were true that the French government were prepared only to sell off a minor stake, then the company's long-term development might surely be compromised in such a partnership scenario. As it was, the European Commission had begun a competition enquiry in January 1998 into the rudimentary linkages that Air France had laboured hard to build up with the USA's Delta and Continental Airlines.

In mid-June 1998 it was thought likely that, in a sale, the airline would be valued at FFr. 33 billion billion, equivalent to some 45-50 per cent of sales revenue, Lufthansa and BA being valued at about 60 per cent. Selling off a 20 per cent stake would net the French government about FFr. 4 billion, which it was thought likely to retain. Most commentators also reckoned that the government would not be able to assist Air France with its much-needed capital investment programme for fleet upgrading over the next five years. The cost of this was put at FFr. 40 billion.

The retention of the government stake would, it was thought, almost certainly impede the company's ability to raise equity on the stock market and to improve the productivity of its 36,170 workforce.[7] Nor would it do anything to assist the embryonic links that Air France had formed with its two American friends. These were, at all events, made all the more tenuous because of the fact that, despite strenuous efforts to the contrary, there was still no replacement for the EU-US *Open Skies* treaty that had lapsed in 1992, mainly as a result of French demands for Air France to be protected.

As if this were not enough, some critics considered that the way the French government had dealt with Air France as its state-owned flag carrier had not just been unfair, but a *farce*. They reckoned that any further agreement by the European Commission to allow further subsidy would be *disgraceful* and *an abuse of power.*[8] This was not without reason. The European Court of Justice (ECJ) itself had examined the European Commission's 1994 decision to allow the French government to subsidise Air France as a restructuring aid, by checking on its legality within the framework of articles 92-94 of the Treaty of Rome.

The case had been brought on behalf of BA, SAS and KLM who regarded the subsidies given as amounting to trade discrimination. The ECJ's tribunal of first instance delivered its judgement on the 26th June 1998. This exonerated both the French government and the Commission from any wrongdoing in respect of the subsidy itself, but found some of the Commission's reasoning suspect.[9] The Commission itself put matters to rights when, on the 22nd July, it re-approved the 1994 package.

AIR FRANCE: OPEN SKIES

There was, in addition, the question of European airline deregulation, the *Open Skies* policy, to consider.

European airline deregulation had, in fact, consisted of a suite of reforms to the pricing and routing aspects of airline operation in the EU, whereby route sharing by two carriers with controlled prices would end by a specified date. The process had been agonisingly slow, starting in December 1987 and ending on the first of April 1997 with an agreement to allow airlines to operate anywhere in 17 European countries without fare or route restrictions. There was, however, no *big bang* formula in the EU, as there had been in the US, leading to free competition. The reason was the traditional manner in which many European countries safeguarded their flag carriers, even if it meant (in the eyes of critics) inefficiency and, for the consumer, a mixture of high prices and limited choice.

But, as a result of *Open Skies,* the number of carriers in the EU had risen from 99 in 1987 to 150 in 1997. And competition had patently increased. Nevertheless, only six per cent of EU routes had three carriers in direct competition in 1997 and 80 per cent of routes were still in monopoly hands. Prices were still considered by the European Commission to be too high, especially as compared with the US.

Additionally, there were two difficult problems to deal with. First, that of new competitor airlines' access to valuable time slots (for take-off and landing) at EU airports, a basic factor which governed aspects of competitiveness. Second, the still thorny issue of the potential for incumbent major national airlines to indulge in predatory pricing against possible new (and cheaper) entrants to their routes. Both these issues were as yet unresolved. Indeed, the FFr 53 billion in subsidies paid by EU governments to their airlines over the period 1993-97 subsidies could well have been construed as a way of inhibiting the entry of low-cost competitors into the market.

Airline	Share of take-off and landing slots at Heathrow airport (%)
British Airways	39
British Midland	13
Lufthansa	5
Air France	3
SAS	3
Alitalia	2

TABLE 2: LEADING EUROPEAN AIRLINES' SLOTS
AT HEATHROW (1997)
Source: *The European* 20-26/7/98

To safeguard its position, British Airways had pursued a successful strategy of buying its way further into the EU market by acquiring stakes in regional services such as Delta Air in Germany and TAT and Air Liberté in

France. This was achieved in the face of massive French opposition. It is to be noted also that neither carrier was affected by the Air France strike. Air France had countered the move by acquiring Air Inter and integrating the two airlines within France.

Other carriers had indulged heavily in franchising (i.e., allowing regional carriers to use a major's brand name) and by code-sharing on connecting flights. This occurs when an airline sells a seat on another carrier's flight but issues a ticket carrying its own code, the advantage being that *it can sell tickets to destinations it does not serve*. IATA figures indicate that there were ten such alliances in 1983 and 363 by mid June 1997.

Cross-holdings among airlines and the creation of low-priced substitute carriers by the majors were among other ways of competing in the European market place. However, EU regulations limited the purchase of a stake in an EU airline by a foreign owner to 49.9 per cent, whilst the corresponding figure for the USA was 25 per cent.

AIR FRANCE: THE TRANSATLANTIC PICTURE

The Lex column in *The Financial Times* of the fifth of October had no doubt of the way things should go for international airlines. It stated that "the era of loss-making national flag carriers offering appalling returns to shareholders is ending. Staying out in the cold while powerful cross-border business share alliances is becoming an unattractive prospect".[10] Where was Air France in all this?

Air France was, in fact, trying to negotiate membership of a brand-new alliance, but as a late-comer. Called *Wings*, the alliance consisted of an ambitious tie-up among Europe's Air France, Alitalia, KLM and Virgin Atlantic and the US' Northwest and was entirely typical of the shifting sands of the alliance business. (See Exhibit 2 on page 535.) The intention was to build on the longstanding KLM-Northwest relationship and extend it to compete with the *Star* alliance (Lufthansa, SAS, United Airlines, Air Canada, Thai Airways and Varig of Brazil) and *Oneworld*. (See Appendix 1 on page 541.) As long as real mergers remained politically taboo, considered Lex, such alliances were "a decent second best" strategy because they reduced the cost base by spreading marketing and ticketing costs over greater volume.

The elusive prize in all this was capturing global business travellers, high-worth individuals (called by the Star Alliance *global mobiles),* and the general aim was to tie them into an airline alliance to cover their entire journey. Additionally, analyst Michael Skapinker reckoned that "the large alliances are not only trying to win over individual business travellers, they are attempting to persuade their employers, and their travel agents, to book all tickets with them".[11]

"A Boston Consulting Group study found that only one third of the intercontinental alliances in place in 1992 were in existence three years later. Alliances within the same region had a slightly higher survival rate: 59 per cent lasted three years. As hard as they try to maintain their partnerships, airlines from different countries have their own histories, cultures and ways of operating"

EXHIBIT 2: A HIGH FAILURE RATE FOR AIRLINE LINK-UPS?
Source: Flights in Formation, Michael Skapinker, *The Financial Times*, 10/1/98

So far as Europe and the USA were concerned, the player with the biggest fleet was *Oneworld*. Actually cementing the planned merger between the two airline giants at the heart of *Oneworld* would bring them a 60 per cent share of the lucrative transatlantic route and it was this fact that was causing concern in mid 1998 to regulators in Washington and Brussels. The counter-argument, namely that the *Star Alliance* already enjoyed a *global* 20 per cent market share, cut little ice. The commercial negotiations for the merger having been completed, the deal hung on the extent to which both parties were perceived to be intent on anti-competitive behaviours and, if so in fact, how this could be countered in the best interests of consumers and competitors.

Indeed, the European competition commissioner Karel van Miert was still not persuaded of the British government's position, namely that all was fair so long as the deal was agreed between the US and the UK and so long as BA sold off 168 take-off and landing slots at Heathrow. (See Table 2, on page 533.)

Element	1995-6	1996-7	1997-8
Sales turnover (FFr m)	52,500	55,602	60,716
Net profit (FFr m)	(2,410)	(147)	1,874

TABLE 3: AIR FRANCE'S FINANCIAL PERFORMANCE (1995-8)
Source: Company data

In fact, the tension that was evident in the relationship between the U.S. and the EU over the transatlantic airline business went much further than the practicalities of the *Oneworld* link-up. There were issues of reciprocal market access, *neo-mercantilist* state interventionism and genuine liberalisation of the world market to face up to. The leader in *The Financial Times* had long been clear about the right direction in which to travel. It declared on the eighth of July 1996:

> *"The EU should propose opening its single aviation market full to US carriers... in return for comparable access to US domestic routes. This would ensure fairer and more open competition than the patchwork of domestic deals sewn up by the US in Europe. The two sides should also abolish their anachronistic restrictions on the foreign ownership of airlines. They should also align their competition policies to keep markets open, rather than to promote the airlines' interests".*

In early June 1998, the main issue in all of this, so far as a strike-bound Air France was concerned, was the likelihood that Karel van Miert would, after all, give the final go-ahead to the BA-AA *Oneworld* merger. The atmosphere in Paris in early July 1998, when the decision was expected, was very tense. It was already known at this time that the Air France pilots' action had cost the company in excess of FFr. 300m.

STRIKING WHILE THE IRON IS HOT

From the start, both the strike and the pilots' hostility to the changes proposed by management were solid. An effective pay *cut* in exchange for shares in an airline, which had not shown abundant signs of profitability for years and was scheduled for part privatisation, did not seem to inspire confidence. Especially, when it was known that Air France pilots earned, on average, 19 per cent more than Lufthansa's pilots and 40 per cent more than BA's. [12]

"Lionel Jospin will today (June 1) celebrate his first year as French prime minister buoyed by record poll ratings, a growing economy and the implosion of the country's centre-right opposition. With unemployment falling below the politically significant figure of three million and France qualified for economic and monetary union, the biggest clouds on the horizon are murmurs of discontent from his Green and Communist coalition partners"

EXHIBIT 3: A GOOD SCORECARD FOR LIONEL JOSPIN?
Source: Derided Jospin's first year in office proves a triumph,
Adam Sage, *The Times*, 1/6/98

A week into the strike, the government was showing a phlegmatic stance, however. "The World Cup will go ahead as normal," prime minister Lionel Jospin had declared. The French "do not need to take a 'plane to go to the matches and nor do the Europeans, while there will be plenty of other airlines to bring everyone here instead of Air France".[13]

The strike came to an end on the tenth of June. The acrimony went on, however, with another dispute between Air France and the pilots over salary payment during the strike days. This time the management-union fall-out hinged on the definition of what was actually involved in striking. Jean-Cyril Spinetta, the PDG of Air France, had repeatedly said that strikers would not be paid and that anyone not turning in for work was deemed to be a striker. For SNPL, the pilots union, this was not enough. A notice entitled the striking pilots' checklist was issued on the 28th May. It read :

"The employer does not have the right to ask you if you are on strike (keep the telegram and do not reply to it). It is not up to you to declare yourself a striker. There is no such thing as an intentional striker. Only the fact of not carrying out a tour of duty proves you are a striker – and only for the period of the tour of duty".

Then there was the problem of the hostility of other unions towards the pilots' action. Right at the start of the strike, the main unions at Air France, the FO and the CFDT, had refused to give it their blessing. In fact they stated with considerable bitterness that the actions of the 3,200 pilots were putting the livelihoods of the company's employees at considerable risk. In the words of Francois Duval, general secretary of FO-Air France, they were simply putting their own interest before what he called *l'intérêt collectif.*

There was undeniably, however, a huge communal sigh of relief in management ranks on the tenth of June when the strike came to an end. Indeed, there was pleasure that the key principle of pay reduction in exchange for share options for *volunteers* was seen to have been conceded by the union, even if M. Spinetta said he did not know how many pilots would sign up for it.

The agreement amounted to the fact that pilot pay would effectively be cut to allow it to "converge" with that of competitors. The basic offer was for a pilot who wished to forgo 2-3 per cent of annual salary throughout their careers in exchange for an equivalent value of shares graded according to seniority and priced attractively. Pilots who wanted to forgo pay of FFr. 12,000 per year instead would also be compensated in this way. Those who were unwilling to take part would have their *pay frozen for seven years, except for promotion.*[14] In return, the company had agreed to pay all pilots the same rates of pay, subject to rank but independent of experience.

It was now time for management to turn to the other pressing matter, the partial privatisation of Air France. Success in this would represent a major turnaround for a company which, in 1993, had been virtually bankrupt. As previously mentioned, it had been Christian Blanc who had retrieved the situation, winning major productivity deals from Air France staff but failing later with his highly unpopular two-level pilot pay plan.

> In the absence of justification drawn from the national interest, we are not in favour of the privatisation of the common patrimony represented by the big public corporations in the competitive sector. For all that, we know that adaptations will be necessary to maintain our rank among the most developed nations of the world and to move closer to our European partners".

EXHIBIT 4: LIONEL JOSPIN IS LUKEWARM ON STATE SELL-OFFS
Source: Market turmoil raises questions about privatisation, David Owen,
The Financial Times, 14/1/98

There was certainly no shortage of knowledge of how the world airline business was developing. Commentator Lois Jones expressed it succinctly by saying, "Size does matter. The announcement of the formation of *Oneworld* is the latest step in the evolution of the airline business into two or three *megagroups*. Once a fiercely nationalistic industry dominated by flag carriers, the airline business is going global".[15] It was also thought that, so long as the alliances were pre-occupied with marketing advances and neither price-fixing nor code-sharing on a multilateral, alliance-wide basis, there would be need for regulatory involvement. But it was obvious that the day was not far off when competition would exist not between individual airlines but among global mega-groups.

One big question was whether the French government's strategy in respect of selling a minority stake would help or hinder its plans to belong to such a mega-group.

The about-turn came, however, when Odile Chamussy of the French transport ministry shrugged off worries regarding the plan to sell off 20 per cent of Air France to private investors by the end of 1998 (including the pilots' reservations). She indicated that up to 49 per cent of the company would, in fact, be privately owned by mid 1999. "The steps leading to the opening of capital are going ahead normally," she said.

As for Rene Philippeau, president of SNPL-Air Inter, the union that had negotiated the deal, he had no doubt of the immediate outcome of all of it.

"Nous avons" he said "fait dix jours de grève pour rien".[16] As for Air France, it had lost FFr 1.7 billion in revenues and FFr 1.3 billion in net profit over the strike.

However, by the end of the year, Odile Chamussy's predictions were coming true as Jean-Cyril Spinetta, Air France's PDG, announced that the sell-off would take place, after all, in early 1999. The ownership stake would be about 49 per cent, it would bring in about FFr 4 billion to the government and the pilots would end up with an ownership state of about 7 per cent in the company.[17]

AIR FRANCE TRIUMPHANT

There appeared to be much rejoicing among top management in Air France in early 1999, as the company seemed to be dealing successfully with two of the main challenges it faced.

The first issue to be resolved was the implementation of the Loi Aubry. On the ninth of January a deal was signed by the unions, representing the 35,000 ground staff within the company. It involved a triennial agreement to cut the working week and to take on new staff. François Cabrera, leader of the CFDT union, was particularly pleased that the weekly working time reduction (39 hours to 35 hours) involved both no loss of pay and an overall drop in the level of what was known as *precarité*, i.e. part-time work of all types. It also provided excellent opportunities for *prerérétraite progressive* (early retirement).

The second matter was the sell-off of the first stake in the company by the French government on the 22nd February 1999. The share prices agreed for the individual and institutional shareholders (FFr91.8 and 93.1, respectively) valued the company at just over Ffr20 billion. The plan was for the privatised stake to rise from the 21.2 per cent sold in February to 47 per cent by March 2003. It is noteworthy that Jean-Claude Grayssot told investors at his press conference on the tenth of January 1999 that the State's continued ownership of a majority share in the company gave *une certaine garantie*.[18]

However wildly elated they were at the ten-fold level of oversubscription for the shares, neither the French government nor Air France's directors could have been anything but still anxious at the pilots' continued reaction to the share-and-salary plan their negotiators had agreed to.. The salary increases the pilots were to forgo in the coming years (some Ffr 1.29 billion) were certainly being used as planned to provide their eventual 6.8 per cent stake in the company, but they had not been allowed any premium on the price to be paid by the individual shareholders. And they felt they had been *dupé*.[19]

And there was the other matter of the airline alliance still to settle. As of the end of October 1999, Air France was still isolated and in a weak position. Its link-up with Delta Airways was fine in itself, but the tandem, unlike its competitors, still had neither a Europe-wide network nor a partner in Asia.

* * * * * * * * * * * * * * * * * *

APPENDIX 1 – AIRLINE ALLIANCES: ALL UP IN THE AIR

	Sales ($bn)	Passengers (m)	Aircraft fleet	Employees
Oneworld alliance				
American Airlines	18.6	81	641	111.500
British Airways	14.2	41.0	276	60.575
Quantas	6.1	18.6	98	30.080
Cathay Pacific	4.0	10.2	64	15,747
Canadian Airlines	2.2	8.6	78	14.233
TOTAL	**45.1**	**159.4**	**1,157**	**220,986**
Possible partners				
Iberia	3.6	16.07	113	20.000
Japan Airlines	9.9	31.36	137	18.127
TOTAL	**58.6**	**206.83**	**1,407**	**259,113**
Star Alliance				
United Airlines	17.4	84.2	562	91.779
Lufthansa	13.4	44.4	231	58.204
SAS	5.1	20.8	170	20.500
Air Canada	4.0	14.0	166	21.215
Varig	3.2	10.7	92	18.203
Thai International	3.1	14.4	74	24.186
TOTAL	**46.2**	**188.5**	**578**	**210,000**
Possible partners				
Singapore Airlines	5.0	12.0	86	28.196
TOTAL	**51.2**	**200.5**	**664**	**238,196**
Qualiflyer alliance				
Swissair	7.4	16.9	61	16,883
Sabena	2.0	9.5	70	9.500
Austrian Airlines	1.6	3.9	35	4.149
TAP Air Portugal	1.2	4.4	31	8.000
THY Turkish Airlines	1.3	10.3	66	8.958
AOM	0.6	3.4	24	1,020
Possible partners				
Air France	10.2	33.5	200	46.385
Delta Air Lines	13.6	101.15	543	63,441
TOTAL	**37.9**	**183.05**	**1030**	**158,336**
Transatlantic Excellence				
KLM	6.7	14.7	121	26.811
Northwest Airlines	10.2	54.7	405	50,000
Possible partners				
Air France	10.2	33.5	200	46.385
Alitalia	5.1	24.6	131	18,676
Continental Airlines	7.2	40.0	332	40,000
TOTAL	**29.2**	**167.5**	**1,189**	**181,872**

Source: *The European* 28/9-4/10/98

REFERENCES

1   Air France : Lionel Jospin intervient, *Le Monde*, 7-8/6/98
2   Strike-hit French take pride in union rights, Jon Henley, *The Guardian*, 5/6/98
3   As 2
4   Les couacs du gouvernement : Jean Pierre Chevenement, *Le Figaro*, 4/6/98
5   Impact limite sur le Mondial, *Le Figaro*, 4/6/98
6   Mounting wave of air and rail strikes threatens World Cup chaos, Jon Henley, *The Guardian*, 4/6/98
7   Gayssot leaves Air France stranded, Paula Hawkins, *The European*, 2-8/3/98
8   Unfair subsidies and the farce of Air France, William Davis, *The Evening Standard*, 8/6/98 and Abuse of Power, *The Times*, 23/7/98
9   Nouvelle decision de Bruxelles sur Air France avant la fin de l'annee, Philippe Lemaitre, *Le Monde* 27/6/98
10   Lex column, *The Financial Times*, 5/10/98
11   Flights in formation, Michael Skapinker, *The Financial Times*, 10/1/98
12   La greve a Air France menace le Mondial, *Le Monde* 2/6/98
13   France ready for long haul over air strike, Ben Macintyre, *The Times*, 8/6/98
14   Shares-for-wages deal for Air France pilots, Robert Graham, *The Financial Times*, 14/10/98
15   Clubbable class books slots for take-off, Lois Jones, *The European*, 28/9-4/10/98
16   Les pilotes et la direction d'Air France s'estiment satisfaits de l'accord de sortie de conflit, *Le Monde,* 12/6/98 . "We have had 10 days on strike for nothing".
17   Floating will lift Air France staff, Carl Mortishead, *The Times*, 22/12/98
18   Le prix retenu pour l'action Air France volorise la compagnie à 20.5 milliards de francs, Francois Bostnavaron, *Le Monde*, 11/2/99
19   As 18.

THE WORLD OF DEUTSCHE BANK

Abstract:

This case covers the context in which Deutsche Bank made a mould-breaking take-over bid for Bankers Trust of America. It allows us to appraise the massive changes affecting the world's financial services industry and reflect on the wisdom of the Bank's chosen strategy.

Questions:

(1)   Review the key drivers in the operating environment for international financial services. Which factors exerted the most pressure ?

(2)   Discuss the extent to which M&A activity is the natural consequence of such pressures

(3)   How justifiable is Deutsche Bank's decision to take over Bankers Trust? Is it a good move? How does it fit in with the *Allfinanz* logic?

(4)   Will Deutsche Bank cope easily with the challenges?

Case Timing: 1998-9

AN ANXIOUS TIME

In early December 1998, the biggest anxiety for whizz-kid dealers in London's leading investment banks seemed to be the size of their year-end bonuses. Because of the volatile market conditions during the year, some of the equity dealers had put in what the City called a *stellar* performance and thus qualified for a big pay-out. Colleagues who dealt in debt, however, often on the same team as the equity dealers, had typically suffered large losses. Hence, in such banks as Merrill Lynch and J.P Morgan, unseemly infighting had occurred among dealers as to who was to receive what, since the normal way of allocating bonus was to average the pay-out among team members. The problem was made all the greater by the fact that this year's bonus was likely to be only half the level of 1997. This had been a record £1b, enough to satisfy everyone.

1998 had, in fact, seen the worst of the economic meltdowns in Asia and Russia and, for debt dealers, had turned into an *annus horribilis*. So far as those handling equity were concerned, however, it was quite the opposite. In the ten days prior to the end of November, global merger and acquisition deals amounting to no less than £135 billion had been struck, whilst the total for the year up to this date was a staggering £1.356 trillion. This was quite enough, as Table 1 indicates, to smash the record for 1997.

	1997	1998
Net income (in billions)	$0.57	$1.90
Trading profits (in billions	$2.02	$1.95
Provisions for losses on loans and advances (in billions	$1.24	$0.85
Cost/income ratio*	75.3%	78.1%
Return on equity, before tax	6.4%	24.8%
Planned capital increase **	$3.37 billion	

* Typically 65% in US Banks

** Price of Deutsche Bank shares on Xetra Dax in Frankfurt was 75 Euros in Mid-January 1998 and 45 Euros in mid-January 1999.

TABLE 1: DEUTSCHE BANK FINANCIALS
Source: Deutsche Bank Stands poised for a reserve,
The Wall Street Journal, 19/3/99.

But there was no discord about year-end bonuses among those working in Britain for Bankers Trust. They had been assured by Deutsche Bank, the new owners of this American investment bank, that their bonuses were still on track. The worry of Bankers Trust's 2,400 employees was, by contrast, which of them would still have a job in 1999.

Deutsche Bank's announcement on December 1 that about 3,000 City posts were to go was also greeted with gloom by many of its own staff of 6,200. It mattered little to those facing redundancy that Deutsche Bank was now, after its strategic thrust into the US market, the biggest bank in the world.

MERGER MANIA

Perhaps the biggest reason for the existence of such bonuses for staff in investment banks, whether questionable or not, was the merger and acquisition (M&A) mania that had engulfed many leading industries in 1998. Both the pace of change and the sums of money involved were awesome and unprecedented. In the first half of the year, for instance, there had been two spectacular mergers, the £100 billion pharmaceutical link-up between Glaxo Wellcome and Smith Klein Beecham and the $166 billion Citigroup banking marriage between Travellers Group and Citicorp, the parent company of Citibank.

Later in the year it was the turn of Daimler Benz and Chrysler, BP and Amoco and Exxon and Mobil. "The tide" wrote analysts Kirstie Hamilton and John Waples "was not even stemmed by the wild months of September and October, when bond and stock markets plunged, junk-bond markets almost closed and central bankers worried that more and more currencies would be toppled by the world-wide panic".[1]

For those investment banks able to profit from the M & A passion, the prospects for an *annus mirabilis* were excellent as, typically, advisory fees amounted to some ten per cent of the overall cost of M&A transactions. The winning banks in the European contest are shown in Table 2, above. This indicates that the total value of M&A deals struck in 1997 and 1998 was £378.4 and £713.9 billion, respectively. In spite of this, a report issued by the US' Securities Industry Association showed that US investment banks stood to make 18 per cent *less* net profit from their global trades than in 1997,[2] with competition clearly hotting up.

It should be noted, in passing, that M&A success for a specific investment bank depended not only on the perceived quality of the bank as a whole, but also on the quality of its advisory teams and, most particularly, on the ability of the leaders of such teams. The 1998 list of so-called *megadealers* included such luminaries as Goldman Sachs' Chris French and Bob Bradway of Morgan Stanley, the latter described by a colleague as a "Harvard MBA manual made flesh".[3]

M&A Adviser	Rank in 1998	Total value of deals (£bn)	
		1998	1997
Morgan Stanley Dean Witter	1	162.9	83.2
Goldman Sachs	2	131.8	60.0
J.P. Morgan	3	88.4	44.9
Merrill Lynch	4	77.3	18.8
Credit Suisse First Boston	5	65.0	44.5
Deutsche Bank	6	47.0	16.8
Warburg Dillon Read	7	43.1	65.3
Schroder	8	37.6	18.7
Chase Manhattan	9	30.5	-
Rothschild	10	30.3	26.2

TABLE 2: TOP 10 EUROPEAN M&A ADVISERS
Source: US Takeover, Kirstie Hamilton and John Waples,
The Sunday Times, 20/12/1998. Note £1 = $1.65

Deal-makers such as these were so important that there existed a sort of transfer market where rival banks sought to outbid each other, firstly, to hire and, secondly, to retain winners. With rewards as high as those existing in the boom market of 1998, it is little wonder that the loyalty of outstanding corporate-finance practitioners to their current employers would be under even more strain than usual. Of course, the fact that it was American merchant banks that now dominated the European M&A scene, was held responsible for much of the *big bucks* pay scenario and the *footloose* business culture which impelled dealers to move from bank to bank in search of better rewards.

There were many other drivers for the 1998 global M&A mania than the existence of *top-dollar* advisory teams in leading American investment houses. For the oil industry, for example, M&A activity was a product of sheer necessity, the economics of the global business having shifted dramatically with onset of global turbulence in 1997 and the inability of OPEC to maintain output agreements in the face of falling demand. The result was, as expected, over-capacity and intense price rivalry. To preserve margins in the oil industry, oil majors needed, therefore, to cut costs and that inevitably meant a further *oligopolisation* of the industry. The ramifications of this for the financial services industry were clear.

So far as the automobile industry was concerned, the example of the Daimler Benz-Chrsyler takeover also exemplified the logic of the need to handle huge research and development and marketing expenses more successfully, as well as to achieve a higher strategic capacity for global market management, manufacturing logistics and product innovation. Nevertheless, the macro-environmental pressure on the two companies to come together was just as evident as any industry-specific rationale. Even the largest producers in this sector of industry were heavily exposed to both unstable global capital flows, especially involving hot money and hedge fund speculation, and the possibility of a wave of economic deflation flowing from the economic woes of Asia Pacific

The global financial services industry was, similarly, faced with such pressures. It was also confronted with the results of an adverse economic climate that had shown signs of an unexpected worsening in 1998. Indeed, the situation had seemed so difficult that, in December 1998, the International Monetary Fund announced the convening, for the first time since the Bretton Woods conference of 1944, of its policy-making Interim Committee. Members were to meet in January 1999 to discuss emergency reforms to the IMF against a background of highly negative World Bank data. These revealed, among other minuses a halving of GDP growth in the 36 developing countries (4.8 per cent in 1997 down to 2.0 per cent in 1998) which had hitherto served as one of the major engines of world economic growth in the 1990s.

Perhaps even worse, on the day the IMF move was announced there was evidence of panic on Wall Street as the world's leading aerospace company, Boeing, announced 48,000 redundancies worldwide as a result of the worsening business climate. In the words of analyst Larry Elliott :

> *"The suckers' rally of the past two months has come to an end. The lay-offs at Boeing brought home an uncomfortable truth, namely that the earnings growth which the (Wall Street) stock market bulls used to justify rocketing share prices simply is not coming through. Far from rising exponentially, profits have been dropping for the past year and are now declining at an annual rate of six per cent".*[4]

In the USA itself there was, however, a division of opinion as to the way that economy would develop in 1999. On the one hand, it was true that, in late 1998, there had been strong growth in the service jobs sector (especially computing) which was more than offsetting weaknesses in the manufacturing sector. Also, the three reductions in interest rates implemented by the Federal Reserve as a strategy to preserve global economic growth, were reducing business costs appreciably. On the other hand, there was solid evidence that the US economy, the world's largest, might be beginning to overheat and that margins were "being squeezed by over-capacity, rising employment costs and a deceleration in productivity growth." [5]

Country	Imports ($bn, 1997)	Exports ($bn, 1997)
UK	0.7	9.1
USA	6.2	7.5
Germany	9.4	11.1
France	8.2	8.2

TABLE 3: TRADE IN FINANCIAL SERVICES
Source: World Bank, IMF

Quite apart from the international economic scene and its strategic implications, the global financial services industry had had yet another concern to face up to in early 1998, the consequences for this industry worldwide if members of the World Trade Organisation did not soon conclude the deal to liberalise financial services globally. This had been long in the making. The sticking point for many nations was the precise level of access to partners' markets they would have to be given if they opened up their own.

The UK was particularly concerned that its partners would not opt for a City-of-London type of openness, but would "impose discriminatory arrangements based on bilateral reciprocity"[6] instead. Major financiers wanted such a high level of openness, even if it actually encouraged inbound M&A activity. Any restrictions, as Table 3, indicates, might seriously affect the UK's positive balance of trade in financial services.

But for most M&A strategists in the big international banks, the preoccupation in late 1998 was with the dire predictions many pundits were making about future global economic scenarios. These were being put forward, not just in the light of structural factors but, more importantly, the near-collapse of the giant hedge fund Long Term Capital Management (LTCM) and its bail-out by the world's leading banks (under Federal Reserve instructions). This had been done in order to to pre-empt what some observers saw as the equivalent of a global financial holocaust.

Many of these banks had placed complete confidence in the notion that LTCM's two Nobel prize-winning economists had mastered the arcane art of accurately predicting the future. They suffered accordingly, when it collapsed on September the fourth 1998, having lost 44 per cent of its value ($1.8bn). LTCM's failure was due to misjudgements on changes in world interest rates and on Russia. The potential for damaging knock-on effects on the world's economy was so serious that the Federal Reserve had felt it necessary to intervene.

Deutsche Bank's chairman Rolf Breuer was in no doubt that "massive consolidation" in the European banking industry would result from the current pressures.[7] His analysis also isolated the powerful effect on M&A of the arrival of the Euro on January the first 1999, changes in banking technology (e.g., electronic and internet banking) and the disappearance of cultural barriers to cross-border M&A. Globalisation had a lot to answer for, as well.

CONCENTRATING THE MIND

Deutsche Bank strategists had received two powerful illustrations of the M&A developments taking place in the financial services industry in 1998. In this momentous year Union Bank of Switzerland consummated its $80 bn marriage with Swiss Bank Corp to form UBS and the mighty Citigroup was created in the USA from the merger of Travelers Group and Citibank. The two groups had assets of $600bn and $700bn, respectively. Certainly, Rolf Breuer could not ignore the salient facts that the new UBS was now the largest bank in Europe (see Table 4, page 550) and that Citigroup would be a *megabank* with a global reach employing some 162,000 people. The two case studies were powerful lessons in the strategy and mechanics of global banking.

The UBS deal was the equivalent for its two partner banks of *crossing the Rubicon*. For a start, the smaller bank, Swiss Bank Corp, ranked number three in Switzerland had, in fact, swallowed its larger rival, Union Bank of Switzerland, despite ending up with the UBS name.

Whilst the affair of Union Bank's $443m losses in derivatives trading in Asia the previous year had served as an ominous backdrop to the merger, it had not held matters up. Secondly, market valuations of financial stocks were falling steadily throughout 1998 such that, by September, those in the USA and Europe were one-third off their peaks.

Then there was the issue of European Economic and Monetary Union (EMU) to factor into the M&A equation. As analyst Thane Peterson put it "A merger boom in European banking seems inevitable as EMU melds eleven different financial markets into a single $6.3 trillion economy. As companies and customers begin to move money around Europe more freely, banks will have to expand beyond national borders to keep pace".[8]

Bank	Total assets ($bn)	Est 1998 ROE (%)
UBS	754	19.9
Deutsche Bank	596	7.2*
Credit Suisse	479	15.5
Hong Kong Shanghai Bank (HSBC)	472	16.7
Hypovereinsbank	429	9.6
Société Génerale	420	NA
ABN AMRO	414	17.1
Barclays	392	18.3

TABLE 4: EUROPE'S BIGGEST BANKS - SEPTEMBER 1998
Source: *Business Week,* 21/9/1998
Note: Deutsche Bank ROE excludes the Daimler special dividend.

Two additional factors were thought to be particularly important. Firstly, in 1998 many European banks had taken big *hits* as a result of the financial meltdown in Asia Pacific and Russia, either through losses on conventional bank loans (i.e., to other banks and corporates) or loans to governments. In this context, the need for any bank, which was suffering from a high level of net exposure in troubled markets or from bond or other trading losses, to find a partner with a better set of financials was clear.

Whilst, admittedly, most of the bank-advanced credits were government-backed, a virtually illiquid Russia owed $30 billion in loans to Germany and $7 billion to France. The Deutsche, Hypovereinsbank, Dresdner and Commerzbank themselves had a commercial net exposure at the end of September 1998 of about $2 billion, of which 60 per cent had already been written down.

Secondly, it was equally clear that globalisation was exerting a new set of pressures on the financial market place by making international competition more of a reality (see Exhibit 1, page 551). It was a fact that there was unprecedented and growing price competition among banks in Europe, either within countries or across borders, for the business of corporates, who were themselves under great pressure to cut costs, due to both reduced customer loyalty and the need to raise the profitability of many products.

By September 1998, corporate lending had become a low-margin activity under enormous strain and foreign exchange dealing, already suffering from thin margins, was about to be hit with the imminent arrival of the Euro. Even areas where higher fee income had previously been possible (mutual funds and asset management services, for instance), were now heavily contested, despite their previous explosive growth. They would clearly be in an even worse position if a prolonged bear market were to arise out of the economic troubles of 1997 and 1998.

---

* Since World War II the structures and approaches of banking in the US and Continental Europe have diverged even more than before. The dominant model in the latter has been the universal bank capable of handling any financial transaction and with a particular form of customer relationship, known as *relationship banking.* In the U S, by contrast, the Glass Steagall Act separated banks strictly into those which were commercial and those which were investment banks. Now, the Act was scheduled for repeal to allow banks greater flexibility and scope.

* In continental Europe gigantic universal banks, like Deutsche, emerged to exercise a leadership which tended to promote standardised products, especially the debt financing of loyal clients. This was adequate for as long as clients were happy with the services of the *house bank,* the cartel-like pricing of bank products and the shallowness of the pool of equity capital available. In the US, it was, in fact, a different story of banks catering for a mature marketplace with a wide range of sophisticated debt and equity products and needing to please customers who had a natural *capitalistic* preference for equity over debt.

* The natural tendency for take-over bids to be a standard feature of business culture in the US was reinforced by the growth of investment banks whose skills lay in deal-making. In continental Europe, there has been a dearth of such banks, given the traditional cultural antagonism to contested take-overs.

EXHIBIT 1: US vs EUROPEAN BANKING TRADITIONS

In merging to become UBS, the two Swiss partners had definitely followed at least one of the precepts Leonhard Fischer, board member at Dresdner Bank, had applied to his own bank, "We have to expand, become pan-European and define a US strategy or be limited to a niche position".[9] The UBS move had been enthusiastically received by shareholders in February 1998. Already aware of Union Bank's 1997 losses, they were thrilled at the notion that the new UBS would, according to the US Federal Reserve, rank as Number Two in world banking behind the Bank of Tokyo-Mitsubishi.

Even more significantly, it would own the world's fourth largest institutional asset manager, be the world's largest private banker and have one of Europe's premier banks, Warburg Read Dillon, as its investment banking subsidiary.

The declared aim of UBS' new chief executive, Marcel Ospel (former CEO of SBC) was to double UBS' long-term return on equity to between 15 and 20 per cent.

"Our future is not as a bancassurer (like Credit Suisse which bought Winterthur, the giant Swiss insurance company in 1997). We believe that banking and insurance will coverge in a few very select areas such as asset management and financial risk management where there are some synergies. We are determined to build our US business but have no ambition to become a domestic bulge bracket (top tier) player in investment banking at this point in time. Obviously the next thing will be transatlantic deals"[10]

EXHIBIT 2: GERMAN ECONOMY TENDING DOWNWARDS
Source: Germany's GDP spurts but slowing is expected,
Christopher Rhoads, *The Wall St Journal, Europe*, 4-5/12/1998

This intention was reflected in the UBS share price, which had gone up over the period December 1997 (when the takeover was first announced) to May 1998 by 25 per cent. The shareholders seemed equally pleased with the strategy proposed by the dynamic and outsider-driven board of directors. According to Marcel Ospel :

The news in June that the US Federal Reserve had backed the UBS merger was a further fillip to the share price; it was the final regulatory hurdle and had been cleared with ease. Not so the revelation in September that UBS had been forced to write off $690m on its exposure to LTCM. When this giant hedge fund collapsed with liabilities of $3.6 billion, a complicated tax-driven transaction came to light involving LTCM and SBC, which ran counter to the Bank's internal trading rules and seemed suspect to the Swiss Federal Banking Commission.

The impact of the loss itself, and the manner of it, were devastating. With the resignation of Mathis Cabiallavetta, chairman of the former Union Bank, over what were termed "gross shortcomings in risk management", came a fall of one third in the market value of UBS.[11]

One week later, serious questions were also being raised about the possible sale of the Warburg Dillon Read subsidiary by UBS or, at least the possibility of an alignment with its only European-owned rival, Credit Suisse's First Boston.

Each had its woes at the time and the issues were of high relevance to Deutsche Bank. Credit Suisse had just confessed it had been caught out over Russia's default on domestic debt in August and now had exposure of $2.1 billion. UBS was suffering from an increasing shortage of skilled dealers and was believed to have lost $80m in August and September on forex proprietary trading under its division head, Singapore-based Richard Silver. The markets were thus questioning the pretensions, and ability, of the two banks to compete in the world's top league at all, alone. As analyst Clay Harris stated, they were each "bull market darlings as long as the juggernaut of a mergers and acquisitions boom rolled on" but their "inherent volatility" was leading the market to question whether "they can live happily within their parent banks".[12] On the 16th October, Richard Silver resigned with immediate effect.

The Citigroup deal was struck on the sixth of April, some five months after the UBS marriage. It too contained significant messages for Deutsche Bank, coming in the immediate aftermath of mergers between BankAmerica and Nations-Bank and between First Chicago and Bank One, each of which was aimed at creating a pan-American bank. The Citigroup affair was, however, categorically different. The CEOs of the two partners, Sanford Weill and John Reed, were confidently thinking forward to a situation in which Citigroup would access one billion customers worldwide by 2010. As Table 5 suggests, the intention was to put together a true *Allfinanz* model, a one-stop shop for financial services trading under a global brand name.

Financial Services Activity	1997 Revenues in $ billion	
	Citibank	Travelers
Consumer finance	-	1.7
Corporate lending	1.2	-
Credit cards	6.9	NA
Cash management	2.3	-
Investment banking services	4.1	21.5
Life insurance	-	4.4
Private banking	1.1	-
Property & casualty insurance	-	9.9
Retail banking	6.0	

TABLE 5: PIECES OF THE CITIGROUP FINANCIAL
SERVICES JIGSAW
Source: *Business Week*, 20/4/98

This was "a merger that would make big waves".[13] Among other analysts' predictions were the notions that, as a result, banks such as Chase and J. P. Morgan might need to merge or that, once the US had repealed barriers to *Allfinanz* operations, continental insurers like Germany's Allianz might start shopping in the US. "The race was on".[14]

Demographic pressures were widely perceived to lie behind the formation of Citigroup. In the US and western Europe the post-war baby-boomers were entering their peak savings years, their 50s, during which they would invest heavily against retirement. The patent inadequacy of governmental welfare state-type pension plans was obliging even medium-income savers (often with government support), even in welfarist western Europe, to look to private pensions as the key retirement instrument. Inflows into retirement-savings plans run by US mutual funds had already, by mid 1998, brought their assets up to $4.8 trillion, with new money coming in at a 30 per cent annual rate. Notably, the Japanese had over $10 trillion in banks accounts savings that could be moved into mutual funds.

The first key question was, therefore, how could a financial services operator maximise market share in a world, firstly, where a private pensions revolution was occurring and, secondly, where there was a widespread convergence of distribution channels, with, for example, banks selling stocks and insurance agents selling mutual funds?

The second key question was about the habits of the well-heeled financial services consumers, either corporates or private citizens. Technology was certainly speeding the construction of *one-stop shopping* by enabling the creation of sophisticated databases showing the profiles and spending patterns of consumers. But how soon would it be before Europe followed the lead of the US in widespread acceptance of such practices as telephone banking and Internet stock-trading? One estimate by Bill Burnham, analyst at Piper Jaffray, was that 30 per cent of all retail stock transactions were already being done on the Internet in America. The possibilities for the *Allfinanz* operator to create virtual financial services web sites were endless, even if they required very heavy investments in database marketing. But timing of strategic moves was of the essence.

The Citigroup move fitted this framework exactly. But, would the merger, the first between an American insurer and commercial bank in six decades, actually work? Would the two partners be easily able to cross-market products, having given up tribal ways? Would the prior investment bank link-up of Salomon Smith Barney and Travelers actually begin to bear real fruit soon, as Travelers had promised?

These were some of the issues preoccupying Wall Street (and Deutsche Bank strategy planners) as, in October, Citigroup reported a 53 per cent fall in net income for the previous quarter (as on the same period in 1997) to $739m. There was even more anxiety when, at the start of November, Citigroup's president, Jamie Dimon, suddenly resigned. He had been given the task of meshing the divisions of the new group together. Commentator Grant Ringshaw reckoned, not without good reason, that "Dimon's departure is symptomatic of deep problems in the divisions... Citigroup, under the leadership of co-chairmen Sandy Weill and John Reed, has tried to jam together the Salomon Smith Barney (investment banking) and Citibank (commercial banking) businesses too quickly. The result has been a series of bitter battles."[15]

This in-fighting was at considerable variance from the overriding rationale for the deal. This was, in the words of Deryck Maughan, Citigroup VP in charge of group strategy, that:

"The business logic for the deal is more compelling, the more you look at it. We are convinced that we can grow market share, that the forces such as global competition, which created the merger, will continue and that many more banks and securities firms will be pressurised by the marketplace to rationalise. We are all aware that banks and securities companies are not that easy to put together. It requires a degree of finesse. But I think it is right to take the hard decisions up front rather than to allow ourselves to be engaged in culture wars for the next two or three years".[16]

But would it really be a case of *big is beautiful?* Peter Coy, Business Week's associate economics editor, was pessimistic. "Assets" he remarked "can be a heavy weight to bear when they under perform. Weill and Reed are betting that they can gain what is quaintly known as *share of wallet...* But, for all the grand visions, financial supermarkets have an inglorious history".[17]

AND SO TO DEUTSCHE BANK...

In February 1998 Rolf Breuer, Deutsche Bank's chairman, claimed that Deutsche did "not intend to join in the merger mania gripping European banks".[18] Be that as it may, on the 30th November of that year he announced that it was acquiring, subject to American US regulatory approval, the US investment bank, Bankers Trust, for $10.1 billion and that, even after spending $93/share on this purchase, the Bank would still have funds left to "pull off a major deal in Europe".[19] The chairman said he was also looking for a major change in the bank's financial performance. Its return on equity in 1997 had been a meagre 6.4 per cent: by 2001, five years after becoming chairman, he wanted this to be 25 per cent.

Commentators Paula Hawkins and Eric Culp[20] reckoned that the Bankers Trust move was just the sort of "big deal" needed to reverse Deutsche Bank's "decline over the past few years".[21] Certainly, the Bank had been shocked to be pushed into second place in Germany's rankings by the merger of Bayerische Vereinsbank and Bayerische Hypothekenbank. But there had been a string of even worse occurrences recently to cause disquiet.

Perhaps the most significant had been the fact of Deutsche Bank's losing its cherished triple A rating in August 1998 when Fitch IBCA downgraded it to AA+ and Standard & Poor's followed suit. And this for a bank with assets of $570b and capital of $18b! Then there was the matter of the $300m loss caused to the Bank by the criminal activities of a rogue fund manager, Peter Young, whose investment portfolio, on investigation, turned out to be worth far from the superb rating it had previously been given.

Staff defections in the investment side of the business were also a well-publicised problem, and had been ever since Deutsche bank had acquired Morgan Grenfell, the British merchant bank, in 1989 and endured endless and damaging *integration* problems. This move, "a textbook example of the pitfalls of M&A" according to Wall Street Journal's Paul Beckett, was one of the reasons for the loss of the triple A, another being the bank's exposure to the Russian's economic difficulties in 1998.

Perhaps, the results of the Deutsche Morgan Grenfell (DMG) operations could have been anticipated better. DMG had tried to expand its US operation aggressively from 1995 onwards by hiring of 1000 staff each year for several years only to find that, after all, it was not likely to achieve the sort of success targetted - revenues of $2bn by 2000. Not only that, "American investment bankers charged with boosting Deutsche Morgan Grenfell's US presence were *anathema* to their stiffer British and German colleagues who balked at the Americans' lavish expenses".[22] The eventual result was massive redundancies in the cutback that followed.

But it was the Quattrone affair that had loomed largest.

In July, Frank Quattrone, head of Deutsche Bank's high-tech corporate finance team, had quit the bank to join Credit Suisse First Boston, *taking almost his entire team of 131 people with him.* Quattrone's criticism of his German bosses was that they generally failed to act in "Internet time" and that the only thing they really cared about was Germany. "We were" he claimed "off their radar screen".[23] He echoed the view held by many former DMG staff that the German managers were "hierarchical and bureaucratic".[24] Of course, the fact that Quattrone and his team had shifted employers for a total package thought to be as high as $1 billion was important. But it was evidently not as significant as the autonomy he claimed he would enjoy with his new employer "to invest, have our own budget and head count".[25]

The Deutsche Bank takeover of Bankers Trust put all these problems into perspective. It was the largest bank in the world and, as Rolf Breuer himself proudly and polysyllabically put it, "ein richtiges globales Finanzsdienstleistungsunternehmen" (*a truly compelling global financial services company*).[26] It had performed successfully over the period 1994-97, raising its net income from 18.4 to 24.2 billion DM and, in the process, it had shifted the contribution on net commission business from 30.2 per cent to 36.8 per cent, whilst reducing that from net interest to 45.8 per cent from 61 per cent.

Factor	Deutsche Bank	Bankers Trust
Number of employees	66,833	18,286
Total assets ($b)	575	140
Profits ($b)	22.6	3.5
Turnover ($b)	33.5	11.7
Return on Equity (%, 1998) before tax	6.4	11.0
Size ranking in own Domestic market	No2	No8

TABLE 6: HOW THEY COMPARE
Sources: *Datastream, Bloomberg, Bankers Trust*

"Cost synergies" Breuer claimed "is one reason for this merger, but not the most important one. Bankers Trust is a platform on which we shall build an opening in the US".[27] The news lifted trading in banking shares on Wall Street, with Bankers Trust shares shooting up, on the 23rd November, from $77 to $87.
However, note that, at the offer price of $93, the shares were worth just over twice book value, the bank having lost one third of its stock market valuation since the summer. Truth to tell, it had been a bad year for Bankers Trust. Quite apart from posting an unexpectedly high $488m loss in the third quarter, the bank had also been undermined by its involvement in the LTCM bail-out and by having to reveal an $875m exposure to speculative hedge funds.

So what, in fact, would it bring to the party by way of products and expertise? *The Financial Times'* Graham Bowley and Tracy Corrigan thought that the acquisition would "definitely advance DMG's position in the US market. Bankers Trust has expertise in derivatives and a desirable position in the high-yield bond and initial public offerings (IPO) markets". But the DMG-

Bankers combination was not strong enough, in their view, to rival Merrill Lynch or Morgan Stanley Dean Witter. Indeed, Bankers could be looked upon, in the worst case scenario, as "an undifferentiated competitor in a business that is rife with over-capacity." [28]

Pros	Cons
Deutsche gets a proper foothold in the US market - realising a dream. Increases its abilities in the areas of high-yield debt, equity under-writing and asset management	Commercial banks often find relationships with investment banks very difficult. Their cultures are basically antagonistic. Neither bank is known for innovatory management.
Bankers gets access to Deutsche Bank capital for expansion which it needs after its huge losses in 1998.	Bankers is not a top-tier underwriter or M&A adviser. Deutsche Bank is not widely recognised as a leading U.S. commercial banks.

TABLE 7: PROS AND CONS OF DEUTSCHE'S STRATEGY

Analyst Mark Hoge of Credit Suisse First Boston was much more sceptical. "I'm worried" he declared "that Deutsche is getting a little out of its depth. It could get messy".[29] His comments were based on two areas of concern: the financing of the deal and the management of the personnel involved. The first was planned to be accomplished by selling new shares worth about £1.5 billion, as well as using cash and bonds. On top of the acquisition cost, Deutsche Bank would have to write off goodwill ($5bn) and spend heavily on restructuring charges ($1bn).

> *"DAG and HBV, the two German banking unions, are threatening to disrupt the carefully planned start of the single currency on Jan 1st 1999 by threatening an overtime ban by their 470,000 members... They are claiming, on the basis of the German system of national agreements, a 6.5 per cent pay increase, a shorter working week (35 hours rather than 39) and an immediate ban on redundancies. They are strongly opposed to the banks' requirement that Saturday should be treated as a normal working day and that the bonus given annually to many bank employees, one month's extra pay (the so-called 13th month), be scrapped.*

EXHIBIT 3: LIFE IN THE SLOW TRACK?
Source: German bank unions threaten Euro launch, David Gow,
Mark Milner and Jill Treanor, *The Guardian*, 14/12/98

It was thought that Deutsche Bank would not need capital from its investments in German industry – its 20 per cent plus stake in Daimler Benz, for example, which it was known to be wanting to liquidate when the German government relaxed the capital gains tax regulations. But there was worry in Frankfurt on the matter of the financing of the deal and a certain amount of scepticism also about Deutsche Bank's strategy.

So far as the staff issue was concerned, it was clear at the outset that strategic synergy would necessarily mean redundancies. One initial estimate was that between 5,000 and 10,000 staff would go in New York and London, reducing the pay bill by some $1.5bn. This was not the largest problem expected by Deutsche Bank, however. It was how to *retain* those staff thought crucial to the success of the new group. When Bankers Trust bought the Baltimore broker Alex Brown in 1997, it set aside $200m to fund "a management retention plan", i.e., to pay loyalty bonuses.

Financial Results	1997	1998
Net Income (billion marks)	1.02	3.38
Trading Profit (billion marks)	3.6	3.47

TABLE 7: DEUTSCHE BANK'S FINANCIALS
Source: Deutsche Bank is ready for French call,
The Wall St. Journal, Europe, 19-20/3/1999.

Deutsche Bank's integration committee started to select the best staff soon after the acquisition bid was made. It was faced with estimates that it would cost as much as $1bn to build a first-class investment banking team. Vital to the operation were Frank Newman, chairman of Bankers Trust, whose take-home pay in 1998 had been $55m, and Mary Cirillo, head of the group's global custody business. They were to receive bonuses of $10m each. Other staff who were to be retained would share in bonuses worth $380. Such bonuses were colloquially known in the investment banking business as *golden handcuffs*.[30]

The biggest question in the minds of the architects of the strategy was, of course, not just one of teams and teamwork. It was whether Deutsche Bank's new financing initiative to raise equity capital to buy out Bankers Trust would succeed as well as it was hoped. The advertisement for the new issue spoke glowingly, after all, of the bank's improved cost-efficiency, its strengthened position as a leading European Bank and its Weltweite Wachstumstrategie (world-wide growth strategy) involving the Bankers Trust takeover.[31]

* * * * * * * * * * * * * * * * * * * *

APPENDIX 1

	1998	1997
Post Tax Income (DMm)	2431	1493
Total Assets (DMb)	1215	1043
Cost/Income Ratio (%)	73	73
Share Price (DM)		
High	162.20	104.30
Low	108.80	71.32
Employees (and branches)		
in Germany	48130	49086
	(1572)	(1584)
and abroad	26024	27055
	(716)	(771)
Earnings per share (DM)	4.57	2.95
No of shares outstanding (Ave m.)	532	505

Source: *Deutsche Bank at a Glance*, Deutsche Bank, 72-020/02   09/1998

REFERENCES

1   US Take-over, Kirstie Hamilton and John Waples, *The Sunday Times*, 20/12/1998

2   Wall Street in $2.2bn profits fall, Oliver August, *The Times*, 29/12/1998

3   As 1

4   The buck pops here, Larry Elliott, *The Guardian*, 7/12/1998

5   As 4

6   WTO risk to financial markets, Guy de Jonquieres, *The Financial Times*, 16/10/1997

7   Breuer sees European banking shake-up, *The Financial Times*, 11/9/1998

8   Bank eat bank, Thane Peterson, *Business Week*, 21/9/1998

9   As 8

10   Profile Marcel Ospel, William Hall & Clay Harris, *The Financial Times*, 25 May 1998

11   UBS chairman resigns in fall-out from LTCM crisis, Phillip Coggan & Clay Harris, *The Financial Times*, 3/10/1998

12   National champions were more bruised than most, Clay Harris, *The Financial Times*, 13/10/1998

13   This merger will make big waves, Stanley Reed, Kerry Capell & Thane Peterson, *Business Week*, 20/4/1998

14   As 13

15   Can Citigroup be saved from the storm, Grant Ringshaw, *The Sunday Telegraph*, 8/11/1998

16   As 15

17   Great Big Company. Great Big Mistake, Peter Coy, *Business Week*, 20/4/1998

18   Deutsche's voyage of the damned, Paula Hawkins and Eric Culp, *The European*, 16-22/2/1998

19   Deutsche builds empire, Jill Treanor and Lisa Buckingham, *The Guardian*, 1/12/1998

20   As 18

21   Deutsche Bank push into US market set to be a bumpy ride, Paul Beckett, *The Wall Street Journal, Europe*, 27-28/11/1998

22   Europeans at the gate, Garth Alexander, *The Sunday Times*, 6/12/1998

23   As 22

24   As 22

25   Die Deutsche Bank wird mit dem Kauf von Bankers Trust zur grossten Bank der Welt, *Frankfurter Allgemeine Zeitung*, 24/11/1998

26   As 19

27   Deutsche refuses to give up its American dream, Graham Bowley and Tracy Corrigan, *The Financial Times*, 21/10/1998

28   Is Deutsche Bank "out of its depth?", Thane Peterson and Gary Silverman, *Business Week*, 7/12/1998

29   As 28

30   As 19

31   Die neuen Aktien den Deutsche Bank, *Frankfurter Allgemeine Zeitung*, 14/4/1999

RUSSIA AT THE CROSSROADS

Abstract:

Russia at the Crossroads deals with the tableau of circumstances and events that covered the period between the momentous decision by the Russian government to renege on some of its financial obligations in August 1998 and the resignation of president Yeltsin on the eve of the millennium. The case study enables the reader to probe the political and economic conditions of Russia at this time and draw conclusions as to, firstly, the viability of the Russian government's *perestroika* thrust towards economic reforms and, secondly, the possibility that Russia may be able to make a new beginning with the ending of the Yeltsin reign.

Questions:

(1) On the basis of case data, explain in detail why Russia was in turmoil over the period 1998-2000 and how Russian business was reacting to the turmoil.

(2) If you were a member of the IMF team, would you be inclined to persist in aiding Russia? Why? Why not? What conditions might you set for any future loan?

(3) Does Vladimir Putin, in your view, represent *a new beginning*?

Case Timing: 1998-2000

A MEETING OF MINDS?

"The realistic way out of this crisis for Russia is for aliens from another planet to land and sort everything out".[1]

This bitter comment from Yevgeny Yasin, former Russian economics minister, did little more than echo the unreal atmosphere surrounding the Moscow summit between US president Bill Clinton and his Russian counterpart Boris Yeltsin on the first of September 1998. There was certainly a lot of sorting out to do, economically and politically, in Russia because the country was in crisis, if not in chaos, and time was short.

It was, without doubt, one of the strangest presidential get-togethers that could have been imagined. Bill Clinton had arrived at the height of the impeachment crisis in the US over the Monica Lewinsky affair. As for Boris Yeltsin, he was fighting against chronic ill health and for what remained of his formal presidential role and powers, against a background of political and economic *mayhem,* and, on the face of it, losing.

It was only the previous day that the Russian parliament, the Duma, had rejected by a large majority the main plank of the Yeltsin plan for coping with the chaos, the re-nomination of Viktor Chernomyrdin as prime minister. It seemed unimportant that he had been dismissed by the president from this very office as a failure only five months before. Nor, for that matter, that the largest groups in the Duma, the Communists and the Nationalists, had associated Chernomyrdin specifically with the apparent economic débâcle resulting from the Yeltsin market reform strategy.

As if that were not enough, on that day the Dow Jones index fell by 512 points to close at its lowest level since November 1997. Wall Street worries about the world economic crisis also had an impact on European stock markets to force prices substantially down there. Russia's difficulties, in fact, seemed to be only amplifying the dire economic news that was coming from Asia Pacific and South America.

The previous how-to-turn-Russia-round *headache* was rapidly becoming a *migraine* for all those contemplating investment in a country which had, until relatively recently, been tipped as one of the world's best long-term economic growth prospects.

564

RUSSIA DEFAULTS

For Western banks already involved in Russia, as, for example, bond investors, there was much to consider as the political impasse facing president Yeltsin had become increasingly visible. Minds were being concentrated even before the peremptory replacement of the reformist ministers in the previous government (Messrs Kiryenko, Chubais and Nemtsov) and certainly before shock-horror news that broke on the 17th August 1998.

On this day, contrary to all previous pronouncements, the Russian government declared that it was devaluing the rouble and that it had imposed a 90-day moratorium on the repayment of some foreign debts by Russian banks. It also froze all payments on a total of $40 billion in Treasury bonds. This catastrophic event took place against a background of knowledge that lending by western banks to central and eastern Europe, including Russia, had risen by $2.7 billion in the second quarter of the year, after an increase of $3.3 billion in the first. Stock markets round the world reacted immediately.

Russia's problems were now totally exposed, the big issue being, of course, the extent of Russia's indebtedness. It was in hock to the IMF, the German government and the Western banking system in general. What was worse was that the country's economic slide was taking place in the face of aid that had been supplied to ensure the exact opposite, Russia's turnaround and growth in line with the principles of *perestroika* and *glasnost.*

Add in popular opposition to the privileged power and wealth position of the so-called *oligarchy* of industrial magnates that had seized control of a swathe of Russia's key privatised firms, and it is a case of confusion worse confounded. And, if that was not enough, there was always Russia's nuclear arsenal of 11,000 weapons to keep western governments and the global financial markets worried.

MONEY MATTERS

The Group of Seven leading industrial countries, under the chairmanship of Tony Blair, the UK prime minister, had scheduled a speedy meeting to deal with the Russian challenge. The European Commission was urgently lobbying EU finance ministers to adopt a common EU-G7 approach to give a more positive message than the standard IMF policy position. This had long been, of course, that more IMF aid would be extended only in return for more fundamental economic reforms. Indeed, EU finance commissioner, Yves Thibault de Silguy, feared that a failure to help now might hand the Communists in the Duma a political victory which could lead to a defiance of

IMF guidelines and even the *re-nationalisation* of key privatised elements in Russian industry.

The Commission was obviously concerned not only with Russia, but worried that current market turmoil might, in some way, affect the launch of Europe's single currency on the first of January, 1999.

So far as the IMF was concerned, its director, Michel Camdessus, and Viktor Chernomyrdin, the Russian prime minister, had already begun emergency talks on the 26th August in the Ukraine. The topic, as ever, was aid. This time the discussions centred on the already-announced re-scheduling of debt, the free fall taking place on the stock market and the crashing rouble.

The IMF was, itself, in difficulty, however. Having agreed a new conditional $22.6 billion rescue package for Russia in July and already paid over $4.8 billion, it was pledged to supply a $4.3 billion tranche on September 15th. But the IMF itself was running out of money. The key question was, would it now hand out the funds?

Month in 1998	Event
February	Oil prices dropped to below $15 per barrel, the lowest price since 1994
March	President Yeltsin replaced Viktor Chemomyrdin with banker Sergei Kiriyenko
May	The Russian central bank uses up scarce foreign exchange to back the rouble as pressure mounts
July	IMF granted a $22.6 billion credit over two years in return for promises of tough reforms
August 17	Despite promises to hold the value of the rouble, it was devalued. Government announced a 90-day moratorium on short-term debt repayments. All trading in government bills and bonds was frozen.
August 23	Kiryenko government arbitrarily sacked after five months in office.
August 25	Announcement of rouble debt restructuring plan, worth $32b. Treasury bills for longer-term lower rate rouble bonds, These were approximately equivalent to 15-30% of their original value. No change made, however, in the repayment schedule for Russia's $1 40 billion dollar-denominated debt. Major worries about this remained.
August 26	Central Bank stated it could no longer use reserves to maintain the rouble's value. Rouble slid. By the end of the year the rouble was trading at 20.62 to the $.

TABLE 1: 1998 CASE CHRONOLOGY – THE RAKE'S PROGRESS?

Since July 1997 alone the IMF had, in fact, loaned a total of $35 billion in aid to South Korea, Indonesia and Thailand. Now, as the world's lender of last resort, it was looking to the US Congress for a further injection of funds to replenish its almost exhausted coffers. In return, the Congress, bearing in mind that America had 18 per cent of the votes in the IMF, wanted to know urgently what Russia planned to do to tackle what Congress saw as Russia's main inter-dependent problems, its rampant budget deficit and chronic inability to collect taxes.

Congress was also aware of the significant fact that, over the period 1993-7, capital inflow to Russia stood at $58 billion, whilst outflows amounted to $66 billion. In fact, a 45 per cent increase in the IMF's general resource base had been agreed as recently as autumn 1997, but Congress had refused to pay up.

The crux of all the concern was the possibility of a further Russian default. It was now looking as if only a re-negotiation of government debt and more support for the rouble and the balance of payments would help. The country's plight was severe. Since the start of 1998 the decline in share values on Moscow's embryonic stock market had amounted to 80 per cent, giving it a value equal to that of the British supermarket chain, J. Sainsbury. Moreover, although the decision in mid-August had been to let the rouble fall by some seven per cent, it had, by mid-September, been devalued *de facto* in the market-place by 20 per cent.

THE EXPOSURE PROBLEM

How big was the exposure problem? Cumulatively, and since the advent of *perestroika*, the developed nations had lent some $88 billion to Russia, of which loans backed by the German government amounted to $30 billion.[2] According to the US investment bank Brown Brothers Harriman, US banks had about $7.6 billion of debt outstanding of which Chase Manhattan accounted for $500m, the Bank of America $412m and Citicorp $420m.[3] The top four German banks had exposures, said Salomon Smith Barney, of $2 billion in total.[4] In terms of individual bank difficulties arising directly from the Russian experience, it is noteworthy that Deutsche Bank had just had its treasured triple A rating downgraded by Standard and Poor's.

Two hedge funds were also known to be in great difficulties at the time, the epic saga of LTCM coming to light only later. High Risk Opportunities was believed to be facing bankruptcy at the start of September, as a result of borrowing heavily to invest in the high-yielding rouble-denominated Treasury bills (GKOs), which had been made subject to the repayment moratorium by the Russian authorities and, in fact, arbitrarily swapped for longer-term securities.

(See Table 1 on page 566.) Quantum, the hedge fund run by financier George Soros, was also in very serious trouble with losses of $2 billion. Incidentally, it was he who had helped precipitate the crisis by writing to *The Financial Times* on the 13th August in the following vein:

> *"The meltdown in Russian financial markets has reached a terminal phase. The trouble is that the action that is necessary to deal with a banking crisis is diametrically opposed to the action that has been agreed with the IMF to deal with the budget crisis. The best solution would be to introduce a currency board after a modest devaluation. The alternatives are default or hyperinflation"*

It should not be forgotten, however that the one highly positive aspect of the Yeltsin regime had been to bring down inflation from 1526 per cent to 15 per cent in the previous five years. To the typical Russian Man-in-Gorky Street this mattered not at all, of course. His problems were *now*. And all he could see was intense political infighting between the leading Duma factions, the nationalist Zhirinovsky, the Communist Zuyganov, and the weakened president and growing economic misery. The big question was whether the new prime minister, Yevgeny Primakov, who was appointed with Duma support on the 11th September 1998, instead of Yeltsin's first nominee, Viktor Chernomyrdin, would do any better.

Western mutual funds, too, were caught in the maelstrom. Two UK operators, Regent Pacific and Baring Asset Management, had suspended trading until the funds assets could again, as was said, be properly valued. Fleming Russia Securities' Rupert Rucker spoke for many in the sector when he said:

> *"It's all very depressing. No one is going to see a return in the foreseeable future. However, a Russian equity market will survive. They have genuinely privatised, there are shareholders and they can't go back to Communism. Companies will need to raise capital and the only place they can do it is in the stock market".* [5]

So anxious about the overall situation was the UK's Financial Services Authority (FSA), that it began forcing UK banks to hand over information about their exposure to *derivatives*, as well as trades in bills and bonds, in the Russian context. What was, perhaps, perplexing about this level of worry was the fact that Russia had a relatively small economy. It ranked only 14th in the world in GDP terms.

On the other hand, it was not just Russia that was at stake. As commentator Bill Jamieson pointed out:

> *"Russia is yet another piece falling into a spreading jigsaw of global depression – and it is uncomfortably close to Europe. Already almost half the*

world's GDP and more than 3 billion people are caught up in a spreading chaos of collapsing stock-markets, melting currencies and spiralling global bad debt, now reckoned at over $2 trillion". [6]

Nonetheless, Gunter Rexrodt, German economics minister, had no doubts about his country's position. "Wir lassen Russland nicht fallen" ("We will not let Russia fall"), he said. In his view, an unstable Russia would be much more dangerous and expensive than one on the path to market reforms. The risks to the German economy posed by Russia? *Beherrschbar* ("manageable") he declared.[7]

THE ECONOMICS OF THE MADHOUSE?

There is no gainsaying that Russia was, and is, a very rich country. Most of the wealth was and is, however, in extractive industries and *underground*. Truth to tell, so far as Russia's commodity wealth was concerned, the situation was very difficult despite the fact that Russia was the world's third largest producer of oil.

Since 1997 the world price of gas and oil had, in fact, fallen substantially. Indeed it was only in 2000 that it would rise again, and then substantially. The price fall up to 2000 had had the effect of gravely compromising the partial privatisation of Russian oil companies like Gazprom (5 per cent) and Rosneft (75 per cent) on which the government had been banking. The administration was, it must be said, more intent on raising instant revenue than on satisfying western calls for steps towards a market economy. The price fall had also strongly contributed to a grave 4.5 per cent fall in Russia's GDP in the fiscal year to July 1998, after a slight growth in the previous year.

In late 1998 Russia, as a leading exporter of precious metals like platinum and palladium, was, in fact, caught in the grip of a 20-year price low, according to the global Commodity Research Bureau's index of 17 key commodity prices. The market forces continuing to push prices lower were, firstly, the slump in demand from Asia, and secondly, the need for weaker countries like Russia to continue to increase sales, if necessary by dropping prices. Falling export revenues inevitably meant less ability to buy much-needed imports, of tea, sugar and grain, for example, in which there was a global supply glut. The problems were drearily circular. To cap it all, the price of gold, normally a secure haven in times of global economic difficult, itself fell to a 19-year low on the 28th August.

Russia's external state debts were enormous. In mid-1998 it owed a sovereign debt of $150 billion, a sum equal to 30 per cent of the country's GDP, having inherited from the collapse of the USSR a burden of $90 billion. As for internal debt, this added up to about $51 billion.

Many commentators thought that one way of dealing with the slide in global equity markets was to create greater liquidity by reducing interest rates. This would, firstly, reduce the cost of debt to manufacturing industry and, secondly, allow investors to borrow more cheaply to buy shares. So far as the US was concerned, it might also halt the rise in the value of the dollar. As the world's leading economy, its monetary posture was reckoned to be pivotal. Thus, in early September 1998 pressure was known to be mounting on Alan Greenspan, chairman of the US' Federal Reserve, to cut interest rates. The problem was that, the last time this was done in the US (in 1987), monetary policy had been loosened too much and damaging global inflationary pressures had been unleashed. Having himself warned repeatedly since 1996 that the US stock market was suffering from what he called *irrational exuberance*, Greenspan was not thought likely to err on the side of generosity in reducing US interest rates. But, it must be said that, on the 29th August, the Nikkei index in Japan slipped again. This time to a 12-year low of 13,915.

EXHIBIT 1: SIREN VOICES

It was this latter that was, in August, the bone of contention between the Russian government and external creditor banks. They had invested in some $17 billion of short-term, high-yield rouble-denominated Treasury bills (GKOs) and Federal bonds (OFZs) to help finance Russia's budget deficit – 6.8 per cent of GDP in 1997, according to Goldman Sachs, only to find that the August debt re-scheduling had, as Table 1 page 566 points out, cost them dear. But it is worth counter-balancing, yet again, the fact of Russia's short-term financial weakness with the equally significant fact of the country's *immense* reserves of oil, gas, aluminium, copper, and strategic materials like manganese, vanadium and cobalt.

FEARS OF A BANKING CRASH

The re-scheduling plan was only part of the crisis measures that the new government had carried out on the 17th August to alleviate its urgent liquidity crisis. The other key plank, as we have seen, was the devaluation of the rouble. President Yeltsin had, it is true, consistently and vehemently denied before the event that there was any such prospect, re-emphasising this only as recently as the 14th August.

> "The fact is that, despite its collapsing economy, the Kremlin has somehow managed to continue pouring enormous sums into its strategic forces and weapons programmes. For example, during this decade, even as some Russian workers were going unpaid, Moscow deployed a new mobile "Topol M2" ICBM, refitted its Typhoon class submarines to accommodate SS-N 24/26 missiles, implemented a stealth fighter programme and built a fifth generation Borei class ballistic submarine. Even a partial list of such expensive military investments totals around $10 billion – a sum representing half of the (last) ill-fated IMF facility".

EXHIBIT 2: RUSSIA STILL IN THE MILITARY GAME
Source: Abandon the unsustainable firewall between financial policy and national security, Roger Robinson, *The Wall Street Journal, Europe*, 28-29/8/98

Indeed, on the date of the announcement, the government went out of its way to avoid any reference to devaluation, speaking instead of a widening of the corridor within which the rouble could fluctuate. This did not impress the financial *cognoscenti* in the Moscow population. Within minutes of the change, queues started forming at the capital's banks demanding dollars for roubles or, failing that, removing roubles from bank accounts. The money markets took full note: the rouble slumped even further.

Such behaviours brought fears of a banking crash. The collapse of Bank Imperial, Russia's 13th largest, on the 26th August did nothing to build confidence. Nor did the trenchant attacks mounted by analysts such as the *International Herald Tribune's* Michael Wines. Under a banner headline "Corralling Russia's Cowboy Banks" he wrote:

"It was a brief but wild ride for Russia's cowboy banks, which are saddled up to a crumbling economy and headed for disaster. They gave a government easy credit and got hooked on the returns. Then their flight to the dollar made things worse. Now the Russian banking system is insolvent, the victim of mismanagement, bad bets on the rouble and investments in near-worthless government bonds".[8]

It should come as no surprise in view of such comments that, immediately the government announced the nationalisation of SBS-Agros Bank, Russia's third largest, on the 27th August, four banks indicated they would merge and, within two days of the news, another three said they would act thus. Their collective bad debt exposure was put at \$4 billion and these were the best-placed of the country's 1,300 banks to weather the storms. (See Table 2.) None of these changes involved a switch in the position of the biggest bank, the state-owned Sberbank, whose assets amounted to over \$31 billion and which was regarded as too important to be other than safe.

Russian banks, as Michael Wines pointed out, are not "banks as Westerners know them". Most Russians did not trust them or use them, preferring to keep savings at home (out of sight of the taxman) or in Sberbank. Some of the larger ones were the cash dispensers for their super-rich owners' giant corporate holdings, some of the smaller were more, allegedly, in the nature of money launderers or currency speculators. By western standards all were under-capitalised and an estimated 80 per cent were in danger of going under. Among the critical tasks facing the government at the start of September was, therefore, providing finance to the banks to stem the run on them that was taking place.

Bank & Group	Business Ties	claimed assets (\$bn)
Inkombank	Chocolate, paper, metals, aircraft	5.59
National Reserve Bank	Gazprom & govt. securities etc.	1.64
Avtobank	Corporate banking	1.40
Alfa Bank	Cement, oil, real estate & food retailing	1.18
Group A Total		**9.81**
Uneximbank	Metals, oil, foreign trade & pensions	3.77
Menatep	Oil, mining, paper, textiles, chemicals, media	3.06
Most	Media, construction, investment	1.43
Group B Total		**8.26**

TABLE 2: KEY MERGED RUSSIAN BANK GROUPS
Source: Brunswick Warburg, IHT, 29-30/8/98

RUNNING THE SYSTEM

How did society operate in such a precarious situation? The answer is quite simple: by running a non-cash or *virtual* economy. For many ordinary citizens in Russia, the key difficulty was not so much the forlorn hope of trying to withdraw savings from a bank, nor even of passing shops selling designer clothes that could never be afforded, but of existing without pay. (See Exhibit 3.)

According to analyst Robin Lodge, "In a cash-starved economy, the value of the rouble holds little sway. Hardship and shortages have taught Russian citizens how to survive with no money."[9] This was done by self-reliance (e.g., growing your own vegetables, wherever possible) and barter. It was commonplace in Russia to see people selling factory products, pots and pans, cuddly toys, underwear, that workers had been given in lieu of wages at the factory in the street or by the roadside. It was also done by moonlighting: a double job was standard practice wherever and whenever it could be done.

However, the hardship facing ordinary Russian citizens, as of September the first 1998, was of a different magnitude from what it had been during the Gorbachov-Yeltsin reform period to date. According to Al Breach of the Russian-European Centre for Economic Policy, Russia was *bankrupt* and, if things did not get better, there would be *starvation come winter.* [10]

> *"The bank will re-open in half an hour" said Irena Zhumatova, a pensioner, jealously guarding her number one position in the queue. "They are out to lunch. My savings are in roubles. I think the bank still has them. If I get them back, I am going to spend them quickly – on anything. There's no point in keeping roubles now"*

EXHIBIT 3: DOWN TO THE WIRE
Source: Muscovites stop counting the rouble,
Tom Whitehouse, *The Guardian*, 27/8/98

Like society generally, industry, too, operated the barter system as a way of avoiding the use of cash, and the tax liabilities associated with the use of finance that could be tracked by tax inspectors. The power station providing no-invoice electricity to the mine in exchange for no-invoice coal, for instance. So widespread had been this practice that the new job of barter negotiator had emerged *within* Russia. These were people who arranged invoice-less deals between partners who otherwise would go out of business because they either lacked cash or couldn't raise credit. (See Exhibit 4 on page 575.)

Of course, the other way of playing the game was by *never settling your bills*. This, like barter, was endemic in Russia since, all it required was good faith on the part of the players. All it needed was that no-one ever expected cash payment, all acquiesced in the system and no bills were ever paid in cash. Indeed, Russian banks had produced variants of ordinarily dependable payment instruments like bills of exchange *(veksels),* some of which were passed from firm to firm as cash equivalents but never encashed. Not paying wages in such conditions was not abnormal.

Those who are astounded by this practice need to recognise that, under the 70-year long period of Soviet Communism in the USSR, managers had been able to hone both their bartering and non-cash management skills to the highest possible degree. The business climate then was one of state planning of all manufacturing and financial accounting without reference to corporate profitability. In such a context the unconvertible rouble became less a store of value than a form of bargaining chip or a *counter*. For many, the issue now was whether such times could ever return; for some, the question was whether they should. These were, typically, workers and pensioners who had had the previous security of their known world removed and replaced by a get-rich-quick, IOU society in which they were heavy losers.

The Communist Party in the Duma, led by Gennady Zyuganov, and the Nationalists, led by Vladimir Zhirinovsky, had long been a thorn in Yeltsin's flesh in this matter. They had been the losers in the *perestroika* process. Many sought a return to a sort of economic control world, a sort of *Gosplan* for the millenium.

A QUESTION OF OLIGARCHY

"Moscow", wrote Russian analyst Patricia Krantz in early 1998, "has to halt its lurch toward crony capitalism". She was referring to the phenomenon whereby a small number of Russian super-rich industrial magnates (so called *oligarchs)* had managed to craft huge bank-industry empires for themselves by acquiring elements of once state-owned firms as they were privatised by the government. These oligarchs, "politically well-connected entrepreneurs" in her phraseology, had espoused the *chaebol-keiretsu* style of conglomerate management typical of Asia Pacific and were ruling the privatised industry roost.[11] This style of operation resulted, said Krantz, in a "closed and directed type of economic management" in Russia and certainly not in the US' market-driven, open style.

The phenomenon, and the players in it, were consistently criticised in the western media and Russia alike. What offended was the alleged rapaciousness and scandalous behaviour of leading commercial magnates. Certainly, Boris Nemtsov, Russian deputy prime minister in the Chernomyrdin and Kiriyenko administrations, called their activities "semi-bandit capitalism".[12]

Steel Industry

About a quarter of Russia's steelworkers are employed in antiquated open hearth plants which are only ten per cent as productive as US mills. These completely uneconomic mills are all out of cash and cannot pay their energy bills, but continue to operate because local governments, fearing massive unemployment and social unrest, prevent energy companies from cutting off their power. The low cost or free energy naturally has to mean that government forgives them their taxes.

Aluminium Industry

The Achinsk ore combine in Siberia is a major source of alumina and a creator of massive profits for its owners, a private monopoly. The world market price of aluminium is high, the plant's production costs are relatively low yet it makes a loss. How? Because of *tolling*. The ore is, in fact, sold through a variety of "intermediate" companies to the mine that refines the ore into aluminium, rather than being sold directly. This ensures that, by the time the ore actually reaches the refiner (Krasnoyarsk Aluminium), the price is close to world levels. Who owns the intermediate companies which charge the *tolls* as the ore moves to the trackway to the refiner? Managers at Achinsk and Krasnoyarsk. Where can they be situated? Anywhere. Where are the profits actually made? Outside Russia.

Food Retailing Industry

Roughly one third of Russian food sales now go through new types of food retailing enterprises that did not exist in Soviet times. Yet they are hardly more productive than the famously inefficient *gastronomes* which required each customer to make three visits to two counters to buy something. These new types are not supermarkets, however. Why? Because supermarkets have to pay eight per cent tax on sales and other vendors one per cent. Under such circumstances, multinationals will not bring international best practice in merchandising, high productivity and low employment levels, to Russia. The tax regime is even more of a barrier than bureaucratic red-tape, corruption of public officials and even physical threats from organised crime.

EXHIBIT 4: RUSSIA AS IT IS

Source: Why the West Can't Help Russia, William Lewis, *The Wall Street Journal, Europe*, 29-30/10/99 and Offshore Accounts Swell While Russian Treasury Loses Out, Jonathan Steele, *The Guardian*, 22/12/99

So who were they and what had they done? The leading Russian magnate was Vladimir Potanin. Since 1990 he had created a commerce-industry monolith which the Russian stock market valued in late 1997 at $32 billion. His breakthrough had come when he helped implement a plan in 1995 whereby his bank, Uneximbank, made loans to the Russian government in exchange for shares in companies which the government was privatising. The project had been agreed jointly by Vladimir Potanin and Anatoly Chubais, another deputy prime minister colleague of Boris Nemtsov, although it became widely known as the Chubais *loans for shares* plan. It brought solace to a cash-strapped government and rich pickings to the Potanin group. After only two years in operation Uneximbank had become the largest private bank in Russia.

Potanin's master stroke had been the acquisition of a 25 per cent stake in Russia' crown jewel, the telecommunications giant, Svyazinvest. To win control he outsmarted his rivals by enlisting the support of George Soros and by paying $ 1.8 billion. This happened in early 1997.

The formative period for Potaninin and his main rivals, Boris Berezovsky of the highly-diversified Logovaz group, Mikhail Khodorovsky, owner of Menatep Bank and MOST Bank's Vladimir Gusinsky, ran, however, from November 1995 to January 1996. During this time, these three went on a spending spree, purchasing metal, oil and mining companies from the government. The loans for shares deal had been concluded on the *never-never land* basis that, once the government had repaid the loans to the banks advancing them, the banks would be obligated to return the shares to the government. Grigory Yavlinsky, political leader of Yabloko, one of the moderate parties in the Duma, said that these "robber baron" moves had resulted in "an oligarchic system based on semi-criminal relations".[13]

Certainly, there was merit in this argument as both Potanin and Berezovsky, said at the time to be one of the richest men in the world, were known to have poured money into President Yeltsin's election campaign in 1996. Indeed, the former was appointed first deputy prime minister with responsibility for economic policy when the campaign succeeded.

Was Vladimir Potanin unhappy with what he had achieved? No. He had simply, he said, "brought normal management to sizeable companies and broken the control of the *Red Directors* (i.e., former directors of state-owned companies). We created a precedent whereby the enterprise was sold to an investor, not a manager". [14]

The devaluation of the rouble and the default on rouble-denominated bonds on August 17th 1998 may not have detracted from the power position of some of the magnates, even if it did untold damage to Potanin's status. Those who controlled Russia's leading oil companies, Rem Vyakhirev (RAO Gazprom) and Vagit Alekperov (Lukoil), fell into this bracket, also. They were still sitting on assets which could be sold abroad for hard currency, even if their dollar value was currently falling.

But the crash had a bombshell impact on the operations of the Gusinsky media empire (NTV television channel and MOST bank). Fortunately for him, according to *The Wall Street Journal,* he had already switched his place of residence, by the time of the Yeltsin-Clinton summit, from Russia to an unnamed European country. Intriguingly, Boris Berezovsky was also outside Russia when, much later, on the sixth of April 1999, a warrant was issued for his arrest by the office of Yuri Skuratov, Russia's Procurator-general. The charge was "money laundering and illegal commercial activity".

Conglomerate owners Mikhail Khodorovsky and Vladimir Potanin had not followed Vladimir Gusinsky's lead, however. They were still fighting desperately to limit the damage at their banks, the former having pledged shares in the oil company AO Yukos, in exchange for loans from foreign banks. As Menatep could not repay the loans, it had lost control of the 30 per cent of Yukos it once so proudly owned.

NIL DESPERANDUM?

However, it seemed that not all was beyond redemption. On the 19th November 1998, a week after the moratorium expired, it was announced that Russian and foreign banks had reached a deal over the frozen treasury debt that needed to be re-structured. The talks, led by Deutsche Bank, had been very difficult but a framework seemed finally to have been agreed which permitted foreign creditors to repatriate roubles into dollars at some future time. The foreign banks were to receive "a ten per cent cash payment in roubles, 20 per cent in non-coupon securities tradable for tax debts or stakes in Russian banks, and the remaining 70 per cent of the money owed in interest bearing, rouble-denominated securities".[15] The Russian negotiators wished, it was said, that creditors would exchange roubles for dollars in one year's time and were very interested in one of the western bankers requirements, that the rouble-denominated securities they would receive would be indexed to inflation. However high the hopes for the deal, the fact was that, by the end of 1999, only 72 per cent of the western banks involved had acquiesced to it.

To crown everything, there was a statement from the architect of *glasnost* and *perestroika,* the former Russian president Mikhail Gorbachov, that he had lost all his savings (some £48,000) in the August 1998 crash. "All my money is gone" he told the German Bunte magazine.[16]

The man eventually chosen to steer Russia through its post-devaluation traumas was Yevgeni Primakov, erstwhile Soviet apparatchik and successful foreign minister. However, among the new prime minister's first actions to deal with the crisis was a plan to print roubles to pay off the wage backlog and to meet other government obligations. Printing too many roubles brought with it the danger of a repetition of the hyperinflation, which it was thought Russia had conquered. Yevgeni Primakov had, nevertheless, to buy time. "Russia" said *The Herald Tribune's* leader on the 9th November 1998 "is headed into a winter of deprivation and discontent" in which "prices are skyrocketing while pensions and wages are stagnant, if they are paid at all".[17] Another action which brought heavy criticism was the way he promised to prop up favoured enterprises and, hence, did little to tackle the oligarchs who were still refusing to pay their taxes.

The US was committed to providing $625m worth of food to tide Russia over the winter but it was keenly interested in whether he could develop "a programme that would pull Russia back from the brink without abandoning democracy and economic reform".[18] Printing some 30 billion roubles ($1.6 billion) over the August – December period in order to help fill a fourth quarter budget deficit of 70 billion roubles was hardly a way of keeping the USA happy, however. The move was also thought unlikely to improve the chances of a resumption of the frozen IMF lending programme or a brand-new IMF loan, either.

Nor did the new budget that the Russian government crafted in December 1998. After the process had long been delayed in the Duma, the intention was now to actually steer the budget through and to meet the tight deficit target set by the IMF as a precondition for any further lending. Nor did the rejection of the latest restructuring deal by the committee of foreign creditors holding frozen short-term Russian Treasury debt. The final deal was said to offer claimants like Deutsche and Credit Suisse First Boston only five cents on the dollar!

Raising servicemen's pay by 62 per cent from the first of January 1999 and proposing a major cut in VAT, "one of the few taxes in Russia that enjoys a relatively high degree of compliance,"[19] did not seem to raise confidence either. Perhaps, not surprisingly, as on this day Russia failed to make a payment of $362m in interest on Soviet-era debt, a failure accompanied by a government announcement of an investigation by its Federal Security Service into the *disappearance* in August 1998 of billions of dollars.

This came only three months after Yuri Skuratov, Russia's Prosecutor General, had accused Sergei Dubinin, former chairman of the Central Bank, and the Bank itself of having *misused* a large part of the $4.8 billion IMF loan money. It is interesting to reflect on the fact that President Yeltsin attempted, at this time, i.e., in early April 1999, to sack Skuratov, against the outright opposition of the Duma, on grounds of immorality, the Prosecutor General having been on shown on nation-wide TV in bed with two prostitutes, in a secretly shot video. As we have seen, he had been investigating the business activities of Boris Berezovsky and the alleged illegal export of some of Russia's hard currency reserves. President Yeltsin had not been amused.

It all amounted to a dramatic change in the approach that Yevgeni Primakov, as foreign minister had recommended to Mikhail Gorbachov in 1991. Then it had been a case of *doing drastic things* to advance market reform. Now, the advice to Boris Yeltsin in March 1999 was that Russia could not go on *waiting for the market environment to solve its problems.*[20] But, even amid widespread fears of what US Treasury Secretary Robert Rubin called the potential destabilisation of Russia, and well-founded suspicion that much of the $4.8 billion loan already handed over out of the IMF's $22 billion rescue programme had, indeed, been *siphoned off improperly*, the USA was still prepared to back the IMF. Lending the money was, Rubin asserted, the right risk for the world's taxpayers.[21]

It was a view that was repeated at the end of March 1999 when the Michel Camdessus, head of the IMF, announced that, as a result of a Russian agreement to create a budget surplus in 1999, lending would resume. Georgy Boos, Russian tax minister, was more than delighted. *"We'll get as much as we need"* he declared.[22]

But the IMF was not quite as generous as he had hoped. For a start the IMF loan would now "effectively go from one IMF account in Washington to another, *not entering Russia*"[23] Secondly, the loan of $3.1 billion over the coming 12 months was less than the $3.8 billion Russia was scheduled to repay the IMF before the end of 1999. Thirdly, the loan was strictly conditional on the approval of the opposition-led Duma to new tax and banking system reforms. It was all a tall order for a government that announced on the 20th April 1999 that it would be unable to meet the $1.3 billion payment due on its dollar-denominated domestic debt, i.e., the Minfin and Series 3 bonds. And for a country with a black market making up 40 per cent of the economy and with a GDP, at $190 billion, one fifth the size of China's.

A NEW BEGINNING?

But the IMF arrangements were fated to be thrown into the melting pot by the dramatic news that came from the Kremlin on the 12th May 1999, that the government of Yevgeni Primakov had been sacked. It was the third administration that President Yeltsin had dismissed in the last eighteen months and the most popular. The key issue was whether the Duma, divided as it was among the three warring factions of the Communists (leader, Gennady Zyuganov), the Nationalists (leader, Vladimir Zhirinovsky) and the liberal Yabloko party (leader, Grigory Yavlinsky), would now unite against President Yeltsin. If they had, the outcome would have been momentous, the potential for a vote to impeach the Russian president. The charges were far removed from those unsuccessfully levelled at President Clinton and concerned political grievances built up by President Yeltsin's political enemies. One of these was that he had initiated the collapse of the Soviet Union.

But it was not to be as, in August 1999, President Yeltsin abruptly replaced Yevgeni Primakov with Vladimir Putin. For once the choice seemed to be an inspired one. With a 17-year career in espionage behind him, having been head of the FSB, the successor to the KGB, Putin began to restore the reputation of government. His key attraction was the vigour with which he was prepared to prosecute the war that Russia was waging in Chechnya. Indeed, by the end of 1999, as Exhibit 2 (page 571) suggests, he was beginning to be regarded as a phenomenon.

"Despite mounting Russian losses, the Chechnya campaign is still popular at home. It has made Putin the army's man, admired by an officer corps that considers itself to be the country's last hope for stability. He has impressed Moscow's elite with his mastery of detail, foreign leaders with his languages and foreign bankers with his business-like tone on finance and corruption. For the first time since *perestroika* in the 1980s, one man has the overwhelming backing of the media, the Duma's disparate blocs and even of the truculent intelligentsia"

EXHIBIT 5: THE VLADIMIR PUTIN PHENOMENON
Source: The spy who came into the fold, Giles Whittell,
The Times, 1/1/2000

Such was his success that, in December 1999, the Kremlin-backed Unity party, scored a major success in the Duma elections with 25 per cent of the popular vote, equalling the performance of the Communists. This was the best performance ever achieved and a spectacular improvement on the 9.9 per cent of the vote won in the 1995 election by Viktor Chernomyrdin's government-supported Our House is Russia party. It was followed by the equally spectacular resignation of Boris Yeltsin as Russian president on the eve of the millennium. He went a proud man, having brought, he said, the first ten years of democracy to Russia. He went also a reassured man, as the Putin government had given him and his family total immunity from prosecution.

But would the new leader, now prime minister but tipped to become president, be able to transform the economy of Russia? This was a country with what critics asserted was "half a market-place and less than half a rule of law,"[24] "a half-mended economy and a badly fractured society".[25] The *Frankfurter Allgemeine* reckoned that the Chechnya war had brought him to power, but it would be the economy that would keep him there, that was his *Achillesferse* (Achilles heel).[26] The problem was that he did not seem to have any programme beyond that of the Internet outline he put out over Christmas 1999. Yes, he would protect democratic liberties, but *Russia's realities* demanded that the regime did not continue to make the mistake of relying on Western reform models. Yes, Russia did need the backing of international institutions and the trust of investors, but Russian society still needed the *protection of the State*. Yes, Russia agreed that wars are bad, but it did not accept that the US should dictate to Russia on how it should deal with terrorism, or launch its nuclear weapons, or cope with the spread of Islamic separatism. Dirigisme, or state leadership, is implicit in each of these areas. His policies were, therefore, likely to be a far cry from those of the early 1990s when thrusting reformers like Anatole Chubais were urgently seeking the advice of American free marketeers like Harvard's Jeffrey Sachs.

And had the Russian economy itself improved in 1999? Data published in the McKinsey *Global Institute Report* (October 1999) indicated that, by this time, Russia's GDP had plummeted by more than 30 per cent since 1994 and stood at a paltry 15 per cent of the US level. News of alleged criminality on money laundering and malversion, involving an off-shore financial organisation in Jersey (Fimaco) and the Bank of New York, were still rife. As before, they involved the Russian Central Bank, the IMF and senior members of the Russian government. In August, Russia's second largest retail bank defaulted on loan repayments but, whereas the government had withdrawn the banking licences of Uneximbank and Menatep in similar circumstances, this bank, the nationalised SBS-Agros, was too important to Russia's agricultural sector to be allowed to fail.

On the other hand, the oil price had risen, inflation was low (despite the devaluation of the rouble) as wage pressures were not significant and domestic output had risen as imports had fallen. With a GDP rise of 1.5 per cent it had been the best year for Russia since the break up of the USSR in 1991. Some stock prices were strongly up by mid-year. Certainly, Russia was still faced with the need to re-schedule debt repayment and get even more help from the IMF, which, in August 1999, restarted its *supposedly conditional* Russian loan programme. But Goldman Sachs thought in July 1999 that things were really getting better. A circular entitled *From Russia With Love* spelled out that the investment bank recommended all asset classes. "Russia's second attempt at capitalism is only just beginning" it declared.

And Goldman Sachs could well have been right. Vladimir Putin's maiden speech to the Duma on January 18th 2000 indicated that much-needed reforms to the tax-collection system would be introduced and that there would be a private landholding law. The government was planning for ratification of labour and civil court procedures, which were provided for within the constitution, but had not implemented before. But any Russia-watchers who were overcome with enthusiasm at these promises could well bear in mind the sceptical comment made in the Goldman Sachs report, *Russia is never a normal place to do business*".[27]

* * * * * * * * * * * * * * * * * * *

REFERENCES

1   Peril in Russia's quick fix, James Meek, *The Guardian*, 31/8/98
2   Who will be burned by the Russian inferno, Bill Jamieson, *The Sunday Telegraph*, 30/8/98
3   Huge trading losses cast doubt on bank marriages, *The Guardian*, 31/8/98
4   Credit Suisse : the perils of pioneering, *Business Week*, 7/9/98
5   West counts the cost of Russian crisis, Gavin Lumsden and Matthew Barbour, *The Times*, 31/8/98
6   As 4
7   Rexrodt : Wir lassen Russland nicht fallen, *Frankfurter Allgemeine Zeitung*, 19/8/98
8   Corralling Russia's Cowboy Banks, Michael Wines, *The International Herald Tribune*, 29-30/8/98
9   Hardship and shortages have taught citizens how to survive with no money", Robin Lodge, *The Times*, 28/8/98
10 Russians stare into the abyss, Jean Mackenzie, *The Times*, 29/8/98
11   How Russia can avoid the Asian abyss, *Business Week*, 19/1/98
12 Picking Russia's private plums, *The Guardian* editorial, 20/8/97
13   Most powerful man, Patricia Krantz, *Business Week*, 24/11/97
14 As 13
15 Russia, Foreign banks reach debt deal, Mark Whitehouse, *The Wall Street Journal, Europe*, 20-21/11/98
16 Russia "mislaid" billions in cash, Anna Blundy, *The Times*, 30/12/98
17   Russian Hardship, *The International Herald Tribune*, 9/11/98
18 As 17
19 Russia approves budget but figures are questioned, Andrew Higgins, *The Wall Street Journal, Europe*, 11-12/12/98
20 Primakov, A Russian for all Seasons, *The International Herald Tribune*, 20-21/3/99
21 Rubin says Russian turmoil poses world-wide threat, *The Wall Street Journal*, 19-20/3/99
22 IMF pays to save Russia's skin and its own face, James Meek, *The Guardian*, 30/3/99
23 IMF sets tough rules in new loan to Russia, Michael Phillips and Mark Whitehouse, *The Wall Street Journal, Europe*, April 30-May 1 1999
24 Yeltsin's Masterstroke, *The Times* editorial, 1/1/2000
25 The Putin Machine, *The Times* editorial, 3/1/2000
26 Vladimir Putin's Achillesfers ist die Okonomie, *Frankfurter Allgemeine Zeitung*, 4/1/2000
27 Western banks put faith in Russian revival, Richard Beeston, *The Times* 6/8/99

STRATEGY ANALYSIS FRAMEWORK

1. A BASIC FRAMEWORK FOR STRATEGY STUDIES

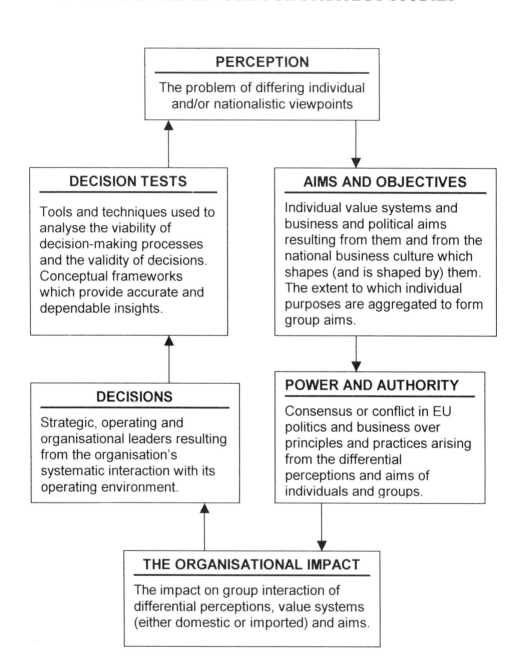

PERCEPTION

The problem of differing individual and/or nationalistic viewpoints

DECISION TESTS

Tools and techniques used to analyse the viability of decision-making processes and the validity of decisions. Conceptual frameworks which provide accurate and dependable insights.

AIMS AND OBJECTIVES

Individual value systems and business and political aims resulting from them and from the national business culture which shapes (and is shaped by) them. The extent to which individual purposes are aggregated to form group aims.

DECISIONS

Strategic, operating and organisational leaders resulting from the organisation's systematic interaction with its operating environment.

POWER AND AUTHORITY

Consensus or conflict in EU politics and business over principles and practices arising from the differential perceptions and aims of individuals and groups.

THE ORGANISATIONAL IMPACT

The impact on group interaction of differential perceptions, value systems (either domestic or imported) and aims.

2. A SIMPLE 10-POINT STRATEGY ANALYSIS FRAMEWORK

(1) Initial determination of the company's aims and objectives (e.g. growth, increase in profitability etc.)
(2) Examination of the level of difficulty and risk posed to the company now and in future by its
   - macro environment, using a PESTLE analysis
   - micro (or industry) environment using stakeholder analysis and Porter's Five Forces framework
   - technology level as opposed to the technology level of competitors
(3) Review of the past strategy pursued by the firm in order to evaluate the success that has been achieved, against the competitive background, on the basis of the three components of corporate strategy :
   - generic strategy. Has the firm made any change in its basic economic approach? Is it still, for example, a *mass* producer or has it specialised (i.e., changed to being a *class* producer)?
   - product-market scope. What has been the direction of travel in the past in terms of changes in the company's products and markets?
   - value-chain positioning. Has the company gone into a strategic alliance or joint venture to try to achieve its goals in company with others. Has it similarly merged with or acquired competitors doing the same work as itself (i.e., at the same point in the value chain) or integrated forwards (towards the market-place) or backwards (by buying a supplier)? Or has it depended on organic growth entirely?
(4) Examination of the strengths and weaknesses of the company today, in relation to (1) and (2) using
   - A core competence analysis, matching the company's *core competencies* to the *critical success factors* that need to be achieved
   - A Boston Box analysis to work out the make-up of the company's product portfolio in terms of cash contribution and growth potential
   - A financial analysis to establish the profitability, activity, liquidity and solvency of the company and its present financial strength
   - A functional analysis to work out the degree of functional capability the firm has.
(5) Specification of the opportunities and threats in the environment and the extent to which the company can deal with them in order to achieve (1) – or a revised version of (1) – on the basis of (4)
(6) Use of (4) and (5) to evaluate the future strategic possibilities of the firm in the light of:
   - Scenarios for the state of the likely future macro- and micro-environments facing the firm
   - Tests of the viability and robustness of any strategic moves that might be made
(7) Selection of the optimum strategy moves – a combination of generic, product-market scope and value chain positioning to achieve (1) – and their setting within a draft Strategic Plan, with a time line and milestones
(8) Consideration of the likely organisational impact of the strategy (structure, culture, systems, style, resources) and production of a Business Transformation Plan
(9) Implementation of the strategy
(10) Checking on the successful implementation of the Strategic and Business Transformation Plans and loop-back to (1)

3. STRATEGIC CHOICE

Ansoff's P-M Scope Approach: Same or Different product/service or market?	Porter's Generic Strategy Approach: Do we make 'Mass' or 'Class' products/services?	Porter's Value Chain Approach: Do we work Alone or in Company?
Productivity improvement Market penetration	Differentiation	Expansion of current value chain position by merger, takeover & alliance
Market development Product development	Cost leadership	Forward or backward integration
Product deletion Diversification	Focus	Divestment

4. VALUE-ADDED CHAIN ANALYSIS

Elements in the Value-Added Chain within a particular industry	Stage	Description of the extent to which a company within this industry is integrated, on the basis of ownership of elements in the value-added chain and on the basis of geography and coverage [local, national EC, international].		
Extraction of raw materials used in	1			
The production of semi-finished components used in	2	Alcan strategy in the global aluminium industry	Pernod Ricards' strategy in the drinks industry	Siemens' strategy in the electronics industry
The production of finished components used in	3			
The assembly of finished products which are	4			
Transported to	5			
Distribution channels [Wholesale & retail] for the purpose of	6			
Consumption	7			

NOTE

[1] A highly integrated company is one which owns [as does, for example, Alcan] and controls all the services involved in Stages 1-6 [for, in this case, aluminium]. It has, over time, followed strategies of forward and/or backward integration [buying up its customers and/or its suppliers]. It has expanded geographically from an initial local/national position to operate internationally. The extent to which trans-border oligopolisation [the creation of major international industry-specific groups where once there were individual smaller competitors] is taking place through cross-border mergers and acquisitions [CBAs] in the EU is of great interest.
Clearly the greater the extent of trans-border oligopolisation [TBO] within a global industry, the higher the level of ownership concentration.

[2] The analysis of the strengths and weaknesses of a particular company plus the appraisal of the opportunities and threats facing it [SWOT analysis] is bound up with analysis of the company's position in the value-added chain, in any in-depth strategic appraisal. One categorisation of products which is useful in this regard was that proposed by the Boston Consultancy Group in Long Range Planning [Feb. 1977] which divides products into 'stars' [products with high growth rate and high market share], 'cash cows' [low-high], question-mark products [high-low] and 'dogs' [low-low].

5. RIDING THE BUSINESS CYCLE

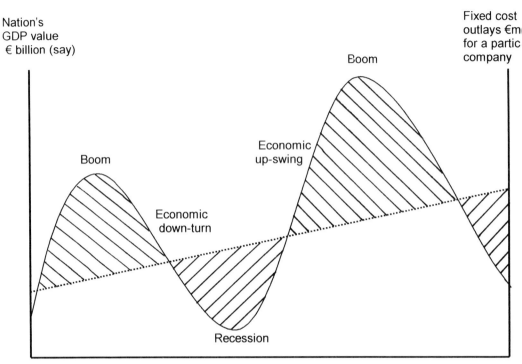

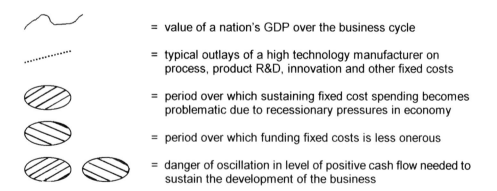

= value of a nation's GDP over the business cycle

= typical outlays of a high technology manufacturer on process, product R&D, innovation and other fixed costs

= period over which sustaining fixed cost spending becomes problematic due to recessionary pressures in economy

= period over which funding fixed costs is less onerous

= danger of oscillation in level of positive cash flow needed to sustain the development of the business

6. POWER ANALYSIS FRAMEWORK

Company's Market-place Muscle

What is the extent of a company's control over its industrial market place [local, national, EU, international] based on its competitive strength and capabilities in R&D [technology], production [output and/or quality], marketing financial resources and purchasing power? Is the cost of assets a critical factor in this industry? To what extent does the company control the value added chain in its industry?

Monopoly [Monopsony] – one seller [buyer]

Duopoly [Duopsony] – two sellers [buyers]

Oligopoly [Oligopsony] – several dominant sellers [buyers]

Monopolistic Competition – many sellers, each with a differentiated, possibly branded, product

---

Pure Competition – no product differentiation

NOTE:
(1) force field analysis – to discover the pressures exerted by 'players' in a given industry; this can be very illuminating. One of the most useful forms of this is Michael Porter's 'Five Forces' approach. This considers the extent of natural rivalry within any industry as affected by such elements as substitute products and ease of entry/exit. Implicit in the analysis is the market power enjoyed by players with economics of scale[low unit costs as a function of large-scale production, marketing etc.] or access to critically-scarce resources [new technology] or a degree of market protection given by government legislation.
(2) Another form of power analysis is that of Stakeholder Analysis. Here one is concerned with the roles that participants in a certain relationship play [positive or negative force] in terms of their objectives and their power.
(3) The macro analysis of the playing field in which a company is working is provided through a PESTLE (political, economic, social, technological, legal and ecological) appraisal.
(4) The power possessed by a company varies also according to its size and the nature of its ownership (public, private, state-owned).

7. THE MILITARY METAPHORS OF STRATEGY

FRONTAL ATTACK	Aimed at capturing the 'commanding heights' or the 'centre of the stage'. All resources are committed. No holds barred.
PRE-EMPTIVE STRIKE	You hit your opponent before he can hit you. A 'fait accompli'. Use of surprise/shocks. Mastery in the use of time.
WAR OF ATTRITION	Grinding the opponent down by allowing him no breathing space and cutting off his supply of resources. A 'scorched earth' policy is a variant of this. Allies vital.
PROPAGANDA	Use all methods of propaganda - making grandiose claims/threats, using smear tactics to frighten your opponent. Actually or artificially 'upping the ante', raising the temperature. Personal attacks/innuendo. Fabricatio Falsi v Suppressio Veri. [Manufacture of lies v suppression of the truth].
STONEWALLING	The rejection of the opponent's viewpoint and a complete unwillingness to compromise with much emotional bluster. Procrastinate. Play for time.
BLUFFING	Pretending that you have greater resources than you have. Hyperbole and exaggeration are used to enlarge your apparent power relative to your opponent and affect his perceptions of the costs and benefits of action alternative. Playacting.
YIELDING	Recognising 'no-win' situations. Parleying; going to arbitration. Selling defeats and 'victories for common sense', etc. Giving in gracefully. Damage limitation.
LINE OF LEAST RESISTANCE	Keep your head down. Adopt a low profile. Hope the problem will go away. Do just enough to show you are still in the fight. Going through the motions.

8. STRATEGIC DECISION CONCEPTS

SOURCE	CONTRIBUTION	REF
L V Bertalanffy	Produced a basic model of the working of 'ecosystems' in the natural world. These are characterised by a state of equilibrium among their constituent parts and are known as 'open systems'. Disturbances of the equilibrium set up forces which lead to the restoration of a change equilibrium.	1
F E Emery & E L Trist	See the organisation as operating within a 'socio-technical system', influencing and being influenced by the environment. 'The primary task of managing an enterprise as a whole is to relate the total system to its environment and internal regulation *per se*.'	2
S Beer	Described the elements characterising systems as boundaries, interacting and mutually interdependent parts, feedback and equilibrium.	3
N Weiner	Analysed cybernetics, the science of communication and control which deals with the phenomena of information feedback systems which are part of living organisms and their work activities.	4
H Simon	Programmed [repetitive and routine dealt with by proven methods] v non-programmed ['novel, unstructured and consequential', with no cut and dried solutions] where there is no possibility of algorithmic [machine-like processing] handling.	5
W Mackenzie	Decision, indecision [a decision not to make up your mind just yet], non-decision [a decision not to decide], a decision by default [a decision made without your participation, wilful or otherwise].	6
I Ansoff	Strategic [long-term, crucial interface decisions] v operating [short-term, 2nd order functional activity decisions] v administrative [internal procedures & organisation structure].	7

9. STRATEGIC THINKING IN THE 1990s

☐ Henry Mintzberg [8]

"In my metaphor of *emergent strategy*, managers are craftsmen and strategy is their clay. Like the potter, they sit between a past of corporate capabilities and a future of market opportunities." (Mintzberg H. And Waters J, Of strategies deliberate and emergent, *Strategic Management Journal*, (1985))

☐ Gary Hamel and CK Prahalad: [9]

" Core competencies are the collective learning in the organisation, especially how to coordinate diverse production skills and integrate multiple streams of technologies". They are the reflection of a flexible and high-value *strategic architecture* within the organisation and allow the development of both the company's *strategic intent* and the *foresight to make strategy happen*. Strategy itself is more *lucky for*esight and the *product of a serendipitous cocktail* than it is the result of mechanistic thinking. (*Competing for the Future*, Gary Hamel and CK Prahalad,, Harvard University Press, 1994)

☐ Peter Senge: [10]

"As the world becomes more inter-connected and business becomes more complex and dynamic, work must become more *learningful*. It is no longer sufficient to have one person learning for the organisation..It's just not possible any longer to figure it out from the top and have everybody else following the orders of *the grand strategist*. The organisations that will truly excel in the future will be the organisations that discover how to tap people's commitment and capacity to learn continuously at all levels in an organisation" (Peter Senge, *The Fifth Discipline, The Art & Practice of the Learning Organisation*, Doubleday, New York, 1990)

☐ James Champy and Michael Hammer: [11]

Business process reengineering – "the fundamental rethinking and radical redesign of business processes to achieve dramatic reductions in critical measures of performance such as cost, service, quality and speed" – is the essence of their wider vision of a corporate revolution. But it has gone down in history generally as simply another version of Frederick Taylor's Scientific Management approach. In fact BPR tended to de-personalise management and has become accepted as a short-hand term for *the mindless down-sizing* of large companies. (*Reengineering the Corporation*, James Champy & Michael Hammer, Harper Business, New York, 1993)

10. THE CONCEPT OF EXPECTED VALUE

	OPTION A		OPTION B	
Pay-offs and Chances	Forecast Result based on est. 60% information	Forecast Result based on est. 70% information	Forecast Result based on est. 60% information	Forecast Result based on est. 70% information
a. Results of policy if it works £	100	110	500	550
b. Chances of success	.7	.75	.3	.2
c Results of policy if it fails £	-50	-55	-250	-280
d. Chances of failure	.3	.25	.7	.8
e Expected Value of Option [(a x b) - (c x d)]	55	68.75	-25	-134

Explanation: The strategy setters have 2 options, A or B. If it is successful, B will produce a much better result than A, but conversely its chances of success are much less. It is more risky. The expected value indicates that A is much more viable than B. In fact with B, the chances are you'll lose money. It can be seen that improving the knowledge on which the decision is based has demonstrated that B is even less viable than it was first thought and that A is more attractive. In fact, as a gambler, you would be prepared to consider paying up to £13.75 [£68.75 - £55] for the extra information on option A since, by obtaining it, you have improved the pay-off.

Note the possibility of applying Sensitivity Analysis [how much of a difference would it make to the decision if probabilities were out by a factor of 25%] in this situation.

To be certain of a successful forecast you need 100% correct information, not as estimated here 60% or 70%. Note that, however sure you are of your forecast, it can always be spoilt by unforecastable events.

[b] + [d] = 1 [certainty].

11. EXAMPLE OF USE OF DECISION TREE ANALYSIS

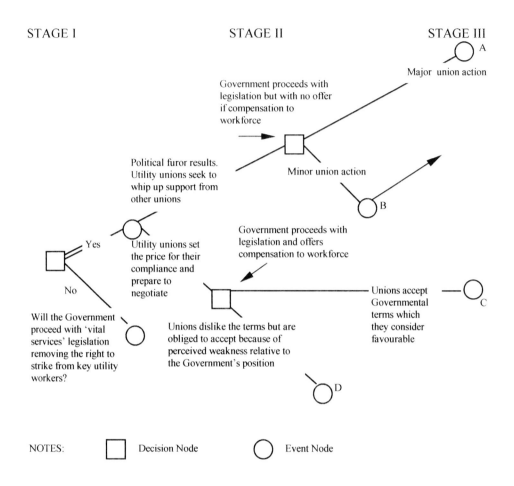

STAGE I   STAGE II   STAGE III

A
Major union action

Government proceeds with
legislation but with no offer
if compensation to
workforce

Political furor results.
Utility unions seek to
whip up support from
other unions

Minor union action

B

Yes   Utility unions set
         the price for their
         compliance and
No   prepare to
         negotiate

Government proceeds with
legislation and offers
compensation to workforce

Unions accept
Governmental
terms which
they consider
favourable

C

Will the Government
proceed with 'vital
services' legislation
removing the right to
strike from key utility
workers?

Unions dislike the terms but are
obliged to accept because of
perceived weakness relative to
the Government's position

D

NOTES: ☐ Decision Node   ◯ Event Node

A, B, C, D: Results of Outcomes in cost-benefit terms both economic and political.
The outcomes are reviewed in terms of the probability of occurrence.

This example assumes the [1] neither the European commission nor the UK's EU
partners can take action to block the move and [2] that such political opposition as
they do represent is disregarded. Neither assumption may be, in fact, correct.

12. DECISION MATRIX ANALYSIS

		Choices available to organisation A		'Expected Value' Result for B
		Action option 1	Action option 2	
Choices available to organisation B	Action option 1	-4 [a]	+3 [b]	-1 [g]
	Action option 2	+2 [c]	-4 [d]	-2 [h]
Expected Value Result for A		+2 [e]	+1 [f]	0 [i]

Explanation: in all power play situations involving two or more players, the decisions made by one should logically involve an understanding of others' available options, purposes and aims and level of rationality. Normally we assume both rationality [irrationality or non-rationality would make for random decisions] and, in each player, the maximum pursuit of self-interest or maximum utility. Matrix analysis is a tool which enables us to estimate, in advance of making a decision, the likely payoffs for the involved players and, hence, the likelihood of particular combinations of moves.

In this example [a] and [d] are expected gains or losses for B, and, conversely, losses or gains for A. If B chooses option 1, the best case scenario is a win of 3 [b] and a loss of 4 [a]; if, by contrast, B selects option 2, then the worst case scenario is a loss of 4 and a win of 2. On this basis, with all the assumptions made, B would select option 1 rather than option 2, given that they are likely to lose on both. In other words [g] is better than [h], so option 1 is the policy of choice. This, of course, is based on the expectation that A will choose the best move he can.

The game represented here is a "Zero-sum [i], i.e., the winner's game is counterbalanced by the loser's loss. Clearly, this is not an adequate representation of real life which, in most case, is far from being "Zero-sum".

13. RISK RETURN TRADE-OFF ANALYSIS

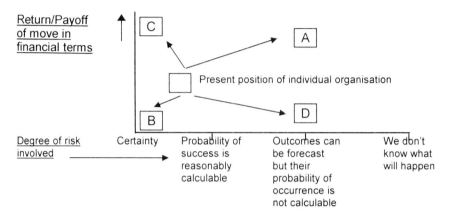

A = A highly risky, speculative move aimed at improving the current pay-off.

B = A low-risk, high-safety move which is sure to succeed but will not improve the current pay-off.

C = A sure-fire success, if you can get it!

D = An idiotic move.

Note: A better return in economic terms could be any improvement in elements of the key equation governing business financial success i.e.

$$\frac{\text{Profit}}{\text{Capital Employed}} = \frac{\text{Profit}}{\text{Sales}} \times \frac{\text{Sales}}{\text{Capital Employed}}$$

: Although D looks preposterous it may be the move chosen by the organisation on grounds of internal power-play or the maintenance of doctrinal purity etc. Not all decision-makers act rationally.

: Strategic moves [i.e. those concerned with the long-term and with critical product-market, make-or-buy, choice-of-technology issues] can be analysed within such a framework by appraising the direction the move would take the firm in. [North West = stronger probability of higher success].

: Note that pay-off success is rarely measurable in single value terms. Improved 'utility' could comprise a mixture, in business terms, of sacrificing short-term profitability for long-term market domination, for instance.

: There are many decisional criteria e.g. efficiency [improving the ratio of outputs to inputs by volume or value], effectiveness [achieving the highest possible % of the target aimed at, whatever the target], economy [doing the best possible job with constrained resources], equity [achieving a fair result for all concerned]. These must be considered in evaluating success levels.

14. BARTLETT AND GHOSHAL CORPORATE CLASSIFICATION SCHEME [12]

☐ THE MULTINATIONAL

This is a firm which consists essentially of firms which are local or regional, often with their own names, which are organised on the basis of federal decentralisation. This means they have quite considerable autonomy as to how they achieve centrally set aims. Management using expatriates from the home country is the prime method of securing cohesion. The International Firm can be said to be at a lower stage of development along this pathway

☐ THE GLOBAL FIRM

Here the story is one of very tight control by the central hub of all strategic decisions, as well as those involving resource allocation. The world is seen as one market and individual countries merely as platforms for supply and/or demand, the in-built thrust being always for more and more scale economies and cost advantages. The company has one name only.

☐ THE TRANSNATIONAL

The typical format for this company is the ACT LOCAL – THINK GLOBAL approach. The search is one in it to find the very best combination of responsiveness to local market conditions with the optimum efficiency in product and supply. A high premium is placed on knowledge management (i.e., the best possible deployment and use of organisational learning) within such firms. They need to be very fast movers.

15. LIMITS ON RATIONALITY IN STRATEGIC DECISION-MAKING

Limitations on a Rational Approach to Strategy Setting

Herbert Simon

The simple model of classical economic man [all-knowing and with ample technocratic skills] is inadequate as a basis for understanding the decision-making processes involved in complex policy problems. Here 'goals and values' may be simple or complex, consistent or inconsistent; the facts may be real or supposed; the inferences may be valid or spurious. (13)

Whilst a logical approach to making the decision may be followed [procedural rationality], it does not suffer from 'bounded rationality' [perceptual and cognition variations, data and computational limitations]. (14)

Hence organisational decisions are concerned with 'satisficing' [satisfy and suffice] rather than with 'maximising' [the ideal solution]. (15)

Charles Lindblom

In public and business policy matters there is almost always controversy over what the problem is, let alone the solution. Such controversy puts 'a limit on analytic policy-making' and provides an entry point for politics, either macro or organisational, and other 'irrationalities'. (16)

As a comprehensive and wholly reliable knowledge of means-ends relationships is unattainable, a completely 'rational-deductive' approach to policy-making is impossible. (17)

In fact, pragmatism, expediency and disjointed incrementalism ['muddling through'] are the real hallmarks of policy-making in the public sector where opportunity for 'search' - for alternatives - is limited, goals are not clear cut and where the wide acceptability of policies depends on a 'satisficing' solution. (18)

Bold strategic thrusts are more observable in the business policy area save in those cases where industrial strategies are much affected by short-termist financial concerns.

Note also the existence of a range of logical fallacies - errors in a chain of argument [premises - conclusions] that do exist in policy-making. For example assumptions taken for granted ["a priori"] but found, in fact to be unwarranted; non sequiturs, like the after-this-therefore-because-of-this [post hoc ergo propter hoc] fallacy; or arguments based not on reason but on the opponent's character [argumentum ad hominem], or on a specious authority [ad verecundiam] or on 'the sympathy vote' [ad misericordiam] or on popular [but unreliable] opinion [ad populum].

Continued on following page

	'Muddling Through' is not enough
Aaron Wildavsky Amitai Etzioni Yehezkel Dror	These three writers strongly resist the elemental defeatism inherent in the 'muddling through' approach diagnosed by Lindblom. Aaron Wildavsky, for example, advocates the need for in-depth 'strategic' analysis of policy situations as a key factor to avoid the simplistic uses of valuable tools such as Planning-Programming-Budge;ing and Zero-based Budgeting. (19) Amitai Etzioni's 'Mixed Scanning' approach has such a purpose, namely to ensure the isolation of a range of policy options [and their inputs and outputs] rather than just a few. He highlights the differences that should be seen to exist between fundamental and incremental decisions. (20) Yehezkel Dror, in similar vein, stresses the need for 'selective rationalism' [i.e. as much rationality and comprehensiveness as possible], as well as a structured approach [termed 'metapolicy'] to policy making. (21) For him, the process should not be simply about 'Partisan Mutual Adjustment' - compromises among groups involved in a policy-struggle. [e.g. the UK's current 'dialogue' with the Commission and its European partners over the European Monetary Union.]
Michael Porter	Characterises strategic business choice as essentially bipolar. Either a company works on its costs profile, to achieve competitive advantage on an economic basis or it focuses heavily on differentiating its product as a 'niche player'. Whichever approach is used, the company needs to be aware of the extent to which structural industry forces [power of suppliers and buyers; challenge of substitute products, technology and new entrants] shape the nature of competition. (22)

601

16. SELECTED CONCEPTS FROM POWER THEORY STUDIES

SOURCE	CONCEPT	EXPLANATION	REF
T Hobbes	Power Urge	Power is needed and sought not necessarily for an improvement in living standards but for preservation of the standards already reached.	23
N Machiavelli	Statecraft	Believed that the art of Government largely depends on an appropriate blend of force and craft [guile], and that the ruler should be morally indifferent to the means used for political purposes so long as they are successful in their main object - the maintenance and, if possible, extension of political power itself. Key elements on this blend are pragmatism, expendiency, manipulation and coercion	24
M Weber	Authority	Postulated three main sources of authority [the claimed "right" to act in a certain way or to control others]: tradition [the status quo sanctified by the past]; the rational-legal system [the country's legislative arrangements conferring power and authority on organisational personnel]: charisma [the highly personal qualities of a 'leader'].	25
R Blake & J Mouton	Power Spectrum	Power acquisition is seen as a key factor in human relationships. The spectrum ranges from powerlessness through collaboration [power sharing] to competition [battle over who dominates]. A '1/0 power ratio' signifies that the manager has total work control of the subordinate.	26
A Etzioni & D Selznick	Leadership Types	Distinguished among 'officials' [who control because of their hierarchical position], 'informal leaders' [who possess charismatic qualities] and 'formal leaders' [who should possess both].	27
A Etzioni	Sources of Power	Contrasts three forms of power: coercive ["stick"], utilitarian ["money or advancement reward"] and normative ["symbolic" as in use of appeals to patriotism, sense of duty, etc.].	28
J Caroll	Neotic Authority	he power and authoritative influence that comes from the individual's possession of important knowledge that is not widely available and is badly needed	29

Continued on following page

Continued from previous page

SOURCE	CONCEPT	EXPLANATION	REF
K Lewin	"Gate-keeping"	Power achieved by persons in an organisation as a function of their position in a communication channel ['gates' manned by 'gatekeepers'].	30
P Bachrach & M Baratz	"Agenda-Setting"	The process whereby power is exercised within, or between, groups to achieve the suppression of the discussion of [and decision-making about] issues which powerful elements do not want raised.	31
C Wright Mills	Power Elite	Analyses the extent to which organisations and policy making are dominated by 'power elites' [cliques, cabals, gangs] who have decisive control over resources, the operating system or rewards.	32
R Dahl	Polyarchy	Our system of 'democratic' decision-making is not pluralistic [allowing access by all concerned parties] but polyarchical [dominated by powerful groups who are in competition].	33
E Latham	Policy & Power Relationships	Policies are seen as the outcome of the resultant power balance arising from the competition among groups with conflicting interests, aims and objectives.	34

17.   SELECTED CONCEPTS FROM BUREAUCRACY THEORY STUDIES

SOURCE	CONCEPT	EXPLANATION	REF
L Gulick & L Urwick	Administration Activities	Administration seen as being composed of planning, organising, staffing, directing co-ordinating, reporting, budgeting	35
J Mooney & A Reilley	Organisation Principles	Outlined principles governing organisation structures as; co-ordinative [span of control], scalar [hierarchy], functional [division of labour] and staff/line	36
T Burns & G M Stalker	Models of Organisations	Organisation structure and management style seen as dependent on the nature of work done and the degree of environmental stability. The model is "closed" [formal] when the environment is stable and the work routine; "open" [informal] when the environment is turbulent and the work innovative.	37
H Wilensky	Culture impact	Attitudes, values, goals or participants and the work system itself are heavily affected by the socio-political culture of the nation	38
E Goffman	Total Institutions	Researched and depersonalising effect of rule-bound "closed community" organisations	39
R Merton	Indoctrination	Traced the extent to which the training/development socialisation of bureaucratic administrator can amount to a pathological indoctrination.	40
I Jarvis	Groupthink	Concurrence-seeking behaviour becomes so dominant in a cohesive in-group that it can over-ride rational considerations of actions. Members can back stupid ideas out of fear of ostracism; the greater the group tyranny, the greater the amount of "group think"	41
R Cyert & J March	Theory of the Firm	Organisations don't have objectives; people do. The "organisation's objectives" are a negotiated consensus [at a given time] of the aims of influential participants. When an organisation becomes stabilised [external/internal change decreases], goals become 'displaced'. Sub-optimisation occurs. Means rather than ends are emphasised. Organisation drift occurs, by contrast, in unstable conditions	42

Continued on following page

Continued from previous page

SOURCE	CONCEPT	EXPLANATION	REF
G Tullock	Bureaucracy as Feudalism	Visualises bureaucracy as a medieval society with the reference politician interacting with spectators, allies, peers, courtiers, barons and the sovereign.	43
A Downs	Personality types	Divided administrators in bureaucracies into climbers, conservers, zealots, advocates and [the decision-making level] statesmen	44
G Tullock	Hierarchical Distortion	The possibility of communicating 'noise-free' information varies according to the size of the organisation and the levels of hierarchy	45
FE Emery & E L Trist	Strategies and Environments	Researched the degree to which the strategies adopted by an organisation - competition, bargaining, coalition - are a function of their operating environment - placid, dynamic, turbulent	46
D Macgregor	Theories 'X' and 'Y'	The employee has relatively little interest in his work and even less involvement, "carrots and sticks" are the main weapon for achieving results [Theory 'X']. Theory 'Y' suggests, to the contrary, that such crudity will not work.	47

605

18. SELECTED CONCEPTS FROM MOTIVATION THEORY STUDIES

SOURCE	TYPES OF THINKING	REF
J D Steinbrunner	"Grooved" thinking occurs in organisations which are well-established and have a regular-patterned work load. There is in such organisations a "highly stable pattern of reaction", and "short-time frame" and a "low level of abstraction". There is a tendency for members to "bread a particular short-range component out of a complex policy problem and make decisions solely in that context", or perhaps, to become pathologically obsessive about low-level tasks, e.g. administrative tidiness, systematic procedures, "Theoretical thinking", by contrast, is the product of extensive belief patterns and a generalised, highly deductive belief system. It involves the ability to think in abstract terms	62
Elliott Jacques	Bureaucracies are seen as having five different work strata, each characterised by the mixture of conceptual [thinking] and practical [doing] work performed. They are: 1. Perceptual Motor Concrete 2. Imaginal concrete 3. Imaginal scanning 4. Conceptual modelling 5. Intuitive theory The work done at stratum 1 level is routine 'hewing of wood and drawing of water'. The stratum 5 level demands little by way of concrete motor skills but requires high conceptual ability. The time horizon may be distant and the issue one of principles rather than practices	63
Henry Mintzberg	"Thus we end up with a vicious circle in our society. An irrational obsession with 'rationality' produces a society of large bureaucratic organisations run by a 'professional' management that proves this superficial, sometimes immoral; that drives out human commitment which, in turn, leads to the politicisation of organisations. This should destroy them, but it does not for they turn around and use their political power to sustain themselves artificially. Organisations, thereby, get larger, more bureaucratic and more politicised".	64

Continued from previous page

SOURCE	CONCEPT	EXPLANATION	REF
W Whyte	Organisation Man	An organisational automaton whose only purpose is to serve the rigid bureaucracy in which he works	57
W Bennis	Typology of Man	Classifies mankind [in what he sees as a post-bureaucratic world] into: militants [who wish to mutilate/destroy the existing system], apocalyptics [who, "with verbal ferocity, burn everything in sight"], regressors ["fruitless exercises in nostalgia"], retreators [those who hope the problem will go away], technocrats ["full steam ahead"] and liberals	58
D Macgregor	"Cosmology"	The particular way in which each of us construes the "reality" around us. We each have our own personal "cosmology" - picture of the outside world	59
H Mintzberg	Adhocracy	Organisation Structure needs to be adaptable in terms of a rapidly changing corporate environment. Derived from work by Alvin Toffler	60
K Ohmae	Genba	Innovation and improvement can only come from where the action [genba] in the organisation really is.	61

607

19. THINKING ABOUT THINKING

SOURCE	TYPES OF THINKING	REF
J D Steinbrunner	"Grooved" thinking occurs in organisations which are well-established and have a regular-patterned work load. There is in such organisations a "highly stable pattern of reaction", and "short-time frame" and a "low level of abstraction". There is a tendency for members to "bread a particular short-range component out of a complex policy problem and make decisions solely in that context", or perhaps, to become pathologically obsessive about low-level tasks, e.g. administrative tidiness, systematic procedures, "Theoretical thinking", by contrast, is the product of extensive belief patterns and a generalised, highly deductive belief system. It involves the ability to think in abstract terms	62
Elliott Jacques	Bureaucracies are seen as having five different work strata, each characterised by the mixture of conceptual [thinking] and practical [doing] work performed. They are: 1. Perceptual Motor Concrete 2. Imaginal concrete 3. Imaginal scanning 4. Conceptual modelling 5. Intuitive theory The work done at stratum 1 level is routine 'hewing of wood and drawing of water'. The stratum 5 level demands little by way of concrete motor skills but requires high conceptual ability. The time horizon may be distant and the issue one of principles rather than practices	63
Henry Mintzberg	"Thus we end up with a vicious circle in our society. An irrational obsession with 'rationality' produces a society of large bureaucratic organisations run by a 'professional' management that proves this superficial. Sometimes immoral. That drives out human commitment which in turn leads to the politicisation of organisations. This should destroy them, but it does not for they turn around and use their political power to sustain themselves artificially. Organisations thereby get larger, more bureaucratic and more politicised".	64
John Kenneth Galbrath	Compelled belief: A belief which people are forced into accepting, either by physical circumstances of by indoctrination. They do not necessarily internalise the belief but they act as if they do. The reward - punishment system gives little alternative but dangerous dissidence [e.g. Rumanian life under Nicolae Ceaucescu]. Convenient belief: Popular, but not necessarily well-founded, notions.	65

20. EUROPEAN UNION REALITIES

Nature of Change	Setting up the EU as a Free Trade Region in Which Economic Efficiency Rules		Setting up the EU as a Political & Economic Union	
Achievement level	Done	In hand	Under active consideration even if, on present grounds unlikely in the short term, from the UK viewpoint.	Necessary, but merely at present conjectural from the UK Labour government perspective.
Macro-Economic/ Macro-political	Abolition of Internal Tariffs and Exchange controls. Some harmonisation of technical standards. Reduction of protectionist practices. Some involvement by Commission in merger control and determining state industry aid. Increase in Regional Aid. Anti-dumping intervention.	Public Procurement. Deregulation of transport. Merger control policy. Trade negotiations with UK and Japan. Note that UK left ERM in September 1992. Expansion of EU.	Tax harmonisation - indirect, capital. UK joining EMU in first wave - European Central Bank. Common currency. Common foreign policy.	Tax harmonisation: Direct, Federal Euro-Parliament Government. Harmonised EU foreign policy.
Industry	Massive trans-border oligopolisation. Standardisation of industrial systems; R&D, manufacturing. EU Directives on Unit Trust, Banking & Insurance to regulate their workings. Change in Common Agricultural Policy. EU funded R&D expansion.	More merger and takeover bids. More regulatory frameworks. Tolerance of EU mergers which might not be accepted nationally.	European Company Statute, including worker representation on supervisory management boards.	Standardised system of company ownership designed to maximise shareholder value and minimise protectionism.
Social	Freedom of movement, goods, service, capital. Mutual recognition of qualifications.	UK opt out clause on Maastricht's Social Chapter. Policy reversed by Labour Government elected in 1997 in Britain.	Standardised work contracts under Maastrict's Employment Chapter.	Common Social Security System.

21. POLAR PRINCIPLES IN POLITICAL IDEOLOGY

Totalitarian Communism	Market-place Capitalism
Perception of the need for economic autarchy [self-sufficiency] or, failing that, separation for the state in question, for self-perpetuation purposes	Perception of the impossibility of isolating or insulating the country in question from the outside world, and hence, of the desirability of free trade.
Need for comprehensive and universal provision of all social services within a tightly controlled access and administration system: state-run. Involves central control of pricing - availability of all commodities, including housing, food and fuel. Little private ownership.	Need for provision of some social services on the basis of individual need. Private charity provision is regarded as an important adjunct. Price of food, housing, fuel etc. is predominantly left to the market place. Maximum private ownership permitted, if not encouraged.
Tight control over all aspects of economic performance [industrial location, investment, subsidies etc.] within a comprehensive state plan framework. This specifies the nature of all industrial development [heavy industry v consumer product] in future. All assets owned by state.	Control over the economy rests on the basis of appropriate fiscal monetary tools and does not comprise intervention in most industrial sectors. Their ownership, economic performance, price levels etc. are not seen as a matter for government involvement. Desirability of free enterprise and competition at all times. Privatisation of state-owned companies.
Citizens are actively politicised [e.g. membership of the Communist Party is desirable] and conformity to the political order is required. Dissident, revanchist tendencies are punished.	Citizens are left, politically, to their own devices. They are free to vote at elections [or not]; join political parties [or not]. Pluralism is a fact of life.
The Party [or more correctly, its autocratic or oligarchic representatives] rules all.	Ability to pay is a key to personal power. Big business plays its part.
= Life in a Zoo	= Life in a Jungle
THE ABSOLUTE NEED FOR STATE [AND MORE APPROPRIATELY ITS AUTOCRATIC/OLIGARCHIC LEADERS] TO CONTROL ALL ASPECTS OF ECONOMIC, SOCIAL AND POLITICAL LIFE.	THE ABSOLUTE NEED TO PRESERVE INDIVIDUALITY AND INDIVIDUAL FREEDOMS-ECONOMIC AND SOCIAL-EVEN AT THE COST OF INEQUALITY. MARKET FUNDAMENTALISM RULES.
Example: Brezhnevite USSR	Example: Mrs Thatcher's Britain

REFERENCES

1   L. V. Bertalanffy, "The Theory of Open Systems in Physics and Biology", *Science*, Vol.1, 11, 1950

2.   F. E. Emery & E. L. Trist, "Socio-technical Systems", *10th International Meeting of the Institute of Management Sciences,* Paris: September, 1959

3.   Stafford Beer, *Cybernetics and management,* N.Y: John Wiley & Sons, 1964

4.   Norbert Wiener, *Cybernetics,* N.Y.: John Wiley & Sons, 1948

5.   Herbert Simon, *The New Science of Management Decision,* N.Y: Harper & Row, 1960

6.   W Mackenzie, *Power, Violence and Decision,* London: Peregrine Books, 1975

7.   Igor Ansoff, *Corporate Strategy*, Harmondsworth, Middx: Penguin Books, 1968

8.   Henry Mintzberg and J. Waters, Of Strategies Deliberate and Emergent, *Strategic Management Journal*, 1985

9.   Gary Hamel and C.K. Prahalad, *Competing for the future*, Boston, Mass: Harvard University Press, 1994

10.   Peter Senge, *The Fifth Discipline: the Art and Practice of the Learning Organisation*, N.Y: Doubleday, 1990

11.   James Champy and Michael Hammer, *Re-engineering the Corporation,* N.Y: Harper Business, 1995

12.   Christopher Bartlett and Sumantra Ghoshal, *Managing Across Borders*, Boston, Mass: Harvard Business School, 1989

13.   Herbert Simon, "Theories of Decision Making in Economics & Behavioural Science", *American Economic Review,* vol. 49, No.3

14.   Herbert Simon, "Theories of Bounded Rationality", in C.B. McGuire & R. Rander (eds), *Decisions, and Organisations*, Amsterdam: New Holland, 1972

REFERENCES

15.   Herbert Simon, "A Behavioural Model of Rational Choice", *Quarterly Journal of Economics*, 1955

16.   Charles Lindblom, *The Policy Making Process,* New York: Prentice Hall, 1968

17.   David Braybrook and Charles Lindblom, *A Strategy of Decisions*, New York: Free Press, 1963

18.   Charles Lindblom, "The Science of Muddling Through", *Public Administration Review*, 1959 and "Still Muddling, Not Yet Through", *Public Administration Review*, Vol. 29, No. 6, 1979

19.   Aaron Wildavsky and Arthur Hammond, "Comprehensive v Incremental Budgeting in the Dept. of Agriculture", *Admin. Science Quarterly*, 10th December 1965

20.   Amitai Etzioni, "Mixed Scanning: a 'Third' Approach to Decision Making", *Public Administration Review*, vol. 28.

21.   Yehezkel Dror, *Public Policy Making Re-examined*, N.Y: Chandler, 1968

22.   Michael Porter, *Competitive Strategy*, N.Y: Free Press, 1980

23.   Thomas Hobbes, *Leviathan*

24.   Niccolo Machiavelli, *The Prince*

25.   Max Weber, *The Theory of Social and Economic Organisation, Oxford:* Oxford University Press, 1947 [First published in German in 1922.]

26.   Robert Blake and Jane Mouton, *Group Dynamics: Key to Decision Making,* Houston: Gulf Publishing Co., 1961

27.   Amitai Etzioni and David Selznick (eds), *Complex Organisations: a Sociological Reader,* N.Y: Holt Rhinehart Winston, 1961

28.   Amitai Etzioni, "Mixed Scanning: a 'Third' Approach to Decision-making", *Public Admin. Review*, Vol.28.

29.   James Caroll, "Neotic Authority", *Public Admin. Review* 29, 1969

REFERENCES

30.   Kurt Lewin, Gatekeeping, in *Readings in Social Psychology,* E. Maccoby, T. Newcomb and E. Hartley (eds) New York: Holt Rhinehart Winston, 1958

31.   Peter Bachrach and Morton Baratz, *Power and Poverty,* N.Y: Oxford University Press, 1979

32.   C. Wright Mills, *The Power Elite,* N.Y: Oxford University Press, 1957

33.   Robert Dahl, *Polyarchy,* Newhaven, Conn: Yale University Press, 1971

34.   Earl Latham, Power Balance, in *The Group Basis of Politics in Political Behaviour,* Heinz Eylau, Samual Eldesveld and Morris Janowits (eds), New York: Free Press, 1956

35.   Luther Gulick and Lyndall Urwick, *Papers on the Science of Administration,* N.Y: Institute of Public Administration, 1937

36.   James Mooney and Alan Reilley, *The Principle of Organisation,* New York: Harper and Bros., 1939

37.   Tom Burns and G. M. Stalker, *The Management of Innovation,* London: Tavistock Institute, 1961

38.   Harold Wilensky, *Organisational Intelligence,* New York: Basic Books, 1967

39.   Irving Goffman, "The Characteristics of Total Institutions", Walter Reed (ed.), *Institute of Research Symposium on Preventative and Social Psychiatry,* Washington, DC: US Government Printing Office, 1957

40.   Robert Merton, "Bureaucratic Structure and Personality", *Social Forces,* 18, 1940

41.   Irving Jarvis, *Psychology Today,* N.Y: Ziff Davis, 1971

42.   Richard Cyert and James March, *A Behavioural Theory of the Firm,* Englewood Cliffs, N.J: Prentice Hall, 1967

43.   Gordon Tullock, *Politics of Bureaucracy,* Washington: Public Affairs Press, 1965

44.   Anthony Downs, *Inside Bureaucracy,* Boston, Mass: Little Brown, 1967

REFERENCES

45.   as 43.

46.   F. E. Emery & E. L. Trist, "The Causal Texture of Organisational Environments", in Walter Hill & Douglas Egan (eds), *Readings in Organisation Theory: a Behavioural Approach*, Boston, Mass: Allyn & Baron, 1966

47.   Douglas Macgregor, *The Human Side of Enterprise, N.Y:* McGraw Hill, 1961.

48.   A Wayne, R Leys, "The Value Framework of Decision Making" in *Concepts and Issues in Administrative Behaviour,* S Manilick and E Van Ness, Englewood-Cliffs, NJ: Prentice Hall, 1962

49.   William Guth and Renato Tagiuri, "Personal Values and Corporate Strategy", *Harvard Business Review,* September-October 1965

50.   Herbert Simon, *Administrative Behaviour: a Study of Decision-making Processes in Administrative Organisation,* N.Y: Free Press, 1947

51.   Abraham Maslow, *Motivation and Personality,* NY: Harper & Brothers, 1954

52.   Frederick Herzberg, *Work and the Nature of Man,* Cleveland, Ohio: World Publishing Co., 1965

53.   Frederick Taylor, *Principles of Scientific Management,* NY: Harper and Row, 1911 [Reprint 1949]

54.   Fritz Roethlisberger and William Dickson, *Management and the Workers,* Boston, Mass: Harvard University Press, 1939

55.   Robert Bales, *Interaction Process Analysis,* Cambridge, Mass: Addison Wesley Press, 1950

56.   Alvin Gouldner, "Cosmopolitans and Locals: Towards an Analysis of Latent Social Roles", *Administrative Science Quarterly,* December 1957 and March 1958

57.   William Whyte, *The Organisation Man,* N.Y: Simon and Schuster, 1956

58.   Warren Bennis, "A Funny Thing Happened on the Way to the Future", *American Psychologist,* Vol.25, No.7, 1970

59.   Douglas Macgregor, *The Professional Manager,* N.Y.: McGraw Hill, 1967

REFERENCES

60.   Henry Mintzberg, Organisation Design: Fashion or fit?, *Harvard Business Review*, 1981

61.   Kenichi Ohmae in T Peters and R Waterman, *The Pursuit of Excellence*, N.Y: Harper & Row, 1982

62.   J D Steinbrunner, *The Cybernetic Theory of Decision,* N.J: Princeton University Press, 1974

63.   E Jacques, *A General Theory of Bureaucracy, London:* Heinemann, 1976

64.   Henry Mintzberg, "Mintzberg on Management", *The Observer* 31.12.1989

International Business Culture
second edition

Terry Garrison

This book is an ambitious and unusual attempt to meet a need in an increasingly important management field: cross cultural teamwork. Its focus is not on the popular aspects of different behaviours typically exhibited in teamwork involving people from different nations, but on the rationales for those behavioural stances. The book throws little light on the question *what ?,* but strongly illuminates the question *why?* It distinguishes between the super-structure of a nation's business culture and the bedrock.

The bedrock is difficult to pin down. It deals with what we call the issue of *where these people are coming from.* It focuses on key factors, often invisible, and always difficult for a foreigner to make out, which shape and predetermine the visible superstructure, like those of a nation's politics, economics, even its religions, which tend to be under-researched, yet are of vital importance for those involved in international management.

The book's main aim is to show why an understanding of a nation's business culture bedrock is vital, to indicate which factors are of major importance in cross-cultural work and to offer contemporary case studies that illustrate clearly how bedrock factors impact. It is a book for the practitioner. An original feature is the Triangle Test ©, a method for use by members of international teams to help raise questions with their partners about important differences of attitude, viewpoint and values.

The 21 case studies range widely, from European mergers to economic crises, from business corruption to government restructuring and cover, literally, the entire business world. Useful for MBA students doing inter-culture analysis courses and for executives in cross-national project teams.

Sewn paperback, 352 pages, ISBN 1 85450 232 8, £14.95